Web Data Management

The Internet and World Wide Web have revolutionized access to information. Users now store information across multiple platforms from personal computers, to smartphones, to Web sites such as YouTube and Picasa. As a consequence, data management concepts, methods, and techniques are increasingly focused on distribution concerns. That information largely resides in the network, as do the tools that process this information.

This book explains the foundations of XML, the Web standard for data management, with a focus on data distribution. It covers the many facets of distributed data management on the Web, such as description logics, that are already emerging in today's data integration applications and herald tomorrow's semantic Web. It also introduces the machinery used to manipulate the unprecedented amount of data collected on the Web. Several "Putting into Practice" chapters describe detailed practical applications of the technologies and techniques.

Striking a balance between the conceptual and the practical, the book will serve as an introduction to the new global information systems for Web professionals as well as for master's level courses.

Serge Abiteboul is a researcher at INRIA Saclay and ENS Cachan and cofounder of the start-up Xyleme. His previous books include the textbook *Foundations of Databases*.

Ioana Manolescu is a researcher at INRIA Saclay, and the scientific leader of the LEO team, joint between INRIA and University Paris XI.

Philippe Rigaux is a Professor of Computer Science at the Conservatoire National des Arts et Métiers. He has coauthored six books, including *Spatial Databases (2001)*.

Marie-Christine Rousset is a Professor of Computer Science at the University of Grenoble.

Pierre Senellart is an Associate Professor in the DBWeb team at Télécom ParisTech, the leading French engineering school specializing in information technology.

WEB DATA MANAGEMENT

Serge Abiteboul
INRIA Saclay – Île-de-France

Ioana Manolescu
INRIA Saclay – Île-de-France

Philippe Rigaux
CNAM, France

Marie-Christine Rousset
University of Grenoble, France

Pierre Senellart
Télécom ParisTech, France

CAMBRIDGE
UNIVERSITY PRESS

CAMBRIDGE
UNIVERSITY PRESS

Shaftesbury Road, Cambridge CB2 8EA, United Kingdom

One Liberty Plaza, 20th Floor, New York, NY 10006, USA

477 Williamstown Road, Port Melbourne, VIC 3207, Australia

314–321, 3rd Floor, Plot 3, Splendor Forum, Jasola District Centre, New Delhi – 110025, India

103 Penang Road, #05–06/07, Visioncrest Commercial, Singapore 238467

Cambridge University Press is part of Cambridge University Press & Assessment, a department of the University of Cambridge.

We share the University's mission to contribute to society through the pursuit of education, learning and research at the highest international levels of excellence.

www.cambridge.org
Information on this title: www.cambridge.org/9781107012431

First published 2012

A catalogue record for this publication is available from the British Library

Library of Congress Cataloging-in-Publication data
Web data management / Serge Abiteboul... [et al.].
     p. cm.
   Includes bibliographical references and index.
   ISBN 978-1-107-01243-1 (hardback)
   1. Web databases. 2. Database management. 3. Electronic commerce.
   I. Abiteboul, S. (Serge)
   QA76.9.W43.W4154 2011
   005.7402854678–dc23   2011037996

ISBN   978-1-107-01243-1   Hardback

Additional resources for this publication at http://webdam.inria.fr/Jorge/

Contents

Introduction

The Internet and the Web have revolutionized access to information. Individuals are depending more and more on the Web to find or publish information, download music and movies, and interact with friends in social networking Web sites. Following a parallel trend, companies go more and more toward Web solutions in their daily activity by using Web services (e.g., agenda) as well as by moving some applications into the cloud (e.g., with Amazon Web services). The growth of this immense information source is witnessed by the number of newly connected people, by the interactions among them facilitated by the social networking platforms, and above all by the huge amount of data covering all aspects of human activity. With the Web, information has moved from data isolated in very protected islands (typically relational databases) to information freely available to any machine or any individual connected to the Internet.

Perhaps the best illustration comes from a typical modern Web user. She has information stored on PCs, a personal laptop, and a professional computer, but also possibly on some server at work, on her smartphone, in an e-book, and so on. Also, she maintains information in personal Web sites or social network Web sites. She may store pictures in Picasa, movies in YouTube, bookmarks in Firefox Sync, and the like. So, even an individual is now facing the management of a complex distributed collection of data. On a different scale, public or private organizations also have to deal with information produced and stored in different places, or collected on the Web, either as a side effect of their activity (e.g., worldwide e-commerce or auction sites) or because they directly attempt to understand, organize and analyze data collected on the Web (e.g., search engines, digital libraries, or Web intelligence companies).

As a consequence, a major trend in the evolution of data management concepts, methods, and techniques is their increasing focus on distribution concerns: Since information now mostly resides in the network, so do the tools that process this information to make sense of it. Consider for instance the management of internal reports in a company. Typically, many collections of reports may be maintained in different local branches. To offer a unique company-wide query access to the *global* collection, one has to integrate these different collections. This leads to data management within a wide area network. Because of slow communications, the company may prefer to maintain such a large collection in a unique central repository. (This is not always possible for organizational reasons.) If the collection is a massive data set, it may rapidly outrange the capacity of a single computer. One may then choose to distribute the collection *locally* on a cluster of machines. Indeed, one may even prefer this solution simply because buying a cluster of cheap computers may be much cheaper than buying a single high-end machine with the same throughput as the cluster. This leads to data management within a local area network, with very fast communication. An extreme example that combines both aspects is Web search: The global collection is distributed on a wide area network (all documents on the Web) and the index is maintained on a local area network (e.g., a Google farm).

The use of global-area-network distribution is typical for Web data: Data relevant for a particular application may come from a large number of Web servers. Local-area-network distribution is also typical because of scalability challenges raised by the quantity of relevant data as well as the number of users and query load. Mastering the challenges opened by data distribution is the key to handling Web-scale data management.

MOTIVATION FOR THE BOOK

Distributed data management is not a new idea. Research labs and database companies have tackled the problem for decades. Since System R* or SDD-1, a number of distributed database systems have been developed with major technical achievements. There exist for instance very sophisticated tools for distributed transaction processing or parallel query processing. The main achievements in this context have been complex algorithms, notably for concurrency control (e.g., commit protocols), and global query processing through localization.

Popular software tools in this area are ETLs (for extract, transform, and load). To support performance needs, data are imported using ETLs from operational databases into warehouses and replicated there for local processing (e.g., OLAP or online analytical processing). Although a lot of techniques have been developed for propagating updates to the warehouse, this is much less frequently used. Data in warehouses are refreshed periodically, possibly using synchronization techniques in the style of that used for version control systems.

With the Web, the need for distributed data management has widely increased. Also, with Web standards and notably standards for Web services, the management of distributed information has been greatly simplified. For example, the simple task of making a database available on the network that was typically requiring hours with platforms such as Corba, can now be achieved in minutes. The software that is needed is widely available and often with free licenses. This is bringing back to light distributed data management.

The ambition of this book is to cover the many facets of distributed data management on the Web. We will explain the foundations of the Web standard for data management, XML. We will travel in logical countries (e.g., description logic) that provide foundations for the Semantic Web, which is emerging in modern data integration applications. We will show the beauty of software tools that everyone is already using today, for example Web search engines. And finally, we will explain the impressive machinery used nowadays to manipulate an unprecedented amount of data.

We are witnessing an emergence of a new global information system created, explored, and shared by the whole of humankind. This book aims to expose the recent achievements that help make this system usable.

SCOPE AND ORGANIZATION OF THE BOOK

Databases are a fantastic playground where theory and systems meet. The foundation of relational databases was first-order logic, and at the same time, relational systems are among the most popular software systems ever designed. In this book, theory and systems will also meet. We will encounter deep theory (e.g., logics for describing knowledge, automata for typing trees). We will also describe elegant algorithms and data structures such as PageRank or Distributed Hash Tables. We believe that all these aspects are needed to grasp the reality of Web data management.

We present this material in different core chapters that form, in our opinion, the principles of the topic. They include exercises and notes for further reading. We also see as essential putting this material into practice, so that it does not remain too abstract. This is realized in PiP (for Putting into Practice) chapters. For instance, after we present the abstract model for XML in core chapters, we propose a PiP for XML APIs (Application Programming Interfaces for XML), and one for EXIST (an Open Source XML database). The approach is followed for the other topics addressed by the book. Our main concern is to deliver content that reaches a good balance between the conceptual aspects that help make sense of the often unstructured, heterogeneous, and distributed content of the Web and the practical tools that let practitioners acquire a concrete experience. Also, because software or environments typically evolve faster than core material, the PiP chapters are complemented by teaching material that can be found on a Web site.

The book is organized in three parts. The first part covers Web data modeling and representation, the second is devoted to semantic issues, and the last one delves into the low levels of Web scale data handling systems. We next detail these three parts.

Part 1: Modeling Web Data

The HTML Web is a fantastic means of sharing information. But HTML is fully oriented toward visual presentation and keyword search, which makes it appropriate for humans but much less so for access by software applications. This motivated the introduction of a *semistructured data model*, namely XML, which is well suited for both humans and machines. XML describes *content* and promotes machine-to-machine communication and data exchange. XML is a generic data exchange format that can be easily specialized to meet the needs of a wide range of data uses.

Because XML is a universal format for data exchange, systems can easily exchange information in a wide variety of fields, from bioinformatics to e-commerce. This universality is also essential to facilitate data integration. A main advantage (compared to previous exchange formats) is that the language comes equipped with an array of available software tools such as parsers, programming interfaces, and manipulation languages that facilitate the development of XML-based applications. Last but not least, the standard for distributed computation over the Internet is based on Web services and on the exchange of XML data.

This part proposes a wide but concise picture of the state-of-the-art languages and tools that constitute the XML world. We do not provide a comprehensive view of the specifications, but rather explain the main mechanisms and the rationales behind the specifications. After reading this part, the reader should be familiar enough with the semistructured data approach to understand its foundations and be able to pick up the appropriate tools when needed.

Part 2: Web Data Semantics and Integration

On the Web, given a particular need, it may be difficult to find a resource that is relevant to it. Also, given a relevant resource, it is not easy to understand what it provides and how to use it. To solve such limitations and facilitate interoperability, the Semantic Web vision has been proposed. The key idea is to also publish *semantic descriptions* of Web resources. These descriptions rely on *semantic annotations*, typically on logical assertions that relate resources to some terms in predefined *ontologies*.

An ontology is a formal description providing human users or machines a shared understanding of a given domain. Because of the logic inside, one can reason with ontologies, which is a key tool for integrating different data sources, providing more precise answers, or (semiautomatically) discovering and using new relevant resources.

In this part, we describe the main concepts of the Semantic Web. The goal is to familiarize the reader with ontologies: what they are, how to use them for query answering, how to use them for data integration.

Part 3: Building Web Scale Applications

At this stage of the book, we know how to exchange data and how to publish and understand semantics for this data. We are now facing the possibly huge scale of Web data. We will present main techniques and algorithms that have been developed for scaling to huge volumes of information and huge query rates. The few numbers that one may want to keep in mind are billions of Web documents, millions of Web servers, billions of queries per month for a top Web search engine, and a constant scale-up of these figures. Even a much smaller operation, such as a company-wide center, may have to store millions of documents and serve millions of queries.

How do you design software for that scale?

We will describe the basics of full-text search in general, and Web search in particular. Indexing is at the core of Web search and distributed data access. We will consider how to index huge collections in a distributed manner. We will also present specific techniques developed for large-scale distributed computing.

This part puts an emphasis on existing systems, taken as illustrative examples of more generic techniques. Our approach to explain distributed indexing techniques, for instance, starts from the standard centralized case, explains the issues raised by distribution, and shows how these issues have been tackled in some of the most prominent systems. Because many of these technologies have been implemented in Open Source platforms, they also form the basis of the PiP chapters proposed in this part.

INTENDED AUDIENCE

The book is meant as an introduction to the fascinating area of data management on the Web. It can serve as the material for a master course. Some of it may also be used in undergraduate courses. Indeed, the material in this book has already been tested, at both the undergraduate and graduate levels. The PiP chapters are meant to be the basis of labs or projects. Most of the material deals with well-established concepts, languages, algorithms, and tools. Occasionally, we included more speculative material issued from ongoing research dedicated to the emergence of this vision. This is to better illustrate important concepts we wanted to highlight. The book's content can thus also serve as an academic introduction to research issues regarding Web data management.

Among other viewpoints, one can view the Web as a very large library. In our travel within Web territories, we will be accompanied by a librarian, Jorge. This is in homage to Jorge Luis Borges whose short story *The Library of Babel* introduces a library preserving the whole human of knowledge.

COMPANION WEB SITE

A companion Web site for this book, available at http://webdam.inria.fr/Jorge/, contains electronic versions of this book, as well as additional materials (extra chapters, exercise solutions, lecture slides, etc.) pertaining to Web data management. In particular, all examples, data sets, and software used in the PiP chapters are available there.

ACKNOWLEDGMENTS

We would like to thank the following people who helped us to collect, organize, and improve the content of this book: Stanislav Barton (Internet Memory Foundation), Michael Benedikt (Oxford Univ.), Véronique Benzaken (Univ. Paris–Sud), Balder ten Cate (UCSC), Irini Fundulaki (FORTH Institute), Alban Galland (INRIA Saclay), François Goasdoué (Univ. Paris–Sud), David Gross-Amblard (INRIA Saclay), Fabrice Jouanot (Univ. Grenoble), Witold Litwin (Univ. Paris–Dauphine), Laurent d'Orazio (Univ. Clermont-Ferrand), Fabian Suchanek (INRIA Saclay), and Nicolas Travers (CNAM).

We are also grateful to the students at CNAM, ENS Cachan, Grenoble, Paris–Sud, and Télécom ParisTech who followed portions of this course and helped, through their questions and comments, to improve it.

This book has been developed as part of the Webdam project. The Webdam project is funded by the European Research Council under the European Community's Seventh Framework Programme (FP7/2007–2013), ERC grant Webdam, agreement 226513.

PART 1

Modeling Web Data

1

Data Model

The Web is a media of primary interest for companies who change their organization to place it at the core of their operation. It is an easy but boring task to list areas where the Web can be usefully leveraged to improve the functionalities of existing systems. One can cite in particular B2B and B2C (business to business or business to customer) applications, G2B and G2C (government to business or government to customer) applications or digital libraries. Such applications typically require some form of typing to represent data because they consist of programs that deal with HTML text with difficulties. Exchange and exploitation of business information call as well for a more powerful Web data management approach.

This motivated the introduction of a semistructured data model, namely XML, that is well suited both for humans and machines. XML describes *content* and promotes machine-to-machine communication and data exchange. The design of XML relies on two major goals. First it is designed as a generic data format, apt to be specialized for a wide range of data usages. In the XML world for instance, XHTML is seen as a specialized XML dialect for data presentation by Web browsers. Second XML "documents" are meant to be easily and safely transmitted on the Internet, by including in particular a self-description of their encoding and content.

XML is the language of choice for a generic, scalable, and expressive management of Web data. In this perspective, the visual information between humans enabled by HTML is just a very specific instance of a more general data exchange mechanism. HTML also permits a limited integrated presentation of various Web sources (see any Web portal for instance). Leveraging these capabilities to software-based information processing and distributed management of data just turns out to be a natural extension of the initial Web vision.

The chapter first sketches the main traits of semistructured data models. Then we delve into XML and the world of Web standards around XML.

1.1 SEMISTRUCTURED DATA

A semistructured data model is based on an organization of data in labeled trees (possibly graphs) and on query languages for accessing and updating data. The

3

labels capture the structural information. Since these models are considered in the context of data exchange, they typically propose some form of data serialization (i.e., a standard representation of data in files). Indeed, the most successful such model, namely XML, is often confused with its serialization syntax.

Semistructured data models are meant to represent information from very structured to very unstructured kinds, and, in particular, irregular data. In a structured data model such as the relational model, one distinguishes between the type of the data (*schema* in relational terminology) and the data itself (*instance* in relational terminology). In semistructured data models, this distinction is blurred. One sometimes speaks of schema-less data although it is more appropriate to speak of self-describing data. Semistructured data may possibly be typed. For instance, tree automata have been considered for typing XML (see Chapter 3). However, semistructured data applications typically use very flexible and tolerant typing; sometimes no typing at all.

We next present informally a standard semistructured data model. We start with an idea familiar to Lisp programmers of association lists, which are nothing more than label-value pairs and are used to represent record-like or tuple-like structures:

> {name: "Alan", tel: 2157786, email: "agb@abc.com"}

This is simply a set of pairs such as (name, "Alan") consisting of a label and a value. The values may themselves be other structures as in

> {name: { first : "Alan", last : "Black"},
> tel: 2157786,
> email: "agb@abc.com"}

We may represent this data graphically as a tree. See, for instance, Figures 1.1 and 1.2. In Figure 1.1, the label structure is captured by tree edges, whereas data values reside at leaves. In Figure 1.2, all information resides in the vertices.

Such representations suggest departing from the usual assumption made about tuples or association lists that the labels are unique, and we allow duplicate labels as in

> {name: "Alan", tel: 2157786, tel: 2498762 }

The syntax makes it easy to describe sets of tuples as in

> { person: {name: "Alan", phone: 3127786, email: "alan@abc.com"},
>   person: {name: "Sara", phone: 2136877, email: "sara@xyz.edu"},
>   person: {name: "Fred", phone: 7786312, email: "fd@ac.uk"} }

Furthermore, one of the main strengths of semistructured data is its ability to accommodate variations in structure (e.g., all the Person tuples do not need to have the same type). The variations typically consist of missing data, duplicated fields, or minor changes in representation, as in the following example:

> {person: {name: "Alan", phone: 3127786, email: "agg@abc.com"},
> person: &314

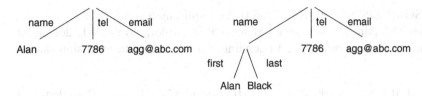

Figure 1.1. Tree representation, with labels on edges.

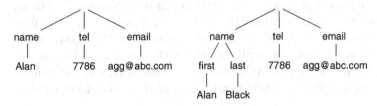

Figure 1.2. Tree representation, with labels as nodes.

```
        {name: { first : "Sara",  last : "Green"          },
         phone: 2136877,
         email: "sara@math.xyz.edu",
         spouse: &443                                      },
person: &443
        {name: "Fred",  Phone: 7786312, Height: 183,
         spouse: &314                                      }}
```

Observe how identifiers (here &443 and &314) and references are used to represent graph data. It should be obvious by now that a wide range of data structures, including those of the relational and object database models, can be described with this format.

As already mentioned, in semistructured data, we make the conscious decision of possibly not caring about the type the data might have and serialize it by annotating each data item explicitly with its description (such as name, phone, etc.). Such data is called *self-describing*. The term "serialization" means converting the data into a byte stream that can be easily transmitted and reconstructed at the receiver. Of course, self-describing data wastes space, since we need to repeat these descriptions with each data item, but we gain interoperability, which is crucial in the Web context.

There have been different proposals for semistructured data models. They differ in choices such as labels on nodes *vs.* on edges, trees *vs.* graphs, ordered trees *vs.* unordered trees. Most importantly, they differ in the languages they offer. Two quite popular models (at the time of writing) are XML, a de facto standard for exchanging data of any kind, and JSON ("Javascript Object Notation"), an object serialization format mostly used in programming environments. We next focus on XML, an introduction to JSON being given in Section 20.3.

1.2 XML

XML, the eXtensible Mark-up Language, is a semistructured data model that has been proposed as the standard for data exchange on the Web. It is a simplified version of SGML (ISO 8879). XML meets the requirements of a flexible, generic, and platform-independent language, as presented earlier. Any XML document can be serialized with a normalized encoding, for storage of transmission on the Internet.

Remark 1.2.1 It is well-established to use the term "XML document" to denote a hierarchically structured content represented with XML conventions. Although we adopt this standard terminology, please keep in mind that by "document" we mean both the content and its structure, but not their specific representation, which may take many forms. Also note that "document" is reminiscent of the SGML application area, which mostly focuses on representating technical documentation. An XML document is not restricted to textual, human-readable data, and can actually represent any kind of information, including images, of references to other data sources.

XML is a standard for representing data but it is also a family of standards (some in progress) for the management of information at a world scale: XLink, XPointer, XSchema, DOM, SAX, Xpath, XSL, XQuery, SOAP, WSDL, and so forth.

1.2.1 XML Documents

An XML document is a labeled, unranked, ordered tree:

Labeled means that some annotation, the label, is attached to each node.
Unranked means that there is no a priori bound on the number of children of a node.
Ordered means that there is an order between the children of each node.

The document of Figure 1.3 can be serialized as follows:

```
<entry><name><fn>Jean</fn><ln>Doe</ln></name>INRIA<adress><city>
Cachan</city><zip>94235</zip></adress><email>j@inria.fr</email>
</job><purpose>like to teach</purpose></entry>
```

or with some beautification as

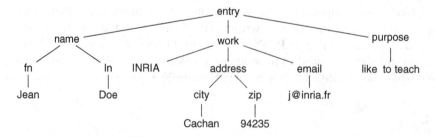

Figure 1.3. An XML document.

```
<entry>
  <name>
    <fn>Jean</fn>
    <ln>Doe</ln> </name>
  <work>
    INRIA
    <adress>
      <city>Cachan</city>
      <zip>94235</zip> </adress>
      <email>j@inria.fr</email> </work>
    <purpose>like to teach</purpose>
</entry>
```

In this serialization, the data corresponding to the subtree with root labeled (e.g., *work*) is represented by a subword delimited by an opening tag <work> and a closing tag </work>. One should never forget that this is just a serialization. The conceptual (and mathematical) view of an XML document is that it is a *labeled, unranked, ordered tree*.

XML specifies a "syntax" and no a priori semantics. So, it specifies the content of a document but not its behavior or how it should be processed. The labels have no predefined meaning unlike in HTLM, where, for example, the label href indicates a reference and img an image. Clearly, the labels will be assigned meaning by applications.

In HTML, one uses a predefined (finite) set of labels that are meant primarily for document presentation. For instance, consider the following HTML document:

```
<h1> Bibliography </h1>
  <p> <i> Foundations of Databases </i>
        Abiteboul, Hull, Vianu
        <br/> Addison Wesley, 1995 </p>
  <p> <i> Data on the Web </i>
        Abiteboul, Buneman, Suciu
        <br/> Morgan Kaufmann, 1999 </p>
```

where <h1> indicates a title, <p> a paragraph, <i> italics and <br/> a line break (
 is both an opening and a closing tag, gathered in a concise syntax equivalent to
</br>). Observe that this is in fact an XML document; more precisely this text is in a particular XML dialect, called XHTML. (HTML is more tolerant and would, for instance, allow omitting the </p> closing tags.)

The presentation of that HTML document by a classical browser can be found in Figure 1.4. The layout of the document depends closely on the interpretation of these labels by the browser. One would like to use different layouts depending on

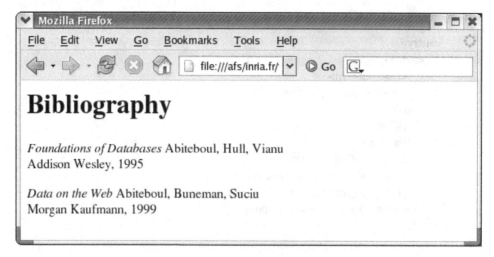

Figure 1.4. HTML presentation.

the usage (e.g., for a mobile phone or for blind people). A solution for this is to separate the content of the document and its layout so that one can generate different layouts based on the actual software that is used to present the document. Indeed, early on, Tim Berners-Lee (the creator of HTML) advocated the need for a language that would go beyond HTML and distinguish between content and presentation.

The same bibliographical information is found, for instance, in the following XML document:

```
<bibliography>
  <book>
    < title > Foundations of Databases </ title >
    <author> Abiteboul </author> <author> Hull </author>
    <author> Vianu </author>
    <publisher> Addison Wesley </publisher>
    <year> 1995 </year> </book>
  <book>...</book>
</bibliography>
```

Observe that it does not include any indication of presentation. There is a need for a stylesheet (providing transformation rules) to obtain a decent presentation such as that of the HTML document. On the other hand, with different stylesheets, one can obtain documents for several media (e.g., also for PDF). Also, the tags produce some semantic information that can be used by applications (e.g., *Addison Wesley is the publisher of the book*). Such tag information turns out to be useful for instance to support more precise search than that provided by Web browser or to integrate information from various sources.

The separation between content and presentation already exists in a precursor of XML, namely SGML. In SGML, the labels are used to describe the structure of the content and not the presentation. SGML was already quite popular at the time XML was proposed, in particular for technical documentation (e.g., Airbus documentation). However, SGML is unnecessarily complicated, in particular with features found in complex document models (such as footnote). XML is much simpler. Like SGML, it is a metalanguage in that it is always possible to introduce new tags.

1.2.2 Serialized and Tree-Based Forms

An XML document must always be interpreted as a tree. However the tree may be represented in several forms, all equivalent (i.e., there exists a mapping from one form to another) but quite different with respect to their use. All the representations belong to one of the following category:

- *Serialized forms*, which are textual, linear representations of the tree that conform to a (sometimes complicated) syntax;
- *Tree-based forms*, which implement, in a specific context (e.g., object-oriented models), the abstract tree representation.

Both categories cover many possible variants. The syntax of the serialized form makes it possible to organize "physically" an XML document in many ways, whereas tree-based forms depend on the specific paradigm and/or technique used for the manipulation of the document. A basic prerequisite of XML data manipulation is to know the main features of the serialized and tree-based representation and to understand the mapping that transforms one form to another.

Figure 1.5 shows the steps typically involved in the processing of an XML document (say, for instance, editing the document). Initially, the document is most often obtained in serialized form, either because it is stored in a file or a database, or because it comes from another application. The *parser* transforms the serialized representation to a tree-based representation, which is conveniently used to process the document content. Once the application task is finished, another, complementary module, the *serializer*, transforms the tree-based representation of the possibly modified document into one of its possible serialized forms.

Strictly speaking, the *syntax* of XML relates to its serialized representation. The syntax can be normalized because a serialized document is meant for data

Figure 1.5. Typical processing of XML data.

exchange in an heterogeneous environment, and must, therefore, be completely independent from a specific context. The tree-based representation is more strongly associated with the application that processes the document, and in particular to the programming language.

We provide a presentation of the XML syntax that covers the main aspects of the serialized representation of an XML document and show their couterpart in terms of a tree-based representation. The serialized syntax if defined by the World Wide Webb Consortium (W3C), and can be found in the XML 1.0 recommendation. Since the full syntax of XML is rather complex and contains many technical detail that do not bring much to the understanding of the model, the reader is referred to this recommendation for a complete coverage of the standard (see Section 1.2.1).

For the tree-based representation, we adopt the DOM (Document Object Model), also standardized by the W3C, which defines a common framework for the manipulation of documents in an object-oriented context. Actually we only consider the aspects of the model that suffice to cover the tree representation of XML documents and illustrate the transformation from the serialized form to the tree form, back and forth. The DOM model is also convenient to explain the semantics of the XPath, XSLT, and XQuery languages, presented in the next chapters.

1.2.3 XML Syntax

Four examples of XML documents (separated by blank lines) are

```
<document/>
```

Document 1

```
<document>
Hello World!
</document>
```

Document 2

```
<document>
 < salutation >
  Hello World!
 </ salutation >
</document>
```

Document 3

```
<?xml version="1.0"
  encoding="utf-8" ?>
<document>
 < salutation  color="blue">
  Hello World!
 </ salutation >
</document>
```

Document 4

In the last one, the first line starting with <?xml is the *prologue*. It provides indications such as the version of XML that is used, the particular coding, possibly indications of external resources that are needed to construct the document.

Elements and Text

The basic components of an XML document are *element* and *text*. The text (e.g., *Hello World!*) is in UNICODE. Thus texts in virtually all alphabets, including, for example, Latin, Hebrew, and Chinese, can be represented. An element is of the form

---

```
<name attr='value' ... > content </name>
```

---

where <name> is the *opening tag* and </name> the *closing tag*.

The content of an element is a list of text or (sub) elements (and gadgets such as comments). A simple and very common pattern is a combination of an element and a textual content. In the serialized form, the combination appears as

---

```
<elt_name>
   Textual   content
</elt_name>
```

The equivalent tree-based representation consists of *two* nodes, one that corresponds to the structure marked by the opening and closing tags, and the second, child of the first, which corresponds to the textual content. In the DOM, these nodes are typed, and the tree is represented as follows:

The **Element** nodes are the internal nodes of a DOM representation. They represent the hierarchical structure of the document. An **Element** node has a *name*, which is the label of the corresponding tag in the serialized form. The second type of node illustrated by this example is a **Text** node. **Text** nodes do not have a name, but a *value* which is a nonstructured character string.

The nesting of tags in the serialized representation is represented by a parent–child relationship in the tree-based representation. The following is a slight modification of the previous examples which shows a nested serialized representation (on the left) and its equivalent tree-based representation (on the right) as a hierarchical organization with two **Element** nodes and two **Text** nodes.

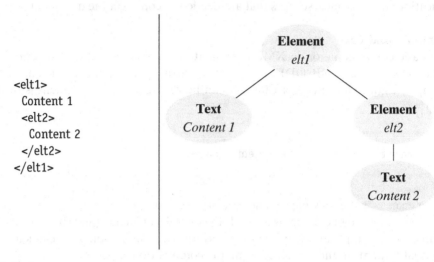

```
<elt1>
  Content 1
  <elt2>
    Content 2
  </elt2>
</elt1>
```

Attributes

The opening tag may include a list of (name,value) pairs called *attributes* as in

```
<report language='fr' date='08/07/07'>
```

Two pairs of attributes for the same element are not allowed to have the same attribute name.

Major differences between the content and the attributes of a given element are that (i) the content is ordered whereas the attributes are not and (ii) the content may contain some complex subtrees whereas the attribute value is atomic.

Attributes appear either as pairs of name/value in opening tag in the serialized form, or as special child nodes of the **Element** node in the tree-based (DOM) representation. The following example shows an XML fragment in serialized form and its counterpart in tree-based form. Note that **Attr** nodes have both a name *and* a value.

```
<elt att1='12' att2='fr'>
  Text1
</elt>
```

Attribute can store content, just as **Text** nodes. In the previous example, the textual content could just be represented as an attribute of the elt element, and conversely attributes could be represented as child elements with a textual content.

This gives rise to some freedom to organize the content of an XML document and adds some complexity to the tree-based representation.

Well-Formed XML Document

An XML document must correctly represent a tree. There exist in a document one and only one element that contains all the others (called the *element root*). An element that is not the root is totally included in its parent. More generally, the tags must close in the opposite order they have been opened. One says of such a document that it is *well-formed*. For instance, <a> <b> </b> </a> is well-formed and <a> <b> </a> </b> is not.

The serialized form often (but not always) begins with the prologue, which takes place in the tree-based representation as a **Document** node. This node has therefore a *unique* **Element** child, which is the *element root* of the document. The following examples illustrates the situation.

```
<?xml version="1.0"
    encoding="utf-8" ?>
<elt>
  Document content.
</elt>
```

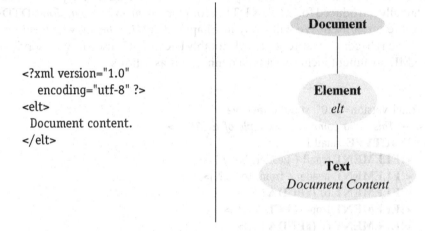

There may be other syntactic objects after the prologue (for instance, processing instructions), which become children of the **Document** node in the tree representation.

The **Document** node is the *root of the document*, which must be distinguished from the *element root*, its only element child. This somehow misleading vocabulary is part of the price to pay in order to master the XML data model.

An important notion (related to the physical nature of a document and not to its logical structure) is the notion of *entity*. Examples of entities are as follows:

```
<!ENTITY chap1 "Chapter 1: to be written">
<!ENTITY chap2 SYSTEM "chap2.xml">
<report> &chap1; &chap2 </report>
```

The content of an entity may be found in the document (as entity chap1), in the local system (as for chap2) or on the Web (with a URI). The content of an entity can be XML. In this case, the document is logically equivalent to the document obtained by replacing the entity references (e.g., &chap1; &chap2) by their content. The content of the entity may also be in some other format (e.g., Jpeg). In such case, the entity is not parsed and treated as an attachment.

Remark 1.2.2 (Details)

1. An *empty* element <name></name> may alternatively be denoted <name/>.
2. An element or attribute name is a sequence of alphanumeric and other allowed symbols that must start with an alphanumeric symbols (or an underscore).
3. The value of attribute is a string with certain limitations.
4. An element may also contain comments and processing instructions.

1.2.4 Typing and Namespaces

XML documents need not typed. They *may* be. The first kind of typing mechanism originally introduced for XML is DTDs, for *Document Type Definitions*. DTDs are still quite often used. We will study in Chapter 3 *XML schema*, which is more powerful and is becoming more standard, notably because it is used in Web services.

An XML document including a type definition is as follows:

```
<?xml version="1.0" standalone="yes" ?>
<!-- This is a comment - Example of a DTD -->
<!DOCTYPE email [
  <!ELEMENT email ( header, body )>
  <!ELEMENT header ( from, to, cc? )>
  <!ELEMENT to (#PCDATA)>
  <!ELEMENT from (#PCDATA)>
  <!ELEMENT cc (#PCDATA)>
  <!ELEMENT body paragraph* >
  <!ELEMENT paragraph (#PCDATA)>
<email>
  <header>
    <from> af@abc.com </from>
    <to> zd@ugh.com </to>
  </header>
  <body>
  </body>
</email>
```

The DOCTYPE clause declares the type for this document. Such a type declaration is not compulsory. Ignoring the details of this weird syntax, this is stating, for instance, that a header is composed of a from element, a to one, and possibly a cc one, that a body consists of a list of paragraphs, and finally that a paragraph is a string.

In general, the list of children for a given element name is described using a regular expression in Backus Neur Form (BNF) specified for that element.

A most important notion is also that of *namespace*. Consider a label such as job. It denotes different notions for a hiring agency or for a (computer) application service provider. Applications should not confuse the two notions. The notion of namespace is used to distinguish them. More precisely, consider the following XML piece of data:

```
<doc xmlns:hire='http://a.hire.com/schema'
     xmlns:asp='http://b.asp.com/schema' >
  ...
  <hire:job> ... </hire:job> ...
  <asp:job> ... </asp:job> ...
</doc>
```

The hire namespace is linked to a schema, and the asp to another one. One can now mix the two vocabularies inside the same document in spite of their overlap.

XML also provides some referencing mechanisms that we will ignore for now.

When a type declaration is present, the document must conform to the type. This may, for instance, be verified by an application receiving a document before actually processing it. If a well-formed document conforms to the type declaration (if present), we say that it is *valid* (for this type).

1.2.5 To Type or Not to Type

The structure of an XML document is included in the document in its label structure. As already mentioned, one speaks of self-describing data. This is an essential difference with standard databases:

In a database, one defines the type of data (e.g., a relational schema) before creating instances of this type (e.g., a relational database). In semistructured data (and XML), data may exist with or without a type.

The "may" (in *may exist*) is essential. Types are not forbidden; they are just not compulsory and we will spend quite some effort on XML typing. But in many cases, XML data often presents the following characteristics:

1. The data are irregular: There may be variations of structure to represent the same information (e.g., a date or an address) or unit (prices in dollars or euros); this is typically the case when the data come from many sources;
2. Parts of the data may be missing, for example, because some sources are not answering, or some unexpected extra data (e.g., annotations) may be found;
3. The structure of the data is not known a priori or some work such as parsing has to be performed to discover it (e.g., because the data come from a newly discovered source);
4. Part of the data may be simply untyped (e.g., plain text).

Another differences with database typing is that the type of some data may be quite complex. In some extreme cases, the size of the type specification may be comparable to, or even greater than, the size of the data itself. It may also evolve very rapidly. These are many reasons why the relational or object database models that propose too rigid typing were not chosen as standards for data exchange on the Web, but a semistructured data model was chosen instead.

1.3 WEB DATA MANAGEMENT WITH XML

XML is a very flexible language, designed to represent contents independently from a specific system or a specific application. These features make it *the* candidate of choice for data management on the Web.

Speaking briefly, XML enables *data exchange* and *data integration*, and it does so *universally* for (almost) all the possible application realms, ranging from business information to images, music, biological data, and the like. We begin with two simple scenarios showing typical distributed applications based on XML that exploit exchange and integration.

1.3.1 Data Exchange

The typical flow of information during XML-based data exchange is illustrated on Figure 1.6. Application *A* manages some internal data, using some specialized data management software (e.g., a relational DBMS). Exchanging these data with another application *B* can be motivated either for publication purposes, or for requiring from *B* some specialized data processing. The former case is typical of *Web publishing* frameworks, where *A* is a *Web server* and *B* a web client (browser, mobile phone, PDF viewer, etc.). The later case is a first step towards distributed data processing, where a set of sites (or "peers") collaborate to achieve some complex data manipulation.

XML is at the core of data exchange. Typically, *A* first carries out some conversion process (often called "XML publishing") which produces an appropriate XML representation from the internal data source(s). These XML data are then consumed by *B* which extracts the content, processes it, and possibly returns an

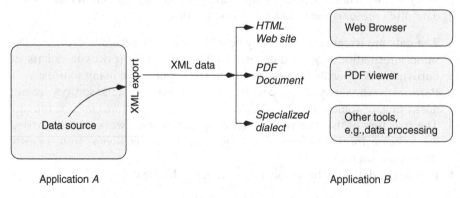

Figure 1.6. Flow of information in XML-based data exchange.

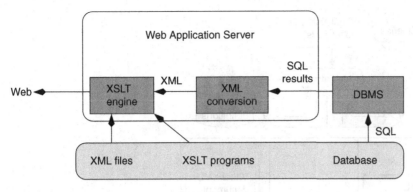

Figure 1.7. Software architecture for Web publishing applications.

XML-encoded result. Several of the aforementioned features of XML contribute to this exchange mechanism:

1. Ability to represent data in a serialized form that is safely transmitted on the Web;
2. Typing of document, which allows A and B to agree on the structure of the exchanged content;
3. Standardized conversion to/from the serialized representation and the specific tree-based representation respectively manipulated by A and B.

For concreteness, let us delve into the details of a real Web Publishing architecture, as shown in Figure 1.7. We are concerned with an application called *Shows* for publishing information about movie showings, in a Web site and in a Wap site. The application uses a relational database. Data are obtained from a relational database as well as directly from XML files. Some specialized programs, written with XSLT (the XML transformation language, see below) are used to restructure the XML data, either coming from files, from the database through a conversion process, or actually from any possible data source. This is the *XML publishing* process mentioned above. It typically produces XHTML pages for a Web site. These pages are made available to the world by a Web server.

The data flow, with successive transformations (from relational database to XML; from XML to a publication dialect), is typical of XML-based applications, where the software may be decomposed in several modules, each dedicated to a particular part of the global data processing. Each module consumes XML data as input and produces XML data as output, thereby creating chains of data producers/-consumers. Ultimately, there is no reason to maintain a tight connection of modules on a single server. Instead, each may be hosted on a particular computer somewhere on the Internet, dedicated to providing specialized services.

1.3.2 Data Integration

A typical problem is the integration of information coming from heterogeneous sources. XML provides some common ground where all kinds of data may be integrated. See Figure 1.8. For each (non-XML) format, one provides a *wrapper* that

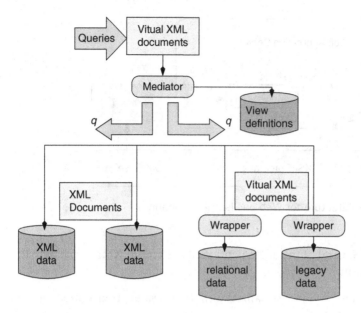

Figure 1.8. Information integration.

is in charge of the mapping from the world of this format to the XML world. Now a query (say an XQuery) to the global XML view is transformed by the mediator (using the view definitions) into queries over the local sources. A source wrapper translates the XML query to the source it receives into a query the source understands. That query is evaluated on the source, and some data are produced. The wrapper translates this data into XML data. The mediator combines the result it receives from all the wrappers to obtain the general result.

1.4 THE XML WORLD

The broad scope of XML is achieved through a spectrum of XML dialects, XML-based standards, and XML-based software. Dialects define specialized structures, constraints, and vocabularies to construct ad hoc XML contents that can be used and exchanged in a specific application area. Languages and softwares on the other hand are *generic*. Together, dialects and languages build an entire world that is at our disposal for developing Web applications.

1.4.1 XML Dialects

Suppose we are working in some particular area, say the industry of plastic. To facilitate the exchange of information, the industry specifies a common type for such exchanges, with the tags that should be used, the structure of the information they contain, and the meaning of the corresponding data. The advantage is that once this is achieved, (i) partners can easily exchange information, (ii) information from different companies can more easily be integrated, and (iii) information of interest can more easily be found. Basically, by doing that, the plastic industry has solved, in part, the problem of the heterogeneity of information sources. It is important to note that the design of such dialect includes the design of a syntax (an XML type) and of a semantics (e.g., the meaning for the different element of the syntax).

We already mentioned the XHTML that serves the same purpose as HTML (describe simple documents) but with an XML syntax. Perhaps the main difference is that all opening tags should be closed. RSS is another popular dialect for describing content updates that is heavily used for blog entries, news headlines, or podcasts. The following document is an example of RSS content published on the WebDam site (http://webdam.inria.fr/):

```
<?xml version="1.0" encoding="UTF-8" ?>

<rss version="2.0">

<channel>
    < title >Webdam Project</title>
    <atom:link href="http://webdam.inria.fr/wordpress/?feed=rss2"
               rel=" self " type=" application / rss+xml" />
    <link>http://webdam.inria.fr/wordpress</link>
    <description >Foundations of Web Data Management</description>
    <pubDate>Wed, 26 May 2010 09:30:54 +0000</pubDate>

    <item>
        < title >News for the beginning of the year</ title >
        < description >The webdam team wish you an happy new year!</description>
        <link>http://webdam.inria.fr/wordpress/?p=475</link>
        <pubDate>Fri, 15 Jan 2010 08:48:45 +0000</pubDate>
        < dc:creator >Serge</ dc:creator >
        <category>News</category>
    </item>

</channel>
</rss>
```

SVG (Scalable Vector Graphics) is an XML dialect for describing two-dimensional vector graphics, both static and animated. SVG is very powerful and can represent quite complex figures such as all the figures found in the present book! The following is a simple example that shows the combination of a surfacic object with some text. The left part is the SVG encoding, the right one shows the graphic representation that can be obtained by a Web browser or by a specialized tool (e.g., Gimp or Inkscape).

```
<?xml version="1.0" encoding="UTF-8" ?>
<svg xmlns="http://www.w3.org/2000/svg">

  <polygon points="0,0  50,0  25,50"
        style="stroke:#660000;  fill :#cc3333;"/>

  <text x="20" y="40">Some SVG text</text>
</svg>
```

Some SVG text

This example shows that data of any kind can be encoded as XML, and exchanged on the Internet between applications that possibly run under different systems, on different computer architectures, and so on. It is also worth noting that, although this SVG example is trivial and easy to understand even without a rendering tool, in general the content of an XML file may be arbitrarily complex and definitely not suitable for inspection by a human being. Some of the SVG representations for complex figures in this book consist of hundreds of lines of abstruse code that can only be manipulated via appropriate software.

As another illustration, (symbolic) music can be represented in XML. The following is a slightly simplified example of a MusicXML document.

```
<?xml version="1.0" encoding="UTF-8" standalone="no"?>

<score-partwise  version="2.0">
  < part-list >
    <score-part  id="P1">
      <part-name>Music</part-name>
    </ score-part >
  </ part-list >
  <part  id="P1">
      < attributes >
        < divisions >1</ divisions>
      </ attributes >
      <note>
        <pitch>
          <step>C</step>
          <octave>4</octave>
        </pitch>
        <duration>4</duration>
      </note>
      <note>
        <pitch>
```

```
        <step>G</step>
        <octave>4</octave>
      </pitch>
      <duration>4</duration>
    </note>
  </part>
</ score-partwise >
```

This encoding can be interpreted by specialized software and rendered as a musical score:

Some other popular XML dialects are MathML (the mathematical mark-up language), an XML dialect for describing mathematical notation and capturing both its structure and content. It aims at integrating mathematical formulae into World Wide Web documents (if one considers only the presentation aspect, it is something like the mathematics in LATEX): See Exercises. XML/EDI is an XML dialect for business exchanges. It can be used to describe, for instance, invoices, healthcare claims, and project statuses. For the moment, the vast majority of electronic commerce transactions in the world are still not using XML, but (pure) EDI, a non-XML format.

There are just too many dialects to mention them all, ranging from basic formats that represent the key/value configuration of a software (look at your Firefox personal directory!) to large documents that encode complex business process. Above all, XML dialects can be created at will, making it possible for each community to define its own exchange format.

1.4.2 XML Standards

The universality of XML brings an important advantage: Any application that chooses to encode its data in XML can benefit from a wide spectrum of standards for defining and validating types of documents, transforming a document from one dialect to another, searching the document for some pattern, manipulating the document via a standard programming language, and so on. These standards are generic to XML and are defined independently from the specificities of a particular dialect. This also enables the implementation of softwares and languages that are generic, as they apply to XML-formatted information whatever the underlying application domain. For the standards, one should also notably mention:

SAX, the Simple API for XML, is an application programming interface (API) providing a serial access to XML documents seen as a sequence of tokens (its serialization).

DOM, the Document Object Model, is an object-oriented model for representing (HTML and) XML document, independently from the programming language.

DOM sees a document as a tree and provides some navigation in it (e.g., move to parent, first child, left/right sibling of a node). A DOM API is available for all popular languages (Java, C++, C#, Javascript, etc.).

XPath, the XML Path Language, is a language for addressing portions of an XML document.

XQuery, is a flexible query language for extracting information from collections of XML documents. It is to a certain extent the SQL for Web data.

XSLT, the Extensible Stylesheet Language Transformations, is a language for specifying the transformation of XML documents into other XML documents. A main usage of XSLT is to define *stylesheet* to transform some XML document into XHTML so that it can be displayed as a Web page. XSLT is covered on the companion Web site.

Web Services, provide interoperability between machines based on Web protocols. See further discussion later in this chapter.

To make the discussion a bit more precise, we consider some of these in slightly more detail.

Programming Interfaces: SAX and DOM

We start with the first two APIs, that provide two distinct ways to see an XML document. See Figure 1.9.

Let us begin with the SAX programming model. A SAX parser transforms an XML document into a flow of events. Examples of events are the start/end of a document, the start/end of an element, an attribute, a text token, a comment, and so forth. To illustrate, suppose that we obtained some relational data in an XML format. SAX may be used, for instance, to load this data in a relational database as follows:

1. When document start is received, connect to the database;
2. When a *Movie* open tag is received, create a new *Movie* record:
   (a) When a text node is received, assign its content to X;
   (b) When a *Title* close tag is received, assign X to *Movie.Title*;
   (c) When a *Year* close tag is received, assign X to *Movie.Year*, and the like;

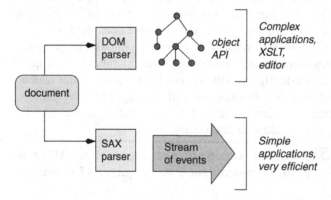

Figure 1.9. Processing an XML document with SAX and DOM.

3. When a *Movie* close tag is received, insert the *Movie* record in the database (and commit the transaction);
4. When document end is received, close the database connection.

SAX is a good choice when the content of a document needs to be examined once (as in the previous example), without having to follow some complex navigation rule that would, for instance, require to turn back during the examination of the content. When these conditions are satisfied, SAX is the most efficient choice as it simply scans the serialized representation. For concreteness, the following piece of code shows a SAX handler written in Java (this example is simplified for conciseness: Please refer to the Web site for a complete version). It features methods that handle SAX events: opening and closing tags; character data.

```java
import org.xml.sax.*;
import org.xml.sax.helpers.LocatorImpl;

public class SaxHandler implements ContentHandler {

    /** Constructor */
    public SaxHandler() {
        super();
    }

    /** Handler for the beginning and end of the document */
    public void startDocument() throws SAXException {
        out.println("Start the parsing of document");
    }

    public void endDocument() throws SAXException {
        out.println("End the parsing of document");
    }

    /** Opening tag handler */
    public void startElement(String nameSpaceURI, String localName,
        String rawName, Attributes attributes) throws SAXException {
        out.println("Opening tag: " + localName);

        // Show the attributes , if any
        if ( attributes.getLength() > 0) {
            System.out.println("  Attributes:  ");
            for (int index = 0;
                    index < attributes.getLength(); index++) {
                out.println("     - " + attributes.getLocalName(index)
                    + " = " + attributes.getValue(index));
            }
        }
    }
```

```
        }

        /** Closing  tag  handler */
        public void endElement(String nameSpaceURI,
                        String localName, String rawName)
            throws SAXException {
            out.print("Closing  tag : " + localName);
            out.println ();
        }

        /** Character  data  handling */
        public void characters (char[] ch, int start ,
                        int end) throws SAXException {
            out.println ("#PCDATA: " + new String(ch, start , end));
        }
    }
```

The other XML API is DOM. A DOM parser transforms an XML document into a tree and, as already mentioned, offers an object API for that tree. A partial view of the class hierarchy of DOM is given in Figure 1.10. We give below a *Preorder* program that takes as argument the name of some XML file and analyzes the document with a DOM parser. The analysis traverses the XML tree in preorder and outputs a message each time an **element** is met. Comments in the code should clarify the details.

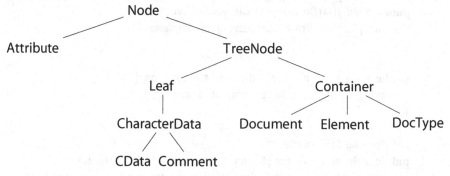

Figure 1.10. DOM class hierarchy.

```
// Import Java  classes
import java.io.*;
import javax.xml.parsers .*;
import org.w3c.dom.*;

/**
 * A DOM class that outputs  all  the  elements  in  preorder
 */
```

```
class DomExample {
  /**
   * The main method.
   */
  public static void main(String args []) {
    // Obtain the document
    File fdom = new File(args [0]);

    // Parser instantiation
    DocumentBuilderFactory factory =
        DocumentBuilderFactory.newInstance();
    DocumentBuilder builder = factory.newDocumentBuilder();

    // Document analysis
    Document dom = builder.parse(fdom);

    // Start the recursive traversal from the root element
    Node elementRoot = dom.getDocumentElement();
    Traversal (elementRoot);
  }

  /**
   * The recursive method.
   */
  private static void Traversal (Node node) {
    String str = new String();
    // Node numbering if it is a text
    if (node.getNodeType() == Node.ELEMENT_NODE) {
      str = "Found element " + node.getNodeName();
      System.out.println ( str + "\n");

      // Recursive cal if node has children
      if (node.hasChildNodes()) {
        // Get the list of children
        NodeList child = node.getChildNodes ();
        // List traversal
        for (int i = 0; i < child.getLength(); i++)
          Traversal ( child.item(i ));
      }
    }
  }
}
```

Several implementation of DOM exist. The example we use here is based on an implementation proposed by the Apache Foundation and a popular DOM parser called Xerces.

Query Languages: XPath, XQuery

Consider a large collection of XML documents, say the archives of the DBLP bibliography. To extract some pieces of information from this collection, a user will typically specify graphically a query. That query may be translated in XPath or XQuery queries in much the same way that a standard graphical query to a relational database is translated to SQL.

In an XML context, queries combine different styles of selection:

1. Queries by keywords as in search engines;
2. Precise queries as in relational systems;
3. Queries by navigation as in Web browsing.

Loosely speaking, XPath is a language that allows the specification of paths between the nodes of an XML document (seen as a tree, as it always should). This specification takes the form of *patterns* that describe more or less tightly a family of paths that comply to the specification. These paths "match" the pattern. An example of XPath pattern query is as follows:

```
document('dblp.xml')//book[publisher = 'Cambridge University Press']
```

It selects the books in the document *dblp.xml* with *Cambridge University Press* for publisher. XPath is at the core of other XML manipulation languages, such as XQuery and XSLT, because it provides a mechanism to navigate in an XML tree.

Here is an example of query with XQuery.

```
for $p in document('dblp.xml')//publisher
let $b := document('dblp.xml')//book[publisher = $p]
where count($b) > 100
return <publisher> $p//name $p//address </publisher>
```

In this query, the variable p scans the list of publishers. For each publisher, variable b contains the sequence of books published by this publisher. The **where** clause filters out the publishers who published fewer than 100 books. Finally, the **return** constructs the result, for each publisher, the name and address.

Web Services

An application on a machine when turned into a Web service can be used by a remote machine. This is the basis of distributed computing over the Internet. Different machines over the network exchange XML data using a particular protocol,

SOAP. They describe their interfaces using yet another language, namely *WSDL* (pronounced wiz-d-l), the Web Services Description Language.

The idea underlying Web services is very simple and will be best explained by an example. Suppose I wrote a program that takes as input a URL and computes the page rank of that page and its classification in some ontology (what it is talking about). Suppose a friend in California wants to use my program. I have to package it, send her all the data (perhaps some databases) the program is using (which may be forbidden by my company). Then we have to solve loads of problems such as software compatibility. It is much simpler to turn my program into a Web service (which takes a couple of minutes) and publish it on a local Web server. My friend can then use it without knowing that I developed it in Java or C++, on Mandrake Linux or Vista, with standard libraries or rather obscure homemade ones.

The core ideas are to exchange (serialized) XML and use a standard protocol for messages. The basis is SOAP, the Service Oriented Architecture Protocol, a protocol for exchanging XML-based messages over the network (typically using HTTP or HTTPS). The most common messaging for SOAP is a Remote Procedure Call (RPC) where a computer (the client) sends a request message to another one (the server); and the server responds by a message to the client. Imagine for instance that you make the following function call from your Client application:

```
pr = getPageRank ("http://webdam.inria.fr /");
```

This call must be shipped to the server. The SOAP protocol encodes the relevant information in XML and transfers the following XML document to the server.

```
<?xml version="1.0" encoding="UTF-8">
<SOAP-ENV:Envelope
 SOAP-ENV:encodingStyle="http://schemas.xmlsoap.org/soap/encoding/"
 xmlns:SOAP-ENV="http://schemas.xmlsoap.org/soap/envelope/"
 xmlns:SOAP-ENC="http://schemas.xmlsoap.org/soap/encoding/"
 xmlns:xsi="http://www.w3.org/1999/XMLSchema-instance"
 xmlns:xsd="http://www.w3.org/1999/XMLSchema">
  <SOAP-ENV:Body>
    <ns1:getPageRank
     xmlns:ns1="urn:PageRankService">
      <param1 xsi:type=" xsd:string ">
        http://webdam.inria.fr/
      </param1>
    </ns1:getPageRank>
  </SOAP-ENV:Body>
</SOAP-ENV:Envelope>
```

Although rather verbose, this SOAP message is simple enough to exhibit the main information that constitutes the remote function call: the server Uniform Resource Name (urn), the function name, and the parameter value. The server then transmits its answer with a SOAP message. This exchange is transparent to the Client: What is exploited here is the capacity of XML to safely encode and exchange data between computers.

Let us finally complete this very brief overview of Web Services by mentionning WSDL, the Web Services Description Language. WSDL is an XML-based language for describing Web services, which specifies the type of their input and output. It can be used, in particular, to generate automatically the correct "stubs" of client applications that takes care of creating the SOAP message that respects the signature (type and number of parameters) of the functions provided by the service.

1.5 FURTHER READING

Before the Web, publication of electronic data was limited to a few scientific and technical areas. With the Web and HTML, it rapidly became universal. HTML is a format meant for presenting documents to humans. However, a lot of the data published on the Web is produced by machines. Moreover, it is more and more the case that Web data are consumed by machines as well. Because HTML is not appropriate for machine processing, *semistructured data models*, and most importantly of a new standard for the Web, namely XML were developed in the 1990s [174]. The use of a semistructured data model as a standard for *data representation* and *data exchange* on the Web brought important improvement to the publication and reuse of electronic data by providing a simple syntax for data that is machine-readable and, at the same time, human-readable (with the help of the so-called stylesheets).

Semistructured data models may be viewed, in some sense, as bringing together two cultures that were for a long while seen as irreconcilable, document systems (with notably SGML [74]) and database systems (with notably relational systems [156]). From a model perspective, there are many similarities with the object database model [39]. Indeed, like XML, the object database model is based on trees, provides an object API, comes equipped with query languages, and offers some form of serialization. As already mentioned, an alternative to XML in some contexts is JSON (see http://www.json.org and the description in Section 20.3), a semistructured model directly derived from the need to serialize the representation of an object that must be exchanged by two programs (typically, a Web browser and a Web server). A main difference is that the very rigorous typing of object databases was abandoned in semistructured data models.

SGML (Standard Generalized Markup Language) is the (complex) 1986 ISO Standard for data storage and exchange. SGML dialects can be defined using DTD. For instance, HTML is such a dialect.

XML is developed and promoted by the World Wide Web Consortium (W3C). XML is a 1998 recommendation of the W3C. Its specification is a couple of dozens of pages long, vs. the hundreds of pages of SGML. It is supported by academic labs such as MIT (U.S.), INRIA (Europe) or Keio University and backed by all the heavy weights of industry notably Oracle, IBM, and Microsoft. The role of W3C is in particular to lead the design of standards where the XML syntax is only the tip of the iceberg. They propose a wide range of them for typing XML [165], querying XML

[182], transforming XML [183], interacting with XML [58], developing distributed applications with XML, etc. See the site of the W3C [161] for more.

The articulation of the notion of semistructured data may be traced to two simultaneous origins, the OEM model at Stanford [8, 132] and the UnQL model at the University of Pennsylvania [134]. See [5] for a first book on the topic.

Specific data formats had been previously proposed and even became sometimes popular in specific domains (e.g. ASN.1 [96]). The essential difference between data exchange formats and semistructured data models is the presence of high-level query languages in the latter. A query language for SGML is considered in [6]. Languages for semistructured data models such as [8, 134] then paved the way for languages for XML [182].

1.6 EXERCISES

1.6.1 XML Documents

Exercise 1.6.1 (well-formed XML documents) *Have you ever written an HTML page? If not, it is time to create your first one: Create a .html home page with your public information: CVs, address, background and hobbies, photos, and so on.*

This page must be a well-formed XHTML document. Use a public XHTML validator to check its well-formedness, and correct any error. Hints: The W3C provides an online validator at http://validator.w3c.org/. You can also add to your browser a validator that checks any page loaded from the Internet (for Firefox, the Web Developer plugin is a good choice).

Exercise 1.6.2 (XML and graphics) *Now, embellish you page with some vector graphics. As a starting point, take the SVG example given in the present chapter, save it in an svg.xml document and add the following instruction somewhere in your XHTML code.*

```
<object data="svg.xml" type="image/svg+xml" width="320" height="240" />
```

Open the page in your browser (of course, the browser should be equipped with an SVG rendering module: Firefox natively supports SVG), and see the graphics displayed in your Web page. Search for some more exciting SVG options and experiment them.

Exercise 1.6.3 *MathML is an XML dialect for the representation of mathematical fomulas in XML. Arithmetic formulas in MathML use a prefix notation, where operators come before their operands. For instance, the prefix notation of*

$$x^2 + 4x + 4$$

is

```
(+ (^ x 2) (* 4 x) 4)
```

When encoded in MathML, this formula is represented by the following document:

```
<?xml version='1.0'?>
<apply>
  <plus/>
  <apply>
    <power/>
    <ci>x</ci>
    <cn>2</cn>
  </apply>
  <apply>
    <times/>
    <cn>4</cn>
    <ci>x</ci>
  </apply>
  <cn>4</cn>
</apply>
```

Note that each parenthesis gives rise to an apply element; operators $+$, $\times$ and, $\wedge$ are, respectively, represented with plus, times and power elements; finally, variables are represented by ci elements, and constants cn elements.

1. *Give the tree for of this MathML document.*
2. *Express the following formulas in MathML*
   - $(x^y + 3xy) \times y$
   - $x^{a+2} + y$
3. *Give the DTD that corresponds to the MathML fragment given above.*

1.6.2 XML Standards

Programming with XML APIs, SAX and DOM, is a good means to understand the features of XML documents. We invite you to realize a few, simple programs, based on examples supplied on our Web site.

These examples are written in Java. You need a SAX/DOM parser: the Xerces open-source parser is easy to obtain, and our programs have been tested with it:

- get the Xerces java archive from http://xerces.apache.org/ and download it sowewhere on your local disk;
- add your Xerces directory to $JAVA_HOME;
- take from our Web site the following files: *SaxExample.java*, *SaxHandler.java*, and *DomExample.java*.

Let us try the SAX program first. It consists of a class, the *handler*, that defines the method triggered when syntactic tokens are met in the parsed XML document (see page 21 for details). The handler class is supplied to the *SAX parser*, which scans the XML document and detects the tokens. Our handler class is in *SaxHandler.java*, and the parser is instantiated and run in *SaxExample.java*. Look at both files; compile them an run *SaxExample*. It takes as input the name of the XML document. For instance, using the *movies.xml* document from our site:

    java SaxExample movies.xml

The DOM example executes the same basic scan of the XML document in pre-order, and outputs the name of each element. Compile it, and run it on the same file:

    java DomExample movies.xml

We also provide a *DomPreorder.java* example that shows a few other features of DOM programming: modification of nodes, and serialization of a DOM object.

For the following exercises, you should download the *dblp.xml* document from the DBLP site: http://www.informatik.uni-trier.de/~ley/db/. The main file is about 700 Mbs, which helps to assess the respective performance of the SAX and DOM approaches.

Exercise 1.6.4 (Performance) *Write a SAX program that counts the number of top-level elements (elements under the element root) in an XML document.*

- *Apply your program to dblp.xml and count the number of references.*
- *Extend your program to count only a subset of the top-level elements, say, journals or books.*

Write the same program in DOM. Run it on dblp.xml and compare the performances.

Exercise 1.6.5 (Tree-based navigation) *Imagine that you need to implement a Navigate program that accesses one or several nodes in an XML documents, referred to by a path in the hierarchy. For instance:*

    java Navigate movies movie title

should retrieve all the <title> nodes from the movies.xml document (nb: This is actually a quite rudimentary XPath evaluator, see the next chapter).

Try to design and implement this program in SAX and DOM. Draw your conclusions.

2

XPath and XQuery

2.1 INTRODUCTION

This chapter introduces XPath and XQuery, two related languages that respectively serve to navigate and query XML documents. XPath is actually a subset of XQuery. Both languages, specified by the W3C, are tightly associated and share in particular the same conceptual modeling of XML documents. Note that the XPath fragment of XQuery has a well-identified purpose (expressing "paths" in an XML tree) and as such can be used independently in other XML processing contexts, such as inside the XSLT transformation language. XQuery uses XPath as a core language for path expressions and navigation.

XQuery is a declarative language and intends to play for XML data the role of SQL in the relational realm. At a syntactical level, it is somewhat inspired from SQL. More importantly, it is expected to benefit from a mixture of physical storage, indexing, and optimization techniques in order to retrieve its result by accessing only a small fraction of its input. XQuery constitutes therefore an appropriate choice when large XML documents or large collections of documents must be manipulated.

In this chapter, we use as running example a *movies* XML database. Each XML document represents one movie and is similar in structure to the sample document shown in Figure 2.1.

We begin the chapter with a bird's-eye view of XQuery principles, introducing the XML data model that supports the interpretation of path expressions and queries, and showing the main features of the two languages. We then consider in more detail XPath and XQuery in a rather informal way. Finally we reconsider XPath more formally, investigating nice connections with first-order logic.

2.2 BASICS

The W3C devoted a great deal of effort (along with heavy documents) to formally define the data model that underlies the interpretation of XPath and XQuery expressions. We just need, for the purpose of this introduction, to understand that

```
<?xml version="1.0" encoding="UTF-8"?>

<movie>
  < title >Spider-Man</ title>
  <year>2002</year>
  <country>USA</country>
  <genre>Action</genre>
  <summary>On a school field trip , Peter Parker (Maguire) is
    bitten by a genetically modified spider . He wakes
    up the next morning with incredible powers. After
    witnessing the death of his uncle (Robertson),
    Parkers decides to put his new skills to use in
    order to rid the city of evil , but someone else
    has other plans. The Green Goblin (Dafoe) sees
    Spider-Man as a threat and must dispose of him. </summary>
  < director  id='21'>
    <last_name>Raimi</last_name>
    <first_name>Sam</first_name>
    <birth_date>1959</birth_date>
  </ director >
  <actor id='19'>
    <first_name>Kirsten</first_name>
    <last_name>Dunst</last_name>
    <birth_date>1982</birth_date>
    <role>Mary Jane Watson</role>
  </actor>
  <actor id='22'>
    <first_name>Tobey</first_name>
    <last_name>Maguire</last_name>
    <birth_date>1975</birth_date>
    <role>Spider-Man / Peter Parker</role>
  </actor>
  <actor id='23'>
    <first_name>Willem</first_name>
    <last_name>Dafoe</last_name>
    <birth_date>1955</birth_date>
    <role>Green Goblin / Norman Osborn</role>
  </actor>
</movie>
```

Figure 2.1. An XML document describing a movie.

XQuery is designed as the database query language for XML sources. As such, it must fulfill some basic requirements, two of the most important being that

1. There exists a well-defined "data model" (i.e., a set of constructs and typing rules that dictate the shape of any information that conceptually constitutes an XML database).
2. The query language is closed (or *composable*) – in plain English, this means that queries operate on instances of the data model and produce instances of the data model.

Let us first consider the corresponding requirements for relational databases. In a relational database, data are represented using two-dimensional "tables." Each table consists of a set of rows with a predefined list of "columns." Given a row and a column, an entry consists of an atomic value of a predefined type specified by the column. This constitutes a simple and effective data model. Regarding the SQL language, each query takes one or several tables as input and produces one table as output. (We ignore here some features such as ordering the rows with **order by** commands.) Even if the query returns a single value, this value is seen as a cell in a one-row, one-column, result table. The closed-form requirement guarantees that queries can be composed to form complex expressions. In other words, one can build complex queries using composition because the output of a query can serve as input to another one.

Let us now consider these requirements in the context of XML. We must be able to model the content of the documents, which is much more flexible and complex than the content of a relational table. We must also model the structure of the database as a set of documents, with possibly quite different contents and structures. And, finally, we need to make sure that any query output is also a collection of XML documents, so that we can compose queries.

A difficulty is that we sometimes want to talk about a tree and we sometimes want to focus on a sequence of trees (the children of a node in a tree). The W3C has therefore introduced a data model which, beyond the usual atomic data types, proposes two constructs: *trees* to model the content of XML documents and *sequences* to represent any ordered collection of "items," an item being either an atomic value or a document.

Another difficulty is that, as we shall see, we sometimes want to talk about collections without duplicates. For instance, the result of the simplest XPath queries is such a collection. Indeed, the specification of XPath 1.0, which is still the most widely implemented version of the language, does not allow arbitrary sequences, but only *node sets*, duplicate-free collections of nodes. So we shall have to carefully distinguish between sequences (ordered lists possibly with duplicates) and duplicate-free collections or node sets.

To conclude this preliminary discussion, we want to stress that XQuery is a functional language based on *expressions*: Any expression takes sequences as inputs and produces a sequence as output. This is probably everything that needs to be remembered at this point. We now illustrate the principles, starting with the tree model of XML documents.

2.2.1 XPath and XQuery Data Model for Documents

In the XQuery model, an XML document is viewed as a tree of *nodes*. Each node in a tree has a *kind*, and possibly a *name*, a *value*, or both. These concepts are important for the correct interpretation of path expressions. Note that this is actually a simplified version of the object-based representation that supports the **Dom** API (see Chapter 1). Here is the list of the important node kinds that can be found in an XML tree:

- **Document**: the *root node* of the XML document, denoted by "/";
- **Element**: element nodes that correspond to the tagged nodes in the document;
- **Attribute**: attribute nodes attached to **Element** nodes;
- **Text**: text nodes (i.e., untagged leaves of the XML tree).

The data model also features **ProcessingInstruction**, **Comment**, and **Namespace** node kinds. The first two can be addressed similarly as other nodes, and the third one is used for technical processing of namespaces that is rarely needed. Therefore, to simplify, we do not consider these node kinds in the following presentation. Another important feature of the XQuery data model is the *data type* that can be attached to element and attribute nodes. This data type comes from an XML Schema annotation (see Chapter 3) of the document. It is a very powerful feature that allows XQuery queries to deal differently with nodes of different declared data types. It also allows for the static verification of a query. However, because of lack of support from implementations, this component of XQuery is sparingly used. Again to simplify, we mostly ignore data types in the remaining of this chapter.

It is worth mentioning that the tree model ignores syntactic features that are only relevant to serialized representations. For instance, literal sections or entities do not appear, since they pertain to the physical representation and thus have no impact on the conceptual view of a document. Entities are supposed to have been resolved (i.e., references replaced by the entity content) when the document is instantiated from its physical representation.

Figure 2.2 shows a serialized representation of an XML document, and Figure 2.3 its interpretation as an XML tree. The translation is straightforward and must be understood by anyone aiming at using XPath or XQuery. Among the few traps, note that the typical fragment <a>v</a> is *not* interpreted as a single node with name a and value v, but as two nodes: an **Element** that bears the name and a **Text** child that bears the value. It is important to keep in mind a few other characteristics that are common to all tree representations and help understand the meaning of expressions:

- The *document order* denotes the order of the nodes when the tree is traversed in pre-order; it is also the order of the serialized representation;
- A tree has a unique **Document** node, called the *root node* of the tree in the following; this root node has a unique child of type **Element**, called the *root element*.

A root node may also have other children such as comments or processing instructions, but as previously mentioned, we ignore them here. Next, for each node in a tree, the concepts of *name* and *value* are defined as follows: (i) an **Element** node

```
<?xml version="1.0"
        encoding="utf-8"?>
<A>
  <B att1='1'>
    <D>Text 1</D>
    <D>Text 2</D>
  </B>
  <B att1='2'>
    <D>Text 3</D>
  </B>
  <C att2="a"
     att3="b"/>
</A>
```

Figure 2.2. Example XML document in serialized form.

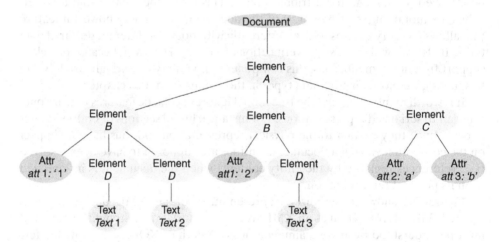

Figure 2.3. Tree representation of the XML document from Figure 2.2.

has a name (i.e., the tag in the serialized representation), but no value; (ii) a **Text** node has a value (a character string), but no name; and (iii) an **Attribute** node has both a name and a value. As we shall see, **Attribute** nodes are special: attributes are not considered as first-class nodes in an XML tree and are addressed in a specific manner.

A term commonly used is "content," which must be distinguished from the notion of "value." Although an **Element** node N has no value, it has a *content*, which is the XML subtree rooted at N. If we consider the serialized representation instead, the content is (equivalently) the part of the document contained between the opening and closing tags of the element. Now one often makes the mistake to see the content of an XML node as the serialized representation. It is important to keep in mind that conceptually it is a tree. To increase the confusion, one sometimes speak of the *textual content* of a node *N*, which is the concatenation of the values of the **Text** nodes, which are descendant of *N*. In others words, the textual content of *N* is obtained from its content by getting rid of all the structural information. This makes sense only when we think of an XML document as structured text.

Although all this may seem confusing at first glance, it is important to be very comfortable with these notions and in particular keep in mind that *the content of a node of an XML tree is the subtree rooted at that node.*

2.2.2 The XQuery Model (Continued) and Sequences

The main construct manipulated by XQuery expressions is the *sequence of items*, a deliberately vague and general structure that covers all kinds of information that can be dealt with in an XML database. An item is either an *atomic value* or a *node*. In the latter case, when the node *N* is an **Element** or a **Document** (i.e., the root node of a document), it represents the whole XML tree rooted at *N*.

Sequences constitute a central concept for XQuery, since a query takes as input one or more sequences and produces as output a sequence.

A sequence may be an enumeration, surrounded with parentheses. The content of a sequence may also be described intentionally (e.g., all integers between 1 and 5).

```
(1, 'a', 1, 'zgfhgf', 2.12)
(1 to 5)
```

Observe that the first sequence mixes integers, characters, character strings, floating numbers. The mixture may also contain nodes and accepts duplicates. Due to the very versatile shape of semistructured information, the data model actually puts almost no restriction on the content of a sequence. An important point is that sequences cannot be embedded inside each other: A sequence is always a flat, ordered, collection of atomic values or nodes. In other words, the following two sequences are identical:

```
(1, (2, 3), (4, 5, 6))
(1, 2, 3, 4, 5, 6)
```

Since querying atomic values is of little interest, a query takes in general as input XML documents or a collection of XML documents. A *collection* is actually nothing other than a persistent sequence of XML documents, which can be referred to by a name. XQuery identifies its input(s) with the following functions:

1. *doc()* takes the URI of an XML document and returns a singleton document tree;

2. *collection*() takes the URI of a collection of XML documents and returns a sequence of trees.

For instance,

---

doc('Spider-Man.xml')
collection ('movies')

The result of *doc('Spider-Man.xml')* is the singleton sequence consisting of the *root node* of the tree representation of the XML content found in Spider-Man.xml. The node kind is **Document**.

As part of our running example, the *movies* collection contains a set of XML documents, each describing a specific movie. The result of *collection('movies')* is the sequence of root nodes of the collection of *movie* documents. In general, the *collection*() function returns a sequence of items. Although its organization is much more flexible, a collection is somehow comparable to tables in the relational model, where items of the collection set play the role of tuples.

The functions *doc*() and *collection*() take as input a URI. They can therefore be used to access a database that is stored either locally or remotely. For instance, the URI *movies* may refer to the database serving all the movie XML documents. In both cases, the output is a sequence of **Document** nodes. Given such sequences available through calls to the *doc*() or *collection*() functions, XPath and XQuery expressions can be expressed to retrieve information from these contents. Such an environment is typically an XML database system (e.g., the EXIST system; see Chapter 5).

2.2.3 Specifying Paths in a Tree: XPath

XPath is a syntactic fragment of XQuery, which forms the basic means of navigating in an XML tree. At its core are *path expressions*, which denote paths in a tree, using a mixture of structural information (node names, node kinds) and constraints on data values. Here is a first example:

---

doc('Spider-Man.xml')/movie/title

An XPath expression consists of *steps*, separated by "/". The preceding expression consists of three steps. The first one returns a singleton with the root node of the document. The second step (movie) returns the children of the root node with name movie. Again, this is a singleton since the root node has only one **Element** child. Finally, the third step (title) returns the sequence of **Element** nodes, of name title, children of the movie element. The sequence of title nodes is the result of the whole XPath expression.

More generally, a path expression is evaluated with respect to a *context node*, which is often (but not always) the root node of some XML document, and its result is a sequence of terminal nodes of the paths that start from the context node and match the expression.

So far, the interpretation is quite similar to the usual navigation in the directory tree of a computer system. XPath is more expressive and permits very flexible navigation in the trees with access to both content and structure of the visited trees. The following example features a *predicate* (i.e., a Boolean expression that must be satisfied for the nodes to be qualified in the result sequence). The interpretation should be clear: one retrieves the nodes corresponding to the actresses of the input document whose last name is Dunst.

doc('Spider-Man.xml')/movie/actor[last_name='Dunst']

One obtains a sequence, with as many actor items as there are matching nodes in the document (here: only one). Note that the item is an **Element** node, *along with its content* (i.e., the subtree at this node). In other word, the (serialized) result is:

```
<actor id='19'>
  <first_name>Kirsten</first_name>
  <last_name>Dunst</last_name>
  <birth_date>1982</birth_date>
  <role>Mary Jane Watson</role>
</actor>
```

The comparison with navigation in file system directories can be extended a little further. Indeed, XPath is not limited to going down the tree, following the "child" axis, but can also access the (unique) parent of a node. The following XPath expression gives all the titles of movies in the movies collection, featuring Kirsten Dunst as an actress.

collection ('movies')/movie/actor[last_name='Dunst']/../ title

To better understand what is going on here, it is probably useful to take a representation of the tree of a specific movie (say, *Spider-Man*), and draw the path that matches the preceding expression (knowing that, as expected, the ".." step denotes the parent of the context node). There exists an equivalent (and maybe more natural) expression:

```
collection ('movies')/movie[actor/last_name='Dunst']/title
```

The power of XPath is however relatively limited in term of node retrieval.[1] Moreover, the result of an XPath expression can only consist of a sequence of nodes from the input document. This is a very severe restriction since it prevents the construction of new XML documents. However, it constitutes a convenient tool for describing classes of paths in XML trees and can be used together with more powerful languages to obtain complex queries.

2.2.4 A First Glance at XQuery Expressions

XQuery is a functional language. An expression is a syntactic construct which operates on a sequence (the input) and produces a sequence (the output). Since the output of an expression can be used as the input of another expression, the combination of expressions yields the mechanism to create very complex queries.

The simplest expression is a literal: Given a sequence S, it returns S. The following is therefore a valid XQuery expression:

```
(1, 'a', 1, 'zgfhgf', 2.12)
```

XQuery becomes more powerful than XPath when it comes to constructing rich output or to expressing complex statements. The following simple examples illustrate the most important features without delving into details.

First, XQuery allows the construction of new documents, whose content may freely mix literal tags, literal values, and results of XQuery expressions. The following shows the construction of an XML document containing the list of movie titles.

```
document {
  < titles >
    { collection ('movies')// title }
  </ titles >
}
```

The *collection*() function is now embedded in an XML literal fragment (formed here of a single root element titles). Expressions can be used at any level of a query, but in order to let the XQuery parser recognize an expression e, which

---

[1] This is all the truer if one restricts the language to the XPath 1.0 fragment, which cannot express much more than these kinds of path expressions. XPath 2.0, with its iteration features described further, is more powerful, but still limited compared to XQuery.

must be evaluated and replaced by its result, the expression *e* must be surrounded by curly braces {} when it appears inside literal elements. Forgetting the braces results in a literal copy of the expression in the result (i.e., it remains uninterpreted). Any number of expressions can be included in a template, thereby giving all freedom to create new XML content from an arbitrarily large number of XML inputs.

Note that, in the preceding query, XPath is used as a core language to denote paths in an existing XML document referred to by the *doc*() expression.

Here is a second example of a powerful XQuery expression that goes far beyond the capabilities of simple path expressions. The following shows a query that returns a list of character string with the title of a movie (published after 2005) and the name of its director.

```
for $m in collection ('movies')/movie
where $m/year >= 2005
return
<film>
  {$m/title/text ()},
  directed by {$m/director/last_name/text()}
</film>
```

The query is syntactically close to the SQL **select-from-where** construct. The **for** clause is similar to the SQL **from**, and defines the range of a variable $m. The **return** clause (in the spirit of SQL **select**) constructs the result, using variable $m as the root of XPath expression. The output obtained from our sample collection, is (disregarding whitespace)

```
<film>A History of Violence, directed by Cronenberg</film>
<film>Match Point, directed by Allen</film>
<film>Marie Antoinette, directed by Coppola</film>
```

Note that the result is a sequence of nodes, and not an XML document.

Expressions based on the **for** clause are called *FLWOR expressions*. This is pronounced "flower" with the "F" standing for **for**, "L" for **let** (a clause not used in the previous example), "W" for **where**, "O"for **order by** (an optional ordering clause), and "R" for **return**. A FLWOR expression must contain at least one (but potentially many) **for** or **let** clause and exactly one **return** clause, the other parts being optional. The expressive power of the language comes from its ability to define variables in flexible ways (**from** and **let**), from supporting complex filtering (**where**) and ordering (**order by**), and allowing the construction complex results (**return**).

2.2.5 XQuery vs XSLT

XQuery is thus a choice language for querying XML documents and producing structured output. As such, it plays a similar role as XSLT, another W3C standardized language for transforming XML documents, which is presented in more detail in the companion Web site of this book, http://webdam.inria.fr/Jorge/. The role of XSLT is to extract information from an input XML document and to transform it into an output document, often in XML, which is also something that XQuery can do. Therefore, both languages seem to compete with one another, and their respective advantages and downsides with respect to a specific application context may not be obvious at first glance. Essentially,

- XSLT is good at *transforming* documents and is, for instance, very well adapted to map the content of an XML document to an XHTML format in a Web application;
- XQuery is good at *efficiently retrieving* information from possibly very large repositories of XML documents.

Although the result of an XQuery query may be XML structured, the creation of complex output is not its main focus. In a publishing environment where the published document may result from an arbitrarily complex extraction and transformation process, XSLT should be preferred.

Note however that, due to its ability to randomly access any part of the input tree, XSLT processors usually store in main memory the whole DOM representation of the input. This may severely impact the transformation performance for large documents. The procedural nature of XSLT makes it difficult to apply rewriting or optimization techniques that could, for example, determine the part of the document that must be loaded or devise an access plan that avoids a full main-memory storage. Such techniques are typical of *declarative* database languages such as XQuery that let a specialized module organize accesses to very large datasets in an efficient way.

We conclude here this introduction to the basics of XQuery. We next visit XPath in more depth.

2.3 XPATH

The term *XPath* actually denotes two different languages for selecting nodes in a tree:

1. XPath 1.0, whose specification was finalized in 1999, is the most widely used version of XPath; implementations exist for a large variety of programming languages, and it is used as an embedded language inside another language in a number of contexts, especially in XSLT 1.0. XPath 1.0 is a simple language for navigating a tree, based on the notion of path expressions, and its expressive power is quite limited, as discussed further. Its data model is somewhat simpler than the XQuery data model discussed earlier in this chapter: node sets instead of sequences, and no data type annotations.

2. XPath 2.0, standardized in 2007, is an extension of XPath 1.0 that adds a number of commodity features, extends the data model to that of XQuery, and adds some expressiveness to the language, with the help of path intersection and complementation operators, as well as iteration features. XPath 2.0 is a proper subset of XQuery, and is also used inside XSLT 2.0. Apart from these two contexts, implementations of XPath 2.0 are rare. With a few technical exceptions, XPath 2.0 is designed to be backwards compatible with XPath 1.0: XPath 1.0 expressions are, mostly, valid XPath 2.0 expressions with the same results.

In this section, we mostly discuss XPath 1.0 and its core aspect, path expressions. We discuss briefly at the end of the section the additional features available in XPath 2.0. As already mentioned, a path expression consists of *steps*. It is evaluated over a list, taking each element of the list, one at a time. More precisely, a step is always evaluated in a specific *context*

$$[\langle N_1, N_2, \ldots, N_n \rangle, N_c]$$

consisting of a *context list* $\langle N_1, N_2, \ldots, N_n \rangle$ of nodes from the XML tree; and *a context node* N_c belonging to the context list, the node that is currently being processed. The result of a path expression, in XPath 1.0, is a *node set*. Here is a subtlety. The term *set* insists on the fact that there is no duplicate. Now to be able to be reused in another step, this set has to be turned into a sequence (i.e., be equipped with an order). We shall see how this is achieved.

2.3.1 Steps and Path Expressions

An XPath *step* is of the form:

axis::node-test$[P_1][P_2]\ldots[P_n]$

Here, *axis* is an *axis name* indicating the direction of the navigation in the tree, *node-test* specifies a selection on the node, and each P_i ($n \geq 0$) is a *predicate* specifying an additional selection condition. A step is evaluated with respect to a *context* and returns a *node set*. The following examples of steps illustrate these concepts:

1. child::A denotes all the **Element** children of the context node that have A for name; child is the axis, A is the node test (it restricts the selected elements based on their names), and there is no predicate. This very frequently used step can be denoted A for short.
2. descendant::C[@att1=1] denotes all the **Element** nodes descendant of the context node, named C and having an **Attribute** node att1 with value 1. Observe how a node test is used to specify the name of the node and a predicate is used to specify the value of an attribute.
3. parent::*[B] denotes the parent of the context node, whatever its name may be (node test *) and checking it has an **Element** child named B. The predicate here checks the existence of a node. Since each node has a single parent, for a context node, the result is a collection of one element (the parent has a B child) or is empty (the test failed).

A path *expression* is of the form:

$$[/]step_1/step2/\ldots/step_n$$

When it begins with "/", it is an *absolute* path expression and the context of the first step is in that case the *root node*. Otherwise, it is a *relative* path expression. For a relative path expression, the context must be provided by the environment where the path evaluation takes place. This is the case, for instance, with XSLT where XPath expressions can be found in *templates*: the XSLT execution model ensures that the context is always known when a template is interpreted, and this context serves to the interpretation of all the XPath expressions found in the template.

The following are examples of XPath expressions:

1. /A/B is an *absolute* path expression, which denotes the **Element** nodes with name B, children of the root element A;
2. /A/B/@att1[. > 2] denotes all the **Attribute** nodes with name att1 of the nodes obtained with the previous expression, whose values are greater than 2.
3. ./B/descendant::text() is a *relative* path expression, which denotes all the **Text** nodes descendant of an **Element** B, itself child of the context node.

In the last two expressions, "." is an abbreviation of the step self::node(), which refers to the context node itself. The axis self represents the "stay-here" navigation, and the node() predicates is true for all nodes.

2.3.2 Evaluation of Path Expressions

The result of a path expression is a sequence of nodes obtained by evaluating successively the steps of the expression, from left to right. A step $step_i$ is evaluated with respect to the context of $step_{i-1}$. More precisely:

- For $i = 1$ (first step): if the path expression is *absolute*, the context is a singleton, the root of the XML tree; otherwise (for *relative* path expressions) the context is defined by the environment.
- For $i > 1$: if $\mathcal{N}_i = \langle N_1, N_2, \ldots, N_n \rangle$ is the result of step $step_{i-1}$, $step_i$ is successively evaluated with respect to the context $[\mathcal{N}_i, N_j]$, for each $j \in [1, n]$.

The result of the path expression is the node set obtained after evaluating the last step. As an example, consider the evaluation of /A/B/@att1. The path expression is absolute, so the context consists of the root node of the tree (Figure 2.4).

The first step, A, is evaluated with respect to this context and results in the element node that becomes the context node for the second step (Figure 2.5).

Next, step B is evaluated, and the result consists of the two children of A named B. Each of these children is then taken in turn as a context node for evaluating the last step @att1.

1. Taking the first element B child of A as context node, one obtains its attribute att1 (Figure 2.6);
2. Taking the second element B child of A as context node, one obtains its attribute att1 (Figure 2.7).

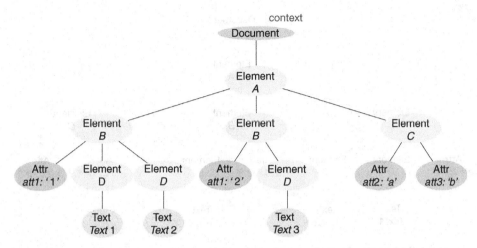

Figure 2.4. First step of the evaluation of /A/B/@att1.

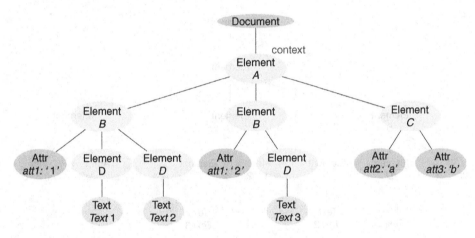

Figure 2.5. Second step of the evaluation of /A/B/@att1.

The final result is the union of all the results of the last step, @att1. This union is a set-theoretic way (i.e., duplicates are eliminated). It is turned into a sequence (i.e., ordered) using an order that, as we shall see, is specified by the axis of the last step.

2.3.3 Generalities on Axes and Node Tests

Given a context list, the axis determines a new context list. For each node in turn, the node test is evaluated filtering out some of the nodes. Then each predicate is evaluated, and the nodes that fail some test are eliminated. This yields the resulting context list.

Table 2.1 gives the list of all XPath axes. Using them, it is possible to navigate in a tree, up, down, right, and left, one step or an arbitrary number of steps. As already mentioned, the axis also determines the order on the set of resulting nodes. It is in

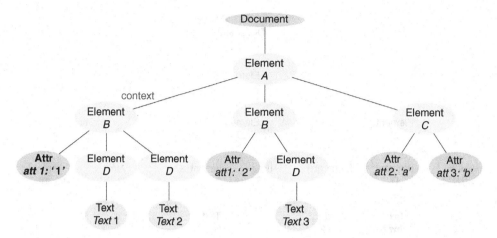

Figure 2.6. Evaluation of @att1 with context node B[1].

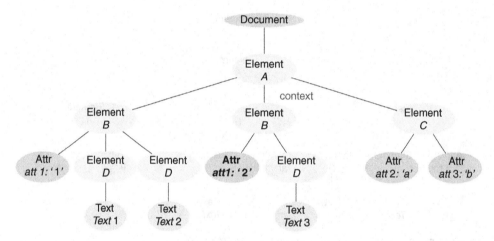

Figure 2.7. Evaluation of @att1 with context node B[2].

most cases the document order. In some cases, it is the *reverse document order*. The rule can be simply remembered as: for *forward* axes, positions follow the document order; for *backward* axes (cf. Table 2.1), they are in reverse order. One can also see that they correspond to how they are "naturally" visited following the navigation from the context node.

An axis is always interpreted with respect to the context node. It may happen that the axis cannot be satisfied because of some incompatibility between the kind of the context node and the axis. An empty node set is then returned. The cases of such "impossible" moves are the following:

■ When the context node is a *document node*: parent, attribute, ancestor, ancestor-or-self, following-sibling, preceding, preceding-sibling.

Table 2.1. XPath Axes	
child	(*default axis*)
parent	Parent node.
attribute	Attribute nodes.
descendant	Descendants, excluding the node itself.
descendant-or-self	Descendants, including the node itself.
ancestor	Ancestors, excluding the node itself. **Backward** axis.
ancestor-or-self	Ancestors, including the node itself. **Backward** axis.
following	Following nodes in *document order* (except descendants).
following-sibling	Following siblings in *document order.*
preceding	Preceding nodes in *document order* (except ancestors). **Backward** axis.
preceding-sibling	Preceding siblings in *document order.* **Backward** axis.
self	Context node itself.

■ When the context node is an *attribute node*: child, attribute, descendant, descendant-or-self, following-sibling, preceding-sibling.

■ When the context node is a *text node*: child, attribute, descendant, descendant-or-self.

We briefly observe next a subtlety. Attributes are not considered as part of the "main" document tree in the XPath data model. An attribute node is therefore not the child of the element on which it is located. (To access them when needed, one uses the attribute axis.) On the other hand, the parent axis, applied to an attribute node, returns the element on which it is located. So, applying the path parent::*/child::* on an attribute node, a node set that does not include the node one started with is returned.

We next detail the different axes. To be able to illustrate, we also use node tests. These will be detailed further.

2.3.4 Axes

Child Axis The child axis denotes the **Element** or **Text** children of the context node. This is the default axis, used when the axis part of a step if not specified. So, child::D is in fact equivalent to D. See Figure 2.8.

Parent Axis The parent axis denotes the parent of the context node. The result is always an **Element** or a **Document** node, or an empty node-set (if the parent does not match the node test or does not satisfy a predicate). One can use as node test an element name. The node test * matches all names. The node test node() matches all node kinds. These are the standard tests on element nodes. For instance:

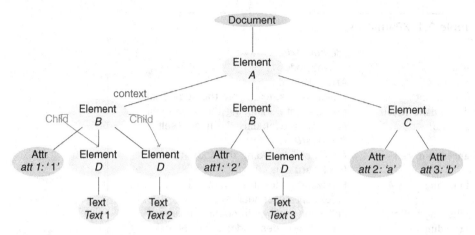

Figure 2.8. The child axis.

■ if the context node is one of the B elements, the result of parent::A is the root element of our sample document; one obtains the same result with parent::* or parent::node();

■ if the context node is the root element node, then parent::* returns an empty set, but the path parent::node() returns the root node of the document.

The expression parent::node() (the parent of the context node) may be abbreviated as "..."

Attribute Axis The attribute axis retrieves the attributes of the context node. The node test may be either the attribute name, or @* which matches all attribute names. So, assuming the context node is the C element of our example,

■ @att1 returns the attribute named att1;

■ @* returns the two attributes of the context node.

Descendant Axis The descendant axis denotes all nodes in the subtree of the context node, *except* the **Attribute** nodes. The node test text() matches any **Text** node. Assume for instance that the context node is the first B element in the document order (Figure 2.9). Then

■ descendant::node() retrieves *all* nodes descendants of the context node, except attributes (Figure 2.9);

■ descendant::* retrieves all **Element** nodes, whatever their name, which are descendant of the context node;

■ descendant::text() retrieves all **Text** nodes, whatever their name, which are descendant of the context node.

Observe that the context node is not a descendant of itself. If one wants it in the resulting context list, one should use instead descendant-or-self.

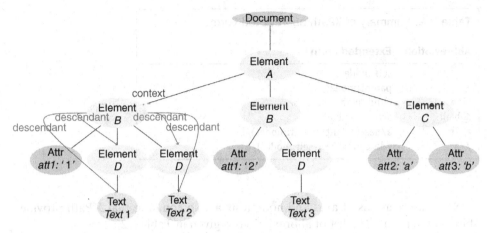

Figure 2.9. Result of descendant::node().

Ancestor Axis The ancestor axis denotes all ancestor nodes of the context node. The result of ancestor::node(), when the context node is the first B element, consists of both the element root and the root node. Again, if one wants the context node to belong to the result, one should use ancestor-or-self instead.

Following and Preceding Axes The following and preceding axes denote, respectively, all nodes that follow the context node in the document order, or that precede the context node, with the exception of descendant or ancestor nodes. **Attribute** nodes are *not* selected.

Sibling Axes The *siblings* of a node N are the nodes that have the same parent as N. XPath proposes two axes: following-sibling and preceding-sibling, which denote, respectively, the siblings that follow and precede the context node in document order. The node test that can be associated with these axes are those already described for descendant or following: a node name (for **Element**), * for all names, text() or node(). Note that, as usual, the sibling axes do not apply to attributes.

2.3.5 Node Tests and Abbreviations

Node tests are closely related to the kinds of the nodes. Their usage is therefore constrained to the kind of nodes returned by axis. Node tests are of the following forms:

- node() matches any node, except attributes;
- text() matches any **Text** node;
- * matches any named node (i.e., any **Element** node, or any **Attribute** for the attribute axis);
- ns:* or ns:blah match elements or attributes in the namespace bound to the prefix ns; the second form also imposes the exact name.

Table 2.2. Summary of XPath abbreviated Forms

Abbreviation	Extended Form
.	self::node()
..	parent::node()
blah	child::blah
@blah	attribute::blah
a//b	a/descendant-or-self::node()/b
//a	/descendant-or-self::node()/a

Some associations of axes and node tests are so common that XPath provides abbreviated forms. The list of abbreviations is given in Table 2.2.

2.3.6 Predicates

Predicates are optional Boolean expressions built with *tests* and Boolean connectors (and, or). Negation is expressed with the *not()* Boolean function. A *test* may take one of the following forms:

■ an XPath expression; the semantics is that the resulting node set is nonempty;
■ a comparison or a call to a Boolean function.

Predicates, the last components of an XPath expression step, provide the means to select nodes with respect to content of the document, whereas axis and node test only address the structural information. The processor first creates a sequence of nodes from the axis and the node test. The nodes in the sequence are then tested for each predicate (if any), one predicate after the other. Only those nodes for which each predicate holds are kept.

In order to understand the meaning of a precidate, we must take into account the context of the step evaluation. Recall that an XPath step is *always* evaluated with respect to the context of the previous step. This context consists of a context list, and a context node from this list. The size of the context list is known by the function *last()*, and the position of the context node in the list by *position()*.

It is very common to use these functions in predicates. For instance, the expression:

```
//B/descendant :: text()[position() = 1]
```

denotes the first **Text** node descendant of each node B. Figure 2.10 shows the result. Using the position is so common that when the predicates consists of a single number n, this is assumed to be an abbreviation for *position()* $= n$. The previous expression is therefore equivalent to

```
//B/descendant :: text()[1]
```

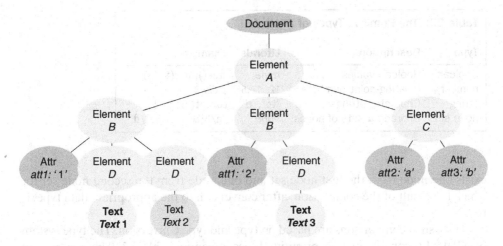

Figure 2.10. Result of //B/descendant::text()[position()=1].

Expression //B[last()] denotes therefore the last element B in the document (it is an abbreviation for //B[position()=last()]). A predicate on a position must be carefully interpreted with respect to the context when the *position*() and *last*() functions are evaluated. It should be clear, for instance, that the following expressions all give different results (look at our example document, and try to convince yourself!):

1. //B[1]//text(),
2. //B[1]//text()[1],
3. //B//text()[1], and
4. //B/D/text()[1].

Conversions in XPath
Since a predicate often consists in some test on the value or on the content of some document node(s), its evaluation may require a *conversion* to the appropriate type, as dictated by the comparator or the constant value used in the predicate expression. Consider for instance the following examples:

- B/@att1 = 3
- /A/B = /A/C/@att2
- /A/B = /A/C

The first case is a simple (and natural) one. It just requires a conversion of the value of the att1 attribute to a number so that the comparison may take place. Note that this may not always be possible. For instance, if the value of the attribute is "Blah," this string cannot be coerced to be an integer and the comparison simply returns false. The second case is more intricate. Suppose the /A/B expression returns a sequence of nodes and /A/C/@att2 returns a single attribute. Since this expression is perfectly legal in XPath, the language defines type conversion rules to interpret this comparison. Finally the last case is a comparison between two node sets. Here again, a rule that goes far beyond the traditional meaning of the equality operator is used in XPath: the result of the comparison between two node sets is true if there

Table 2.3. The Primitive Types of XPath 1.0

Type	Description	Literals	Examples
Boolean	Boolean values	*none*	true(), not($a=3)
number	Floating-point numbers	12, 12.5	1 div 33
string	Character strings	"to", 'ti'	concat('Hello','!')
node set	Unordered sets of nodes	*none*	/a/b[c=1 or @e]/d

exists one node from the first node set and one node from the second node set for which the result of the comparison, after conversion to the appropriate data type, is true.

Thus, such comparisons are based on type and type conversion. The type system of XPath 1.0 consists of four primitive types, given in Table 2.3. The result of an XPath expression (including constant values) can be *explicitly* converted using the *boolean()*, *number()* and *string()* functions. There is no function for converting to a node set, since this conversion is naturally done in an *implicit* way most of the time. The conversion obeys rules that try, as far as possible, to match the natural intuition.

Conversion to a Boolean

Here are the rules for *converting to a Boolean*:

- A number is true if it is neither 0 nor *NaN*. (*NaN* stands for *Not a Number*. It is a value of the number type representing an undefined or unrepresentable value.)
- A string is true if its length is not 0.
- A node set is true if it is not empty.

An important conversion rule is the one that states that a node set is true if it is nonempty. Consider the following two examples:

- //B[@att1=1]: all nodes B having an attribute att1 with value 1;
- //B[@att1]: all nodes B having an attribute named att1.

In this last example, @att1 is an XPath expression whose result is a node set which is either empty or contains a single node, the att1 attribute. Found in a predicate, it is converted to a Boolean. If, for a B node, the node set resulting from @att1 is nonempty (the current context node has an att1 attribute), the set is converted to the Boolean true.

Converting a Node Set to a String

Here are the rules for *converting a node set to a string*:

- The string value of an element or document node is the concatenation of the character data in all the text nodes that are its children.
- The string value of a text node is its character data.
- The string value of an attribute node is the attribute value.

```
<a toto="3">
  <b  titi ='tutu'><c /></b>
  <d>tata</d>
</a>
```

Figure 2.11. XML file illustrating types conversion.

■ The string value of a node set is the string value of its first item in document order.[2]

These rules are illustrated by the following examples, based on the document of Figure 2.11:

■ boolean(/a/b) is true;
■ boolean(/a/e) is false;
■ string(/) is "tata" (assuming all whitespace-only text nodes are stripped);
■ string(/a/@toto) is "3";
■ string(/a/*) evaluates to the empty string in XPath 1.0; it raises an error in XPath 2.0.

This concludes this presentation of the essential principles of XPath. All the material presented so far is valid for XPath 1.0, which is the specification that is most commonly implemented nowadays. Some features specific to XPath 2.0 are introduced in Section 2.3.7. Note also that the expressiveness of XPath is extended with specific *functions* that provide ad hoc computations. For a large part, these functions are normalized and now belong to the XQuery specification. XML systems often add their own built-on functions, and the ability to create new ones. Chapter 5, devoted to the EXIST system, gives a list of the most useful ones.

2.3.7 **XPath 2.0**

We briefly mention here the most important extensions that the XPath 2.0 language adds to XPath 1.0; since XPath 2.0 is a subset of XQuery, all of these are usable in XQuery:

■ **Improved data model**, tightly associated with XML Schema. XPath 2.0 fully follows the XQuery data model presented earlier, including schema annotations and sequences (the semantics of simple path expressions remain the same, however; in particular the result of a path expression does not contain duplicate nodes and is sorted either in document order or in reverse document order, depending on the last step of the path).

---

[2] This behavior is specific to XPath 1.0. In XPath 2.0, it is an error to cast a sequence of more than one item to a string.

- **More expressive** language features, especially allowing to compute the intersection or set difference of a path operation (respectively, intersect and except), to branch depending on the result of a condition (if(...) then ... else ...), and to iterate over a sequence (for ... return, some ... satisfies and every ... satisfies expressions). The for ... return expression is a restriction of the more general XQuery FLWOR expression. Here is a showcase of some of these new capabilities of the language:

  //a//b intersect //a//c
  if(/a/b) then /a/c else /a/d
  for $x in //a return ($x,$x/..)
  //a[some $x in * satisfies $x = //b]

- **More precise** operators for value comparisons: eq, ne, or le behave similarly as =, !=, and <, except they can only be applied to atomic values, not sequences of length greater than one. In the presence of schema annotations, comparison behaves accordingly to the data types of the operands. A new is operator allows testing node identity.
- **Ease-of-use** with many new built-in functions, including regular expression matching, date and time manipulation, and extraction of distinct values in a sequence.

XPath 2.0 also introduces new node tests:

item() any node or atomic value;
element() any element node;
element(author) any element named author;
element(*, xs:person) any element of type xs:person;
attribute() any attribute.

Finally, XPath 2.0 also permits nested paths expressions: any expression that returns a sequence of nodes can be used as a step. The following expression is for instance valid in XPath 2.0, but not in XPath 1.0.

/book/(author | editor)/name

2.4 FLWOR EXPRESSIONS IN XQUERY

We delve in this section in more detail into the fundamental aspect of XQuery, namely FLWOR expressions. As already mentioned, FLWOR queries are very close, syntactically and semantically, to SQL queries formed with **select**, **from**, **where**, and **order by**. A major difference is that the output of a SQL queries is limited to the creation of flat tuples, whereas XQuery is able to nest query results in order to create complex documents with hierarchical structure.

In its simplest form, a FLWOR expression provides just an alternative to XPath expressions. For instance:

```
let $year:=1960
for $a in doc('Spider-Man.xml')//actor
where $a/birth_date >= $year
return $a/last_name
```

is equivalent to the XPath expression //actor[birth_date>=1960]/last_name.

Actually FLWOR expressions are much more expressive and, in general, cannot be rewritten simply with XPath. Let us now examine in turn the clauses **for**, **let**, **where**, and **return**. The use of **order by** is straightforward: it allows for the ordering of the sequence processed by the **return** clause, in the same way as the SQL keyword of the same name; the ascending or descending character of the order is specified with the **ascending** (default behavior) or **descending** keywords following the sort criterion.

2.4.1 Defining Variables: The for and let Clauses

A FLWOR expression starts with an arbitrary (nonzero) number of **for** and **left** clauses, in whatever order. A **for** clause defines a variable that ranges over a sequence. The sequence may be obtained by many means. Most commonly one uses the result of an XPath expression, and the sequence often consists of nodes with similar structure. However, nothing prevents a variable to range over a heterogeneous sequence that mixes values and nodes of completely unrelated structures. The following variant of the previous query is perfectly legal:

```
for $a in doc('Spider-Man.xml')//*
where $a/birth_date >= 1960
return $a/last_name
```

Note that $a now ranges over *all* the element nodes of the document. The semantics of XQuery states that the result is instantiated only for nodes that feature both a birth_date and a last_name. If only actor nodes have both, the two are equivalent. However, this second query is typically less efficient, in particular if many nodes have one of the two and not the other.

The range of a **for** clause can also be a sequence of values, as in

```
for $i in (1 to 10) return $i
```

As all loops in any language, **for** clauses can be nested:

```
for $i in (1 to 10) return
  for $j in (1 to 2) return $i * $j
```

This expression realizes a *cross product* of the two input sequences. The bindings generated by these expressions consist of all the possible pairs of values. XQuery allows a more concise syntactic variant:

```
for $i in (1 to 10), $j in (1 to 2)
  return $i * $j
```

In all cases, the result of a **for** expression is the sequence of nodes and values obtained by instantiating the content of the **return** clause. In fact, a **for** clause is just an instance of an XQuery expression that returns a sequence. As such, it can be used as the range of another sequence. The following query is valid, and enumerates the multiples of 6 from 6 to 60:

```
for $i in (for $j in (1 to 10) return $j * 2)
  return $i * 3
```

XQuery is a functional language: Any expression takes as input a sequence and returns a sequence. This allows expressions to be nested in one another without restrictions.

The **let** clause is just a simple way of defining a variable and assigning a value to it. The variable just acts as a synonym for its value (which, of course, is a sequence obtained by any convenient means, ranging from literals to complex queries). the following defines $m to be a shorthand for the root element of the *Spider-Man.xml* document.

```
let $m := doc('movies/Spider-Man.xml')/movie
return $m/director/last_name
```

Once defined, a variable can be used as its value. In the following example, the **let** clause could easily be avoided. In general, **let** is essentially a convenient way of referring to a value.

```
let  $m := doc('movies/Spider-Man.xml')/movie
for  $a in $m/actor
return $a/last_name
```

The scope of a variable is that of the FLWOR expression where it is defined. Since XQuery is a pure functional language, variables cannot be redefined or updated within their scope (the same rule holds for XSLT). They are in effect *constants*. This yields sometimes strange behavior, as shown by the following example:

```
let  $j := 0
for  $i in (1 to 4)
   let  $j := $j + $i
return $j
```

One might expect that $j works like an accumulator which stores successively the values $(1, 1+2, 1+2+3, 1+2+3+4)$. But $j instead is redefined at each iteration of the **for** loop, and the resulting sequence is simply $(1, 2, 3, 4)$.

One must consider XQuery variables, just like XSLT variables, as references to values, and not as storage unit whose content can be accessed and replaced. There is indeed nothing like a global register holding some information shared by all expressions. The XQuery user must comply to the functional spirit of the language, and design its operations as trees of expressions that receive and transmit sequences, without any form of side effect. The sequence $(1, 1+2, 1+2+3, 1+2+3+4)$ can be obtained by

```
for  $i in 1 to 4 return sum (1 to $i)
```

2.4.2 Filtering: The Where Clause

The optional **where** clause allows to express conditional statements. It is quite similar to its SQL counterpart. The difference lies in the much more flexible structure of XML documents and in the impact of this flexibility on the interpretation of the **where** statement. A few examples follow. The first one retrieves titles of films in the *movies* collection that are directed by Woody Allen, in lexicographic order.

```
for  $m in collection ("movies")/movie
where $m/director/last_name='Allen'
order by $m/title
return $m/title
```

This first example resembles the use of **where** in SQL. Variable $m ranges over the collection of movies, and each movie is selected if and only if its (unique) director is named Allen.

A first comment is that, at least in the absence of schema, nothing guarantees that the path

movie/director/last_name

is always found in in the *movies* collection. In a relational database context, data always comply to a known schema, and the query parser is always able to determine whether a query matches the schema or not, in which case an error (with explanatory messages) is produced. This is no longer systematically true in an XML database context. If the schema is unknown, the parser accepts any syntactically correct expression and attempts to match the paths in the query with the documents found in the scope of the query. If a path does not exist, then this results either in an evaluation to false (in the **where** clause) or an empty result (in the **return** clause). A downside of this flexibility, from the user point of view, is that mistakes in query expressions will not be rejected by the parser.

Here is another example which is only a small restatement of the previous one. We are looking for movies featuring Kirsten Dunst as an actress.

```
for  $m in collection ("movies")/movie
where $m/actor/last_name='Dunst'
order by $m/title
return $m/title
```

The query is syntactically correct and delivers the expected result. The subtle point here is that the path $m/actor/last_name returns a sequence of nodes (the list of actors in a movie), which is compared to a single value ("Dunst"). This is a specific example for the more general rule for evaluating comparison operators between two sequences: If *at least* one successful matching is found between one element of the left sequence and one element of the right one, then it evaluates to true, else to false. For our example, this can be stated as: "Return those movies for which at least one of the actor names is 'Dunst'."

2.4.3 The return Clause

The **return** clause is a mandatory part of a FLWOR expression and always comes last. It is instantiated once for each binding of the variable in the **for** clause that passed the **where** test. The body of **return** may include arbitrary XQuery expressions, but it often contains literal XML fragments that serve to structure the output of the query. Inside these XML fragments, XQuery expressions must be surrounded with braces so that the parser can identify them. Actually, nesting expressions in a **return** clause is the only means of creating nonflat results, and so complex XML documents. The following examples shows how to output a textual representation of a movie featuring Kirsten Dunst.

A first loop outputs the information that functionally depends on each movie.

```
for $m in collection ("movies")/movie
let $d := $m/director
where $m/actor/last_name='Dunst'
return
  <div>{
  $m/title/text (), ' directed by ',
        $d/first_name/text (), ' ', $d/last_name/text()
  }</div>
```

As it appears inside a literal element, the sequence inside the curly braces is interpreted as a sequence of nodes to be inserted inside the element. Atomic values (strings, numbers, etc.) are converted into text nodes containing this value, and adjacent text nodes are merged. This notation facilitates the production of text mixing literal and dynamic values. The query returns the following result:

```
<div>Marie Antoinette, directed by Sofia Coppola</div>
<div>Spider-Man, directed by Sam Raimi</div>
```

Now we need to add the list of actors. This requires a second FLWOR expression, inside the **return** clause of the first one.

```
for $m in collection ("movies")/movie
let $d := $m/director
where $m/actor/last_name='Dunst'
return
  <div>{
  $m/title/text (), ' directed by ',
        $d/first_name/text (), $d/last_name/text()}, with
  <ol>{
    for $a in $m/actor
      return <li>{concat($a/first_name, ' ', $a/last_name,
                  ' as ', $a/role)}</li>
  }</ol>
  </div>
```

XQuery comes equipped with a large set of functions, namely all functions from XPath 2.0 (see Chapter 5 on EXIST for a short list). The preceding query uses *concat*(), as an alternative of the merging of text nodes used previously. One obtains finally the following output:

```
<div>Marie Antoinette, directed by Sofia Coppola, with
<ol>
<li>Kirsten Dunst as Marie Antoinette</li>
<li>Jason Schwartzman as Louis XVI</li>
</ol>
</div>

<div>Spider-Man, directed by Sam Raimi, with
<ol>
<li>Kirsten Dunst as Mary Jane Watson</li>
<li>Tobey Maguire as Spider-Man / Peter Parker</li>
<li>Willem Dafoe as Green Goblin / Norman Osborn</li>
</ol>
</div>
```

2.4.4 Advanced Features of XQuery

In addition to FLWOR expressions, a number of aspects of the XQuery language are worth mentioning, some of which inherited from XPath 2.0.

Distinct values from a sequence can be gathered in another sequence with the help of the XPath 2.0 function *distinct-values()*. (This loses identity and order.) This is useful to implement grouping à la SQL **group by**. For instance, the query "Return each publisher with their average book price" can be expressed as:

```
for $p in
  distinct-values(doc("bib.xml")//publisher)
  let $a :=
  avg(doc("bib.xml")//book[publisher=$p]/price)
  return
    <publisher>
      <name>{ $p/text() }</name>
      <avgprice>{ $a }</avgprice>
    </publisher>
```

The **if-then-else** branching feature of XPath 2.0 is also often useful, as in the following example that extracts some information about published resources, depending on their kind:

```
for $h in doc("library.xml")//publication
return
  <publication>
    { $h/title,
```

```
      if  ($h/@type = "journal")
      then $h/editor
      else  $h/author }
</publication>
```

The existential and universal quantifier expressions from XPath can be used to express such queries as "Get the document that mentions sailing and windsurfing activities" or "Get the document where each paragraph talks about sailing."

```
for $b in doc("bib.xml")//book
where some $p in $b//paragraph
    satisfies  (contains($p," sailing ")
                   and contains($p,"windsurfing"))
return $b/title
```

```
for $b in doc("bib.xml")//book
where every $p in $b//paragraph
                  satisfies  contains($p," sailing ")
return $b/title
```

Finally, it is possible to define functions in XQuery. Such functions may be recursive. This turns XQuery into a full-fledged, Turing-complete, programming language, which is a major departure from the limited expressive power of a language like XPath. The following example shows how to define and use a function computing the factorial of a positive integer. This example also illustrates the use of primitive XML Schema types, and the fact that XQuery programs need not contain FLWOR expressions.

```
declare namespace my="urn:local";
declare namespace xs="http://www.w3.org/2001/XMLSchema";

declare function my: factorial ($n as xs: integer)
   as xs: integer {
   if ($n le 1) then
     1
   else
     $n * my: factorial ($n - 1)
};

my: factorial (10)
```

We end here this practical introduction to the XPath and XQuery languages. The following section explores the theoretical foundations of the XPath language.

2.5 XPATH FOUNDATIONS

The main role of XPath is the selection of nodes in a tree. Its semantics is defined as some form of guided navigation in the tree browsing for particular nodes on the way. The language is rather elegant and avoids the use of explicit variables. This should be contrasted with a language such as first-order logic (FO for short), elegant in a different way, that is built around the notion of variable. In this section, we highlight a surprisingly deep connection between the navigational core of XPath 1.0, called in the following navigational XPath, and a fragment of FO, namely, FO limited to using at most two variables. We shall also mention other results that highlight the connection between various fragments of XPath 1.0 and 2.0 and FO.

These connections are best seen with an alternative semantics of XPath that proceeds bottom-up (i.e., starting from the leaves of the XPath expression and moving to its root). The "official" semantics that we previously presented suggests simple top-down implementations that turn out to be very inefficient on some queries. Indeed, the first XPath implementations that followed too closely the specification were running on some queries in time that was exponential in the size of the tree. To give an intuition of the issues, we present an example of such a query. Consider the document `<a><d/><d/></a>` and the sequence of XPath "pathological" expressions:

$pathos_0$ /a/d
$pathos_1$ /a/d/parent::a/d
$pathos_2$ /a/d/parent::a/d/parent::a/d
$\dots$

$pathos_i$ /a/d(/parent::a/d)^i

A naive evaluation of these queries that follows closely the top-down semantics we discussed has exponential running time: each addition of a navigation "up" and "down" doubles the time of the evaluation. Important improvements in algorithms for evaluating XPath are now fixing these issues. Indeed it is now known that the complexity of XPath is PTIME for all queries, and good XPath processors do not run in exponential time for any query.

The problem with the evaluation of the previous query comes from an incorrect interpretation of the semantics of XPath. The result of the $pathos_1$ expressions is the node set (d_1, d_2), where d_1 is the first d node and d_2 the second. If the node set is seen as a sequence, as in XPath 2.0, the order is that of the document because the last axis is child. Now, for each i, the result of $pathos_i$ is the same node set with the same order. (And no! $pathos_2$ is not (d_1, d_2, d_1, d_2) because duplicates are eliminated in node sets.)

We next, in turn, (i) introduce a formal relational view of an XML tree, (ii) specify navigational XPath, (iii) reformulate its semantics, (iv) show that this simple fragment can be evaluated in PTIME; and (v) consider connections with first-order logic.

2.5.1 A Relational View of an XML Tree

A common way to efficiently store and query an XML database is to encode it as a relational database, as described in Chapter 4. In a similar manner, we define here a formal view of trees as relational structures, to help define the semantics of navigational XPath.

A tree T can be represented as a relational database (a finite structure in terms of logic) as follows. Each node is given a unique identifier. We have a unary relation L_l for each label l occurring in the tree. The fact $L_l(n)$ indicates that the label of node n is l. Labels stand here for both names and values, to simplify.

We shall use a relation *nodeIds* that contains the set of identifiers of nodes in T. We also have two binary relations *child* and *next-sibling*. Observe that we are using the symbol *child* to denote both the axis and the corresponding relation. We shall do so systematically for all axes. For two node identifiers n and n', *child*(n,n') if n' is the child of n, *next-sibling*(n,n') if n' is the next sibling of n. (They have the same parent and the position of n' is that of n plus 1.) Though *next-sibling* is not an axis available in XPath 1.0, it can be simulated by the expression following-sibling::*[1].

We can define binary relations for the other axes:

- *self* is $\{(n,n) \mid nodeIds(n)\}$;
- *descendant* is the transitive closure of *child*;
- *descendant-or-self* is the union of *self* and *descendant*;
- *following-sibling* is the transitive closure of *next-sibling*;
- *following* is

$$\{(n,q) \mid \exists m \exists p \quad \textit{ancestor-or-self}(n,m) \wedge \textit{following-sibling}(m,p)$$

$$\wedge \textit{descendant-or-self}(p,q)\};$$

- *parent, ancestor, ancestor-or-self, preceding-sibling, previous-sibling, preceding*, are the inverses of, respectively, *child, descendant, descendant-or-self, next-sibling, following-sibling, following*.

Observe that this gives a formal semantics for axes. Note also that relations *nodeIds*, *child*, and *next-sibling* can be constructed in one traversal of the tree and that from them the other axis relations can be constructed in PTIME, for instance using a relational engine including transitive closure.

We use the term *node-set* to denote the powerset of *nodeIds*. An element in *node-set* is thus a set of node identifiers.

2.5.2 Navigational XPath

We consider a fragment of XPath 1.0 that focuses exclusively on its navigational part, namely *NavXPath*. This fragment ignores such things as equalities between path expressions, positions, or aggregate functions such as *count*() or *sum*(). To be able to better highlight the connections with logic, we depart slightly from the XPath syntax. The language is still a fragment of the whole language in that each NavXPath query can easily be translated to an "official" XPath query.

NavXPath expressions are built using the grammar:

$$p \quad ::- \quad step \quad | \quad p/p \quad \quad | \quad p \cup p$$
$$step \quad ::- \quad axis \quad | \quad step[q]$$
$$q \quad ::- \quad p \quad \quad | \quad label() = l \quad | \quad q \wedge q \quad | \quad q \vee q \quad | \quad \neg q$$

where

- p stands for path expression and q for *qualifier* or *filter* (we avoid the term *predicate* here because it has another meaning in first-order logic); and
- *axis* is one of the axes previously defined.

Ignoring the order first, the semantics is formally defined as follows. Since an XPath expression p may be interpreted both as an expression and as a qualifier, we have to be careful when we formally define the semantics and distinguish two semantic functions, one denoted $[.]_p$ (for path expressions) and one $[.]_q$ (for qualifiers). It is important to keep in mind that the semantic function $[.]_p$ maps a path expression p_1 to a binary relation, where $[p_1]_p(n,n')$ states that there exists a path matching p_1 from n to n'. On the other hand, the semantic function $[.]_q$ maps a qualifier q_1 to a unary relation, where $[q_1]_q(n)$ states that node n satisfies q_1. Formally, we have

Expressions		Qualifiers	
$[r]_p$	$:= r$ (for each axis relation r)[3]	$[label() = l]_q$	$:= L_l$ (for each label l)
$[step[q_1]]_p$	$:= \{(n,n') \mid [step]_p(n,n') \wedge [q_1]_q(n')\}$	$[p_1]_q$	$:= \{n \mid \exists n'([p_1]_p(n,n'))\}$
$[p_1/p_2]_p$	$:= \{(n,n') \mid \exists m([p_1]_p(n,m) \wedge [p_2]_p(m,n'))\}$	$[q_1 \wedge q_2]_q$	$:= [q_1]_q \cap [q_2]_q$
$[p_1 \cup p_2]_p$	$:= [p_1]_p \cup [p_2]_p$	$[q_1 \vee q_2]_q$	$:= [q_1]_q \cup [q_2]_q$
		$[\neg q_1]_q$	$:= nodeIds - [q_1]_q$

A path query p_1 applied to a context node n returns a node set, that is $\{n' \mid [p_1]_p(n,n')\}$. Now let us introduce the order. Observe that the semantics so far defined specifies a *set* of nodes. The last axis of the path expression defines the order. Depending on the forward or backward character of the axis, the set is ordered either in document order or backwards.

Clearly, we have departed slightly from the official syntax. For instance, a query such as

$$child[label() = a][q]$$

corresponds to child::a[q] in standardized XPath 1.0. Observe also that the focus is on relative path expressions. It is easy to introduce absolute path expressions: One tests for the root as the (only) node without parent. It is left as an exercise to show that all queries in NavXPath can be expressed in XPath 1.0 and that the translation can be achieved in LINEAR TIME.

---

[3] Do not get confused. The r at the left of $:=$ is the axis name, whereas at the right it is the axis relation.

2.5.3 Evaluation

Using the bottom-up semantics we presented, we consider the evaluation of NavXPath expressions.

Again, let us start by ignoring order. As already mentioned, the *child* and *next-sibling* relations, as well as the L_l-relations for each label l, can be constructed in linear time by one traversal of the documents, using for instance the Dewey notation for identifiers (see Chapter 4). Now *descendant* and *following-sibling* can be computed as the transitive closure of the previous ones, also in PTIME. Then one can show that each NavXPath expression can be expressed as an FO formula or as a relational algebra query over these relations. (This formula can be computed in linear time.) From this, it is easy to see that any NavXPath expression can be evaluated in PTIME in the size of the tree. In fact, one can show that it can be evaluated in PTIME in the size of the tree *and* the expression.

Now consider order. In XML, one typically chooses a node identification scheme that makes it easy to determine which node comes first in document order. So, this ordering phase can be achieved in $O(n' \cdot \log(n'))$, where n' is the size of the result. Remember that the result of a NavXPath expression is a subset of the nodes of the original document. This whole phase is therefore achieved in $O(n \cdot \log(n))$, where n is the size of the document.

We illustrate the construction of the FO formula with an example. In the example, we use an attribute to show that their handling does not raise any particular issue. In the example, a binary relation @a is used for each attribute a occurring in the tree. Similarly, we could have a binary relation *text* for the content of text nodes.

Consider the XPath expression: descendant::a/*[@b=5]/preceding-sibling::*, or, in NavXPath notation:

$$q = descendant[lab() = a]/child[@b = 5]/preceding-sibling$$

Then we have

$$q_1(n,n_1) \equiv descendant(n,n_1) \wedge L_a(n_1)$$

$$q_2(n,n_2) \equiv \exists n_1(q_1(n,n_1) \wedge child(n_1,n_2) \wedge @b(n_2,5))$$

$$q(n,n_3) \equiv \exists n_2(q_2(n,n_2) \wedge following\text{-}sibling(n_3,n_2))$$

To see a second (and last) example, consider the pathological query *pathos₂*:

/a/d/parent::a/d/parent::a/d/parent::a/d

The bottom-up construction yields:

$$d = \{(x',y) \mid (child(x',y) \wedge L_d(y))\}$$

$$parent::a/d = \{(y',y) \mid \exists x'(child(x',y') \wedge L_a(x') \wedge child(x',y) \wedge L_d(y))\}$$

$$d/parent::a/d = \{(x,y) \mid \exists y'(child(x,y') \wedge L_d(y') \wedge \exists x'(child(x',y') \wedge L_a(x')$$
$$\wedge child(x',y) \wedge L_d(y)))\}$$

$$\ldots$$

Observe that we are in a polynomial growth even without using fancy relational query optimization.

The bottom-up semantics specifies a PTIME evaluation algorithm.[4] Of course the resulting algorithm is rather inefficient, and the state of the art in XPath processing does much better. Furthermore, we treated only the navigational part of XPath. It turns out that using clever, typically top-down, algorithms, one can process any XPath query in PTIME both in the size of the tree but also of the query.

2.5.4 Expressiveness and First-Order Logic

In this section, focusing on NavXPath, we present surprising connections with first-order logic as well as stress differences. The binary predicates (relations) allowed in the logic are all axis relations: *child, descendant, following-sibling*, etc.

The translation of NavXPath to FO is straightforward based on the semantics we presented for NavXPath. In fact, it turns out that NavXPath queries correspond to some extend to FO^2. The logic FO^2 is FO limited to two variables, say x and y, which may be reused in different existential or universal quantifiers.

Recall that a NavXPath expression can be interpreted as a binary relation mapping a node n into a set of nodes, or as a logical formula with two free variables. Also, a NavXPath qualifier is interpreted as a Boolean function and so can be interpreted by a first-order logic formula with only one free variable. For instance, consider the path expression d/parent::a/d. Now think about it as a qualifier. Although it may seem we need four variables to express it in logic, one can make do with two:

$$d/parent::a/d(x) = \exists y' \left(child(x,y') \wedge L_d(y') \wedge \exists x'(child(x',y') \wedge L_a(x') \right.$$
$$\wedge \exists y(child(x',y) \wedge L_d(y))))$$
$$\equiv \exists y \left(child(x,y) \wedge L_d(y) \wedge \exists x (child(x,y) \wedge L_a(x) \right.$$
$$\wedge \exists y(child(x,y) \wedge L_d(y))))$$

Check these formulas carefully to convince yourself that they are indeed equivalent. Get a feeling for why it is in general the case that we can express NavXPath qualifiers with FO^2.

The precise theorem that relates FO^2 and NavXPath is a bit intricate because, to move to XPath expressions as opposed to qualifiers, we already need variables to account for the source and target. But every FO^2 formula can be expressed in XPath, and every qualifier can be expressed in FO^2.

Although translations between XPath and FO^2 exist, one may wonder about the size of the results. It is known that for some FO^2 queries, the equivalent NavXPath expressions have exponential size. For the other direction, the translation of an XPath qualifier can be done in polynomial time.

---

[4] This is because of the restrictions coming with NavXPath; more powerful fragments of XPath 1.0 cannot easily be evaluated with a bottom-up approach.

Since it is known that some FO queries require more than two variables, there are FO queries that cannot be expressed in NavXPath. For instance, the following query cannot be expressed in NavXPath: There is a path from some a node to a descendant a node that traverses only b nodes. Indeed, this query cannot be expressed in XPath 1.0.

2.5.5 Other XPath Fragments

NavXPath covers only the navigational core of XPath 1.0; in particular, it is impossible to express queries about the value equalities of nodes of the tree such as

$$movie[actor/@id = director/@id]/title$$

It is possible to define a formal extension of NavXPath that adds this capability. The characterization of this language in terms of first-order logic is less clear, however. It has been shown that it is a proper subset of FO^3 over the previously mentioned relations, as well as binary relations that express value comparisons. As already mentioned, query evaluation remains PTIME in terms of data-and-query complexity.

XPath 2.0 is a much more powerful language than XPath 1.0, with the intersection and complementation operators, the iteration features, and so on. Its navigational core has the same expressive power as the whole of FO. Evaluating a navigational XPath 2.0 query is, however, a PSPACE-complete problem in data-and-query complexity.

2.6 FURTHER READING

XPath

XPath 1.0 is a W3C recommendation [163] that was released in November 1999. The relative simplicity of the language makes the recommendation quite readable to application programmers, in contrast to other W3C recommendations that describe more involved technologies.

There exists a large number of implementations for XPath 1.0. Here are a few examples freely available for various programming languages:

libxml2: Free *C* library for parsing XML documents, supporting XPath.
java.xml.xpath: *Java* package, included with JDK versions starting from 1.5.
System.Xml.XPath: Standard *.NET* classes for XPath.
XML::XPath: Free *Perl* module, includes a command-line tool.
DOMXPath: *PHP* class for XPath, included in PHP5.
PyXML: Free *Python* library for parsing XML documents, supporting XPath.

XPath is also directly usable for client-side programming inside all modern browsers, in JavaScript.

The W3C published in January 2007 a recommendation [168] for the XPath 2.0 language. This document is not self-contained, it refers to two additional recommendations, one for describing the data model [170], and the other to describe all operators and functions [172]. An excellent reference book to the XPath 2.0 language (and to XSLT 2.0) is [108], by Michael Kay, the author of the SAXON XSLT and XQuery processor.

The large number of extensions that were brought to the language, especially in connection to XML schema annotations, make it a much more complex language, with far fewer implementations. In essence, there are no implementations of XPath 2.0 outside of XQuery and XSLT 2.0 implementations.

XQuery

XQuery was standardized along XPath 2.0, and its recommendation [169] is also dated January 2007. In addition to the recommendations on its data model and functions, cited previously, there are separate documents that describe its semantics [171] as well as its serialization features [173]. The reference information is thus spread across five documents, not counting the recommendations of XML itself, XML namespaces, and XML schemas, which does not help readability. More didactic presentations of the language can be found in [121, 178].

There are a large number of XQuery implementations, both as stand-alone processors and as part of a XML database management system. Among the freely available (most of which provide support for the core language, but have no support for external XML schemas), let us cite:

SAXON: In-memory Java and .NET libraries; the open-source version has no support of external XML schemas, but it is still a very convenient tool.

GNU QEXO: A very efficient open-source processor that compiles XQuery queries into Java bytecode; it does not support all features of the language.

QIZX: Java libraries for both a stand-alone processor and a native XML database; open and free versions have limitations.

EXIST: An open-source XML database management system, with a very user-friendly interface.

MONETDB: An in-memory column-oriented engine for both SQL and XQuery querying; among the fastest.

An interesting benchmarking of some freely available XQuery processors is [123]. The W3C maintains a list of XQuery processors at
http://www.w3.org/XML/Query/#implementations.

XPath Foundations

The literature on XPath expressiveness, complexity, and processing is quite impressive. The material of this section borrows a lot from the article "XPath Leashed" [24] that is an in-detail discussion of expressiveness and complexity of various fragments of XPath 1.0. Efficient algorithms for processing XPath queries are presented in [76]. Another interesting survey of expressiveness and complexity results can be found in [154], which is one of the few research works that look at the expressiveness of XPath 2.0. XQuery is a Turing-complete language, but its core can also be analyzed with respect to first-order logic, as is done in [25].

2.7 EXERCISES

Most of the following exercises address the principles of XPath or XQuery. They are intended to check your understanding of the main mechanisms involved in XML documents manipulation. These exercises must be completed by a practical experiment with an XPath/XQuery evaluator. You can refer to the list of XPath and XQuery implementations in Section 2.6. The EXIST XML database, in particular, is simple to install and use. Chapter 5 proposes several exercises and labs with EXIST.

The exercises that follow refer to a few XPath functions whose meaning should be trivial to the reader: *count()* returns the cardinality of a node-set, *sum()* converts the nodes of a node-set in numbers, and sums them all, *name()* returns the name (label) of a node, etc. Chapter 5 gives a list of common XPath/XQuery functions.

Exercise 2.7.1 *Consider the XML document shown in Figure 2.12. We suppose that all text nodes containing only whitespace are removed from the tree.*

1. *Give the result of the following XPath expressions:*
   (a) //e/preceding::text()
   (b) count(//c|//b/node())
2. *Give an XPath 1.0 expression for the following queries, and the corresponding result:*
   (a) *Sum of all attribute values.*
   (b) *Text content of the document, where every "b" is replaced by a "c" (Hint: use function translate(s, $x_1 x_2 \cdots x_n$, $y_1 y_2 \cdots y_n$) that replaces each x_i by y_i in s).*
   (c) *Name of the child of the last "c" element in the tree.*

Exercise 2.7.2 *Explain the difference between the following two XPath expressions:*

- ▪ *//c[position() = 1]*
- ▪ */descendant::c[position() = 1]*

Give an example of a document for which both expressions yield a different result.

Exercise 2.7.3 *Explain the following expressions, and why they are not equivalent.*

- ▪ *//lecture[name='XML']*
- ▪ *//lecture[name=XML]*

Give an instance that yields the same result.

```
<a>
  <b><c /></b>
  <b id="3" di="7">bli <c /><c><e>bla</e></c></b>
  <d>bou</d>
</a>
```

Figure 2.12. Sample document for Exercise 2.7.1.

Exercise 2.7.4 (node tests) *Give the appropriate combination of axis and node tests to express in XPath the following searches.*

■ *select all nodes which are children of an A node, itself child of the context node;*
■ *select all elements whose namespace is bound to the prefix* xsl *and that are children of the context node;*
■ *select the root element node;*
■ *select the* B *attribute of the context node;*
■ *select all siblings of the context node, itself included (unless it is an attribute node);*
■ *select all* blah *attributes wherever they appear in the document.*

Exercise 2.7.5 (predicates) *Give the results of the following expressions when applied to our example document (Figure 2.3).*

1. *//B[1]//text(),*
2. *//B[1]//text()[1],*
3. *//B//text()[1], and*
4. *//B/D/text()[1].*

Exercise 2.7.6 *For each of the following XPath expressions, explain its meaning and propose an abbreviation whenever possible.*

■ *child::A/descendant::B*
■ *child::*/child::B*
■ *descendant-or-self::B*
■ *child::B[position()=last()]*
■ *following-sibling::B[1]*
■ *//B[10]*
■ *child::B[child::C]*
■ *//B[@att1 or @att2]*
■ **[self::B or self::C]*

Exercise 2.7.7 (XQuery and recursion) *We get back to MathML documents. Recall that arithmetic formulas are written in prefix notation (see Exercise 1.6.3). In this exercise, we adopt the following restrictions: The only operators are <plus/> and <times/>), and these operators are binary.*

1. *Give an XQuery expression that transforms an apply expression in infix form. For instance, applied to the following document:*

```
<apply>
  <times/>
  <ci>x</ci>
  <cn>2</cn>
</apply>
```

*the query returns "x * 2".*

2. *Assume now that the infix expression can be expressed as a function eval($op, $x, $y), where $op is an operation, $x and $y two operands. XQuery makes it possible to call recursively any function. Give the query that transforms a MathML expression in infix form. For instance, applied to the following document*

```
<apply>
  <times/>
  <apply>
    <plus/>
    <ci>x</ci>
    <cn>2</cn>
  </apply>
  <ci>y</ci>
</apply>
```

*the query should return "(x + 2) * y".*

Exercise 2.7.8 *Show that all NavXPath queries can be expressed in XPath 1.0 and that the transformation can be achieved in* LINEAR TIME.

Exercise 2.7.9 *At the end of Section 2.5, it is stated that the query "there is a path from some a node to a descendant a node that traverses only b nodes" cannot be expressed in XPath 1.0. Can you find an XPath 2.0 expression for this query?*

3

Typing

In this chapter, we discuss the typing of semistructured data. Typing is the process of describing, with a set of declarative rules or constraints called a *schema*, a class of XML documents, and verifying that a given document is *valid* for that class (we also say that this document is valid *against* the type defined by the schema). This is, for instance, used to define a specific XML vocabulary (XHTML, MathML, RDF, etc.), with its specificities in structure and content, that is used for a given application.

We first present motivations and discuss the kind of typing that is needed. XML data typing is typically based on finite-state automata. Therefore, we recall basic notion of automata, first on words, then on ranked trees, finally on unranked trees (i.e., essentially on XML). We also present the main two practical languages for describing XML types, DTDs, and XML Schema, both of which endorsed by the W3C. We then briefly describe alternative schema languages with their key features. In a last section, we discuss the typing of graph data.

One can also consider the issue of "type checking a program," that is, verifying that if the input is of a proper input type, the program produces an output that is of a proper output type. In Section 3.5, we provide references to works on program type checking in the context of XML.

3.1 MOTIVATING TYPING

Perhaps the main difference with typing in relational systems is that typing is not compulsory for XML. It is perfectly fine to have an XML document with no prescribed type. However, when developing and using software, types are essential, for interoperability, consistency, and efficiency. We describe these motivations next and conclude the section by contrasting two kinds of type checking, namely dynamic and static.

Interoperability Schemas serve to document the interface of software components and provide therefore a key ingredient for the interoperability between programs: A program that consumes an XML document of a given type can assume that the program that has generated it has produced a document of that type.

Consistency Similar to dependencies for the relational model (primary keys, foreign key constraints, etc.), typing an XML document is also useful to protect data against improper updates.

Storage Efficiency Suppose that some XML document is very regular, say, it contains a list of companies, with, for each, an ID, a name, an address, and the name of its CEO. This same information may be stored very compactly, for instance, without repeating the names of elements such as address for each company. Thus, a priori knowledge on the type of the data may help improve its storage.

Query Efficiency Consider the following XQuery query:

```
for $b in doc("bib.xml")/bib//*
where $b/*/zip = '12345'
return $b/title
```

Knowing that the document consists of a list of books and knowing the exact type of book elements, one may be able to rewrite the query:

```
for $b in doc("bib.xml")/bib/book
where $b/address/zip = '12345'
return $b/title
```

that is typically much cheaper to evaluate. Note that in the absence of a schema, a similar processing is possible by first computing from the document itself a *data guide* (i.e., a structural summary of all paths from the root in the document). There are also other more involved *schema inference* techniques that allow attaching such an *a posteriori* schema to a schemaless document.

Dynamic and Static Typing

Assume that XML documents (at least some of them) are associated with schemas and that programs use these schemas. In particular, they verify that processed documents are valid against them. Most of the time, such verification is dynamic. For instance, a Web server verifies the type when sending an XML document or when receiving it. Indeed, XML data tend to be checked quite often because programs prefer to verify types dynamically (when they transfer data) than risking to run into data of unexpected structure during execution.

It is also interesting, although more complicated, to perform static type checking (i.e., verify that a program receiving data of the proper input type only generates data of the proper output type). More formally, let note $d \models T$ when a document d is valid against a type T. We say that a type T_1 is *more specific* than a type T_2 if all documents valid against T_1 are also valid against T_2, that is,

$$\forall d \, (d \models T_1 \Rightarrow d \models T_2).$$

Let T_i be an *input type* and f be a program or query that takes as input an XML document and returns an XML document. This f might be an XPath or XQuery query, an XSLT stylesheet, or even a program in a classical programming language. Static typing implies either static verification or static inference, defined as follows:

Verification: Is it true that $\forall d \models T_i, f(d) \models T_o$, for some given *output type T_o*?
Inference: Find the *most specific T_o* such that $\forall d \models T_i, f(d) \models T_o$.

Note that in a particular case, we have no knowledge of the input type, and the inference problem becomes: Find the *most specific T_o* such that $f(d) \models T_o$.

The notion of *smallest output type* depends of the schema language considered. Assume for instance that types are described as regular expressions on the tag sequences[1] and consider the following XQuery query:

```
for $p in doc("parts.xml")//part[color="red"]
return <part><name>$p/name</name><desc>$p/desc</desc></part>
```

Assuming no constraint on the input type, it is easy to see that the type of the result is described by the following regular expression:

(<part> <name> *any* </name> <desc> *any* </desc> </part>)*

where *any* stands for any well-formed tag sequence. The regular language described by this regular expression is also the smallest one that describes the output of the query, since any document in this language can be generated as the output of this query.

Verifying or inferring an output type for a program is in all generality an undecidable problem, even for XPath queries and a simple schema language such as DTDs. Even when the verification problem is decidable, a smallest output type might not exist. Consider, for instance, the XQuery program:

```
let $d:=doc("input.xml")
for $x in $d//a, $y in $d//a
return <b/>
```

Suppose that the input is <input> <a/> <a/> </input>. Then the result is

---

[1] As shall be seen later in this chapter, typical schema languages for XML are more adapted to the tree structure of the document because they are defined in terms of regular tree languages rather than of regular string languages.

```
<b/><b/><b/><b/>
```

In general, the result consists in n^2 b-elements for some $n \geq 0$. Such a type cannot be described by DTDs or XML schemas. One can approximate it by regular expressions but not obtain a "best" result

$$<b/>^*$$
$$\epsilon + <b/> + <b/>^4 <b/>^*$$
$$\epsilon + <b/> + <b/>^4 + <b/>^9 <b/>^*$$

...

3.2 AUTOMATA

XML was recently introduced. Fortunately, the model can benefit from a theory that is well established, automata theory. We briefly recall some standard definitions and results on automata over words. Then we mention without proof how they extend to ranked trees with some limitations. As previously mentioned, XML is based on unranked trees, so we finally consider unranked trees.

3.2.1 Automata on Words

This is standard material. We recall here briefly some notation and terminology.

Definition 3.2.1 *A finite-state word automaton (FSA for short) is a 5-tuple* $(\Sigma, Q, q_0, F, \delta)$ *where*

1. Σ *is a finite alphabet;*
2. Q *is a finite set of states;*
3. $q_0 \in Q$ *is the initial state;*
4. $F \subseteq Q$ *is the set of final states; and*
5. δ, *the transition function, is a mapping from* $(\Sigma \cup \{\epsilon\}) \times Q$ *to* 2^Q.

Such a nondeterministic automaton accepts or rejects words in Σ^*. A word $w \in \Sigma^*$ is accepted by an automaton if there is a path in the state space of the automaton, leading from the initial state to one of the final states and compatible with the transition functions, such that the concatenation of all labels from $\Sigma \cup \{\epsilon\}$ along the path is w. The set of words accepted by an automaton A is denoted $L(A)$. A language accepted by an FSA is called a *regular* language. They can alternatively be described as regular expressions built using concatenation, union and Kleene closure (e.g., $a(b+c)^*d$).

Example 3.2.2 Consider the FSA A with $\Sigma = \{a,b\}$, $Q = \{q_0, q_1, q_2, q_3\}$, $F = \{q_2\}$, $\delta(a, q_0) = \{q_0, q_1\}$, $\delta(b, q_1) = \{q_0\}$, $\delta(\epsilon, q_1) = \{q_2\}$, $\delta(\epsilon, q_2) = \{q_3\}$, $\delta(\epsilon, q_3) = \{q_3\}$. Then *abaab* is not in $L(A)$, whereas *aba* is in $L(A)$.

An automaton is *deterministic* if (i) it has no ϵ-transition (i.e., $\delta(\epsilon,q) = \emptyset$ for all q); and (ii) there are no multiple transitions from a single pair of symbol and state (i.e., $|\delta(a,q)| \leq 1$ for all (a,q)).

The following important results are known about FSAs:

1. For each FSA A, one can construct an equivalent deterministic FSA B (i.e., a deterministic FSA accepting exactly the same words). In some cases, the number of states of B is necessarily exponential in that of A. This leads to another fundamental problem that we will ignore here, the problem of state minimization, i.e., the problem of finding an equivalent deterministic automaton with as few states as possible.
2. There is no FSA accepting the language $\{a^i b^i \mid i \geq 0\}$.
3. Regular languages are closed under complement.
   (To see this, consider an automaton A. Construct a deterministic automaton that accepts the same language but never "blocks" (i.e., that always reads the entire word). Let Q be the set of states of this automaton and F its set of accepting states. Then the automaton obtained by replacing F by $Q - F$ for accepting states, accepts the complement of the language accepted by A.)
4. Regular languages are closed under union and intersection.
   (Given two automata A, B, construct an automaton with states $Q \times Q'$ that simulates both. For instance, an accepting state for $L(A) \cap L(B)$ is a state (q, q'), where q is accepting for A and q' for B.)

3.2.2 Automata on Ranked Trees

Automata on words are used to define word languages, that is, subsets of Σ^* for some alphabet Σ. Similarly, it is possible to define *tree automata* whose purpose is to define subsets of the set of all trees. For technical reasons, it is easier to define tree automata for ranked trees (i.e., trees whose number of children per node is bounded). We will explain in Section 3.2.3 how the definitions can be extended to unranked trees.

Word automata defined in the previous section process a string from left to right. It is easy to define a notion of right-to-left automaton, and also easy to see that in terms of accepted languages, there is absolutely no difference between left-to-right and right-to-left automata. For trees, there is a difference between top-down and bottom-up automata. Intuitively, in a top-down automaton, we have a choice of the direction to go (e.g., to choose to go to the first child or the second), whereas in bottom-up automata, similarly to word automata, the direction is always prescribed.

Bottom-Up Tree Automata. Let us start with the example of bottom-up automata for binary trees. Similarly to word automata, a bottom-up automaton on binary trees is defined by

1. A finite *leaf* alphabet $\mathcal{L}$;
2. A finite *internal* alphabet Σ, with $\Sigma \cap \mathcal{L} = \emptyset$;
3. A set of states Q;
4. A set of accepting states $F \subseteq Q$;

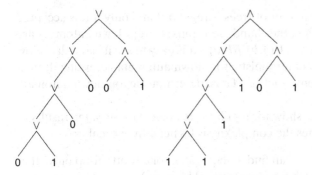

Figure 3.1. Two binary trees.

5. A transition function δ that maps:
   - a leaf symbol $l \in \mathcal{L}$ to a set of states $\delta(l) \subseteq 2^Q$;
   - an internal symbol $a \in \Sigma$, together with a pair of states (q,q') to a set of states $\delta(a,q,q') \subseteq 2^Q$.

The transition function specifies a set of state for the leaf nodes. Then if $\delta(a,q,q')$ contains q'', this specifies that if the left and right children of a node labeled a are in states q,q', respectively, then the node *may move* to state q''.

Example 3.2.3 (Boolean circuit) Consider the following bottom-up automaton: $\mathcal{L} = \{0,1\}$, $\Sigma = \{\vee,\wedge\}$, $Q = \{f,t\}$, $F = \{t\}$, and $\delta(0) = \{f\}$, $\delta(1) = \{t\}$, $\delta(\wedge,t,t) = \{t\}$, $\delta(\wedge,f,t) = \delta(\wedge,t,f) = \delta(\wedge,f,f) = \{f\}$, $\delta(\vee,f,f) = \{f\}$, $\delta(\vee,f,t) = \delta(\vee,t,f) = \delta(\vee,t,t) = \{t\}$. The tree of the left of Figure 3.1 is accepted by the bottom-up tree automata, whereas the one on the right is rejected. More generally, this automaton accepts and/or trees that evaluate to true.

The definition can be extended to ranked trees with symbols of arbitrarily arity in a straightforward manner. An ϵ-transition in the context of bottom-up tree automata is of the form $\delta(a,r) = r'$, meaning that if a node of label a is in state r, then it may move to state r'. We can also define deterministic bottom-up tree automata by forbidding ϵ-transition and alternatives (i.e., some $\delta(a,q,q')$ containing more than one state).

Definition 3.2.4 *A set of trees is a regular tree language if it is accepted by a bottom-up tree automata.*

As for automata on words, one can "determinize" a nondeterministic automata. More precisely, given a bottom-up tree automata, one can construct a deterministic bottom-up tree automata that accepts the same trees.

Top-Down Tree Automata In a top-down tree automaton, transitions are of the form $(q,q') \in \delta(a,q'')$ with the meaning that if a node labeled a is in state q'', then this transition moves its left child to state q and its right child to q'. The automaton accepts a tree if *all* leaves can be set in accepting states when the root is in some given initial state q_0. Determinism is defined in the obvious manner.

It is not difficult to show that a set of trees is regular if and only if it is accepted by a top-down automata. On the other hand, deterministic top-down automata are weaker. Consider the language $L = \{f(a,b), f(b,a)\}$. It is easy to see it is regular. Now one can verify that if there is a deterministic top-down automata accepting it, then it would also accept $f(a,a)$, a contradiction. Thus, deterministic top-down automata are weaker.

Generally speaking, one can show for regular tree languages the same results as for regular languages (sometimes the complexity is higher). In particular:

1. Given a tree automata, one can find an equivalent one (bottom-up only) that is deterministic (with possibly an exponential blow-up).
2. Regular tree languages are closed under complement, intersection and union (with similar proofs than for word automata).

3.2.3 Unranked Trees

We have defined in Section 3.2.2 tree automata (and regular tree languages) over the set of *ranked trees* (i.e., trees where there is an a priori bound of the number of children of each node). But XML documents are unranked (take for example XHTML, in which the number of paragraphs <p> inside the body of a document is unbounded).

Reconsider the Boolean circuit example from Example 3.2.3. Suppose we want to allow and/or gates with arbitrary many inputs. The set of transitions of a bottom-up automaton becomes infinite:

$$\delta(\wedge,t,t,t) = t, \quad \delta(\wedge,t,t,t,t) = t, \quad \ldots$$
$$\delta(\wedge,f,t,t) = f, \quad \delta(\wedge,t,f,t) = f, \quad \ldots$$
$$\delta(\vee,f,f,f) = f, \quad \delta(\vee,f,f,f,f) = f, \quad \ldots$$
$$\delta(\vee,t,f,f) = t, \quad \delta(\vee,f,t,f) = t, \quad \ldots$$

So an issue is to represent this infinite set of transitions. To do that, we can use regular expressions on words.

Example 3.2.5 Consider the following regular word languages:

$$And_1 = tt^* \quad And_0 = (t+f)^* f (t+f)^*$$
$$Or_0 = ff^* \quad Or_1 = (t+f)^* t (t+f)^*$$

Then one can define infinite sets of transitions:

$$\delta(\wedge, And_1) = \delta(\vee, Or_1) = t, \quad \delta(\wedge, And_0) = \delta(\vee, Or_0) = f$$

One can base a theory of unranked trees on that principle. Alternatively, one can build on ranked trees by representing any unranked tree by a binary tree where the left child of a node represents the first child and the right child, its next sibling in the original tree, as shown in Figure 3.2.

Let F be the one-to-one mapping that encodes an unranked tree T into $F(T)$, the binary tree with first-child and next-sibling. Let F^{-1} be the inverse mapping that

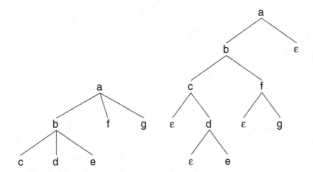

Figure 3.2. An unranked tree and its corresponding ranked one.

"decodes" binary trees thereby encoded. One can show that for each unranked tree automata A, there exists a ranked tree automata accepting $F(L(A))$. Conversely, for each ranked tree automata A, there is an unranked tree automata accepting $F^{-1}(L(A))$. Both constructions are easy.

As a consequence, one can see that unranked tree automata are closed under union, intersection, and complement.

Determinism Last, let us consider determinism for unranked tree automata. We cannot build on the translation to ranked tree automata as we did for union, intersection, and complement. This is because the translation between ranked and unranked trees does not preserve determinism. So, instead we define determinism directly on bottom-up tree automata over unranked trees.

Let us define more precisely the machinery of these automata, and first the nondeterministic ones. The automata over unranked trees are defined as follows. An automata A includes a finite alphabet Σ of labels, a finite set Q of states, and a set F of accepting states. For each $a \in \Sigma$, it includes an automaton A_a over words that takes both its word alphabet and its states in Q. Consider a tree T with labels in Σ. Suppose its root is labelled a and that it has $n \geq 0$ subtrees, $T_1, ..., T_n$, in that order. Then A may reach state q on input T if there exists $q_1, ... q_n$ such that:

- For each i, A may reach the state q_i on input T_i.
- A_a may reach state q on input $q_1 ... q_n$.

The automaton A accepts T if q is accepting.

Now for the automaton A to be deterministic, we need to prevent the possibility that it may reach two states for the same input tree. For this, we require A_a to be deterministic for each a.

3.2.4 Trees and Monadic Second-Order Logic

There is also a logical interpretation of regular tree languages in terms of *monadic second-order logic*. One can represent a tree as a logical structure using identifiers for nodes. For instance, the tree of Figure 3.3, where "1(a)" stands for "node id 1,

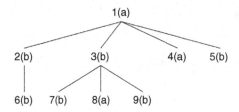

Figure 3.3. A tree with node identifiers listed.

label a", is represented by

$$E(1,2), E(1,3), \ldots, E(3,9)$$

$$S(2,3), S(3,4), S(4,5), \ldots, S(8,9)$$

$$a(1), a(4), a(8)$$

$$b(2), b(3), b(5), b(6), b(7), b(9)$$

Here, the predicate $E(x,y)$ denotes the *child* relation, whereas the predicate $S(x,y)$ represents the *next-sibling* relation.

The syntax of *monadic second-order logic* (MSO) is given by

$$\varphi \ :- \ x = y \mid E(x,y) \mid S(x,y) \mid a(x) \mid \ldots \mid \varphi \wedge \varphi \mid \varphi \vee \varphi \mid \neg\varphi \mid \exists x \varphi \mid \exists X \varphi \mid X(x)$$

where x is an atomic variable and X a variable denoting a set. $X(x)$ stands for $x \in X$. Observe that in $\exists X \varphi$, we are quantifying over a set, the main distinction with first-order logic where quantification is only on atomic variables. The term *monadic* means that the only second-order variables are unary relations, that is, sets.

MSO is a very general logical languages for trees. For instance, we can capture in MSO the constraint: "each a node has a b descendant." This is achieved by stating that for each node x labeled a, each set X containing x and closed under descendants contains some node labeled b. Formally,

$$\forall x \, a(x) \rightarrow (\forall X \, X(x) \wedge \beta(X) \rightarrow \exists y \, X(y) \wedge b(y))$$

where $\beta(X) = \forall y \forall z \, (X(y) \wedge E(y,z) \rightarrow X(z))$.

We state a last result in this section because it beautifully illustrates the underlying theory. We strongly encourage the reader to read further about tree automata and about monadic second-order logic.

Theorem 3.2.6 A set L of trees is regular if and only if $L = \{T \mid T \models \varphi\}$ for some monadic second-order formula φ (i.e., if L is definable in MSO).

3.3 SCHEMA LANGUAGES FOR XML

In this section, we present actual languages that are used to describe the type of XML documents. We start with DTDs, that are part of the specification of XML, and then move to the other schema language endorsed by the W3C, XML Schema. We finally discuss other existing schema languages, highlighting the differences with respect to DTDs and XML Schema.

3.3.1 Document Type Definitions

DTD stands for "Document Type Definition." An integral part of the XML speci-fication, this is the oldest syntax for specifying typing constraints on XML, still very much in use. To describe types for XML, the main idea of DTDs is to describe the children that nodes with a certain label may have. With DTDs, the labels of children of a node of a given label are described by regular expressions. The syntax, inherited from SGML, is bizarre but rather intuitive.

An example of a DTD is as follows:

```
<!ELEMENT populationdata (continent*) >
<!ELEMENT continent (name, country*) >
<!ELEMENT country (name, province*)>
<!ELEMENT province ((name|code), city*) >
<!ELEMENT city (name, pop) >
<!ELEMENT name (#PCDATA) >
<!ELEMENT code (#PCDATA) >
<!ELEMENT pop (#PCDATA) >
```

The comma is the concatenation operator, indicating a sequence of children, whereas "–" is the union operator that expresses alternatives. "*" indicates an arbitrary number of children with that structure; #PCDATA just means "textual con-tent." In DTDs, the regular expressions are supposed to be *deterministic*. In brief, the XML data can be parsed (and its type verified) by a deterministic finite-state automaton that is directly derived from the regular expression. For instance, the expression

$$(a+b)^*a$$

(in DTD syntax, ((a|b)*,a)) is not deterministic since when parsing a first a, one doesn't know whether this is the a of $(a+b)^*$ or that of the last a. On the other hand, this expression is equivalent to

$$(b^*a)^+$$

(in DTD syntax, ((b*,a)+)) that is deterministic.

Under this restriction, it is easy to type-check some XML data while scanning it (e.g., with a SAX parser). Observe that such a parsing can be sometimes performed with a finite-state automaton but that sometimes more is required. For instance, consider the following DTD:

```
<!ELEMENT part (part*) >
```

The parser reads a list of *part* opening tags. A stack (or a counter) is needed to remember how many where found to verify that the same number of closing tags is found.

The reader may be a bit confused by now. Is this language regular (an automaton suffices to validate it) or not? To be precise, if we are given the tree, a tree automaton suffices to check whether a document satisfies the previous DTD. On the other hand, if we are given the serialized form of the XML document, just the verification that the document is well-formed cannot be achieved by an automaton. (It requires a stack as $a^n b^n$ does.)

Observe that we do want the kind of recursive definitions that cannot be verified simply by an FSA. On the other hand, DTDs present features that are less desired, most importantly, they are not closed under union:

DTD_1:

<!**ELEMENT** used (ad*) >
<!**ELEMENT** ad (year, brand) >

DTD_2:

<!**ELEMENT** new (ad*) >
<!**ELEMENT** ad (brand) >

$L(DTD_1) \cup L(DTD_2)$ cannot be described by a DTD although it can be described easily with a tree automaton. The issue here is that the type of *ad* depends of its parent. We can approximate what we want:

<!**ELEMENT** ad (year?, brand) >

But this is only an approximation. It turns out that DTDs are also not closed under complement.

What we need to do is to decouple the notions of type and that of label. Each type corresponds to a label, but not conversely. So, for instance, we may want two types for ads, with the same label:

```
car:   [car]   (used|new)*
used:  [used]  (ad1*)
new:   [new]   (ad2*)
ad1:   [ad]    (year, brand)
ad2:   [ad]    (brand)
```

With such decoupling, we can prove closure properties. This is leading to XML Schema, described in the next section, that is based on decoupled tags with many other features.

DTDs provide a few other functionalities, such as the description of the type of attributes, a mechanism for including external files and for defining local macros, or the possibility of declaring an attribute value as unique (ID) in the whole document or refers to one of these unique values (IDREF). These ID and IDREF attribute types can be used to create "pointers" from one point of the document to another, as investigated in Section 3.4. XML documents can include in-line description of their DTDs, as well as refer to external DTDs to indicate their type. Thus, XHTML documents typically contain such a declaration (before the opening tag of the root element and after the optional XML declaration):

```
<!DOCTYPE html
    PUBLIC "-//W3C//DTD XHTML 1.0 Strict//EN"
        "http://www.w3.org/TR/xhtml1/DTD/xhtml1-strict.dtd">
```

Here, html is the name of the root element, -//W3C//DTD XHTML 1.0 Strict//EN is a *public identifier* for this DTD (that Web browsers can for instance use to identify the particular HTML dialect a document is written in) and http://www.w3.org/TR/xhtml1/DTD/xhtml1-strict.dtd is the *system identifier*, a URL to the DTD.

A final annoying limitation of DTDs, overcome in XML Schema, is their unawareness of XML namespaces. Because XML namespaces are very much used in practice, this considerably limits the usefulness of DTDs. In brief, it is impossible to give a DTD for an XML document that will remain valid when the namespace prefixes of this document are renamed. Let us explain this further. An XML document making use of namespaces is usually conceptually the same when the prefix used to refer to the namespace is changed.[2] For instance, the following three documents are usually considered to be syntactic variants of the same:

```
<a xmlns="http://toto.com/"><b /></a>
<t:a xmlns:t="http://toto.com/"><t:b /></t:a>
<s:a xmlns:s="http://toto.com/"><s:b /></s:a>
```

These documents can be distinguished using advanced features (*namespace nodes*) of XML programming interfaces and languages (DOM, SAX, XPath, XSLT, XQuery, etc.), but it is very rarely done or useful. As DTDs have been introduced at the same time that XML itself, they predate the introduction of namespaces in XML. A side-effect of this is that it is impossible to write a DTD all three documents above are valid against. In XML Schema (as well as in other modern schema languages for XML), this is directly supported.

3.3.2 XML Schema

XML Schema is an XML-based language for describing XML types proposed by the W3C. Despite criticism for being unnecessarily complicated, this is the primary

---

[2] There are exceptions to that, when the namespace prefix is also used in attribute values or text content, such as in XSLT or XML Schema, but they are rare.

```
<?xml version="1.0" encoding="utf-8"?>
<xs:schema xmlns:xs="http://www.w3.org/2001/XMLSchema">
  <xs:element name="book">
    <xs:complexType>
      <xs:sequence>
        <xs:element name="title" type=" xs:string "/>
        <xs:element name="author" type="xs:string"/>
        <xs:element name="character"
                    minOccurs="0" maxOccurs="unbounded">
          <xs:complexType>
            <xs:sequence>
              <xs:element name="name" type="xs:string"/>
              <xs:element name="friend-of" type=" xs:string "
                          minOccurs="0" maxOccurs="unbounded"/>
              <xs:element name="since" type="xs:date"/>
              <xs:element name=" qualification " type=" xs:string "/>
            </xs:sequence>
          </xs:complexType>
        </xs:element>
      </xs:sequence>
      < xs:attribute  name="isbn" type=" xs:string "/>
    </xs:complexType>
  </xs:element>
</xs:schema>
```

Figure 3.4. Simple XML schema.

schema language for XML documents (disregarding DTDs), notably because of its support and use in other W3C standards (XPath 2.0, XSLT 2.0, XQuery 1.0, WSDL for describing Web services, etc.). In essence, XML schemas are very close to deterministic top-down tree automata but, as already mentioned, with many practical gadgets. It uses an XML syntax, so it benefits from XML tools such as editors and type checkers.

An example XML schema is given in Figure 3.4. XML schemas first include the definition of simple elements with atomic types, where the common types are xs:string, xs:decimal, xs:integer, xs:boolean, xs:date, xs:time. For instance, one can define

```
<xs:element name="lastname" type="xs:string"/>
<xs:element name="age" type="xs:integer"/>
<xs:element name="dateborn" type="xs:date"/>
```

And corresponding data are

```
<lastname>Refsnes</lastname>
<age>34</age>
<dateborn>1968-03-27</dateborn>
```

One can also define attributes as, for instance in

```
< xs:attribute  name="lang" type="xs:language"/>
```

with for corresponding data

```
<lastname lang="en-US">Smith</lastname>
```

One can impose restrictions of simple elements as in

```
<xs:element name="age">
  <xs:simpleType>
    < xs:restriction  base=" xs:integer ">
      <xs:minInclusive  value="0"/>
      <xs:maxInclusive  value="100"/>
    </ xs:restriction >
  </xs:simpleType>
</xs:element>
```

Other restrictions are enumerated types, patterns defined by regular expressions, etc.

XML schemas also allow defining *complex elements* that possibly correspond to subtrees of more that one nodes. A complex element may be empty, contain text, other elements or be "hybrid" (i.e., contain both some text and subelements).

One can define the content of complex elements as in

```
<xs:element name="person">
  <xs:complexType>
    <xs:sequence>
      <xs:element name="firstname" type=" xs:string "/>
      <xs:element name="lastname" type="xs:string "/>
    </xs:sequence>
```

```
    </xs:complexType>
  </xs:element>
```

It is also possible to specify a type and give it a name.

```
<xs:complexType name="personinfo">
  <xs:sequence> <xs:element name="firstname" type=" xs:string "/>
  <xs:element name="lastname" type="xs:string"/> </xs:sequence>
</xs:complexType>
```

Then we can use this type name in a type declaration, as in

```
<xs:element name="employee" type="personinfo" />
```

One should also mention some other useful gadgets:

1. It is possible to import types associated to a namespace.

```
<xs:import nameSpace = "http://... "
  schemaLocation = "http://... " />
```

2. It is possible to include an existing schema.

```
<xs:include schemaLocation="http://..." />
```

3. It is possible to extend or redefine an existing schema.

```
<xs:redefine schemaLocation="http://..." />
  ... Extensions ...
</ xs:redefine >
```

There are more restrictions on XML schemas, some rather complex. For instance, inside an element, no two types may use the same tag. Some of them can be motivated by the requirement to have efficient type validation (i.e., that the top-down tree automaton defined by the schema is deterministic). The main difference

```
<!ELEMENT book (title, author, character*) >
<!ELEMENT title (#PCDATA) >
<!ELEMENT author (#PCDATA) >
<!ELEMENT character (name,friend-of*,since,qualification)>
<!ELEMENT name (#PCDATA) >
<!ELEMENT name friend-of (#PCDATA) >
<!ELEMENT since (#PCDATA) >
<!ELEMENT qualification (#PCDATA) >

<!ATTLIST book isbn CDATA #IMPLIED >
```

Figure 3.5. Example DTD, corresponding to the XML schema of Figure 3.4.

with DTDs (besides some useful gadgets) is that the notions of types and tags are decoupled.

XML Schema also allows going beyond what is definable by tree automata with *dependencies*: It is possible to define *primary keys* (<xs:key />) and *foreign keys* (<xs:keyref />, in a similar way as keys on relational databases. This extends and complements the xs:ID and xs:IDREF datatypes that XML Schema inherits from DTDs.

To conclude and contrast DTDs with XML Schema, consider again the XML Schema from Figure 3.4. A corresponding DTD is given in Figure 3.5. In this example, the only difference between the DTD and the XML schema is that the DTD is unable to express the datatype constraint on since.

3.3.3 Other Schema Languages for XML

DTDs and XML Schema are just two examples of schema languages that can be used for typing XML documents, albeit important ones because of their wide use and their endorsement by the W3C. We briefly present next other approaches.

RELAX NG RELAX NG (REgular LAnguage for XML Next Generation) is a schema language for XML, spearheaded by the OASIS consortium, and is a direct concurrent to XML Schema, with which it shares a number of features. The most striking difference is at the syntax level, since RELAX NG provides, in addition to an XML syntax, a non-XML syntax, which is much more compact and readable than that of XML Schema. As an example, here is a RELAX NG schema equivalent to the XML Schema of Figure 3.4:

```
element book {
  element title { text },
  element author { text },
  element character {
    element name { text },
```

```
        element friend-of { text }*,
        element since { xsd:date },
        element qualification { text }
    }*,
    attribute isbn { text }
}
```

It is also possible to define named types and reuse them in multiple places of the schema, like with named XML Schema types. The built-in datatypes of RELAX NG are much less rich than what exists in XML Schema, but RELAX NG offers the possibility of using XML Schema datatypes, as shown in the previous example with the datatype xsd:date. RELAX NG is also much more convenient to use when describing unordered content and does not have the same determinism restrictions as XML Schema.

Schematron Schematron is a schema language that is built on different principles as XML Schema or RELAX NG. A Schematron schema is an XML document built out of rules, each rule being an arbitrary XPath expression that describes a constraint to be respected. Schematron is not designed as a stand-alone schema language able to fully describe the structure of a document, but can be used in addition to another schema language to enforce constraints that are hard or impossible to express in this language. Thus, the following Schematron schema ensures that there are as many a elements as b elements as c elements in a whole document:

```
<schema xmlns="http://purl.oclc.org/dsdl/schematron">
  <pattern>
    <rule context="/">
      <assert test="count(//a) = count(//b) and count(//a) = count(//c)">
        Invalid number of characters.
      </assert>
    </rule>
  </pattern>
</schema>
```

Such a constraint on a document is impossible to impose with DTDs, XML schemas, or RELAX NG schemas.

General Programming Languages. In some XML processing contexts, the facilities offered by schema languages for XML are not enough to ensure that a document conforms to a precise type. This might be because the syntax rules are too complex to express in schema languages, or because they deal with syntactic features of XML documents not available in the data model that XML "Validator" use. For instance, the W3C XHTML Validitor checks whether the character set declared in a <meta http-equiv="Content-Type" /> tag conforms to the one used in the textual serialization of the document, which is impossible to do using XML schema languages.

In these cases, a program in a general programming language, such as C, Java, or Perl, possibly with a DOM or SAX XML parser can be used to enforce these extra constraints. Obviously, one loses the advantages of a declarative approach to XML typing.

3.4 TYPING GRAPH DATA

Using the ID and IDREF attribute types in DTDs, or the `<xs:key />` and `<xs:keyref />` XML Schema elements, it is possible to define XML types where one node of the tree references another node in the tree, moving this way from trees to graphs. In this section, we very briefly present a graph data model and mention alternative approaches to typing graph data.

3.4.1 Graph Semistructured Data

Prior to XML trees and ID/IDREF links, different models have been proposed for describing graph data. We next mention one.

Definition 3.4.1 *(Object Exchange Model) An OEM is a finite, labeled, rooted graph* (N, E, r) *(simply* (E, r) *when N is understood) where*

1. *N is a set of nodes;*
2. *E is finite ternary relation subset of* $N \times N \times \mathcal{L}$ *for some set* $\mathcal{L}$ *of labels,* $(E(s, t, l)$ *indicates there is an edge from s to t labeled l);*
3. *r is a node in the graph.*

It should also be stressed that many other graph data models have been considered. In some sense, RDF (see Chapter 7) is also such a graph data model.

3.4.2 Graph Bisimulation

A typing of a graph may be seen in some sense as a classification of its nodes, with nodes in a class sharing the same properties. Such a property is that they "point to" (or are "pointed by") nodes in particular classes. For instance, consider Figure 3.6. A set of nodes forms the class *employee*. From an *employee* node, one can follow *workson*, *leads*, and possibly *consults* edges to some nodes that form the class *project*. This is the basis for typing schemes for graph data based on "simulation" and "bisimulation."

A *simulation* S of (E, r) with (E', r') is a relation between the nodes of E and E' such that

1. $S(r, r')$ and
2. if $S(s, s')$ and $E(s, t, l)$ for some s, s', t, l, then there exists t' with $S(t, t')$ and $E'(s', t', l')$.

The intuition is that we can simulate moves in E by moves in E'.

Given $(E, r), (E', r')$, S is a *bisimulation* if S is a simulation of E with E' and S^{-1} is a simulation of E' with E.

To further see how this relates to typing, take a very complex graph E. We can describe it with a "smaller" graph E' that is a bisimulation of E. There may be several bisimulations for E including more and more details. At one extreme, we have the graph consisting of a single node with a self loop. At the other extreme, we have the graph E itself. This smaller graph E' can be considered as a type for the original graph E. In general, we say that some graph E has type E' if there is a bisimulalation of E and E'.

3.4.3 Data Guides

Another way to type graph data is through *data guides*. Sometimes we are interested only in the paths from the root. This may be useful for instance to provide an interface that allows to navigate in the graph. Consider the OEM graph in Figure 3.6. There are paths such as

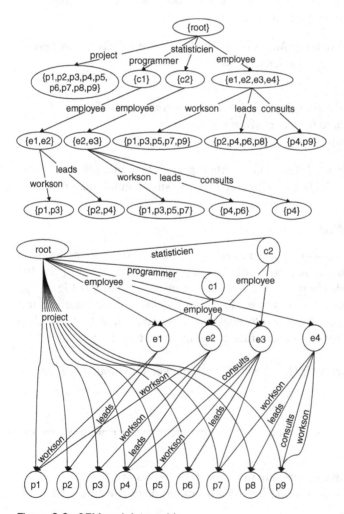

Figure 3.6. OEM and data guide.

programmer
programmer employee
programmer employee workson

It turns out that in general, the set of paths in an OEM graph is a regular language. For instance, for Figure 3.6, the set of paths can be described by the regular language

- Programmer employee leads workson workson?
- Statistician employee leads workson^2 consults?
- Employee leads workson workson?
- Employee leads workson^2 consults?
- Project

A deterministic automaton accepting it is called a *data guide*. A main issue in practice is that the automaton that is obtained "naturally" from the graph is "very" nondeterministic and that the number of states may explode when it is turned into a deterministic automaton.

Observe that the data guide gives some information about the structure of the graph, but only in a limited way: for instance, it does not distinguish between

t1 = r (a (b) a (b d))
t2 = r (a (b b d))

that have the same data guide. Note that a document of type t1 has two *a* elements whereas a document of type *t2* only has one. Furthermore, suppose the *b*s have IDs. Then the document of type *t*1 specifies which of the two *b* elements is related to the *d* element whereas the second one does not.

3.5 FURTHER READING

Schema Inference and Static Typing

Several algorithms for inferring schemas from example documents have been proposed, [27] for DTDs and [28] for XML Schema are recent references that also review other approaches. The problem of static typechecking for XML is reviewed in [125, 152].

Automata

The idea that regular tree languages form the proper basis for typing XML was first proposed in [93]. Finite-state automata theory is at the core of computer science. We suggest to the readers not familiar with the topic to do additional reading. There are numerous texbooks (e.g., [91]). For everything pertaining to tree automata and regular tree languages, a freely available reference is [48].

Schema Languages for XML

DTDs are defined in the W3C Recommendation for XML [174]. The specification of XML Schema is split into three documents: an introductory primer [165], the main part describing the structure of a schema [166], and a description of the built-in datatypes [167]. RELAX NG is defined by an OASIS specification [127] and a separate document [128] defines its compact, non-XML, syntax. Both specifications are also integrated in an ISO standard [97] that is part of the freely available *Document Schema Definition Language* standard. Schematron is defined in another part of this standard [98]. An interesting comparison of schema languages for XML is presented in [89], along with many practical advice on XML document processing.

Typing Languages

A very influencial XML-tranformation language, namely XDuce, is presented in [92]. Its type checker is based on tree-automata type checking. The language XDuce was then extended to the programming language CDuce [26].

Typing Graph Data

For more details about typing semistructured data in general, including graphs, see [5]. Data guides for semistructured data have been proposed in [75]. A query language for the OEM model is proposed in [9].

3.6 EXERCISES

Exercise 3.6.1 *Show how to construct a right-to-left word automaton that accepts the same language as a given left-to-right word automaton.*

Exercise 3.6.2 *Show that the languages accepted by nondeterministic bottom-up tree automata and nondeterministic top-down tree automata are the same.*

Exercise 3.6.3 *The DBLP Computer Science Bibliography, http://www.informatik. uni-trier.de/~ley/db/, maintained by Michael Ley, provides bibliographic information on major computer science journals and proceedings. DBLP indexes more than one million articles as of 2010. The whole content of the DBLP bibliography is available for download from http://dblp.uni-trier.de/xml/ in an XML format, valid against a DTD available at http://www.informatik.uni-trier.de/~ley/db/about/dblp. dtd.*

Retrieve the DBLP DTD from the aforementioned URL, and give a document that validates against it and uses all elements and attributes of the DTD.

Exercise 3.6.4 *Consider the following XML document:*

```
<Robots>
    <Robot type="Astromech">
        <Id>R2D2</Id>
        <maker>Petric Engineering</maker>
        <components>
            <processor>42GGHT</processor>
            <store>1.5 zetabytes</store>
        </components>
```

```
      </Robot>
      <Robot type="Protocol">
      <Id>C-3PO</Id>
      <maker>Xyleme Inc</maker>
         <components>
            <processor>42GGHT</processor>
            <store>100 exabytes</store>
         </components>
      </Robot>
   </Robots>
```

Give a DTD, XML schema, or RELAX NG schema that validate families of robots such as this one.

Exercise 3.6.5 *Consider the following four sets of documents:*

C_1: `<a> <b> <c>x</c> </b> <d> <e>y</e> </d> </a>`
C_2: `<a> <b> <c>x</c> </b> <b> <e/> </b> </a>`
C_3: `<a> <b> <c>x</c> </b> <b/> </a>`
C_4: `<a> <b> <c/> </b> <b> <c>x</c> <c/> </b> </a>`

where x and y stand for arbitrary text nodes. Call these sets C_1, C_2, C_3, C_4.
Questions:

1. *For each $C_i \in \{C_1, C_2, C_3, C_4\}$, give a DTD (if one exists) that accepts exactly C_i. Otherwise, explain briefly what cannot be captured.*
2. *For each $C_i \in \{C_1, C_2, C_3, C_4\}$, is there an XML schema that accepts exactly C_i? If yes, you do not need to give it. Otherwise, explain briefly what cannot be captured.*
3. *Summarize your results of the first two questions in a table of the form:*

	C_1	C_2	C_3	C_4
DTD	yes/no	yes/no	yes/no	yes/no
XML Schema	yes/no	yes/no	yes/no	yes/no

4. *Each time you answered "no" in the previous question, give the schema (DTD or XML Schema, according to the case) that is as restrictive as you can and validates C_i.*
5. *Give a DTD that is as restrictive as you can and validates the four sets of documents (i.e., $\cup_{i=1}^{4} C_i$).*
6. *Describe in words (10 lines maximum) an XML Schema as restrictive as you can that validates the four sets of documents (i.e., $\cup_{i=1}^{4} C_i$).*

Exercise 3.6.6 *Consider the trees with nodes labeled f of arity 1 and g of arity 0. Consider the constraint: "all paths from a leaf to the root have even length." Can this constraint be captured by (i) a nondeterministic bottom-up tree automaton, (ii) a deterministic one, (iii) a top-down deterministic tree automaton?*
   Same question if f is of arity 2.

Exercise 3.6.7 *([48]) Consider the set T of trees with nodes labeled f of arity 2, g of arity 1, and a of arity 0. Define a top-down nondeterministic tree-automaton, a bottom-up one, and a bottom-up deterministic tree-automaton for $G = \{f(a,u), g(v)) \mid u, v \in T\}$. Is it possible to define a top-down deterministic tree automaton for this language?*

4

XML Query Evaluation

In previous chapters, we presented algorithms for evaluating XPath queries on XML documents in PTIME with respect to the combined size of the XML data and of the query. In this context, the entire document is assumed to fit within the main memory. However, very large XML documents may not fit in the memory available to the query processor at runtime. Since access to disk-resident data is orders of magnitude slower than access to the main memory, this dramatically changes the problem. When this is the case, performance-wise, the goal is not so much in reducing the algorithmic complexity of query evaluation but in designing methods reducing the number of disk accesses that are needed to evaluate a given query. The topic of this chapter is the efficient processing of queries of disk-resident XML documents.

We will use extensively depth-first tree traversals in the chapter. We briefly recall two classical definitions:

preorder: To traverse a nonempty binary tree in preorder, perform the following operations recursively at each node, starting with the root node: (1) Visit the root, (2) traverse the left subtree, (3) traverse the right subtree.
postorder: To traverse a nonempty binary tree in postorder, perform the following operations recursively at each node, starting with the root node: (1) Traverse the left subtree, (2) traverse the right subtree, (3) visit the root.

Figure 4.1 illustrates the issues raised by the evaluation of path queries on disk-resident XML documents. The document represents information about some auctions. It contains a list of items for sale, as well as a collection of the currently open auctions. A page size has been chosen, typically reasonably small so that one can access some small unit of information without having to load too much data. A very simple method has been used to store the document nodes on disk. A preorder traversal of the document, starting from the root, groups as many nodes as possible within the current page. When the page is full, a new page is used to store the nodes that are encountered next, and so on. Each thick-lined box in the figure represents a page. Observe, that a node may be stored in a different page than its parent. When this is the case, the "reference" of the child node in the parent page may consist of

(i) the ID of the page that stores the child node and (ii) the offset of the child node in that separate page.

We now consider the processing of simple queries on the document in Figure 4.1:

- /auctions/item requires the traversal of two disk pages;
- /auctions/item/description and
  /auctions/open_auctions/auction/initial
  both require traversing three disk pages;
- //initial requires traversing all the pages of the document.

These examples highlight the risk of costly disk accesses even when the query result is very small. As a consequence, there is a risk of very poor performance on documents stored in such a naïve persistent fashion. Indeed, the example was meant to illustrate that navigation on disk-resident structures may be costly and should be avoided. This is indeed a well-known principle since the days of object-oriented databases.

How can one avoid navigation? Two broad classes of techniques have been proposed.

Smart fragmentation: Since XML nodes are typically accessed by a given property (most often their names and/or their incoming paths), fragmentation aims at decomposing an XML tree into separate collections of nodes, grouped by the value of an interesting, shared property. The goal is to group nodes that are often accessed simultaneously so that the number of pages that need to be accessed in order to process a given query is globally reduced. We present the main approaches for fragmentation in Section 4.1.

Rich node identifiers: Even on a well-fragmented store, some queries may require combining data from more than one stored collection. This can be seen as "stitching" back together separated fragments, and amounts to performing some joins on the identifiers of stored nodes. To make stitching efficient, sophisticated node identifier schemes have been proposed. We present some in Section 4.2 and discuss interesting properties they provide. We present XML query evaluation techniques exploiting node identification schemes in Section 4.3.

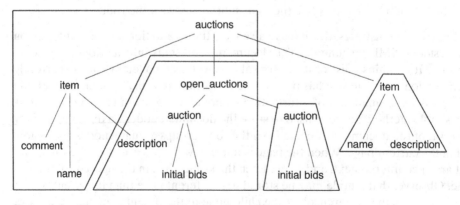

Figure 4.1. Simple page-based storage of an XML tree.

4.1 FRAGMENTING XML DOCUMENTS ON DISK

A set of simple alternatives have been explored for fragmenting XML documents, and they can all be conceptualized with the help of some set of relations. The evaluation of XML queries then turns into a sequence of two steps: translating the XML query into a relational (XML) query and evaluating the relational query on the tables representing the XML document content.

To illustrate fragmentation approaches, we will rely on the sample auction document in Figure 4.2, where we show an integer that allows identifying the node next to each node.

The simplest approach considers a document to be a collection of edges, stored in a single **Edge(pid, cid, clabel)** relation. Here, **cid** is the ID of some node (child node), **pid** stands for the ID of its parent, and **label** is its label (the label of the child node). For instance, part of the document in Figure 4.2 is encoded by the relation shown in Figure 4.3.

Let us now explain the processing of XPath queries relying on such a store. Here and throughout the section, we consider the evaluation of an XPath query up to the point where the identifiers of the result nodes are known. It is then usually straightforward to retrieve the full XML elements based on their identifiers.

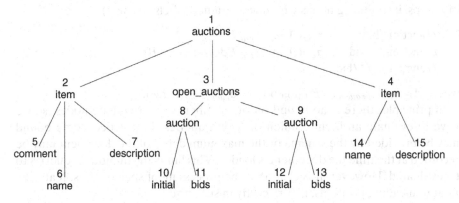

Figure 4.2. Sample XML document with simple node identifiers.

pid	cid	clabel
-	1	auctions
1	2	item
2	5	comment
2	6	name
2	7	description
1	3	open_auctions
3	8	auction
...	...	...

Figure 4.3. Partial instance of the *Edge* relation for the document in Figure 4.2.

■ The query //initial can now be answered by evaluating the expression:

$$\pi_{cid}(\sigma_{clabel=initial}(Edge))$$

The *Edge* storage is quite beneficial for queries of this form (i.e., //a for some node label a), since, with the help of an appropriate index on *Edge.clabel*, one can evaluate such queries quite efficiently.

■ The query /auctions/item translates to the expression:

$$\pi_{cid}((\sigma_{clabel=auctions}(Edge)) \bowtie_{cid=pid} (\sigma_{clabel=item}(Edge)))$$

Observe that the two nodes in the query translate to two occurrences of the *Edge* relation. Similarly, queries such as

/auctions/item/description and

/auctions/open_auctions/auction/initial

require joining several instances of the *Edge* table. Such queries become problematic when the size of the query increases.

■ Now consider a query such as //auction//bid. In the absence of schema information, the distance between the XML nodes matching auction and their descendants matching bid is unknown. Therefore, such queries lead to a union of simpler queries of different-lengths, where the // has been replaced with chains of / steps, introducing nodes with unconstrained labels (using *):

//auction/bid	$\pi_{cid}(A \bowtie_{cid=pid} B)$
//auction/*/bid	$\pi_{cid}(A \bowtie_{cid=pid} Edge \bowtie_{cid=pid} B)$
//auction/*/*/bid	$\cdots$

where $A = \sigma_{clabel=auctions}(Edge)$ and $B = \sigma_{clabel=bid}(Edge)$.

In principle, there is no bound on the number of intermediate nodes, so we have to evaluate an infinite union of XPath queries. In practice, some bound may be provided by the schema or the maximum depth of the document may be recorded at the time the document is loaded. This limits the number of queries to be evaluated. However, it is clear that the processing of such queries, featuring // at nonleading positions, is very costly in such a setting.

Tag Partitioning A straightforward variation on the above approach is the *tag-partitioned Edge* relation. The *Edge* relation is partitioned into as many tag-based relations as there are different tags in the original document. Each such relation stores the identifiers of the nodes, and the identifiers of their respective parents. (There is no need to store the label in such a partitioned table, since it is the same for all its nodes.) Figure 4.4 illustrates tag-partitioning for the document in Figure 4.2.

Clearly, the tag-partitioned *Edge* store reduces the disk I/O needed to retrieve the identifiers of elements having a given tag, since it suffices to scan the corresponding tag-partitioned relation. However, the partitioning of queries with // steps in nonleading position remains as difficult as it is for the *Edge* approach.

Path Partitioning The *Path-partitioning* fragmentation approach aims at solving the problem raised by // steps at arbitrary positions in a query. The idea is roughly

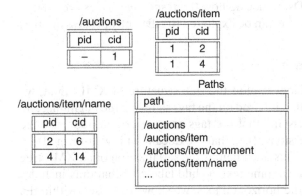

Figure 4.4. Portions of the tag-partitioned *Edge* relations for the document in Figure 4.2.

/auctions

pid	cid
–	1

/auctions/item

pid	cid
1	2
1	4

/auctions/item/name

pid	cid
2	6
4	14

Paths

path
/auctions
/auctions/item
/auctions/item/comment
/auctions/item/name
...

Figure 4.5. Relations resulting from the path-partitioned storage of the document in Figure 4.2.

to encode the data guide (see Section 3.4.3) of the XML data set in a set of rela-tions. There is one relation for each distinct parent-child path in the document, e.g., /auctions/item/name. There is also an extra table, namely path containing all the unique paths. Figure 4.5 illustrates the resulting relations for the document in Figure 4.2.

Based on a path-partitioned store, a linear query such as //item//bid can be evaluated in two steps:

- Scan the **path** relation and identify all the parent-child paths matching the given linear XPath query;
- For each of the paths thus obtained, scan the corresponding path-partitioned table.

On a path-partitioned store, the evaluation of XPath queries with many branches will still require joins across the relations. However, the evaluation of // steps is simplified, thanks to the first processing step, performed on the path relation. For very structured data, this relation is typically small, much smaller than the data set itself. Thus, the cost of the first processing step is likely negligible, while the performance benefits of avoiding numerous joins are quite important. However, for some data, the path relation can quite large and, in pathological cases, even larger than the data.

4.2 XML NODE IDENTIFIERS

We have seen that, within a persistent XML store, each node must be assigned a unique identifier (or ID, in short). Such an identifier plays the role of a primary key to the node, which allows distinguishing it from other nodes even if they have the same label and pairwise identical children. In a fragmented store, moreover, these identifiers are essential to be able to reconnect nodes according to their relationships and to reconstruct the original XML document.

Going beyond these simple ID roles, we show next that it is very useful to encapsulate in identifiers some knowledge of the element's position within the original document. Indeed, with particular node identifiers, it even becomes possible, just by considering two XML node IDs, to decide how the respective nodes are related in the document. We will see how this can be exploited to efficiently process queries.

4.2.1 Region-Based Identifiers

Typically, the identifiers we consider exploit the tree structure of XML. First, we present an identification scheme that is based on the tags signaling the beginning and the end of XML elements. We assume that the tags are properly nested (just like parentheses in arithmetical expressions) (i.e., that the document is well-formed).

Figure 4.6 shows an example. This document is the serialization of an XML tree with a root labeled a, which includes some text, a child labeled b that only includes text, followed by some text. On the horizontal axis, we show the offset, within the XML file, at which begin tags, such as <a>, and end tags, such as </a>, respectively, are encountered. In the figure, the a element is the root of the document; thus, its begin tag starts at offset 0. The b element starts at offset 30 in the file and finishes at offset 50. Observe that due to the well-formedness of an XML document, an element's begin tag must follow the begin tags of its ancestors. Similarly, an element's end tag must precede the end tags of its ancestors.

The so-called region-based identifier scheme simply assigns to each XML node n, the pair composed of the offset of its begin tag, and the offset of its end tag. We denote this pair by $(n.begin, n.end)$. In the example in Figure 4.6:

- the region-based identifier of the <a> element is the pair $(0, 90)$;
- the region-based identifier of the <b> element is pair $(30, 50)$.

Comparing the region-based identifiers of two nodes n_1 and n_2 allows deciding whether n_1 is an ancestor of n_2. Observe that this is the case if and only if:

- $n_1.start < n_2.start$ and
- $n_2.end < n_1.end$.

Thus, by considering only the identifiers $n_1 = (0, 90)$ and $n_2 = (30, 50)$, and without having to access the respective nodes or any other data structures, one can decide that the element identified by n_1 is an ancestor of the element identified by n_2. Contrast this simple decision procedure with the costly navigation required to answer a similar question on the page-fragmented storage shown in Figure 4.1!

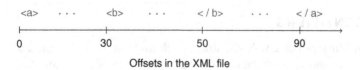

Figure 4.6. Region-based identifiers.

Region-based node identifiers are the simplest and most intuitive structural XML IDs. The simple variant presented using offsets in the serialized XML file can be implemented easily, since one only needs to gather offsets inside the file corresponding to the serialized document. However, for the purpose of efficiently evaluating tree pattern queries, one does not need to count all characters in the file, but only the information describing how elements are structurally related in the XML tree. Popular variants of region-based identifiers based on this observation include the following:

(Begin tag, end tag): Instead of counting characters (offsets), count only opening and closing tags (as one unit each) and assign the resulting counter values to each element. Following this scheme, the `<a>` element in Figure 4.6 is identified by the pair $(1,4)$, while the `<b>` element is identified by the pair $(2,3)$.

The pair (begin tag, end tag) clearly allows inferring whether an element is an ancestor of another by simple comparisons of the ID components.

(Pre, post): The *(pre, post)* identifiers are computed as follows:

- Perform a preorder traversal of the tree. Count nodes during the traversal and assign to each node its corresponding counter value. This would assign the so-called *pre number* of 1 to the a-node, and the pre number of 2 to the b-node.
- Perform a post-order traversal of the tree. Count nodes during the traversal and assign to each node its corresponding counter value, called *post number*. For instance, the post number of `<a>` in Figure 4.6 is 2, and the post number of `<b>` is 1.

The (pre, post) IDs still allow inferring whether an element n_1 is an *ancestor* of another one n_2 (i.e., if $n_1.pre \leq n_2.pre$ and $n_2.post \leq n_1.post$).

It is also useful to be able to decide whether an element is *a parent* of another. The following variant allows to do so:

(Pre, post, depth): This scheme adds to the (pre, post) pair an integer representing the depth, or distance from the document root, at which the corresponding individual node is found. An element identified by n_1 is the parent of an element identified by n_2, if and only if the following conditions hold:

- n_1 is an ancestor of n_2 and
- $n_1.depth = n_2.depth - 1$.

For illustration, Figure 4.7 shows the XML document of the running example, with nodes adorned with (pre, post, depth) identifiers.

Region-based identifiers are quite compact, as their size only grows logarithmically with the number of nodes in a document.

4.2.2 Dewey-Based Identifiers

Another family of identifiers borrows from the well-known Dewey classification scheme, widely used, for example, in libraries long before computers and databases took over the inventories. The principle of Dewey IDs is quite simple: The ID of a node is obtained by adding a suffix to the ID of the node's parent. The suffix should

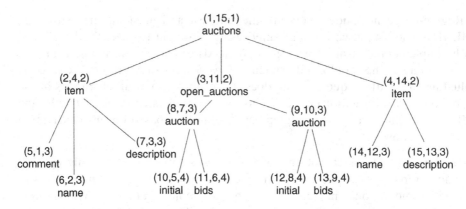

Figure 4.7. Sample XML document with (pre, post, depth) node identifiers.

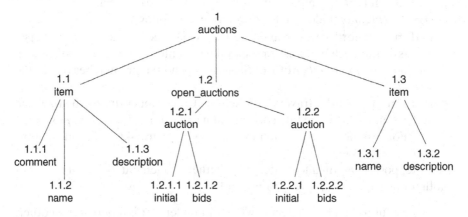

Figure 4.8. Sample XML document with Dewey node identifiers.

allow distinguishing each node from all its siblings that are also constructed starting from the same parent ID. For instance, the root may be numbered 1, its first child 1.1, its second child 1.2 and so on. For example, Figure 4.8 shows our sample XML document with the nodes adorned with Dewey node IDs.

Dewey IDs encapsulate structural information in a much more explicit way than region IDs. We illustrate some aspects next. Let n_1 and n_2 be two identifiers of the form $n_1 = x_1.x_2.\ldots.x_m$ and $n_2 = y_1.y_2.\cdots.y_n$. Then:

- The node identified by n_1 is an ancestor of the node identified by n_2 if and only if n_1 is a prefix of n_2. When this is the case, the node identified by n_1 is the parent of the node identified by n_2 if and only if $n = m + 1$.
- Dewey IDs also allow establishing other relationships such as preceding-sibling and before (respectively, following-sibling, and after). The node identified by n_1 is a preceding sibling of the node identified by n_2 if and only if (i) $x_1.x_2.\ldots.x_{m-1} = y_1.y_2.\ldots.y_{n-1}$; and (ii) $x_m < y_n$.
- Given two Dewey IDs n_1 and n_2, one can find the ID of the *lowest common ancestor (LCA)* of the corresponding nodes. The ID of the LCA is the longest common prefix of n_1 and n_2. For instance, in Figure 4.8, the LCA of the nodes

identified by 1.2.1.1 and 1.2.2.2 is 1.2. Determining the LCA of two nodes is useful, for instance, when searching XML documents based on a set of keywords. In this context, the user does not specify the size or type of the desired answer, and the system may return the smallest XML subtrees containing matches for all the user-specified keywords. It turns out that such smallest XML subtrees are exactly those rooted at the LCA of the nodes containing the keywords.

As just discussed, Dewey IDs provide more information than region-based IDs. The main drawback of Dewey IDs is their potentially much larger size. Also, the fact that IDs have lengths that may vary a lot within the same document complicates processing.

4.2.3 Structural Identifiers and Updates

Observe that identifier of a node for all the forms mentioned in Section 4.2.2 may change when the XML document that contains this node is updated. For instance, consider a node with Dewey ID 1.2.2.3. Suppose we insert a new first child to node 1.2. Then the ID of node 1.2.2.3 becomes 1.2.3.3.

In general, offset-based identifiers need to change even if a simple character is added to or removed from a text node in the XML document, since this changes the offsets of all nodes occurring in the document *after* the modified text node. Identifiers based on the (start, end) or (pre, post) model, as well as Dewey IDs, are not impacted by updates to the document's text nodes. One may also choose to leave them unchanged when removing nodes or even full subtrees from the document. Using any of the three methods mentioned above, if we leave the identification unchanged when subtrees are removed, we introduce gaps in the sequence of identifiers of the remaining nodes. However, these gaps do not affect in any way the computation of structural joins.

The management of insertions, on the other hand, is much more intricate. When inserting an XML node n_{new}, the identifiers of all nodes occurring after n_{new} in the preorder traversal of the tree, need to change. Depending on the ID model, such changes may also affect the IDs of n_{new}'s ancestors. The process of reassigning identifiers to XML nodes after a document update is known as *relabeling*.

In application scenarios where XML updates are expected to be frequent, relabeling may raise important performance issues.

4.3 XML QUERY EVALUATION TECHNIQUES

We present in the next section techniques for the efficient evaluation of XML queries, and in particular for tree pattern queries.

4.3.1 Structural Join

The first techniques concern structural joins and can be seen as foundational to all the others. Structural joins are physical operators capable of combining tuples from two inputs, much in the way regular joins in the relation case do, but based on a structural condition (thus the name). Formally, let p_1 and p_2 be some partial evaluation plans in an XML database, such that attribute X in the output of p_1, denoted

$p_1.X$, and attribute Y from the output of p_2, denoted $p_2.Y$, both contain structural IDs. Observe that the setting is very general, that is, we make no assumption on how p_1 and p_2 are implemented, which physical operators they contain, and so on. Let $\prec$ denote the binary relationship "isParentOf" and $\prec\!\!\prec$ denote the binary relationship "isAncestorOf." Formally then, the structural join of p_1 and p_2 on the condition that $p_1.X$ be an ancestor of $p_2.Y$ is defined as

$$p_1 \bowtie_{X \prec\!\!\prec Y} p_2 = \{(t_1, t_2) \mid t_1 \in p_1, t_2 \in p_2, t_1.X \prec\!\!\prec t_2.Y\}$$

and the structural join on the parent relation $\prec$ is similarly defined by

$$p_1 \bowtie_{X \prec Y} p_2 = \{(t_1, t_2) \mid t_1 \in p_1, t_2 \in p_2, t_1.X \prec t_2.Y\}$$

We have seen that expressive node IDs allow deciding just by comparing two IDs whether the respective nodes are related or not. Now, what is needed is an efficient way of establishing how the nodes from *sets* of tuples are related (i.e., how to efficiently evaluate a join of the form $p_1 \bowtie_{X \prec\!\!\prec Y} p_2$). Efficiency for a join operator means reducing its CPU costs, and avoiding incurring memory and I/O costs. For our discussion, let $|p_1|$ denote the number of tuples output by p_1, and $|p_2|$ the number of tuples output by p_2.

One can consider the following different kinds of joins:

Nested loop join: The simplest physical structural join algorithms could proceed in *nested loops*. One iterates over the output of p_1 and, for each tuple, one iterates over the output of p_2. However, this leads to CPU costs in $O(|p_1| \times |p_2|)$, since each p_1 tuple is compared with each p_2 tuple.

Hash join: As in traditional relational database settings, one could consider *hash joins* that are often called upon for good performance, given that their CPU costs are in $O(|p_1| + |p_2|)$. However, hash-based techniques cannot apply here because the comparisons that need to be carried are of the form "is id_1 an ancestor of id_2?" which do not lead themselves to a hash-based approach.

Stack-based join: To efficiently perform this task, operators for *stack-based* structural joins have been proposed originally for *(start, end)* ID scheme. They can be used for other labeling schemes as well. We discuss these joins next.

To be able to use stack-based joins, the structural IDs must allow efficiently answering the following questions:

1. Is id_1 the identifier of the parent of the node identified by id_2? The same question can be asked for ancestor.
2. Does id_1 start after id_2 in preorder traversal of the tree? In other words, does the opening tag of the node identified by id_1 occur in the document after the opening tag of the node identified by id_2?
3. Does id_1 end after id_2? In other words, does the closing tag of the node identified by id_1 occur in the document after the closing tag of the node identified by id_2?

Assuming each of these questions can be answered fast, say in constant time, based on the values of id_1 and id_2, stack-based structural joins can be evaluated in $\Omega(|p_1| + |p_2|)$, which is very efficient. Intuitively, we start with the two lists of

$< \text{root}_{(1,5)} > < \text{list}_{(2,4)} > < \text{list}_{(3,3)} > < \text{para}_{(4,2)} > < \text{para}_{(5,1)}/ > < /\text{para} >$

$< /\text{list} > < /\text{list} > < /\text{root} >$

Ordered by ancestor ID (list ID)		Ordered by descendantID (para ID)	
(2,4)	(4,2)	(2,4)	(4,2)
(2,4)	(5,1)	(3,3)	(4,2)
(3,3)	(4,2)	(2,4)	(5,1)
(3,3)	(5,1)	(3,3)	(5,1)

Figure 4.9. Sample XML snippet and orderings of the (list ID, para ID) tuples.

identifiers. Condition (1) allows deciding whether a pair (i,j) with i from one list and j from the other is a solution. Because of Conditions (2) and (3), we can just scan the two lists (keeping some running stacks) and do not have to consider *all* such (i,j) pairs.

More precisely, two algorithms have been proposed, namely, StackTreeDescendant (or STD in short) and StackTreeAncestor (or STA in short). The algorithms are quite similar. They both require the input p_1 tuples sorted in the increasing order[1] of $p_1.X$, and the input p_2 tuples in the increasing order of $p_2.Y$. The difference between STD and STA is the order in which they produce their output: STD produces output tuples sorted by the ancestor ID, whereas STA produces them sorted by the descendant ID.

To see why the two orders do not always coincide, consider the XML snippet shown in Figure 4.9, with the *(start, end)* IDs appearing as subscripts in the opening tags. In the figure, we show the (ancestor, descendant) ID pairs from this snippet, where the ancestor is a list, and the descendant is a paragraph (labeled "para").

Observe that the second and third tuples differ in the two tuple orders. This order issue is significant, since both STD and STA require inputs to be ordered by the IDs on which the join is to be made. Thus, when combining STD and STA joins in larger query evaluation plans, if the order of results in one join's output is not the one required by its parent operator, Sort operators may need to be inserted, adding to the CPU costs, and delaying the moment when the first output tuple is built. We now introduce the STD algorithm by means of an example, leaving STA as further reading.

Figure 4.10 shows a sample XML document with *(start, end)* IDs shown as subscripts of the nodes. In this example, the structural join to be evaluated must compute all pairs of (ancestor, descendant) nodes such that the ancestors are labeled b and the descendants are labeled g.

Figure 4.10 shows a sequence of snapshots during STD execution, with arrows denoting transitions from one snapshot to the next one.

In each snapshot, the first table shows the inputs (i.e., the ordered lists of IDs of the b nodes), respectively, of the g nodes. The algorithm's only internal data structure is a stack, in which *ancestor* node IDs are all successively pushed, and from which they are popped on later.

---

[1] This is the lexicographical order, i.e. $((i,j) < (i',j')$ if $i < i'$ or if $i = i'$ and $j < j')$.

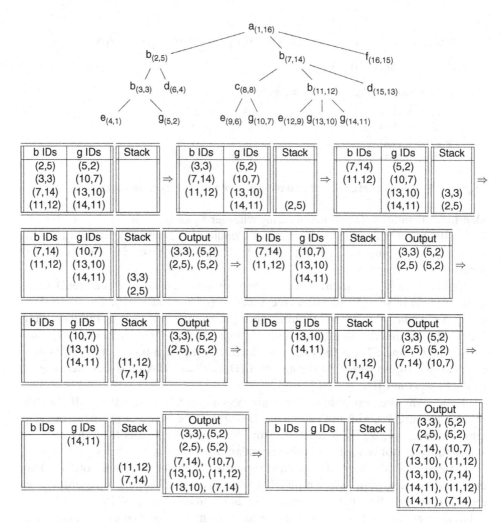

Figure 4.10. Sample XML tree, and successive snapshots of the inputs and stack during the execution of a StackTreeDescendant (STD) structural join.

STD execution starts by pushing the ancestor (i.e., *b* node) ID on the stack, namely (2,5). Then, STD continues to examine the IDs in the *b* ancestor input. As long as the current ancestor ID is a descendant of the top of the stack, the current ancestor ID is pushed on the stack, without considering the descendant IDs at all. This is illustrated by the second *b* ID, (3,3) pushed on the stack, since it is a descendant of (2,5). The third ID in the *b* input, (7,14), is not a descendant of current stack top, namely (2,5). Therefore, STD stops pushing *b* IDs on the stack and considers the current descendant ID to see if it has matches *on the stack*. It turns out that the first *g* node, namely (5,2), is a descendant of both *b* nodes on the stack, leading to the first two output tuples. Observe that the stack content does not change when output is produced. This is because there may be further descendant IDs to match these ancestor IDs on the stack.

Importantly, *a descendant ID that has been compared with ancestor IDs on the stack and has produced output tuples can be discarded after the comparisons*. In other words, we are certain that this descendant has encountered *all its ancestors from the ancestor stream*. This is because of the way in which ancestor IDs are pushed on the stack (push as long as they are ancestors of each other). Indeed, all the ancestors of a given g node, for instance, are on a single vertical path in the document; therefore, they are guaranteed to be on the stack when the lowermost g element encounters some descendants in the descendant input. In our example, once the (5,2) node ID has lead to producing output, it is discarded.

As the STD execution continues, the g ID (10,7) encounters no matches on the stack. Moreover, (10,7) occurs in the original document *after* the nodes on the stack. Therefore, *no descendant node ID yet to be examined can have ancestors on this stack*. This is because the input g IDs are in document order. Thus, if the current g ID is after the stack nodes, all future g IDs will also occur "too late" to be descendants of the nodes in the current stack. Therefore, at this point, the stack is emptied. This explains why *once an ancestor ID has transited through the stack and has been popped away, no descendant ID yet to be examined could produce a join result with this ancestor ID*.

The previous discussion provides the two reasons for the efficiency of STD:

- A single pass over the descendants suffices (each is compared with the ancestor IDs on the stack only once);
- A single pass over the ancestors suffices (each transits through the stack only once).

Thus, the STD algorithm can apply in a streaming fashion, reading each of its inputs only once and thus with CPU costs in $\Omega(|p_1| + |p_2|)$.

Continuing to follow our illustrative execution, the ancestor ID (7,14) is pushed on the stack, followed by its descendant (in the ancestor input) (11,12). The next descendant ID is (10,7) which produces a result with (7,14) and is then discarded. The next descendant ID is (13,10), which leads to two new tuples added in the output, and similarly the descendant ID (14,11) leads to two more output tuples.

Observe in Figure 4.10 that, true to its name, the STD algorithm produces output tuples sorted by the descendant ID.

4.3.2 Optimizing Structural Join Queries

Algorithm STD allows combining two inputs based on a structural relationship between an ID attribute of one plan and an ID attribute of the other. Using STD and the similar STA, one can compute matches for larger query tree patterns, by combining sets of identifiers of nodes having the labels appearing in the query tree pattern.

This is illustrated in Figure 4.11, which shows a sample tree pattern and a corresponding structural join plan for evaluating it based on collections of identifiers for a, b, c, and d nodes. The plan in Figure 4.11(b) is a first attempt at converting the logical plan into a physical executable plan. In Figure 4.11(b), the first logical structural join is implemented using the STD algorithm, whose output will be sorted by b.ID. The second structural join can be implemented by STD (leading to an output ordered by c.ID) or STA (leading to an output ordered by b.ID), but in both cases, the output of this second structural join is not guaranteed to be sorted by

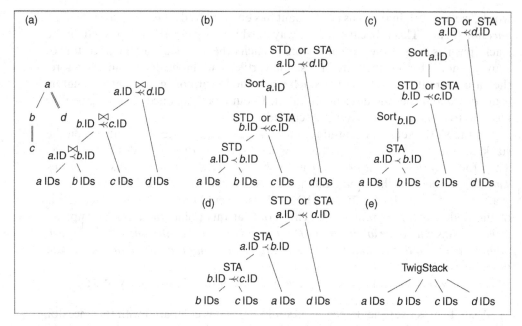

Figure 4.11. Tree pattern query and a corresponding logical structural join plan (a); possible physical plans (b)–(e).

a.ID. Therefore, a Sort operator is needed to adapt the output of the second join to the input of the third join, which requires its left-hand input sorted by a.ID.

The plan in Figure 4.11(c) uses STA instead of STD for the first structural join (between a.ID and b.ID). This choice, however, is worse than the one in Figure 4.11(b) because a Sort operator is needed after the first join to reorder its results on b.ID, and a second Sort operator is needed to order the output of the second physical join, on a.ID. The Sort operators are blocking (i.e., they require completely reading their input before producing their first output tuple). Therefore, they increase the time to the first output tuple produced by the physical plan and the total running time.

In contrast to the plans in Figures 4.11(b) and 4.11(c), the plan in Figure 4.11(d) allows evaluating the same query and does not require any Sort operator. Observe, however, that the plan does not apply joins in the same order as the other ones in Figure 4.11. In general, it turns out that for any tree pattern query, there exist some plans using the STD and STA physical operators, and which do not require any Sort (also called *fully pipelined plans*). However, one cannot ensure *a fully pipelined plan for a given join order*. For instance, in Figure 4.11, the reader can easily check that no fully pipelined plan exists for the join order $a \prec b$, $b \prec\!\!\!\prec c$, $a \prec\!\!\!\prec d$.

This complicates the problem of finding an efficient evaluation plan based on structural joins because two optimization objectives are now in conflict:

- ■ Avoiding Sort operators (to reduce the time to the first output, and the total running time) and
- ■ Choosing the join order that minimizes the sizes of the intermediary join results.

Algorithms for finding efficient, fully pipelined plans are discussed in [181].

4.3.3 Holistic Twig Joins

Section 4.3.2 showed how, in a query evaluation engine including binary structural join operators, one can reduce the total running time by avoiding Sort operators and reduce the total running time and/or the size of the intermediary join results by chosing the order in which to perform the joins.

A different approach toward the goals of reducing the running time *and* the size of the intermediary results consists in devising a new (logical and physical operator, more precisely, an *n*-ary structural join operator, also called a *holistic*) twig join. Such an operator builds the result of a tree pattern query in a single pass over all the inputs in parallel. This eliminates the need for storing intermediary results and may also significantly reduce the total running time.

Formally, let q be a tree pattern query having n nodes, such that for $1 \leq i \leq n$, the i-th node of the pattern is labeled a_i. Without loss of generality, assume that q's root is labeled a_1. For each node labeled a_i, $2 \leq i \leq n$, we denote by a_i^p is the parent of a_i in q.

We first define the *logical* holistic twig join operator. Assume available a set of logical sub-plans $lp_1, lp_2, \ldots, lp_n$ such that for each i, $1 \leq i \leq n$, the plan lp_i outputs structural IDs of elements labeled a_i. The logical holistic structural join of $lp_1, lp_2, \ldots, lp_n$ based on q, denoted $\bowtie_q (lp_1, lp_2, \ldots, lp_n)$, is defined as

$$\sigma_{(a_2^p \ll a_2) \wedge (a_3^p \ll a_3) \wedge \cdots \wedge (a_n^p \ll a_n)}(lp_1 \times lp_2 \times \cdots \times lp_n)$$

In this expression, we assumed that all edges in q correspond to the ancestor-descendant relationship. To account for the case where the edge between a_i and a_i^p is parent-child, one needs to replace the atom $a_i^p \ll a_i$ in the selection, by $a_i^p \prec a_i$.

We now turn to discussing efficient *physical* holistic twig join operators. For ease of explanation, we first present an algorithm called PathStack, for evaluating *linear* queries only, and then generalize to the TwigStack algorithm for the general case.

Algorithm PathStack   The algorithm uses as auxiliary data structures one stack S_i for each query node n_i labeled a_i. During execution, PathStack pushes IDs of nodes labeled a_i in the corresponding stack S_i. At the end of the execution, each stack S_i holds exactly those IDs of nodes labeled a_i, which participate to one or more result tuples.

PathStack works by continuously looking for the input operator (let's call it iop_{min}, corresponding to the query node n_{min} labeled a_{min}) whose first ID has the smallest *pre* number among all the input streams. This amounts to finding the first element (in document order) among those not yet processed, across all inputs. Let's call this element e_{min}.

Once e_{min} has been found, PathStack inspects all the stacks, looking for nodes of which it can be guaranteed that they will not contribute to further query results. In particular, this is the case for any nodes *preceding* e_{min} (i.e., ending before the start of e_{min}). It is easy to see that such nodes cannot be ancestors of e_{min} nor of any of the remaining nodes in any of the inputs because these remaining nodes have a starting position even bigger than e_{min}'s. PathStack pops all such entries, from all stacks.

PathStack then pushes the current n_{min} entry on $S_{a_{min}}$, if and only if suitable ancestors of this element have already been identified and pushed on the stack of

a^p_{min}, the parent node of a_{min} in the query. If this is the case and a new entry is pushed on $S_{a_{min}}$, importantly, a pointer is stored *from the top entry in $S_{a^p_{min}}$, to the new (top) entry in $S_{a_{min}}$*. Such pointers record the connections between the stack entries matching different query nodes and will be used to build out result tuples (as discussed later). Finally, PathStack advances the input operator iop_{min} and resumes its main loop, identifying again the input operator holding the first element (in document order) not yet processed, and so on.

When an entry is pushed on the stack corresponding to the query *leaf*, we are certain that the stacks contain matches for all its ancestors in the query, matches that are ancestors of the leaf stack entry. At this point, two steps are applied:

1. Result tuples are built out of the entries on the stacks, and in particular of the new entry on the stack of the query leaf;
2. This new entry is popped from the stack.

Figure 4.12 illustrates the algorithm through successive snapshots of the input streams and stacks, for the sample document shown at left in the figure. The first execution snapshot is taken at the start: All stacks are empty, and all streams are set to their first element. The search for the iop_{min} operator is done by comparing the top elements in all the streams. In this case, the smallest element ID is (2,14) in the stack of a; therefore, n_{min} is set to this node, and n_{min} is pushed on the correspondint stack S_a. The stream of a advances to the next position, and we seek again for the new iop_{min}, which turns out to be the stream of b IDs. The new value of n_{min} is the b node identified by (3,13); this node is therefore pushed on the b stack and the pointer from (2,14) to (3,13) records the connection between the two stack entries (which corresponds to a structural connection in the document). The b stream is advanced again, and then iop_{min} is found to be the a stream, leading to pushing (4,12) on the a stack.

At this point, we must check the entries in the stacks corresponding to descendants of a, and possibly prune "outdated" entries (nodes preceding the newly

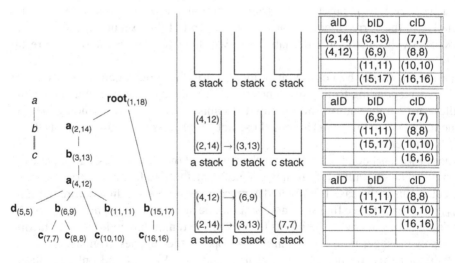

Figure 4.12. Sample tree pattern, XML document, and stacks for the PathStack algorithm.

pushed a in the document). In our case, there is only one entry in the b stack. Comparing its ID, (3,13) with the ID (4,12) of the newly pushed a element, we decide that the (3,13) entry should be preserved in the b stack for the time being.

After advancing the a stream, PathStack's data structures take the form shown in the middle snapshot at right in Figure 4.12.

The process is repeated and pushes the (6,9) identifier on the b stack. No entry is eliminated from the c stack since it is still empty. The algorithm then pushes the identifiers (7,7) on the c stack and connects it to the current to p of the b stack, namely (6,9). This is the situation depicted at the bottom right of Figure 4.12.

Observe that (7,7) is a match of the c node which is a leaf in the query. Thus, at this point, the following result tuples are built out of the stacks, based on the connections between stack entries:

aID	bID	cID
(2,14)	(3,13)	(7,7)
(2,14)	(6,9)	(7,7)
(4,12)	(6,9)	(7,7)

The (7,7) entries are then popped from their stack, and (8,8) takes its place, leading similarly to the result tuples:

aID	bID	cID
(2,14)	(3,13)	(8,8)
(2,14)	(6,9)	(8,8)
(4,12)	(6,9)	(8,8)

Now, the smallest element not yet processed is identified by (10,10) in the stream of c elements. This element is *not* pushed in the c stack because it is not a descendant of the current top of the b stack (namely, (6,9)).

Continuing execution, the b element identified by (11,11) is examined. It leads to expunging from the stacks all entries whose end number is smaller than 11, and in particular, the b entry (6,9). (11,11) is then pushed on the b stack. When (15,17) is read from the b stream, all existing a and b entries are popped; however, (15,17) is not pushed due to the lack of a suitable ancestor in the a stack. Finally, (16,16) is not pushed, by a similar reasoning.

The algorithm has two features of interest:

■ No intermediary result tuples: Results are built directly as n-tuples, where n is the size of the query. This avoids the multiplication, say, of every a element by each of its b descendants, before learning whether or not any of these bs had a c descendant.

■ Space-efficient encoding of results: Thanks to the pointer structures and to the way the algorithm operates, the total size of the entries stored on the stacks at any point in times is bound by $|d| \times |q|$; however, such stack entries allow encoding up to $|d|^{|q|}$ query results, a strong saving in terms of space (and thus, performance).

Algorithm TwigStack This algorithm generalizes PathStack with support for multiple branches. The ideas are very similar, as the main features (no intermediary

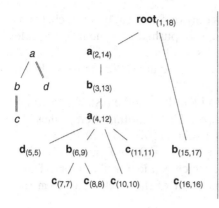

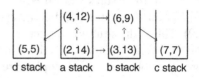

a ID	b ID	c ID	d ID
(2,14)	(3,13)	(7,7)	(5,5)
(4,12)	(6,9)	(8,8)	
	(11,11)	(10,10)	
	(15,17)	(16,16)	

Figure 4.13. Sample tree pattern, XML document, and stacks for the TwigStack algorithm.

results and space-efficient encoding of twig query results) are the same. Figure 4.13 shows a twig (tree) pattern query derived from the linear query of Figure 4.12 by adding a lateral c branch. The document is the same in both figures.

At right in Figure 4.13, we show the input streams at the beginning of the execution (top right) as well as a snapshot of the stacks at the moment during execution when (7,7) has been pushed on the c stack. Now that there is a match for each query leaf node, the following tuples are output:

a**ID**	b**ID**	c**ID**	d**ID**
(2,14)	(3,13)	(7,7)	(5,5)
(2,14)	(6,9)	(7,7)	(5,5)
(4,12)	(6,9)	(7,7)	(5,5)

One can show [37] that if the query pattern edges are only of type ancestor/ descendant, TwigStack is I/O and CPU optimal among all sequential algorithms that read their inputs in their entirety.

4.4 FURTHER READING

The XML storage, indexing, and query processing area is still very active and has witnessed a wide variety of techniques and algorithms.

Interval-based node IDs were first proposed in the context of efficient relational storage for XML documents in XRel [185] and XParent [105]. As pointed out in the original structural join paper [15], they are, however, inspired by known works in information retrieval systems, which assign positional identifiers to occurrences of words in text and are closely related to the Dietz numbering scheme [57]. Dewey-style XML identifiers were used, for instance, in [146].

Compact labeling of trees is now a mature topic, see [2, 106].

Simple region and Dewey-based ID schemes suffer when the document is updated, since this may require extensive node relabeling. ORDPATH IDs [130] offer a remedy to this problem. An ORDPATH ID is a dot-separated sequence of labels, in the style of Dewey, but using integer labels and playing on the odd/

even character of the numbers to allow inserting nodes at any place without relabeling any existing node. ORDPATHs were implemented within the Microsoft SQL Server's XML extension. Other interesting node identifier schemes, trading between compactness, efficient query evaluation, and resilience to updates, are described in [119,181] and, among the most recent works, in [184].

Stack-based structural joins operators have been proposed in [15]. Heuristics for selecting the best join order in this context are presented in [181]. The TwigStack algorithm is presented in [37]. Numerous improvements have been subsequently brought to TwigStack, mainly by adding B-Tree style indexes on the inputs. This enables skipping some of the input IDs, if it can be inferred that they will not contribute to the query result.

Given the robustness of relational database management systems, many works have considered using relational DBMSs to store and query XML documents. The first works in this area are [67, 147]. An interesting line of works starting with [81–83] considered the efficient handling of XML data in relational databases relying on (start, end) identifiers. The special properties satisfied by such IDs (and which are due to the nested nature of XML documents) is exploited in these works to significantly speed up the processing of XPath queries and, more generally, of (XQuery) tree pattern queries. These works also provide an extensive approach for faithfully translating XML queries expressed in XPath and XQuery, into relational algebra (endowed with minimal extensions). In a more recent development, this algebraic approach has been compiled to be executed by the MONETDB column-based relational store [32].

Manipulating XML documents within relational databases and *jointly with relational data* has been considered quite early on in the industrial world. The ISO standard SQL/XML [99] is an extension to the SQL language, allowing a new elementary data type xml. A relation can have columns of type xml, which can be queried using XPath/XQuery invoked by a built-in function, within a regular SQL query. SQL/XML also provides facilities for declaratively specifying a mapping to export relational data in an XML form.

4.5 EXERCISES

The following exercises will allow you to derive a set of results previously established in the literature, which have been used to efficiently implement tree pattern query evaluation.

Exercise 4.5.1 *(inspired from [83])*
Recall the notions of pre, post, and level numbers assigned to nodes in an XML document:

■ *The pre number of node n, denoted n.pre, is the number assigned to n when n is first reached by a preorder traversal of the document;*
■ *The post number of node n, denoted n.post, is the number assigned to n when n is first reached by a postorder traversal of the document;*
■ *The level number of node n is 0 if n is the root element of the document; otherwise, it is the number of edges traversed on the path from the root element to n.*

Moreover, we denote by size(n) the number of descendants of a node n. We denote the height of a document d by h(d).

1. *Prove that for any XML node n*

   $$n.pre - n.post + size(n) = n.level$$

2. *Let n be an XML node and n_{rl} be the rightmost leaf descendant of n. In other word, n_{rl} is attained by navigating from n to its last child r_1 (if it exists), from r_1 to its last child r_2 (if its exist) and so on, until we reach a childless node, i.e. the leaf n_{rl}. Prove that*

   $$n_{rl}.pre \leq h(d) + n.post$$

3. *Using the answer for point 2 show that for any descendant m of a node n*

   $$n.pre \leq m.pre \leq h(d) + n.post$$

4. *Let n_{ll} be the leftmost leaf descendant of n. Node n_{ll} is attained from n by moving to the first child l_1 of n (if such a child exists), then from l_1 to its first child l_2 (if such a child exists) and so on, until we reach a leaf (which is n_{ll}). Show that*

   $$n_{ll}.post \geq n.pre - h(d)$$

5. *Using the answer in point 4. show that for any node m descendant of a node n:*

   $$n.pre - h(d) \leq m.post \leq n.post$$

6. *Assume an XML storage system based on the following relations:*

Doc(ID, URL, h)	For each document, its internal ID, its URL, and its height
Node(docID, pre, post, level, label)	For each XML node, the ID of its document, its pre, post and level numbers, and its label

Let dID be the identifier of a document d, and npre, npost and nlevel be the pre, post, and level numbers of an XML node $n \in d$. Write the most restrictive (selective) SQL query retrieving the pre numbers and labels of all n descendants in d.

Exercise 4.5.2 *(inspired from [181]) We consider a tree pattern query evaluation engine based on structural identifiers and binary structural joins (implemented by the STA and STD operators). For any node label l, we denote by l**ID** a relation storing the structural identifiers of all nodes labeled l. Recall that a physical plan without any Sort operator is termed a fully pipelined plan. For instance, $STA_{a \ll b}(a**ID**, STA_{b \prec c}(b**ID**, c**ID**))$ is a fully pipelined plan for the query $//a//b/c$.*

1. *Let q_{flat} be a "flat" XPath query of the form $/r[.//a_1][.//a_2] \cdots [.//a_k]$. Propose a fully pipelined plan for evaluating q_{flat}.*

2. *For the same query q_{flat}, consider the following the join order ω_1: First verify the predicate $r \ll a_1$, then the predicate $r \ll a_2$, then $r \ll a_3$ and so on, until the*

last predicate $r \nll a_k$. *Is there a fully pipelined plan for evaluating* q_{flat} *respecting the join order* ω_1?

3. *Let* q_{deep} *be a "deep" XPath query of the form* $/r//a_1//a_2 \cdots //a_k$. *Propose a fully pipelined plan for evaluating* q_{deep}.

4. *For the query* q_{deep} *introduced earlier, let* ω_2 *be a join order that starts by verifying the* $r \nll a_1$ *predicate, then the predicate* $a_1 \nll a_2$, *then the predicate* $a_2 \nll a_3$ *and so on, until the last predicate* $a_{k-1} \nll a_k$. *Is there a fully pipelined plan for evaluating* q_{deep} *respecting the join order* ω_2? *If yes, provide one. If not, explain why.*

5. *For the same query* q_{deep}, *now consider the join order* ω_3, *which starts by verifying the predicate* $a_{k-1} \nll a_k$, *then the predicate* $a_{k-2} \nll a_{k-1}$ *and so on, until the predicate* $r \nll a_1$. *Is there a fully pipelined plan for evaluating* q_{deep} *respecting the join order* ω_3? *If yes, provide one. If not, explain why.*

6. *Show that, for any XPath query* q, *there is at least a fully pipelined plan for evaluating* q.

7. *Propose an algorithm that, given a general XPath query* q *and a join order* ω, *returns a fully pipelined plan respecting the join order* ω *if such a plan exists, and returns failure otherwise.*

Exercise 4.5.3 *(inspired from [37]) Consider a tree pattern query* q *and a set of stacks such as those used by the PathStack and TwigStack algorithms. Propose an algorithm, which, based on stack entries containing matches for all nodes in* q, *computes the tuples corresponding to the full answers to* q:

- *In the case where* q *is a linear path query (algorithm PathStack);*
- *In the general case where* q *is a twig pattern query (algorithm TwigStack).*

5

Putting into Practice: Managing an XML Database with EXIST

This chapter proposes some exercises and projects to manipulate and query XML documents in a practical context. The software used in these exercises is EXIST, an open-source native XML database that provides an easy-to-use and powerful environment for learning and applying XML languages. We begin with a brief description on how to install EXIST and execute some simple operations. EXIST provides a graphical interface that is pretty easy to use, so we limit our explanations below to the vital information that can be useful to save some time to the absolute beginner.

5.1 PREREQUISITES

In the following, we assume that you plan to install EXIST in your Windows or Linux environment. You need a *Java Development Kit* (JDK) for running the EXIST java application (version 1.5 at least). If you do not have a JDK already installed, get it from the Sun site (try searching "download JDK 1.5" with Google to obtain an appropriate URL) and follow the instructions to set up your Java environment.

Be sure that you can execute Java applications. This requires the definition of a JAVA_HOME environment variable, pointing to the JDK directory. The PATH variable must also contain an entry to the directory that contain the Java executable, $JAVA_HOME/bin.

1. Under Windows: Load the configuration panel window; run the *System* application; choose *Advanced* and then *Environment variables*. Create a new variable JAVA_HOME with the appropriate location, and add the $JAVA_HOME/bin path to the PATH variable.
2. Under Linux: As before, use the exact command depending on your shell language. For instance, with *bash*, put the following in the *.bashrc* file:

    ```
    export JAVA_HOME=your_path_to_java export
    PATH=$PATH:$JAVA_HOME/bin
    ```

3. Under MacOS X, the Java environment should be natively configured.

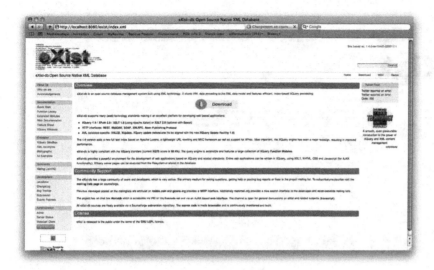

Figure 5.1. The home page of a local EXIST server.

Check that you can run the *java* program. If yes you are ready to install EXIST.

5.2 INSTALLING EXIST

EXIST (software, documentation, and many other things) can be found at http://www.exist-db.org/.

The software consists of a Java archive which can be downloaded from the home page. Assume its name is *exist.jar* (actually the archive name will contain the version as well). Run the installation package with the following command:

```
java -jar exist.jar
```

Just follow the instructions, which ask in particular for the EXIST installation directory (referred to as 'EXIST home' in the following). Once the installation is completed, you can start the EXIST server as follows:

Linux, Mac OS X and other Unix systems. Move to the EXIST home directory, and type either bin/startup.sh or bin/startup.bat. If something goes wrong, look at the *README* file.

Windows. The installation procedure creates an EXIST menu and shorcuts in the desktop. Simply use them to start/stop the server.

When the server is up and running, it waits for HTTP requests on the port 8080.[1] So, using any Web browser, you can access to the EXIST interface (Figure 5.1) at the URL http://localhost:8080/exist/.

---

[1] This is the default port. You can change it in the *jetty.xml* file in the subdirectory *tools/jetty* of EXIST.

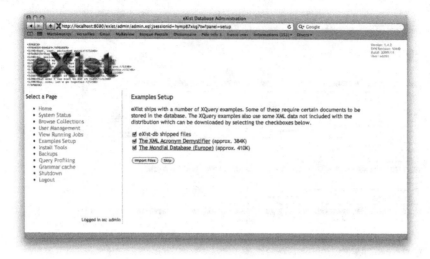

Figure 5.2. Loading XQuery examples in EXIST.

From this interface, you can carry out administration tasks, get the documentation, and run a few predefined client applications. Look at the *QuickStart* part of the documentation for further information on the configuration of EXIST.

5.3 GETTING STARTED WITH EXIST

EXIST comes with a predefined set of XML samples which can be loaded in the database. To start using these example applications, you must log in to the EXIST administration page. Enter the username "admin" and leave the password field empty.[2] Next, choose *Examples Setup* from the menu on the left. Click on the "Import Data" button to start the setup and begin downloading example data from the Internet (Figure 5.2).

The import creates so-called "collections." A collection can be used to store a set of documents sharing the same schema, but it can be itself organized recursively in subcollections for more flexible document sets organizations. Loading the example creates several collections, including:

1. *library*: a bibliographic RDF document, *biblio.rdf*;
2. *mondial*: administrative information on several countries;
3. *shakespeare*: a few plays from William Shakespeare.

You can access these collections from the "Browse collections" option of the admin menu. You can also create a new collection with the form at the bottom of the page. Do the following:

---

[2] The installation tool sometimes requires a password to set up EXIST, in which case access to the administration page is protected by this password.

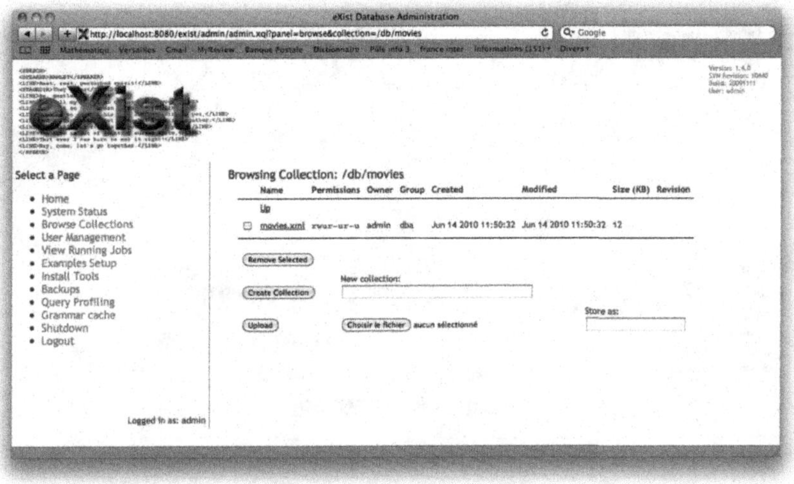

Figure 5.3. The *movies* collection, containing a *movies.xml* sample document.

1. Create a *movies* collection;
2. Add to the *movies* collection the document *movies.xml*, which can be downloaded from our site.

EXIST stores now *movies.xml* in its repository, and you can search, update, or transform the document. Figure 5.3 shows the Web interface that you should obtain.

Now, get back the home page, and choose the "XQuery Sandbow" option. It provides a simple interface that allows to enter XQuery (or XPath) expressions, and displays the result. Check the following XPath/XQuery query:

```
/movies
```

This shows the content of the *movies* elements found in *all* the collections stored under the /db root element of EXIST (which plays the role of a global root for all the documents stored in the repository). Figure 5.4 shows how to run XPath queries with the sandbox: The interface shows the result sequence in the bottom window.

You can restrict the search to a specific documents (or set of documents) with the *document()* function. Here is an example:

```
document('/db/movies/movies.xml')/movies/movie[year=2005]
```

The *collection()* function allows to refer to a collection, as in

```
collection('movies')/movies/movie[year=2005]
```

You are now ready to play with XPath and XQuery, using the sandbox. The next section proposes exercises.

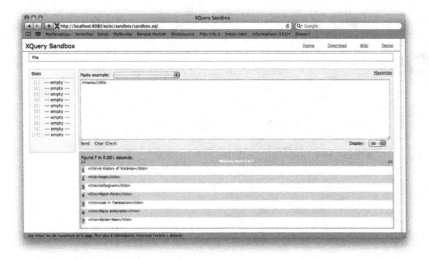

Figure 5.4. Running the /movies//title XPath query in the sandbox.

5.4 RUNNING XPATH AND XQUERY QUERIES WITH THE SANDBOX

5.4.1 XPath

Get the *movies.xml* and *movies_refs.xml* documents from the book's Web site, and insert them into EXIST. Look at the document structure: in the first one, each movie is represented as one element, including the director's and actors' names. In the second one the document consists of two lists, one for movies, one for actors, the former referencing the latter.

Express the following queries in XPath 1.0, on both documents (*Note*: *movies.xml* does not require joining the two lists, which makes expressions easier).

1. All title elements.
2. All movie titles (i.e., the textual value of title elements).
3. Titles of the movies published after 2000.
4. Summary of '*Spider-Man*'.
5. Who is the director of *Heat*?
6. Titles of the movies featuring Kirsten Dunst.
7. Which movies have a summary?
8. Which movies do *not* have a summary?
9. Titles of the movies published more than 5 years ago.
10. What was the role of Clint Eastwood in *Unforgiven*?
11. What is the *last* movie of the document?
12. Title of the film that immediatly precedes *Marie Antoinette* in the document?
13. Get the movies whose title contains a "V" (*Hint*: Use the function *contains*()).
14. Get the movies whose cast consists of exactly three actors (*Hint*: Use the function *count*()).

5.4.2 XQuery

Exercise 5.4.1 *Get the movies_alone.xml and artists_alone.xml documents from the book's Web site. They contain, respectively, the list of movies with references to artists and the list of artists. It might be simpler to first express complex queries over the movies.xml document, which contains all the data in one file, before reformulating them over these two documents.*

*For convenience, you may define a variable for each of these document with a **let** at the beginning of each query:*

```
let $ms:=doc("movies/movies_alone.xml"),
    $as:=doc("movies/ artists_alone .xml")
```

Express the following XQuery queries:

1. *List the movies published after 2002, including their title and year.*
2. *Create a flat list of all the title-role pairs, with each pair enclosed in a "result" element. Here is an example of the expected result structure:*

```
< results >
    < result >
        < title >Heat</ title >
        <role>Lt. Vincent Hanna</role>
    </ result >
    < result >
        < title >Heat</ title >
        <role>Neil McCauley</role>
    </ result >
</ results >
```

3. *Give the title of movies where the director is also one of the actors.*
4. *Show the movies, grouped by genre. Hint: Function distinct-values() removes the duplicates from a sequence. It returns atomic values.*
5. *For each distinct actor's id in movies_alone.xml, show the titles of the movies where this actor plays a role. The format of the result should be:*

```
<actor>16,
< title >Match Point</ title >
< title >Lost in Translation </ title >
</ actor>
```

Variant: Show only the actors which play a role in at least two movies (hint: function count() returns the number of nodes in a sequence).

6. *Give the title of each movie, along with the name of its director. Note: This is a join!*
7. *Give the title of each movie, and a nested element <actors> giving the list of actors with their role.*
8. *For each movie that has at least two actors, list the title and first two actors, and an empty "et-al" element if the movie has additional actors. For instance:*

```
< result >
< title >Unforgiven</ title >
<actor> Clint  Eastwood as  William  ' Bill '  Munny</actor>
<actor>Gene Hackman as Little  Bill  Daggett</actor>
< et-al />
</ result >
```

9. *List the titles and years of all movies directed by Clint Eastwood after 1990, in alphabetic order.*

5.4.3 Complement: XPath and XQuery Operators and Functions

XPath proposes many operators and functions to manipulate data values. These operators are mostly used in predicates, but they are also important as part of the XQuery language which inherits all of the XPath language. We briefly describe the most important ones here, all from XPath 1.0. XPath 2.0 widely extends the library of available functions.

Operators

- Standard arithmetic operators: +, -, *, div, mod.
  Warning! div is used instead of the usual /.
  Warning! "-" is also a valid character inside XML names; this means an expression a-b tests for an element with name a-b and does not compute the subtraction between the values contained in elements a and b. This subtration can be expressed as a - b.
- Boolean operators: or, and, as in @a and c=3.
- Equality operators: =, != that can be used for strings, Booleans, or numbers.
  Warning! //a!=3 means: there is an a element in the document whose string value is different from 3.
- Comparison operators: <, <=, >=, > as in $a<2 and $a>0.
  Warning! They can only be used to compare numbers, not strings.
  Warning! If an XPath expression is embedded in an XML document (this is the case in XSLT), < must be used in place of <.
- Set-theoretic union of node sets: | as in node()|@*.

Note that $a is a *reference* to the variable a. Variables cannot be defined in XPath 1.0, they can only be referred to.

Node Functions   The following functions apply to node sets.

■ count($s) and sum($s) return, respectively, the *number of items* and the *sum of values* in the node set $s.
■ local-name($s), namespace-uri($s), and name($s), respectively, return the *name without namespace prefix*, *namespace URI*, and *name with namespace prefix*, of the node argument; if $s is omitted, it is taken to be the context item.

String Functions.   The following functions apply to character strings.

■ concat($s_1,...,$s_n) *concatenates* the strings $s_1, ..., $s_n.
■ starts-with($a,$b) returns true if the string $a *starts with* the string $b.
■ contains($a,$b) returns true if the string $a *contains* the string $b.
■ substring-before($a,$b) returns the *substring* of $a that precedes the first occurrence of $b in $a.
■ substring-after($a,$b) returns the *substring* of $a that follows the first occurrence of $b in $a.
■ substring($a,$n,$l) returns the *substring* of $a of length $l starting at the $n-th position of $a. (One starts counting from 1). If $l is omitted, the *substring* of $a of length $l starting at the $n-th position of $a is returned.
■ string-length($a) returns the *length* of the string $a.
■ normalize-space($a) *removes* all leading and trailing *white-space* from $a, and *collapses* each white-space sequence to a single white space.
■ translate($a,$b,$c) returns the string $a, where all occurrences of a character from $b has been *replaced* by the character at the same place in $c.

Boolean and Number Functions

■ not($b) returns the *logical negation* of the Boolean $b.
■ floor($n), ceiling($n), and round($n) round the number $n to, respectively, the *next lowest*, *next greatest*, and *closest* integer.

5.5 PROGRAMMING WITH EXIST

In this Section, we give some examples of the programming interfaces (API) provided by EXIST. They can be used to access an XML repository from an application program. Two interfaces are shown: The first one, XML:DB, is a JDBC-like component that can be introduced in a Java application as a communication layer with EXIST; the second one provides the Web services of EXIST.

Along with XPath and XQuery, these APIs constitute a complete programming environment which supports projects proposed in Section 5.6.3.

5.5.1 Using the XML:DB API with EXIST

Documents stored in EXIST can be accessed from a Java application. EXIST provides an implementation of the XML:DB API specification, which is to XML databases what JDBC is to relational databases.

```java
import org.xmldb.api.DatabaseManager;
import org.xmldb.api.base. Collection ;
import org.xmldb.api.base.CompiledExpression;
import org.xmldb.api.base.Database;
import org.xmldb.api.base.Resource;
import org.xmldb.api.base. ResourceIterator ;
import org.xmldb.api.base.ResourceSet;
import org.xmldb.api.modules.XMLResource;

public class ExistAccess {
    protected static
    String DRIVER = "org. exist .xmldb.DatabaseImpl";
    protected static
    String URI = "xmldb:exist:// localhost :8080/ exist /xmlrpc";
    protected static String collectionPath = "/db/movies/";
    protected static String resourceName = "Heat.xml";

    {public static void main(String[] args) throws Exception

    // initialize database driver
    Class cl = Class .forName(DRIVER);
    Database database = (Database) cl .newInstance();
    DatabaseManager.registerDatabase (database );

    // get the collection
    Collection  col =
        DatabaseManager.getCollection (URI + collectionPath );

    //get the content of a document
    System.out. println ("Get the content of " + resourceName);
    XMLResource res = (XMLResource)col.getResource(resourceName);
    if ( res == null){
        System.out. println ("document not found!");
    }
    else{
        System.out. println ( res .getContent ());
    }

    }

}
```

Figure 5.5. First example: Retrieving a document.

```
import org. exist .xmldb.XQueryService;
import org.xmldb.api.DatabaseManager;
import org.xmldb.api.base.Collection;
import org.xmldb.api.base.CompiledExpression;
import org.xmldb.api.base.Database;
import org.xmldb.api.base.Resource;
import org.xmldb.api.base.ResourceIterator;
import org.xmldb.api.base.ResourceSet;
import org.xmldb.api.modules.XMLResource;

public class ExistQuery {
    protected static
        String DRIVER = "org.exist.xmldb.DatabaseImpl";
    protected static
        String URI = "xmldb:exist://localhost :8080/ exist /xmlrpc";
    protected static String collectionPath = "/db/movies";
    protected static String resourceName = "movies.xml";

    public static void main(String[] args) throws Exception{

        // initialize database driver
        Class cl = Class.forName(DRIVER);
        Database database = (Database) cl.newInstance();
        DatabaseManager.registerDatabase(database);

        // get the collection
        Collection col =
            DatabaseManager.getCollection(URI + collectionPath);

        //query a document

        String xQuery=
            "for $x in doc('" + resourceName + "')// title  "
            + "return data($x)";
        System.out.println("Execute xQuery = " + xQuery);

        // Instantiate a XQuery service
        XQueryService service =
            (XQueryService) col.getService("XQueryService", "1.0");
        service .setProperty("indent", "yes");

        // Execute the query, print the result
        ResourceSet result = service .query(xQuery);
        ResourceIterator i = result . getIterator ();
        while(i .hasMoreResources()) {
            Resource r = i .nextResource();
            System.out.println((String)r .getContent());
        }
    }
}
```

Figure 5.6. Second example: Query a collection.

We give a few examples of Java programs that connect to EXIST, access documents, and perform XQuery queries. You can get these files from our site (see Figure 5.5 and 5.6). You need a Java programming environment (*Java Development Kit*) with the JAVA_HOME environment variable properly set, and JAVA_HOME/bin directory added to the PATH environment variable.

To use the EXIST API, the following archives must be put in your CLASSPATH.

1. *exist.jar*, found in EXIST_HOME or EXIST_HOME/lib;
2. *xmldb.jar*, *xmlrpc-1.2-patched.jar*, and *log4j-1.2.14.jar*, found in EXIST_HOME/ lib/core.

These archives are sufficient to compile and run our examples. For more complex Java programs, some other archives might be necessary (e.g., the XERCES parser or the XALAN XSLT processor). They can usually be found in EXIST_HOME/lib

You can find many explanations and examples on Java programming with EXIST at

http://exist.sourceforge.net/devguide.html.

5.5.2 Accessing EXIST with Web Services

If you do not want to use Java, or if the architecture of your application makes the embedding of XQuery calls in your code unsuitable, you can use the Web Service layer of EXIST to send queries and get result. This is actually an excellent example of the advantage of a well-defined query language as an interface to a remote data source, and serves as a (small) introduction to the world of distributed computing with web services.

EXIST runs a server on a machine, and the server opens several communication port to serve requests that might come from distant locations. Several protocols are available, but the simple one is based on REST (representational state transfer), a service layer implementation that completely relies on HTTP.

Recall that a Web service allows a Client to send a function call to a server without having to deal with data conversion and complicated network communication issues. In the case of REST-style services, the function call is encoded as a URL, including the function parameters, and transmitted to the server with an HTTP GET or POST request. The REST servers send back the result in HTTP. REST services are quite easy to deal with: The client application just needs an HTTP client library, available in all programming languages. Moreover, the service can easily be tested with a browser by sending "manual" URL.

Here is a first example: The following GET query retrieves the *movies.xml* document from your local EXIST repository:

http:// localhost :8080/ exist / rest /db/movies/movies.xml

Note that this is a "pseudo-url": There is nothing on your local disk that resembles directory path */exist/rest/db/movies/movies.xml*. Actually,

1. The REST service is located at */exist/rest/*; thanks to a URL rewriting mechanism, any GET request that begins with this address is redirected to the service;
2. The remaining part of the URL, *db/movies/movies.xml*, is a parameter sent to the service; it must denote either a collection or a document.

In summary, a REST query such as the preceding one is tantamount to a *document()* or *collection()* call sent to EXIST. The service accepts other parameters, and in particular the _query parameter whose value may be an XPath or XQuery expression. Try the following URL:

http:// localhost :8080/ exist / rest /db/movies?_query=//title

You should get the result of the XPath query collection('movies')//title.

Remark 5.5.1 *REST services are called via GET or POST requests. In the case of GET, all the values must be URL encoded. This is automatically done by a browser (or any HTTP client) when the URL is a link in an HTML page, but be careful when you directly enter the URL.*

Here is a selected list of parameters accepted by the EXIST REST service (for details, please refer to the *Developer's guide* on the EXIST Web site).

- _xsl=XSL Stylesheet. Applies an XSLT stylesheet to the requested resource. If the _xsl parameter contains an external URI, the corresponding external resource is retrieved. Otherwise, the path is treated as relative to the database root collection and the stylesheet is loaded from the database.
- _query=XPath/XQuery Expression. Executes a query specified by the request.
- _encoding=Character Encoding Type. Sets the character encoding for the resultant XML. The default value is UTF-8.
- _howmany=Number of Items. Specifies the number of items to return from the resultant sequence. The default value is 10.
- _start=Starting Position in Sequence. Specifies the index position of the first item in the result sequence to be returned. The default value is 1.
- _wrap=yes | no. Specifies whether the returned query results are to be wrapped into a surrounding <exist:result> element. The default value is yes.
- _source=yes | no. Specifies whether the query should display its source code instead of being executed. The default value is no.

5.6 PROJECTS

The following projects are intended to let you experiment with XML data access in the context of an application that needs to manipulate semistructured data. In all cases, you must devise an architecture that fulfills the proposed requirements, the only constraint being that the data source model *must* be XML. Of course, you are invited to base your architecture on an appropriate combination of the XML tools and languages presented in this book and during the classes: XPath, XSLT (see the resources available on the companion Web site of this book), XQuery, and Java APIs or REST services.

5.6.1 Getting Started

The minimal project is a very simple Web application that allows you to *search* some information in an XML document and then displays this information in a user-friendly way. You can use the *movies.xml* document or any other XML resource.

The application must be accessible from a Web browser (e.g., Firefox) or from a smartphone browser (e.g., a mobile phone: take one of the many mobile phone simulators on the Web). Here are the requirements:

1. There must be a form that proposes to the user a list of search criteria: (fragment of) the title, list of genres, director and actors names, years, and keywords that can be matched against the summary of the movie;
2. When the user submits the form, the application retrieves the relevant movies from the XML repository and displays the list of these movies in XHTML;
3. In the previous list, each movie title should be a link that allows to display the full description of the movie.

This is a simple project. It can be achieved by a single person in limited time. In that case you are allowed to omit other markup languages (but doing it will result in a better appreciation!).

5.6.2 Shakespeare Opera Omnia

The project is based on the Shakespeare's collection of plays shipped with the EXIST software. The application's purposes can be summarized as follows: Browsing through a play in order to analyze its content, read some specific parts and maybe find related information.

Basically, it consists in writing a small Web application devoted to navigating in a play and extracting some useful information. Here are a few precise requirements:

1. Show the part of a given character, for a given act and/or a given scene;
2. Show the table of contents of the play, along with the organization in acts and scenes and the characters present in each scene;
3. Show a full summary of the play, including the author, list of characters, stages requirements, and so on.

The Web application should be presented in a consistent way, allowing users to switch from one summary to another. It should be possible to navigate from the table of contents to the full description of a scene, from the description of the scene to a character, and from anywhere to the full summary. This list is by no way restrictive. Any other useful extract you can think of will raise the final appreciation! Finally, the Web application should be available on a traditional browser, as well as on a smartphone.

The project must be conducted in two steps:

1. Write a short description of the architecture and design of your XML application; then run some limited tests showing that you know how to put each

tool at the right place where it communicates correctly with the rest of the application;

2. Embark on the development after the design has been validated.

5.6.3 MusicXML Online

This is an exploratory project, since there are no guarantees that all the ideas presented here can be implemented in a reasonable amount of time. The project is also focused on a specific area: music representation and manipulation. So, it should be chosen only by people with both musical inclination and appetite for not yet explored domains.

Music is traditionally distributed on the Web via audio files, described by a few meta-data (author, style, etc.). A quite different approach consists in distributing an accurate content description based on a digital score. The MusicXML DTD serves this purpose. It allows the user to represent the music notation of any piece of music (voice, instruments, orchestra, etc.). The goal of the projet is to specify a Web portal distributing music scores and to investigate the functionalities of such a portal.

The following is a list of suggestions, but the project is really open to new directions. Other ideas are welcome, but please talk first to your advisor before embarking in overcomplicated tasks.

Data

It is not that difficult to find data (e.g., digital music scores). Look for instance at *http://icking-music-archive.org/*. A collection is also available from your advisor, but you are encouraged to search resources on the Web. Any kind of music could do, from full symphony to a voice-piano/guitar reduction of folk songs. You can look for digital score produced by tools such as *Finale* or *Sibelius*. From these digital scores, it is possible to export MusicXML files.

Core Functions

The basic requirement is to be able to store XML music sheets in EXIST and to display the music on demand. Displaying scores can be achieved with the Lilypond software (*http://lilypond.org/*), along with a convertor (musicxml2ly) from MusicXML to Lilypond format. Putting all these tools together is probably the first thing you should do.

It would be useful to extract some important parts from the MusicXML document. For instance, you can extract the lyrics from a song, as well as the melody. A basic search form to extract lyrics and/or melody based on a simple pattern (i.e., a keyword or a musical fragment) would be welcome.

Advanced Options

Here is now a list of the possible additional functionalities that could be envisaged. You are free to limit yourself to a state-of-the-art of the possible solutions, to implement (in a simple way) some of them, or both.

1. **Input**: How can we enter music (e.g., a song) in a database, and how can we query music (e.g., with a keybard simulator, by whistling, by putting your iPod in front of a microphone, etc.);

2. **Ouput**: OK, we can print a score; but what if we we want to *listen* music? Can we transform an XML document to a MIDI document? Yes, this is possible with Lilypond: You are encouraged to investigate further.

Finally, the Web application should be available on a traditional browser, as well as on a smartphone.

This remains, of course, about XML and its multiple usages. You must devise a convenient architecture, using appropriately all the tools together, that will enable the functionalities of your application.

6

Putting into Practice: Tree Pattern Evaluation Using SAX

In this chapter, we learn how to build an evaluation engine for tree-pattern queries, using the SAX (*S*imple *A*PI for *X*ML) programming model. We thereby follow a dual goal: (i) improve our understanding of XML query languages and (ii) become familiar with SAX, a stream parser for XML, with an event-driven API. Recall that the main features of SAX were presented in Section 1.4.2.

6.1 TREE-PATTERN DIALECTS

We will consider tree-pattern languages of increasing complexity. We introduce them in this section.

C-TP This is the dialect of *conjunctive tree-patterns*. A *C-TP* is a tree, in which each node is labeled either with an XML element name, or with an XML attribute name. C-TP nodes corresponding to attributes are distinguished by prefixing them with @ (e.g., @color). Each node has zero or more children, connected by edges that are labeled either / (with the semantics of child) or // (with the semantics of descendant). Finally, the nodes that one wants to be *returned* are marked.

As an example, Figure 6.1 shows a simple XML document d where each node is annotated with its preorder number. (Recall the definition of this numbering from Section 4.2.) Figure 6.2 shows a C-TP pattern denoted t_1 and the three tuples resulting from "matchings" of t_1 into d. A *matching* v is a mapping from the nodes in the tree pattern to the nodes in the XML tree that verifies the following conditions: For each nodes n, m,

- If n is labeled l for some l, $v(n)$ is an element node labeled l; if n is labelled @l, $v(n)$ is an attribute node labelled @l;
- If there is a / edge from n to m, $v(n)$ is a parent of $v(m)$; if there is a // edge from n to m, $v(n)$ is an ancestor of $v(m)$.

In Figure 6.2, the nodes that we want to be returned are marked by boxes surrounding their labels. Observe that a result is a tuple of nodes denoted using their preorder

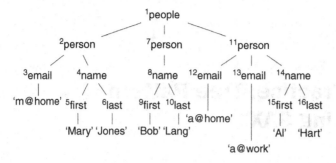

Figure 6.1. A sample document.

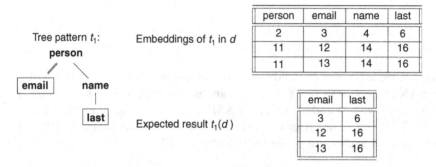

Tree pattern t_1:   Embeddings of t_1 in d

person	email	name	last
2	3	4	6
11	12	14	16
11	13	14	16

Expected result $t_1(d)$

email	last
3	6
12	16
13	16

Figure 6.2. A C-TP and its result for a sample document.

numbers. For now, assume that C-TPs return tuples of preorder numbers. In real-world scenarios, of course, we may also want to retrieve the corresponding XML subtrees, and at the end of this chapter, the reader will be well-equipped to write the code that actually does it.

Before moving on and extending our language of tree-pattern queries, we next observe an important aspect of the language. For that consider the following three queries:

Query q_1:
for $p in //person[email]
                [name/last]
return ($p//email,
        $p/name/last)

Query q_1':
for $p in //person
return ($p//email, $p/name/last)

Query q_2:
for $p in //person[name/last]
return ($p//email,
        $p/name/last)

Which one do you think corresponds to the tree-pattern query t_1? Well, it is the first one. In q_1, the for clause requires the elements matching $p to have both an e-mail descendant, and a descendant on the path name/last. Similarly, to obtain a matching from t_1 and d, we need matches on both paths. In contrast, consider the more relaxed query q_1' that would output the last name of a person element without an email, or the email of a person element without last name. Last, query q_2 requires a last name but no e-mail. This motivates an extension of the language we consider next.

TP   The dialect TP is a superset of C-TP, extending it to allow optional. Syntactically, TP distinguishes between two kinds of edges, compulsory and optional. In a nutshell, the semantics of TP is defined as follows. Matchings are defined as for C-TP. The only difference is that for an optional child edge from n to m, two cases can be considered:

- If $v(n)$ has some child $v(m)$ such that there is a matching from the subtree of the query rooted at m and the subtree of d rooted at $v(m)$, then v extends such a matching from the m-subtree to the $v(m)$-subtree.
- Or $v(n)$ has no such child, then v has a null value for m and all its descendants.

And similarly for descendant.

As an example, Figure 6.3 shows the TP pattern t_2 corresponding to Query 2. It resembles t_1 but the edge between the person and email nodes is optional (denoted by the dashed lines in the figure). As the figure shows, the second person element from the document in Figure 6.1 lacks an e-mail, which leads to a matching tuple with a null. As a consequence, one of the tuples in $t_2(d)$ contains a null email.

To conclude this section, we consider three somehow orthogonal extensions of both TP and C-TP. Figure 6.4 shows the extended tree pattern t_3, t_4 and t_5, together with their equivalent queries, respectively, q_3, q_4, and q_5, and their results for the sample document in Figure 6.1. The three extensions are:

Star (*) patterns: We allow labels to be not only element or attribute names but also "*" that are interpreted as wildcards matched by any element or attribute.

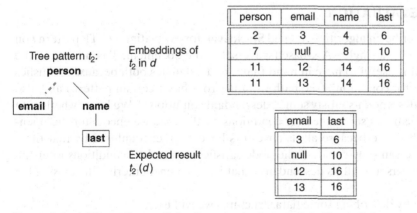

Figure 6.3. A TP and its result for the sample document in Figure 6.1.

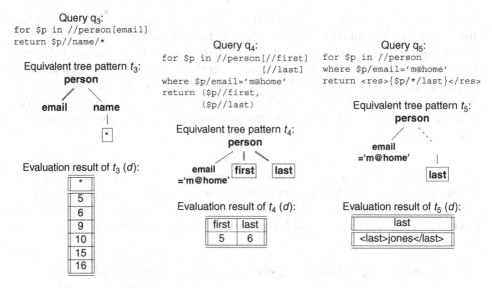

Figure 6.4. Extended patterns.

Value predicate patterns: We can impose a constraint on nodes using some predicates. For instance, we can impose the value of an e-mail (e.g., email = m@home).

Patterns returning full elements: Finally, we can request the tree pattern to not only return the preorder values of nodes but the entire corresponding subtrees. For simplicity, we do not introduce any explicit graphical notation for requesting that in answers. In Figure 6.4, the result of $t_5(d)$ assumes that "full answers" are requested.

From a practical perspective of XML querying, all these extensions are interesting. In particular, C-TP with all the extensions corresponds to a large and useful subset of XPath, whereas its counterpart building on TP is at the core of an important expressive fragment of XQuery. We first consider the evaluation of C-TP; then we look at extensions.

6.2 CTP EVALUATION

We now describe an algorithm, named **StackEval**, for evaluating a C-TP pattern t on a document d in a single SAX-based traversal of the document. To understand the algorithm, it is useful to have in mind that a node matches both because it satisfies some "ancestor condition" (the path from the root has a certain pattern) and also because its descendants satisfy some "descendant conditions." We know whether an XML node satisfies some ancestor conditions by the time we encounter the opening tag of the node because all its ancestors have been encountered by that time. However, we can only decide if the node satisfies descendant conditions after the complete traversal of all its descendants, that is, when encountering the closing tag of the node. We start by describing some data structures we will use:

■ When a node n_d in document d is found to satisfy the *ancestor conditions* related to a node n_t in t, a Match object is created to record this information. A Match holds the following:

  ■ the start number of node n_d (an integer);

  ■ an internal state flag, whose value can be either open or closed;

  ■ (ancestor conditions) the Match parent that corresponds to a match between the parent (or an ancestor) of n_d, and the parent of n_t in the tree pattern query (If the edge above n_t is a parent edge, then parent can only correspond to the parent node of n_d. Otherwise, parent may be built from the parent or another ancestor of n_d);

  ■ (descendant conditions) the (possibly empty) array of matches that were created out of n_d's children or descendants, for each child of n_t in the query (Such matches for n_t children are mapped in the children structure on the PatternNode children of n_t);

  ■ a pointer st to a TPEStack (standing for tree pattern query evaluation stack), As we will see, we associate a TPEStack to each node in the pattern. Then st points to the stack associated to the pattern node n_t.

■ For each node p in the tree pattern, a TPEStack is created, on which the matches corresponding to this pattern node are pushed as they are created. Observe that a TPEStack contains a "regular" Stack in which Match objects are pushed and from which they are popped. The extra structure of a TPEStack serves to connect them to each other according to the structure or the query. More specifically, each TPEStack corresponding to a pattern node p points to

  ■ the TPEStack spar corresponding to the parent of p, if p is not the pattern root;

  ■ a set childStacks of the TPEStacks corresponding to the children of p, if any.

■ The Match and TPEStack structures are interconnected (i.e., each Match points to the (unique) TPEStack on which the Match has been pushed upon creation).

The main features of the Match and TPEStack classes are summarized in Figure 6.5. In our discussion of the algorithms, unless otherwise specified, we use the term "stack" to refer to a TPEStack.

The StackEval algorithm The algorithm evaluates C-TP queries based on the SAX XML document processing model. More specifically, the query evaluation algorithm runs suitable handlers of the methods:

    startElement   (String nameSpaceURI, String localName, String rawName, Attribute attributes)

    endElement   (String nameSpaceURI, String localName, String rawName)

described in Section 1.4.2. For simplicity, within startElement we only use the localName and Attributes, whereas from the parameters of endElement we only use localName. As a consequence, the evaluation algorithm we describe does not take into account namespaces. Extending it to include the support of namespaces does not raise interesting algorithmic issues.

The StackEval class (Figure 6.6) contains the stack corresponding to the query root. It also stores an element counter called currentPre, from which pre number

```
class Match {
    int start;
    int state;
    Match parent;
    Map <PatternNode, Array<Match>> children;
    TPEStack st;

    int getStatus() {...}
}
```

```
class TPEStack {
    PatternNode p;
    Stack <Match> matches;
    TPEStack spar;

    Array <TPEStack> getDescendantStacks(); {...}
    // gets the stacks for all descendants of p
    push(Match m){ matches.push(m); }
    Match top(){ return matches.top(); }
    Match pop(){ return matches.pop(); }
}
```

Figure 6.5. Outline of the Match and TPEStack classes.

will be assigned to new Match objects. Finally, it stores a stack of all pre numbers of elements currently open but whose end has not been encountered yet.

The startElement handler is notified that an element with a given localName and a set of attributes has just started. The handler seeks to identify the stack (or stacks) associated with query nodes, which the newly started element may match. To this purpose, it enumerates all the stacks created for the query (by getting all descendants of the root stack), and for each stack it checks two conditions. The first condition is that the label of the starting node matches the label of the query nodes for which the stacks were created. A second condition applies in the case of a stack s created for a query node p having a parent in the query: we push a new match on s if and only if there is an open match on the parent stack of s, namely p.spar. Such an open match signifies that the newly started element appears in the right context (i.e., all the required ancestors have been matched above this element). In this case, a Match is created with the current pre number (which is incremented). The Match is open by default when created. Finally, the currentPre and preOfOpenNodes are updated to reflect the new element.

Since tree patterns may also require matches in XML attributes, the next lines in the startElement handler repeat the previously described procedure for each of the attributes whose presence is signaled in the same call to startElement.

The endElement handler (Figure 6.7) plays a dual role with respect to the startElement one. Ancestor conditions for a potential query node match are enforced by startElement when the element starts; descendant conditions are checked by

```
class StackEval extends DocumentHandler {
    TreePattern q;
    TPEStack rootStack; // stack for the root of q
    // pre number of the last element which has started:
    int currentPre = 0;
    // pre numbers for all elements having started but not ended yet:
    Stack <Integer> preOfOpenNodes;

    startElement(String localName, Attribute attributes){
        for(s in rootStack.getDescendantStacks()){
            if(localName == s.p.name && s.spar.top().status == open){
                Match m = new Match(currentPre, s.spar.top(), s);
                // create a match satisfying the ancestor conditions
                // of query node s.p
                s.push(m); preOfOpenNodes.push(currentPre);
            }
            currentPre ++;
        }
        for (a in attributes){
            // similarly look for query nodes possibly matched
            // by the attributes of the currently started element
            for (s in rootStack.getDescendantStacks()){
                if (a.name == s.p.name && s.par.top().status == open){
                    Match ma = new Match(currentPre, s.spar.top(), s);
                    s.push(ma);
                }
            }
        }
        currentPre ++;
    }
}
```

Figure 6.6. StartElement handler for the StackEval tree-pattern evaluation algorithm.

endElement when the element's traversal has finished, because at this time, all the descendants of the XML node for which the match was created have been traversed by the algorithm. Thus, we know for sure what parts of the queries could be matched in the descendants of the current node. The endElement handler plays two roles:

■ Prune out of the stacks those matches, which satisfied the ancestor constraints but not the descendant constraints;
■ Close all Match objects corresponding to the XML element, which has just finished (there may be several such matches, if several query nodes carry the same label). Closing these Matches is important as it is required in order for future tests made by the startElement handler to work.

```
class StackEval{ ...
   endElement(String localName){
      // we need to find out if the element ending now corresponded
      // to matches in some stacks
      // first, get the pre number of the element that ends now:
      int preOflastOpen = preOfOpenNodes.pop();
      // now look for Match objects having this pre number:
      for(s in rootStack.getDescendantStacks()){
         if (s.p.name == localName && s.top().status == open &&)
            s.top().pre == preOfLastOpen){
            // all descendants of this Match have been traversed by now.
            Match m = s.pop();
            // check if m has child matches for all children
            // of its pattern node
            for (pChild in s.p.getChildren()){
               // pChild is a child of the query node for which m was created
               if (m.children.get(pChild) == null){
                  // m lacks a child Match for the pattern node pChild
                  // we remove m from its Stack, detach it from its parent etc.
                  remove(m, s);
               }
            }
            m.close();
         }
      }
   }
}
```

Figure 6.7. EndElement handler for the StackEval tree-pattern evaluation algorithm.

Instructions   Based on the previous explanation:

1. Implement an evaluation algorithm for C-TP tree patterns. At the end of the execution, the stacks should contain only those Match objects that participate to complete query answers.
2. Implement an algorithm that computes the result tuples of C-TP tree patterns, out of the stacks' content.

6.3 EXTENSIONS TO RICHER TREE PATTERNS

Once this is implemented, the reader might want to consider implementing the extensions previously outlined. For all these extensions, a single traversal of the document suffices.

More precisely, one can consider:

1. Extend the evaluation algorithm of Section 6.2 to "*" wildcards. For this, Stack objects are allowed to be created for *-labeled query tree nodes. Also the startElement and endElement handlers are adapted.
2. Extend the evaluation algorithm to optional nodes, by modifying the tests performed in endElement (looking for children which the Match should have) to avoid pruning a Match if only optional children are missing.
3. Extend the algorithm developed in (2.) to handle optional nodes, by filling in partial result tuples with nulls as necessary.
4. Extend the evaluation algorithm to support value predicates, by (i) implementing a handler for the characters(...) SAX method, in order to record the character data contained within an XML element and (ii) using it to compare the text values of XML elements for which Match objects are created, to the value predicates imposed in the query.
5. Extend the algorithm in (2.) to return subtrees and not only preorder numbers. The subtrees are represented using the standard XML syntax with opening/closing tags.

Web Data Semantics and Integration

7

Ontologies, RDF, and OWL

7.1 INTRODUCTION

The vision of the Semantic Web is that of a world-wide distributed architecture where data and services easily interoperate. This vision is not yet a reality in the Web of today, in which given a particular need, it is difficult to find a resource that is appropriate to it. Also, given a relevant resource, it is not easy to understand what it provides and how to use it. To solve such limitations, facilitate interoperability, and thereby enable the Semantic Web vision, the key idea is to also publish *semantics descriptions* of Web resources. These descriptions rely on *semantic annotations*, typically on logical assertions that relate resources to some terms in predefined *ontologies*. This is the topic of the chapter.

An ontology is a formal description providing human users a shared understanding of a given domain. The ontologies we consider here can also be interpreted and processed by machines thanks to a logical semantics that enables reasoning. Ontologies provide the basis for sharing knowledge, and, as such, they are very useful for a number of reasons:

Organizing data. It is very easy to get lost in large collections of documents. An ontology is a natural means of "organizing" (structuring) it and thereby facilitates browsing through it to find interesting information. It provides an organization that is flexible, and that naturally structures the information in multidimensional ways. For instance, an ontology may allow browsing through the courses offered by a university by topic or department, by quarter or time, by level, and so forth.

Improving search. Ontologies are also useful for improving the accuracy of Web search. Consider a typical keyword search, say "jaguar USA." The result is a set of pages in which these intrinsically ambiguous English terms occur. Suppose instead that we use precise *concepts* in an ontology, say car:jaguar country:USA. First, one doesn't miss pages where synonyms are used instead of the query terms (e.g., United States). Also, one doesn't recover pages where one of the terms is used with a different meaning (e.g., pages that talk about the jaguar animal).

Data integration. Ontologies also serve as semantic glue between heterogeneous information sources (e.g., sources using different terminologies or languages). Consider for instance a French-American university program. The American data source will speak of "students" and "course," whereas the French one will use "étudiants" and "cours." By *aligning* their ontologies, one can integrate the two sources and offer a unique bilingual entry point to the information they provide.

An essential aspect of ontologies is their potential, because of the "logic inside", to be the core of *inferencing* components. What do we mean by inferencing in our setting? Consider for instance a query that is posed to the system. It may be the case that the query has no answer. It is then useful to infer why this is the case, to be able, for instance, to propose a more general query that will have some answers. On the other hand, the query may be too vague and have too many answers, and it may be helpful to propose more specific queries that will help the user to state what he really wants were precisely. In general, automatic inferences, even very simple ones, can provide enormous value to support user navigation and search, by guiding in a possibly overwhelming ocean of information. Inferencing is also an essential ingredient for automatically integrating different data sources. For instance, it is typically used to detect inconsistencies between data sources and resolve them, or to analyze redundancies and optimize query evaluation.

The inferencing potential of ontologies is based on their logical formal semantics. As we will see, languages for describing ontologies can be seen as fragments of first-order logic (FOL). Since inference in FOL is in general undecidable, the "game" consists in isolating fragments of FOL that are large enough to describe the semantics of resources of interest for a particular application, but limited enough so that inference is decidable and, even more, feasible in reasonable time.

Not surprisingly, we focus here on Web languages. More precisely, we consider languages that are already standards of the W3C or on the way to possibly becoming such standards (i.e., recommendations of that consortium). Indeed, in the first part of this chapter, we consider RDF, RDFS, and OWL. Statements in these languages can be interpreted with the classical model-theoretic semantics of first-order logic.

In the second part, we study more formally the inference problem for these languages. Checking logical entailment between formulas, possibly given a set of axioms, has been extensively studied. Since the problem is undecidable for FOL, we focus on decidable fragments of FOL that are known under the name of *description logics*. Description logics provide the formal basis of the OWL language recommended by the W3C for describing ontologies. They allow expressing and reasoning on complex logical axioms over unary and binary predicates. Their computational complexity varies depending on the set of constructors allowed in the language. The study of the impact of the choice of constructors on the complexity of inference is the main focus of the second part of the chapter.

We start with an example for illustrating what an ontology is, and the kind of reasoning that can be performed on it (and possibly on data described using it). Then, we survey the RDF(S) and OWL languages. Finally, we relate those languages to FOL, and in particular to description logics, to explain how the constructors used to describe an ontology may impact the decidability and tractability of reasoning on it.

7.2 ONTOLOGIES BY EXAMPLE

An ontology is a formal description of a domain of interest based on a set of *individuals* (also called entities or objects), *classes* of individuals, and the *relationships* existing between these individuals. The logical statements on memberships of individuals in classes or relationships between individuals form a base of *facts* (i.e., a *database*). Besides, logical statements are used for specifying knowledge about the classes and relationships. They specify constraints on the database and form the *knowledge base*. When we speak of ontology, one sometimes thinks only of this knowledge that specify the domain of interest. Sometimes, one includes both the facts and the constraints under the term ontology.

In this chapter, we use as running example, a university ontology. In the example, the terms of the ontology are prefixed with ":" (e.g., the individual :Dupond or the class :Student). This notation will be explained when we discuss namespaces.

The university ontology includes classes (e.g., :Staff, :Student, :Department, or :Course). These classes denote natural *concepts* that are shared or at least understood by users familiar with universities all over the world. A class has a set of *instances* (the individuals in this class). For example, :Dupond is an instance of the class :Professor. The ontology also includes relationships between classes, that denote natural relationships between individuals in the real world. For instance, the university ontology includes the relationship (e.g., :TeachesIn). Relationships also have instances, for example, TeachesIn(:Dupond,:CS101) is an instance of :TeachesIn that has the meaning that Dupond teaches CS101. Class or relationship instances form the database.

Let us now turn to the knowledge base. Perhaps the most fundamental constraint considered in this context is the subclass relationship. A class C is a subclass of a class C' if each instance of C is also an instance of C'. In other words, the set of instances of C is a subset of the set of instances of C'. For instance, by stating that the class :Professor is a subclass of the class :AcademicStaff, one expresses a knowledge that is shared with the university setting: all professors are members of the academic staff. Stating a subclass relationship between the class :AcademicStaff and the class :Staff expresses that all the members of the academic staff, in particular the professors, belong to the staff of the university. So, in particular, from the fact that :Dupond is an instance of the class :Professor, we also know that he is an instance of :AcademicStaff and of :Staff.

It is usual to represent the set of subclass statements in a graphical way by a *class hierarchy* (also called a *taxonomy*). Figure 7.1 shows a class hierarchy for the university domain.

Besides the class hierarchy, a very important class of ontology constraints allows fixing the domains of relationships. For instance,

- :TeachesIn(:AcademicStaff, :Course) indicates that if one states that "X :TeachesIn Y", then X belongs to :AcademicStaff and Y to :Course;
- :TeachesTo(:AcademicStaff, :Student) and :Leads(:Staff,:Department) similarly indicate the nature of participants in different relationships.

A wide variety of other useful constraints are supported by ontology languages. For instance,

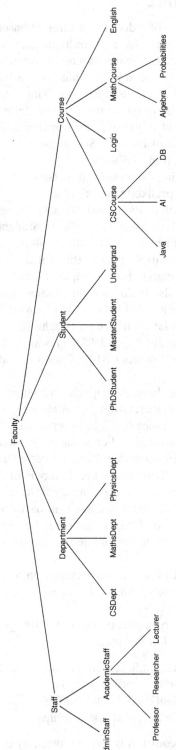

Figure 7.1. A class hierarchy.

- Disjointness constraints between classes such as the classes :Student and :Staff are disjoint, (i.e., a student cannot belong to the staff).
- Key constraints (for binary relations) such as each department must have a unique manager.
- Domain constraints such as only professors or lecturers may teach undergraduate courses.

We will show how to give a precise (formal) semantics to these different kinds of constraints based on logic. The use of logic enables *reasoning*. For instance, from the fact that Dupond leads the CS department and the university ontology, it can be logically inferred that :Dupond is in :Professor and :CSDept is in :Department. Indeed, such a reasoning based on ontologies and *inference rules* is one of the main topics of this chapter. But before delving in the technicalities of inference, we devote the remainder of the section to illustrating the usefulness of inference.

Inference is first very useful for query answering. For instance, consider the query "Who are the members of the academic staff living in Paris?" Suppose Professor :Dupond lives in Paris. He should be in the answer. Why? Because he lives in Paris and because he is a professor. Note, however, that the only explicit facto we may have for :Dupond are that he lives in Paris and that he is a professor. A query engine will have to use the formula that states that professors are members of the academic staff and *inference* to obtain Dupond in the answer. Without inference, we would miss the result.

Inference helped us in the previous example derive new facts such as Dupond is a member of the academic staff. It can also serve to derive new knowledge (i.e., new constraints even in absence of any fact). For instance, suppose that we add to the class hierarchy of Figure 7.1, the subclass relationship between :PhDStudent and :Lecturer. Then, it can be inferred that :PhDStudent is also a subclass of the class :Staff. At the time one is designing such an ontology, it is useful to be aware of such inference. For instance, membership in the staff class may bring special parking privileges. Do we really mean to give such privileges to all PhD students?

Furthermore, suppose that the ontology specifies the (already mentioned) disjointness relationship between the classes :Staff and :Student. Then, from this constraint and the subclass relationship between :PhDStudent and :Student, it can be inferred that the class :PhDStudent is empty. This should be understood as an anomaly: Why would a specification bother to define an empty class? Highlighting in advance such anomalies in ontologies is very important at the time the ontology is defined because this may prevent serious errors at the time the ontology is actually used in an application.

A last illustration of the use of ontologies pertains to integration. Consider again an international university program. Suppose U.S. students may follow some courses in France for credits. Then we need to integrate the French courses with the American ones. Statement such as "FrenchUniv:Cours is a subclass of :Course" serves to map French concepts to American ones. Now a student in this international program who would ask the query "database undergraduate" may get as answers *Database 301* and *L3, Bases de données*.

These are just examples to illustrate the usefulness of inference based on ontologies. In the next section, we describe the languages and formalisms that can be used to represent ontologies. In Section 7.4, we will be concerned with inference algorithms that are sound and complete with respect to the logical formal semantics, that is, algorithms guaranteeing to infer all the implicit information (data or knowledge) deriving from the asserted facts, relationships and constraints declared in the ontology.

7.3 RDF, RDFS, AND OWL

We focus on three ontology languages that have been proposed for describing Web resources. We first consider the language RDF, a language for expressing facts (focusing primarily on the database). The other two languages allow constraining RDF facts in particular application domains: RDFS is quite simple, whereas OWL is much richer. We start by reviewing common terminology and notions central to this context.

7.3.1 Web Resources, URI, Namespaces

A *resource* is anything that can be referred to: a Web page, a fragment of an XML document (identified by an element node of the document), a Web service, an identifier for an entity, a thing, a concept, a property, and so on. This is on purpose very broad. We want to be able to talk about and describe (if desired) anything we can identify. A URI may notably be a URL that any (human or software) agent or application can access. In particular, we need to talk about specific ontologies. The ontology that is used in the example of this chapter is identified by the URL:

http://webdam.inria.fr/Jorge/OntologiesChapter/Examples#

The instance Dupond in this ontology has URI:

http://webdam.inria.fr/Jorge/OntologiesChapter/Examples#Dupond

To avoid carrying such long URIs, just as in XML (see Chapter 1), we can use namespaces. So, for instance, we can define the *namespace* jorge: with the URL of the example ontology. Then the instance Dupond in the ontology jorge: becomes jorge:Dupond. This is just an abbreviation of the actual URI for Dupond in that ontology.

The examples we will present are within the jorge ontology. When denoting individuals or relationships in this ontology, we will use the notation :Name instead of jorge:Name, considering that jorge is the default namespace. For example, the RDF triplet ⟨ :Dupond, :Leads, :CSDept ⟩ expresses in RDF the fact that :Dupond leads :CSDept. Remember that these are only abbreviations; for example,

http://webdam.inria.fr/Jorge/OntologiesChapter/Examples#Dupond

abbreviates to

Jorge:Dupond

abbreviates to

> :Dupond

One can publish standard namespaces to be used by all those interested in particular domain areas. In this chapter, we will use the following standard namespaces:

rdf: A namespace for RDF. The URI is:

> http://www.w3.org/1999/02/22-rdf-syntax-ns#

rdfs: A namespace for RDFS. The URI is:

> http://www.w3.org/2000/01/rdf-schema#

owl: A namespace for OWL. The URI is:

> http://www.w3.org/2002/07/owl#

dc: A namespace for the Dublin Core Initiative. The URI is:

> http://dublincore.org/documents/dcmi-namespace/

foaf: A namespace for FOAF. The URI is:

> http://xmlns.com/foaf/0.1/.

In each case, at the URL, one can find an ontology that, in particular, specifies a particular vocabulary. Dublin Core is a popular standard in the field of digital libraries. The Friend of a Friend (FOAF) initiative aims at creating a "social" Web of machine-readable pages describing people, the links between them and the things they create and do. We will encounter examples of both.

7.3.2 RDF

RDF (Resource Description Framework) provides a simple language for describing *annotations* about Web resources identified by URIs. These are facts. Constraints on these facts in particular domains will be stated in RDFS or OWL.

RDF Syntax: RDF Triplets

In RDF, a fact expresses some metadata about a resource that is identified by a URI. An RDF fact consists of a *triplet*. A triplet is made of a *subject*, a *predicate*, and an *object*. It expresses a *relationship* denoted by the *predicate* between the *subject* and the *object*. Intuitively, a triplet $\langle a\ P\ b \rangle$ expresses the fact that b is a value of *property* P for the subject a. (In general, a may have several values for property p.) Don't get confused by the terminology: a relationship, a predicate, a property, are three terms for the same notion. The relationship $\langle a\ P\ b \rangle$ uses the predicate P, and expresses that the subject a has value b for property P.

In a triplet, the subject, but also the predicate, are URIs pointing to Web resources, whereas the object may be either a URI or a *literal* representing a *value*.

In the latter case, a triplet expresses that a given subject has a given value for a given property. RDF borrows from XML the literal data types such as strings and integers, thanks to the predefined RDF data type rdf:Literal. One can include an arbitrary XML value as an object of an RDF triplet, by using the predefined RDF data type rdf:XMLLiteral.

In RDF, one can distinguish between individuals (objects) and properties (relationships). This is not mandatory, but it can be done using two rdf keywords (i.e., keywords defined in the rdf namespace): rdf:type and rdf:Property. For instance, one can declare that the term :Leads is a property name by the triplet ⟨ :Leads rdf:type rdf:Property ⟩.

Then data are specified using a set of triplets. These triplets may be represented either in a tabular way, as a *triplet table* or as a *RDF graph*.

Representing a set of triplets as a directed *graph* is convenient to visualize all the information related to an individual at a single node by bringing it together. In such a graph, each triplet is represented as an edge from its subject to its object. Figures 7.2 and 7.3 visualize, respectively, the tabular form and the RDF graph corresponding to some set of triplets.

This is almost all there is in RDF. Trivial, no? There is one last feature, the use of blank nodes to capture some form of unknown individuals. A *blank node* (or anonymous resource or bnode) is a subject or an object in an RDF triplet or an RDF graph that is not identified by a URI and is not a literal. A blank node is referred to by a notation _:p where p is a local name that can be used in several triplets for stating several properties of the corresponding blank node.

⟨ :Dupond :Leads :CSDept ⟩
⟨ :Dupond :TeachesIn :UE111 ⟩
⟨ :Dupond :TeachesTo :Pierre ⟩
⟨ :Pierre :EnrolledIn :CSDept ⟩
⟨ :Pierre :RegisteredTo :UE111 ⟩
⟨ :UE111 :OfferedBy :CSDept ⟩

Subject	Predicate	Object
:Dupond	:Leads	:CSDept
:Dupond	:TeachesIn	:UE111
:Dupond	:TeachesTo	:Pierre
:Pierre	:EnrolledIn	:CSDept
:Pierre	:RegisteredTo	:UE111
:UE111	:OfferedBy	:CSDept

Figure 7.2. An RDF triplet table.

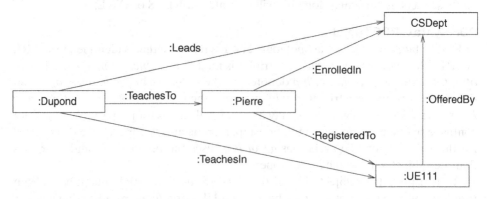

Figure 7.3. An RDF graph.

Example 7.3.1 *The following triplets express that Pierre knows someone named "John Smith" who wrote a book entitled Introduction to Java.*

:Pierre	foaf:knows	_:p
_:p	foaf:name	"John Smith"
_:p	wrote	_:b
_:b	dc:title	"Introduction to Java"

The predicates foaf:knows and foaf:name belong to the FOAF vocabulary. The predicate dc:title belongs to the Dublin Core vocabulary.

We have used here an abstract syntax of RDF. One can clearly describe in a number of ways using a "concrete" syntax. For instance, there exists an RDF/XML syntax for describing RDF triplets. We now turn to the semantics that is, as we will see, quite simple as well.

RDF Semantics

A triplet $\langle s\ P\ o \rangle$ without blank node is interpreted in first-order logic (FOL) as a fact $P(s,o)$ (i.e., a grounded atomic formula), where P is the name of a predicate and s and o denotes constants in the FOL language.

Blank nodes, when they are in place of the *subject* or the *object* in triplets, are interpreted as *existential variables*. Therefore, a set of RDF triplets (represented with a triplet table or an RDF graph or in RDF/XML syntax), possibly with blank nodes as subjects or objects, is interpreted as a conjunction of positive literals in which all the variables are existentially quantified.

Giving a FOL semantics to triplets in which the predicates can be blank nodes is also possible but a little bit tricky and is left out of the scope of this chapter (see Section 7.5).

Example 7.3.2 *Consider again the four triplets that we used to express that Pierre knows someone named "John Smith" who wrote a book entitled* Introduction to Java. *They are interpreted in FOL by the following positive existential conjunctive formula, where the prefixes (foaf:, dc:, _: and :) for denoting the constants, predicates and variables have been omitted for readability.*

$\exists p \exists b [knows(Pierre,p) \wedge name(p, "John\ Smith") \wedge wrote(p,b)$

$\wedge\ title(b, "Introduction\ to\ Java")]$

7.3.3 RDFS: RDF Schema

RDFS is the *schema language* for RDF. It allows specifying a number of useful constraints on the individuals and relationships used in RDF triplets. In particular, it allows declaring objects and subjects as *instances* of certain *classes*. In addition, *inclusion statements* between classes and properties make it possible to express semantic relations between classes and between properties. Finally, it is also possible to semantically relate the "domain" and the "range" of a property to some classes. These are all very natural constraints that we consider next.

Syntax of RDFS

The RDFS statements can be themselves expressed as RDF triplets using some specific predicates and objects used as RDFS keywords with a particular meaning. We have already seen the rdf:type predicate. This same keyword is used to declare that an individual i is an instance of class C with a triplet of the form ⟨i rdf:type C⟩.

Example 7.3.3 *The following triplets express that :Dupond is an instance of the class :AcademicStaff, :UE111 of the class :Java and :Pierre is an instance of the class :MasterStudent.*

> :Dupond   rdf:type   :AcademicStaff
> :UE111   rdf:type   :Java
> :Pierre   rdf:type   :MasterStudent

RDFS provides a new predicate rdfs:subClassOf to specify that a class is a subclass of another one. One can use it in particular to disambiguate terms. For instance, by specifying that :Java is a subclass of :CSCourse, one say that, in the context of this particular ontology, by Java, we mean exclusively the CS programming language. Subclass relationships between classes, and thus a class hierarchy, can be declared as a set of triplets of the form ⟨ C rdfs:subClassOf D ⟩. The class hierarchy of Figure 7.1 can be described in RDFS by a set of RDF triplets, an extract of which is given in Figure 7.4.

Similarly, RDFS provides a predicate rdfs:subPropertyOf to express structural relationships between properties. We could state for instance with the triplet

⟨:LateRegisteredTo rdfs:subPropertyOf:RegisteredTo⟩

that the relationship :LateRegisteredTo is more specific than the relationship :RegisteredTo. So, suppose that we know

⟨:Alice:LateRegisteredTo:UE111⟩

Then we can infer that also

⟨:Alice:RegisteredTo:UE111⟩

A property *P* (between subjects and objects) may be seen as a function that maps a subject *s* to the set of objects related to *s* via *P*. This functional view motivates calling the set of subjects of a property *P*, its *domain*, and the set of objects, its *range*.

:Java	rdfs:subClassOf	:CSCourse
:AI	rdfs:subClassOf	:CSCourse
:BD	rdfs:subClassOf	:CSCourse
:CSCourse	rdfs:subClassOf	:Course
:Logic	rdfs:subClassOf	:Course
:MathCourse	rdfs:subClassOf	:Course
:English	rdfs:subClassOf	:Course
:Algebra	rdfs:subClassOf	:MathCourse
:Probabilities	rdfs:subClassOf	:MathCourse

Figure 7.4. Some RDFS declarations for the class hierarchy of Figure 7.1.

Restricting the domain and the range of a property is also possible in RDFS using two other new predicates rdfs:domain and rdfs:range and triplets of the form:

$$\langle P \text{ rdfs}: \text{domain} C \rangle$$

and

$$\langle P \text{ rdfs}: \text{range} D \rangle$$

Example 7.3.4 *Some domain and range constraints on properties in the ontology of the university domain mentioned in Section 7.2 can be expressed in RDFS by the set of RDF triplets given in Figure 7.5.*

RDFS Semantics

Accordingly to the FOL semantics of RDF presented before, the RDFS statements can be interpreted by FOL formulas. Figure 7.6 gives the logical semantics of the RDFS statements by giving their corresponding FOL translation. The figure also gives the corresponding DL notation, to be explained further on.

Observe that these statements all have the same general form:

$$\forall \ldots (\cdots \Rightarrow \ldots)$$

Such constraints are very useful in practice and are very adapted to inferencing. They are called *tuple-generating dependencies*. Intuitively, each such rule may be thought of as a factory for generating new facts: no matter how (with which valuations of the variables) you can match the left part of the arrow, you can derive the right part. Underneath this inference are the notion of *pattern*, that is, of a fact where some of the individuals are replaced by variables (i.e., placeholder) and that of *valuation*. An example of a pattern is :TeachesIn(X, Y), where X, Y are variables. A valuation v may map X to :Dupond and Y to :UE111. It transforms the pattern :TeachesIn(X, Y) into the fact :TeachesIn(:Dupond, :UE111).

:TeachesIn	rdfs:domain	:AcademicStaff	:TeachesIn	rdfs:range	:Course
:TeachesTo	rdfs:domain	:AcademicStaff	:TeachesTo	rdfs:range	:Student
:Leads	rdfs:domain	:Staff	:Leads	rdfs:range	:Department

Figure 7.5. Some RDFS declarations of domain and range constraints for the university domain.

RDF and RDFS Statements	FOL Translation	DL Notation
i rdf:type C	$C(i)$	$i : C$ or $C(i)$
i P j	$P(i,j)$	$i P j$ or $P(i,j)$
C rdfs:subClassOf D	$\forall X (C(X) \Rightarrow D(X))$	$C \sqsubseteq D$
P rdfs:subPropertyOf R	$\forall X \forall Y (P(X,Y) \Rightarrow R(X,Y))$	$P \sqsubseteq R$
P rdfs:domain C	$\forall X \forall Y (P(X,Y) \Rightarrow C(X))$	$\exists P \sqsubseteq C$
P rdfs:range D	$\forall X \forall Y (P(X,Y) \Rightarrow D(Y))$	$\exists P^- \sqsubseteq D$

Figure 7.6. RDFS logical semantics.

The FOL translation that we presented suggests inference rules that can be used "operationally" to derive new RDF triplets. This is what is called the *operational semantics* of RDFS. One starts with a set of facts, RDF triplets, and constraints. When the body of a rule matches some knowledge we have, the head of the rule specifies some knowledge we can infer. To illustrate, consider the inference rule for rdfs:subClassOf:

if ⟨ r rdf:type A ⟩ and ⟨ A rdfs:subClassOf B ⟩ **then** ⟨ r rdf:type B ⟩

where r, A, and B are variables.

This means that **if** we know two triplets matching the patterns ⟨ r rdf:type A ⟩ and ⟨ A rdfs:subClassOf B ⟩ for some values of r, A, B, **then** we can infer the triplet ⟨ r rdf:type B ⟩ with the values of r, B taken to be those of the match.

Or more formally, if there exists a valuation v such that we know

⟨$v(r)$ rdf:type $v(A)$⟩

and

⟨$v(A)$ rdfs:subClassOf $v(B)$⟩

then we can infer

⟨$v(r)$ rdf:type $v(B)$⟩

Of course, triplets that have been inferred can be themselves used to infer more triplets.

We also need rules to capture the operational semantics of rdfs:subPropertyOf, rdfs:domain and rdf:range constraints:

if ⟨ r P s ⟩ **and** ⟨ P rdfs:subPropertyOf Q ⟩ **then** ⟨ r Q s ⟩
if ⟨ P rdfs:domain C ⟩ **and** ⟨ x P y ⟩   **then** ⟨ x rdf:type C ⟩
if ⟨ P rdfs:range D ⟩ **and** ⟨ x P y ⟩   **then** ⟨ y rdf:type D ⟩

An important issue is that of the *soundness* and *completeness* of the operational semantics defined by the preceding four inference rules. Let $\mathcal{A}$ be a set of RDF triplets and $\mathcal{T}$ be a set of associated RDFS triplets (expressing constraints on facts in $\mathcal{A}$). The operational semantics is *sound* if any fact f inferred from $\mathcal{A}$ and $\mathcal{T}$ by the rules (denoted: $\mathcal{A} \cup \mathcal{T} \vdash f$) is a logical consequence of the facts in $\mathcal{A}$ together with the constraints in $\mathcal{T}$ (denoted: $\mathcal{A} \cup \mathcal{T} \models f$).

The soundness of the operational semantics is easy to show, just because our rules are very close to the constraints imposed by the RDFS statements. More formally, it can be shown by induction on the number of rules required to infer f (details are left as an exercise).

It is a little bit more difficult to show that the operational semantics is *complete* (i.e., for any fact f, if $\mathcal{A} \cup \mathcal{T} \models f$, then $\mathcal{A} \cup \mathcal{T} \vdash f$). We prove it by contrapositive (i.e., we show that if $\mathcal{A} \cup \mathcal{T} \nvdash f$, then $\mathcal{A} \cup \mathcal{T} \nmodels f$). We consider the set of constants appearing in the facts in $\mathcal{A}$ as the domain of an interpretation I, which is built as follows from the set of facts obtained by applying the rules to the set of triplets in $\mathcal{A} \cup \mathcal{T}$:

- For each class C, $I(C) = \{i | \mathcal{A} \cup \mathcal{T} \vdash C(i)\}$.
- For each property R, $I(R) = \{(i,j) | \mathcal{A} \cup \mathcal{T} \vdash R(i,j)\}$.

if ⟨ P rdfs:domain A ⟩ **and** ⟨ A rdfs:subClassOf B ⟩
  then ⟨ P rdfs:domain B ⟩
if ⟨ P rdfs:range C ⟩ **and** ⟨ C rdfs:subClassOf D ⟩
  then ⟨ P rdfs:range D ⟩
if ⟨ A rdfs:subClassOf B ⟩ **and** ⟨ B rdfs:subClassOf C ⟩
  then ⟨ A rdfs:subClassOf C ⟩
if ⟨ P rdfs:subPropertyOf Q ⟩ **and** ⟨ Q rdfs:subPropertyOf R ⟩
  then ⟨ P rdfs:subPropertyOf R ⟩

Figure 7.7. The inference rules for RDFS constraints.

It is easy to verify that I is a model of $\mathcal{A} \cup \mathcal{T}$ (details are left as an exercise). Now, let f be a fact such that $\mathcal{A} \cup \mathcal{T} \nvdash f$. By construction of I, since f is not inferred by the rules, f is not true in I. Therefore, I is a model of $\mathcal{A} \cup \mathcal{T}$ in which f is not true (i.e., $\mathcal{A} \cup \mathcal{T} \nvDash f$).

It is important to note that the completeness we just discussed concerns the inference of *facts* (possibly with blank nodes). For extending the completeness result to the inference of *constraints*, we need additional inference rules (described in Figure 7.7) to account for the combination of range and domain constraints with the subclass relationship, and also for expressing the transitivity of the subclass and subproperty constraints. The proof is left as an exercise (see Exercise 7.6.1).

The RDFS statements are exploited to saturate the RDF triplets by adding the triplets that can be inferred with the rules. Then the resulting set of RDF triplets can be queried with a query language for RDF (e.g., SPARQL). This will be explained in the next chapter.

7.3.4 OWL

OWL (the Web Ontology Language and surprisingly not the Ontology Web Language) extends RDFS with the possibility to express additional constraints. Like RDFS, OWL statements can be expressed as RDF triplets using some specific predicates and objects used as OWL keywords with a particular meaning. In this section, we describe the main OWL constructs. Like RDFS, we provide their FOL semantics and, in anticipation of the next section, the corresponding DL notation.

There are many constructs expressible in OWL that provide considerable modeling flexibility and expressiveness for the Semantic Web. Providing an operational semantics for all the OWL constructs is an open issue. However, most of the OWL constructs come from DL. Therefore, we get for free all the positive and negative known results about reasoning in DLs. This allows better understanding inferences when considering facts described with RDF triplets and constraints in OWL.

OWL offers a number of rich semantic constructs, namely class disjointness, functional constraint, intentional class definition, class union and intersection, and the like. We consider them in turn.

Expressing class disjointness constraints
OWL provides a predicate owl:disjointWith to express that two classes C and D are disjoint using the triplet: ⟨ C owl:disjointWith D ⟩.

Although very natural, this constraint cannot be expressed in RDFS. For instance, in our example, we can state the triplet: ⟨ :Student owl:disjointWith :Staff ⟩.

The following table provides the logical semantics of this construct.

OWL Notation	FOL Translation	DL Notation
C owl:disjointWith D	$\forall X(C(X) \Rightarrow \neg D(X))$	$C \sqsubseteq \neg D$

Observe the use of negation in the logical formulas. This is taking us out of tuple generating dependencies. Such rules are not used to produce new facts but for ruling out possible worlds as inconsistent with what we know of the domain of interest.

Functional Constraints

In OWL, it is possible to state that a given relationship between A and B is in fact a *function* from A to B (resp. from B to A). One can also state that a property is the *inverse* of another, or that a property is *symmetric*. Observe the use of equality in the logical formulas.

OWL Notation	FOL Translation	DL Notation
P rdf:type owl:FunctionalProperty	$\forall X \forall Y \forall Z$ $(P(X,Y) \wedge P(X,Z) \Rightarrow Y = Z)$	$(funct\, P)$ or $\exists P \sqsubseteq (\leq 1 P)$
P rdf:type owl:InverseFunctionalProperty	$\forall X \forall Y \forall Z$ $(P(X,Y) \wedge P(Z,Y) \Rightarrow X = Z)$	$(funct\, P^-)$ or $\exists P^- \sqsubseteq (\leq 1 P^-)$
P owl:inverseOf Q	$\forall X \forall Y (P(X,Y) \Leftrightarrow Q(Y,X))$	$P \equiv Q^-$
P rdf:type owl:SymmetricProperty	$\forall X \forall Y (P(X,Y) \Rightarrow P(Y,X))$	$P \sqsubseteq P^-$

Recall that a triplet ⟨*a P b*⟩ is viewed in the model-theoretic interpretation as a pair in relation P. An owl:FunctionalProperty thus expresses that the first attribute of P is a *key*, while an owl:InverseFunctionalProperty expresses that its second attribute is a *key*. Note that a property may be both an owl:FunctionalProperty and an owl:InverseFunctionalProperty. It would be the case for instance for the property hasIdentityNo that associates identification numbers to students in the university example.

Example 7.3.5 *In the university example, the constraint that every department must be led by a unique manager is expressed in OWL by adding the triplet:*

:Leads rdf:type owl:InverseFunctionalProperty

to the RDFS triplets we already have for the domain and range constraints for :Leads. See Figure 7.5.

Intentional Class Definitions

A main feature of OWL is the intentional definition of new classes from existing ones. It allows expressing complex constraints such as *every department has a unique manager who is a professor*, or *only professors or lecturers may teach to undergraduate students*.

The keyword owl:Restriction is used in association with a blank node class, that is being defined (without being given a name), and some specific restriction properties (owl:someValuesFrom, owl:allValuesFrom, owl:minCardinality, owl:maxCardinality) used for defining the new class. The blank node is necessary because the expression of each restriction requires a set of triplets that are all related to the same class description.

Example 7.3.6 *The following set of triplets defines the blank (i.e., unnamed) class describing the set of individuals for which all the values of the property :Leads come from the class :Professor:*

_:a	rdfs:subClassOf	owl:Restriction
_:a	owl:onProperty	:Leads
_:a	owl:allValuesFrom	:Professor

The constraint that every department can be led only by professors is then simply expressed by adding the following triplet (involving the same blank class _:a):

: *Department rdfs:subClassOf _:a*

Note that the constraint that *every department must be led by a unique manager who is a professor* is actually the conjunction of the above constraint and of the functionality constraint of :Leads.

Also with restriction, one can use the owl:someValuesFrom keyword on a property P to produce a class description denoting the set of individuals for which *at least one* value of the property P comes from a given class *C* using:

_:a	rdfs:subClassOf	owl:Restriction
_:a	owl:onProperty	P
_:a	owl:someValuesFrom	C

Finally, the owl:minCardinality and owl:maxCardinality restrictions allow expressing constraints on the number of individuals that can be related by a given property P.

Example 7.3.7 *The following triplets describe the class (denoted by the blank node _:a) of individuals having at least three registrations and the class (denoted by the blank node _:b) of individuals having at most six registrations.*

_:a	rdfs:subClassOf	owl:Restriction
_:a	owl:onProperty	RegisteredTo
_:a	owl:minCardinality	3
_:b	rdfs:subClassOf	owl:Restriction
_:b	owl:onProperty	RegisteredTo
_:b	owl:maxCardinality	6

The constraint that each student must be registered to at least 3 courses and atmost 6 courses is then simply expressed by adding the two following triplets (involving the same blank classes _:a and _:b):

:Student	rdfs:subClassOf	_:a
:Student	rdfs:subClassOf	_:b

OWL Notation	FOL Translation	DL Notation
_:a owl:onProperty P _:a owl:allValuesFrom C	$\forall Y(P(X,Y) \Rightarrow C(Y))$	$\forall P.C$
_:a owl:onProperty P _:a owl:someValuesFrom C	$\exists Y(P(X,Y) \wedge C(Y))$	$\exists P.C$
_:a owl:onProperty P _:a owl:minCardinality n	$\exists Y_1 \ldots \exists Y_n(P(X,Y_1) \wedge \ldots \wedge P(X,Y_n) \wedge$ $\bigwedge_{i,j \in 1..n, i \neq j}(Y_i \neq Y_j))$	$(\geq n P)$
_:a owl:maxCardinality n	$\forall Y_1 \ldots \forall Y_n \forall Y_{n+1}$ $(P(X,Y_1) \wedge \ldots \wedge P(X,Y_n) \wedge P(X,Y_{n+1})$ $\Rightarrow \bigvee_{i,j \in 1..n+1, i \neq j}(Y_i = Y_j))$	$(\leq n P)$

Figure 7.8. Logical semantics of the OWL restriction constructs.

The logical semantics of these different class descriptions defined by restrictions can be given in FOL either as open formulas with one free variable or as DL concepts using DL constructors. This is summarized in Figure 7.8, where X denotes a free variable.

Union and Intersection

The owl:intersectionOf and owl:unionOf constructs allow combining classes. The intersection of (possibly unnamed) classes denotes the individuals that belong to both classes; whereas the union denotes the individuals that belong to some. Note that the argument of those two constructs is in fact a *collection*, for which we use the standard shortcut notation of lists, as illustrated in the following example by the list (:Professor, :Lecturer) declared as the argument of owl:unionOf.

Example 7.3.8 *The constraint that only professors or lecturers may teach to undergraduate students can be expressed in OWL as follows:*

_:a	rdfs:subClassOf	owl:Restriction
_:a	owl:onProperty	:TeachesTo
_:a	owl:someValuesFrom	:Undergrad
_:b	owl:unionOf	(:Professor, :Lecturer)
_:a	rdfs:subClassOf	_:b

In the spirit of union, and like union requiring logical disjunction, the owl:oneOf construct allows describing a class by enumerating its elements as a collection. This corresponds to the following FOL and DL semantics.

OWL Notation	FOL Translation	DL Notation
owl:intersectionOf $(C,D...)$	$C(X) \wedge D(X)...$	$C \sqcap D...$
owl:unionOf $(C,D...)$	$C(X) \vee D(X)...$	$C \sqcup D...$
owl:oneOf $(e,f...)$	$X=e \vee X=f...$	oneOf $\{e,f,...\}$

Class and Property Equivalence

The construct owl:equivalentClass allows stating that two classes are equivalent (i.e., that there are inclusions both ways). Similarly, owl:equivalentProperty allows stating that two properties are equivalent. Strictly speaking, those two constructs do not add expressivity to RDFS. In fact, ⟨ C owl:equivalentClass D ⟩ can be expressed in RDFS by the two triplets: ⟨ C rdfs:subClassOf D ⟩ and ⟨ D rdfs:subClassOf C ⟩.

As explained in the next section, OWL constructs are all syntactic variants of description logic constructors.

7.4 ONTOLOGIES AND (DESCRIPTION) LOGICS

First-order logic is the formal foundation of the OWL ontology Web language. First-order logic (also called predicate logic) is especially appropriate for knowledge representation and reasoning. In fact, ontologies are simply knowledge about classes and properties. From a logical point of view, classes are unary predicates while properties are binary predicates, and constraints are logical formulas asserted as axioms on these predicates (i.e., asserted as true in the domain of interest).

From the early days of computer science, the problem of automatic deduction in FOL has been extensively studied. The main result that any computer scientist should know is that *the implication problem in FOL is not decidable but only recursively enumerable*, which is stated briefly as *FOL is recursively enumerable*. That means that there exists an algorithm that given some formula φ enumerates all the formulas ψ such φ implies ψ. On the other hand, there does not exist any general algorithm (i.e., a systematic machinery) that, applied to two any input FOL formulas φ and ψ, decides where φ implies ψ. Observe that φ implies ψ if and only if there is no model for $\varphi \wedge \neg\psi$. Thus, the seemingly simpler problem of deciding whether a FOL formula is satisfiable is also not decidable.

A lot of research has then been devoted to exhibit *fragments* of FOL that are decidable (i.e., subsets of FOL formulas defined by some restrictions on the allowed formulas, for which checking logical entailment between formulas, possibly given a set of axioms, can be performed automatically by an algorithm). In particular, *description logics (DLs)* are decidable fragments of first-order logic allowing reasoning on complex logical axioms over unary and binary predicates. This is exactly what is needed for handling ontologies. Therefore, it is not surprising that the OWL constructs have been borrowed from DLs. DLs cover a broad spectrum of class-based logical languages for which reasoning is decidable with a computational complexity that depends on the set of constructs allowed in the language.

Research carried out on DLs provides a fine-grained analysis of the trade-off between expressive power and computational complexity of sound and complete reasoning. In this section, we just give a minimal background on the main DLs' constructs and the impact of their combinations on the complexity of reasoning. This should first help practitioners to choose among the existing DL reasoners the one that is the most appropriate for their application. Also, for researchers, it should facilitate further reading of advanced materials about DLs.

7.4.1 Preliminaries: The DL Jargon

A DL knowledge base is made of an intentional part (the Tbox) and an assertional part (the Abox). The Tbox defines the ontology serving as conceptual view over the data in the Abox. In DLs, the classes are called *concepts*, and the properties are called *roles*.

A Tbox $\mathcal{T}$ is a set of *terminological axioms* that state inclusions or equivalences between (possibly complex) concepts ($B \sqsubseteq C$ or $B \equiv C$) and roles ($R \sqsubseteq E$ or $R \equiv E$), while an Abox $\mathcal{A}$ is a set of *assertions* stating memberships of individuals in concepts ($C(a)$) and role memberships for pairs of individuals ($R(a,b)$). The legal DL knowledge bases $\langle \mathcal{T}, \mathcal{A} \rangle$ vary according to the DL *constructs* used for defining complex concepts and roles and to the restrictions on the axioms that are allowed in the Tbox and the assertions allowed in the Abox. As said in the previous section, the DL *constructs* are the OWL *constructs*, denoted with a different syntax. The ingredients for constructing a DL knowledge base are thus:

- A *vocabulary* composed of a set **C** of *atomic concepts* (A, B,...), a set **R** of *atomic roles* (P, Q,...), and a set **O** of *individuals* (a, b, c,...),
- A set of *constructs* used for building complex concepts and roles from atomic concepts and roles,
- A language of *axioms* that can be stated for constraining the vocabulary in order to express domain constraints.

Example 7.4.1 *Student* ⊓ Researcher *is a complex concept built from the two atomic concepts Student and Researcher using the conjunction construct (which is denoted owl:intersectionOf in OWL). This complex concept can be related to the atomic concept PhDStudent by an inclusion axiom:*

PhDStudent $\sqsubseteq$ Student ⊓ Researcher

or by an equivalence axiom:

PhDStudent $\equiv$ Student ⊓ Researcher

The difference between inclusion and equivalence axioms will be clearer when we will define the formal semantics underlying DLs. From a modeling point of view, the equivalence axioms are used to define new concepts (such as *PhD-Student*) from existing concepts (such as *Student* and *Researcher*). Concepts can be defined by restricting a role using either the *value restriction* construct $\forall R.C$ (denoted owl:allValuesFrom in OWL) or the *existential restriction* construct $\exists R.C$ (denoted owl:someValuesFrom in OWL). For example, we can define the concept *MathStudent* as follows:

MathStudent $\equiv$ *Student* ⊓ ∀*RegisteredTo.MathCourse*

to specify that Math students are exactly those who are registered to Math courses only. However, if we define the concept *MathStudent* instead as follows:

MathStudent $\equiv$ *Student* ⊓ ∃*RegisteredTo.MathCourse*

any student who is registered in at least one Math course will be considered a Math student.

The inclusion axioms express relations between concepts. The simplest relations are the inclusion relations between *atomic* concepts or roles, which correspond to the subClassOf and to the subPropertyOf relations of RDFS. For example, if *MathCourse* and *Course* are atomic concepts in the vocabulary, and *LateRegisteredTo* and *RegisteredTo* are atomic roles in the vocabulary, the following inclusion axioms express that *MathCourse* is a more specific concept than (i.e., a subclass of) *Course*, and that *LateRegisteredTo* is a more specific role than (i.e., a subproperty of) *RegisteredTo*:

MathCourse ⊑ Course

LateRegisteredTo ⊑ RegisteredTo

General inclusion axioms (calleds GCIs) consist of inclusions between *complex* concepts. For example, the following GCI expresses the constraint that *only professors or lecturers may teach to undergraduate students* (which is expressible in OWL by a set of five triplets, as seen in Section 7.3.4):

∃TeachesTo.Undergrad ⊑ Professor ⊔ Lecturer

Such a constraint can interact with other constraints expressed in the Tbox, or in the Abox. For instance, suppose that we have in the Tbox (i.e., in the ontology) the following inclusion axioms stating that researchers are neither professors nor lecturers, that only students are taught to, and that students that are not undergraduate students are graduate students:

Researcher ⊑ ¬Professor

Researcher ⊑ ¬Lecturer

∃TeachesTo⁻ ⊑ Student

Student ⊓ ¬Undergrad ⊑ GraduateStudent

Based on the logical semantics, which will be detailed below, the following constraint can be inferred:

Researcher ⊑ ∀TeachesTo.GraduateStudent

Suppose now that the Abox contains the following assertions on the individuals *dupond* and *pierre*:

TeachesTo(dupond,pierre)

¬GraduateStudent(pierre)

¬Professor(dupond)

The new fact *Lecturer(dupond)* can be logically inferred from those facts and the above constraints in the Tbox.

The underlying reasoning leading to such inferences is quite elaborate and requires a complex algorithmic machinery to make it automatic. It is the focus of the remaining of this section.

FOL Semantics of DL

Reasoning in DLs is based on the standard logical semantics in terms of FOL interpretations of individuals as constants, of concepts as subsets, and of roles as binary relations.

An *interpretation* consists of a nonempty *interpretation domain* Δ^I and an *interpretation function* I that assigns an element to each individual in **O**, a subset of Δ^I to each atomic concept **C**, and a binary relation over Δ^I to each atomic role in **R**. Usually, in DL, the so-called *unique name assumption* holds and thus *distinct* individuals are interpreted by *distinct* elements in the domain of interpretation.

The semantics of complex concepts using those constructs is recursively defined from the interpretations of atomic concepts and roles as follows:

- $I(C_1 \sqcap C_2) = I(C_1) \cap I(C_2)$
- $I(\forall R.C) = \{o_1 \mid \forall o_2 [(o_1, o_2) \in I(R) \Rightarrow o_2 \in I(C)]\}$
- $I((\exists R.C) = \{o_1 \mid \exists o_2.[(o_1, o_2) \in I(R) \wedge o_2 \in I(C)]\}$
- $I(\neg C) = \Delta^I \setminus I(C)$
- $I(R^-) = \{(o_2, o_1) \mid (o_1, o_2) \in I(R)\}$

Satisfaction is defined as follows:

- An interpretation *I satisfies* (i.e., is a *model* of) an class inclusion axiom $B \sqsubseteq C$, resp. $B \equiv C$, if $I(B) \subseteq I(C)$, resp. $I(B) = I(C)$.
- *I satisfies* a relationship inclusion axiom $R \sqsubseteq E$, resp. $R \equiv E$, if $I(R) \subseteq I(E)$, resp. $I(R) = I(E)$.
- *I satisfies* the membership assertion $C(a)$, resp. $R(a,b)$, if $I(a) \in I(C)$, resp., $(I(a), I(b)) \in I(R)$.
- *I satisfies* or is *model of a knowledge base* $\mathcal{K} = \langle \mathcal{T}, \mathcal{A} \rangle$ if it is a model of all the statements both in $\mathcal{T}$ and $\mathcal{A}$. A knowledge base $\mathcal{K}$ is *satisfiable* (or *consistent*) if it has at least one model.

Finally, a knowledge base $\mathcal{K}$ *logically entails* a (terminological or assertional) statement α, written $KB \models \alpha$, if every model of $\mathcal{K}$ is a also model of α.

Reasoning Problems Considered in DLs

The main reasoning problems that have been extensively studied in the DL community are satisfiability (i.e., consistency) checking of DL knowledge bases, and also instance checking and subsumption checking. They are formally defined as follows.

- *Satisfiability checking:* Given a DL knowledge base $\mathcal{K} = \langle \mathcal{T}, \mathcal{A} \rangle$, is $\mathcal{K}$ satisfiable?
- *Subsumption checking:* Given a Tbox $\mathcal{T}$ and two concept expressions C and D, does $\mathcal{T} \models C \sqsubseteq D$?
- *Instance checking:* Given a DL knowledge base $\mathcal{K} = \langle \mathcal{T}, \mathcal{A} \rangle$, an individual e and a concept expression C, does $\mathcal{K} \models C(e)$?

Instance checking and subsumption checking are logical entailment problems that can in fact be reduced to (un)satisfiability checking *for DLs having full negation in their language* (i.e., for DLs in which the constructor $\neg$ can apply to any complex concept in the axioms of the Tbox). The reason is that, based on the logical semantics, we have the following equivalences (in which a is a new individual that we introduce):

- $\mathcal{T} \models C \sqsubseteq D \Leftrightarrow \langle \mathcal{T}, \{(C \sqcap \neg D)(a)\} \rangle$ is unsatisfiable.
- $\langle \mathcal{T}, \mathcal{A} \rangle \models C(e) \Leftrightarrow \langle \mathcal{T}, \mathcal{A} \cup \{\neg C(e)\} \rangle$ is unsatisfiable.

For simple DLs in which the constructor of negation is not allowed, instance checking can be reduced to subsumption checking by computing the *most specific concept* satisfied by an individual in the Abox. Given an Abox $\mathcal{A}$ of a given DL and an individual e, the *most specific concept* of e in $\mathcal{A}$ (denoted $msc(\mathcal{A}, e)$) is the concept expression D in the given DL such that for every concept C in the given DL, $\mathcal{A} \models C(e)$ implies $D \sqsubseteq C$. Clearly, once $msc(\mathcal{A}, e)$ is known, we have

$$\langle \mathcal{T}, \mathcal{A} \rangle \models C(e) \Leftrightarrow \mathcal{T} \models msc(\mathcal{A}, e) \sqsubseteq C$$

We now focus on some representative DLs. We start with $\mathcal{ALC}$ (Section 7.4.2), which is the basis of the most expressive DLs, and in particular those that led to OWL. Reasoning in these expressive DLs (and thus in OWL) is decidable but at the price of some high complexity often prohibitive in practice. We then survey DLs for which reasoning is polynomial: first $\mathcal{FL}$ and $\mathcal{EL}$ in Section 7.4.3, and finally the most recent DL-LITE family in Section 7.4.4, which provides a good trade-off between expressiveness and efficiency.

7.4.2 $\mathcal{ALC}$: The Prototypical DL

$\mathcal{ALC}$ is often considered as the prototypical DL because it corresponds to a fragment of FOL that is easy to understand, and also because it is a syntactic variant of the basic modal logic K (see references). $\mathcal{ALC}$ is the DL based on the following constructs:

- *Conjunction* $C_1 \sqcap C_2$,
- *Existential restriction* $\exists R.C$,
- *Negation* $\neg C$.

As a result, $\mathcal{ALC}$ also contains de facto

- The *disjunction* $C_1 \sqcup C_2$ (which stands for $\neg(\neg C_1 \sqcap \neg C_2)$),
- The value restriction (since $\forall R.C$ stands for $\neg(\exists R.\neg C)$),
- The top $\top$ and bottom $\bot$ (standing, respectively, for $A \sqcup \neg A$ and $A \sqcap \neg A$).

An $\mathcal{ALC}$ Tbox may contain GCIs such as

$\exists TeachesTo.Undergrad \sqsubseteq Professor \sqcup Lecturer$

An $\mathcal{ALC}$ Abox is made of a set of facts of the form $C(a)$ and $R(a, b)$ where a and b are individuals, R is an atomic role, and C is a possibly complex concept.

Since $\mathcal{ALC}$ allows full negation, subsumption and instance checking in $\mathcal{ALC}$ can be trivially reduced to satisfiability checking of $\mathcal{ALC}$ knowledge bases, as seen previously.

The algorithmic method for reasoning in $\mathcal{ALC}$ (and in all expressive DLs extending $\mathcal{ALC}$) is based on tableau calculus, which is a classical method in logic for satisfiability checking. The *tableau method* has been extensively used in DLs both for proving decidability results and for implementing DL reasoners such as Fact, Racer, and Pellet, respectively implemented in C++, Lisp-like, and Java).

We just illustrate here the tableau method on a simple example, and refer the reader to Section 7.5 for pointers to more detailed presentations. Consider an $\mathcal{ALC}$ knowledge base whose Tbox $\mathcal{T}$ is without GCIs (i.e., $\mathcal{T}$ is made of concept definitions only). For instance,

$$\mathcal{T} = \{C_1 \equiv A \sqcap B, C_2 \equiv \exists R.A, C_3 \equiv \forall R.B, C_4 \equiv \forall R.\neg C_1\}$$

Let us consider the following associated Abox $\mathcal{A}$:

$$\mathcal{A} = \{C_2(a), C_3(a), C_4(a)\}$$

For checking whether the knowledge base $\langle \mathcal{T}, \mathcal{A} \rangle$ is satisfiable, we first get rid of the Tbox by recursively unfolding the concept definitions. This is always possible for Tbox composed of a set of acyclic equivalence axioms of the form $A \equiv C$, where A is an atomic concept appearing in the left-hand side of exactly one equivalence axioms (no multiple definition). We obtain the following Abox, which is equivalent to $\langle \mathcal{T}, \mathcal{A} \rangle$:

$$\mathcal{A}' = \{(\exists R.A)(a), (\forall R.B)(a), (\forall R.\neg(A \sqcap B))(a)\}$$

We now apply a preprocessing that consists in transforming all the concepts expressions in $\mathcal{A}'$ into *negation normal form* so that the negation construct applies to only atomic concepts. This transformation can be done in polynomial time. The result is the following equivalent Abox $\mathcal{A}''$:

$$\mathcal{A}'' = \{(\exists R.A)(a), (\forall R.B)(a), (\forall R.(\neg A \sqcup \neg B))(a)\}$$

The tableau method tries to build a finite model of $\mathcal{A}''$ by applying tableau rules to extend it. There is one rule per construct (except for the negation construct). From an extended Abox which is *complete* (no rule applies) and *clash-free* (no obvious contradiction), a so-called *canonical interpretation* can be built, which is a model of the initial Abox.

More precisely, the tableau rules applies to a set of Aboxes, starting from $\{\mathcal{A}''\}$. The rules picks one Abox and replaces it by finitely many new Aboxes. New Aboxes containing a clash (i.e., two contradictory facts $A(e)$ and $\neg A(e)$) are simply deleted. The algorithm terminates if no more rules apply to any Abox in the set. The returned answer is then *yes* (the input Abox is satisfiable) if the set is not empty, and *no* otherwise.

The tableau rules for $\mathcal{ALC}$ (applied to an Abox $\mathcal{A}$ in the set of Aboxes) are the following:

- ■ *The $\sqcap$-rule*:
  Condition: $\mathcal{A}$ contains $(C \sqcap D)(a)$ but not both $C(a)$ and $D(a)$.
  Action: Add $\mathcal{A}' = \mathcal{A} \cup \{C(a), D(a)\}$.
- ■ *The $\sqcup$-rule*:
  Condition: $\mathcal{A}$ contains $(C \sqcup D)(a)$ but neither $C(a)$ nor $D(a)$.
  Action: Add $\mathcal{A}' = \mathcal{A} \cup \{C(a)\}$ and $\mathcal{A}'' = \mathcal{A} \cup \{D(a)\}$.
- ■ *The $\exists$-rule*:
  Condition: $\mathcal{A}$ contains $(\exists R.C)(a)$, but there is no c such that $\{R(a,c), C(c)\} \subseteq \mathcal{A}$.
  Action: Add $\mathcal{A}' = \mathcal{A} \cup \{R(a,b), C(b)\}$ where b is a new individual name.
- ■ *The $\forall$-rule*:
  Condition: $\mathcal{A}$ contains $(\forall R.C)(a)$ and $R(a,b)$ but not $C(b)$.
  Action: Add $\mathcal{A}' = \mathcal{A} \cup \{C(b)\}$.

The result of the application of the tableau method to $\mathcal{A}'' = \{(\exists R.A)(a), (\forall R.B)(a),$ $(\forall R.(\neg A \sqcup \neg B))(a)\}$ gives the following Aboxes:

$$\mathcal{A}''_1 = \{(\exists R.A)(a), (\forall R.B)(a), (\forall R.(\neg A \sqcup \neg B))(a), R(a,b), A(b), B(b), \neg A(b)\}$$

$$\mathcal{A}''_2 = \{(\exists R.A)(a), (\forall R.B)(a), (\forall R.(\neg A \sqcup \neg B))(a), R(a,b), A(b), B(b), \neg B(b)\}$$

They both contain a clash. Therefore, the original $\mathcal{A}''$ is correctly decided unsatisfiable by the algorithm.

The interest of the tableau method is that it is "easily" extensible to new constructs and new constraints. For instance, in order to extend the previous tableau method to $\mathcal{ALC}$ with GCIs, we first observe that a finite set of GCIs $\{C_1 \sqsubseteq D_1, \ldots, C_n \sqsubseteq D_n\}$ can be encoded into one GCI of the form $\top \sqsubseteq C$ where C is obtained by transforming $(\neg C_1 \sqcup D_1) \sqcap \cdots \sqcap (\neg C_n \sqcup D_n)$ in negation normal form, and we add the following tableau rule:

■ *The GCI-rule* for $\top \sqsubseteq C$:
  Condition: $\mathcal{A}$ contains the individual name a but not $C(a)$.
  Action: Add $\mathcal{A}' = \mathcal{A} \cup \{C(a)\}$.

The subtle point is that by adding this rule, the termination of the tableau method is not guaranteed, as it can be seen just by considering the Abox $\{P(a)\}$ and the GCI $\top \sqsubseteq \exists R.P$. The clue is to add a blocking condition for stopping the generation of new individual names and to prevent the tableau rules for applying to blocked individuals. An individual y is blocked by an individual x such as the set of concepts describing y is included in the set of concepts describing x. In our example, from the Abox obtained by applying the GCI rule to $\{P(a)\}$, we stop at the clash-free Abox $\mathcal{A} = \{P(a), (\exists R.P)(a), R(a,b), P(b), (\exists R.P)(b), R(b,c), P(c)\}$ since the individual c is blocked by the individual b. The canonical interpretation I of a clash-free Abox $\mathcal{A}_n$ to which no more rules apply is obtained by defining as domain of interpretation Δ^I the set of all the individual appearing in the corresponding Abox and

■ For each atomic concept A: $I(A) = \{e \in \Delta^I \mid A(e) \in \mathcal{A}_n\}$.
■ For each atomic role R: $I(R) = \{(e,f) \in \Delta^I \times \Delta^I \mid R(e,f) \in \mathcal{A}_n\} \cup \{R(f,f) \mid f \text{ is blocked}$ by e such that $R(e,f) \in \mathcal{A}_n\}$.

It can be shown that this canonical interpretation is in fact a model of the corresponding clash-free Abox, and therefore of the original Abox which is therefore satisfiable.

The tableau method shows that the satisfiability of $\mathcal{ALC}$ knowledge bases is decidable but with a complexity that may be exponential because of the disjunction construct and the associated $\sqcup$-*rule*.

7.4.3 Simple DLs for Which Reasoning Is Polynomial

$\mathcal{FL}$ and $\mathcal{EL}$ are two minimal DLs for which subsumption checking is polynomial for Tboxes without GCIs. For such simple Tboxes, as already mentioned previously, by concept unfolding, we can get rid of the Tbox, and the subsumption checking problem becomes: given two concept expressions C and D, does $\models C \sqsubseteq D$ (i.e., for any individual x, does $C(x)$ implies $D(x)$)?

The constructs allowed in $\mathcal{FL}$ are *conjunction* $C_1 \sqcap C_2$, *value restrictions* $\forall R.C$ and also *unqualified existential restriction* $\exists R$. Satisfiability is trivial in $\mathcal{FL}$: Every $\mathcal{FL}$ knowledge base is satisfiable. Subsumption checking between two concept expressions C and D can be done in quadratic time by a *structural subsumption* algorithm *IsSubsumed?*(C, D), which consists in

- Normalizing the concept expressions. The normal form of a $\mathcal{FL}$ concept expression is obtained by
  - flattening all nested conjunctions, that is, by applying exhaustively the rewriting rule to the concept expression: $A \sqcap (B \sqcap C) \rightarrow A \sqcap B \sqcap C$;
  - pushing value restrictions over conjunctions, that is, by applying exhaustively the rewriting rule to the concept expression: $\forall R.(A \sqcap B) \rightarrow \forall R.A \sqcap \forall R.B$.

  For example, the normalization of $\forall R.(A \sqcap \forall S.(B \sqcap \forall R.A))$ returns the expression: $\forall R.A \sqcap \forall R.\forall S.B \sqcap \forall R.\forall S.\forall R.A$.

  The application of these rewriting rules preserves logical equivalence; hence, the subsumption is preserved by the normalization. (The proof is left as an exercise.)
- Comparing recursively the structure of the normalized expressions $C_1 \sqcap \cdots \sqcap C_n$ and $D_1 \sqcap \cdots \sqcap D_m$ as follows: *IsSubsumed?*(C, D) return *true* if and only if for all D_i
  - if D_i is an atomic concept or an unqualified existential restriction, then there exists a C_j such that $C_j = D_i$;
  - if D_i is a concept of the form $\forall R.D'$, then there exists a C_j of the form $\forall R.C'$ (same role) such that *IsSubsumed?*(C', D').

By induction on the number of nesting of the $\forall$ constructs, it is easy to prove that the foregoing algorithm runs in $O(|C| \times |D|)$, where $|C|$ denotes the size of the concept expression C defined by the number of the constructs $\sqcap$ and $\forall$ appearing in it.

The structural subsumption is *sound* since when *IsSubsumed?*(C, D) returns true, then it holds that $I(C) \subseteq I(D)$ for every interpretation I. Take any conjunct D_i of D: Either it appears as a conjunct C_j of C, and by definition of the logical semantics of the conjunction construct $I(C) \subseteq I(C_j) = I(D_i) \subseteq I(D)$; or it is of the form $\forall R.D'$, and there exists as conjunct of C of the form $\forall R.C'$ such that *IsSubsumed?*(C', D'); Then, by induction $I(C') \subseteq I(D')$ and by definition of the logical semantics of the $\forall$ construct, $I(\forall R.C') \subseteq I(\forall R.D')$, and thus by the conjunction semantics, $I(C) \subseteq I(C_j) \subseteq I(D_i) \subseteq I(D)$.

The *completeness* of the structural subsumption is a little bit harder to prove: It must be shown that, whenever $I(C) \subseteq I(D)$ for all interpretations I, then the algorithm *IsSubsumed?*(C, D) returns *true*. The proof is done by contrapositive, that is, by showing that anytime *IsSubsumed?*(C, D) returns *false*, then there exists an interpretation assigning an element of the domain to C and not to D (i.e., $C \not\sqsubseteq D$). The proof relies on the fact that anytime *IsSubsumed?*(C, D) returns *false*, there exists a conjunct D_i of D that has no correspondent conjunct in C. In this case, we can build an interpretation I in which all the conjuncts in C are assigned to subsets containing a given element e, and in which D_i is assigned to the empty set: $e \in I(C)$ and $e \notin I(D)$.

As an exercise, by applying the above algorithm, check that

$$\forall R.(\forall S.B \sqcap \forall S.\forall R.A) \sqcap \forall R.(A \sqcap B) \sqsubseteq \forall R.(A \sqcap \forall S.(B \sqcap \forall R.A))$$

For $\mathcal{FL}$ general Tboxes (i.e., Tboxes including general concept inclusions (GCIs), subsumption checking becomes intractable even for Tboxes containing inclusion axioms between atomic concepts only. In this case, subsumption checking is co-NP complete (by reduction from the inclusion problem for acyclic finite automata).

The constructs allowed in $\mathcal{EL}$ are *conjunctions* $C_1 \sqcap C_2$ and *existential restrictions* $\exists R.C$. As for $\mathcal{FL}$, any $\mathcal{EL}$ knowledge base is satisfiable. Subsumption checking in $\mathcal{EL}$ is polynomial even for general Tboxes (i.e., Tboxes including GCIs). The subsumption algorithm for $\mathcal{EL}$ can also be qualified as a structural algorithm, although it is quite different from the "normalize and compare" algorithm for $\mathcal{FL}$ concept expressions described previously. In fact, it relies on the representation of $\mathcal{EL}$ concept expressions as labeled trees (called description trees), in which nodes are labeled with sets of atomic concepts, while edges are labeled with atomic roles. It is shown that an $\mathcal{EL}$ concept expression C is subsumed by an $\mathcal{EL}$ concept expression D if there is an homomorphism from the description tree of D to the description tree of C. Checking subsumption corresponds then to checking the existence of an homomorphism between trees. This problem is known to be NP-complete for graphs but to be polynomial for trees. Taking into account GCIs in the Tbox can be done by extending accordingly the labels of the description trees.

Therefore, if we can say for short that **subsumption checking is polynomial for** $\mathcal{EL}$, We have to be more cautious for $\mathcal{FL}$: We just can say that subsumption checking between two $\mathcal{FL}$ concept expressions (w.r.t. an empty Tbox) is polynomial.

As explained previously, instance checking can be reduced to subsumption checking by computing the *most specific concept* of a constant e in $\mathcal{A}$ (denoted $msc(\mathcal{A}, e)$). The problem is that in $\mathcal{FL}$ or $\mathcal{EL}$ the most specific concepts do not always exist. A solution for checking whether $C(e)$ is entailed from an $\mathcal{FL}$ or $\mathcal{EL}$ knowledge base is to adapt the tableau method: First, the tableau rules corresponding to the constructs allowed in $\mathcal{FL}$ and $\mathcal{EL}$ can be applied to saturate the original Abox; then the negation of $C(e)$ is injected, and the tableau rules are applied, including possibly the ⊔-rule, since the ⊔ construct can be introduced by negating $\mathcal{FL}$ or $\mathcal{EL}$ concept expressions; $C(e)$ is entailed from the original knowledge base if and only if all the resulting Aboxes contain a clash.

If we combine the constructs of $\mathcal{FL}$ and $\mathcal{EL}$, namely *conjunction* $C_1 \sqcap C_2$, *value restrictions* $\forall R.C$, and *existential restrictions* $\exists R.C$, we obtain the new DL called $\mathcal{FLE}$ for which even checking subsumption between two concept expressions is NP-complete.

In fact, since the DL *existential restrictions* and *value restrictions* correspond to the OWL restrictions **owl:oneValuesFrom** and **owl:allValuesFrom** (see Figure 7.8), that means that the combination of those restrictions that are quite natural from a modeling point of view may lead to intractability for automatic inferencing.

7.4.4 The DL-LITE Family: A Good Trade-off

The DL-LITE family has been recently designed for capturing the main modeling primitives of conceptual data models (e.g., Entity-Relationship) and object-oriented formalisms (e.g., basic UML class diagrams[1]), while remaining reasoning tractable in presence of concept inclusion statements and a certain form of negation.

The constructs allowed in DL-LITE are *unqualified existential restriction* on roles ($\exists R$) and on inverse of roles ($\exists R^-$), and the negation.

The axioms allowed in a Tbox of DL-LITE are concept inclusion statements of the form $B \sqsubseteq C$ or $B \sqsubseteq \neg C$, where B and C are atomic concepts, or existential restriction ($\exists R$ or $\exists R^-$).

DL-LITE$_\mathcal{F}$ and DL-LITE$_\mathcal{R}$ are then two dialects of DL-LITE that differ from some additional allowed axioms:

- a DL-LITE$_\mathcal{R}$ Tbox allows role inclusion statements of the form $P \sqsubseteq Q$ or $P \sqsubseteq \neg Q$, where P and Q are atomic roles or inverse of atomic roles
- a DL-LITE$_\mathcal{F}$ Tbox allows functionality statements on roles of the form (*funct P*) or (*funct P^-*). An interpretation I *satisfies* a functionality statement (*funct R*) if the binary relation $I(R)$ is a function, that is, $(o,o_1) \in I(R)$ and $(o,o_2) \in I(R)$ implies $o_1 = o_2$.

It is worth noticing that negation is only allowed in the right-hand sides of inclusion statements. Inclusion axioms with negation in the right-hand side are called *negative inclusions* (for short *NIs*), whereas the inclusion axioms without negation are called *positive inclusions* (for short *PIs*).

It can be shown that subsumption checking is polynomial both for DL-LITE$_\mathcal{R}$ and DL-LITE$_\mathcal{F}$ Tboxes, and that their combination (denoted DL-LITE$_{\mathcal{R}\mathcal{F}}$) is PTIME-complete. The subsumption algorithm is based on computing the *closure* of the Tbox (i.e., the set of all PIs and NIs that can be inferred from the original Tbox). Checking $\mathcal{T} \models C \sqsubseteq D$ consists then in checking whether $C \sqsubseteq D$ belongs to the closure of $\mathcal{T}$. Satisfiability checking and instance checking also rely on exploiting the closure. In fact, they are particular cases of the most general problem of answering conjunctive queries over DL-LITE knowledge bases, for which the DL-LITE family has been designed. Answering conjunctive queries over ontologies is a reasoning problem of major interest for the Semantic Web, the associated decision problem of which *is not reducible* to (un)satisfiability checking or to subsumption or instance checking. This problem has been studied quite recently, and we will dedicate a whole chapter to it (Chapter 8). In particular, we will see that the DL-lite family groups DLs that have been specially designed for guaranteeing query answering to be polynomial in data complexity.

It is noticeable that DL-LITE$_\mathcal{R}$ has been recently incorporated into the version OWL2 of OWL as the profile called OWL2 QL. This profile is an extension of RDFS.

---

[1] See http://www.omg.org/uml.

7.5 FURTHER READING

We refer to existing books (e.g., [16, 20]) for a full presentation of RDF, RDFS, and OWL.

We use an abstract compact syntax for RDF, RDFS, and OWL statements, instead of their verbose XML notation. The usage of the XML syntax for RDF, RDFS or OWL is mainly for exchanging metadata and ontologies in a standard format. XML namespaces and XML tools for parsing, indexing, transforming, browsing can be used for that purpose. Several tools such as Jena [104] are now widely available and used to store, manage, and query RDFS data. We will discuss a query language for RDF, namely SPARQL, in Chapter 8.

RDFS (without blank nodes) can be seen as a fragment of $DL\text{-}Lite_R$, which is a DL of the $DL\text{-}Lite$ family described in [38]. The $DL\text{-}Lite$ family has been designed for enabling tractable query answering over data described w.r.t. ontologies. We will consider the issue of querying with ontologies in Chapter 8.

The readers interested in the translation in FOL of the full RDFS (possibly with blank nodes in place of properties) are referred to [36].

A set of RDFS triplets can also be formalized in conceptual graphs [47] that are graphical knowledge representation formalisms that have an FOL semantics for which reasoning can be performed by graph algorithms (such as projection). The formalization of RDFS in conceptual graphs have been studied in [23].

At the moment, in contrast with RDFS, there is very little usage of tools supporting reasoning over OWL statements. The only available reasoners are description logic reasoners such as FaCT [62], RACER [138], or Pellet [148].

Readers interested in a comprehensive summary of the complexity results and reasoning algorithms on Description Logic are referred to [22]. There is a close relation between some Description Logic (in particular $\mathcal{ALC}$) and modal logics [30], which have been extensively studied in Artificial Intelligence.

Satisfiability checking in $\mathcal{ALC}$ (and thus also subsumption and instance checking) has been shown EXPTIME-complete. Additional constructs like those in the fragment OWL DL of OWL, which corresponds to DLs[2] do not change the complexity class of reasoning (which remains EXPTIME-complete). In fact, OWL DL is a syntactic variant of the so-called $\mathcal{SHOIN}$ DL, which is obtained from $\mathcal{ALC}$ by adding *number restrictions* $(\geq nP)$, *nominals* $\{a\}$, and *inverse roles* P^- of atomic roles. Nominals make it possible to construct a concept representing a singleton set $\{a\}$ (a nominal concept) from an individual a. In addition, some atomic roles can be declared to be *transitive* using a role axiom $Trans(P)$, and the Tbox can include *role inclusion* axioms $R_1 \sqsubseteq R_2$.

The semantics of those additional constructs and axioms is defined from the interpretations of individuals, atomic concepts, and roles as follows ($\sharp\{S\}$ denotes the cardinality of a set S):

- $I((\geq nP)) = \{d \in \Delta^I \mid \sharp\{e \mid (d,e) \in I(P)\} \geq n\}$;
- $I(P^-) = \{(o_2,o_1) \mid (o_1,o_2) \in I(P)\}$;
- $I(\{a\}) = \{I(a)\}$.

---

[2] OWL Full is undecidable.

An interpretation I *satisfies* a role transitivity statement (*Trans P*) if the binary relation $I(P)$ is transitive, that is, $(o, o_1) \in I(P)$ and $(o_1, o_2) \in I(P)$ implies $(o, o_2) \in I(P)$.

$\mathcal{SHIQ}$ extends $\mathcal{SHOIN}$ with so-called *qualified number restrictions* $(\geq nP.C)$ whose semantics is defined by the following interpretation rule:

$$I((\geq nP.C)) = \{d \in \Delta^I \mid \sharp\{e \mid (d,e) \in I(P) \wedge e \in I(C)\} \geq n\}.$$

Relating the ontology modeling OWL language to DLs is of primary importance since it allows to understand the cost to pay if we want to automatically exploit constraints requiring a given combination of OWL constructs. In particular, we know (from the EXPTIME-completeness of $\mathcal{ALC}$) that *in the worst case* an inference algorithm may take an exponential time for reasoning on a set of constraints expressed using full negation, conjunction, existential and value restriction. In practice, however, the existing DL reasoners such as FaCT, RACER, and Pellet have acceptable performances for dealing with expressive ontologies of reasonable size. The reason is that the constraints expressed in real-life ontologies usually do not correspond to the pathological cases leading to the worst-case complexity.

7.6 EXERCISES

Exercise 7.6.1 *Show that the inference rules of Figure 7.7 are complete for the logical entailment of constraints expressible in RDFS. More precisely, let $\mathcal{T}$ be a set of RDFS triplets expressing logical constraints of the form $A \sqsubseteq B$, $P \sqsubseteq R$, $\exists P \sqsubseteq A$ or $\exists P^- \sqsubseteq B$, where A and B denote classes while P and Q denote properties. Show that for every constraint $C \sqsubseteq D$ of one of those four previous forms, if $\mathcal{T} \models C \sqsubseteq D$, then the RDFS triplet denoting $C \sqsubseteq D$ is inferred by applying the inference rules of Figure 7.7 to $\mathcal{T}$.*

Exercise 7.6.2 *$\mathcal{AL}$ is the Description Logic obtained from $\mathcal{FL}$ by adding negation on atomic concepts.*

1. *Based on the logical semantics, prove that the concept expression $\forall R.A \sqcap \forall R.\neg A$ is subsumed by the concept expression $\forall R.B$, for any atomic concept B.*
2. *Show that the structural subsumption algorithm is not complete for checking subsumption in $\mathcal{AL}$.*
   Indication: Apply the algorithm IsSubsumed?$(\forall R.A \sqcap \forall R.\neg A, \forall R.B)$.
3. *Apply the tableau method for checking that $\forall R.A \sqcap \forall R.\neg A$ is subsumed by the concept expression $\forall R.B$.*
   Indication: Apply the tableau rules to the Abox $\{(\forall R.A \sqcap \forall R.\neg A)(a), (\exists R.\neg B)(a)\}$.

Exercise 7.6.3 *Based on the logical semantics, show the following statements:*

1. *$\forall R.(A \sqcap B) \equiv \forall R.A \sqcap \forall R.B$.*
2. *$\exists R.(A \sqcap B) \not\equiv \exists R.A \sqcap \exists R.B$.*
3. *$\exists R.(A \sqcap B) \sqsubseteq \exists R.A \sqcap \exists R.B$.*
4. *$\exists R.A \sqcap \forall R.B \sqsubseteq \exists R.(A \sqcap B)$.*

8

Querying Data Through Ontologies

8.1 INTRODUCTION

As we saw in the previous chapter, ontologies form the backbone of the Semantic Web by providing a conceptual view of data and services available worldwide via the Web. We discussed the RDF language for describing knowledge, and a family of languages, called description logics, that provide formal foundations for ontologies and in particular for the OWL ontology language recommended by the W3C.

In this chapter, the focus is on querying RDF data. Since massive volumes of RDF sources are more and more present on the Web, specifying queries for RDF data that can be evaluated efficiently is becoming every day more and more important.

We will see that the set of query answers strongly depends on the semantic context. We will study query answering when the ontology is specified in RDFS and then when the ontology is specified in DL-LITE. The ontology language DL-LITE belongs to the DL family. It has been designed as a trade-off between the ability to describe a wide range of domains of interest and query evaluation efficiency. More precisely, we will focus on two important fragments of DL-LITE, namely DL-LITE$_\mathcal{R}$ and DL-LITE$_\mathcal{F}$.

We will observe that the problem of answering queries through ontologies is quite different from that of answering database queries for the following two essential reasons:

Implicit facts: In a DBMS setting, all the facts are explicit. For instance, the constraint "Every PhD student is a student" enforces that, before inserting a value v in the *PhDStudent* table, this value is also inserted in the *Student* table (if not already there). In an ontology context, someone may be a student not explicitly but because of the constraint used as an inference rule. In addition, the implicit facts may be incompletely known, coming from constraints such as "A professor teaches at least one master course." From a fact such as *Professor(dupond)*, one can infer the two facts *Teaches(dupond,x)* and *MasterCourse(x)* for some unknown value x. Such partially known implicit facts may however be useful for answering queries such as "Give me all the persons who teach a master course."

Inconsistency: In a DBMS setting, the constraint "each course must have a single responsible" is also viewed as a law that cannot be violated. An update of the corresponding table that would violate this law would simply be rejected. In an ontology context, such local verifications are not sufficient for checking data inconsistency. Because of data incompleteness, this may require intricate reasoning on different constraints and data distributed over different tables. For instance, if in addition of the previous key constraint, it is declared that "only professors can be responsible for courses they must teach," "a master course is taught by a single teacher," and "lecturers are not professors," the presence of the three following facts in different tables of the database makes it inconsistent: *Lecturer(jim)*, *TeachesIn(jim,ue431)*, and *MasterCourse(ue431)*. The reason is that because of the constraint "only professors can be responsible for courses they must teach," we can infer that the course *ue431* must have a responsible x who is unknown but for whom we have partial information: S/he is a professor, and s/he teaches in the course *ue431*. Without knowing x, the fact that she is a professor is sufficient to infer that $x \neq jim$ (since *jim* is a lecturer and thus not a professor). Therefore, the course *ue431* is taught by two distinct teachers, which is forbidden for a master course.

From this, it should be clear that query answering through ontologies is more complicated than in classical databases. We have to reason to find which inferences may participate in answering a given query. We also have to reason to verify the consistency of our knowledge.

8.2 QUERYING RDF DATA: NOTATION AND SEMANTICS

In this section, we set the stage for querying RDF data. We also discuss the impact of ontologies (knowledge on the domain of interest) on the answers. To simplify, we ignore here blank nodes.

Figure 8.1 is an enhanced version of the university example that we will use throughout this chapter. The first column provides RDF data in the triple syntax, whereas the second column shows the corresponding facts in FOL.

RDF triples can be asserted in a very flexible way and almost without constraints. The association of some ontology is not a requirement. Users can update a collection of RDF statements freely by just adding/removing triples. The only reserved word in the RDF vocabulary is rdf:type that is used to relate constant names to types (i.e., classes in domain of interest or unary predicates in FOL world).

Let us now consider querying a set of RDF facts, for which the query language SPARQL has been proposed. We briefly consider it next.

SPARQL (pronounced "sparkle") is an acronym standing for *SPARQL Protocol And RDF Query Language*. It is a W3C recommendation as of 2008. Although it does borrow some features from XQuery (functions and operators), it is based on the graph model underlying RDF data.

For instance, the following query expresses in SPARQL the search of all the individuals who are enrolled in a department led by a Professor.

Subject	Predicate	Object	FOL Semantics
dupond	Leads	infoDept	Leads(dupond,infoDept)
dupond	rdf:type	Professor	Professor(dupond)
durand	ResponsibleOf	ue111	ResponsibleOf(durand,ue111)
durand	Leads	csDept	Leads(durand,csDept)
paul	TeachesTo	pierre	TeachesTo(paul,pierre)
paul	rdf:type	PhdStudent	PhDStudent(paul)
paul	EnrolledIn	infoDept	EnrolledIn(paul, infodept)
pierre	EnrolledIn	infoDept	EnrolledIn(pierre, infodept)
pierre	rdf:type	Undergrad	Undergrad(pierre)
pierre	RegisteredTo	ue111	Registered(pierre, ue111)
ue111	OfferedBy	infoDept	OfferedBy(ue111,infoDept)
ue111	rdf:type	CSCourse	CSCourse(ue111)
jim	EnrolledIn	csDept	EnrolledIn(jim, csDept)
csDept	rdf:type	TeachingDept	TeachingDept(csDept)

Figure 8.1. RDF triple syntax and its FOL semantics.

---

select x **where** x EnrolledIn y, z Leads y, z rdf:type Professor

---

We used here an SQL-like syntax. There exists competing syntaxes for expressing SPARQL queries. The corresponding query in FOL notation is

$$q(x) : - \exists y \exists z [EnrolledIn(x,y) \land Leads(z,y) \land Professor(z)]$$

This is a *conjunctive query*, that is, an FOL formula without negation or disjunction, of the form

$$q(x_1,...,x_m) : - \exists y_1,...,y_n R_1(u_1) \land \cdots \land R_p(u_p)$$

where each u_i is a vector of variables in $\{x_1,...,x_m,y_1,...,y_n\}$ or constants, and each variable x_i appears in the body of the query (i.e., for each $x \in \{x_1,...,x_m\}$, there exists u_i such that $x \in u_i$).

In the remainder of this chapter, we use conjunctive queries as the query language for RDF. From the example, it should be clear that all we say is relevant to SPARQL. We use a (standard) simplified notation for conjunctive queries. We omit the existential quantifiers and denote the connector $\land$ by a comma. Observe that this does not introduce any ambiguity. In particular, all variables not occurring in the "head of the query" (i.e., in $q(x_1,...,x_m)$) are understood as existentially quantified. The variables in $x_1,...,x_m$ are said to be *distinguished*.

In this simplified form, the example SPARQL query becomes

---

q(x) :- EnrolledIn(x,y), Leads(z,y), Professor(z)

Now consider a query in the general form:

$$q(x_1,...,x_m) :- R_1(u_1),...,R_p(u_p)$$

with existential variables $y_1,...,y_n$. Following the standard FOL semantics, the evaluation of the query consists in finding valuations v of the variables for which the closed fact $R_i(v(u_i))$ "holds" for each i. The corresponding answer is then $q(v(x_1),...,v(x_m))$. Equally, we may say that $(v(x_1),...,v(x_m))$ is an answer for the query q. When the query is unary (i.e., it has a single distinguished variable), we either say "$q(a)$ is an answer" or "a is an answer for q."

An essential issue is in the meaning of "holds" in the previous informal definition.

Inference with Data Only   In the simplest case, a fact $R_i(v(u_i))$ holds if it is a known fact (explicitly stated in the data store). For instance, consider the previous conjunctive query in the University example. The evaluation of the query $q(x)$ against the facts of Figure 8.1 returns {*paul*, *pierre*} as its answer set. To see why *paul* is an answer, we just check that, by mapping the distinguished variable to the constant *paul*, and the existential variables y and z respectively to the constants *infoDept* and *dupond*, all the conjuncts in the query definition are satisfied by facts in the database. The same holds if the distinguished variable x is instantiated with the constant *pierre*.

More Inference Using an Ontology   Now, let us assume that a fact $R_i(v(u_i))$ holds if it is a known fact or if it is a consequence of the known facts by taking the ontological statements into account. Suppose now that we also have the knowledge that someone responsible for a class has to be a professor, that is, in DL syntax

$\exists ResponsibleOf \sqsubseteq Professor$.

Additional answers can then be inferred. For instance, for the query $q(x)$, the additional answer *jim* is obtained. It would come from the presence in the data of the facts *EnrolledIn(jim, csDept)*, *Leads(durand, csDept)*, and from the fact *Professor(durand)*, which, without being explicitly stated in the data, is logically entailed from the fact *ResponsibleOf(durand, ue111)* and $\exists ResponsibleOf \sqsubseteq Professor$.

To see why, we just have to consider the FOL semantics of this DL statement:

$\forall x \forall y[ResponsibleOf(x,y) \Rightarrow Professor(x)]$.

This logical implication indeed allows inferring the fact *Professor(durand)* from the fact *ResponsibleOf(durand, ue111)*.

More subtly, we can get answers from *partially instantiated* facts that can be logically entailed by the knowledge base. Suppose that we know that a professor teaches at least one course, that is in DL syntax:

$Professor \sqsubseteq \exists TeachesIn$.

and consider the query $q(x) :- TeachesIn(x,y)$.

From the explicit ground fact *Professor(durand)* and the constraint $Professor \sqsubseteq \exists TeachesIn$, we know that $TeachesIn(durand,v)$ holds for some unknown value v. The valuation of v may vary in the different "worlds" satisfying the constraint. This is, however, sufficient to infer that answer $q(durand)$ is true in all these possible worlds.

Formal Definition of Answer Set   Recall that $\varphi \models \psi$ (i.e., φ *implies* ψ) if each interpretation making φ true also makes ψ true, or equivalently, every model of φ is a model of ψ. We next provide a formal definition of the *answer set* of a query for a DL knowledge base, that captures the general setting where data (the Abox $\mathcal{A}$) is associated to an ontology (the Tbox $\mathcal{T}$) to form a DL *knowledge base* $\mathcal{K} = \mathcal{T} \cup \mathcal{A}$. A *query* to the knowledge base is a conjunctive query using class or property predicates from the given knowledge base with the proper arity. (Class predicates have arity one and property predicates arity 2.)

A valuation v of a set of variables $\{z_1,...,z_p\}$ is a substitution (denoted $\{z_1/a_1,...,z_p/a_p\}$) that assigns each variable z_i to a constant a_i (two distinct variables may be assigned to a same constant). Given two valuations v and v' of two disjoint sets of variables $\{z_1,...,z_p\}$ and $\{v_1,...,v_k\}$, $v \circ v'$ denotes the valuation assigning the variables z_i to the corresponding constants in v, and the variables v_j to the corresponding constants in v'.

We can now formally define the notion of answers.

Definition 8.2.1 *Let* $q(x_1,...,x_m)$ $:-$ $R_1(u_1),...,R_p(u_p)$ *be a query to a knowledge base* $\mathcal{K}$. *An answer is a ground fact* $q(v(x_1),...,v(x_m))$ *for some valuation v of the distinguished variables such that in every model of $\mathcal{K}$ there exists a valuation v' of the existential variables for which* $R_i(v \circ v'(u_i))$ *is true for each i. The answer set of q for* $\mathcal{K}$ *is the set of all such answers. It is denoted* $q(\mathcal{K})$.

Consider again the previous university query example. We have seen that its answer set varies depending on the knowledge base against which it is evaluated. In particular, if $\mathcal{A}$ is the set of facts of Figure 8.1 and $\mathcal{T}$ is $\{\exists ResponsibleOf \sqsubseteq Professor\}$, we have

- $q(\mathcal{A}) = \{paul, pierre\}$.
- $q(\mathcal{A} \cup \mathcal{T}) = \{paul, pierre, jim\}$.

Boolean Queries   To conclude this section, we consider a particular interesting case of queries, that of Boolean queries. The *arity* of a query is the number of its distinguished variables. A query of arity 0, i.e., a query of the form $q() : ...$, is called a *Boolean query*. Note that there is a single possible answer, namely $q()$. In this case, we see that as a positive answer to the query (i.e., as *true*). If the answer set is empty, we see that as *false*.

To see an example, consider the query

```
q'() :- Student(x), TeachesTo(x,y)
```

This Boolean query asks whether there exists a student teaching to other students. Suppose $\mathcal{T}' = \{PhDStudent \sqsubseteq Student\}$. Then we can distinguish two cases:

- $q'(\mathcal{A}) = \emptyset$, and the answer is no.
- $q'(\mathcal{A}, \mathcal{T}') = \{q'()\}$, and the answer is yes.

In the second case, the fact *Student(paul)*, although not in the Abox $\mathcal{A}$, can be inferred from the fact *PhDStudent(paul)* in $\mathcal{A}$ and the inclusion statement *PhDStudent* $\sqsubseteq$ *Student* in $\mathcal{T}'$. Together with the fact *TeachesTo(paul,pierre)* present in the Abox, it makes the body of the query q' satisfied.

8.3 QUERYING THROUGH RDFS ONTOLOGIES

In this section, we consider RDF data without blank nodes (that can be seen as an Abox), associated to an RDFS ontology (that can be seen as a very simple Tbox). RDF data and RDFS statements can be denoted and stored as triples. However, the important point is that RDFS statements have a logical semantics that can be operationalized as a set of inference rules (see Section 7.3). We illustrate here how this can be used to answer queries.

Figure 8.2 is an example of an RDFS ontology that can be associated with the RDF data in Figure 8.1. The RDFS statements composing the ontology are given in three notations: the triple notation, the DL notation, and the corresponding FOL notation.

As already said, these RDFS statements can be used to infer new triples (i.e., new facts) from the RDF database. For example, the RDF triple $\langle durand\ ResponsibleOf\ ue111 \rangle$ in Figure 8.1 corresponds to the fact *ResponsibleOf* $(durand, ue111)$, and the RDFS statement $\langle ResponsibleOf\ \text{rdfs:domain}\ Professor \rangle$ corresponds to the logical rule: $ResponsibleOf(X, Y) \Rightarrow Professor(X)$. The condition of this rule can be mapped with the fact *ResponsibleOf(durand,ue111)* by the substitution {X/durand, Y/ue111}, and thus the corresponding instantiation of the conclusion *Professor(durand)* can be inferred. This new fact can in turn trigger a rule such as $Professor(X) \Rightarrow AcademicStaff(X)$, thereby allowing the inference of additional facts such as *AcademicStaff(durand)*.

More generally, RDFS statements correspond to rules that can be applied in a forward-chaining manner to the initial set of facts until saturation (i.e., until no more fact can be inferred). It is important to see that the variables in the head of rule all occur in the body. In other words, no variable is quantified existentially. So rules always infer new ground facts. Such rules are said to be *safe*. We will use unsafe rules when we consider DL-LITE, which will render query processing more complicated.

The simple forward-chaining Algorithm 1 starts with the set of initial facts and repeats inference steps until saturation.

Figure 8.3 shows the facts resulting from the application of Algorithm 1 to the facts of Figure 8.1 and the rules of Figure 8.2.

To answer queries from RDF facts associated to an RDFS ontology, one can proceed as follows. First, one computes all the inferred facts (in a bottom-up manner) with the previous algorithm. Each step of the loop can be computed, for instance, using a standard relational query engine. This yields a new database consisting of the set of all the facts (asserted or inferred). Then one can evaluate the query directly on that database using a standard relational query engine.

RDFS Notation	DL Notation	FOL Notation
⟨AcademicStaff rdfs:subClassOf Staff⟩	$AcademicStaff \sqsubseteq Staff$	$AcademicStaff(X) \Rightarrow Staff(X)$
⟨Professor rdfs:subClassOf AcademicStaff⟩	$Professor \sqsubseteq AcademicStaff$	$Professor(X) \Rightarrow AcademicStaff(X)$
⟨Lecturer rdfs:subClassOf AcademicStaff⟩	$Lecturer \sqsubseteq AcademicStaff$	$Lecturer(X) \Rightarrow AcademicStaff(X)$
⟨PhDStudent rdfs:subClassOf Lecturer⟩	$PhDStudent \sqsubseteq Lecturer$	$PhDStudent(X) \Rightarrow Lecturer(X)$
⟨PhDStudent rdfs:subClassOf Student⟩	$PhDStudent \sqsubseteq Student$	$PhDStudent(X) \Rightarrow Student(X)$
⟨TeachesIn rdfs:domain AcademicStaff⟩	$\exists TeachesIn \sqsubseteq AcademicStaff$	$TeachesIn(X,Y) \Rightarrow AcademicStaff(X)$
⟨TeachesIn rdfs:range Course⟩	$\exists TeachesIn^- \sqsubseteq Course$	$TeachesIn(X,Y) \Rightarrow Course(Y)$
⟨ResponsibleOf rdfs:domain Professor⟩	$\exists ResponsibleOf \sqsubseteq Professor$	$ResponsibleOf(X,Y) \Rightarrow Professor(X)$
⟨ResponsibleOf rdfs:range Course⟩	$\exists ResponsibleOf^- \sqsubseteq Course$	$ResponsibleOf(X,Y) \Rightarrow Course(Y)$
⟨TeachesTo rdfs:domain AcademicStaff⟩	$\exists TeachesTo \sqsubseteq AcademicStaff$	$TeachesTo(X,Y) \Rightarrow AcademicStaff(X)$
⟨TeachesTo rdfs:range Student⟩	$\exists TeachesTo^- \sqsubseteq Student$	$TeachesTo(X,Y) \Rightarrow Student(Y)$
⟨Leads rdfs:domain AdminStaff⟩	$\exists Leads \sqsubseteq AdminStaff$	$Leads(X,Y) \Rightarrow AdminStaff(X)$
⟨Leads rdfs:range Dept⟩	$\exists Leads^- \sqsubseteq Dept$	$Leads(X,Y) \Rightarrow Dept(Y)$
⟨RegisteredIn rdfs:domain Student⟩	$\exists RegisteredIn \sqsubseteq Student$	$RegisteredIn(X,Y) \Rightarrow Student(X)$
⟨RegisteredIn rdfs:range Course⟩	$\exists RegisteredIn^- \sqsubseteq Course$	$RegisteredIn(X,Y) \Rightarrow Course(Y)$
⟨ResponsibleOf rdfs:subPropertyOf TeachesIn⟩	$ResponsibleOf \sqsubseteq TeachesIn$	$ResponsibleOf(X,Y) \Rightarrow TeachesIn(X,Y)$

Figure 8.2. An RDFS ontology expressed in different notations.

Asserted Facts	Inferred Facts
Leads(dupond,infoDept)	AdminStaff(dupond)
Professor(dupond)	Dept(infoDept)
ResponsibleOf(durand,ue111)	AcademicStaff(dupond)
Leads(durand,csDept)	Professor(durand)
TeachesTo(paul,pierre)	Course(ue111)
PhDStudent(paul)	AcademicStaff(durand)
EnrolledIn(paul, infodept)	AdminStaff(durand)
EnrolledIn(pierre, infodept)	Dept(csDept)
Undergrad(pierre)	AcademicStaff(paul)
Registered(pierre, ue111)	Student(pierre)
OfferedBy(ue111,infoDept)	Student(paul)
CSCourse(ue111)	Student(pierre)
EnrolledIn(jim, csDept)	Lecturer(paul)
TeachingDept(csDept)	AcademicStaff(paul)
	Staff(paul)
	Staff(dupond)
	Staff(durand)

Figure 8.3. Inferred facts from RDF facts and an associated RDFS ontology.

Algorithm 1. The *Saturation* algorithm
Saturation$(\mathcal{A}, \mathcal{T})$
Input: An Abox $\mathcal{A}$ and an RDFS Tbox $\mathcal{T}$
Output: The set of facts that are inferred: Δ_0
(1) $F \leftarrow \mathcal{A}$
(2) $\Delta_0 \leftarrow \mathcal{A}$
(3)   **repeat** $\Delta_1 \leftarrow \emptyset$
(4)   **foreach** rule *condition* $\Rightarrow$ *conclusion* in $\mathcal{T}$,
(5)   **if** there exists a substitution σ such that $\sigma.condition \in \Delta_0$
(6)   **and** $\sigma.conclusion \notin F$
(7)   **add** $\sigma.conclusion$ to Δ_1
(8) $F \leftarrow F \cup \Delta_1$
(9) $\Delta_0 \leftarrow \Delta_1$
(10)   **until** $\Delta_1 = \emptyset$

For example, the standard evaluation against the set of (asserted + inferred) facts in Figure 8.3 of the query

$$q(x) :- Enrolled(x,y), Leads(z,y), Professor(z)$$

(searching for individuals enrolled in a department led by a Professor) returns *{paul,pierre,jim}* as its answer set. If we evaluate the same query against the set of asserted facts only, we do not find the answer *jim*.

Complexity Analysis It is interesting to estimate both the maximum number of inferred triples and the worst-case time complexity for inferring them. Of course, this depends on the number of asserted triples (i.e., the size of the data) and also on the number of axioms in the ontology (i.e., the size of the ontology).

Let M be the number of facts in the Abox and N the number of axioms in the Tbox. From the presence of some initial fact $C(a)$, one can derive a number of new facts $C'(a)$ for some class C'. Note that the number of such $C'(a)$ is bounded by the number of axioms in the ontology (i.e., it is less than N). Now consider some initial fact $R(a,b)$. From it, one can derive some facts $R'(a,b)$ or $R'(b,a)$ as well as some facts $C'(a)$ or $C'(b)$ for some R' and C'. Again, one can observe that for a particular $R(a,b)$, the number of new facts one can derive is bounded by the number of axioms in the ontology, i.e., it is less than N. Since the number of initial facts is M, the number of facts one can derive is bounded by $M \times N$. Observe in particular that it is linear in the number of database facts.

Now consider the worst-case time complexity for inferring them by the Algorithm 1. We have to perform at most $M \times N$ iterations. Each iteration can be performed in polynomial time. So the algorithm is in PTIME. One can show more precisely that it is in $0((M \times N)^2)$.

8.4 ANSWERING QUERIES THROUGH DL-Lite ONTOLOGIES

In this section, we consider two important fragments of the DL-LITE ontology language of the DL family. As we will see, querying is feasible for these two languages even though they provide a quite rich framework for describing semantics. We study querying through ontologies expressed in these two fragments.

8.4.1 DL-Lite

A DL-LITE ontology may contain axioms corresponding (up to the syntax) to those allowed in an RDFS ontology. Besides, it may contain other axioms, of three kinds: positive inclusions (PI for short), negative inclusions (NI), and key constraints (Key). Figure 8.4 shows examples of these three kinds of DL-LITE axioms with their corresponding FOL semantics. These constraints are not expressible in RDFS.

We next consider in turn these new kinds of axioms.

Positive Inclusion and Incompleteness A *positive* inclusion axiom is an expression of one of the following forms:

	DL Notation	**Corresponding Logical Rule**
PI	$Professor \sqsubseteq \exists TeachesIn$	$Professor(X) \Rightarrow \exists Y TeachesIn(X,Y)$
	$Course \sqsubseteq \exists RegisteredIn^-$	$Course(X) \Rightarrow \exists Y RegisteredIn(Y,X)$
NI	$Student \sqsubseteq \neg Staff$	$Student(X) \Rightarrow \neg Staff(X)$
Key	$(funct\ ResponsibleOf^-)$	$ResponsibleOf(Y,X) \wedge ResponsibleOf(Z,X) \Rightarrow Y = Z$

Figure 8.4. Examples of DL-LITE axioms not expressible in RDFS.

DL Notation	Corresponding Logical Rule
$B \sqsubseteq \exists P$	$B(X) \Rightarrow \exists Y P(X,Y)$
$\exists Q \sqsubseteq \exists P$	$Q(X,Y) \Rightarrow \exists Z P(X,Z)$
$B \sqsubseteq \exists P^-$	$B(X) \Rightarrow \exists Y P(Y,X)$
$\exists Q \sqsubseteq \exists P^-$	$Q(X,Y) \Rightarrow \exists Z P(Z,X)$
$P \sqsubseteq Q^-$ or $P^- \sqsubseteq Q$	$P(X,Y) \Rightarrow Q(Y,X)$

where P and Q denote properties and B denotes a class. Recall that P^- denotes the *inverse* of P (i.e., $P^-(x,y)$ iff $P(y,x)$ for all x,y).

Observe that expressions of the form $\exists P \sqsubseteq B$ belong to DL-LITE since they already are in RDFS. Expressions of the form $P \sqsubseteq Q$ (so equivalently $P^- \sqsubseteq Q^-$) also belong to DL-LITE for the same reason.

It is important to note that the logical rules corresponding to PI axioms expressible in DL-LITE are *not* necessarily safe (as opposed to RDFS, which uses only safe rules). Consider the rule

$$\forall X (Professor(X) \Rightarrow \exists Y (TeachesIn(X,Y)))$$

The variable Y is existentially quantified. As already mentioned, the main issue is that, as a consequence, such an axiom does not produce new facts (i.e., ground atoms) from initial facts, but only an *incomplete* information in the form of atoms that may be partially instantiated. For example, from the fact *Professor(durand)*, the previous axiom permits to infer that there exists some course(s) y that *durand* teaches. In other words, we know that there exists some fact of the form *TeachesIn(durand,y)* that is true, but we do not know the value of y. This makes it difficult to apply the bottom-up approach described in Section 8.3. Such an approach is not appropriate for answering queries through DL-LITE ontologies.

Negative Inclusion and Inconsistencies   A *negative* inclusion axioms is an expression that takes one of the forms:

DL Notation
$B_1 \sqsubseteq \neg B_2$
$R_1 \sqsubseteq \neg R_2$

where

- B_1 and B_2 are either classes or expressions of the form $\exists P$ or $\exists P^-$ for some property P.
- where R_1 and R_2 are either properties or inverses of properties.

The corresponding logic rules are left as an exercise. An example of NI (expressing the constraint "Students do not teach courses") and the corresponding logical rule are as follows:

DL Notation	Corresponding Logical Rule
$Student \sqsubseteq \neg \exists TeachesIn$	$Student(X) \Rightarrow \neg \exists Y TeachesIn(X,Y)$
	or equivalently, $\exists Y TeachesIn(X,Y) \Rightarrow \neg Student(X)$

NIs express disjointness constraints between classes or between properties, and thus introduce negation in the language. Therefore, the knowledge base against

DL Notation	**Corresponding Logical Rule**
(funct P)	$P(X,Y) \wedge P(X,Z) \Rightarrow Y = Z$
(funct P⁻)	$P(Y,X) \wedge P(Z,X) \Rightarrow Y = Z$

Figure 8.5. Functionality axioms expressible in DL-LITE and not in RDFS.

which the queries have to be evaluated may be *inconsistent* (i.e., a model of the corresponding theory may not exist). Note that this is not possible with RDFS ontologies: we showed an algorithm that computed a model (indeed the smallest model).

For example, adding the NI *Student* ⊑ ¬*Staff* to the ontology of Figure 8.2 leads to the inconsistency of the knowledge base made of the facts in Figure 8.1 and of the axioms in the ontology of Figure 8.2 enriched with that NI. The reason is that from the fact *PhDStudent(paul)*, and the inclusion axiom *PhdStudent* ⊑ *Student*, we can infer the fact *Student(paul)*, and in turn the literal ¬*Staff(paul)* from the NI *Student* ⊑ ¬*Staff*. On the other hand, the fact *Staff(paul)* can be inferred from the fact *PhDStudent(paul)* and the inclusion axioms *PhdStudent* ⊑ *Lecturer*, *Lecturer* ⊑ *AcademicStaff*, and *AcademicStaff* ⊑ *Staff*.

Key Constraints and More Inconsistencies Key constraints are expressed by functionality axioms of the form *(funct P)* or *(funct P⁻)*, where *P* is a property and *P⁻* denotes the inverse property of *P*. Figure 8.5 shows their logical semantics in the form of logical rules.

Observe that key constraints may also lead to inconsistencies. This is the case if we attempt to equate two distinct constants (e.g., durand and dupond). For instance, the axiom *(funct ResponsibleOf⁻)* expresses that a course must have a unique professor responsible for it. Therefore, a knowledge base containing this axiom and the two facts:

ResponsibleOf(durand, ue111) and *ResponsibleOf(dupond, ue111)*

would be inconsistent. This is because we assume implicitly that an individual is denoted by a single constant. This natural (in practice) assumption is called in logic the *unique name assumption*.

We will consider the following two fragments of DL-LITE:

DL-LITE$_\mathcal{R}$ is obtained by extending the axioms of RDFS with the PI and NI axioms.
DL-LITE$_\mathcal{F}$ is obtained by extending the axioms of RDFS with key constraints, the PI and NI axioms, but excluding inclusion between properties. Note that, since DL-LITE$_\mathcal{F}$ does not permit us to express inclusion between properties, RDFS is not included in DL-LITE$_\mathcal{F}$.

One may wonder why one would choose such a convoluted language. Why not simply extend RDFS with the three kinds of axioms? This is because functional constraints interact with inclusion constraints in intricate ways. Query evaluation when they are all present is much more complex. This will be illustrated by an example in Section 8.4.4.

From the previous discussion, there are two fundamental differences between query answering in the context of RDFS and of DL-LITE knowledge bases:

Inconsistency: RDFS does not permit expressing any form of negation, so an RDFS knowledge base is always consistent. On the other hand, a DL-LITE knowledge base may be inconsistent. Thus, answering queries through DL-LITE ontologies requires that we make sure the data are consistent with respect to the constraints expressed in the ontology.

Incompleteness: The rules corresponding to RDFS axioms are safe thereby allowing the simple bottom-up algorithm we described. On the other hand, axioms in DL-LITE may correspond to unsafe rules. Thus a bottom-up approach may infer atoms that are not ground (i.e., some incomplete facts). Therefore, we will have to use a top-down approach for evaluating the queries that is more appropriate than the bottom-up approach.

In Section 8.4.2, we show an algorithm for checking consistency of a DL-LITE knowledge base, and in Section 8.4.3, an algorithm for answering conjunctive queries posed to a DL-LITE knowledge base. The particularity of these two algorithms is that they work in two-steps:

1. In a first step, we reason with the Tbox alone (i.e., the ontology without the data) and some conjunctive queries;
2. In the second step, we evaluate these conjunctive queries against the data in the Abox.

Separating ontology reasoning from data processing is typically a desired feature (when possible). In particular, such an approach has the practical interest that it makes it possible to use an SQL engine for the second step, thus taking advantage of well-established query optimization strategies supported by standard relational data management systems. In the first step, we deal with the Tbox only, typically of much smaller size.

In Section 8.4.4, we show by an example that DL-LITE$_{\mathcal{R}}$ and DL-LITE$_{\mathcal{F}}$ are two maximal fragments of the DL-LITE family for which reformulating queries into SQL is possible: combining constraints expressible in DL-LITE$_{\mathcal{R}}$ and DL-LITE$_{\mathcal{F}}$ may result in an *infinite* number of nonredundant SQL reformulations for some queries.

8.4.2 Consistency Checking

Toward consistency checking, the first step uses the Tbox alone. It consists of computing the *deductive closure* of the Tbox (i.e., all the inclusion axioms that are logically entailed by the axioms declared in the Tbox. More precisely, the deductive closure (closure for short) of a DL-LITE Tbox is defined as follows.

Definition 8.4.1 (closure of a Tbox) *Let $\mathcal{T}$ be a DL-LITE$_{\mathcal{F}}$ or a DL-LITE$_{\mathcal{R}}$ Tbox. The closure of $\mathcal{T}$, denoted by $cl(\mathcal{T})$, is inductively defined as follows:*

1. *All the statements in $\mathcal{T}$ are also in $cl(\mathcal{T})$.*
2. *If $B_1 \sqsubseteq B_2$ and $B_2 \sqsubseteq B_3$ are in $cl(\mathcal{T})$, then $B_1 \sqsubseteq B_3$ is in $cl(\mathcal{T})$.*

3. If $R_1 \sqsubseteq R_2$ and $\exists R_2 \sqsubseteq B$ are in $cl(\mathcal{T})$, then $\exists R_1 \sqsubseteq B$ is in $cl(\mathcal{T})$.
4. If $R_1 \sqsubseteq R_2$ and $\exists R_2^- \sqsubseteq B$ are in $cl(\mathcal{T})$, then $\exists R_1^- \sqsubseteq B$ is in $cl(\mathcal{T})$.
5. If $R_1 \sqsubseteq R_2$ and $R_2 \sqsubseteq R_3$ are in $cl(\mathcal{T})$, then $R_1 \sqsubseteq R_3$ is in $cl(\mathcal{T})$.
6. If $R_1 \sqsubseteq R_2$ is in $cl(\mathcal{T})$, then $R_1^- \sqsubseteq R_2^-$ is in $cl(\mathcal{T})$.
7. If $B_1 \sqsubseteq B_2$ and $B_2 \sqsubseteq \neg B_3$ (or $B_3 \sqsubseteq \neg B_2$) are in $cl(\mathcal{T})$, then $B_1 \sqsubseteq \neg B_3$ is in $cl(\mathcal{T})$.
8. If $R_1 \sqsubseteq R_2$ and $\exists R_2 \sqsubseteq \neg B$ (or $B \sqsubseteq \neg \exists R_2$) are in $cl(\mathcal{T})$, then $\exists R_1 \sqsubseteq \neg B$ is in $cl(\mathcal{T})$.
9. If $R_1 \sqsubseteq R_2$ and $\exists R_2^- \sqsubseteq \neg B$ (or $B \sqsubseteq \neg \exists R_2^-$) are in $cl(\mathcal{T})$, then $\exists R_1^- \sqsubseteq \neg B$ is in $cl(\mathcal{T})$.
10. If $R_1 \sqsubseteq R_2$ and $R_2 \sqsubseteq \neg R_3$ (or $R_3 \sqsubseteq \neg R_2$) are in $cl(\mathcal{T})$, then $R_1 \sqsubseteq \neg R_3$ is in $cl(\mathcal{T})$.
11. If $R_1 \sqsubseteq \neg R_2$ or $R_2 \sqsubseteq \neg R_1$ is in $cl(\mathcal{T})$, then $R_1^- \sqsubseteq \neg R_2^-$ is in $cl(\mathcal{T})$.
12. (a) In the case in which $\mathcal{T}$ is a DL-LITE$_\mathcal{F}$ Tbox, if one of the statements $\exists R \sqsubseteq \neg \exists R$ or $\exists R^- \sqsubseteq \neg \exists R^-$ is in $cl(\mathcal{T})$, then both such statements are in $cl(\mathcal{T})$.
    (b) In the case in which $\mathcal{T}$ is a DL-LITE$_\mathcal{R}$ Tbox, if one of the statements $\exists R \sqsubseteq \neg \exists R$, $\exists R^- \sqsubseteq \neg \exists R^-$, or $R \sqsubseteq \neg R$ is in $cl(\mathcal{T})$, then all three such statements are in $cl(\mathcal{T})$.

Observe that although all axioms should be considered to construct this closure, only negative inclusions and key constraints can raise an inconsistency. The set of all the negative inclusions and key constraints in $cl(\mathcal{T})$ is called the *NI-closure*. For example, consider the Tbox of Figure 8.6 made of the RDFS ontology shown in Figure 8.2 enriched with the PIs and NI shown in Figure 8.4. The NI-closure of that Tbox is shown in Figure 8.7.

DL Notation	FOL Notation
$AcademicStaff \sqsubseteq Staff$	$AcademicStaff(X) \Rightarrow Staff(X)$
$Professor \sqsubseteq AcademicStaff$	$Professor(X) \Rightarrow AcademicStaff(X)$
$Lecturer \sqsubseteq AcademicStaff$	$Lecturer(X) \Rightarrow AcademicStaff(X)$
$PhDStudent \sqsubseteq Lecturer$	$PhDStudent(X) \Rightarrow Lecturer(X)$
$PhDStudent \sqsubseteq Student$	$PhDStudent(X) \Rightarrow Student(X)$
$\exists TeachesIn \sqsubseteq AcademicStaff$	$TeachesIn(X,Y) \Rightarrow AcademicStaff(X)$
$\exists TeachesIn^- \sqsubseteq Course$	$TeachesIn(X,Y) \Rightarrow Course(Y)$
$\exists ResponsibleOf \sqsubseteq Professor$	$ResponsibleOf(X,Y) \Rightarrow Professor(X)$
$\exists ResponsibleOf^- \sqsubseteq Course$	$ResponsibleOf(X,Y) \Rightarrow Course(Y)$
$\exists TeachesTo \sqsubseteq AcademicStaff$	$TeachesTo(X,Y) \Rightarrow AcademicStaff(X)$
$\exists TeachesTo^- \sqsubseteq Student$	$TeachesTo(X,Y) \Rightarrow Student(Y)$
$\exists Leads \sqsubseteq AdminStaff$	$Leads(X,Y) \Rightarrow AdminStaff(X)$
$\exists Leads^- \sqsubseteq Dept$	$Leads(X,Y) \Rightarrow Dept(Y)$
$\exists RegisteredIn \sqsubseteq Student$	$RegisteredIn(X,Y) \Rightarrow Student(X)$
$\exists RegisteredIn^- \sqsubseteq Course$	$RegisteredIn(X,Y) \Rightarrow Course(Y)$
$ResponsibleOf \sqsubseteq TeachesIn$	$ResponsibleOf(X,Y) \Rightarrow TeachesIn(X,Y)$
$Professor \sqsubseteq \exists TeachesIn$	$Professor(X) \Rightarrow \exists Y TeachesIn(X,Y)$
$Course \sqsubseteq \exists RegisteredIn^-$	$Course(X) \Rightarrow \exists Y RegisteredIn(Y,X)$
$Student \sqsubseteq \neg Staff$	$Student(X) \Rightarrow \neg Staff(X)$

Figure 8.6. A DL-LITE Tbox.

DL Notation	FOL Notation
$Student \sqsubseteq \neg Staff$	$Student(X) \Rightarrow \neg Staff(X)$
$PhDStudent \sqsubseteq \neg Staff$	$PhDStudent(X) \Rightarrow \neg Staff(X)$
$\exists TeachesTo^- \sqsubseteq \neg Staff$	$TeachesTo(Y,X) \Rightarrow \neg Staff(X)$
$\exists RegisteredIn \sqsubseteq \neg Staff$	$RegisteredIn(X,Y) \Rightarrow \neg Staff(X)$
$Lecturer \sqsubseteq \neg Student$	$Lecturer(X) \Rightarrow \neg Student(X)$
$Lecturer \sqsubseteq \neg PhDStudent$	$Lecturer(X) \Rightarrow \neg PhDStudent(X)$
$Lecturer \sqsubseteq \neg \exists TeachesTo^-$	$Lecturer(X) \Rightarrow \neg \exists Y[TeachesTo(Y,X)]$
$Lecturer \sqsubseteq \neg \exists RegisteredIn$	$Lecturer(X) \Rightarrow \neg \exists Y[RegisteredIn(X,Y)]$
$Professor \sqsubseteq \neg Student$	$Professor(X) \Rightarrow \neg Student(X)$
$Professor \sqsubseteq \neg PhDStudent$	$Professor(X) \Rightarrow \neg PhDStudent(X)$
$Professor \sqsubseteq \neg \exists TeachesTo^-$	$Professor(X) \Rightarrow \neg \exists Y[TeachesTo(Y,X)]$
$Professor \sqsubseteq \neg \exists RegisteredIn$	$Professor(X) \Rightarrow \neg \exists Y[RegisteredIn(X,Y)]$
$AcademicStaff \sqsubseteq \neg Student$	$AcademicStaff(X) \Rightarrow \neg Student(X)$
$AcademicStaff \sqsubseteq \neg PhDStudent$	$AcademicStaff(X) \Rightarrow \neg PhDStudent(X)$
$AcademicStaff \sqsubseteq \neg \exists TeachesTo^-$	$AcademicStaff(X) \Rightarrow \neg \exists Y[TeachesTo(Y,X)]$
$AcademicStaff \sqsubseteq \neg \exists RegisteredIn$	$AcademicStaff(X) \Rightarrow \neg \exists Y[RegisteredIn(X,Y)]$
$Staff \sqsubseteq \neg Student$	$Staff(X) \Rightarrow \neg Student(X)$
$Staff \sqsubseteq \neg PhDStudent$	$Staff(X) \Rightarrow \neg PhDStudent(X)$
$Staff \sqsubseteq \neg \exists TeachesTo^-$	$Staff(X) \Rightarrow \neg \exists Y[TeachesTo(Y,X)]$
$Staff \sqsubseteq \neg \exists RegisteredIn$	$Staff(X) \Rightarrow \neg \exists Y[RegisteredIn(X,Y)]$
$\exists TeachesTo \sqsubseteq \neg Student$	$TeachesTo(X,Y) \Rightarrow \neg Student(X)$
$\exists TeachesTo \sqsubseteq \neg PhDStudent$	$TeachesTo(X,Y) \Rightarrow \neg PhDStudent(X)$
$\exists TeachesTo \sqsubseteq \neg \exists TeachesTo^-$	$TeachesTo(X,Y) \Rightarrow \neg \exists Z[TeachesTo(Z,X)]$
$\exists TeachesTo \sqsubseteq \neg \exists RegisteredIn$	$TeachesTo(X,Y) \Rightarrow \neg \exists Z[RegisteredIn(X,Z)]$
$\exists TeachesIn \sqsubseteq \neg Student$	$TeachesIn(X,Y) \Rightarrow \neg Student(X)$
$\exists TeachesIn \sqsubseteq \neg PhDStudent$	$TeachesIn(X,Y) \Rightarrow \neg PhDStudent(X)$
$\exists TeachesIn \sqsubseteq \neg \exists TeachesTo^-$	$TeachesIn(X,Y) \Rightarrow \neg \exists Z[TeachesTo(Z,X)]$
$\exists TeachesIn \sqsubseteq \neg \exists RegisteredIn$	$TeachesIn(X,Y) \Rightarrow \neg \exists Z[RegisteredIn(X,Z)]$

Figure 8.7. The NI-closure of the Tbox in Figure 8.6.

This example shows that it is possible to infer an important number of new NIs. In fact, we have to compute *all* the consequences. But as we will see there is at most a polynomial number of consequences.

We use three propositions for analyzing the consistency problem: one for evaluating the complexity of evaluating the closure and the last two for showing the logical soundness and completeness of this closure. Finally, a fourth proposition will show how to use these results for data consistency checking.

Proposition 8.4.2 (size of the closure of a Tbox and complexity of its computation)
Let T be a DL-LITE$_F$ *or a* DL-LITE$_R$ *Tbox.*

1. *The number of statements in $cl(T)$ is at most polynomial in the size of T.*
2. *$cl(T)$ can be computed in polynomial time in the size of T.*

Proof (sketch). (1.) Follows from the form the statements are allowed in a DL-LITE$_F$ or a DL-LITE$_R$ Tbox.

For (2.), consider the items (2.) to (12.) in Definition 8.4.1. These are *closure rules* that are exhaustively applied to the Tbox until saturation. Let $T_0 = T$. For each i, let Δ_i be the set of statements that can be derived from T_i directly using the closure rules (2.) to (12.). Let $\mathcal{T}_{i+1} = \mathcal{T}_i \cup \Delta_i$. Clearly, for each i, $\mathcal{T}_i \subseteq cl(\mathcal{T})$, so its size is polynomial in the size of $\mathcal{T}$.

Now since the size of $\mathcal{T}_i$ is polynomial in the size of $\mathcal{T}$, each step of the computation can clearly be performed in PTIME. Since the number of steps is less than the number of statements in $cl(\mathcal{T})$, the entire computation can be performed in PTIME.
□

The next proposition states the soundness of the closure.

Proposition 8.4.3 (soundness of the closure of a Tbox) *For each $\mathcal{T}$, $\mathcal{T} \equiv cl(\mathcal{T})$. In other words, for each Abox $\mathcal{A}$ satisfying a Tbox $\mathcal{T}$, $\mathcal{A}$ also satisfies $cl(\mathcal{T})$.*

Proof (sketch). $cl(\mathcal{T}) \models \mathcal{T}$, since $\mathcal{T}$ is included in $cl(\mathcal{T})$. Clearly, the application of each closure rule is sound. So for each i, $\mathcal{T}_i \models \mathcal{T}_{i+1}$. By induction, $\mathcal{T} = \mathcal{T}_0 \models \mathcal{T}_i$ for each i. Thus, $\mathcal{T} \models cl(\mathcal{T})$, so $\mathcal{T} \equiv cl(\mathcal{T})$. □

The next proposition establishes the completeness of the closure of a Tbox $\mathcal{T}$: $cl(\mathcal{T})$ contains all the PIs, NIs, and key constraints that are logically entailed by that Tbox (up to equivalence).

Proposition 8.4.4 (completeness of the closure of a Tbox) *Let $\mathcal{T}$ be a DL-LITE$_\mathcal{F}$ or a DL-LITE$_\mathcal{R}$ Tbox. Then*

1. *Let $X \sqsubseteq Y$ be a NI or a PI. If $\mathcal{T} \models X \sqsubseteq \neg X$,*
   then $X \sqsubseteq \neg X \in cl(\mathcal{T})$;
   otherwise, $\mathcal{T} \models X \sqsubseteq Y$ iff $X \sqsubseteq Y \in cl(\mathcal{T})$ or $\neg Y \sqsubseteq \neg X \in cl(\mathcal{T})$.
2. *$\mathcal{T} \models (funct\ R)$ iff $(funct\ R) \in cl(\mathcal{T})$ or $\exists R \sqsubseteq \neg \exists R \in cl(\mathcal{T})$.*

Proof (sketch). We build a canonical interpretation I of the classes and properties appearing in $\mathcal{T}$ as follows: For each X such that $X \sqsubseteq \neg X \in cl(\mathcal{T})$, $I(X) = \emptyset$; for the other classes or properties, we associate a constant (respectively a pair of constants) with each class (respectively each property) and initialize their interpretations with those (pairs of) constants. Then, we complete these interpretations by applying the positive inclusions in $cl(\mathcal{T})$ as logical rules in a bottom up manner until saturation. For instance, if $A \sqsubseteq \exists P$ is in $cl(\mathcal{T})$, from the initial state where a is $I(A)$, and (p_1, p_2) is in $I(P)$, we add a new constant p_3 in the domain of interpretation and the pair (a, p_3) in $I(P)$. Now, if $\exists P \sqsubseteq \exists Q$ is also in $cl(\mathcal{T})$, we add two new constants p_4 and p_5 in the domain and the pairs (a, p_4) and (p_1, p_5) to $I(Q)$.

Clearly, by construction, I is a model of each PI in $\mathcal{T}$. It is also a model of each NI $X \sqsubseteq \neg Y$ in $\mathcal{T}$. Suppose that this not the case: There would exist a constant x which is in $I(X)$ and in $I(Y)$. By construction of I, a chain of positive inclusions in $cl(\mathcal{T})$ would exist between X and Y and thus $X \sqsubseteq Y$ would be in $cl(\mathcal{T})$, and therefore $X \sqsubseteq \neg X$ would be in $cl(\mathcal{T})$ too, and in this case $I(X)$ would be empty, which contradicts that I is not a model of $X \sqsubseteq \neg Y$.

To prove (1.), if $\mathcal{T} \models X \sqsubseteq \neg X$, in every model of $\mathcal{T}$, X must be empty, in particular in I. By construction of I, this means that $X \sqsubseteq \neg X \in cl(\mathcal{T})$. Otherwise, consider a PI $X \sqsubseteq Y$ such that $\mathcal{T} \models X \sqsubseteq Y$. Since I is a model of $\mathcal{T}$, $I(X) \subseteq I(Y)$. By construction of I, this means that there exists a chain of positive inclusions in $cl(\mathcal{T})$ between X and Y and thus $X \sqsubseteq Y$ is in $cl(\mathcal{T})$.

Consider now a NI $X \sqsubseteq \neg Y$ such that neither $X \sqsubseteq \neg Y$ nor $Y \sqsubseteq \neg X$ belong to $cl(\mathcal{T})$. Let us define the interpretation J such that

■ $J(Z) = \emptyset$ for each class or property Z appearing in the right-hand side of a NI in $cl(\mathcal{T})$ of the form $X \sqsubseteq \neg U$ or $U \sqsubseteq \neg X$,

■ $J(A) = D$ (where D is the whole domain of interpretation) for the other classes, and $J(P) = D \times D$ for the other properties.

In particular $J(X) = D$ (since $X \sqsubseteq \neg X$ is not in $cl(\mathcal{T})$), and $J(Y) = D$ (since neither $X \sqsubseteq \neg Y$ nor $Y \sqsubseteq \neg X$ belong to $cl(\mathcal{T})$). Clearly, J is a model of $\mathcal{T}$, but it is not a model of $X \sqsubseteq \neg Y$. Therefore, $\mathcal{T} \not\models X \sqsubseteq \neg Y$. This ends the proof of (1.).

For proving (the contraposite of) (2.), we adapt the preceding canonical interpretation I by initializing with $\{(p,q),(p,r)\}$ the interpretation of all the properties R such that neither $(functR)$ nor $\exists R \sqsubseteq \neg \exists R$ belong to $cl(\mathcal{T})$. And we show that the resulting interpretation I' is a model of $\mathcal{T}$ in which the constraints of functionality of such R is not satisfied.   □

Finally, the last proposition establishes that checking consistency can be reduced to check whether the data in $\mathcal{A}$ satisfy every NI in the closure.

Proposition 8.4.5 (consistency checking using NI-closure) *Let $\mathcal{T}$ be a* DL-LITE$_\mathcal{F}$ *or a* DL-LITE$_\mathcal{R}$ *Tbox. Let $\mathcal{A}$ be an Abox associated to $\mathcal{T}$. $\langle \mathcal{T}, \mathcal{A} \rangle$ is unsatisfiable iff there exists a NI or a key constraint in the closure of $\mathcal{T}$ which is violated by some facts of $\mathcal{A}$.*

Proof (sketch). For every constant a appearing in the Abox $\mathcal{A}$, we define $\mathcal{A}(a)$ as the set of facts extracted from $\mathcal{A}$ as follows:

■ If $A(a) \in \mathcal{A}$, then $A(a)$ is added in $\mathcal{A}(a)$;

■ If $P(a,b) \in \mathcal{A}$, then $(\exists P)(a)$ is added in $\mathcal{A}(a)$ and $(\exists P^-)(b)$ is added in $\mathcal{A}(b)$.

We first show that if $\langle \mathcal{T}, \mathcal{A} \rangle$ is unsatisfiable, there exists a constant a such that $\langle \mathcal{T}, \mathcal{A}(a) \rangle$ is unsatisfiable. In fact we show the contrapositive: suppose that for every constant a, $\langle \mathcal{T}, \mathcal{A}(a) \rangle$ is satisfiable: for each a, there exists an interpretation I_a satisfying the inclusions in $\mathcal{T}$ and all the facts in $\mathcal{A}(a)$. It is easy to show that the interpretation I defined on the union of domains of interpretations as follows is a model of $\langle \mathcal{T}, \mathcal{A} \rangle$ (which is then satisfiable):

■ For every class or property X: $I(X) = \bigcup_a I_a(X)$

■ For every constant a: $I(a) = I_a(a)$

Then, since each $\mathcal{A}(a)$ is a conjunction of facts of the form $X(a)$, if $\langle \mathcal{T}, \mathcal{A} \rangle$ is unsatisfiable, there exists a constant a such that $\mathcal{T}, X_1(a) \wedge \cdots \wedge X_n(a)$ is unsatisfiable. Therefore, $\mathcal{T}, \exists x(X_1(x) \wedge \cdots \wedge X_n(x))$ is unsatisfiable. This entails $\mathcal{T} \models \forall x(\neg X_1(x) \vee \cdots \vee \neg X_n(x))$, which in DL notation corresponds to: $\mathcal{T} \models X_1 \sqsubseteq \neg X_2 \sqcup \cdots \sqcup \neg X_n$. Because of the form of the inclusion allowed in DL-LITE, there must exist i such that $\mathcal{T} \models X_1 \sqsubseteq \neg X_i$. According to Proposition 8.4.4, this entails that the corresponding NI $X_1 \sqsubseteq \neg X_i$ is in the closure of $\mathcal{T}$ and that $\mathcal{A}$ violates it (since it includes $X_1(a)$ and $X_i(a)$).

Conversely, it is easy to show that if a NI in the closure of $\mathcal{T}$ is violated by some facts in the Abox, then $\langle \mathcal{T}, \mathcal{A} \rangle$ is unsatisfiable. If it were not the case, since according to Proposition 8.4.3 $\mathcal{T}$ and $cl(\mathcal{T})$ have the same models, there would be a model in which all the NIs in the closure of $\mathcal{T}$ would be satisfied by the facts in $\mathcal{A}$.   □

The second step of consistency checking, after the NI-closure is computed, does not require any further computation on the Tbox $\mathcal{T}$. This second step simply consists in evaluating against the Abox $\mathcal{A}$ (seen as a relational database) a Boolean query corresponding to each *negated* NI in the NI-closure of the Tbox. If one of those Boolean queries is evaluated to *true* against $\mathcal{A}$, it means that some data in the Abox $\mathcal{A}$ violates the corresponding NI, and therefore the knowledge base $\mathcal{K} = \langle \mathcal{T}, \mathcal{A} \rangle$ is inconsistent.

For example, consider the NI: $\exists TeachesTo \sqsubseteq \neg PhDStudent$. Its corresponding FOL formula φ and its negation are:

$$\forall x, y'\, TeachesTo(x, y') \Rightarrow \neg PhDStudent(x) \qquad \varphi$$
$$\exists x, y'\, TeachesTo(x, y') \wedge PhDStudent(x) \qquad \neg \varphi$$

and the corresponding Boolean query is

$$q_{unsat}() :- TeachesTo(x, y'), PhDStudent(x)$$

(i.e., the direct translation of the negation of the NI).

Consider the evaluation of the q_{unsat} query against the Abox $\mathcal{A}$ of Figure 8.1. It evaluates to *true*: Consider valuation v with $v(x) = pierre$, $v(y') = paul$, and the facts

$$PhDStudent(paul) \text{ and } TeachesTo(paul, pierre)$$

Thus, the knowledge base $\mathcal{K}$ made of the Tbox of Figure 8.6 and the Abox of Figure 8.1 is inconsistent.

The transformation of NIs into Boolean queries that correspond to their negation is described in Definition 8.4.6.

Definition 8.4.6 (transformation of NIs into Boolean queries) *The transformation δ of NIs into Boolean queries corresponding to their negation is defined as follows:*

$$
\begin{aligned}
\delta(B_1 \sqsubseteq \neg B_2) \;=\; & q_{unsat} :- \gamma_1(x), \gamma_2(x) \text{ such that} \\
& \gamma_i(x) = A_i(x) \text{ if } B_i = A_i \\
& \gamma_i(x) = P_i(x, y_i) \text{ if } B_i = \exists P_i \\
& \gamma_i(x) = P_i(y_i, x) \text{ if } B_i = \exists P_i^- \\
\delta(R_1 \sqsubseteq \neg R_2) \;=\; & q_{unsat} :- \rho_1(x, y), \rho_2(x, y) \text{ such that} \\
& \rho_i(x, y) = P_i(x, y) \text{ if } R_i = P_i \\
& \rho_i(x, y) = P_i(y, x) \text{ if } R_i = P_i^- \\
\delta((funct\ P)) \;=\; & q_{unsat} :- P(x, y), P(x, z), y \neq z \\
\delta((funct\ P^-)) \;=\; & q_{unsat} :- P(x, y), P(z, y), x \neq z
\end{aligned}
$$

This second step of consistency checking is summarized in the *Consistent* Algorithm (Algorithm 2). In the algorithm, for each NI clause α, the query $q_{unsat, \alpha}$

Subject	Predicate	Object	FOL Semantics
dupond	Leads	infoDept	Leads(dupond,infoDept)
dupond	rdf:type	Professor	Professor(dupond)
durand	ResponsibleOf	ue111	ResponsibleOf(durand,ue111)
durand	Leads	csDept	Leads(durand,csDept)
paul	TeachesTo	pierre	TeachesTo(paul,pierre)
pierre	EnrolledIn	infoDept	EnrolledIn(pierre, infodept)
pierre	rdf:type	Undergrad	Undergrad(pierre)
pierre	RegisteredTo	ue111	Registered(pierre, ue111)
ue111	OfferedBy	infoDept	OfferedBy(ue111,infoDept)
ue111	rdf:type	CSCourse	CSCourse(ue111)
jim	EnrolledIn	csDept	EnrolledIn(jim, csDept)
csDept	rdf:type	TeachingDept	TeachingDept(csDept)

Figure 8.8. $\mathcal{A}'$: an Abox consistent w.r.t the Tbox of Figure 8.6.

is an SQL query computing the Boolean conjunctive queries $\delta(\alpha)$. Also, $db(\mathcal{A})$ denotes the $\mathcal{A}$ set in a relational database.

Algorithm 2. The *Consistent* algorithm
Consistent$(\mathcal{T}, \mathcal{A})$
Input: a KB $\mathcal{K} = \langle \mathcal{T}, \mathcal{A} \rangle$
Output: *true* if $\mathcal{K}$ is satisfiable, *false* otherwise
(1) $q_{unsat} = \emptyset$ (i.e., q_{unsat} is *false*)
(2)   **foreach** $\alpha \in cln(\mathcal{T})$ **let** $q_{unsat} = q_{unsat} \cup q_{unsat,\alpha}(db(\mathcal{A}))$
(3)
(4)   **if** $q_{unsat} = \emptyset$ **return** *true*
(5)   **else return** *false*

It is important to emphasize that this two-step approach for consistency checking does not require any inference on the data. The only inferences concern the Tbox and consist in computing the deductive closure of its axioms, from which the NI-closure (denoted $cln(\mathcal{T})$ in the Algorithm) is extracted.

Consider the Abox $\mathcal{A}'$ obtained from the inconsistent Abox $\mathcal{A}$ in Figure 8.1 by deleting the fact *PhDStudent(paul)*. The knowledge base made of the Abox $\mathcal{A}'$ in Figure 8.8 and the Tbox $\mathcal{T}$ in Figure 8.6 is consistent. (See Exercise 8.6.4.)

8.4.3 Answer Set Evaluation

In the previous section, the negative constraints played the main role. Once we know the knowledge base is consistent and move to query answering, the positive constraints take over.

Answering queries to a DL-LITE knowledge base is done in two steps. The first step is the query reformulation, which consists in translating the original query q into a set Q of queries. The second step consists in evaluating the queries in Q over the Abox (again seen as a relational database). The beauty of the approach is that this will provide the answer set. Of course, simply evaluating q over the Abox would possibly yield an incomplete answer. Completeness is achieved by the "reasoning" in the reformulation step. During this step, we access only the Tbox and not the data.

The query reformulation step is performed by the *PerfectRef* (Algorithm 3, Figure 8.10). It consists in reformulating the initial query by using the PIs in $\mathcal{T}$ as rewriting rules. The intuition is that PIs are seen as logical rules that are applied in backward-chaining to query atoms in order to expand them (in a resolution style). In databases, this is called a *chase*.

The queries we consider (i.e., the conjunctive queries), consist of several atoms. In general, because of the existential variables, new variables are introduced in queries. So we could be lead to generate more and more queries with new variables. It turns out that we will be able to control this process and generate only a finite number of distinct queries. This is due to the limitations of the constraints allowed in the Tbox. As outlined in Section 8.4.4, as soon as we allow the combination of key constraints with inclusions of properties, we may generate an infinite number of nonredundant queries.

Consider a PI rule $\alpha \Rightarrow \beta$. Applicability of the rule to an atom of a query is defined as follows:

- ■ It is *applicable to an atom $A(x)$* of a query if A occurs in β.
- ■ It is *applicable to an atom $P(x_1,x_2)$* of a query if
  - $\alpha \Rightarrow \beta$ is a role inclusion assertion and P or P^- occurs in β;
  - $x_2 = \_$ and β is $\exists P$;
  - $x_1 = \_$ and β is $\exists P^-$.

As usual, $\_$ denotes here an unbounded existential variable of a query.

The following definition defines the result $gr(g,I)$ of the *goal reduction* of the atom g using the PI I, which is at the core of *PerfectRef*.

Definition 8.4.7 (backward application of a PI to an atom) *Let I be an inclusion assertion that is applicable to the atom g. Then, $gr(g,I)$ is the atom defined as follows:*

if	$g = A(x)$	and	$I = A_1 \sqsubseteq A,$	then $gr(g,I) = A_1(x);$
if	$g = A(x)$	and	$I = \exists P \sqsubseteq A,$	then $gr(g,I) = P(x,\_);$
if	$g = A(x)$	and	$I = \exists P^- \sqsubseteq A,$	then $gr(g,I) = P(\_,x);$
if	$g = P(x,\_)$	and	$I = A \sqsubseteq \exists P,$	then $gr(g,I) = A(x);$
if	$g = P(x,\_)$	and	$I = \exists P_1 \sqsubseteq \exists P,$	then $gr(g,I) = P_1(x,\_);$
if	$g = P(x,\_)$	and	$I = \exists P_1^- \sqsubseteq \exists P,$	then $gr(g,I) = P_1(\_,x);$
if	$g = P(\_,x)$	and	$I = A \sqsubseteq \exists P^-,$	then $gr(g,I) = A(x);$
if	$g = P(\_,x)$	and	$I = \exists P_1 \sqsubseteq \exists P^-,$	then $gr(g,I) = P_1(x,\_);$
if	$g = P(\_,x)$	and	$I = \exists P_1^- \sqsubseteq \exists P^-,$	then $gr(g,I) = P_1(\_,x);$
if	$g = P(x_1,x_2)$	and	either $I = P_1 \sqsubseteq P$ or $I = P_1^- \sqsubseteq P^-$	then $gr(g,I) = P_1(x_1,x_2);$
if	$g = P(x_1,x_2)$	and	either $I = P_1 \sqsubseteq P^-$ or $I = P_1^- \sqsubseteq P$	then $gr(g,I) = P_1(x_2,x_1).$

The subtle point of *PerfectRef* is the need of simplifying the produced reformulations, so that some PIs that were not applicable to a reformulation become applicable to its simplifications. A simplification amounts to unify two atoms of a reformulation using their *most general unifier* and then to switch the possibly new unbounded existential variables to the anonymous variable denoted _.

Let us illustrate the reformulation step of the following query using the PIs in the Tbox $\mathcal{T}$ of Figure 8.6:

---

q(x):- TeachesIn(x,y), RegisteredIn(z,y), Student(z).

Figure 8.9 shows the result returned by *PerfectRef(q(x),$\mathcal{T}$)*.

We detail here the inference chain leading to some reformulations that are particularly interesting for getting answers for q from the data in the Abox $\mathcal{A}'$ of Figure 8.8. This also illustrates the need of the simplification step. The reformulation

---

q4(x):- TeachesIn(x,y), RegisteredIn(_,y)

---

is obtained

- By the backward application to the atom *Student(z)* of $q(x)$ of the PI: $\exists RegisteredIn \sqsubseteq Student$, which leads to the reformulation

  $q'(x) :- TeachesIn(x,y), RegisteredIn(z,y), Registered(z,\_)$

  in which the anonymous variable _ appearing in the atom *Registered(z,_)* denotes the unbounded existential variable produced by the backward application of the PI,
- followed by a simplification step, consisting in unifying the two redundant atoms in the body of q': the atom *Registered(z,y)* is kept instead of the atom *Registered(z,_)* because y is an existential variable which is bounded within the body of q'. But now, the existential variable z is unbounded within the body of q': it is replaced by the anonymous variable _.

In turn, $q_4(x)$ can be reformulated by the backward application of the PI *Course* $\sqsubseteq \exists RegisteredIn^-$ to the atom *RegisteredIn(_,y)*, which results in the reformulation $q_{11}(x)$:

---

q11(x):- TeachesIn(x,y), Course(y)

Then, the reformulation $q_{12}(x)$ is produced by the backward application of the PI $\exists$ *TeachesIn*$^- \sqsubseteq Course$, and the simplification by unification of the two atoms followed by the replacement of the existential variable y, now unbounded, with the anonymous variable _.

Initial query

q(x):- TeachesIn(x,y), RegisteredIn(z,y), Student(z)

Reformulations	Applied PI	Reformulated Query
$q_1(x)$:- ResponsibleOf(x,y), RegisteredIn(z,y), Student(z)	*ResponsibleOf* ⊑ *TeachesIn*	q(x)
$q_2(x)$:- TeachesIn(x,y), RegisteredIn(z,y), PhDStudent(z)	*PhDStudent* ⊑ *Student*	q(x)
$q_3(x)$:- TeachesIn(x,y), RegisteredIn(z,y), TeachesTo(_,z)	*∃TeachesTo⁻* ⊑ *Student*	q(x)
$q_4(x)$:- TeachesIn(x,y), RegisteredIn(_,y)	*∃RegisteredIn* ⊑ *Student*	q(x)
$q_5(x)$:- ResponsibleOf(x,y), RegisteredIn(z,y), PhDStudent(z)	*PhDStudent* ⊑ *Student*	$q_1(x)$
$q_6(x)$:- ResponsibleOf(x,y), RegisteredIn(z,y), TeachesTo(_,z)	*∃TeachesTo⁻* ⊑ *Student*	$q_1(x)$
$q_7(x)$:- ResponsibleOf(x,y), RegisteredIn(_,y)	*∃RegisteredIn* ⊑ *Student*	$q_1(x)$
$q_8(x)$:- ResponsibleOf(x,y), RegisteredIn(z,y), PhDStudent(z)	*ResponsibleOf* ⊑ *TeachesIn*	$q_2(x)$
$q_9(x)$:- ResponsibleOf(x,y), RegisteredIn(z,y), TeachesTo(_,z)	*ResponsibleOf* ⊑ *TeachesIn*	$q_3(x)$
$q_{10}(x)$:- ResponsibleOf(x,y), RegisteredIn(_,y)	*ResponsibleOf* ⊑ *TeachesIn*	$q_4(x)$
$q_{11}(x)$:- TeachesIn(x,y), Course(y)	*Course* ⊑ *∃RegisteredIn⁻*	$q_4(x)$
$q_{12}(x)$:- TeachesIn(x,_)	*∃TeachesIn⁻* ⊑ *Course*	$q_{11}(x)$
$q_{13}(x)$:- ResponsibleOf(x,_)	*ResponsibleOf* ⊑ *TeachesIn*	$q_{12}(x)$
$q_{14}(x)$:- Professor(x)	*Professor* ⊑ *∃TeachesIn*	$q_{12}(x)$

Figure 8.9. A query and its reformulations obtained by *PerfectRef* applied to the Tbox of Figure 8.6.

191

```
q12(x):- TeachesIn(x,_)
```

Finally, the reformulations $q_{13}(x)$ and $q_{14}(x)$ are obtained from the backward application of the PIs *ResponsibleOf* $\sqsubseteq$ *TeachesIn* and *Professor* $\sqsubseteq$ $\exists$*TeachesIn* respectively.

```
q13(x):- ResponsibleOf(x,_)
```

```
q14(x):- Professor (x)
```

It is important to notice that the answers *durand* and *dupond* are obtained for the initial query $q(x)$ thanks to those reformulations $q_{13}(x)$ and $q_{14}(x)$: They would not be returned by the standard evaluation of the query $q(x)$ against the Abox $\mathcal{A}'$ of Figure 8.8.

The *PerfectRef* algorithm is described in Figure 8.10, in which:

- The notation $q[g/gr(g,I)]$ (Line 7) denotes the replacement of the atom g in the body of the query q with the result $gr(g,I)$ of the backward application of the PI I to the atom g,
- The operator *reduce*(q,g,g') (Line 10) denotes the simplification of the body of q obtained by replacing the conjunction of its two atoms g and g' with their *most general unifier* (if g and g' can be unified),
- The operator τ (Line 10) replaces in the body of a query all the possibly new *unbounded* existential variables with the anonymous variable denoted _.

Figure 8.9 shows the result returned by *PerfectRef*$(q(x),\mathcal{T})$, where $q(x)$ is the query of the previous example, and $\mathcal{T}$ is the Tbox of Figure 8.6. The second column makes explicit the PI used for obtaining the corresponding reformulation. Note that equivalent reformulations can be produced by different inferences, such as for example the reformulations $q_4(x)$ and $q_7(x)$.

Although we will not prove it here, the following properties hold:

soundness. All the facts computed using *PerfectRef* are correct query answers.
completeness. All query answers are obtained.
complexity. Since we touch the data only for the evaluation of FOL queries, the worst-case complexity is PTIME in the size of the Abox. The number of reformulations is PTIME in the size of the Tbox. Therefore, the complexity evaluating a query against a DL-LITE$_{\mathcal{R}}$ or DL-LITE$_{\mathcal{F}}$ knowledge base is PTIME in the size of the knowledge base.

Algorithm 3. The *PerfectRef* algorithm

PerfectRef(q,T)

Input: a conjunctive query q and a Tbox T

Output: a union of conjunctive queries: PR

(1) $PR := \{q\}$

(2)   **repeat**

(3) $PR' := PR$

(4)   **foreach** $q \in PR'$

(5)   (a) **foreach** $g \in q$

(6)   **if** a PI $I \in T$ is applicable to g

(7) $PR := PR \cup \{qg/gr(g,I)\}$

(8)   (b) **foreach** $g_1, g_2 \in q$

(9)   **if** g_1 et g_2 sont unifiables

(10) $PR := PR \cup \{\tau(reduce(q,g_1,g_2))\}$

(11)   **until** $PR' = PR$

Figure 8.10.

8.4.4 Impact of Combining DL-LITE$_\mathcal{R}$ and DL-LITE$_\mathcal{F}$ on Query Answering

In this section, we exhibit an example showing that the interaction of key constraints (the specificity of DL-LITE$_\mathcal{F}$) with inclusion constraints between properties (the specificity of DL-LITE$_\mathcal{R}$) may lead to a reformulation of a query into an *infinite* number of conjunctive rewritings, each one likely to bring additional answers. This makes an algorithmic approach such as the one we used for DL-LITE$_\mathcal{R}$ and DL-LITE$_\mathcal{F}$ in isolation incomplete for query answering when DL-LITE$_\mathcal{R}$ and DL-LITE$_\mathcal{F}$ are combined together.

Consider a Tbox made of the following inclusion axioms, in which R and P are two properties and S is a class:

$R \sqsubseteq P$

$(functP)$

$S \sqsubseteq \exists R$

$\exists R^- \sqsubseteq \exists R$

Let us consider the following query:

$q(x) :- R(z,x)$

The following query expression is a valid reformulation for the query q:

$r_1(x) :- S(x_1), P(x_1,x)$

To see this, we observe that from the fact $S(x_1)$ and the PI $S \sqsubseteq \exists R$, it can be inferred that there exists y such that $R(x_1,y)$ holds, and thus $P(x_1,y)$ holds too (since $R \sqsubseteq P$). From the functionality constraint on P and the conjunct $P(x_1,x)$ in the body of r_1, we can now infer that $y = x$, and thus that $R(x_1,x)$ holds. Therefore, $\exists z R(z,x)$ is logically entailed by $\exists x_1 S(x_1) \wedge P(x_1,x)$, that is, $r_1(x)$ is contained in the query $q(x)$, and thus is a valid reformulation of the query $q(x)$.

It turns out that the situation is even more subtle. Surprisingly, this reformulation $r_1(x)$ is not the only one. In fact there exists an *infinite* number of different reformulations for $q(x)$. Let $k \geq 2$. The following query is a *valid reformulation* of $q(x)$:

$$r_k(x) :- S(x_k), P(x_k, x_{k-1}), \ldots, P(x_1, x)$$

To show that $r_k(x)$ is logically contained in $q(x)$, we exploit again the axiom of functionality of P and the inclusion axiom between R and P: From the fact $S(x_k)$ and the PI $S \sqsubseteq \exists R$, it can be inferred that there exists y_k such that $R(x_k, y_k)$ holds, and thus $P(x_k, y_k)$ holds too (since $R \sqsubseteq P$). Since P is functional, we get $y_k = x_{k-1}$, and thus $R(x_k, x_{k-1})$ holds. Now, based on the PI $\exists R^- \sqsubseteq \exists R$, there exists y_{k-1} such that $R(x_{k-1}, y_{k-1})$ holds, and with the same reasoning as before, we get $y_{k-1} = x_{k-2}$, and thus $R(x_{k-1}, x_{k-2})$ holds. By induction, we obtain that $R(x_1, x)$ holds, that is, $r_k(x)$ is logically contained in the query $q(x)$.

One can also show that for each k, there exists an Abox such that the reformulation r_k returns answers that are not returned by the reformulation $r_{k'}$ for $k' < k$. Thus, there exists an infinite number of nonredundant conjunctive reformulations.

It can be shown that if we combine key constraints and inclusions of properties in a restricted way, this problem can be avoided. For instance, if key constraints are forbidden on properties involved in the right-hand side of an inclusion axiom, there is a finite number of nonredundant conjunctive reformulations and they can be found by the *PerfectRef* algorithm.

8.5 FURTHER READING

The spreading of RDF data on the Web and the importance of queries for such data is illustrated by the Billion Triple Track of the Semantic Web Challenge.[1] The idea is to "do something" efficiently with one billion of RDFS triples.

RDFS Reasoners for RDFS like the Jena2 ontology API [104], which implements the forward-chaining algorithm we described, are available online and can be downloaded, A SPARQL [175] engine included in the same programmatic Jena environment enables storing and querying datasets made of (asserted + inferred) triples. In fact, since RDFS statements are also stored as RDF triplets, SPARQL can also be used to query the schema, and not just the RDF data. For guaranteeing the completeness of the answers to a schema query, all the inference rules that we gave in Figure 7.7 (in the section describing RDFS) must be taken into account, and not only the subset that we considered in the forward-chaining algorithm.

We mentioned the practical advantage of separating the computation over a Tbox from that over the Abox. This is useful also from a theoretical point of view. This gives a bound on the data complexity (the complexity in terms of the Abox only) of consistency checking and of query answering. We showed that they can be performed using FOL queries and it is known [9, 159] that evaluating FOL queries over a relational database is in LOGSPACE in the size of the database.

[1] http://challenge.semanticweb.org/.

DL-lite   DL-LITE$_\mathcal{R}$ has been recently incorporated into the version OWL2 [176] of OWL as the profile called OWL2 QL. The proof that the *PerfectRef* Algorithm computes the *whole* answer is shown in [38]. It follows that the complexity of query answering by reformulation in these fragments of DL-LITE is polynomial in the size of the Tbox, and in LOGSPACE in the size of the Abox.

A major result in [38] is that DL-LITE$_\mathcal{R}$ and DL-LITE$_\mathcal{F}$ are two maximal fragments of the DL-Lite family supporting tractable query answering over large amounts of data. It has been shown in [38] that consistency checking and instance recognition (which a particular case of query answering), while being LOGSPACE both for DL-LITE$_\mathcal{R}$ and DL-LITE$_\mathcal{F}$ Tboxes, are PTIME-COMPLETE for the languages that combine the axioms of both (denoted DL-LITE$_{\mathcal{R}\mathcal{F}}$). This complexity result shows it is unlikely that an approach based on query reformulation would provide a complete query-answering algorithm for DL-LITE$_{\mathcal{R}\mathcal{F}}$.

QuOnto ([13]) is a JAVA tool implementing the DL-LITE family of ontology representation languages. It permits the declaration of an ontology as a DL-LITE Tbox, the construction of an associated Abox that can be stored and as a MySQL database. The consistency checking of the resulting DL-LITE knowledge base, and query answering by reformulation are the core functionalities of QuOnto, based on the implementation in Java of the algorithms presented in this chapter.

Datalog^{+-}   Recent research [11, 12] has extended the Datalog database query language toward query answering over ontologies. This has resulted in a unifying framework based on a family of expressive extensions of Datalog, called Datalog^{+-}, that captures DL-LITE$_\mathcal{R}$ and DL-LITE$_\mathcal{F}$.

8.6 EXERCISES

Exercise 8.6.1 *With the university example, find a new query that has a different answer:*

1. *On the RDF data vs. the RDF data together with the RDFS ontology.*
2. *On the RDF data vs. the RDF data together with the DL-LITE ontology.*

Exercise 8.6.2 *Prove that the Saturation algorithm runs in $0((M \times N)^2)$.*

Exercise 8.6.3 *Prove that the rules used for computing the TBox closure are sound.*

Exercise 8.6.4 *Consider Abox $\mathcal{A}$ in Figure 8.1 and $\mathcal{A}'$ obtained by deleting the fact PhDStudent(paul), and the Tbox $\mathcal{T}$ in Figure 8.6. Show that*

1. *The knowledge base $\mathcal{A} \cup \mathcal{T}$ is inconsistent.*
2. *The knowledge base $\mathcal{A}' \cup \mathcal{T}$ is consistent.*

Exercise 8.6.5 *Give the FOL rule corresponding to the different cases of negative inclusion axioms.*

9

Data Integration

9.1 INTRODUCTION

The goal of data integration is to provide a uniform access to a set of autonomous and possibly heterogeneous data sources in a particular application domain. This is typically what we need when, for instance, querying the *deep web* that is composed of a plethora of databases accessible through Web forms. We would like to be able with a single query to find relevant data no matter which database provides it.

A first issue for data integration (that will be ignored here) is social: The owners of some data set may be unwilling to fully share it and be reluctant to participate in a data integration system. Also, from a technical viewpoint, the difficulty comes from the lack of interoperability between the data sources, that may use a variety of formats, specific query-processing capabilities, different protocols. However, the real bottleneck for data integration is logical. It comes from the so-called *semantic heterogeneity* between the data sources. They typically organize data using different schemas even in the same application domain. For instance, each university or educational institution may choose to model students and teaching programs in its own way. A French university may use the social security number to identify students and the attributes NOM, PRENOM, whereas the Erasmus database about European students may use a European student number and the attributes FIRSTNAME, LASTNAME, and HOME UNIVERSITY.

In this chapter, we study data integration in the *mediator* approach. In this approach, data remain exclusively in data sources and are obtained when the system is queried. One sometimes uses the term *virtual* data integration. This is in contrast to a *warehousing* approach where the data is extracted from the data sources ahead of query time, transformed, and loaded in the warehouse. At query time, the warehouse is accessed but the data sources are not. Warehouse approaches are typically preferred for very complex queries (e.g., for data mining). On the other hand, to have access to "fresh" information, a mediator approach is preferred since it avoids having to propagate in real time, data source updates to the warehouse. Figure 9.1 illustrates these two approaches of data integration.

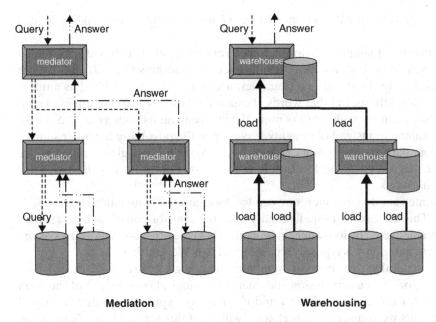

Figure 9.1. Virtual versus materialized data integration.

In the *mediator* approach, one starts by designing a global schema (also called *mediated* schema) that serves as a unique entry point on which global queries are posed by users. A main issue is then to specify the relationships, namely *semantic mappings*, between the schemas of the data sources and the global schema. Based on these mappings, one can answer queries over the global schema using queries over the data sources. Typically, query answering in the mediator approach is performed as follows. First, independently of the data in the sources, the user's query posed over the global schema is transformed into *local queries* that refer to the schemas of the data sources. A *global query* combines the data provided by sources. Queries are optimized and transformed into query plans. The local query plans are executed and their results combined by the global query plan.

In the following, for presentation purposes, we consider that the global schema and the schemas of the data sources to integrate are all relational. In practice, each nonrelational data source (e.g., XML or HTML) is abstracted as a relational database with the help of a *wrapper*. Wrappers are small programs that translate local relational queries into appropriate requests understood by specific data sources, and transform their results into relations. The role of wrappers is to allow the mediator to see each data source as relational, no matter which actual format it uses.

Let us consider in more detail the specification of semantic mappings between the data sources and the global schema. Let S_1, ..., S_n be the local schemas of n preexisting data sources. To simplify the presentation, let us assume that each local schema S_i is made of a single relation that we denote also S_i. The relations S_1, ..., S_n are called the *local* relations. Suppose the global schema G consists of the *global* relations G_1, ..., G_m. The goal is to specify semantic relations between the local relations S_i and the global relations G_j. The G_j are logically (intentionally) defined by the S_i.

An example of simple relationship (not very interesting) is based on equality (e.g., $G_1 = S_1$). One can find more complicated relationships (e.g., $G_2 = S_1 \cup S_2$ or $G_3 = S_1 \bowtie S_3$). In these last two examples, a global relation is defined as a query over the local relations. In other words, the global relation is a *view* of the local relations. Indeed, one typically prefers more flexible constraints such as $G_3 \supseteq S_1 \bowtie S_3$. Using containment instead of equality leaves open the possibility for other sources of providing data about G_3 (e.g., $G_3 \supseteq \sigma_{A="yes"}(S_4)$). Because global relations are constrained by views of the local relations, one uses the term *global-as-view* for such specifications.

In a somewhat dual manner, one can use *local-as-view* constraints such as: $S_4 \subseteq G_1 \bowtie G_3$. This leaves even more flexibility since the contribution of each data source can be specified (e.g., by its owner) independently of the other sources of the system. This kind of autonomy is typically well adapted to a Web setting.

More generally, to express semantic mappings between $\{S_1,...,S_n\}$ and $\{G_1,...,G_m\}$, one can use inclusion statements (i.e., logical constraints) of the form $v(S_1,...,S_n) \subseteq v'(G_1,...,G_m)$, where v and v' are query expressions called views. All the constraints we consider in this chapter will be of this general form. Now, given an instance I of $\{S_1,...,S_n\}$ (i.e., an instance of the data sources), we don't know the instance J of the global schema. But we know that

$$v(I(S_1),...,I(S_n)) \subseteq v'(J(G_1),...,J(G_m))$$

So, the story of mediator systems is essentially a story of logical constraints and incomplete information. In this general setting, given I, an *answer* to a global query q is a fact $q(a)$ that is true in any instance J that together with I satisfies the mapping constraints (i.e., a fact we can be sure of as a logical consequence of both the data stored in I and of the logical constraints expressed by the mappings). Not surprisingly, query answering is thus a complex reasoning problem that in general may be undecidable. We focus on two particular decidable cases, for which rewriting algorithms have been designed and implemented. They are based on semantic mappings that capture typical constraints found in many applications:

Global-as-view (GAV for short). The semantic mappings are of the form

$$V_i(S_1,...,S_n) \subseteq G_i$$

also equivalently denoted

$$G_i \supseteq V_i(S_1,...,S_n)$$

where each V_i is a view over the local schemas (i.e., a query built on local relations).

Local-as-view (LAV for short). The semantic mappings are of the form

$$S_i \subseteq V_i(G_1,...,G_m)$$

where each V_i is a view over the global schema (i.e., a query built on global relations).

In our development, we will consider conjunctive queries. Using negation in queries greatly complicates the issues. In the next section, we recall some standard material on *containment* of conjunctive queries (i.e., of the queries at the heart of our formal development). In Sections 9.3 and 9.4, we study GAV and LAV mediators, respectively. For each of these languages, we describe appropriate query rewriting algorithms. In Section 9.5, we show the impact on query rewriting of adding DL-LITE constraints in the global schema. Finally, in Section 9.6, we lay the basis of a peer-to-peer approach for data integration. In contrast with the mediator approach which offers a unique entry point to data, peer-to-peer data management systems (PDMS for short) are decentralized data integration systems.

9.2 CONTAINMENT OF CONJUNCTIVE QUERIES

In this section, we recall some basic notions on comparing conjunctive queries that we will use in the following.

We recall that a *conjunctive query* is an expression of the form:

$$q(x_1,...,x_n) :- A_1(\vec{u}_1),...,A_k(\vec{u}_k)$$

where each A_i is a relation and $\vec{u}_1,...,\vec{u}_k$ are vectors of constants and variables. Furthermore, we require that each x_i occurs in some $\vec{u}_i$. $q(x_1,...,x_n)$ is called the *head* and $A_1(\vec{u}_1),...,A_k(\vec{u}_k)$ the *body* of the query. The x_i variables are called *distinguished*. The other variables are called *existential*.

Given an instance I of the relations appearing in the body of the query, an *answer* is a tuple $\langle v(x_1),...,v(x_n)\rangle$ for some valuation v of the variables in the query, such that for each i, $A_i(v(\vec{u}_i))$ holds in I. We denote $q(I)$ the set of answers.

We sometimes denote this query $q(x_1,...,x_n)$ when its body is understood. Observe that the interpretation of such a conjunctive query in logical terms is:

$$\{x_1,...,x_n \mid \exists y_1,...,\exists y_m(A_1(\vec{u}_1) \wedge \cdots \wedge A_k(\vec{u}_k))\}$$

where $y_1,...,y_m$ are the variables not occurring in the head.

The data integration techniques rely on *conjunctive query containment*. This problem has been extensively studied because it is at the core of query optimization. We use known techniques that we recall next.

A query q_1 is contained in q_2, denoted $q_1 \subseteq q_2$, if for each I, $q_1(I) \subseteq q_2(I)$. It is known that the containment between a conjunctive query q_1 and a conjunctive query q_2 can be tested by finding a "homomorphism" from q_2 to q_1.

Definition 9.2.1 *Let $q_1(x_1,...,x_n)$ and $q_2(y_1,...,y_n)$ be two conjunctive queries. A (conjunctive query) homomorphism from q_2 to q_1 is a mapping ψ from the variables of q_2 to the variables of q_1 such that*

1. *For each i, $\psi(y_i) = x_i$ and*
2. *For each atom $R(\vec{u}_i)$ in the body of q_2, $R(\psi(\vec{u}_i))$ is in the body of q_1.*

Example 9.2.2 *Consider the following queries:*

- $q_1(x_1,x_1') : -A_1(x_1,x_2,x_3), A_2(x_1',x_2,x_3)$
- $q_2(y_1,y_1') : -A_1(y_1,y_2,y_3), A_2(y_1',y_2,y_3')$

Consider a mapping ψ such that $\psi(y_i) = x_i$ for each i, $\psi(y_1') = x_1'$ and $\psi(y_3') = x_3$. Then the required conditions hold, and it follows that $q_1 \subseteq q_2$. Intuitively, q_2 joins A_1 and A_2 on the second attribute, whereas q_1 also joins on the third one. The additional condition induces the containment.

The following proposition states that the existence of a homomorphism is a necessary and sufficient condition for query containment.

Proposition 9.2.3 (homomorphism theorem) *Let q_1 and q_2 be two conjunctive queries. Then q_1 is contained in q_2 if and only if there exists a homomorphism from q_2 to q_1.*

This provides a simple algorithm for testing conjunctive query containment. In the general case, deciding whether a conjunctive query is contained in another one is NP-complete in the size of the two queries. In fact, in many practical cases, there are polynomial-time algorithms for query containment.

Algorithm 4 checks whether a query q_1 is contained in a query q_2.

Algorithm 4. The *Query containment algorithm*
$QC(q_1, q_2)$
Input: Two conjunctive queries:
   $q_1(\vec{x}) :\text{-} g_1(\vec{x_1}), \ldots, g_n(\vec{x_n})$
   $q_2(\vec{y}) :\text{-} h_1(\vec{y_1}), \ldots, h_m(\vec{y_m})$
Output: Yes if $q_1 \subseteq q_2$; no otherwise
(1)   **freeze** q_1: construct a canonical instance $D_{can} = \{g_i(v(\vec{x_i})) \mid 1 \leq i \leq n\}$
(2)   for some valuation v mapping each variable in q_1
(3)   to a distinct constant
(4)   **if** $v(\vec{x}) \in q_2(D_{can})$ **return** yes
(5)   **else return** no.

Example 9.2.4 *Consider the queries of Example 9.2.2. The canonical instance D_{can} is $A_1(a,b,c), A_2(a',b,c)$. It is easily verified that $q_2(D_{can}) = (a,a')$, which is $v(x,x')$.*

9.3 GLOBAL-AS-VIEW MEDIATION

The main advantage of GAV is its conceptual and algorithmic simplicity. The global schema is simply defined using views over the data sources and specifies how to obtain tuples of the global relation G_i from tuples in the sources.

Definition 9.3.1 (GAV mapping) *A GAV mapping is an expression of the form:*
$R(x_1,\ldots,x_n) \supseteq q(x_1,\ldots,x_n)$, *where* $q(x_1,\ldots,x_n) :\text{-} A_1(\vec{u_1}),\ldots,A_k(\vec{u_k})$ *is a conjunctive query of the same arity as R. The semantics of this mapping is*

$$\forall x_1,\ldots,x_n(\exists y_1,\ldots,y_m(A_1(\vec{u_1}),\ldots,A_k(\vec{u_k}) \Rightarrow R(\vec{u})))$$

where $y_1,\ldots,y_m$ are of variables occurring in the body of the rule and not its head.

We write alternatively this GAV mapping as:

$$R(x_1,...,x_n) \supseteq A_1(\vec{u}_1),...,A_k(\vec{u}_k)$$
$$R(x_1,...,x_n) \supseteq q(x_1,...,x_n)$$
$$R \supseteq q$$

by omitting information that is either not needed or that is clear from the context. When we want to stress which are the existential variables, we write it $R(\vec{x}) \supseteq q(\vec{x}, \vec{y})$ where $\vec{y}$ is the vector of existential variables.

Example 9.3.2 *Consider the following four data sources:*

■ *The source relation S1 is a catalog of teaching programs offered in different French universities with master programs.*

S1.Catalogue(nomUniv, programme)

■ *The source relation S2 provides the names of European students enrolled in courses at some university within the Erasmus exchange program:*

S2.Erasmus(student, course, univ)

■ *The source relation S3 provides the names of foreign students enrolled in programs of some French university:*

S3.CampusFr(student, program, university)

■ *The source relation S4 provides the course contents of international master programs:*

S4.Mundus(program, course)

Now, suppose we define a global schema with the following unary and binary relations:

MasterStudent(studentName),   University(uniName),
MasterProgram(title),   MasterCourse(code),
EnrolledIn(studentName, title),   RegisteredTo(studentName, uniName).

These relations are defined in terms of the local *relations by the following GAV mappings:*

$MasterStudent(N) \supseteq S2.Erasmus(N,C,U), S4.Mundus(P,C)$
$MasterStudent(N) \supseteq S3.CampusFr(N,P,U), S4.Mundus(P,C)$
$University(U) \supseteq S1.Catalogue(U,P)$
$University(U) \supseteq S2.Erasmus(N,C,U)$
$University(U) \supseteq S3.CampusFr(N,P,U)$
$MasterProgram(T) \supseteq S4.Mundus(T,C)$
$MasterCourse(C) \supseteq S4.Mundus(T,C)$
$EnrolledIn(N,T) \supseteq S2.Erasmus(N,C,U), S4.Mundus(T,C)$
$EnrolledIn(N,T) \supseteq S3.CampusFr(N,T,U), S4.Mundus(T,C)$
$RegisteredTo(N,U) \supseteq S3.CampusFr(N,T,U)$

Note that in a warehousing approach, one would simply evaluate all the queries that define the global view, and populate the warehouse using standard relational query evaluation. In a mediator approach, we try to only derive data that is relevant to a specific query posed on the global view by a user. We show how to rewrite a global query into queries over the local relations and combine their results. This is achieved by a technical trick that consists in *unfolding* the atoms of the global query.

Observe the first two mappings. They specify (using joins) how to obtain tuples of the unary relation MasterStudent. Now consider the following global query asking for universities with registered master students:

```
q(x) :- RegisteredTo(s,x), MasterStudent(s)
```

The rewriting of this query into source queries is obtained by *unfolding* (i.e., by replacing each atom that can be matched with the head of some view, by the body of the corresponding view). (For readers familiar with logic programming, this is some very simple form of resolution.)

In the example, there is a single mapping whose head can be matched with *RegisteredTo(s,x)*, and two mappings that match *MasterStudent(s)*. Thus, we obtain the following two unfoldings:

```
q1(x) :- S3.CampusFr(s,v1,x), S2.Erasmus(s,v2,v3), S4.Mundus(v4,v2)
q2(x) :- S3.CampusFr(s,v5,x), S3.CampusFr(s,v6,v7), S4.Mundus(v6,v8)
```

Observe that q2 can be simplified. Replacing the conjunction of its first two atoms by the single atom S3.CampusFr(s,v6,x) leads to an equivalent query. We thus obtain the following two GAV rewritings of the initial query:

```
r1(x) :- S3.CampusFr(s,v1,x), S2.Erasmus(s,v2,v3), S4.Mundus(v4,v2)
r2(x) :- S3.CampusFr(s,v6,x), S4.Mundus(v6,v8)
```

The result is obtained by computing r1 $\cup$ r2. Now, observe that each r_ℓ is a conjunctive query. It can be optimized using standard query optimization to obtain an optimized physical query plan. Of course, the choice of the particular physical query plan that is selected depends on the statistics that are available and the capabilities of the sources. For instance, a plan may consist in querying S3 and then for each value a of v6 (i.e., a particular university program), asking the query q(X) :- S4.Mundus(a,X) to S4.

We now formalize the simple and intuitive notion of query unfolding.

Definition 9.3.3 (query unfolding) *Let* $q(\vec{x}) :- G_1(\vec{z}_1), \ldots, G_n(\vec{z}_n)$ *be a query and for each i,* $G_i(\vec{x}_i) \supseteq q_i(\vec{x}_i, \vec{y}_i)$ *be a GAV mapping. An* unfolding *of q is the query u obtained from q by replacing, for each i, each conjunct* $G_i(\vec{z}_i)$ *by* $q_i(\psi_i(\vec{x}_i, \vec{y}_i))$ *where* ψ_i *is a function that maps* $\vec{x}_i$ *to* $\vec{z}_i$, *and the existential variables* $\vec{y}_i$ *to new fresh variables.*

The renaming of the existential variables into fresh ones is necessary to avoid the introduction of unnecessary constraints in the unfolding. Indeed, consider an existential variable y occurring in two distinct atoms, say G_i and G_j. Then, the two atoms should be understood as $\exists...y...G_i(\vec{z}_i)$ and $\exists...y...G_j(\vec{z}_j)$. The scopes of y in both are disjoint and nothing requires that the two occurrences of y take the same value, hence the renaming using fresh variables.

Example 9.3.4 *Suppose we have the two mappings:*

$$F(x,y) \supseteq S(x,z), S(y,z) \qquad G(x) \supseteq S(x,y)$$

and the query $q(x) :- F(x,y), G(y)$. Then we get the following unfolding:

$$q(x) :- S(x,v_1), S(y,v_1), S(y,v_2)$$

The variable v_1 corresponds to the renaming of the existential variable z in the view defining F, whereas v_2 comes from the renaming of the existential variable y in the view defining G.

We next establish that each unfolding of a query computes a part of the desired results, and that their union computes the whole set of answers. To do so, we use two propositions. The first one ignores unfolding and focuses on the "materialization" of the global relations.

Proposition 9.3.5 *Let $S_1,...,S_n$ be a set of source relations; $G_1,...,G_m$ a global schema defined by a set $\mathcal{G}$ of GAV mappings over $S_1,...,S_n$; and I be an instance over $S_1,...,S_n$. Let J be the instance over $G_1,...,G_m$ defined by, for each j,*

$$J(G_j) = \cup\{V(I) \mid G_j \supseteq V(S_1,...,S_n) \in \mathcal{G}\}$$

Then for each query q over $G_1,...,G_m$, the answer of q is $q(J)$.

Proof (sketch). Let u be an answer. Then, by definition, $q(u)$ is true in each instance J' over $G_1,...,G_m$ such that I and J' together satisfy the mappings. In particular, u belongs to $q(J)$. Conversely, let u be in $q(J)$. Let J' be an instance such that I and J' together satisfy the mappings. Since J' satisfies the mappings, $J \subseteq J'$. Since conjunctive queries are monotone, $q(J) \subseteq q(J')$. Thus, $u \in J'$. Since u belongs to all such J', u is an answer. □

The second proposition deals with unfoldings.

Proposition 9.3.6 *Let $\mathbf{S}$ be a set of source relations and $\mathbf{G}$ a set of global relations defined by a set $\mathcal{G}$ of GAV mappings over $\mathbf{S}$. Consider the query $q(\vec{z}) :- G_{i_1}(\vec{z}_{i_1}),...,G_{i_n}(\vec{z}_{i_n})$ over $\mathbf{G}$ and the set $\{r_\ell\}$ of unfoldings of q given $\mathcal{G}$. Then for each I over $S_1,...,S_n$, the answer of q is given by $\cup r_\ell(I)$.*

Proof (sketch). Let J be as in Proposition 9.3.5. By the same proposition, it suffices to show that $q(J) = \cup r_\ell(I)$.

Soundness: Let $u \in \cup r_\ell(I)$. Then u is $r_\ell(I)$ for some unfolding r_ℓ. Suppose r_ℓ results from the unfolding defined by selecting for each j, the mapping $G_{i_j}(\vec{x}_{i_j}) \supseteq q_{i_j}(\vec{x}_{i_j}, \vec{y}_{i_j})$. It follows that $u \in q(\{\vec{u}_1\},...,\{\vec{u}_n\})$ where for each j, $\vec{u}_j$ is derived by $G_{i_j}(\vec{x}_{i_j}) \supseteq q_{i_j}(\vec{x}_{i_j}, \vec{y}_{i_j})$. Thus, each $\vec{u}_j$ is in $J(G_{i_j})$ and $u \in q(J(G_{i_1}),...,J(G_{i_n})) = q(J)$. Therefore, $\cup r_\ell(I) \subseteq q(J)$.

Completeness: Conversely, consider u in $q(J)$. Then, there exists $\vec{u}_1$ in $J(G_{i_1}),...,\vec{u}_j$ in $J(G_{i_j}),...,\vec{u}_n$ in $J(G_{i_n})$ such that $u \in q(\{\vec{u}_1\},...,\{\vec{u}_n\})$. By construction of J, for each

j there is some mapping $G_{i_j}(\vec{x}_{i_j}) \supseteq q_{i_j}(\vec{x}_{i_j}, \vec{y}_{i-1})$ such that $\vec{u}_j$ is in $q_{i_j}(\vec{x}_{i_j}, \vec{y}_{i-1})$. Consider the unfolding r_ℓ defined by selecting for each j, this particular mapping. One can verify that u is $r_\ell(I)$. Hence, $u \in \cup r_\ell(I)$ and $q(J) \subseteq \cup r_\ell(I)$.

$\square$

We can compute the answer using the unfoldings (also called the GAV rewritings). These unfoldings can be simplified by removing redundant conjuncts that may have been introduced by the technique. This simplification relies on checking conjunctive query containment. Given a conjunctive query with body $A_1(\vec{u}_1), ..., A_m(\vec{u}_m)$, we verify whether each query obtained by removing some $A_i(\vec{u}_i)$ is equivalent to the initial one. If yes, the atom is redundant and can be removed. We keep doing this until the query is "minimal." This simplification test is costly, but the resulting query may be much less expensive to evaluate that the initial one.

We must evaluate all the unfoldings to obtain the complete answer. If we are aware of some constraints on the local schemas or on the global one, this can be further simplified. For instance, the constraints may imply that the result of a particular unfolding is empty, in which case this particular unfolding needs not be evaluated. Also, the constraints may imply that the result of some unfolding, say r_ℓ, is always included in another one. Then r_ℓ need not be evaluated. For instance, in the previous example, if it is known that students obtained from the source *S2* are European students, whereas those obtained from the source *S3* are non-European students, we can be sure that the GAV rewriting r_ℓ obtained by unfolding will not provide any answer. This requires expressing and exploiting disjointness constraints over the local relations. Inclusion constraints on local relations would, on the other hand, permit to detect in advance that a given query plan provides answers that are redundant with those obtained by another query plan.

A main limitation of GAV is that adding or removing data sources to the integration system may require deeply revising all the views defining the global schema. In a Web context where sources may come and go, for example, because of (non)availability of servers, this is really too constraining. The LAV approach does not suffer from this disadvantage.

9.4 LOCAL-AS-VIEW MEDIATION

The LAV approach takes a dual approach. The local relations are defined as views over global relations. The goal is to define the global schema in such a way that individual definitions do not change when data sources join or leave the integration system except for the definitions of the sources that are involved in the change.

Definition 9.4.1 (LAV mapping) *A LAV mapping is a mapping of the form:* $S \subseteq q$, *for some conjunctive query* $q(x_1, ..., x_n) :\text{-} A_1(\vec{u}_1), ..., A_k(\vec{u}_k)$ *over the global relations. Its semantics is*

$$\forall x_1, ..., x_n [S(x_1, ..., x_n) \Rightarrow (\exists y_1, ..., y_m A_1(\vec{u}_1), ..., A_k(\vec{u}_k))]$$

where $y_1, ..., y_m$ *are the existential variables.*

Again, $S(x_1, ..., x_n)$ is called the *head* of the view, whereas $A_1(\vec{u}_1), ..., A_k(\vec{u}_k)$ is called the *body* of the view.

Example 9.4.2 *We define the global schema as consisting of the following relations:*

Student(studentName),	*EuropeanStudent(studentName),*
University(uniName),	*NonEuropeanStudent(studentName),*
FrenchUniversity(uniName),	*EuropeanUniversity(uniName),*
NonEuropeanUniversity(uniName),	*Program(title),*
MasterProgram(title),	*EnrolledInProgram(studentName,title),*
Course(code),	*EnrolledInCourse(studentName,code),*
PartOf(code, title),	*RegisteredTo(studentName, uniName),*
OfferedBy(title, uniName).	

The four data sources considered in the previous example can be described by the following LAV mappings:

m1: S1.Catalogue(U,P) $\subseteq$ *FrenchUniversity(U), Program(P), OfferedBy(P,U),*
    OfferedBy(P',U), MasterProgram(P')

m2: S2.Erasmus(S,C,U) $\subseteq$ *Student(S), EnrolledInCourse(S,C), PartOf(C,P),*
    OfferedBy(P,U), EuropeanUniversity(U),
    EuropeanUniversity(U') RegisteredTo(S,U'),
    U $\neq$ *U'*

m3: S3.CampusFr(S,P,U) $\subseteq$ *NonEuropeanStudent(S), Program(P),*
    EnrolledInProgram(S,P), OfferedBy(P,U),
    FrenchUniversity(U), RegisteredTo(S,U)

m4: S4.Mundus(P,C) $\subseteq$ *MasterProgram(P), OfferedBy(P,U),*
    OfferedBy(P,U'), EuropeanUniversity(U),
    NonEuropeanUniversity(U'), PartOf(C,P)

LAV mappings enable quite fine-grained descriptions of the contents of data sources. For example, we are able to specify precisely the students that can be found in the Erasmus source: they are European students enrolled in courses of a given (European) university that is different from their home (European) university in which they remain registered.

LAV mappings express loose coupling between local and global relations, which is important for flexibility and robustness when the participating data sources change frequently. If we are interested in Master students, we do not need to know in advance (unlike the GAV approach) how to join two sources. We just define them as a global query:

MasterStudent(E) :-   Student(E), EnrolledInProgram(E,M),
                       MasterProgram(M).

The local sources that must be queried and combined to get the Master students will be discovered by the rewriting process. Recall that, in the GAV approach, they were predefined by the two mappings given in Example 9.3.2.

The price to pay for the flexibility of LAV compared to GAV is that the rewritings are more complicated to find. We describe three algorithms that achieve this rewriting. The Bucket algorithm and the Minicon algorithm follow the same approach. They first determine the local relations that are *relevant* to the query; then they consider their combinations as *candidate* rewritings and verify whether they are indeed correct. Minicon is actually an optimization of Bucket that avoids the last verification step by a trickier first step. The third algorithm, namely the Inverse Rules algorithm, follows a completely different approach: it consists in transforming the logical rules supporting the LAV mappings (which are unsafe rules) into a set of safe rules with a single global relation. The global query is unfolded using these rules.

9.4.1 The Bucket Algorithm

The principle of the Bucket algorithm is quite simple. It proceeds in three steps:

1. Construct for each atom g of the global query body its *bucket*, which groups the view atoms from which g can be inferred;
2. Build a set of *candidate* rewritings that are obtained by combining the view atoms of each bucket;
3. Check whether each candidate rewriting is valid.

Bucket Creation

Let g be a query atom. The atoms in *bucket(g)* are the heads of mappings having in their body an atom from which g can be inferred. Intuitively, data comes from source relations, and a (global) query atom is satisfied by (local) data only if it can be matched to a (global) atom in the body of a mapping whose head can be matched to source facts. A match between g and some atom in the body of a mapping is thus an indication that the corresponding data source provides a relevant information for this particular query.

There is an extra constraint that has to be considered to guarantee that g can indeed be logically inferred, as illustrated next. In fact, the bucket of a query atom g includes a view atom v only if an atom in the body of v can be matched with g by a variable mapping such that the variables mapped to the *distinguished* variables of g are also *distinguished* variables in the view defining the mapping.

Let us illustrate this on an example. Consider the LAV mappings of Example 9.4.2, and the global query:

q(x) :- RegisteredTo(s,x), EnrolledInProgram(s,p), MasterProgram(p)

Let us consider the query atom g= RegisteredTo(s,x), in which the variable x is *distinguished*.

We can find two mappings (m2 and m3) in which a body atom can be matched to RegisteredTo(s,x).

First, consider the mapping m3:

m3: S3.CampusFr(S,P,U) ⊆ NonEuropeanStudent(S), Program(P),
                          EnrolledInProgram(S,P), OfferedBy(P,U),
                          FrenchUniversity(U), RegisteredTo(S,U)

The atom RegisteredTo(s,x) matches the atom RegisteredTo(S,U) with the variable mapping $\{S/s, U/x\}$, where U is *distinguished* in the view defining the mapping (it occurs in the head of this LAV mapping).

Therefore, applying the variable mapping $\{S/s, U/x\}$ to the head S3.CampusFr(S,P,U) of the mapping m3 enforces the matching of RegisteredTo(S,U) with the query atom RegisteredTo(s,x), and then:

S3.CampusFr(s,v1,x) $\wedge$ FOL(m3) $\models$ $\exists s$RegisteredTo(s,x)

Thus, S3.CampusFr(s,v1,x) is added in *Bucket(g)*. Note that v1 is simply a fresh variable mapped to the variable P appearing in S3.CampusFr(S,P,U) but not in the variable mapping $\{S/s, U/x\}$.

On the other hand, consider the mapping m2:

m2: S2.Erasmus(S,C,U) $\subseteq$ Student(S), EnrolledInCourse(S,C), PartOf(C,P),
$\qquad\qquad\qquad\qquad\quad$ OfferedBy(P,U), EuropeanUniversity(U),
$\qquad\qquad\qquad\qquad\quad$ EuropeanUniversity(U') RegisteredTo(S,U'), U $\neq$ U'

The match this time is between $g =$ RegisteredTo(s,x) and RegisteredTo(S,U') by the variable mapping $\{S/s, U'/x\}$. The difference with the previous situation is that the variable U' is *existentially* quantified in the view defining the mapping. Applying the variable mapping $\{S/s, U'/x\}$ to the head S2.Erasmus(S,C,U) of the mapping m2 *do not* enforce the matching of RegisteredTo(S,U') in its body with the query atom RegisteredTo(s,x).

More formally:

S2.Erasmus(s,v2,v3) $\wedge$ FOL(m2) $\not\models$ $\exists s$RegisteredTo(s,x).

To see why, consider the LAV mapping m2 and its logical meaning FOL(m2):

FOL(m2): $\forall S \forall C \forall U$ [S2.Erasmus(S,C,U) $\Rightarrow$ $\exists$ P $\exists$ U' (
$\qquad\qquad$ EuropeanStudent(S) $\wedge$ EnrolledInCourse(S,C) $\wedge$
$\qquad\qquad$ PartOf(C,P) $\wedge$ OfferedBy(P,U)
$\qquad\qquad$ $\wedge$ EuropeanUniversity(U) $\wedge$ RegisteredTo(S,U') $\wedge$ U $\neq$ U')]

From the fact that S2.Erasmus(s,v2,v3), it follows that

$\exists s \exists U'$RegisteredTo(s,U').

However, this is a strictly weaker statement than $\exists$ s RegisteredTo(s,x) where x is fixed. We prove this next. Consider an instance I over the domain $\Delta = \{s, v2, v3, v4, v5, x\}$ defined by

$\quad I(\text{S2.Erasmus}) = \{\langle s, v2, v3\rangle\}$ $\quad I(\text{EuropeanStudent}) = \{s\}$
$\quad I(\text{EnrolledInCourse}) = \{\langle s, v2\rangle\}$ $\quad I(\text{PartOf}) = \{\langle v2, v4\rangle\}$
$\quad I(\text{OfferedBy}) = \{\langle v4, v3\rangle\}$ $\quad I(\text{EuropeanUniversity}) = \{v3, v5\}$
$\quad I(\text{RegisteredTo}) = \{\langle s, v5\rangle\}$

By the valuation that instantiates, respectively, the variables S to the constant s, C to the constant v2, U to the constant v3, P to the constant v4, and U' to the constant v5, we see that I satisfies the fact S2.Erasmus(s,v2,v3) and the formula FOL(m2), but that $\exists$ s RegisteredTo(s,x) is not satisfied in I.

As a consequence, S2.Erasmus(s,v2,v3) does not belong to the bucket and

Bucket(RegisteredTo(s,x)) = $\{$S3.CampusFr(s,v1,x)$\}$.

Algorithm 5. The *Bucket* algorithm

Bucket(g, q, M)

Input: An atom $g = G(u_1,...,u_m)$ of the query q and a set of LAV mappings

Output: The set of view atoms from which g can be inferred

(1) $Bucket(g) : \emptyset$

(2)   **for each** LAV mapping $S(\vec{x}) \subseteq q(\vec{x}, \vec{y})$

(3)   **if** there exists in $q(\vec{x}, \vec{y})$ an atom $G(z_1,...,z_m)$ such that

(4) z_i is distinguished for each i such that u_i is distinguished in q;

(5)   **let** ψ the variable mapping $\{z_1/u_1,...., z_m/u_m\}$

(6)   extended by mapping the head variables in $\vec{x}$ not

(7)   appearing in $\{z_1,...,z_m\}$ to new fresh variables;

(8)   **add** $S(\psi(\vec{x}))$ to $Bucket(g)$;

(9)   **return** $Bucket(g)$;

Algorithm 5 constructs the buckets. Proposition 9.4.3 is a logical characterization of the view atoms put in the buckets of the atoms of the global query.

Proposition 9.4.3 *Let $G(u_1,...,u_m)$ be an atom of the global query. Let $\vec{u}$ be the (possibly empty) subset of existential variables in $\{u_1,...,u_m\}$. Let $m: S(\vec{x}) \subseteq q(\vec{x}, \vec{y})$ be a LAV mapping. Then*

$$S(\vec{v}), FOL(m) \models \exists \vec{u} G(u_1,...,u_m)$$

iff there exists a view atom in $Bucket(g)$ that is equal to $S(\vec{v})$ (up to a renaming of the fresh variables).

The proof is tedious and left as an exercise.

In the worst case, the Bucket algorithm applied to each atom of a query has a time complexity in $O(N \times M \times V)$ and produces N buckets containing each at most $M \times V$ view atoms, where N is the size of the query, M is the maximal size of the LAV mappings, and V is the number of LAV mappings.

Returning to the example, we obtain by the Bucket algorithm, the following buckets for the three atoms of the query q.

RegisteredTo(s,x)	EnrolledInProgram(s,p)	MasterProgram(p)
S3.CampusFr(s,v1,x)	S3.CampusFr(s,p,v2)	S1.Catalogue(v3,v4)
		S4.Mundus(p,v5)

Construction of Candidate Rewritings

The *candidate* rewritings of the initial global query are then obtained by combining the view atoms of each bucket. In the worst case, the number of candidate rewritings is in $O((M \times V)^N)$. For instance, in our example, we obtain two *candidate* rewritings for the query q:

```
r1(x) :- S3.CampusFr(s,v1,x), S3.CampusFr(s,p,v2), S1.Catalogue(v3,v4)
r2(x) :- S3.CampusFr(s,v1,x), S3.CampusFr(s,p,v2), S4.Mundus(p,v5)
```

A *candidate* rewriting may not be a valid rewriting of the query. By Proposition 9.4.3, we only know that each candidate rewriting entails each atom of the query *in isolation* (i.e., without taking into account the possible bindings of the existential variables within the query).

It turns out that, in our example, the first candidate rewriting r1 is not a valid rewriting of the query *q*: the body of *q* is not logically entailed by the conjunction of the view atoms in the body of r1.

To see why, we first apply to each view atom in the body of r1 the corresponding LAV mapping to obtain the logical global expression (i.e., built on global relations). This step is called *expanding* r1, and its result, the *expansion* of r1. In our case, the expansion of r1 is the following query expression:

```
Exp_r1(x) :- NonEuropeanStudent(s), Program(v1), EnrolledInProgram(s,v1),
             OfferedBy(v1,x), FrenchUniversity(x), RegisteredTo(s,x),
             Program(p), EnrolledInProgram(s,p), OfferedBy(p,v2),
             FrenchUniversity(v2), RegisteredTo(s,v2),
             FrenchUniversity(v3), Program(v4), OfferedBy(v4,v3),
             OfferedBy(v5,v3), MasterProgram(v5)
```

Note that new existential variables may be introduced by the expansion of some view atoms. For instance, the LAV mapping defining S1.Catalogue(v3,v4) contains the existential variable denoted P′ in the LAV mapping definition. Such variables are renamed with new fresh variables to avoid unnecessary constraints between the variables. In our example, this corresponds to variable v5 in the body of Exp_r1(x).

To check whether a rewriting is correct, it suffices to check with the Conjunctive Query Containment algorithm whether the query Exp_r1(x) is *contained* in the query q(x). For each variable v, let the corresponding constant (i.e., $\psi(v)$), be "v". The canonical database obtained from r1 is given in Figure 9.2.

The evaluation of q(x) over this canonical database yields an empty result because there is no way of assigning the existential variables s and p to constants of the canonical database that satisfies the binding of the existential variable p between the two last atoms of the body of the query.

Expanding the rewriting r2 and checking that it is contained into the query q is left in exercise. This shows that among the two candidate rewritings, only r2 is a valid rewriting:

NonEuropean-Student	Program	EnrolledIn-Program	OfferedBy	French-University	RegisteredTo	Master-Program
"s"	"v1"	("s", "v1")	("v1", "x")	"x"	("s", "x")	"v5"
	"p"	("s", "p")	("p", "v2")	"v2"	("s", "v2")	
	"v4"		("v4", "v3")	"v3"		
			("v5", "v3")			

Figure 9.2. The canonical database resulting from freezing r1.

```
r2(x)  :- S3.CampusFr(s,v1,x),  S3.CampusFr(s,p,v2),S4.Mundus(p,v5)
```

Remark 9.4.4 In spite of the apparent redundancy of the two first atoms, this rewriting cannot be simplified to

```
r2.1(x)  :- S3.CampusFr(s,p,x),  S4.Mundus(p,v5)
```

It is true that r2.1(x) is contained into r2(x). However, the two queries are not equivalent. For some data sets, it may be the case that there is a student s and a university x such that (based on S3.CampusFr), s is registered in x and also enrolled in a Mundus master program offered by another university. The containment would hold under a constraint that would forbid a student to be registered in more than one universities.

One can prove that each rewriting finally obtained does indeed provide answers and that their union constitutes the complete answer.

9.4.2 The Minicon Algorithm

The idea underlying Minicon is to avoid putting in a bucket an atom that will only generate invalid rewritings. As we saw in the discussion of Bucket, the reason for an atom to be useless is that its binding of a variable does not match with the binding of other occurrences of that variable. This explains why a candidate rewriting (like r1) is not valid.

We now illustrate the Minicon algorithm by example. Consider the query q:

```
q(x)  :- U(y,z),  R(x,z),  T(z,y),  R(y',x)
```

and the two LAV mappings:

$$V1(u,v) \subseteq T(w,u), U(v,w), R(v,u)$$
$$V2(u,v,v') \subseteq T(w,u), U(v,w), R(v',w)$$

Minicon proceeds in two steps that correspond to the first two steps of Bucket.

First Step of Minicon: Creation of MCDs

Minicon scans each atom in the query, but instead of creating buckets for them, it builds MCDs (short name for *Minicon Descriptions*). The first iteration of Minicon determines the relevance of the different LAV mappings to rewrite the first query atom U(y,z):

■ The Bucket algorithm would put V1(v1,y) in the bucket of U(y,z) (where v1 is a fresh variable) because the variable mapping $\{v/y, w/z\}$ allows the match between the atom U(v,w) in the expansion of V1(u,v) and the query atom U(y,z).

Minicon does not consider the query atom U(y,z) in isolation. Instead, since the variable w is *existential* in the view defining the mapping, and mapped to the variable z that has several occurrences in the query, it checks whether the variable mapping $\{v/y, w/z\}$ also *covers all* the query atoms involving variable z (i.e., can be extended to also match R(x,z) and T(z,y)). Because variable w is *existential* in the expansion of V1(u,v) (i.e., w does not appear in the head of the mapping), it is the only way to enforce the several occurrences of z in the query to be mapped to by the same variable w. Here, matching the query atom R(x,z) with an atom of the form R(_,w) in the expansion of V1(v1,y) is not possible: There does not exist such an atom in the expansion of V1(v1,y). Therefore, no MCD is created from V1 for covering the query atoms including an occurrence of the variable z.

▪ When considering V2, though Minicon starts from the same variable mapping $\{v/y, w/z\}$ to match U(v,w) in the expansion of V2(u,v,v′) and the query atom U(y,z), the situation is different for checking whether it can be extended to cover the other query atoms R(x,z) and T(z,y) containing occurrences of the variable z. Extending the variable mapping $\{v/y, w/z\}$ to match R(x,z) with the atom R(v′,w) is possible by adding the variable mapping v'/x. Now, extending the variable mapping $\{v/y, w/z, v'/x\}$ to match T(z,y) with the atom T(w,u) is also possible by adding the variable mapping u/y. The resulting variable mapping is $\{v/y, w/z, v'/x, u/y\}$. And, V2(y,y,x) is retained as a rewriting of the corresponding part of the query: an MCD is created for it, in addition to the positions of the atoms in the query it covers:

MCD1 = (V2(y,y,x)), {1,2,3})

The last iteration of building MCDs corresponds to the last query atom: R(y′,x). The LAV mapping V1 has in its expansion the atom R(v,u) that can be matched to it by the variable mapping $\{v/y', u/x)\}$. Since the distinguished variable x in the query is assigned to the distinguished variable (same condition as for adding to a bucket), and since the existential variable y′ of the query atom has a single occurrence in the query, the following MCD is created:

MCD2 = ((V1(x,y′), {4})

In contrast, there is no MCD created for R(y′,x) with the second LAV mapping: In the variable mapping $\{v'/y', w/x)\}$ that allows to match the query atom R(y′,x) with the atom R(v′,w) in the expansion of V2, the distinguished variable x in the query is assigned to the variable w, which is not distinguished in the expansion of of V2. As for adding a view atom in a bucket, an MCD is created for a query atom g *only* if the variables mapped to the distinguished variables of g are also distinguished variables in the view defining the mapping.

Second Step of Minicon: Combination of the MCDs
The second step of Minicon replaces the combination of the buckets by the combination of the MCDs. More precisely, the rewritings are obtained by combining MCDs that cover mutually disjoint subsets of query atoms, while together covering all the atoms of the query.

Because of the way in which the MCDs were constructed, the rewritings obtained that way are guaranteed to be valid. No containment checking is needed, unlike in the Bucket algorithm. In our example, we would therefore obtain as single rewriting of q(x):

---

r(x) :- V2(y,y,x), V1(x,y')

9.4.3 The Inverse Rules Algorithm

This algorithm takes a radically different approach. It transforms the LAV mappings into GAV mappings (called inverse rules) so that the complex operation of query rewriting using LAV mappings can then be replaced by the much simpler operation of query unfolding. A LAV mapping is replaced by several GAV mappings, one for each atom in the body of the rule. The subtlety is to keep bindings between the different occurrences of the same existential variable in the body. This is realized using a simple trick from first-order logic, namely by introducing *Skolem functions*.

Let us explain the Inverse Rules algorithm on the example we used for Minicon. A first important point that distinguishes it from the Bucket and Minicon algorithms is that the Inverse Rules algorithm is independent of the query. It only considers as input the set of LAV mappings:

$$V1(u,v) \subseteq T(w,u), U(v,w), R(v,u)$$
$$V2(u,v,v') \subseteq T(w,u), U(v,w), R(v',w).$$

Consider the first LAV mapping and recall that its logical meaning mapping is the formula:

$$\forall u \forall v [V1(u,v) \Rightarrow \exists w (T(w,u) \wedge U(v,w)) \wedge R(v,u))]$$

Suppose we know that (a,b) belongs to the source relation V1. From the fact V1(a,b), we can infer the fact R(b,a), that is, the tuple (b,a) is in the extension of the global relation R, and thus, for instance, b is an answer for the global query q(x) :- R(x,y).

But we can infer much more. We can also infer that there exists some constant d1 such that T(d1,a) and U(b,d1) are both true. We do not know the exact value of that constant d1, but we know it exists and that, in some way, it depends on the constants a,b. Since this dependency comes from the first rule, we denote this unknown d1 value: f1(a,b).

Creating the Inverse Rules   This motivates the construction of three following GAV mappings for which we give also the FOL translation.

$$IN11 : V1(u,v) \subseteq T(f1(u,v),u) \quad FOL(IN11) : \forall u \forall v [V1(u,v) \Rightarrow T(f1(u,v),u)]$$
$$IN12 : V1(u,v) \subseteq U(v,f1(u,v)) \quad FOL(IN12) : \forall u \forall v [V1(u,v) \Rightarrow U(v,f1(u,v))]$$
$$IN13 : V1(u,v) \subseteq R(v,u) \quad\quad FOL(IN13) : \forall u \forall v [V1(u,v) \Rightarrow R(v,u)]$$

They are called the *inverse rules* of the corresponding LAV mapping.

In the previous rules, the symbol f1 is a Skolem function of arity 2, and f1(u,v) is a Skolem term denoting some constant that depends on the values instantiating the variables u,v. Given two distinct Skolem terms (e.g., f1(1,2) and f1(2,v3)), we cannot tell whether they refer to the same constant or not.

The Inverse Rules algorithm just scans the LAV mappings and creates n GAV mappings for each LAV mapping having n atoms. The result of this algorithm applied to the second LAV mappings in the example is

IN21 : V2(u,v,v′) ⊆ T(f2(u,v,v′),u)
IN22 : V2(u,v,v′) ⊆ U(v,f2(u,v,v′))
IN23 : V2(u,v,v′) ⊆ R(v′,f2(u,v,v′))

Obtaining the Rewritings by Unfolding   The rewritings of any global query is now obtained by unfolding the query atoms using the (Inverse Rules) GAV mappings corresponding to the initial set of LAV mappings. The unfolding operation here is a bit trickier than the unfolding defined in Definition 9.3.3, because of the Skolem terms. In Definition 9.3.3, the unfolding was based on matching each query atom G(x1,...,xm) with an atom (in the right-hand side of a GAV mapping) of the form G(z1,...,zm) by equating each pair (zi, xi) of variables. Proposition 9.3.6 showed that unfolding each atom of the query *in isolation* builds valid rewritings of the query (i.e., conjunctions of view atoms, which logically implies the conjunction of the query atoms). It is not the case anymore when atoms in the right-hand side of GAV mappings contain Skolem terms.

The *unification* of two atoms with functions is more complex than just equating variables, and it may fail. It may require the substitution of some variables with functional terms (in our case, Skolem terms). This may make impossible unifying the other atoms of the query with atoms in the right-hand side of GAV mappings.

Let us illustrate on our example the subtleties of unfolding queries in presence of functional terms. Consider again the same query q:

q(x) :- U(y,z), R(x,z), T(z,y), R(y′, x).

The query atom U(y,z) can be unified with the atom U(v,f1(u,v)) in the right-hand side of the GAV mappings IN12 using a so-called *most general unifier (mgu)*. In this case, the mgu is the substitution:

$\sigma = \{y/v1, v/v1, z/f1(v2,v1), u/v2\}$

where v1 and v2 are new fresh variables introduced in order to avoid name conflict between variables that would generate unnecessary constraints. The substitution σ is a unifier of the two expressions U(y,z) and U(v,f1(u,v)) because the replacement in the two expressions of the occurrences of the variables y, v, z, and u by the corresponding term (variable or Skolem term) in σ results in two identical expressions:

$\sigma(U(y,z)) = \sigma(U(v,f1(u,v)))$

This substitution, which makes the unfolding of the first query atom possible, now constrains the other occurrences in the query of the variables y and z for the unfolding of the other query atoms. After the application of σ to the whole body of the query and the unfolding of the first query atom made possible by σ, we obtain the following (partial) query rewriting:

$$pr1(x) \text{ :- } V1(v2,v1), \; R(x,f1(v2,v1)), \; T(f1(v2,v1),v1), \; R(y',x).$$

The unfolding of the second atom $R(x,f1(v2,v1))$ yields $V1(f1(v2,v1),x)$, and we obtain the (partial) rewriting:

$$pr2(x) \text{ :- } V1(v2,v1), \; V1(f1(v2,v1),x), \; T(f1(v2,v1),v1), \; R(y',x).$$

It is useless to continue unfolding the remaining query atoms of $pr2(x)$. As soon as a given unfolding has produced a view atom with Skolem terms, we can be sure that the evaluation of the query plan under construction will not produce any answer: There is no way to match $V1(f1(v2,v1),x)$ with any fact in the data source which are of the form $V1(a,b)$ where a,b are constants. Since we don't know $f1(v2,v1)$, there is absolutely no reason to believe that it is equal to a.

Using the inverse rule IN23 to unfold $R(x,f1(v2,v1))$ does not help because unifying $R(x,f1(v2,v1))$ and $R(v',f2(u,v,v'))$ fails because of the two different Skolem functions. Thus, the (partial) rewriting issued from unfolding $U(y,z)$ using the inverse rule IN12 is abandoned.

Let us try now to unfold $U(y,z)$ using IN22 made possible by the substitution

$$\sigma' = \{y/v1, \; v/v1, \; z/f2(v2,v1,v3), \; u/v2, \; v'/v3\}$$

We obtain the following (partial) query rewriting:

$$pr'1(x) \text{ :- } V2(v2,v1,v3), \; R(x,f2(v2,v1,v3)), \; T(f2(v2,v1,v3),v1), \; R(y',x)$$

Now, unfolding $R(x,f2(v2,v1,v3))$ using the inverse rule IN23 is possible thanks to the substitution

$$\sigma'' = \{v'/x, v3/x, u/v2, v/v1\}$$

This leads to the (partial) rewriting:

$$pr'2(x) \text{ :- } V2(v2,v1,x), \; V2(v2,v1,x), \; T(f2(v2,v1,x),v1), \; R(y',x)$$

in which one of the first two atoms can be dropped.

Now, we examine the unfolding of the query atom $T(f2(v2,v1,x),v1)$, which requires checking whether $T(f2(v2,v1,x),v1)$ and $T(f2(u,v,v'),u)$ are unifiable. This is the case thanks to the substitution $\{v2/v3, u/v3, v1/v3, v/v3, v'/x\}$, which leads to the (partial) rewriting:

$$pr'3(x) \;:\text{-}\; V2(v2,v1,x),\; V2(v3,v3,x),\; R(y',x)$$

Again, we can remove the first atom that is redundant and obtain the equivalent (partial) rewriting:

$$pr'4(x) \;:\text{-}\; V2(v3,v3,x),\; R(y',x)$$

Finally the unfolding of $R(y',x)$ using IN23 leads to the final rewriting:

$$r1(x) \;:\text{-}\; V2(v3,v3,x),\; V1(x,y')$$

9.4.4 Discussion

The three algorithms have the same (worst-case) complexity and they guarantee to provide the correct answer. Some experiments have shown that in practice Minicon outperforms both Bucket and Inverse Rules. The main advantage of the Inverse Rules algorithm over the Bucket and Minicon algorithms is that the step producing the inverse rules is done independently of the queries. Furthermore, the unfolding step can also be applied to *Datalog* queries (i.e., to *recursive* queries).

The common limitation of the three algorithms is that they do not handle additional knowledge (ontology statements) that can be known about the domain of application. In the next section, we see how to extend both the local-as-views and global-as-views approaches with DL-LITE ontologies (i.e., we consider global schemas that include constraints expressed as DL-LITE axioms).

9.5 ONTOLOGY-BASED MEDIATORS

We first show a negative result: as soon as we add functionality constraints over the global schema, the number of conjunctive rewritings of a query to be considered, may become infinite. This is a severe limitation for extending the LAV or GAV approaches since such constraints are rather natural. So these approaches to data integration fail when we consider the DL-LITE$_\mathcal{F}$ dialect of previous chapters. On the positive side, we show how to extend the GAV and LAV approaches to constraints expressible in DL-LITE$_\mathcal{R}$.

9.5.1 Adding Functionality Constraints

We illustrate with an example the problem raised by taking into account functionality constraints in the global schema. Let us consider a global schema with one unary relation C and two binary relations R and $R1$. In both R and $R1$, we impose that the first attribute is a key. Let us consider two LAV mappings:

> V1: $S(P,N) \subseteq R(P,A), R1(N,A)$
> V2: $V(P) \subseteq C(P)$

and the following query:

> $q(x) :\text{-} R(x,z), R(x_1,z), C(x_1).$

The three previous algorithms (Bucket, Minicon, and Inverse Rules) would return no rewriting at all for q. The proof is left as an exercise. However, we next show that the following rewriting is valid:

> $r_1(x) :\text{-} S(x,v_1), S(x_1,v_1), V(x_1)$

To prove it, we expand $r_1(x)$ and show that the resulting expansion *together with the logical axiom expressing the functionality of R1* logically implies the conjunction of atoms in the body of the query. The expansion of $r_1(x)$ is

> $Exp\_r_1(x) :\text{-} R(x,y_1), R1(v_1,y_1), R(x_1,y'_1), R1(v_1,y'_1), C(x_1)$

Now, if we ignore the functional dependencies, it is not true that $Exp\_r_1 \subseteq q$. But knowing them, the inclusion holds. Indeed, the logical axiom expressing the functionality of $R1$ is

> $\forall y \forall z1 \forall z2 [R1(y,z1) \wedge R1(y,z2) \Rightarrow z1 = z2]$

Therefore, it can be inferred from $R1(v_1,y_1)$ and $R1(v_1,y'_1)$ in the body of $Exp\_r_1(x)$ that $y_1 = y'_1$, and, thus,

> $Exp\_r_1(x) :\text{-} R(x,y_1), R1(v_1,y_1), R(x_1,y_1), R1(v_1,y_1), C(x_1)$

Hence, $Exp\_r_1 \subseteq q$ with ψ mapping x, x_1, z to x, x_1, y_1, respectively. Thus, $r_1(x)$ is a *valid rewriting* of $q(x)$.

It is important to note that to properly check containment, the standard query containment algorithm seen in the previous section would have to be modified in a standard manner to take into account functional dependencies. Intuitively, one would have to proceed pretty much as we did in the example, equating variables as implied by the functional dependencies.

It turns out that the situation is even more subtle. Surprisingly, this rewriting $r_1(x)$ is not the only one. In fact there exists an infinite number of different rewritings for $q(x)$. Let $k \geq 2$. The following query is a *valid rewriting* of $q(x)$:

> $r_k(x) : S(x,v_k), S(x_k,v_k), S(x_k,v_{k-1}), S(x_{k-1},v_{k-1}), \ldots, S(x_2,v_1), S(x_1,v_1), V(x_1)$

The expansion of $r_k(x)$ is

$$
\begin{aligned}
Exp\_r_k(x) :\text{-} \quad & R(x,y_k), & & R1(v_k,y_k), \\
& R(x_k,y'_k), & & R1(v_k,y'_k), \\
& R(x_k,y_{k-1}), & & R1(v_{k-1},y_{k-1}), \\
& R(x_{k-1},y'_{k-1}), & & R1(v_{k-1},y'_{k-1}), \\
& \dots, & & \dots \\
& R(x_2,y_1), & & R1(v_1,y_1), \\
& R(x_1,y'_1), & & R1(v_1,y'_1), & & C(x_1)
\end{aligned}
$$

To show that this expansion is logically contained in q, we exploit the axioms of functionality of both R and $R1$. Since $R1$ is functional, we get: $y_k = y'_k$, and since R is functional, we get: $y'_k = y_{k-1}$. By induction, we obtain $y_k = y'_k = y_{k-1} = y'_{k-1} = \cdots = y_1 = y'_1$, and in particular: $y_k = y'_1$. Thus, $Exp\_r_k \subseteq q(x)$. This implies that $r_k(x)$ is a *valid rewriting* of $q(x)$.

One can also show that for each k, each such rewriting may return answers that are not returned with $k - 1$. Thus, there exists an infinite number of nonredundant conjunctive rewritings. The reader familiar with Datalog will observe that this infinite collection of rewritings can be captured in Datalog by the following *recursive* rewriting:

$$
\begin{aligned}
& r(x) :\text{-} S(x,v),S(x_1,v),V(x_1) \\
& r(x) :\text{-} S(x,v),P(v,u),S(x_1,u),V(x_1) \\
& P(v,u) :\text{-} S(z,v),S(z,u) \\
& P(v,u) :\text{-} S(z,v),S(z,w),P(w,u)
\end{aligned}
$$

The question of building automatically such conjunctive rewritings is out of the scope of this book (see Section 9.7).

9.5.2 Query Rewriting Using Views in DL-LITE$_{\mathcal{R}}$

Querying data through DL-LITE$_{\mathcal{R}}$ ontologies was detailed in Chapter 8. It has been shown how the positive and negative constraints expressed in the ontology are exploited both for data consistency checking and for query answering. In particular, the first step of query answering is the *query reformulation* step, which is performed by the *PerfectRef* algorithm: Using the positive constraints, called the PIs, it computes a set of *reformulations*, which are then evaluated over the data to produce the answer set of the original query. The negative constraints, called the NIs, are used to check data consistency, by translating each (declared or entailed) NI into a Boolean conjunctive query q_{unsat} that must be evaluated over the data.

In this section, we show how to extend both the LAV and GAV approaches to rewrite queries in term of views when the global schema includes some DL-LITE$_{\mathcal{R}}$ Tbox.

Two observations explain how this can be realized:

1. First, one can obtain the answer set of a query $q(\vec{x})$ by computing the union of the answer sets returned by the evaluation over the local data sources of the (GAV or LAV) *relational rewritings* of each *reformulation* of $q(\vec{x})$ as computed by PerfectRef($q(\vec{x}), PI$).

2. The rewritings that are obtained may be inconsistent with the negative constraints NI declared or inferred in the Tbox. Therefore, the consistency of each rewriting $r(\vec{x})$ has to be checked. This can be done by checking containment between the Boolean query $\exists \vec{x}\, Exp\_r(\vec{x})$ (where $Exp\_r(\vec{x})$ is the expansion of $r(\vec{x})$) and each of the Boolean queries q_{unsat} obtained from the NIs.

These two observations follow from the completeness of the *PerfectRef* and *Consistent* algorithms for DL-LITE$_\mathcal{R}$ presented in Chapter 8, and that of the rewriting algorithms of Sections 9.3 and 9.4; namely *Unfolding* for GAV and *Minicon*, *Bucket*, or *Inverse Rules* for LAV.

The argument may be somewhat too abstract for some readers. We next illustrate these two points with examples. We use the global schema considered in Example 9.4.2, enriched with the DL-LITE$_\mathcal{R}$ Tbox of Figure 9.3. Note in particular that we add the subclass *College* of the class *University*, the subproperty *EnrolledInCollege* of the property *RegisteredTo*, for which the domain is declared as being the class *MasterStudent*. In addition, we add the property *EnrolledInMasterProgram* that we declare as a subproperty of the property *EnrolledInProgram*. Finally, we declare a mandatory property for the class *College*: any college must have students enrolled in it.

GAV and DL-LITE$_\mathcal{R}$

We revisit Example 9.3.2 by adding the data source S5 giving the list of French so-called *Grandes Ecoles*. Its local schema is made of the local relation: S5.GrandeEcole(nomEcole). According to this new source and also to the enriched global schema of Figure 9.3, we add the following GAV mappings to the ones already considered in Example 9.3.2:

    College(U) ⊇ S5.GrandeEcole(U)
    EuropeanStudent(N) ⊇ S2.Erasmus(N,C,U)
    NonEuropeanStudent(N) ⊇ S3.CampusFr(N,P,U)

Consider again the global query looking for universities with registered master students:

    q(x) :- RegisteredTo(s,x), MasterStudent(s)

It is left as an exercise to show that the application of the *PerfectRef(q(x), PI)* algorithm returns, in addition to q(x) itself, the reformulation:

    q1(x) :- College(x)

By unfolding q(x), we obtain the same two rewritings as in Example 9.3.2:

DL Notation | **FOL Notation**

PIs:

DL Notation	FOL Notation
$MasterStudent \sqsubseteq Student$	$MasterStudent(X) \Rightarrow Student(X)$
$EuropeanStudent \sqsubseteq Student$	$EuropeanStudent(X) \Rightarrow Student(X)$
$NonEuropeanStudent \sqsubseteq Student$	$NonEuropeanStudent(X) \Rightarrow Student(X)$
$College \sqsubseteq University$	$College(X) \Rightarrow University(X)$
$FrenchUniversity \sqsubseteq University$	$FrenchUniversity(X) \Rightarrow University(X)$
$EuropeanUniversity \sqsubseteq University$	$EuropeanUniversity(X) \Rightarrow University(X)$
$NonEuropeanUniversity \sqsubseteq University$	$NonEuropeanUniversity(X) \Rightarrow University(X)$
$\exists EnrolledInCollege \sqsubseteq MasterStudent$	$EnrolledInCollege(X,Y) \Rightarrow MasterStudent(X)$
$College \sqsubseteq \exists EnrolledInCollege^-$	$College(X) \Rightarrow \exists Y EnrolledInCollege(Y,X)$
$EnrolledInCollege \sqsubseteq RegisteredTo$	$EnrolledInCollege(X,Y) \Rightarrow RegisteredTo(X,Y)$
$MasterStudent \sqsubseteq \exists EnrolledInMasterProgram$	$MasterStudent(X) \Rightarrow \exists Y EnrolledInMasterProgram(X,Y)$
$\exists EnrolledInMasterProgram^- \sqsubseteq MasterProgram$	$EnrolledInMasterProgram(X,Y) \Rightarrow MasterProgram(Y)$
$EnrolledInMasterProgram \sqsubseteq EnrolledInProgram$	$EnrolledInMasterProgram(X,Y) \Rightarrow EnrolledInProgram(X,Y)$

NIs:

DL Notation	FOL Notation
$NonEuropeanStudent \sqsubseteq \neg EuropeanStudent$	$NonEuropeanStudent(X) \Rightarrow \neg EuropeanStudent(X)$
$NonEuropeanUniversity \sqsubseteq \neg EuropeanUniversity$	$NonEuropeanUniversity(X) \Rightarrow \neg EuropeanUniversity(X)$
$NonEuropeanUniversity \sqsubseteq \neg FrenchUniversity$	$NonEuropeanUniversity(X) \Rightarrow \neg FrenchUniversity(X)$

Figure 9.3. A DL-LITE$_\mathcal{R}$ Tbox enriching the global schema of Example 9.4.2.

```
r1(x) :- S3.CampusFr(s,v1,x), S2.Erasmus(s,v2,v3), S4.Mundus(v4,v2)
r2(x) :- S3.CampusFr(s,v6,x), S4.Mundus(v6,v8)
```

By unfolding the reformulation q1(x), we get the additional rewriting:

```
r3(x) :- S5.GrandeEcole(x)
```

It is important to note that even if we had the GAV mapping

$$\text{College}(U) \supseteq \text{S5.GrandeEcole}(U)$$

the rewriting r3(x) would not have been obtained without reformulated first the initial query q(x) into q1(x).

Now, in contrast with the standard GAV approach, we have to check the consistency of each of these rewritings. To do so:

- We first compute the closure of the NI and we translate them into Boolean queries q_{unsat} (as explained in detail in Section 8.4). This is independent of the rewritings and can be performed at compile time given the Tbox. From the Tbox in Figure 9.3, we obtain only three Boolean queries q_{unsat}:

$$q_{unsat}^1 :\text{- NonEuropeanStudent}(x), \text{EuropeanStudent}(x)$$
$$q_{unsat}^2 :\text{- NonEuropeanUniversity}(x), \text{EuropeanUniversity}(x)$$
$$q_{unsat}^3 :\text{- NonEuropeanUniversity}(x), \text{FrenchUniversity}(x)$$

- At query time, we check the consistency of each rewriting by applying the *Consistent* algorithm to the canonical instance obtained by expanding each rewriting and freezing its variables (as explained in detail in Section 8.4).

We illustrate the consistency check by checking the consistency of the rewriting r1(x). First, its expansion replaces each of its local atoms $S(\vec{z})$ with the conjunction of global atoms of the form $G(\vec{z})$ that can be produced by a GAV mapping $G(\vec{x}) \supseteq S(\vec{x})$, if such GAV mappings exist. For expanding r1(x), we apply the following GAV mappings:

$$\text{NonEuropeanStudent}(N) \supseteq \text{S3.CampusFr}(N,P,U)$$
$$\text{University}(U) \supseteq \text{S3.CampusFr}(N,P,U)$$
$$\text{RegisteredTo}(N,U) \supseteq \text{S3.CampusFr}(N,P,U)$$
$$\text{EuropeanStudent}(N) \supseteq \text{S2.Erasmus}(N,C,U)$$
$$\text{University}(U) \supseteq \text{S2.Erasmus}(N,C,U)$$
$$\text{MasterProgram}(T) \supseteq \text{S4.Mundus}(T,C)$$
$$\text{MasterCourse}(C) \supseteq \text{S4.Mundus}(T,C)$$

As a result, we obtain the following expansion for r1(x):

```
Exp_r1(x) :- NonEuropeanStudent(s), University(x), RegisteredTo(s,x),
             EuropeanStudent(s), University(x), MasterProgram(v4),
             MasterCourse(v2)
```

We then apply the *Consistent* algorithm. For this, we evaluate q^1_{unsat}, q^2_{unsat} and q^3_{unsat} over the body of Exp_r1(x) seen as a relational database (i.e., we freeze its atoms to obtain a canonical instance). Query q^1_{unsat} returns *true*, so an inconsistency has been detected and the rewriting r1(x) is rejected.

LAV and DL-LITE$_\mathcal{R}$

We revisit Example 9.4.2 by adding the same data source S5 as in Section 9.5.2. The GAV mapping is also a LAV mapping: S5.GrandeEcole(U) ⊆ College(U).

Consider again the global query considered in Section 9.4.1:

```
q(x) :- RegisteredTo(s,x), EnrolledInProgram(s,p), MasterProgram(p)
```

It is left as an exercise to show that the application of the *PerfectRef(q(x), PI)* algorithm returns, in addition to q(x) itself, the following reformulation:

```
q1(x) :- College(x)
```

By applying the Minicon algorithm[1] to the initial query q(x), we obtain the following rewriting (as shown in Section 9.4.1):

```
r2(x) :- S3.CampusFr(s,v1,x), S3.CampusFr(s,p,v2),S4.Mundus(p,v5)
```

By applying the Minicon algorithm to the reformulation q1(x) of the initial query, we obtain the additional rewriting:

```
r3(x) :- S5.GrandeEcole(x)
```

---

[1] The same holds for the Bucket or Inverse Rules algorithm.

As for the extended GAV approach, the consistency of LAV rewritings is not guaranteed because of the NIs in the Tbox. We follow the same approach: At compile time, the closure of the NIs is computed and each (declared or inferred) NI is compiled into a Boolean query q_{unsat}. At query time, each of these q_{unsat} queries is evaluated over the canonical instance corresponding to each rewriting.

9.6 PEER-TO-PEER DATA MANAGEMENT SYSTEMS

In contrast with the centralized mediator model, a peer-to-peer data management system (PDMS for short) implements a decentralized view of data integration, in which data sources collaborate without any central authority. In a PDMS, each collaborating data source can also play the role of a mediator, so it is at the same time a data server and a client for other data sources. Thus, each participant to the system is a *peer*, and there are mappings relating data from the different peers. A PDMS architecture is therefore very flexible in the sense that there is no need for a global schema defining in advance a set of terms to which each data source needs to adhere. Over time, data sources can join or leave the PDMS just by adding or removing mappings between them. PDMS are inspired by P2P file-sharing systems but they enable answering fine-grained queries. As in the mediator model, answering queries is performed by reformulating queries based on the mappings, but in a decentralized manner.

Each peer in a PDMS has a peer schema composed of peer relations and peer mappings that relate its schema to the schemas of other peers. To avoid confusing relations from different peers, we assume that each relation of peer p is of the form $r@p$ for some local relation name r. A query to a PDMS is posed using the peer schema of one of the peers. A query is asked to a particular peer, as a query over his particular schema. It is reformulated using the peer mappings into a set of queries that may refer to other peer relations. This captures the intuition that we want to use the information available in the entire P2P system to answer the query.

For designing the mappings, the distinction made in the mediator model between local and global relations does not make sense anymore, since each peer relation may play the role at different times both of a local relation and of a global relation. Therefore, the notions of GAV and LAV mappings are relaxed to the more appropriate symmetric notion of GLAV mappings.

Definition 9.6.1 (GLAV mapping) *Let S@i and S@j be the peer schemas of two peers i and j. A GLAV mapping between these two peers is an inclusion axiom of the form: $q_i(\vec{x}) \subseteq q_j(\vec{x})$, where $q_i(\vec{x})$ and $q_j(\vec{x})$ are conjunctive queries over the peer schema S@i, S@j, respectively.*

Let $q_i(\vec{x}, \vec{y}_i)$ and $q_j(\vec{x}, \vec{y}_j)$ be the bodies of $q_i(\vec{x})$ and $q_j(\vec{x})$, respectively. The semantics of the GLAV mapping $q_i(\vec{x}) \subseteq q_j(\vec{x})$ is: $\forall \vec{x}[\exists \vec{y}_i \, q_i(\vec{x}, \vec{y}_i) \Rightarrow \exists \vec{y}_j \, q_j(\vec{x}, \vec{y}_j)]$.

In database terms, a GLAV mapping $q_i(\vec{x}) \subseteq q_j(\vec{x})$ expresses the answers obtained by asking $q_i(\vec{x})$ at peer i should also be considered as answers to $q_j(\vec{x})$ asked at peer j. Note that with this semantics, each local query is assumed to be *incompletely* answered with local data since external data may bring in new information to it. As already mentioned, such an open-world assumption is fully appropriate for Web data.

We next show one negative and one positive result for PDMSs. In Section 9.6.1, we show that in general, answering queries with GLAV mappings is undecidable, so without further restriction, answering queries in a PDMS is undecidable. In Section 9.6.2, we show that if we restrict the peer mappings to be DL-LITE$_\mathcal{R}$ inclusion axioms, a decentralized version of the algorithm for DL-LITE$_\mathcal{R}$ can be used to answer queries in DL-LITE$_\mathcal{R}$ PDMSs.

9.6.1 Answering Queries Using GLAV Mappings Is Undecidable

We show that the *Dependency Implication Problem* (more precisely, the problem of the implication of an inclusion dependency from a set of inclusion and functional dependencies) can be reduced to the *GLAV Query Answering Problem* (i.e., the problem of answering queries in presence of GLAV mappings). Since the *Dependency Implication Problem* is known to be undecidable, this shows that the *GLAV Query Answering Problem* is also undecidable.

The reduction technique is standard for proving undecidability results. We first recall how it works and also recall the *Dependency Implication Problem*. We believe that these notions are important to know beyond the scope of this book. Finally, we use a reduction to show the undecidability of answering queries using GLAV mappings.

Reduction from a Decision Problem B to a Decision Problem B$'$

Let B be a Boolean function over a set X. The *decision problem B* is *decidable* if there exists an algorithm (in any computation model equivalent to Turing machines) that terminates on any input $x \in B$ and returns "true" *if and only if* $B(x)$ is true.

Let B, B' be two decision problems. A *reduction* from B to B' is an algorithm f computing a function (also denoted f) from X to X' such that $B(x)$ is true $\Leftrightarrow B'(f(x))$ is true.

It is immediate to see that if there is a reduction f from B to B':

- If B' is decidable, then B is also decidable. Suppose B' is decidable. Let $f_{B'}$ be an algorithm that, given some $x' \in X'$, decides whether $B'(x')$ holds. Then for each x, $B(x)$ is true if $f_{B'}(f(x))$ is true. This provides an algorithm for deciding for any x if $B(x)$ is true.
- (The contrapositive) If B is undecidable, then B' is also undecidable.

The Dependency Implication Problem

We recall the class of dependencies that are used. Let R be a relation of arity n. Then:

Functional dependencies: A *functional dependency* over R is an expression $R : i_1, ..., i_m \to j$, where $1 \leq i_1, ..., i_m, j \leq n$, for $n = arity(R)$. An instance I over R satisfies $R : i_1, ..., i_m \to j$ if for each tuples $\langle a_1, ..., a_n \rangle$, $\langle b_1, ..., b_n \rangle$ in I,

if for each $k \in [1...m], a_{i_k} = b_{i_k}$, then $a_j = b_j$.

Inclusion dependencies: An *inclusion dependency* over R_1, R_2 is an expression $R_1 : i_1...i_m \subseteq R_2 : j_1...j_m$, where the i_k are distinct, the j_k are distinct, $1 \leq i_1...i_m \leq arity(R_1)$, $1 \leq j_1, ..., j_m \leq arity(R_2)$. An instance I over $\{R_1, R_2\}$ satisfies $R_1 :$

$i_1...i_m \subseteq R_2 : j_1...j_m$ if for each tuple $\langle a_1,...,a_n \rangle$ in $I(R_1)$, there exists a tuple $\langle b_1,...,b_{n'} \rangle$ in $I(R_2)$ such that for each k, $1 \leq k \leq m$, $a_{i_k} = b_{j_k}$.

We will use the following known result:

Theorem 9.6.2 (undecidability of the *Dependency Implication Problem*) Let $\mathbf{R} = \{R_1,...,R_n\}$ be a relational schema. Given a set Σ of functional and inclusion dependencies and an inclusion dependency σ over relations in $\mathbf{R}$, one cannot decide whether $\Sigma \models \sigma$ (i.e., whether each instance over $\mathbf{R}$ satisfying Σ also satisfies σ).

The problem is undecidable when Σ contains both functional and inclusion dependencies. Note that the implication problem is decidable for functional dependencies alone, and for inclusion dependencies alone. Undecidability arises when they are considered together.

Undecidability of the GLAV Query Answering Problem

The *GLAV Query Answering Problem* is to decide, given a PDMS $\mathcal{N}$ defined using a set of GLAV mappings and a query asked at one of the peers, whether some particular tuple is in its answer.

Let us define a reduction from the *Dependency Implication Problem* to the *GLAV Query Answering Problem*. If we show that such a reduction exists, since the *Dependency Implication Problem* is undecidable, this will show that the *GLAV Query Answering Problem* is undecidable.

Surprisingly, we can show the reduction for a PDMS with a single peer. To do that, we will use some GLAV mapping of the form $q@P \supseteq q'@P$, where both sides of the mapping involve the same peer. Note that the undecidability still holds if such "self" mappings are forbidden. Indeed, we can simulate such a mapping by using "clones" of relations. For instance, suppose that we want to enforce the mapping $R@P(x_1,...,x_n) \supseteq R'@P(y_1,...,y_n)$. Then we can use a dummy site $\widehat{P}$ and a copy $\widehat{R@P}$ of $R@P$ with the mappings:

$$R@P(x_1,...,x_n) \supseteq \widehat{R@P}(x_1,...,x_n)$$
$$\widehat{R@P}(x_1,...,x_n) \supseteq R@P(x_1,...,x_n)$$
$$\widehat{R@P}(x_1,...,x_n) \supseteq R'@P(y_1,...,y_n)$$

So, in the rest of this proof, we consider a single peer, say P, with possibly self mappings. To simplify a relation $R@P$ is simply denoted R.

Let (Σ,σ) be an instance over $\{R_1,...,R_n\}$ of the *Dependency Implication Problem* with Σ a finite set of functional and inclusion dependencies, and σ an inclusion dependency. We build a PDMS $\mathcal{N}$ defined as follows:

- For each relation R_i, the peer P has a relation R_i.
- For each inclusion dependency $R_1 : i_1...i_m \subseteq R_2 : j_1...j_m$ in Σ, we add the GLAV mapping $q_1 \subseteq q_2$, where

$$q_1(x_1,...,x_m) :- R_1(\vec{u})$$
$$q_2(x_1,...,x_m) :- R_2(\vec{v})$$

where $\vec{u}$ has x_k in position i_k for each k and some existential variable x_j^i in each other position j; and similarly for $\vec{v}$ and j_k.

■ For each functional dependency $R_i : i_1...i_m \rightarrow j$ in Σ, we add the GLAV mapping $q \subseteq q'$ where q, q' are defined by

$$q(x_{i_1},...,x_{i_k},x_j,x'_j) \quad :- \quad R_i(x_1,...,x_k), R_i(x'_1,...,x'_k), x_{i_1} = x'_{i_1},...,x_{i_k} = x'_{i_k}$$
$$q'(x_{i_1},...,x_{i_k},x_j,x'_j) \quad :- \quad R_i(x_1,...,x_k), R_i(x'_1,...,x'_k), x_{i_1} = x'_{i_1},...,x_{i_k} = x'_{i_k}, \mathbf{x_j} = \mathbf{x'_j}$$

for some distinct sets $x_1,...,x_k$ and $x'_1,...,x'_k$ of variables.

It is easy to see that the GLAV mappings force each R_i to satisfy the functional dependencies of R_i, and each R_i, R_j to satisfy the inclusion dependencies between R_i and R_j.

Let us assume that $\sigma = R_i : i_1 \subseteq R_j : j_1$ for some R_i of arity n. (This is without loss of generality since the implication is already undecidable when σ is unary).

Let $Ext(R_i)$ be the set of tuples t of arity n with values in $[1...n]$ such that

■ $t[i_1] = 1$, for every tuple t in $Ext(R_i)$,
■ each tuple t in $Ext(R_i)$ represents an equality pattern between values in tuples of size n.

For instance if $n = 3$ and $i_1 = 2$, $Ext(R_i) = \{\langle 1,1,1 \rangle, \langle 1,1,2 \rangle, \langle 2,1,1 \rangle, \langle 2,1,2 \rangle, \langle 2,1,3 \rangle\}$.

We construct an instance $(\mathcal{N}, Ext(R_i), q)$ of the *GLAV Query Answering Problem* where q is the query defined by $q(x) :- R_j(y_1,...,x,...y_k)$ where the distinguished variable x is in position j_1, and the existential variables y_i are pairwise distinct.

We show that $\Sigma \models \sigma$ iff 1 is an answer to q in the PDMS $\mathcal{N}$ in which the only data is $Ext(R_i)$.

$(\Rightarrow)$ Suppose that $\Sigma \models \sigma$. Let I be a model of $Ext(R_i)$ satisfying the GLAV mappings of $\mathcal{N}$. By construction of those GLAV mappings, I is a model of Σ. Because $\Sigma \models \sigma$, I is a model of σ, and thus for each tuple $\langle a_1,...,a_n \rangle$ in $I(R_i)$, there exists a tuple $\langle b_1,...,b_k \rangle$ in $I(R_j)$ such that $a_{i_1} = 1 = b_{j_1}$. Therefore, $I \models \exists y_1,...,y_k R_j(y_1,...,1,...,y_k)$ (i.e., $I \models q(1)$). Thus, 1 is an answer to q given the GLAV mapping of $\mathcal{N}$ and the extension $Ext(R_i)$.

$(\Leftarrow)$ Conversely, suppose that 1 is an answer to q given the GLAV mapping of $\mathcal{N}$ and the extension $Ext(R_i)$. Note that 1 is also an answer to q if the extension of R_i is reduced to any tuple of the original $Ext(R_i)$. Suppose that $\Sigma \not\models \sigma$: There exists an interpretation I that satisfies Σ in which σ is not satisfied. This means that there exists a tuple $\langle e_1,...,e,...e_n \rangle$ (where e is in position i_1) in $I(R_i)$ such that there does not exists a tuple in $I(R_j)$ with the value e in position j_1. Let t be the tuple of $Ext(R_i)$, which corresponds to the equality pattern between values of $\langle e_1,...,e,...e_n \rangle$. By extending I to interpret each value of t by the element e_i at the same position in $\langle e_1,...,e,...e_n \rangle$, we obtain a new interpretation I' that satisfies Σ and thus each GLAV mapping of $\mathcal{N}$, and $R_i(t)$. Since 1 is an answer to q given the GLAV mapping of $\mathcal{N}$ and $R_i(t)$, $I' \models q(1)$ (i.e., $I'(1) \in I'(R_j[j_1])$). Since $I'(1) = e$ and $I'(R_j) = I(R_j)$, it means that there exists a tuple in $I(R_j)$ with the value e in position j_1, which contradicts our assumption that σ is not satisfied in I. Hence, $\Sigma \models \sigma$.

9.6.2 Decentralized DL-LITE$_\mathcal{R}$

If we restrict the GLAV mappings in a PDMS to be inclusion statements that are expressible in DL-LITE$_\mathcal{R}$, we get what we will call a DL-LITE$_\mathcal{R}$ PDMS. The decidability of query answering over a DL-LITE$_\mathcal{R}$ PDMS results from the algorithmic machinery described in the previous chapter for answering queries over DL-LITE$_\mathcal{R}$ knowledge bases. Given a query posed to a given peer, the application of the *PerfectRef* algorithm to the set of all the GLAV mappings in the PDMS provides a set of reformulations. The union of the answer sets obtained by evaluating each reformulation provides the answer set of the initial query. Note that a reformulation is of the form:

$$R_1@i_1(\vec{z_1}),\ldots,R_k@i_k(\vec{z_k})$$

where the different conjuncts $R_j@i_j(\vec{z_j})$ may refer to relations of different peer schemas. Therefore, the evaluation of each reformulation may require the interrogation of different peers and the combination of the answers returned by each such sub-queries.

This provides a centralized algorithm for computing the reformulations of answering queries over a *decentralized* DL-LITE$_\mathcal{R}$ knowledge base. We next present a *decentralized* algorithm that computes exactly the same thing, that is, we present a decentralized version of the *PerfectRef* algorithm seen in Chapter 8 in order to deploy effectively DL-LITE$_\mathcal{R}$ PDMSs that avoids having to centralize all the GLAV mappings.

We denote *PerfectRef^i(q)* the reformulation algorithm running on the peer P_i applied to a query q (asked to the peer P_i). The main procedure is the decentralized reformulation of each atom of the query using the positive inclusion statements that are distributed over the whole PDMS. Let us denote *AtomRef^i(g)* the reformulation algorithm running on the peer P_i to reformulate the atom g (built on a relation of the schema of the peer P_i).

Within each peer P_i we distinguish the *local* positive inclusion axioms of the form $C_i \subseteq D_i$ where C_i and D_i are built over relations in the schema of the peer P_i, from the *mappings* which are positive inclusion mappings of the form $C_j \subseteq D_i$ or $D_i \subseteq C_j$ where C_j denotes a relation of another peer P_j (while D_i refers to a relation in the schema of the peer P_i).

Let us denote *LocalRef(g,PI$_i$)* the result of the reformulation of the atom g using the set PI_i of local positive inclusion atoms of the peer P_i. We refer to the previous chapter (Definition 8.4.7, Section 8.4) for the computation of *LocalRef(g,PI$_i$)* by backward application of the local PIs.

We just recall here that $gr(g,I)$ denotes the reformulation of the atom g using the positive inclusion axiom I. We also recall that the atoms g that can be found as conjunct of a query q over a DL-LITE$_\mathcal{R}$ PDMS are of the following forms:

- $A@i(x)$ where $A@i$ is a unary relation in the schema of a peer P_i and x is an (existential or qualified) variable
- $P@i(x,\_)$, $P@i(\_,x)$ or $P@i(x,y)$ where $P@i$ is a binary relation in the schema of a peer P_i, and $\_$ denotes an unbounded existential variable of the query, while

x and y denote qualified variables or existential variables which are bounded in the query.

Running the algorithm $AtomRef^i$ on the peer P_i for reformulating the atom g consists first in computing the set $LocalRef(g, PI_i)$ of local reformulations of g, and then, for each mapping m with a peer P_j applicable to a local reformulation g', in triggering the application of $AtomRef^j(gr(g', m))$ on P_j (by sending a message to P_j). Other peers P_k may be solicited in turn to run locally $AtomRef^k$.

A loop may occur if a request of reformulation of an atom g initiated by a given peer P generates a branch of requests reaching a peer P', which in turn requests P to reformulate g. Such loops can be easily handled by transmitting with every request the *history* of the current reasoning branch. More precisely, an history *hist* is a sequence $[(g_k, P_k), \ldots, (g_1, P_1)]$ of pairs (g_i, P_i), where g_i is an atom of a peer P_i such that for each $i \in [1 \ldots k-1]$, g_{i+1} is a reformulation of g_i using a mapping between P_i and P_{i+1}.

This is summarized in Algorithm 6, which is the atom reformulation algorithm with history running on Peer i.

Algorithm 6. The *decentralized* algorithm with history for reformulating atoms

$AtomRefHist^i(g, hist)$

Input: An atom g in the vocabulary of the peer P_i, an history *hist*
Output: The set of its reformulations in the PDMS: R
(1) $R \leftarrow \emptyset$
(2)   **if** $(g, P_i) \in hist$ **return** R
(3)   **else**
(4)   Let PI_i be the local PIs of the peer P_i
(5)   Let M_i be the mappings between the peer P_i and other peers
(6)   **for each** $g' \in LocalRef(g, PI_i)$
(7)   **for each** mapping $m \in M_i$ between P_i and a peer P_j applicable to g'
(8) $R \leftarrow R \cup AtomRefHist^j(gr(g', m)), (g, P_i)|hist)$

Algorithm 7 is the atom reformulation algorithm (denoted $AtomRef^i$) running on peer P_i, which just calls $AtomRefHist^i$ with an empty history.

Algorithm 7. The *decentralized* algorithm for reformulating atoms

$AtomRef^i(g)$

Input: An atom g in the vocabulary of the peer P_i
Output: The set of its reformulations in the PDMS
(1) $AtomRefHist^i(g, \emptyset)$

The decentralized version of the *PerfectRef* algorithm that computes all the reformulations of a conjunctive query q is provided in Algorithm 8. With the centralized version the main difference is that the simplification of the produced reformulations (which is required for making some PIs applicable) are delayed after (decentralized) computation of the reformulations of all the atoms in the query.

We recall here the notation used for denoting the simplification of some atoms within a query under reformulation, which were introduced in the previous chapter when describing the *PerfectRef* algorithm:

- The notation $q[g/gr(g,I)]$ denotes the replacement of the atom g in the body of the query q with the result $gr(g,I)$ of the backward application of the PI I to the atom g.
- The operator $reduce(q,g,g')$ denotes the simplification of the body of q obtained by replacing the conjunction of its two atoms g and g' with their *most general unifier* (if g and g' can be unified),
- The operator τ replaces in the body of a query all the possibly new *unbounded* existential variables with the anonymous variable denoted $\_$.'

For each atom in the query, it computes first (in the decentralized manner explained previously) the set of all of its reformulations, and then a first set of reformulations of the original query by building all the conjunctions between the atomic reformulations (denoted $\oplus_{i=1}^n AtomRef^i(g_i)$ at Line 5). These reformulations are then possibly simplified by unifying some of their atoms (Lines 8 to 11), and the reformulation process is iterated on these newly produced reformulations until no simplification is possible (general loop starting on Line 4).

Algorithm 8. The decentralized *PerfectRef* algorithm running on the peer P_i

$PerfectRef^i(q)$

Input: a conjunctive query q over the schema of the peer P_i

Output: a set of reformulations of the query using the union of PIs and mappings in the PDMS

(1) $PR := \{q\}$
(2) $PR' := PR$
(3)   **while** $PR' \neq \emptyset$
(4)   (a) **foreach** $q' = g_1 \wedge g_2 \wedge \cdots \wedge g_n \in PR'$
(5) $PR'' := \oplus_{i=1}^n AtomRef^i(g_i)$
(6) $PR' := \emptyset$
(7)   (b) **foreach** $q'' \in PR''$
(8)   **foreach** $g_1', g_2' \in q''$
(9)   **if** g_1' and g_2' unify
(10) $PR' := PR' \cup \{\tau(reduce(q'',g_1',g_2'))\}$
(11) $PR := PR \cup PR' \cup PR''$
(12)   **return** PR

One can prove that the decentralized algorithm computes the same set of facts as the centralized one, and thus is correct. The proof results (1) from the observation that the centralized version of *PerfectRef* (in which $AtomRef^i(g_i)$ is computed by iterating the one-step application of PIs on each atom g_i of the query) produces the same results than the original *PerfectRef*, and (2) from the completeness of $AtomRef^i(g_i)$ ensuring the decentralized computation of all the reformulations of g_i.

9.7 FURTHER READING

The Bucket and Minicon algorithms can be extended ([113, 137]) to handle (union of) conjunctives queries with *interpreted predicates*. When a query q includes interpreted predicates, finding all answers to q given the LAV mappings is co-NP hard in the size of the data. This complexity result shows that answering such queries cannot be fully realized with a finite set of conjunctive rewriting (unlike what we showed here in absence of interpreted predicates). The Inverse Rule algorithm does not handle interpreted predicates but is able to build *recursive* query plans for data integration [59].

A survey on answering queries using views can be found in [87], and a survey on query containment for data integration systems in [124].

More material can be found on PDMS in [86, 88].

Distributed reasoning in a peer-to-peer setting has been investigated in [14] as a basis for querying distributed data through distributed ontologies [1, 73]. The subtle point that we have not treated in this chapter concerns consistency checking. In contrast with the centralized case, the global consistency of the PDMS cannot be checked at query time since the queried peer does not know all the peers in the PDMS. However, it can get the identifiers of the peers involved in a reformulation of the query. Then the (local) consistency of the union of the corresponding knowledge bases can be checked in a decentralized manner. The important point is that it can be shown that this local consistency is sufficient to guarantee that the answers obtained by evaluating the reformulations (computed by the decentralized algorithm that we have described) are *well founded*.

The undecidability of the *Dependency Implication Problem* is shown in [42] even if σ is a unary inclusion dependency. More on this topic may be found in [9]).

9.8 EXERCISES

Exercise 9.8.1 *By applying the query containment algorithm (see Algorithm 4), determine which query is contained in which one among the three following queries. Are there equivalent queries? (two queries q and q' are equivalent if q is contained in q' and q' is contained in q.)*

$q1(x)$:- $A(x,y)$, $B(x,y')$, $A(y,z')$

$q2(x)$:- $A(x,y')$, $A(y',z)$, $B(x,x)$

$q3(x)$:- $B(x,y)$, $A(x,y')$, $B(z,z')$, $A(y',u)$

Exercise 9.8.2 *Consider a global schema defined by the following relations:*
emp(E): E is an employee
phone(E,P): E has P as phone number
office(E,O): E has O as office
manager(E,M): M is the manager of E

dept(E,D): D is the department of E

Suppose that the three following data sources are available for providing data:

Source1 provides the phone number and the manager for some employees. It is modeled by the local relation s1(E,P,M).

Source2 provides the office and the department for some employees. It is modeled by the local relation s2(E,O,D).

Source3 provides the phone number of employees of the 'toy' department. It is modeled by the local relation s3(E,P).

1. *Model the content of these sources by GAV mappings.*
2. *Model the content of these sources by LAV mappings.*
3. *Consider the global query asking for Sally's phone number and office:*

$$q(x,y) :- phone('sally', x), office('sally', y)$$

   Compute the reformulation of the query in terms of local relations:
   - *By applying the query unfolding algorithmto the GAV mappings of Question 1.;*
   - *By applying the Bucket algorithm to LAV mappings of Question 2..*
   Which algorithm is easier?
4. *Now Source1 disappears (becomes unavailable) and is replaced by a new source that provides the phone number of their manager for some employees. Do the updates in the GAV and LAV mappings that are required to take into account these changes. What is the approach (GAV or LAV) for which updating the mappings between the global and local relations is easier?*

Exercise 9.8.3 *Consider the three following LAV mappings.*
V1(x) ⊆ cite(x,y), cite(y,x)
V2(x,y) ⊆ sameTopic(x,y)
V3(x,y) ⊆ cite(x,z), cite(z,x), sameTopic(x,z)

1. *Provide the FOL semantics of these LAV mappings.*
2. *Suppose that the global relation cite(x,y) means that the paper x cites the paper y, and that the global relation sameTopic(x,y) means that the two papers x and y have the same topic. Suppose that each LAV mapping models the content of different available data sources. Express with an English sentence which information on papers each data source provides.*
3. *Apply in turn the Bucket, Minicon, and Inverse Rule algorithms to compute the different rewritings of the following query asking for papers that cite and are cited by a paper having the same topic:*

$$q(u) :- cite(u,v), cite(v,u), sameTopic(u,v)$$

10

Putting into Practice: Wrappers and Data Extraction with XSLT

Besides languages to extract information such as XPath or XQuery, languages for *transforming* XML documents have been proposed. One of them, XSLT, is very popular. The goal of this PiP is to expose the reader to this aspect of XML and to languages based on tree-pattern rewriting. A presentation of XSLT is beyond the scope of this book. The reader can read the present PiP to get a feeling on standard tasks that are commonly performed with XSLT programs. Of course, realizing the project that is described requires a reasonable understanding of the language. Such an understanding can be obtained, for instance, from the companion Web site of the book, i.e., at http://webdam.inria.fr/Jorge/. More references on XSLT may be found there.

XSLT is an XML transformation language. Its principles are quite different from that of XQuery, although they may roughly serve the same purpose: accessing and manipulating XML content and producing an XML-formatted output. In practice, XQuery is used to extract pieces of information from XML documents, whereas XSLT is often used to restructure documents, typically for publishing them in different forms, different dialects. We show in the present PiP chapter how XSLT can serve to write simple "wrappers" for XML pages. This is taking us back to data integration. To integrate a number of data sources, the first step is typically to wrap them all into a uniform schema. Since most data source now export XML, the wrapping technique considered here can be used in a wide variety of contexts. We focus in the PiP on HTML pages from the Web, after transforming them into XML.

Any XSLT processor can be used for the exercises of this chapter. Using an XSLT 2.0 processor, however, will make things much easier: features such as grouping or regular expression matching are of great help in writing wrappers. Therefore, we recommend, for instance, the open-source version of SAXON that is available at http://saxon.sourceforge.net/ and on the companion Web site. Applying a stylesheet yin.xsl to a document yang.xml with SAXON is done with the following command line:

```
java -cp saxon8.jar net.sf.saxon.Transform yang.xml yin.xsl
```

10.1 EXTRACTING DATA FROM WEB PAGES

We first focus on the extraction of data from Web pages:

1. Choose a Web site that presents semistructured information about some
   entities such as products, movies, books, or persons. You should choose a
   collection of pages where data follow a fixed template. To simplify your task,
   properties of these entities should (at least partly) be clearly presented within
   the structure of the Web page, as in

   <li> Chez Chen Chinese food, excellent Beijing

   Duck</li>

   rather than simply given in text:

   Chez Chen. Chinese food, excellent Beijing Duck

   Here are a few ideas, but you can also select your favorite Web sites:

   - The Internet Movie Database (IMDb, http://www.imdb.com/)
   - Amazon (http://www.amazon.com/) or any other e-commerce Web site
   - Ethnologue (http://www.ethnologue.com/), a resource on all languages of
     the world
   - The Mathematics Genealogy Project (http://genealogy.math.ndsu.nodak.
     edu/) that gives the scientific adviser of a given researcher in mathematics
     and related fields
   - DBLP (http://www.informatik.uni-trier.de/~ley/db/), or some other
     research publication database
   - The Yellow Pages service, or other kinds of phone directories

   A solution is proposed on the companion Web site. More precisely, we
   provide Web pages, wrappers, and extracted data for the IMDb Web site.
   Depending on your experience in XSLT, you may wish to study them before
   implementing your own wrapper, refer to them as you progress, or consult
   them after finishing the exercises to compare the approaches.

2. Select in the Web site you chose a few pages with the same structure presenting different entities. Save these Web pages on disk. Make sure your browser
   does not try reformatting the Web page: request saving the *Web page only* or
   only the HTML.

3. With rare exceptions, HTML pages from the Web, even when supposedly
   written in XHTML, the XML-ized variant of HTML, are not well-formed
   XML documents and cannot be directly transformed by an XSLT processor.
   We will use the open-source *tidy* utility, available as a command-line tool[1] or
   through a Web interface,[2] to transform HTML Web pages from the wild into
   well-formed XML documents valid against the XHTML DTD.

   To do this cleanly, we need to set up some options, notably to remove the
   document type declaration in the output and to replace all named references
   with numeric references. This is necessary so that the XSLT processor will

---

[1] http://tidy.sourceforge.net/.
[2] http://infohound.net/tidy/.

not need to perform complex tasks such as downloading and analyzing the XHTML DTD. If you use the command line, the syntax is

```
tidy -q -asxhtml --doctype omit
   --numeric-entities yes file.html > file.xhtml
```

If you use the Web interface, be sure to set the same options. Do this on all the Web pages you saved. Do not be rebuked by the (usually high) number of warnings!

4. The documents are now ready to be processed. Before doing something too elaborate, write a minimalistic XSLT stylesheet that for instance outputs the title (that can be retrieved with /html/head/title) of the XHTML documents you want to process. Remember that XHTML elements live in the XHTML namespace http://www.w3.org/1999/xhtml. You should therefore either declare an XHTML namespace associated with some prefix and use this prefix before every element name in XPath expressions, or (only in XSLT 2.0) use the xpath-default-namespace attribute of the **< xsl:stylesheet >** element to specify the default namespace used in XPath expressions. Test the stylesheet.

5. You should now decide what information to extract from the Web pages. Do not be overly ambitious, start with simple things (e.g., for movies, title, and name of the director). You can do this in an iterative manner (extracting one piece of information at a time, testing it, and then adding another one). Design a DTD for the XML document that will contain the extracted information.

6. For each piece of information, look into the XHTML source for robust ways of identifying where the information is located, using an XPath pattern (since we will use this pattern in a match attribute of a template, the context node does not need to be the document root). Element names, *class* attributes, position predicates, and the like, are especially useful. For example,

> if the movie title is given inside a <span class=" title "> </span> element,
> the pattern span[@class='title'] can be used.

Write then a template definition in your stylesheet that makes use of this XPath expression to produce a new output element containing the extracted information. Because of the restrictions on the kind of axes that may occur in a match attribute, it may be necessary to put part of the pattern there and part of it in an **<xsl:value−of** select=" " **/>.**

In some cases, there is not enough XHTML structure to precisely identify the location of a particular property. When this happens, "regular expressions" can be used in the template definition to only extract only relevant data. For regular expressions,

- ■ XPath 2.0 provides the tokenize() function and
- ■ XSLT 2.0, the <xsl:analyze-string> element.

7. Run your template on each XHTML document and check that each time the output document is valid against the DTD you designed. If not, adapt your stylesheet accordingly.

8. We are now going to modify the stylesheet (and the DTD) a little bit so that it processes all Web pages at a time, resulting in a single output document containing all information. Create a file list.xml listing all your XHTML documents with the following structure:

```
< files >
  < file  href="a.xhtml" />
  < file  href="b.xhtml" />
  < file  href="c.xhtml" />
</ files >
```

Modify the stylesheet so that it takes as input document this list.xml file and processes in turn (using the document() function) each referenced file. The result should be an XML document data.xml collecting extracted information from all different Web pages. Adapt the DTD as needed.

10.2 RESTRUCTURING DATA

Up to now, the data we obtained closely follows the structure of the original Web source: each item is described one after the other, with all its properties. But it is often needed to restructure extracted information (e.g., to present a list of movies without their cast, and then a list of actors referencing all movies this actor has played in). We now write a second XSLT program to restructure data in this way.

1. Choose one of the properties of your items according to which data will be regrouped (e.g., actors of movies, publication year of books) This will be called the *grouping key*. The final XML file you need to produce should have a structure similar to what follows:

```
<data>
  <item id="id1">
    <property1> ... </property1>
    <property2> ... </property2>
  </item>
  ...
  <item id="id9">
    <property1> ... </property1>
  </item>
  <grouping-key name="...">
    <item-ref  ref="id3" />
    <item-ref  ref="id7" />
  </grouping-key>
  <grouping-key name="...">
    <item-ref  ref="id2" />
```

```
        </grouping-key>
    </data>
```

In other words, all items are listed one after the other as before, but the values of the grouping key are not listed among their properties. They are listed separately after the item descriptions, and items that share a given grouping key value are referred to in the description of this grouping key. Write a DTD for the final document. Obviously, choose more explicit element names than grouping-key or item.

2. Write an XSLT stylesheet that transforms the XML document previously obtained into an identical document, with two exceptions:
   - Elements representing items now have an id attribute that uniquely identifies them (one can use the XSLT function generate-id() for that);
   - Information about the grouping key is removed from the document.

3. Modify this stylesheet to add after the list of items the list of all values of the grouping key, without duplicates. This can be easily done in XSLT 2.0 with the **<xsl:for–each–group>** element. In XSLT 1.0, this is more intricate. It can be done, for instance, by expressing in XPath the fact that a specific occurrence of the grouping key value is the first in the document.

4. Add to each element representing the value of a grouping key the list of items that have this specific value. Test that the resulting document is valid against the DTD you have designed.

11

Putting into Practice: Ontologies in Practice (by Fabian M. Suchanek)

This chapter proposes exercises to manipulate and query real-world RDFS ontologies, and especially YAGO. YAGO was developed at the Max Planck Institute in Saarbrücken in Germany. At the time of this writing, it is the largest ontology of human quality that is freely available. It contains millions of entities such as scientists, and millions of facts about these entities such as where a particular scientist was born. YAGO also includes knowledge about the classes and relationships composing it (e.g., a hierarchy of classes and relationships).

11.1 EXPLORING AND INSTALLING YAGO

Go to the YAGO Web site, http://mpii.de/yago, click on the *Demo* tab and start the textual browser. This browser allows navigating through the YAGO ontology.

1. Type "Elvis Presley" in the box. Then click on the Elvis Presley link. You will see all properties of Elvis Presley, including his biographic data and his discography.
2. You can follow other links to explore the ontology. Navigate to the wife of Elvis Presley, Priscilla.
3. The ontology is held together by a taxonomy of classes. Its top class is called "entity". Verify this by repeatedly following type and subClassOf links.
4. Go back to Elvis Presley. Navigate to one of his songs. You will see the date the song was recorded. Can you find all songs together with their record dates? Why would this be a tedious endeavor?

Then, to install YAGO on your machine, make sure that you have Java installed and around 5 GB free disk space. Proceed as follows:

1. Download the YAGO ontology. YAGO is available at the project homepage http://mpii.de/yago. We also provide a version of YAGO on the Web site of this book, http://webdam.inria.fr/Jorge/. There are multiple versions of the ontology; the easiest is to download the Jena TDB store, that can be directly

queried. Select the smallest dataset available. Save the file on your hard drive and unzip it. This may take some time.

2. Download the YAGO converters from the same site. Unzip the file to your hard drive.

You are all set, YAGO is installed on your machine and is ready for querying!

11.2 QUERYING YAGO

YAGO is expressed in RDFS. In RDFS, the facts and the ontological statements are written as triples. These triples can be queried using SPARQL, the standard querying language for RDFS facts. SPARQL was introduced in Chapter 8. The query engine of YAGO uses the Jena framework http://openjena.org/. Jena is an open-source project that has grown out of work with the HP Labs Semantic Web Program. Jena ships with YAGO, so that we only need to download and install YAGO.

To query YAGO, open a terminal window, navigate to the folder where the converters live and run the SPARQL script (called yago2sparql.bat on Windows and yago2sparql.sh on Unix). You will be invited to type SPARQL queries for YAGO. For ease of notation, the following namespaces are already defined:

```
PREFIX rdf: <http://www.w3.org/1999/02/22-rdf-syntax-ns#>
PREFIX rdfs: <http://www.w3.org/2000/01/rdf-schema#>
```

In addition, the default namespace, referred to as simply ":", is already set to the namespace of YAGO, http://www.mpii.de/yago/resource/. We can ask for simple YAGO facts through SPARQL queries of the form

```
SELECT ?V WHERE { A R B }
```

Here, ?V is a variable name, as indicated by the question mark. The SELECT clause may contain several variables separated with whitespace. A and B are entities (with proper namespace prefix) and R is a relation (also with proper namespace prefix). Each of these components may also be a variable. The WHERE clause possibly contains multiple triples, separated by a dot. Try out the following:

1. Ask

```
SELECT ?x WHERE { :Elvis_Presley rdf:type ?x }
```

This query lists all classes that Elvis Presley is an instance of. (Be sure to type all characters in the query exactly as written here.) Note that the results show the full URI of the entities, not the equivalent short form with namespace prefixes.
2. Can you modify the query so that it lists all facts with Elvis Presley in the position of the subject, not just the ones with the rdf:type relation? You should find facts about his songs, his wife, his birth date, and the movies he acted in.
3. List all the entities that Elvis created (with the relation :created). Now list only those of them that were created on 1974-03-20. Use the relation :wasCreatedOnDate and remember to put quotes around the literal 1974-03-20.

Your query should retrieve the entity :Good_Times_(Elvis_Presley_album). Can you imagine why the entity is not simply called :Good_Times?

4. Knowing that rdfs:label is the relation between an entity and its name, retrieve all entities that are called "Good Times."

5. Write another query to list all entities called "Good Times" together with their creator. Compare the results of this query to the results of the previous query. Verify that not all of the entities have a creator. Can you imagine why this is the case, even though every entity was certainly created? What does this imply for the notion of negation in SPARQL?

6. Write another query to retrieve all classes that Elvis Presley is an instance of. Is Elvis an instance of the class singer? Can you imagine why?

In YAGO, the ontological statements expressing the subclass and subproperty relations as well as the range and domain restrictions of properties are stored as RDFS triples. However, the semantics of these statements is not taken into account. In particular, the facts that follow from the RDFS entailment rules (see Chapter 7) are not derived. To derive these facts, one can use the saturation algorithm given in Chapter 8. It is possible, using the converters, to generate a Jena store of YAGO that includes (some of) these derived facts. This requires, however, downloading the YAGO2 ontology in its default format, and the conversion process can be a lenghty one.

Enter a blank line to quit the SPARQL interface.

11.3 WEB ACCESS TO ONTOLOGIES

11.3.1 Cool URIs

An ontology refers to an entity through a URI. YAGO, for example, refers to the entity of Elvis Presley as http://mpii.de/yago/resource/Elvis_Presley. Another ontology may use a different identifier to refer to that entity. The DBpedia ontology, for instance, refers to Elvis as http://dbpedia.org/resource/Elvis_Presley. In general, these URIs (i.e., identifiers) do not have to be URL (i.e., locators). In other words, they do not have to refer to Web pages. In principle, when a URI is entered in a browser, one might simply get an error message. However, some ontologies implement the "Cool URI" protocol[1] of the W3C. This means that each URI in the ontology is actually understood by a Web server that is configured to respond to a request of this URI. (In other words, each such URI is also an URL.) This allows a machine to retrieve fragments of the ontology from the server. Let us try this out:

1. If you do not have a UNIX-based operating system, search online for a version of the tool wget that works with your operating system. There should be a free version available. Download and install this tool. wget allows accessing a URL and downloading its content – much like a Web browser does it.

2. Open a terminal and type

---

[1] http://www.w3.org/TR/cooluris/.

wget -O elvis .html http://dbpedia.org/resource/ Elvis_Presley

This accesses the URI as a URL, just like a Web browser. If you look into elvis.html, you will see the Wikipedia page of Elvis.

3. Now we tell wget to ask the server specifically for RDFS files:

wget -O elvis . rdfs --header "Accept: application /rdf+xml"
http://dbpedia.org/resource/ Elvis_Presley

The file elvis.rdfs should now contain everything YAGO knows about Elvis Presley. The file format is RDF, encoded in XML.

4. These facts in the answer contain again other URIs. Find one of Elvis's albums in the answer. Then use another wget command to retrieve information about that album.

By following the URIs in the results, a machine can navigate the entire ontology.

11.3.2 Linked Data

As we have seen, different ontologies can use different URIs to refer to the same entity. The Linked Data Project, found at http://linkeddata.org/, tries to establish links between such synonymous URIs. Such a link takes the form of an RDFS statement. The predicate is sameAs of the OWL namespace:

http://mpii.de/yago/resource/ Elvis_Presley
owl:sameAs http://dbpedia.org/resource/ Elvis_Presley

These links allow jumping from one ontology to another. If both ontologies implement the Cool URI protocol, a machine can gather information about one entity from multiple servers. Let us try this out: Go to the Web site of the *Sig.ma* semantic Web search engine, http://sig.ma/. This engine gathers information from different ontologies about a given entity. It uses sameAs links, Cool URIs, and RDFa annotations hidden in HTML pages.[2] This leads to a lot of data, but potentially also very noisy data. Ask Sig.ma for

http://mpii.de/yago/resource/ Elvis_Presley .

You can also try out keywords (such as "United States"). See how Sig.ma gathers data from multiple ontologies. The Linked Data Project was pioneered by the DBpedia ontology, which is therefore a hub in this Web of data.

---

[2] http://www.w3.org/TR/rdfa-syntax/

Putting into Practice: Mashups with YAHOO! PIPES and XProc

Mashups are Web applications that integrate and combine data from multiple Web sources to present them in a new way to a user. This chapter shows two different ways to construct mashup applications in practice: YAHOO! PIPES, a graphical user interface for building mashups, and XProc, a W3C language for describing workflows of transformations over XML documents. Pros and cons of either approach will be made clear as one follows the indicated steps. The goal will be to present information about news events, each event being accompanied by its localization displayed on a map. For that purpose, we integrate three sources of information:

1. A Web feed about current events in the world, in RSS format (e.g., CNN's top stories at http://rss.cnn.com/rss/edition.rss). Any such RSS feed is fine, though English is preferable to ensure precision of the geolocalization.
2. A geolocalization service. We use information from the GeoNames[1] geographical database, and specifically their RSS to GeoRSS converter, whose API is described at http://www.geonames.org/rss-to-georss-converter.html.
3. A mapping service. We use Yahoo! Maps.[2]

12.1 YAHOO! PIPES: A GRAPHICAL MASHUP EDITOR

YAHOO! PIPES[3] allows creating simple mashup applications (simply called *pipe*) using a graphical interface based on the construction of a pipeline of boxes connected to each other, each box performing a given operation (fetching information, annotating it, reorganizing it, etc.) until the final output of the pipeline. It can be used by nonprogrammers, though defining complex mashups still requires skill and experience with the platform. The mashup we want to build is demonstrated at http://pipes.yahoo.com/webdam/geolocalized_news: it asks the user for a feed URL, and displays with markers on a map the result of the geolocalization of each news item.

---

[1] http://www.geonames.org/.
[2] http://maps.yahoo.com/.
[3] http://pipes.yahoo.com/.

1. Go to the YAHOO! PIPES website and either log in using an existing Yahoo!
   account or create a free account. Once you follow the links for creating a pipe,
   you will be presented with the interface of the graphical editor: on the left, a
   list of all boxes that can be used inside a pipe; in the center, the workspace
   where you can build your pipe; in the bottom part, a debugger shows the
   output of the currently selected box.
2. Drag a "Fetch Feed" box on the workspace. Enter the URL in the box and
   connect it to the "Pipe Output" box at the bottom of the workspace by drag-
   ging a link from the output port of the initial box (shown as a circle on its
   bottom border) to the input port of the final box. Save your pipe and click on
   "Run pipe..." to see the result.
3. We are going to add some geolocalization information by using the "Location
   Extractor" operator of YAHOO! PIPES, which should be put in the middle of
   the two existing boxes. Save and run the pipe.
4. The location extractor of YAHOO! PIPES is not always as precise or complete
   as GeoNames. Study the documentation of the RSS to GeoRSS converter
   REST API. Use this API by trying to form URLs directly in your browser
   until you fully understand how it works. Then integrate it into your pipe by
   using a "URL Builder" whose output port is connected to the *url* parameter
   of the existing "Fetch Feed" box. Compare the results to what you had before.
5. To give a final touch to your pipe, add a "URL input" box to ask the user for
   the URL of the feed to be geolocalized. Save and test.

You can decide to publish your pipe to give other users access to it; if you want
to keep playing with YAHOO! PIPES, you can try enriching your pipe by retrieving
data from multiple RSS feeds, using a Web search operator to discover feeds dealing
with a given topic, adding to feed items images obtained by querying Flickr with
keywords from the description of the item, and so on. You can also look at the vast
library of published pipes to get some inspiration.

12.2 XPROC: AN XML PIPELINE LANGUAGE

XProc is a W3C Recommendation for describing transformation workflows on
XML documents. Throughout this section, refer to the XProc specification[4] for
more detail about the language. As with YAHOO! PIPES, a workflow is seen
as a pipeline of operations (here called *steps*) that fetch or process information;
these operations heavily rely on other XML standards (XPath, XSLT, XInclude,
XML Schema, XQuery, etc.). In YAHOO! PIPES, connections between boxes are
described in a graphical manner; in XProc they are described using an XML syntax.
Finally, contrary to YAHOO! PIPES, which deals with Web data at large, XProc is
dedicated to the processing of XML data only. Any XProc processor can be used;
we recommend XML CALABASH,[5] a Java implementation that is easy to install and
to use.

---

[4] http://www.w3.org/TR/xproc/.
[5] http://xmlcalabash.com/.

1. Download the skeleton pipeline skeleton.xpl from the book Web site, http://webdam.inria.fr/Jorge/. Test your XProc processor; if you use XML CALABASH and its installation directory is in your path environment variable, you can just type

   ```
   calabash skeleton.xpl > result.html
   ```

   No error message should show (only information messages), and result.html should contain a basic view of CNN's feed.

2. Look at the skeleton.xpl file. The whole pipeline is described inside a top-level <p:pipeline> element. First, a variable is declared; declared variables can be used in XPath expressions further in the file (all values of select attributes are XPath expressions). Then the RSS file is loaded with the help of the standard <p:load> step (again, see the XProc specification for the definition of standard steps). All items of the RSS feed are put into a sequence (<p:for-each>), and this sequence is then wrapped under a common item element (<p:wrap-sequence>); these two steps are arguably not very useful, but this structure will help us in extending this pipeline. Finally, an inline XSLT stylesheet is reformatting the list of items into a table, where each line has a single cell, containing the title of the item and pointing to the corresponding article.

3. Change the <p:load> so that a geolocalized version of the RSS feed is loaded instead of the original one. Once again, refer to the documentation of the API of GeoNames to determine which URL to load. You can use the XPath 2.0 function *encode-for-uri*() to properly encode special characters in a URL.

4. Items should now have geo:lat and geo:long child elements with geolocalization information. Test this by adding in the XSLT stylesheet, after the item's title, two <xsl:value-of> elements that show both coordinates. Test.

5. We now want to filter out items that do not have any geolocalization information (if any). For this purpose, you can modify the select attribute of the <p:iteration-source> to keep only items with geo:long and geo:lat child elements.

6. We will use the Yahoo! Maps Image API[6] to add a map for each news item. Carefully study the API documentation and apply for a Yahoo! Application ID.

7. Replace the <p:identity> step with a <p:load> step that calls the Yahoo! Maps Image API appropriately. Remember you can use any XPath expression inside a select attribute. In the XSLT stylesheet, add a cell:

   ```
   <td><xsl:value-of select="." /></td>
   ```

   before the existing cell to display the URL of the map image. The display of the title and link to the article does not work any more because we discarded the news items to keep only the map image. We are going to fix this later on.

---

[6] http://developer.yahoo.com/maps/rest/V1/.

8. Replace the display of the URL by an HTML <img> element that loads this URL. In XSLT, to input an XPath expression inside an arbitrary attribute, surround the XPath expression with curly braces.
9. To keep in the sequence both map images and information about news items, you will need two <p:for-each> steps and a <p:pack> step to combine the two sequences. Refer to the XProc specification. The <p:pack> step will introduce an extra wrapping element, so remember to adapt the XPath expressions used in the XSLT stylesheets.

PART 3

Building Web Scale Applications

13

Web Search

With a constantly increasing size of dozens of billions of freely accessible documents, one of the major issues raised by the World Wide Web is that of searching in an effective and efficient way through these documents to find those that best suit a user's need. The purpose of this chapter is to describe the techniques that are at the core of today's search engines (such as Google,[1] Bing,[2] or Exalead[3]), that is, mostly keyword search in *very large* collections of text documents. We also briefly touch upon other techniques and research issues that may be of importance in next-generation search engines.

This chapter is organized as follows. In Section 13.1, we briefly recall the Web and the languages and protocols it relies upon. Most of these topics have already been covered earlier in the book, and their introduction here is mostly intended to make the present chapter self-contained. We then present in Section 13.2 the techniques that can be used to retrieve pages from the Web, that is, to *crawl* it, and to extract text tokens from them. First-generation search engines, exemplified by Altavista,[4] mostly relied on the classical information retrieval (IR) techniques, applied to text documents, that are described in Section 13.3. The advent of the Web, and more generally the steady growth of documents collections managed by institutions of all kinds, has led to extensions of these techniques. We address scalability issues in Section 13.3.3, with focus on centralized indexing. Distributed approaches are investigated in Chapter 14. The graph structure of the Web gives rises to *ranking* techniques that very effectively complement information retrieval. We conclude with a brief discussion of currently active research topics about Web search in Section 13.5.

---

[1] http://www.google.com/.
[2] http://www.bing.com/.
[3] http://www.exalead.com/.
[4] http://www.altavista.com/.

13.1 THE WORLD WIDE WEB

Whereas the Internet is a physical network of computers (or *hosts*) connected to each other from all around the world, the World Wide Web, WWW or Web in short, is a logical collection of hyperlinked documents shared by the hosts of this network. A hyperlinked document is just a document with references to other documents of the same collection. Note that documents of the Web may refer both to static documents stored on the hard drive of some host of the Internet and to dynamic documents that are generated on the fly. This means that there is a virtually unlimited number of documents on the Web, since dynamic documents can change at each request. When one speaks of the Web, it is mostly about the *public* part of the Web, which is freely accessible, but there are also various *private* Webs that are restricted to some community or company, either on private *Intranets* or on the Internet, with password-protected pages.

Documents and, more generally, *resources* on the Web, are identified by a *URL* (*Uniform Resource Locator*) which is a character string that follows a fixed format illustrated on the imaginary URL below, with basic components, described next.

$$\underbrace{\text{https://}}_{scheme}\underbrace{\text{www.example.com}}_{hostname}\underbrace{\text{:443}}_{port}/\underbrace{\text{path/to/document}}_{path}\underbrace{\text{?name=foo\&town=bar}}_{query\ string}\underbrace{\text{#first-para}}_{fragment}$$

scheme: Describes the way the resource can be accessed; on the Web, it is generally one of the Web *protocols* (http, https) that are described further.

hostname: This is the domain name of a host, as given by the domain name system (DNS). Frequently on the Web, the hostname of a Web site will start with www., but this is only a common convention, not a rule.

port: TCP port where the server listens on the host; it defaults to 80 for the http scheme and 443 for the https scheme and is rarely present.

path: The logical path of the document; for simple cases, this corresponds to a path leading to the static document in the filesystem of the host.

query string: Additional parameters identifying the resource, mostly used with dynamic documents.

fragment: Identifies a specific part of the document.

Query strings and fragments are optional (and, most of the time, absent) and the path can be omitted, in which case the URL refers to the *root* of the Web host. URLs can also be relative (by opposition to the *absolute URL* shown here), when both the scheme and hostname portions are omitted. A relative URL is to be interpreted in a given URL *context* (for instance, the URL of the current document) and is resolved in a straightforward way: if the context is that of the URL above, the relative URLs /images[5] and data would be resolved, respectively, as https://www.example.com:443/images and https://www.example.com:443/path/to/data in a way similar to (UNIX) relative paths resolution.

---

[5] Note that here /images is considered as a relative URL, because it lacks the scheme and hostname part; the path /images, however, is an absolute path.

```
<!DOCTYPE html PUBLIC
"-//W3C//DTD XHTML 1.0 Strict//EN"
"http://www.w3.org/TR/xhtml1/DTD/xhtml1-strict.dtd">

<html xmlns="http://www.w3.org/1999/xhtml"
      lang="en" xml:lang="en">
  <head>
    <meta http-equiv="Content-Type"
          content="text/html; charset=utf-8" />
    <title>Example XHTML document</title>
  </head>
  <body>
    <p>This is a
      <a href="http://www.w3.org/">link to the
      <strong>W3C</strong>!</a></p>
  </body>
</html>
```

Figure 13.1. Example XHTML document.

The usual format for documents (or, in this case, *pages*) on the Web is HTML (the HyperText Markup Language), though one can find many documents, including hyperlinked documents, in other formats. This is the case for PDF documents (another kind of hyperlinked structure), documents from word-processing softwares, and nontextual, *multimedia* documents such as images and audio files.

HTML is originally a dialect of SGML, the ancestor of XML, but is hardly ever parsed as such. The most common versions found on today's Web are HTML 4.01 and XHTML 1.0, which is a direct XMLization of HTML 4.01, with minor differences. An example XHTML document is given in Figure 13.1. As it is an SGML or XML file, an (X)HTML document is made out of elements, attributes, and text content. Elements carry, between other things, meta-information about the document (e.g., <meta>, <title>), structural information at the document level (e.g., <table>, <ul>, <p>), structural information at the character level (e.g., <strong>, <em>) or references to other media (e.g., <img>, <object>). An element of importance is <a>, which defines a hyperlink to another resource on the Web identified by the URL given as the href attribute. Both relative and absolute links are allowed here. The context of resolution is the URL of the current page, unless it contains a <base> element that indicates another context. HTML pages can also contain other *disguised* hyperlinks in the form of JavaScript code that loads other URLs, of redirection after a timeout with some specific use of the <meta> element, or of Flash or Java applets; all these links are less easy to identify and then less accessible to users and Web robots.

Although HTML pages are primarily seen thanks to a browser (and, most of the time, a graphical browser as Microsoft Internet Explorer or Mozilla Firefox), the HTML code is not supposed to describe the way the page will appear in a browser (it is the role of a styling language like CSS) but the core structure and content of the document in a way accessible to all kind of browsers and a wide variety of *user agents* such as the crawlers that we describe in Section 13.2.1. For this reason, it is important that HTML documents be valid against the W3C specifications; tools

Request	`GET /myResource HTTP/1.1` `Host: www.example.com`

Response	`HTTP/1.1 200 OK`
	`Content-Type: text/html; charset=ISO-8859-1`
	
	`<html>`
	`  <head><title>myResource</title></head>`
	`  <body><p>Hello world!</p></body>`
	`</html>`

Figure 13.2. HTTP request and response examples.

like the W3C validator available at http://validator.w3.org/ can be of help. Sadly, because of a history of browser wars, browser limitations, browser permissiveness, and author laziness, most of the (X)HTML pages on the Web are far from being valid, or even well-formed in the sense of XML well-formedness, accounting for what has been called *tag soup*.

Pages of the Web are accessed using the usual client-server architecture of the Internet: a *Web server* on a remote host accepts requests from a client for a given resource, and provides it to him. Two communication protocols are mainly used for this exchange: HTTP and HTTPS. The latter allows for encryption, authentication, and advanced features such as session tracking; it is essential for e-commerce on the Web and all other sensitive applications, but rarely used for regular documents and will not be discussed further. HTTP, or *HyperText Transfer Protocol*, is a quite simple protocol built on top of the Internet protocols IP (*Internet Protocol*, for addressing) and TCP (*Transmission Control Protocol*, for transportation) that is widely used on the World Wide Web. Figure 13.2 shows an example request and response from, respectively, a Web client and a Web server. The request asks for the resource identified by the path /myResource on host www.example.com and the server answers that the document was found (code 200 OK; other common codes are 404 NOT FOUND or 500 SERVER ERROR) and provides it. The reason why the hostname is given, whereas the server has already been contacted, is that a given server may have several different domain names, with different content (thus, www.google.com and www.google.fr point to the same machine). This *virtual hosting* is one of the novel features of HTTP/1.1 with respect to previous versions. Other features of the HTTP protocol include login and password protection, content negotiation (the content served for a given URL is not fixed and depends on the preference indicated by the client, in terms of file formats or languages), cookies (persistent chunks of information that are stored on the client, e.g., for session management purpose), *keep-alive* requests (several requests can be made to the same server without closing the connection), and more.

13.2 PARSING THE WEB

The first task to build a search engine over the Web is to retrieve and index a significant portion of it. This is done by collecting Web documents through a navigation process called *Web crawling*. These documents are then processed to extract relevant information. In case of text documents, sets of words or *tokens* are collected. Web crawling is introduced in Section 13.2.1. We describe in Section 13.2.2 general text preprocessing techniques that turn out to be useful for document retrieval.

13.2.1 Crawling the Web

Crawling is done by user agents that are called *crawlers*, *(Web) spiders* or *(Web) robots*. Their design raises a number of important engineering issues that will be discussed here.

Discovering URLs

Crawling the Web is basically just starting from a given URL or set of URLs, retrieving and indexing this document, discovering hyperlinks (mostly from the <a> elements of the HTML content) on the document, and repeating the process on each link. There is no real termination condition here, as it is vain to try to retrieve the entire Web (which is actually virtually infinite, as already discussed), but the crawl can be terminated after some delay or after some number of URLs have been discovered or indexed. This is essentially a graph browsing problem, which can be tackled by either *breadth-first* (all pages pointed by a page are indexed before the links they contain are analyzed) or *depth-first* (a referred page is indexed, and its links are extracted in turn, as soon as a link to it is discovered) techniques. Obviously, because of the nonexistence of termination conditions, and the possibility of being lost in *robot traps* (infinite paths in the graph), a breadth-first approach is preferred here; actually, a mix of a breadth-first browsing with depth-first browsing of limited depth of each discovered site can be a good compromise.

There are other sources of URLs for Web crawlers than the ones found on Web pages. Web search engines have access to information about the Web page that a Web user comes from when she reaches the Web site of the search engine, thanks to the Referrer HTTP header. It can be used to discover pages that are not referenced anywhere. Finally, Web masters can provide search engines with *sitemaps*, a file, in XML format, that can be used to list all URLs in a given Web site, along with some meta-information (date of last modification, refresh rate). When this is available and properly used, for example automatically generated by a content management system, the situation is ideal: a Web crawler can get the list of all URLs of a Web site with a single HTTP request.

Deduplicating Web Pages

An important subtask of Web crawling is the identification of duplicate pages in the Web, in order to avoid browsing them multiple times. Trivial duplicates are documents that share the same URL, though it can be written in slightly different ways: this means that a *canonization* of URLs has to be performed, to detect for instance that http://example.com:80/foo and http://example.com/foo/../bar are actually the same resource. The identification of other kind of duplicates, that do not have the same URL, is more intricate but also crucial, since it would not be very interesting for a user to get a list of identical pages as a result to a search engine query. Identical duplicates are easy to identify by hashing, but there are often some little differences between two pages (for instance, a date that is automatically generated at each request by the server, or random content such as *Tips of the day*) that present essentially the same content.

The first approach to detect such near-duplicates is simply to compute the *edit distance* between two documents, that is, the minimal number of basic modifications (additions or deletions of characters or words, etc.) to obtain a document from another one. This is a good notion of similarity between textual documents, and edit distance can be computed with dynamic programming in $O(m \cdot n)$, where m and n are the size of the documents. This does not scale to a large collection of documents, since it is definitely unreasonable to compute the edit distance between every pair of documents found on the Web. An alternative is the use of *shingles*: a shingle is a sequence of tokens (say, words) of a fixed length k (for instance, three consecutive words), as found in a document. Consider the following two simple documents:

$d = $ I like to watch the sun set with my friend.

$d' = $ My friend and I like to watch the sun set.

One can compute the set of shingles of length $k = 2$, disregarding punctuation and putting all tokens in lowercase:

$S = \{$i like, like to, to watch, watch the, the sun, sun set, set with, with my, my friend$\}$

$S' = \{$my friend, friend and, and i, i like, like to, to watch, watch the, the sun, sun set$\}$

The similarity between two documents can then be computed as the proportion of common shingles, using the Jaccard coefficient:

$$J(S, S') = \frac{|S \cap S'|}{|S \cup S'|} = \frac{7}{11} \approx 0.64$$

For a value of k between 2 to 10 depending on the applications, this gives a reasonable way to compare two textual documents (the markup of an HTML page can be either considered as part of the tokens, or disregarded altogether, depending on the granularity wished in the comparison). However, this is still costly to compute, since one has to compute the similarity between every two pair of documents. It is however possible to approximate $J(S, S')$ by storing a *summary* (or *sketch*) of the shingles contained in a document of a fixed size. Let N be a fixed integer, which is the size of the summary that will be kept for each document. The following algorithm can be shown to approximate in an unbiased way the Jaccard similarity between sets of shingles:

1. Choose N different and *independent* hash functions;
2. For each hash function h_i and set of shingles $S_k = \{s_{k1} \ldots s_{kn}\}$, store $\phi_{ik} = \min_j h_i(s_{kj})$;
3. Approximate $J(S_k, S_l)$ as the proportion of ϕ_{ik}'s and ϕ_{il}'s that are equal:

$$J(S_k, S_l) \approx \frac{|\{i : \phi_{ik} = \phi_{il}\}|}{N}$$

Then, in order to test if a document is a near-duplicate of one that has already been found, it is enough to compute its sketch of hashed shingles, and to make N accesses

User-agent: *
Allow: /searchhistory/
Disallow: /search

Figure 13.3. Example robots.txt robot exclusion file.

into a hash table. The larger N is, the better the approximation, but the costlier the computation. It is also possible to repeat the hashing on the set of hashed shingles to obtain a set of hashed *super-shingles*, when one is only interested in *very* similar documents, as is the case for finding near-duplicates.

Crawling Ethics

Going back to crawling per se, there are also some *crawling ethics* to abide to. A *standard for robot exclusion* has been proposed to allow Webmasters to specify some pages not to be crawled by Web spiders (the reasons can be varied: for confidentiality purposes, in order not to put too heavy a load on a resource-intensive Web application, to help robots not to fall into robot traps, etc.). This standard is followed by all major search engines and consists in a /robots.txt file that can be put at the root of every Web server and contains restrictions on what part of the Web site spiders are allowed to crawl.

An example of such a file is given in Figure 13.3. It disallows the crawling of all URLs whose path starts with /search, with the exception of those starting with /searchhistory/, to any robots. Another way of expressing such limitations, at the level of a HTML page this time (which can be useful if a Webmaster does not have control over the document root) is through a <meta name="ROBOTS"> directive in the header of the document, such as

    <meta name="ROBOTS" content="NOINDEX,NOFOLLOW">

which disallows robots to either index or follow links from the current Web page. Available keywords are INDEX, FOLLOW, NOINDEX, NOFOLLOW, with a default of INDEX,FOLLOW. Yet another way of influencing robot crawling and indexing is discussed in Section 13.4.3. A last rule that a spider programmer should respect is to avoid too many requests in a short time to a given host, since that could result in DOS (Denial Of Service) from the host. A good rule of thumb is to wait between 100 ms and 1 s between two successive requests to the same Web server.

Design Issues

Because of this last rule, and because network delays are typically much higher than the time needed to process a Web page, it is crucial to send in parallel a large number of requests to different hosts; this also means that a per-host queue of URLs to be processed has to be managed. This parallel processing is typically performed using a multithreaded environment, although asynchronous input and outputs (with for instance the select POSIX C function) provide the same functionality without the overhead introduced by threads. The *keep-alive* feature of HTTP/1.1 can also be used to chain requests (after some delay) to the same host. In large-scale crawlers for general Web search, the crawling itself will be run in parallel on a number of machines, that have to be regularly synchronized, which raises further issues not discussed here.

Another aspect of crawling is the refreshing of URLs. Though we stated earlier that we did not want to crawl the same URL twice, it can be very important to do so in the context of perpetually changing Web content. Furthermore, it is also important to identify frequently changing Web pages in order to crawl them more often than others. Thus, the main page of an online newspaper should probably be crawled every day or even more often, while it may take up to a month to a large-scale crawler to crawl a significant portion of the Web. The HTTP protocol proposes a way to retrieve a document only if it has been modified since some given date (If-Modified-Since header), but this is often unreliable, even more so in the context of dynamic documents which are regenerated at each request. Changes in Web pages have then to be identified by the crawler, without taking into account minor changes, for instance using techniques described above for identifying near-duplicates. Crawling strategies have to be adapted accordingly.

13.2.2 Text Preprocessing

The techniques described here are general techniques for dealing with text corpora. Depending upon the application, some variant or other has to be applied. Furthermore, the original language or languages of the document have a major impact on the preprocessing made.

Tokenization

Let us consider the set of seven (one-sentence) documents represented in Figure 13.4. We describe next and illustrate on this particular example how to process a collection of text documents in a suitable way to efficiently answer keyword queries.

The first step is to tokenize the initial documents into sequences or *tokens*, or simply words. This is illustrated on our example document set in Figure 13.5. At this stage, interword punctuation is generally removed and case is normalized (unless, obviously, the application requires differently, as may be the case in a search engine dedicated to linguists researching the usage of punctuations). This may seem like a very simple step where it is sufficient to replace whitespaces and punctuation by token separators, but the problem is actually trickier than this.

d_1 The jaguar is a New World mammal of the Felidae family.
d_2 Jaguar has designed four new engines.
d_3 For Jaguar, Atari was keen to use a 68K family device.
d_4 The Jacksonville Jaguars are a professional US football team.
d_5 Mac OS X Jaguar is available at a price of US $199 for Apple's new "family pack".
d_6 One such ruling family to incorporate the jaguar into their name is Jaguar Paw.
d_7 It is a big cat.

Figure 13.4. Example set of documents.

d_1 the$_1$ jaguar$_2$ is$_3$ a$_4$ news$_5$ world$_6$ mammal$_7$ of$_8$ the$_9$ felidae$_{10}$ family$_{11}$
d_2 jaguar$_1$ has$_2$ designed$_3$ four$_4$ new$_5$ engines$_6$
d_3 for$_1$ jaguar$_2$ atari$_3$ was$_4$ keen$_5$ to$_6$ use$_7$ a$_8$ 68k$_9$ family$_{10}$ device$_{11}$
d_4 the$_1$ jacksonville$_2$ jaguars$_3$ are$_4$ a$_5$ professional$_6$ us$_7$ football$_8$ team$_9$
d_5 mac$_1$ os$_2$ x$_3$ jaguar$_4$ is$_5$ available$_6$ at$_7$ a$_8$ price$_9$ of$_{10}$ us$_{11}$ \$199$_{12}$ for$_{13}$ apple's$_{14}$ new$_{15}$ family$_{16}$ pack$_{17}$
d_6 one$_1$ such$_2$ ruling$_3$ family$_4$ to$_5$ incorporate$_6$ the$_7$ jaguar$_8$ into$_9$ their$_{10}$ name$_{11}$ is$_{12}$ jaguar$_{13}$ paw$_{14}$
d_7 it$_1$ is$_2$ a$_3$ big$_4$ cat$_5$

Figure 13.5. Tokenization of document set of Figure 13.4.

- Whereas words are immediately visible in a language such as English, other languages (notably, Chinese or Japanese) do not use whitespace to mark word boundaries. Tokenization of such languages requires much more complex procedures that typically use both advanced linguistic routines and dictionaries. Specifically for Chinese, an alternative is to use individual ideograms as tokens, but this may lead to invalid matches in query answering.

- Some care has to be taken for a number of textual oddities, such as acronyms, elisions, numbers, units, URLs, and e-mail addresses. They should probably be preserved as single tokens in most applications and, in any case, should be dealt with consistently.

- Even in English, tokenization is not always obvious, especially with respect to compound words. An immediate question is whether to consider intraword hyphens as token separator, but the problem is broader. Consider for instance the term *hostname* which can be found in three variant forms: *hostname, host-name,* and *host name.* If we want to be able to use any of these terms to query all three variants, some analysis has to be performed, probably with the help of a lexicon, either to consider *host name* as a single compound word, or to break *hostname* in two tokens. The latter solution will also allow searching for *host* and *name,* which may be appropriate, depending on the context. In languages where compounds are even more easily produced than in English (e.g., German or Russian) such an analysis is indispensable.

Stemming

Once tokens are identified, an optional step is to perform some *stemming* to remove morphological markers from inflected words or, more generally, to merge several lexically related tokens into a single *stem.* Such a step is often needed, for instance to be able to retrieve documents containing *geese* where *goose* is queried, but the degree of stemming varies widely depending upon the application (and upon the considered language, obviously: the notion of stemming does not make much sense in a language without any morphological variations like Chinese). Here is a scale of possible stemming schemes, from finest to coarsest.

Morphological stemming: This consists in the sole removal of bound morphemes (such as plural, gender, tense, or mood) from words. Note that this can be a very complex task in morphologically rich languages such as Turkish or, in a lesser way, French, which require advanced linguistic processing for resolutions of *homographs* (different words that are written in the same way).

d_1 the$_1$ jaguar$_2$ be$_3$ a$_4$ new$_5$ world$_6$ mammal$_7$ of$_8$ the$_9$ felidae$_{10}$ family$_{11}$
d_2 jaguar$_1$ have$_2$ design$_3$ four$_4$ new$_5$ engine$_6$
d_3 for$_1$ jaguar$_2$ atari$_3$ be$_4$ keen$_5$ to$_6$ use$_7$ a$_8$ 68k$_9$ family$_{10}$ device$_{11}$
d_4 the$_1$ jacksonville$_2$ jaguar$_3$ be$_4$ a$_5$ professional$_6$ us$_7$ football$_8$ team$_9$
d_5 mac$_1$ os$_2$ x$_3$ jaguar$_4$ be$_5$ available$_6$ at$_7$ a$_8$ price$_9$ of$_{10}$ us$_{11}$ \$199$_{12}$ for$_{13}$ apple$_{14}$ new$_{15}$ family$_{16}$ pack$_{17}$
d_6 one$_1$ such$_2$ rule$_3$ family$_4$ to$_5$ incorporate$_6$ the$_7$ jaguar$_8$ into$_9$ their$_{10}$ name$_{11}$ be$_{12}$ jaguar$_{13}$ paw$_{14}$
d_7 it$_1$ be$_2$ a$_3$ big$_4$ cat$_5$

Figure 13.6. Document set of Figure 13.4, after tokenization, and stemming.

Consider for instance the famous sentence in French: "Les poules du couvent couvent." (The hens of the monastery brood.) Here, the first *couvent* [monastery] is an uninflected noun, which should stay as is, whereas the second *couvent* [brood] is an inflected form of the verb *couver* [to brood], which should be stemmed accordingly. In English, the situation is simpler and plain procedures that remove final -s, -ed, -ing, etc., with a few adaptations for semiregular (-y/-ies) or irregular (mouse/mice) inflections, can be enough. Some ambiguities remain, as illustrated with the words *rose* or *stocking*, which can be either uninflected nouns, or inflected forms of the verb *to rise* and *to stock*, respectively. Depending upon the application, one may choose either a cautious stemming (that does not remove all morphological markers and will then fail to retrieve some query matches) or a more aggressive one (that will retrieve invalid query matches). Figure 13.6 shows the result of a morphological stemming applied on our running example.

Lexical stemming: Stemming can be pushed further to merge lexically related words from different parts of speech, such as *policy, politics, political,* or *politician.* An effective algorithm for such a stemming in English, Porter's stemming, has been widely used. Further ambiguities arise, with for instance *university* and *universal* both stemmed to *universe.* This kind of stemming can also be coupled to the use of lexicons in order to merge synonyms or near-synonyms.

Phonetic stemming: The purpose of phonetic stemming is to retrieve words despite spelling variations or errors. Soundex is a widely used loose phonetic stemming for English, especially known for its use in U.S. censuses, that stems for instance both *Robert* and *Rupert* to *R163.* As can be seen from this example, it is a very coarse form of stemming and should probably not be used in contexts where the precision of matches is important.

In some circumstances, it can be useful to produce different indexes that use different forms of stemming, to support both exact and approximate queries.

Stop-Word Removal

The presence of some words in documents, such as determiners (*the, a, this,* etc.), function verbs (*be, have, make,* etc.), and conjunctions (*that, and,* etc.), is very common and indexing them increases storage requirements. Furthermore, they are not informative: A keyword query on *be* and *have* is likely to retrieve almost all the (English) documents of the corpus. It is then common to ignore them in queries, and sometimes in the index itself (although it is hard to determine in

d_1 jaguar$_2$ new$_5$ world$_6$ mammal$_7$ felidae$_{10}$ family$_{11}$
d_2 jaguar$_1$ design$_3$ four$_4$ new$_5$ engine$_6$
d_3 jaguar$_2$ atari$_3$ keen$_5$ 68k$_9$ family$_{10}$ device$_{11}$
d_4 jacksonville$_2$ jaguar$_3$ professional$_6$ us$_7$ football$_8$ team$_9$
d_5 mac$_1$ os$_2$ x$_3$ jaguar$_4$ available$_6$ price$_9$ us$_{11}$ 199_{12}$ apple$_{14}$ new$_{15}$ family$_{16}$ pack$_{17}$
d_6 one$_1$ such$_2$ rule$_3$ family$_4$ incorporate$_6$ jaguar$_8$ their$_{10}$ name$_{11}$ jaguar$_{13}$ paw$_{14}$
d_7 big$_4$ cats$_5$

Figure 13.7. Document set of Figure 13.4, after tokenization, stemming, and stop-word removal.

advance whether an information can be useful or not). Figure 13.7 shows a further filtering of our running example that removes stop-words (to be compared with Figure 13.6).

13.3 WEB INFORMATION RETRIEVAL

Once all needed preprocessing has been performed, the (text) document set can be indexed in an *inverted file* (or inverted index) that supports efficient answering to keyword queries. Basically, such an index implements a binary association (i.e., a matrix) between the documents and the terms they contain. Documents are represented by their *ids*, a compact key that uniquely identifies a document. Note that the search system is not required to store the document itself, as long as it can be accessed from an external source using its id. Terms are, as discussed before, stemmed tokens that are not stop-words. An inverted index supports very fast retrieval of the documents (ids) that contain the set of keywords in a query.

We describe next and illustrate on our running example how to index a collection of text documents in a suitable way to efficiently answer keyword queries. This problem and related ones are known as *information retrieval* or, simply, *search* problems. We present the *inverted index* model in Section 13.3.1. We then proceed to the problem of answering keyword queries using such an index. Large-scale indexing and retrieval is introduced in Section 13.3.3 and clustering in Section 13.3.4. We discuss briefly at the end of this section how we can go beyond traditional information retrieval techniques to search the Web.

13.3.1 Inverted Files

An inverted index is very similar to traditional indexes found at the end of printed books, where each term of interest is associated to a list of page numbers. In the IR context, an inverted index consists of a collection of *posting lists* $L(T)$, one for each term t, storing the ids (*postings*) of the documents where t occurs. A (partial) example of inverted index for our example is given in Figure 13.8.

For small-scale applications where the index fits on a single machine, lists of occurrences of documents are usually stored, packed, for each given term, in an *inverted file* that is then mapped to memory (using the POSIX system call mmap).

family	d_1, d_3, d_5, d_6
football	d_4
jaguar	$d_1, d_2, d_3, d_4, d_5, d_6$
new	d_1, d_2, d_5
rule	d_6
us	d_4, d_5
world	d_1
...	

Figure 13.8. Partial inverted index for document set of Figure 13.4.

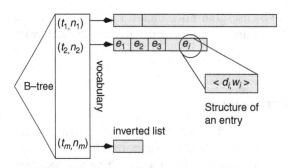

Figure 13.9. Structure of an inverted file

A secondary structure (the *vocabulary*) gives the position of the list for each term in the index. In order to quickly find this position given a term t, the vocabulary can be indexed by, for example, a B-tree.

Figure 13.9 shows the structure of an inverted index. Some details are noteworthy. First, the length of an inverted list is highly variable. This length depends on the number of referred documents in the list, which is high for common terms (t_1 in Figure 13.9), and small for rare ones (t_m in Figure 13.9). In text processing, skewness is the norm and often the handle to strongly accelerate query processing by scanning the shortest lists first. The vocabulary features, therefore, along with each term t_i, the number n_i of documents where t_i occurs.

Second, a list consists of a sequence of homogeneous *entries* that can often be quite efficiently compressed to limit the memory space required by the whole index. A key requirement for efficient compression is the ordering of entries on the document id (represented as an unsigned integer). The basic index illustrated in Figure 13.8 shows an ordering of each on the d_i component, assuming that $d_i < d_j$ when $i < j$.

Here is a first concrete example giving some measures for a basic representation of an inverted index.

Example 13.3.1 Consider an institution that wants to index its collection of e-mails. We assume that the average size of an e-mail is 1,000 bytes and that each e-mail contains an average of 100 words.

A collection of 1 million e-mails occupies 1 GB. It consists in 100×10^6 words. Suppose that, after parsing and tokenization, the number of distinct terms is 200,000. Then:

1. The index consists of 200,000 lists;
2. Each document appears in 80 lists, if we make the (rough) assumption that 20% of the terms in a document appear twice;
3. Each list consists, *on average*, of 400 entries;
4. If we represent document ids as 4-bytes unsigned integers, the *average* size of a list is 1,600 bytes;
5. The whole index contains $400 \times 200,000 = 80,000,000$ entries;
6. The index size is 320 MB (for inverted lists) plus 2,4 MB ($200,000 \times 12$) for the directory.

The index size is generally not negligible. It is more than 30% of the collection size on this example, a ratio that can get even higher when additional information is added in inverted lists, as explained next.

Content of Inverted Lists

Storing the document id is sufficient for Boolean querying (e.g., to determine which document(s) contain a given term). However, applications sometimes require the position of each term in the original document. This is, for instance, the case when phrases can be searched (this is usually done in search engine interfaces by enclosing phrases between quotes), or when the search engine allows operators that need this position information (e.g., the NEAR operator of Altavista, that requires two terms to be close to each other). This information can easily be stored in the index, by simple addition of the positions (as integers) next to the document id in an entry. See Figure 13.10 for an illustration.

When a term appears several times in a document, the sorted list of its positions is stored after the document id. This additional information is likely to increase the size of the inverted file. Storing a list of integers in increasing order allows some effective compression techniques which are discussed in Section 13.3.3.

Note that this space overhead can be avoided at the price of a postprocessing step at run-time. In that case, a phrase query is processed just as a traditional bag-of-words query, and proximity is checked once the document itself has been fetched. This method is however ineffective at large scale, due to the cost of fetching many useless documents.

family	$d_1/11, d_3/10, d_5/16, d_6/4$
football	$d_4/8$
jaguar	$d_1/2, d_2/1, d_3/2, d_4/3, d_5/4, d_6/8 + 13$
new	$d_1/5, d_2/5, d_5/15$
rule	$d_6/3$
us	$d_4/7, d_5/11$
world	$d_1/6$
$\cdots$	

Figure 13.10. Partial inverted index for document set of Figure 13.4, with positions.

Finally, for ranking purposes, a weight w_i is stored along with the document id d_i to represent the relevancy of the document with respect to the term. The value of w_i is discussed next.

Assessing Document Relevance

In traditional databases, the result of a query (say, an SQL query) is the set of tuples that match the query's criterion, without any specific order. This constitutes a major difference with IR queries. The set of documents (ids) that contain a term t is easily found by scanning the list associated with t. But, clearly, some of these documents are more *relevant* to the term than others. Assessing the relevance of documents during the matching process is essential in a system where query results may consist of hundreds of thousands of documents.

Relevance is measured by assigning some *weight* to the occurrence of a term in a document, depending on the relevance and informativeness of the term. A term that appears several times in a document is more relevant for indexing the document than single occurrences. If the term occurs rarely in the whole collection, this further strengthens its relevance. Conversely, a term that occurs frequently in many documents is less discriminative. Based on these principles, a common weighting scheme is *tf–idf*, or *term frequency–inverse document frequency*: this scheme assigns a weight to a term that is proportional to its number of occurrences in the document. It also raises the weight of terms that are present in few documents.

The *term frequency* is the number of occurrences of a term t in a document d, divided by the total number of terms in d. The division normalizes the term frequency to avoid the distorsion that would occur for large documents. In mathematical terms:

$$\text{tf}(t,d) = \frac{n_{t,d}}{\sum_{t'} n_{t',d}}$$

where $n_{t',d}$ is the number of occurrences of t' in d.

The *inverse document frequency* qualifies the importance of a term t in a collection D of documents. A term that is rarely found is more characteristic of a document than another one that is very common. The idf is obtained from the division of the total number of documents by the number of documents where t occurs, as follows:

$$\text{idf}(t) = \log \frac{|D|}{\left|\{d' \in D \mid n_{t,d'} > 0\}\right|}$$

Finally, the mathematical definition for the weight $\text{tfidf}(t,d)$ of term t in document d is the products of these two descriptors:

$$\text{tfidf}(t,d) = \frac{n_{t,d}}{\sum_{t'} n_{t',d}} \cdot \log \frac{|D|}{\left|\{d' \in D \mid n_{t,d'} > 0\}\right|}$$

The first term raises the weight of frequently occurring terms in the given document, whereas the second term negatively depends of the global frequency of the term in the document set. This weighting scheme can then be added to each entry in the index, as shown on Figure 13.11.

family $d_1/11/.13, d_3/10/.13, d_5/16/.07, d_6/4/.08$
football $d_4/8/.47$
jaguar $d_1/2/.04, d_2/1/.04, d_3/2/.04, d_4/3/.04, d_5/4/.02, d_6/8 + 13/.04$
new $d_1/5/.20, d_2/5/.24, d_5/15/.10$
rule $d_6/3/.28$
us $d_4/7/.30, d_5/11/.15$
world $d_1/6/.47$
...

Figure 13.11. Partial inverted index for document set of Figure 13.4, with positions and tf-idf weighting.

Adding the weight or the position has an impact on the index size.

Example 13.3.2 Consider again the e-mails collection of Example 13.3.1. We add the term position and the weight to each entry, resulting in a storage overhead of 8 bytes, assuming a 4-byte representation for each component. The $80,000,000$ entries now occupy $80 \times 12 \times 10^6 = 960$ MB (i.e., almost the size of the whole collection).

13.3.2 Answering Keyword Queries

Given an inverted index built as described in the previous sections, we can answer to keyword queries. This may involve some sophisticated operations if one wants to put the most significant answers on top of the result set. We begin with the simple case of Boolean queries that do not require to rank the result.

Boolean Queries

If we want to retrieve all documents containing a given keyword, we just need to look up the (stemmed) keyword in the index and display the corresponding list of documents; associated weights give an indication of the relevance of each result to the keyword query. Consider now arbitrary multikeyword Boolean queries (containing AND, OR, NOT operators), such as

> (*jaguar* AND *new* AND NOT *family*) OR *cat*

They can be answered in the same way by retrieving the document lists from all keywords appearing in the query and applying the set operations corresponding to the Boolean operators (respectively, intersection, union, and difference for AND, OR, and AND NOT). Assigning a score to each document retrieved by the query is not completely straightforward, especially in the presence of NOT operators. For queries that only contain either the AND or the OR operator, some monotonous functions of the scores (or weights) of all matched terms can be used; a simple and effective way to compute the global score of the document is just to add all scores of matched terms. Another possibility is to use a similarity function, such as cosine (see Section 13.3.4) and compute the similarity between the query and the documents. Queries that give the location of terms relatively to each other (phrase queries or queries with a NEAR operator) can be answered in the same way, by retrieving from the index all matching documents with the associated positions, and checking whether the conditions imposed by the query (such as, position of keyword t should be that of keyword t' minus one for the phrase query "$t\ t'$") are satisfied.

In most applications, it is often desirable to return only a subset of the documents that match a query, since a user cannot be expected to browse through thousands or even millions of documents. This is achieved by *ranking* the result.

Ranked Queries: Basic Algorithm

We consider conjunctive keyword queries of the form:

$$t_1 \text{ AND } \ldots \text{ AND } t_n$$

and let k be a fixed number of documents to be retrieved (e.g., 10 or 50). We describe next two algorithms based on inverted files for top-k queries.

Recall that the inverted lists are sorted on the document id. Starting from the beginning of each list $L_{t_1}, \ldots, L_{t_n}$, a parallel scan is performed, looking for a tuple $[d_i^{(1)}, \ldots, d_i^{(n)}]$ (in other words, a document d_i matching all the terms). We denote by $s(t,d)$ the weight of t in d (e.g., tfidf) and $g(s_1, \cdots, s_n)$ the monotonous function that computes the global score of a document given the weight of each term in the document (e.g., addition). The global score $W_i = g(s(t_1, d_i), \ldots, s(t_n, d_i))$ of d_i is then computed and the pair d_i, W_i inserted in an array. When the parallel scans are finished, the array is sorted on the global score, and the k first documents constitute the output.

The algorithm is linear in the size of the inverted lists (we neglect here the cost of sorting the resulting array, which is in most cases much smaller than the inverted lists). In practice, the efficiency depends on the semantics of the query. If at least one occurrence of each term $t_1, \ldots, t_n$ is required in each document of the result set, then the scan may stop as soon as one of the list is exhausted. However, in general (for a query involving the OR operator), a document can obtain a high global score even if one or several query terms are missing. A semantics that favors the global score and not the presence of each term requires a full scan of the lists.

Fagin's Threshold Algorithm

Fagin's threshold algorithm (TA in short) allows answering top-k queries without having to retrieve and compute the intersection of all documents where each term occurs. We now make the assumption that, in addition to an inverted index that stores lists in increasing documents identifier order, we have another inverted index sorted on the weights. The first index can be used to directly check the weight of a term in a document with binary search. The algorithm is as follows:

1. Let R, the result set, be the empty list.
2. For each $1 \leq i \leq n$:
   (a) Retrieve the document $d^{(i)}$ containing term t_i that has the next largest $s(t_i, d^{(i)})$.
   (b) Compute its global score $g_{d^{(i)}} = g(s(t_1, d^{(i)}), \ldots, s(t_n, d^{(i)}))$ by retrieving all $s(t_j, d^{(i)})$ with $j \neq i$. If the query is a conjunctive query, the score is set to 0 if some $s(t_j, d^{(i)})$ is 0.

family $d_1/11/.13, d_3/10/.13, d_6/4/.08, d_5/16/.07$
new $d_2/5/.24, d_1/5/.20, d_5/15/.10$
...

Figure 13.12. Partial inverted index sorted on tf-idf weighting in descending order.

(c) If R contains fever than k documents, add $d^{(i)}$ to R. Otherwise, if $g_{d^{(i)}}$ is larger than the minimum of the scores of documents in R, replace the document with minimum score in R with $d^{(i)}$.

3. Let $\tau = g(s(t_1, d^{(1)}), s(t_2, d^{(2)}), \ldots, s(t_n, d^{(n)}))$.

4. If R contains at least k documents, and the minimum of the score of the documents in R is greater than or equal to τ, return R.

5. Redo step 2.

We now illustrate this algorithm on our running example with the top-3 query "*new* OR *family*", using the sum of weights as our aggregation function. A first index sorts the inverted lists on the document ids (Figure 13.11), a second one on their weights (Figure 13.12 shows, respectively, the lists for *family* and *new*).

Initially, $R = \varnothing$ and $\tau = +\infty$. The query evaluation must retrieve the $k = 3$ top-ranked document in the result set. Here, $n = 2$ (the query consists of two keywords). We develop a step-by-step progress of TA.

Let $i = 1$. Document $d^{(1)}$ is the first entry in the list L_{family}, hence $d^{(1)} = d_1$. We now need $s(\text{new}, d_1)$, the weight of term *new* in d_1. Note that we cannot afford to scan the entries L_{new} since this would involve a linear cost at each step of the algorithm. This is where a binary search on another inverted list L'_{new} sorted on the document id is useful. One gets $s(\text{new}, d_1) = 0.20$. Finally, the global score for d_1 is $g(s(\text{family}, d_1), s(\text{new}, d_1)) = 0.13 + 0.20 = 0.33$.

Next, $i = 2$, and the highest scoring document for *new* is d_2. Applying the same process, one finds that the global score for d_2 is .24 (note that d_2 does not appear in L_{family}, so its weight for term *family* is 0). The algorithm quits the loop on i with $R = \langle d_1, .33, d_2, .24 \rangle$ and $\tau = 0.13 + 0.24 = 0.37$.

Since the termination condition is not fulfilled, we proceed with the loop again, taking d_3 and d_5 as, respectively, $d^{(1)}$ and $d^{(2)}$. The global score for d_3 is 0.13 and the global score for d_5 is $0.10 + 0.07 = 0.17$. The element $[d_5, 0.17]$ is added to R (at the end) and the threshold τ is now $0.10 + 0.13 = 0.23$. Although R now contains three documents, as required, the termination condition is not met because τ is larger than the minimal score in R. Therefore, it is still possible to find a document whose score is higher than 0.17. Assume for instance a document d at the next position in both lists, with weights 0.09 and 0.12. A last loop concludes that the next candidate is d_6, with a global score of 0.08 and $\tau = 0.08$. The algorithm halts with

$$R = \langle [d_1, 0.33], [d_2, 0.24], [d_5, 0.17] \rangle$$

13.3.3 Large-Scale Indexing with Inverted Files

Inverted files must be able to process keyword-based queries on collections of large documents. As discussed earlier, the basic operation is a sequential scan of a list that retrieves the set of document containing a given term. This operation is linear in the

Table 13.1. Hardware Characteristics		
Type	**Size**	**Speed**
Processor	Cache lines = a few MBs	3–4 GHz; typical processor clock rate $\approx 0,310^{-9}$ s.
Memory	Tens of GBs	Access time $\approx 10^{-9}$ s $- 10^{-8}$ s (10–100 ns)
Disk	Several terabytes	Access time $\approx 5 \times 10^{-3}$ s (5 ms.); max. disk transfer rate $= 100$ MB/s

size of the list, and therefore in the size (number of documents) of the collection. It is also linear in the number of terms in the query. This seems to keep inverted files from being scalable to very large collections. However, the following analysis shows that they actually constitute a quite effective structure.

Table 13.1 summarizes a few important properties of modern hardware. Values are given for a typical data server. The cost of a random disk access (about 5 ms) is several orders of magnitudes larger than an access to main memory (about 100 ns). Most of this cost accounts for positioning the disk head (seek time, or *disk latency*). A sequential read which avoids the seek time can retrieve as much as 100 MB/s from the disk. A typical data server holds tens of gigabytes of main memory, and stores several terabytes of data on disks. Two simple guidelines for the design of efficient large scale systems are: (i) keep data in main memory as much as possible and (ii) write and read, *sequentially* large chunks of contiguous data on disks. Note that the discussion assumes a single data server.

Performance of Inverted Files

Consider an inverted file structure that does not store the position of terms in the lists. An entry is a pair $[d_i, w_i]$. The document id d_i can be represented with a 4-byte unsigned integer, allowing 2^{32} = more than four billions of documents ids. The weight w_i only requires 2 bytes by setting its value to $n_{t,d}$. The tf–idf can then be computed on the fly.

A collection of 1 million documents can therefore be indexed with 1 million of entries that occupy 6 MBs (the size of secondary structures is considered negligible). For a collection of 1 billion documents, a 6 GBs index suffices. Clearly such an index fits in the main memory of any reasonable data server and requires far less storage than the documents themselves. Assume for a moment that the collection contains 10,000 terms uniformly distributed in the documents. Each of the 10,000 lists contains 100,000 entries and occupies 600,000 bytes. Even if the list is on disk, it takes less than 1/100 s. to scan it and process its content. In practice, terms are *not* uniformly distributed, and this makes things even better, as explained later. These figures assume a contiguous storage of inverted lists, which is essential to ensure a high-speed sequential disk-based retrieval.

If the index stores the positions of terms in the list entries, things become less pleasant. In a naive approach, a position is stored with 2 bytes (this limits the size of documents to $2^{16} = 65,536$ positions/terms) or 3 bytes (16,777,216 positions). This constitutes a storage overhead of at least 50% with respect to the position-free index if each term occurs only once, and much more for terms with multiple occurrences in a same document.

What about Web-scale indexing? At the end of 2011, the size of the Web (a continuously changing value) is at least 50 billion pages (see http://www.worldwidewebsize.com/ for an up-to-date estimate), and probably two of three times larger (note that a four-byte storage is no longer sufficient for documents ids). Several hundreds of gigabytes are necessary to index its content with the simplest possible inverted index, without storing the term positions and without replication. For Web-scale applications, such as search engines, the index is distributed over a cluster of machines. Distribution mechanisms are investigated in a dedicated chapter.

Building and Updating an Inverted File

Building inverted files is a complex task because of their large size, and because of the need to preserve the contiguous storage of inverted lists. We first discuss *static construction*, where the collection of documents is known in advance, then *dynamic maintenance* of the index as documents are added or removed.

The basic procedure consists in scanning the documents one by one, creating for each a sorted list of the tokens. One creates a matrix with documents ids in rows and terms in columns, which must then be inverted to obtain a row for each term. For large files, matrix inversion cannot be processed in main memory. Moreover, writing each entry on the disk as soon as it is found would result in a highly fragmented storage.

The index can be created in two passes. The first pass collects information on the frequency of each term t. This determines the size of the inverted list for t, which can then be allocated on the disk. During the second pass, each entry can be written sequentially in the appropriate list. This results in a nonfragmented index.

The drawback of any two-pass approach is that documents must be processed twice. Another strategy relies on a preprocessing step (e.g., sorting). *Sort-based algorithms* first extract triplets $[d, t, f]$ from the collection, then sort the set of triplets on the term-docid pair $[t, d]$. Contiguous inverted lists can be created from the sorted entries.

The most commonly used algorithm for external sorting is an adaptation of the sort/merge main memory algorithm. In the first phase, sorted subfiles called "runs" are created from the data source. Assuming m blocks in main memory, each run occupies m pages and stores a sorted subset of the input. In order to create the runs, one repeats the following sequence of operations (Figure 13.13):

1. The m buffer pages in main memory are filled with triplets $[d, t, f]$ extracted from the documents;
2. The triplets in the m pages are sorted on $[t, d]$ with an internal-memory algorithm (usually quick-sort);
3. The sorted blocks are written onto disk in a new run.

Starting from the runs created in the first phase, the merge phase begins. One block in main memory is assigned to each run file: $m - 1$ runs are merged in a single pass, and the last block in main memory is allocated to the output run.

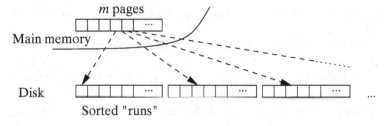

Figure 13.13. The creation of initial runs.

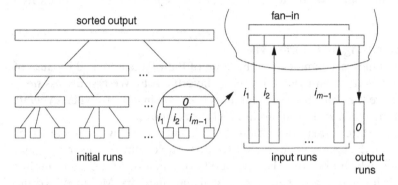

Figure 13.14. The merge phase.

The process is illustrated in Figure 13.14. It can be represented by a tree, each node of the tree corresponding to a single merge operation described in the right part of the figure. One reads the first page of each input run $\{i_1, i_2, \ldots, i_{m-1}\}$ in the main memory buffer (recall that the input runs are sorted). The merge then begins on the data in main memory. The record with the smallest t value is repeatedly picked in one of the $m-1$ blocks and stored in the output block (if several triplets with the same t exist, then the one with the smallest d is chosen). When all the triplets in an input block, say j, have been picked, one reads the following block in run i_j. Once the output block is full it is written in the output run. Eventually, an output run is full ($m \times (m-1)$ blocks have been written in the run), it is ready to be merged at a higher level with other runs obtained from the first-level merge operations and so on.

The merge of runs is done in linear time. Each run is read once and the size of the output is the sum of the sizes of the input runs. Therefore, at each level of the tree, one needs exactly $2n$ I/Os. If the fan-in is $m-1$, there are $O(\log_m n)$ levels in the tree, and we obtain an $\Theta(n \log_m n)$ algorithm.

As a final improvement, *merge-based algorithms* avoid the sort phase by directly constructing sorted inverted lists in main memory. When the memory is full, sorted in-memory lists are flushed on the disk, just like sorted runs in the sort-merge algorithm. When all documents have been processed, the flushed lists that relate to a term t are merged, and the result constitutes the final inverted list for t.

This is illustrated with Figure 13.15. For each document d in the collection, the *parsing* process extracts a set of terms, and a pair $[d, f]$ is inserted in the in-memory

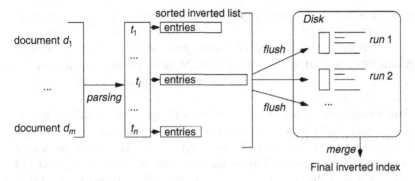

Figure 13.15. The merge-based algorithm.

list L_i for each term t_i. Eventually the allocated memory gets full. A *flush* creates then a "run" on the disk. At the end of collection, several such runs may have been created. A final *merge* operation carries out a merge of the lists associated with each term. One obtains the final inverted index.

This algorithm enjoys several properties that make it widely used in practice. First, it avoids both a double parsing of the input documents and a costly external sort. Second, it is robust enough to behave correctly in the presence of large collections or moderate memory availability. Finally, this algorithm turns out to be useful for evolving collections, as discussed next.

Indexing Dynamic Collections

When new documents are added or removed continuously (which is the standard situation in Web indexing), the inverted index must be updated to reflect the up-to-date knowledge acquired by the crawler, which constantly runs in parallel. Updating the index is typically quite costly since it requires updating the document list of various terms, changing the structure of each list. Actually, applying the naive approach of directly accessing the list for each incoming document would result in awful performances.

The merge-based algorithm provides a solution to the problem. An in-memory index that holds the information related to the new documents is maintained. Searches are performed on the two indexes. When the index becomes full (that is, its size exceeds a given threshold), it can be seen as the last run of a merge-based approach, and a merge with the main index can be processed. During a merge, a copy of the old index must be kept to support the current searches operations. This doubles the space requirements. The preceding description disregards deletions, which can be processed thanks to a small variant (left as an exercise).

Compression of Inverted Lists

Compression of inverted lists is an important feature of text IR systems. It brings several advantages:

1. Compressed files require less disk space;
2. The same amount of information can be read more quickly;
3. A larger part of the inverted index can be kept in main memory.

The price to pay is the need to uncompress the content of the lists when they are accessed. A basic criterion is that the total cost of reading (on disk) a compressed inverted list followed by its decompression should not exceed the cost of reading the uncompressed list. The compression would otherwise jeopardize the query evaluation process. Efficient decompression algorithms exist that take advantage of the very high speed of modern hardwares.

The standard storage size of an integer is 4 bytes (2 bytes for so-called "short" integers). A 4-byte unsigned integer can represent values in the range $[0; 2^{32} - 1] = 4,294,967,296$ (the maximal value is 65,535 for 2-bytes ints). The intuition behind the compression strategies of inverted list is that they can be seen as sequences of positive integers such that the gap between two consecutive entries in the list is typically small. Assume for instance that a term t is represented in the following documents, put in ascending order:

$$[87; 273; 365; 576; 810].$$

Note that we need at least one byte to store the first id, and 2 bytes for the other ones. This sequence of sorted documents id can be equivalently represented by the gaps between two consecutive ids:

$$[87; 186; 92; 211; 234].$$

An immediate advantage of this latter representation is that, since the gaps are much smaller that the absolutes ids, they can be represented (on this particular example) with 1-byte integers. More generally, the following facts help to greatly reduce the necessary storage:

1. Relative gaps tend to be smaller than ids, and thus need *on average* a lot less space than the standard 4-byte storage;
2. For very common terms that appear in many documents, the gap often is the minimal value of 1, with high potential compression.

This representation, called *delta-coding*, is a very simple way to achieve a significant reduction of space requirements. Note, however, that although one may expect a lot of small gaps, we must be ready to face large gaps in the inverted lists of rare terms. The compression method must therefore adapt to these highly variable values, in order to choose the appropriate storage on a case-by-case basis. As mentioned earlier, this method must also support a very quick decompression mechanism.

We present later two efficient compression methods, which, respectively, attempt at using the minimal number of bytes (bytewise compression) or the minimal number of bits (bitwise compression) to represent gaps. Both methods are *parameter-free* in the sense that they do not rely on any assumption on the distribution of gaps, and thus do not require the additional storage of parameters that would describe this distribution. Bitwise compression achieves a (slightly) better compression ratio than bytewise compression, at the price of a higher decompression cost.

Variable Byte Encoding

As the name suggests, *variable byte encoding* (VByte in short) encodes integers on a variable (but integral) number of bytes. The idea of VByte encoding is very simple. Given a positive integer value v, one tests whether d is strictly less than 128. If yes, d can be encoded on the last 7 bits of a byte, and the first bit is set to 1 to indicate that we are done. Otherwise,

1. Take the reminder v' of $v/128$; encode v' as explained above in a byte b;
2. Apply recursively the procedure to $v/128$, this time setting the first bit to 0; concatenate the result with b.

Let, for example, $v = 9$. It is encoded on one byte as 10001001 (note the first bit set to 1). Now consider a larger value, say $v = 137$.

1. The first byte encodes $v' = v \bmod 128 = 9$, thus $b = 10001001$ just as before;
2. Next we encode $v/128 = 1$, in a byte $b' = 00000001$ (note the first bit set to 0).

The value 137 is therefore encoded on two bytes:

00000001 10001001

Decoding is very simple: one reads the bytes $b_n, \ldots, b_2$ with a leading 0, until one finds a byte b_1 with a leading 1. The value is

$$b_n \times 128^{n-1} + \cdots + b_2 \times 128 + b_1$$

The procedure is very efficient because it manipulates full bytes. It is also quite flexible since very large integers (there is no upper bound) can be encoded just as very small ones. The method also achieves a significant amount of compression, typically 1/4 to 1/2 of the fixed-length representation.

Variable Bit Encoding

We next illustrate bit-level encoding with γ-codes. Given an unsigned integer x, the starting point is the binary representation with $\lfloor \log_2 x \rfloor + 1$ bits. For instance, the binary representation of 13 is 1101, encoded with $\lfloor \log_2(13) \rfloor + 1 = 4$ bits. The binary representation is space-optimal, but since its size obviously depends on x, we need to represent this varying length as well to be able to decode the value.

Using γ-codes, the length $\lfloor \log_2 x \rfloor + 1$ is encoded in unary: a length l is represented with $l - 1$ '1' bits terminated by a '0' bit. The value 13 can therefore be represented by a pair (1110, 1101), where 1110, the *length*, is in unary format, followed by the value (called the *offset*, see below) in binary.

γ-codes introduce an optimization based on the following observation: a nonnull value x is of the form $2^{\lfloor \log_2(x) \rfloor} + d$. In terms of binary representation, the first term corresponds to a leading '1', followed by the binary representation of d (the *offset* of x).

Since the first term $2^{\lfloor \log_2(x) \rfloor}$ is determined by the length, which is known from the prefix of the code, we only need to store the value of d in the suffix. So, still taking 13 as an illustration, we put it in the form $2^3 + 5$. We encode the length in unary as before as 1110, and we encode the offset (5) in binary on 3 bits as 101. The

γ-code for 13 is finally

1110101

Decoding first reads the number of leading '1' bits until a '0' is met. This gives us the length of the binary code that follows. On our example, we determine that the length is 3. The value is therefore $2^3 + decode(101) = 8 + 5 = 13$.

The length of a γ-code for a value x is $2 \times \lfloor \log_2(x) \rfloor + 1$, that is, at most twice the minimal possible storage required for x (recall that using this minimum representation is not possible since we need to be able to find the boundaries of each value).

Better compression can only be achieved by using a *model* of the distribution of the values. It turns out that using such a model for inverted list is never done because (i) it leads to a compression/decompression cost which balances the gain of space reduction, and (ii) the maintenance of encoding becomes too complicated if the distribution changes.

Experiments show that bitwise compression achieves a better compression than bytewise (about 10 to 20% better, depending on the data set), at the price of a more expensive pre- and postprocessing of the inverted lists.

13.3.4 Clustering

If one wants to search on the Web some information about the jaguar animal, one is probably not interested in the other meanings of the word *jaguar*, such as the car make or the version of Mac OS X. *Clustering* can be used in such contexts to partition a set of documents (the result of the keyword query) into a set of homogeneous document collections. The result of a clustered search for *jaguar* on the Clusty[6] search engine is shown on Figure 13.16.

One way to achieve such a clustering is the following. Start from some document set that is to be clustered. We shall see this document set in a *document vector space* model, that is the dual of the inverted index model: Documents are described by the terms that occur in them, with associated weighting, and each term is seen as a dimension of a vector space documents live in. The coordinate of a document d in this vector space, along the dimension corresponding to t, will be the weight of t in d (say, tfidf(t,d)). We then consider the *cosine* similarity between two documents d and d', seen as vectors:

$$\cos(d, d') = \frac{d \cdot d'}{\|d\| \times \|d'\|}$$

where $d \cdot d'$ is the scalar product of d and d' and $\|d\|$ the norm of vector d. With this definition (which is a simple extension of the usual cosine function in the Euclidean plane), $\cos(d, d) = 1$ and $\cos(d, d') = 0$ if d and d' are orthogonal, that is, if they do not share any common term.

This is illustrated on Figure 13.17, which shows a two-dimensional vector space built on the terms (jaguar, Mac OS). Documents are represented as normalized vectors with two coordinates representing respectively their scores for each term. The similarity is estimated by the angle between two vectors (and measured by the cosine of this angle). Figure 3.17 shows that d_1 and d_3 share almost the same scores, resulting in a small angle θ and thus in a cosine close to 1.

---

[6] http://clusty.com/.

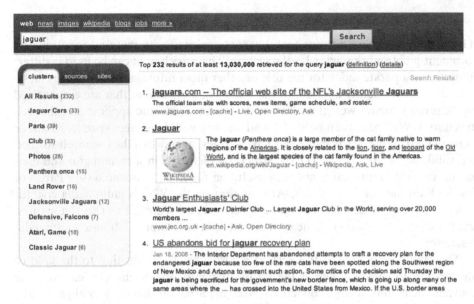

Figure 13.16. Example clustering from Clusty of the results of the query *jaguar*.

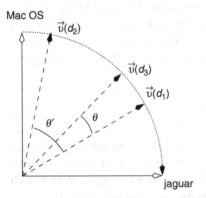

Figure 13.17. Illustration of similarity in the document vector space.

This definition of similarity is all that we need to apply standard clustering algorithms, for instance the following simple agglomerative clustering:

1. Initially, each document forms its own cluster.
2. The similarity between two clusters is defined as the maximal similarity between elements of each cluster.
3. Find the two clusters whose mutual similarity is highest. If it is lower than a given threshold, end the clustering. Otherwise, regroup these clusters. Repeat.

Note that many other more refined algorithms for clustering exist.

13.3.5 Beyond Classical IR

HTML Web pages are not just text, but text enriched with meta-information and document-level and character-level structure. This enrichment can be used in different ways: A separate index for the title or other meta-information of a page can be built and independently queried, or the tokens of a document that are emphasized can be given a higher weight in the inverted index. For some applications, the tree structure of Web pages can be stored and queried with languages such as XPath or XQuery (cf. Chapter 2); because most Web pages, even when they are well-formed and valid, do not really use HTML structural elements in a meaningful and consistent way, this approach is not very useful on the Web as a whole (see Part 2 of this book on the Semantic Web). Also present on the Web is multimedia content such as images or videos. They can be described and searched as text (file names, text present in the context of the content, etc.), or with more elaborate multimedia descriptors.

The material covered in this section is just a brief introduction to the field of Information Retrieval, taken as the art of efficiently and accurately searching for relevant documents in large collections. Note in particular that the techniques introduced here are by no way restricted to Web search, and apply to any collection of documents (e.g., a digital library). The next section is devoted to IR extensions that address the specificities of the Web, namely its graph structure. Modern search engines make also use other kinds of information, especially *query logs*, the list of all queries made by users to the engine, and, in some cases, also consider their selection among the list of results returned. If a user never clicks on a link for a given query, it makes sense to decrease its relevance score.

13.4 WEB GRAPH MINING

As all hyperlinked environments, the World Wide Web can be seen as a directed graph in the following way: Web pages are vertices of the graph, whereas hyperlinks between pages are edges. This viewpoint has led to major advances in Web search, notably with the PageRank and HITS algorithms presented in this section.

Extraction of knowledge from graphs, or *graph mining*, has been used on other graph structures than the Web, for instance on the graph of publications, where edges are the citation links between publications; *cocitation analysis* relies on the observation that two papers that are cited by about the same set of papers are similar. Other graphs susceptible to this kind of analysis include graphs of dictionaries or encyclopedias, or graphs of social networks.

13.4.1 PageRank

Though tf–idf weighting adds some relevance score to a document matching a keyword, it does not distinguish between reference documents that are highly trusted and obscure documents containing erroneous information. The idea of using the graph structure of the Web to assign some score to a document relies in the following idea or variants of it: If a document is linked by a large number of *important* documents, it is itself *important*.

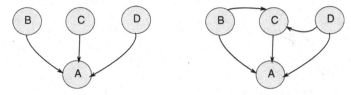

Figure 13.18. PageRank—Basic idea.

PageRank, which was introduced with much success by the founders of the Google search engine, is a formalization of this idea. The *PageRank* of a page i can be defined informally as the probability $pr(i)$ that the random surfer has arrived on page i at some distant given point in the future. Consider for instance the basic graph on the left of Figure 13.18. A random surfer will reach node A at step i if it reaches node B, C or D at step $i-1$. Therefore,

$$pr(A) = pr(B) + pr(C) + pr(D)$$

In less simplistic cases, the surfer may have to choose among several outgoing edges. In that case one assumes that the probability is uniform. Looking at the right part of Figure 13.18, the probability for a surfer residing on node B (or D) to reach node C i 1/2. Hence, the probability to reach C at i given the position at $i-1$ is

$$pr(C) = \frac{1}{2}pr(B) + \frac{1}{2}pr(D)$$

In general, let $G = (g_{ij})$ be the transition matrix of the Web graph (or a large part of it), that we assume to be normalized in the following way:

$$\begin{cases} g_{ij} = 0 & \text{if there is no link between page } i \text{ and } j; \\ g_{ij} = \frac{1}{n_i} & \text{otherwise, with } n_i \text{ the number of outgoing links of page } i. \end{cases}$$

This normalization ensures that the matrix is *stochastic* (all rows sum to 1) and that it describes a *random walk* on the pages of the Web: a *random surfer* goes from page to page, choosing with uniform probability any outgoing link.

Example 13.4.1 Consider the graph of Figure 13.19. Its normalized transition matrix is as follows

$$G = \begin{pmatrix} 0 & 1 & 0 & 0 & 0 & 0 & 0 & 0 & 0 & 0 \\ 0 & 0 & \frac{1}{4} & 0 & 0 & \frac{1}{4} & \frac{1}{4} & 0 & \frac{1}{4} & 0 \\ 0 & 0 & 0 & \frac{1}{2} & \frac{1}{2} & 0 & 0 & 0 & 0 & 0 \\ 0 & 1 & 0 & 0 & 0 & 0 & 0 & 0 & 0 & 0 \\ 0 & 0 & 0 & 0 & 0 & \frac{1}{2} & 0 & 0 & 0 & \frac{1}{2} \\ \frac{1}{3} & \frac{1}{3} & 0 & \frac{1}{3} & 0 & 0 & 0 & 0 & 0 & 0 \\ 0 & 0 & 0 & 0 & 0 & \frac{1}{3} & 0 & \frac{1}{3} & 0 & \frac{1}{3} \\ 0 & \frac{1}{3} & 0 & 0 & 0 & 0 & 0 & 0 & \frac{1}{3} & \frac{1}{3} \\ 0 & \frac{1}{2} & \frac{1}{2} & 0 & 0 & 0 & 0 & 0 & 0 & 0 \\ 0 & 0 & 0 & 0 & 1 & 0 & 0 & 0 & 0 & 0 \end{pmatrix}$$

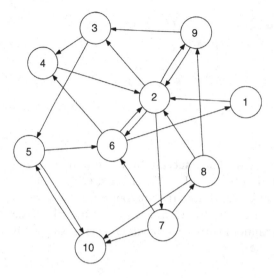

Figure 13.19. Illustration of PageRank—Example graph.

Thus, the probability that a random surfer goes from page 2 to page 6 or, in other words, the probability of transition between nodes 2 and 6 in the random walk on the graph, is $g_{2,6} = \frac{1}{4}$.

Observe that if v denotes the initial position as a column vector (say, a uniform column vector would mean that the random surfer starts with uniform probability on each page), $(G^T)v$ is a column vector indicating the position after one step of the random walk. The PageRank can then be defined as the limit of this process, that is the PageRank of page i is the i-th component of the column vector:

$$\lim_{k \to +\infty} (G^T)^k v$$

if such a limit exists.

Example 13.4.2 Let us continue with the graph of Example 13.4.1. Let v be the uniform column vector of sum 1. This measure over the graph nodes can be displayed as in Figure 13.20. Consider one iteration of the PageRank computation. It amounts to multiplying the matrix of G^T by v, which gives

$$G^T v = \begin{bmatrix} \frac{1}{30} & \frac{19}{60} & \frac{3}{40} & \frac{5}{60} & \frac{3}{20} & \frac{13}{120} & \frac{1}{40} & \frac{1}{30} & \frac{7}{120} & \frac{7}{60} \end{bmatrix}^T$$

$$\approx \begin{bmatrix} 0.033 & 0.317 & 0.075 & 0.083 & 0.150 & 0.108 & 0.025 & 0.033 & 0.058 & 0.117 \end{bmatrix}^T$$

This is the vector of probabilities of reaching a given node after one step, assuming a uniform probability for the initial node.

If we iterate this computation, we converge toward the measure displayed in Figure 13.21, the PageRank measure. Here, node 2 has the highest PageRank score because it is somehow more central in the graph: The probability of reaching node 2 after an arbitrarily long random walk in the graph is the greatest.

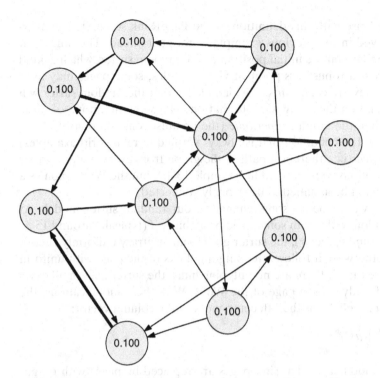

Figure 13.20. Illustration of PageRank—Initial uniform distribution.

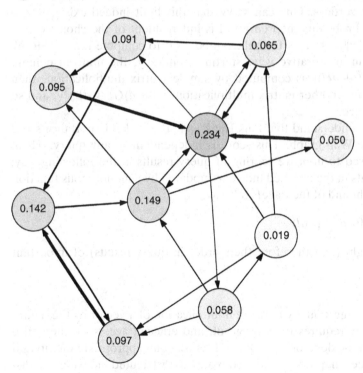

Figure 13.21. PageRank (damping factor of 1) for graph of Figure 13.19.

Some problems arise with this definition of the PageRank score. The convergence that is observed in the previous example is not guaranteed. The limit (if it exists) can be dependent on the initial position of the random surfer, which is kind of disappointing from a robustness point of view. Besides, some pages may have no outgoing links (they are called *sinks*), which means that the random surfer will eventually be blocked on these pages. Note that one can show that none of these problems occurs when the graph is *aperiodic* (the greatest common divisor of the length of all cycles is 1, a condition that is always verified in real-world examples) and *strongly connected* (i.e., there is a path in the graph from every node to every node). These assumptions were verified in Example 13.4.2, but the Web graph as a whole can definitely not be assumed to be strongly connected.

For this reason, we introduce some change in our random surfer model: At each step of the random walk, with some fixed probability d (typically around 15%; $1 - d$ is called the *damping factor*), the surfer goes to an arbitrary uniformly chosen page of the Web; otherwise, it follows the outgoing links of the page with uniform probability as before (and if there are no outgoing links, the surfer goes in all cases to an arbitrary uniformly chosen page of the Web). With these modifications, the PageRank of page i is defined as the i-th component of the column vector:

$$\lim_{k \to +\infty} ((1 - d)G^T + dU)^k v,$$

where G has been modified so that sink pages are replaced by pages with outgoing links to any page of the Web, and U is the matrix with all $\frac{1}{N}$ values where N is the number of vertices. One can show that this limit indeed exists, whenever $d > 0$ (Perron–Frobenius theorem) and is independent of the choice of the vector v, whenever $\|v\| = 1$. This formula can be used to compute the PageRank scores of all pages in an iterative way: starting from, say, the uniform column vector v, $((1 - d)G^T + dU)v$ is computed by simple matrix multiplication, then $((1 - d)G^T + dU)^2 v$ by another matrix multiplication, $((1 - d)G^T + dU)^3 v$, and so forth, until convergence.

It is important to understand that PageRank assigns a *global* importance score to every page of the Web graph. This score is independent of any query. Then, PageRank can be used to improve scoring of query results in the following way: Weights of documents in the inverted index are updated by a monotonous function of the previous weight and of the PageRank, say,

$$\mathrm{weight}(t, d) = \mathrm{tfidf}(t, d) \times \mathrm{pr}(d)$$

thus raising the weight (and therefore their order in query results) of important documents.

Online Computation

The computation of PageRank by iterative multiplication of a vector by the dampened transition matrix requires the storage of, and efficient access to, the entire Web matrix. This can be done on a cluster of PCs using an appropriate distributed storage technique (see Chapters 15 and 16 devoted to distributed indexing and distributed computing). An alternative is to compute PageRank while crawling the Web, on the fly, by making use of the *random walk* interpretation of PageRank. This is what the following algorithm, known as OPIC for Online PageRank Importance Computation, does:

1. Store a global cashflow G, initially 0.
2. Store for each URL u its *cash* $C(u)$ and *history* $H(u)$.
3. Initially, each page has some initial cash c_0.
4. We crawl the Web, with some crawling strategy that accesses repeatedly a given URL.
5. When accessing URL u:
   - we set $H(u) := H(u) + C(u)$;
   - we set $C(u') := C(u)/n_u$ for all URL u' pointed to by u, with n_u the number of outgoing links in u.
   - we set $G := G + C(u)$ and $C(u) := 0$.
6. At any given time, the PageRank of u can be approximated as $\frac{H(u)}{G}$.

It can be shown that this gives indeed an approximation of the PageRank value, whatever the crawling strategy is, as long as a URL is repeatedly accessed. A reasonable strategy is for instance a *greedy* one, to crawl the URL with the largest amount of cash at each step. Finally, much like to the use of the damping factor in the iterative computation of PageRank, convergence can be ensured by adding a virtual node u that is pointed to by each URL and that points to all URLs. In addition to making the storage of the Web matrix unnecessary, such an online algorithm also is more adapted to the case of a changing Web, when pages are added continuously. However, since computation power tends to be cheap and the storage of the content of Web pages already necessitates appropriate storage, search engines currently stick with the classical iterative computation of PageRank.

13.4.2 HITS

The *HITS* algorithm (Hypertext Induced Topic Selection) is another approach proposed by Kleinberg. The main idea is to distinguish two kinds of Web pages: *hubs* and *authorities*. Hubs are pages that point to good authorities, whereas authorities are pages that are pointed to by good hubs. As with PageRank, we use again a mutually recursive definition that will lead to an iterative fixpoint computation. For example, in the domain of Web pages about automobiles, good hubs will probably be portals linking to the main Web page of car makers, that will be good authorities.

More formally, let G' be the transition matrix (this time, not normalized, i.e., with Boolean 0 and 1 entries) of a graph (say, a subgraph of the Web graph). We consider the following iterative process, where a and h are column vectors, initially of norm 1:

$$\begin{cases} a := \frac{1}{\|G'^T h\|} \, G'^T h \\ h := \frac{1}{\|G' a\|} \, G' a \end{cases}$$

If some basic technical conditions on G' hold, we can show that this iterative process converges to column vectors a and h which represent, respectively, the authority and hub scores of vertices of the graph. Kleinberg proposes then the following way of using authority scores to order query results from the Web:

1. Retrieve the set D of Web pages matching a keyword query.
2. Retrieve the set D^* of Web pages obtained from D by adding all linked pages, as well as all pages linking to pages of D.
3. Build from D^* the corresponding subgraph G' of the Web graph.
4. Compute iteratively hubs and authority scores.
5. Sort documents from D by authority scores.

The process is here very different from PageRank, as authority scores are computed for each request (on a subgraph kind of centered on the original query). For this reason, and although HITS give interesting results, it is not as efficient as PageRank, for which all scores can be precomputed and top-k optimization is possible.

13.4.3 Spamdexing

The term *spamdexing* describes all fraudulent techniques that are used by unscrupulous Webmasters to artificially raise the visibility of their Web site to users of search engines. As with virus and antivirus, or spam and spam fighting, spamdexing and the fight against it is an unceasing series of techniques implemented by spamdexers, closely followed by countertechniques deployed by search engines. The motivation of spamdexers is to bring users to their webpages so as to generate revenue from pay-per-view or pay-per-use content (especially in the industries of online gambling and online pornography), or from advertising.

A first set of techniques consists in lying about the document by adding to a page keywords that are unrelated to its content; this may be done either as text present in the page but invisible to users through the use of CSS, JavaScript, or HTML presentational elements, or in the meta-information about the page that can be provided in the <meta name="description"> or <meta name="keywords"> tags in the header. As a result, current search engines tend not to give a strong importance to this kind of meta-information, or even to ignore them altogether. Furthermore, they implement automatic methods to find text hidden to a regular user and ignore it. In some cases, this is even used as a reason to lower the importance of the Web page.

PageRank and similar techniques are subject to *link farm* attacks, where a huge number of hosts on the Internet are used for the sole purpose of referencing each other, without any content in themselves, to raise the importance of a given website or set of Web sites. Countermeasures by search engines include detection of Web sites with empty or duplicate content, and the use of heuristics to discover subgraphs that look like link farms. A collection of algorithms have also been proposed to assign importance scores to Web pages in a way that is more robust to these kind of attacks. TrustRank, for instance, is defined using the same kind of iterative computation as PageRank, except that random jumps toward uniformly selected Web pages are replaced by random jumps to a small subset of "safe" seed pages, to prevent being trapped in link farms; this has the downside of artificially raising the importance of the set of seed pages, and thus of biasing the computation.

An assumption made by the graph mining techniques described earlier is that the addition of a link to a Web page is a form of approval of the content of the linked page, thus raising its importance. While this is mostly true when Web pages are written by a single individual or entity, this does not hold with user-editable content, such as wikis, guestbooks, blogs with comment systems, and so on. Spamdexers have an incentive to use these platforms to add links to their Web sites. They can also exploit security faults in Web applications to achieve the same effect. While most Webmasters take care to control whatever is added to their Web sites and to remove spam content, this cannot be assumed on a global level. A partial solution to this is the possibility of adding a rel="nofollow" attribute to all <a> links that have not been validated or are not approved by the Webmaster (some content management systems and blog platforms automatically add this attribute to any link inside content provided by users). Most current-day Web spiders recognize this attribute and ignore this link.

13.4.4 Discovering Communities on the Web

The graph structure of the Web can be used beyond the computation of PageRank-like importance scores. Another important graph mining technique that can be used on the Web is graph clustering: using the structure of the graph to delimitate homogeneous sets of Web pages (e.g., communities of Web sites about the same topic). The assumption is that closely connected set of pages in a Web page will share some common semantic characteristic.

Various algorithms for graph clustering have been studied, in this context and others (to isolate local networks of interest on the Internet, to find communities of people in social networks, etc.). Let us just present briefly one of them, which has the advantage of being simple to understand. Given a graph, the purpose is to separate it, hierarchically, into smaller and smaller, and more and more homogeneous, communities of nodes. We introduce the notion of *betweenness* of an edge, as the number of shortest paths between any two nodes of the graph that use this edge. The main idea of the algorithm is that edges with high betweenness tend to be connecting distinct communities. The algorithm proceeds by computing the betweenness of all edges (i.e., computing all shortest paths between pairs of nodes) removing the edge with highest betweenness, and then iterating the whole procedure, recomputing all betweenness values at each step. The algorithm ends when enough components of the graph have been separated, or when the highest betweenness is less than a given threshold. This is not a particularly efficient technique (the number of required operations is cubic in the number of nodes). Cubic-time algorithms are not appropriate for the whole graph of the Web, but such an algorithm might be used to cluster subgraphs.

Other graph clustering methods, usually more efficient, rely on another principle, namely that of minimum cut in a transport network. This is a classical algorithmic problem: Given a directed graph with weights (positive numbers) on the edges, one wants to find the set of edges of minimum weight to remove from the graph to separate two given nodes. This can be used to cluster the Web: In order to find the community to which a given Web page belongs, just compute the minimum cut (with some appropriate weighting of the edges) that separate this page from the rest of the Web, represented as a virtual node all pages point to. Such an approach differs from the previous one in that it is more local: We are not looking for a global partition into clusters but for the cluster of a given Web page.

13.5 HOT TOPICS IN WEB SEARCH

We conclude this chapter with some research topics related to the search of information on the Web that are particularly active at the moment of writing.

Web 2.0

Web 2.0 is a *buzzword* that has appeared recently to refer to recent changes in the Web, notably:

- Web applications with rich dynamic interfaces, especially with the help of AJAX technologies (AJAX stands for *Asynchronous JavaScript And XML* and is a way for a browser to exchange data with a Web server without requiring a reload of a Web page); it is exemplified by GMail[7] or Google Suggest[8];
- User-editable content, collaborative work and social networks (e.g., in blogs, wikis such as Wikipedia,[9] and social network Web sites like MySpace[10] and Facebook[11]);
- Aggregation of content from multiple sources (e.g., from RSS feeds) and personalization, that is proposed for instance by Netvibes[12] or YAHOO! PIPES (see Chapter 12).

Though Web 2.0 is more used in marketing contexts than in the research community, some interesting research problems are related to these technologies, especially in the application of graph mining techniques similar to those employed on the graph of the Web to the graph of social network Web sites, and in the works about *mashups* for aggregating content from multiple sources on the Web.

Deep Web

The *deep Web* (also known as *hidden Web* or *invisible Web*) is the part of Web content that lies in online databases, typically queried through HTML forms, and not usually accessible by following hyperlinks. As classical crawlers only follow these hyperlinks, they do not index the content that is behind forms. There are hundreds of thousands of such deep Web services, some of which with very high-quality information: all *Yellow pages* directories, information from the U.S. *Census Bureau*, weather or geolocation services, and so on.

There are two approaches to the indexing of the deep Web. A first possibility is an *extensional* approach, where content from the deep Web is generated by submitting data into forms, and the resulting Web pages are stored in an index, as with classical Web content. A more ambitious *intensional* approach is to try to understand the structure and semantics of a service of the deep Web, and to store this semantic description in an index. A semantic query from a user would then be dispatched to all relevant services, and the information retrieved from them. Whatever

---

[7] http://mail.google.com/.
[8] http://www.google.com/webhp?complete=1.
[9] http://www.wikipedia.org/.
[10] http://www.myspace.com.
[11] http://www.facebook.com/.
[12] http://www.netvibes.com/.

Showing results 1 through 25 (of 94 total) for all:xml

1. **cs.LO/0601085** [abs, ps, pdf, other] :
   Title: **A Formal Foundation for ODRL**
   Authors: **Riccardo Pucella, Vicky Weissman**
   Comments: 30 pgs, preliminary version presented at WITS-04 (Workshop on Issues in the Theory of Security), 2004
   Subj-class: Logic in Computer Science; Cryptography and Security
   ACM-class: H.2.7; K.4.4

2. **astro-ph/0512493** [abs, pdf] :
   Title: **VOFilter, Bridging Virtual Observatory and Industrial Office Applications**
   Authors: **Chen-zhou Cui (1), Markus Dolensky (2), peter Quinn (2), Yong-heng Zhao (1), Francoise Genova (3) ((1)NAO China, (2) ESO, (3) CDS)**
   Comments: Accepted for publication in ChJAA (9 pages, 2 figures, 185kb)

3. **cs.DS/0512061** [abs, ps, pdf, other] :
   Title: **Matching Subsequences in Trees**
   Authors: **Philip Bille, Inge Li Goertz**
   Subj-class: Data Structures and Algorithms

4. **cs.IR/0510025** [abs, ps, pdf, other] :
   Title: **Practical Semantic Analysis of Web Sites and Documents**
   Authors: **Thierry Despeyroux (INRIA Rocquencourt / INRIA Sophia Antipolis)**
   Subj-class: Information Retrieval

5. **cs.CR/0510013** [abs, pdf]:
   Title: **Safe Data Sharing and Data Dissemination on Smart Devices**
   Authors: **Luc Bouganim (INRIA Rocuencourt), Cosmin Cremarenco (INRIA Rocquencourt), Francois, Dang N goc (INRIA Rocquencourt, PRISM - UVSQ), Nicolas Dieu (INRIA Rocquencourt), Phillippe Pucheral (INRIA Rocquencourt, PRISM - UVSQ)**
   Subj-class: Cryptography and Security; Databases

Figure 13.22. Example pages resulting from the submission of a HTML form.

the method, searching the deep Web requires first discovering all relevant forms, and some analysis to understand what data to submit to a form. In the *intensional* approach, deep Web search is also needed to extract information from the pages resulting from the submission of a form, which is the topic of the next section.

Information Extraction

Classical search engines do not try to extract information from the content of Web pages, they only store and index them as they are. This means that the only possible kind of queries that can be asked is keyword queries, and the results provided are complete Web pages. The purpose of Web *information extraction* is to provide means to extract structured data and information from Web pages, so as to be able to answer more complex queries. For instance, an information extractor could extract phone numbers from Web pages, as well as the name of their owner, and provide an automatically built directory service. Information extraction is facilitated by very structured Web pages, such as those that are dynamically generated on response to the submission of an HTML form (e.g., Figure 13.22); a *wrapper* for this kind of dynamic site can be generated, in order to abstract away its interface.

Most research works in information extraction are in a supervised or semisupervised context, where humans pre-annotate Web pages whose content is to be extracted, or where human give some feedback on automatic wrapper construction. Unsupervised approaches rely either on the detection of linguistic or sentence-level patterns that express some concept or relation between concepts (e.g., addresses usually follow some kind of fixed format that can be discovered in corpus; textual patterns like *was born in* year can be found to automatically extract birth dates of individuals) or the detection of structural patterns in the Web page (e.g., repetitive structures such as tables or lists).

13.6 FURTHER READING

We provide references on the material found in this chapter. More information, as well as in-depth coverage of some other parts of this chapter, can be found in [41].

Web Standards

HTML 4.01 [162] is described by a recommendation of the World Wide Web Consortium, an organism that regroups academics and industrials for the development of standards about the World Wide Web, as is XHTML 1.0 [164]. The W3C is working at the time of writing on the successor to both languages, HTML5 [177]. The DNS and HTTP protocols, which are Internet protocols, are published by the Internet Engineering Task Force (IETF) and can be found, respectively, in [94] and [95].

The standard for robot exclusion and sitemaps both have unofficial specifications, not supported by any normalization organization. The former is described in [110]. Sitemaps are an initiative of Google, that has been embraced by other search engines. The specification of sitemaps is available in [149].

Web Parsing and Indexing

Computation of the edit distance between two text documents is a classical problem, and a dynamic algorithm for solving it can be found in textbooks on algorithmics, such as [49]. The Jaccard similarity coefficient has been introduced by the botanist Paul Jaccard for comparing floral populations across areas [100]. Hashing shingles of a document to build a compact sketch that can be used to efficiently detect near-duplicates has been proposed in [35].

The stemming technique described in the text is from Porter [136]. Soundex [157] is a widely used loose phonetic stemming for English.

[189] is a recent and accurate survey on inverted files. From the same authors, the book [179] provides a larger (but less up-to-date) coverage of the field, including a detailed presentation of the most useful text and index compression techniques. The recent book [120] covers information retrieval techniques and supplies on-line material at http://nlp.stanford.edu/IR-book/information-retrieval-book.html. The byte-level compression technique has been developed and experimented in [18, 19, 144]. Experimental results show that byte-level compression is twice as fast as bit-level compression. The compression loss with respect to the latter approach is reported to be approximately 30%. Integer compression methods have been studied for a long time in computer science. The γ code presented here is from [60].

Efficient external memory algorithms to construct index structures that cannot fit in memory is one of the core issues in databases and information retrieval. See for instance [160] for an in-depth survey. The external sort/merge is a standard algorithm implemented in all DBMS (and used, for instance, during non-indexed joins or grouping operations). [90] covers in detail the one-pass construction algorithm outlined in the present chapter.

Fagin's threshold algorithm (TA) that computes the top-k result of a ranked query is from [64]. It improves an earlier algorithm proposed by Fagin in [63].

Graph Mining

PageRank was introduced in [34] by the founders of the Google search engine, Sergey Brin and Lawrence Page. The OPIC algorithm is from [7]. HITS has been proposed by Kleinberg in [109]. TrustRank has been presented by researchers from Stanford University and Yahoo! in [85]. Interestingly, Google registered *TrustRank* as a trademark in 2005, suggesting they might adopt the technology, but the trademark was abandoned in 2008.

The graph clustering algorithm relying on betweenness is the work of two physicists, published in [126]. The idea of using minimum cuts on the Web graph has been proposed in [65, 66]. A large number of graph clustering techniques exist, some of them are reviewed in [143]. One particular technique of interest, particularly interesting because of its efficiency and the availability of an optimized implementation, is MCL, the Markov CLustering algorithm [158].

The Deep Web and Information Extraction

The first study about the amount of content is [33]. Other works [45] have confirmed the fact that an impressive amount of content is hidden to current-day search engines. Google believes in an extensional approach to crawling the deep Web, see [119]. Research works that go toward intensional indexing include [46, 145].

A survey of existing information extraction techniques on the Web can be found in [43]. Unsupervised techniques, which are probably the only relevant at the scale of the whole world, include RoadRunner [51], ExAlg [21], and the various works derived from the MDR system [117, 187].

13.7 EXERCISES

Exercise 13.7.1 *(1) Use Google. For each query, note the number of answers. Query "Bonnie and Clyde," "bonnie clyde," "bonny and Clyde," "Bonnie or Clyde," "bonnieclyde," "Bonnie and Bonnie." (2) Analyze your results. (3) Consider the same queries with AltaVista, Ask Jeeves, Yahoo!, and MSN Search. Compare.*

Exercise 13.7.2 *A user poses a query and ask for the top-10 documents. There are $n = 2$ relevant documents in the result.*

1. *What is the precision?*
2. *The user knows that the collection contains six documents relevant to her query. What is the recall?*
3. *Repeat questions 1 and 2 with $n = 4$.*
4. *What would be a result with recall = 1 and precision = 0.5?*
5. *What would be a result with recall = 0.5 and precision = 1?*

Exercise 13.7.3 *Consider the following documents:*

1. *$d_1 = I$ like to watch the sun set with my friend.*
2. *$d_2 = The$ Best Places To Watch The Sunset.*
3. *$d_3 = My$ friend watches the sun come up.*

Construct an inverted index with tf–idf weights for terms "Best" and "sun." What would be the ranked result of the query "Best and sun"?

Exercise 13.7.4 *Consider the document set example from Figure 13.4. Suppose that we want to index the term be (we consider therefore that it is not a stop-word). Compute the line of the inverted index for term be, with positions and tf–idf weighting.*

Exercise 13.7.5 *Give the pseudo-code of the naive algorithm that builds an inverted index from a large documents collection. Explain why the result is not satisfactory.*

Exercise 13.7.6 *Use Fagin's threshold algorithm to compute the top-2 result of the query:*

   jaguar OR new

on the inverted index of Figure 13.11.

Exercise 13.7.7 *Prove that the Fagin's TA algorithm is correct for monotone aggregation functions (nb: A function g is monotone if $g(x_1, x_2, \ldots, x_n) \leq g(x'_1, x'_2, \ldots, x'_n)$ whenever $x_i \leq x'_i$ for every i.)*

Exercise 13.7.8 *Analyze the time and space complexities of the merge-based algorithm.*

Exercise 13.7.9 *Explain how deletions can be handled in a dynamic inverted index. Hint: Propose a small variant of the dynamic insertion strategy described in the chapter.*

Exercise 13.7.10 (logarithmic merging) *For simplicity, it is implicitly assumed in the text that each inverted list is stored in a separate file. This greatly reduces the complexity of merging operations. In pratice, though, the number of files would be far too large, and efficient index implementation would attempt to limit this number.*

1. *Assume first that the inverted index is maintained as a single file that concatenates all the inverted lists. Describe the merge operation and analyze its complexity (count how many times an entry has to be accessed during the maintenance operations of a file).*
2. *(project) Study the binomial heap structure and propose an adaptation to the problem of merging inverted files. The main idea is to maintain a set of runs in exponentially growing size, leading to an amortized build complexity of $\log |F|(|F|/r)$.*

Exercise 13.7.11 *The inverted list of a term t consists of the following document ids:*

   $[345; 476; 698; 703]$

Apply the VBytes compression technique to this sequence. What is the amount of space gained by the method?

Exercise 13.7.12 *Implement the PageRank algorithm as described in the section for a graph of up to one thousand pages. Then:*

1. *Test it on the graph of Figure 13.19.*
2. *Add a few sinks, and test your algorithm again.*
3. *Pick the page p with the least PageRank. Add some new nodes to simulate a link farm. How many pages do you need to introduce to promote p as the most popular?*

Exercise 13.7.13 *Find a free crawler on the Web and play with it.*

Exercise 13.7.14 *Write a "mini" crawler. Its input is a few words and the URL of a "seed page" (e.g., your homepage). The crawler should crawl, say, one hundred pages, and sort the words based on their number of occurrences. Try different crawling strategies: depth first, breadth first, popular first. Bonus: Use some stemming.*

Exercise 13.7.15 *Choose a few interesting pages (e.g., news, music). Try to find metadata for these pages: author, date, purpose, citation of sources, copyright, etc. How much metadata could be found inside the pages?*

Exercise 13.7.16 *When asked a keyword query, a metasearch engine queries several search engines and aggregates their answers. Find some on the Web (e.g., metacrawler), and test them.*

Exercise 13.7.17 *Find the homepages of the authors of this book. Add pointers to these pages from your own homepage. This will be tested using Google "Find pages that link to page X."*

Exercise 13.7.18 *Here are some document sketches:*

docId	Terms
1	France, Recession, Slowing, IMF
2	USA, Financial, Paulson, Slowing, Crisis
3	Crisis, Government, Slowing, IMF
4	GDP, France, Crisis, Slowing

1. *Create for each term present in documents the corresponding posting list.*
2. *Transform the following sentences into Boolean queries of terms and evaluate them on the posting lists (skip missing terms).*
   - *"The crisis is slowing down"*
   - *"In France, the IMF criticizes the GDP"*
   - *"In the USA, Paulson and the crisis"*
3. *Based on this intuitive process, propose an algorithm that processes a query.*
4. *How can we choose term order to optimize evaluation?*
5. *Very long posting lists take time to process. How can we optimize skipping nonmerging docIds, since posting lists are small?*
6. *Modify the algorithm with this optimization.*

Exercise 13.7.19 *In an inverted index, each posting list must be stored on the disk. Because they are often read, it is essential to compress them. In this exercise, we consider an index of 100,000 distinct terms, over 10 million of documents. Let us say that, on average, each term is associated to 500,000 documents (from 10,000 to 5 million). We are interested in determining how much space the index uses. The physical characteristics of the index are given below:*

- *Dictionary: a term (20 bytes), an idf value (4 bytes), a pointer (8 bytes);*
- *Posting list entry: a docId (X bytes), a tf value (4 bytes).*

Compressing the dictionary

1. *Give the size of the dictionary (i.e., not counting posting lists themselves).*
2. *Propose a term compression method.*
3. *Replace terms by terms identifiers. Give the new size of the dictionary.*
4. *How can we find the term identifier from a given term?*

Compressing the posting lists

1. *According to the number of documents, give the encoding size of a docId.*
2. *Give the average encoding size of each posting list and the global index size.*
3. *Propose a solution to compress document identifiers.*
4. *Compress the following posting list with the previous encoding method: 105, 117, 222, 702, 3002.*
5. *How much storage does the index use if two-fifths of the document identifiers are encoded on a byte and the others on 3 bytes (on average). Do not forget tf values.*

14

An Introduction to Distributed Systems

This chapter is an introduction to very large data management in distributed systems. Here, "very large" means a context where gigabytes (1,000 MB = 10^9 bytes) constitute the unit size for measuring data volumes. Terabytes (10^{12} bytes) are commonly encountered, and many Web companies and scientific or financial institutions must deal with petabytes (10^{15} bytes). In a near future, we can expect exabytes (10^{18} bytes) data sets, with the world-wide digital universe roughly estimated (in 2010) as about 1 zetabytes (10^{21} bytes).

Distribution is the key for handling very large data sets. Distribution is necessary (but not sufficient) to bring *scalability* (i.e., the means of maintaining stable performance for steadily growing data collections by adding new resources to the system). However, distribution brings a number of technical problems that make the design and implementation of distributed storage, indexing, and computing a delicate issue. A prominent concern is the risk of *failure*. In an environment that consists of hundreds or thousands of computers (a common setting for large Web companies), it becomes very common to face the failure of components (hardware, network, local systems, disks), and the system must be ready to cope with it at any moment.

Our presentation covers principles and techniques that recently emerged to handle Web-scale data sets. We examine the extension of traditional storage and indexing methods to large-scale distributed settings. We describe techniques to efficiently process *point queries* that aim at retrieving a particular object. Here there typically is a human being waiting for an answer in front of a screen. So, efficient means a response time in the order of a few milliseconds, a difficult challenge in the presence of terabytes of data. We also consider the *batch analysis* of large collections of documents to extract statistical or descriptive information. This problem is very different. Possibly terabytes of data are streamed into a program. Efficient computation now means hours or even days and a most critical issue is the reliable execution of processes that may run so long, in spite of the many glitches that are likely to affect the infrastructure in such a time frame. We should keep in mind these specificities in the presentation that follows, as they motivate many design choices.

The present chapter introduces the essentials of distributed systems devoted to large-scale data sets. Its material represents by no means an in-depth or accurate coverage of the topic, but merely aims at supplying the neophyte reader with the minimal background. As usual, the Further Reading section points to complementary references.

14.1 BASICS OF DISTRIBUTED SYSTEMS

A *distributed system* is piece of software that serves to coordinate the actions of several computers. This coordination is achieved by exchanging *messages* (i.e., pieces of data conveying information). The system relies on a network that connects the computers and handles the routing of messages.

14.1.1 Networking Infrastructures

We limit the discussion in this chapter to the following two classes of networks: Local Area Networks and P2P Networks.

Local Area Network (LAN) LANs are for instance used in data centers to connect hundreds or even thousands of servers. Figure 14.1 shows the main features of a typical LAN in this context. We roughly distinguish three communication levels:

- First, servers are grouped on "racks," linked by a high-speed cable. A typical rack contains a few dozens of servers.
- Second, a data center consists of one to a large number of racks connected by *routers* (or *switches*) that transfer nonlocal messages.

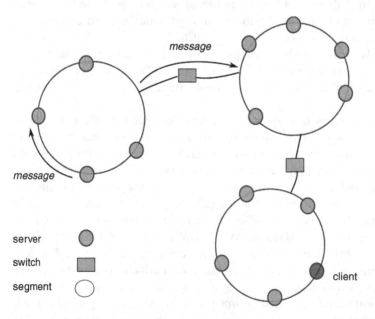

Figure 14.1. A simplified view of a local network.

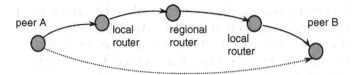

Figure 14.2. Internet networking.

■ A third (slower) communication level, between distinct clusters, may also be considered. It may for instance allow some independent data centers to cooperate (e.g., to consolidate global statistics).

In all cases, servers only communicate via message passing. They do not share storage or computing resources. The architecture is said "shared-nothing".

Example 14.1.1 *At the beginning of 2010, a typical Google data center consists of 100–200 racks, each hosting about 40 servers. The number of servers in such a center is roughly estimated around 5,000. The number of data centers is constantly evolving, and the total number of servers is probably already above one million.*

Peer-to-Peer Network (P2P) A P2P network is a particular kind of *overlay network*, a graph structure build over a native physical network. The physical network we consider here is the Internet. Nodes or "peers" communicate with messages sent over the Internet. The route that connects two peers on the Internet is typically intricate. Typically (Figure 14.2), a message sent by peer A first reaches a local router, that forwards the message to other routers (local, regional, or world-wide) until it is delivered to peer B. By abstracting this complexity, a P2P network imagines a direct link between A and B, as if they were directly connected, as soon as they know the IP addresses of each other. This pseudo-direct connection that may (physically) consist of 10 or more forwarding messages, or "hops," is called an *overlay link*, therefore the term *overlay network*.

Example 14.1.2 *If you are connected to the Internet, you can use the traceroute utility program to inspect the routers involved in the connection between your computer and a site of your choice. For instance: traceroute webdam.inria.fr gives the list of routers on the forwarding Internet path to the Webdam INRIA Web site. Several sites propose a traceroute interface if you do not have access to a console. One can find some (e.g., at traceroute.org).*

For our purposes, we will assimilate nodes to computers running programs of interest to the distributed system. A computer often runs several programs involved in different kinds of services. A process on computer *A* may for instance be in charge of file accesses, while another, running on *A* as well, handles HTTP requests. If we focus on a specific task of the distributed system, there is generally one and only one process that fulfills this task on each computer. This allows blurring the distinction, and we will simply denote as *node* a process running on a computer at a specific location of the network, and in charge of the particular task.

Next, it is often convenient to distinguish *server nodes* from *client nodes*. A server node provides, through cooperation with other server nodes, a service of the distributed system. A client node consumes this service. Nothing prevents a client node to run on the same computer as a server node (this is typically the case in P2P networks), but the point is most often irrelevant to the discussion. In practice, a client node is often a library incorporated in a larger application, that implements the communication protocol with the server nodes. When no ambiguity arises, we will simple use "Client" and "Server" to denote, respectively, a client node and a server node it communicates with.

14.1.2 Performance of a Distributed Storage System

Nodes exchange *messages* following a particular protocol. The Ethernet protocol is the most widely used. It splits messages into small packets of, typically, 1,500 bytes each. At the time of writing, the data transfer rate of a local Ethernet network can (theoretically) reach 1 GB/s. The bandwidth is higher that the maximal disk rate which is at most 100 MB/s. Roughly speaking, it is one order of magnitude faster to exchange in-memory data between two computers connected by a high-speed LAN, than for a single computer to read the same data written on the disk. However, bandwidth is a resource that many participants compete for, and this invites to use it with care in data-intensive applications. The latency (time to initiate an operation) is also cheaper with networks, although the gap is less impressive.

Internet figures for latency and bandwidth are highly varying, as they depend both on the distance between the communicating nodes, and on the network devices involved, particularly at local ends. (For instance, a WiFI connection in an Internet café is a nightmare for data intensive manipulations!) As an illustration, the latency of a connection between INRIA Paris and Stanford University is less than 200 ms, and the bandwidth is 7 MB/s (download) and 3 MB/s (upload). You are encouraged to test these values on your own infrastructure, with the ping command or some of the numerous Web sites. For instance, see

http://www.pcpitstop.com/internet/Bandwidth.asp

The latency of the average Internet path is estimated at 10 ms. The performance of Internet is definitely at least one order of magnitude worse than LANs. Table 14.1 summarizes the values that should be kept in mind.

The following reasoning helps understand the advantage of distributed storage (see Figure 14.3 for an illustration):

Sequential access: Consider a typical 1 TB disk with 100 MB/s maximal transfer rate. It takes 166 minutes (more than 2 hours and a half!) to read the whole content of the disk.

Parallel access: Now imagine the 1 TB data set spread over 100 disks on a same machine. In order to read this data set (i.e., to bring it in the computer's main memory), we must retrieve 10 GB from each disk. This is done, assuming that the disks work in parallel, in a little more that 90 seconds. But, when the size of the data set increases, the CPU of the computer is typically overwhelmed at some point by the data flow and it is slowed down.

Table 14.1. Disk vs Network Latency and Bandwidth

Type	Latency	Bandwidth
Disk	$\approx 5 \times 10^{-3}$s (5 ms);	At best 100 MB/s
LAN	$\approx 1 - 2 \times 10^{-3}$s (1–2 ms);	$\approx$ 1 GB/s (single rack); $\approx$ 100 MB/s (switched)
Internet	Highly variable. Typ. 10–100 ms	Highly variable. Typ. a few MBs

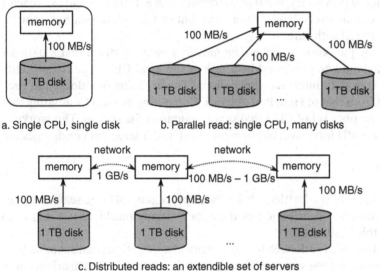

a. Single CPU, single disk   b. Parallel read: single CPU, many disks

c. Distributed reads: an extendible set of servers

Figure 14.3. Distributed data management: Why?

Distributed access: The same disk-memory transfer time can be achieved with 100 computers, each disposing of its own local disk. The advantage now is that the CPU will not be overwhelmed as the number of disks increases.

This is a good basis to discuss some important aspects of data distribution. Note first that we assume that the maximal transfer rate is achieved for each disk. This is only true for *sequential* reads and can only be obtained for operations that fully scan a data set. As a result, the seek time (time to position the head on appropriate disk track) is negligible compared to the transfer time. Therefore, the previous analysis mostly holds for *batch* operations that access the whole collection, and is particularly relevant for applications where most files are written once (by *appending* new content), then read many times. This scenario differs from the classical behavior of a centralized database.

Now consider in contrast a workload consisting of lots of operations, each one randomly accessing a small piece of data in a large collection. (Such a workload is more in the spirit of a database operation where a row in a large table is accessed.) The access may be a read or a write operation. In both cases, we have to perform a random access to a large file and the seek time cannot be ignored. Distribution is here of little help to speed up a single operation. However, if we can afford to replicate the data on many servers, this is an opportunity to balance the query load by distributing evenly read and/or write requests. Architectures for such transactional scenarios can actually be classified by their read/write distribution policy: Distributing writes raises concurrency issues; distributing reads raises consistency issues. We further develop this important point in the following.

Finally, look again at Figure 14.3. The distribution mechanism shows two possible data flows. The first one comes from the disk to the *local* CPU, the second one (shown in dotted arrows) represents exchanges between computers. The performance of network exchanges depends both on the latency and on the network bandwidth. As noted previously, the typical transfer rate is 100 MB/s and can reach 1 GB/s, one order of magnitude higher than disks, but bandwidth is a shared resource that must be exploited with care.

A general principle, known as the *data locality principle*, states that a data set stored on a disk should be processed by a task of the local CPU. The data locality principle is valid for data-intensive applications. The architecture adopted in such cases is different from that of High Performance Computing or Grid Computing that distribute a task across a set of CPU that share a common file system. This works as long as the task is CPU intensive, but becomes unsuited if large data exchanges are involved.

To summarize:

1. Disk transfer rate is a bottleneck for batch processing of large scale datasets; parallelization and distribution of the data on many machines is a means to eliminate this bottleneck;
2. Disk seek time is a bottleneck for transactional applications that submit a high rate of random accesses; replication, distribution of writes, and distribution of reads are the technical means to make such applications scalable;
3. Data locality: when possible, program should be "pushed" near the data they need to access to avoid costly data exchange over the network.

14.1.3 Data Replication and Consistency

Most of the properties required from a distributed system depend on the replication of data. Without replication, the loss of a server hosting a unique copy of some data item results in unrecoverable damages. As already said, replication also brings other advantages, including the ability to distribute read/write operations for improved scalability. However, it raises the following intricate issues:

Performance: Writing several copies of an item takes more time, which may affect the throughput of the system.

Consistency: Consistency is the ability of a system to behave as if the transaction of each user always run in isolation from other transactions and never fails. Consider, for instance, a transaction on an e-commerce site. There is a "basket" that is progressively filled with bought items. At the end the user is directed to a secure payment interface. Such a transaction involves many HTTP accesses and may last an extended period of time (typically, a few minutes). Consistency in this context means that if the user added an item to her basket at some point, it should remain there until the end of the transaction. Furthermore, the item should still be available when time comes to pay and deliver the product.

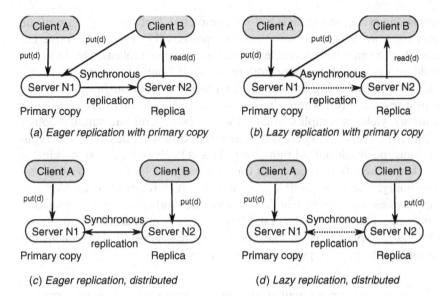

Figure 14.4. Four replication policies in a distributed system.

Data replication complicates the management of consistency in a distributed setting. We illustrate next four typical replication protocols that show the interactions between performance considerations and consistency issues (Figure 14.4). The scenario assumes two concurrent Client applications, A and B, that put/read a data idem d which is replicated on two servers S_1 and S_2. The four cases depicted in Figure 14.4 correspond to the possible combinations of two technical choices: eager (synchronous) or lazy (asynchronous) replication and primary or distributed versioning:

Eager, primary: Consider the first case (a). Here, the replication policy is "eager": a *put(d)* request sent by Client A to Server 1 is replicated at once on Server 2. The request is completed only when both S_1 and S_2 have sent an acknowledgment; meanwhile, A is frozen, as well as any other client that would access d. Moreover, the second design choice in case (a) is that each data item has a primary copy and several (at least one) secondary copies. Each update is first sent to the primary copy.

From an application point of view, such a design offers some nice properties. Because the replication is managed synchronously, a read request sent by Client B always accesses a consistent state of d, whether it reads from S_1 or S_2. And because there is a primary copy, requests sent by several clients relating to a same item can be queued, which ensures that updates are applied sequentially and not in parallel. The obvious downside is that these applications have to wait for the completion of other clients' requests, both for writing and reading.

Async, primary: Case (b) (often referred to as "Master-slave" replication) shows a slightly different design choice. There is still a primary copy, but the replication is asynchronous. Thus, some of the replicas may be out of date with respect to the client's requests. Client B for instance may read on S_2 an old version of item *d* because the synchronization is not yet completed. Note that, because of the primary copy, we can still be sure that the replicas will be *eventually* consistent because there cannot be independent updates of distinct replicas. This situation is considered acceptable in many modern, "NoSQL" data management systems that accept to trade strong consistency for a higher read throughput.

Eager, no primary: Case (c), where there is no primary copy anymore (but eager replication), yields a complex situation where two clients can simultaneously write on distinct replicas, whereas the eager replication implies that these replications must be synchronized right away. This is likely to lead to some kind of interlocking, where both clients wait for some resource locked by another one.

Async, no-primary: The most flexible case is (d) (often referred to as "Master-Master" replication), in which both primary copies and synchronous replication are given up. There is an advantage (often viewed as decisive for web-scale data intensive applications): Client operations are *never* stalled by concurrent operations, at the price of possibly inconsistent states.

Inconsistencies sometimes entailed by asynchronous protocols never occur in centralized database systems whose transactional model guarantees ACID properties. This may however be the preferred choice of distributed systems that favor efficiency and adopt a more permissive consistency model. A pending issue in that case is the management of inconsistent versions, a process often called *data reconciliation*. What happens when the system detects that two replicas have been independently modified? It turns out that the answer is, in most cases, quite practical: Data reconciliation is seen as application-dependent. The system is brought back to a consistent state, possibly by promoting one of the versions as the "current" one, and notifying the client applications that a conflict occurred. Readers familiar with Concurrent Versioning Systems like CVS or Subversion will recognize the optimistic, lock-free mechanism adopted by these tools.

It has been argued that a distributed system cannot simultaneously satisfy consistency and availability while being tolerant to failures ("the CAP theorem," discussed further). Therefore a system designer has to choose which property should be (at least partly) sacrificed. This often leads to giving up strong consistency requirements, in favor of availability and fault tolerance.

In summary, data replication leads to distinguishing several consistency levels, namely:

- *Strong consistency* (ACID properties), requires a (slow) synchronous replication, and possibly heavy locking mechanisms. This is the traditional choice of database systems.
- *Eventual consistency* trades eager replication for performance. The system is guaranteed to converge toward a consistent state (possible relying on a primary copy).
- *Weak consistency* chooses to fully favor efficiency, and never wait for write and read operations. As a consequence, some requests may serve outdated data. Also, inconsistencies typically arise, and the system relies on reconciliation based on the application logic.

Existing database systems are often seen as too heavy and rigid in distributed systems that give up strong consistency to achieve better performance. This idea that the strong consistency requirements imposed by RDBMS are incompatible with distributed data management, is one of the founding principles of the "NoSQL" trend.

14.2 FAILURE MANAGEMENT

In a centralized system, if a program fails for any reason, the simple (and, actually, standard) solution is to abort then restart its transactions. On the other hand, chances to see a single machine fail are low. Things are quite different in the case of a distributed system with thousands of computers. Failure becomes a possibly frequent situation, due to program bugs, human errors, hardware or network problems, among others. For small tasks, it is just simpler to restart them. But for long-lasting distributed tasks, restarting them is often not an acceptable option in such settings, since errors typically occur too often. Moreover, in most cases, a failure affects a minor part of the task, which can be quickly completed providing that the system knows how to cope with faulty components.

Some common principles are met in all distributed systems that try to make them resilient to failures. One of the most important is *independence*. The task handled by an individual node should be independent from the other components. This allows recovering the failure by only considering its initial state, without having to take into account complex relationships or synchronization with other tasks. Independence is best achieved in *shared-nothing* architectures, when both the CPU and the local disk of a server run in isolation of the other components of the servers.

Thanks to replication methods examined earlier, a failure can usually be recovered by replacing the faulty node by a mirror. The critical question in this context is to detect that a system met a failure. Why for instance is a client unable to communicate with a server? This may be because of a failure of the server itself or because the communication network suffers from a transient problem. The client can wait for the failed node to come back, but this runs against availability, since the application becomes idle for an unpredictable period of time.

14.2.1 Failure Recovery

Figure 14.5 recalls the main aspects of data recovery in a centralized data management system, and its extension to distributed settings.

Consider first a client-server application with a single server node (left part). (1) The client issues a *write(a)*. The server does not write immediately *a* in its repository. Because this involves a random access, it would be very inefficient to do so. Instead, it puts *a* in its volatile memory. Now, if the system were to crash or if the memory is corrupted in any way, the write is lost. To prevent such a loss, the server writes in a *log file* (2). A log is a sequential file that supports very fast append operations. When the log manager confirms that the data are indeed on persistent storage (3), the server can send back an acknowledgment to the client (4). Eventually, the main memory data will be flushed in the repository (5).

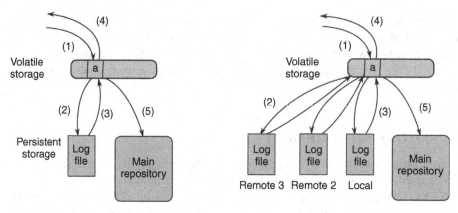

Figure 14.5. Recovery techniques for centralized (left) and replicated architectures (right).

This is a standard recovery protocol, implemented in centralized DBMSs. In a distributed setting, the server must log a write operation not only to the local log file, but also to 1, 2, or more remote logs. The issue is close to replication methods, the main choice being to adopt either a *synchronous* or *asynchronous* protocol.

Synchronous protocol: The server acknowledges the client only when all the remote nodes have sent a confirmation of the successful completion of their *write()* operation. In practice, the client waits until the slowest of all the writers sends its acknowledgment. This may severely hinder the efficiency of updates, but the obvious advantage is that all the replicas are consistent.

Asynchronous protocol: The client application waits only until one of the copies (the fastest) has been effectively written. Clearly, this puts a risk on data consistency, as a subsequent read operation may access an older version that does not yet reflect the update.

The multilog recovery process, synchronous or asynchronous, has a cost, but it brings availability (and reliability). If the server dies, its volatile memory vanishes and its local log cannot be used for a while. However, the closest mirror can be chosen. It reads from its own log a state equivalent to that of the dead server and can begin to answer client's requests. This is standard REDO protocol, described in detail in any classical textbook on centralized databases. We do not elaborate further here.

14.2.2 Distributed Transactions

A *transaction* is a sequence of data update operations that is required to be an "all-or-nothing" unit of work. That is, when a *commit* is requested, the system has to perform *all* the updates in the transaction. We say the transaction has been *validated*. In case of a problem, the system also has the option to perform *nothing* of it. We say the transaction has been *aborted*. On the other hand, the system is not allowed to perform some of the updates and not others (i.e., partial validation is forbidden).

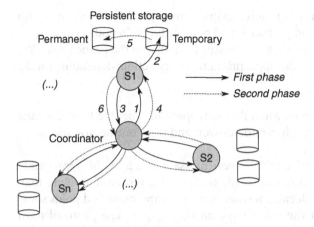

Figure 14.6. The two-phase commit protocol (details are given for the Coordinator-Server 1 communications only).

In a distributed setting, the update operations may occur on distinct servers $\{S_1,\ldots,S_n\}$, called *participants*. A typical case is the eager replication explained earlier. The problem is to find a protocol, implemented and controlled by a distinct node called *coordinator*, that communicates with the participants so that the all-or-nothing semantics is ensured. The main algorithm used to achieve this goal is the *two-phase commit* (2PC) protocol:

1. The coordinator asks each participant whether it is able to perform the required operation with a *Prepare* message.
2. If all participants answered with a confirmation, the coordinator sends a *Decision* message: the transaction is then committed at each site.

Assume for the time being that everything proceeds gracefully, without node failure or network communication problem. In this ideal scenario, a distributed data update transaction conforms to the following workflow (Figure 14.6, with focus on S_1). Initially (1) the Coordinator sends a Prepare message. Each participant then takes appropriate measures to guarantee that it will be able to fulfill its task in the second phase. Typically, updated data stored in volatile memory is written on a safe temporary persistent storage to prevent a loss due to a system crash (2). The participant can then send a confirmation message to the Coordinator (3), either confirm if the participant is ready to commit, or refuse.

The second phase begins when the Coordinator got all the answers from the participating nodes. It sends then a *Decision* message (4) which can either be commit or abort. The rule is that if *at least one* participant refused its part of the transaction, the whole operation must be aborted. If all confirm their readiness, the Coordinator can send a commit. (Although it is not compelled to do so: a refuse is also acceptable.)

In case of commit, each participant copies the data from the temporary area to the main repository (5), else it can simply remove the temporary storage associated to the ongoing transaction. An acknowledgment of success is required for this second round, so that the Coordinator closes the transaction.

Now, the question is: What if a failure occurs somewhere? We can distinguish between network communication problems and node failures. In addition, we have to examine separately the roles of the Coordinator from that of the participants. We start with the latter and examine the appropriate recovery action, depending on the instant of the failure occurrence.

Initial failure: Such a failure occurs when the participant p_i is unable to receive the *prepare* message; in that case, it cannot answer, and the Coordinator aborts the transaction.

Failure in *prepared* state: p_i received the *prepare* message and took the appropriate measures to ensure that it is indeed ready to commit if required to. Note that, at this point, p_i probably allocates resources to the transaction and holds some locks that possibly hinder the overall system throughput. The protocol must ensure that it will eventually (and as soon as possible) receive a decision from the Coordinator, even if it fails, and restart.

Failure in commit or abort state: p_i learned the decision of the Coordinator and is compelled to carry out the operations that do implement this decision, even if it undergoes one or several failures.

Technically speaking, such a distributed protocol must preserve some vital information regardless of the failures that affect a node. For instance, a participant that fails in the *prepared* state must be able to figure out, when it recovers, whether the Coordinator sent its decision. For instance, it could contact the Coordinator to learn the current state. In commit state, a failure may occur while p_i is proceeding with the validation of the transaction. After restart, the validation needs to be reexecuted, which implies that it is implemented as an *idempotent* operation (a property common to all recovery mechanisms).

We now turn our attention to the Coordinator. A first remark is that it must implement the necessary actions to preserve its ability to monitor the distributed transaction, even if it fails. For instance, before sending the *Decision* message, the commit or abort choice must be logged in a safe (persistent) area. Indeed, if the Coordinator fails after sending its decision, it would restart in an undefined status if this information could not be recovered.

In general, if the Coordinator fails, the distributed process may be in an intermediate state which can only be solved if the Coordinator restarts and is able to resume properly the transaction. If, for instance, failure occurs when the Coordinator is sending *prepare* messages, some participants may be informed of the transaction request, while others may not. On restart, the Coordinator should look for pending transactions in its log and re-send the message.

The same approach holds for dealing with Coordinator failure in the various steps of the protocol. The main problem is that the Coordinator may fail permanently, or suffer from network communication problems that leave the process pending for an unbounded time period. Meanwhile, the participants are *blocked* and maintain their locks on the resources allocated to the transaction.

Note that a participant *cannot* decide independently to commit or abort. (We could imagine for instance a timeout mechanism that triggers an abort if the participant is left in a *prepared* state without receiving the decision.) Indeed, it may be the case that the Coordinator sent a commit decision that reached all the participants save one. Aborting this part of the transaction would break the all-or-nothing requirements. Several techniques have been proposed to overcome the blocking nature of the 2PL protocol, including communication among the participants themselves. We invite the reader to consult the last section of the chapter for references.

The 2PL protocol is a good illustration of the difficulty to coordinate the execution of several related processes, in particular in case of failures. Applications that need to execute distributed transactions enter in a mechanism where nodes become *dependent* from one another, and this makes the whole data management much more intricate. Moreover, the mechanism tends to block the operations of other applications and therefore restricts the global throughput of the system. In general, solutions implemented by organizations dealing with Web scale data tend to adopt a nontransactional approach, or at least consistency rules less strict than the standard semantics.

14.3 REQUIRED PROPERTIES OF A DISTRIBUTED SYSTEM

There is a long list of "**-ity" that characterize the good properties of distributed systems: reliability, scalability, availability, and so on. We briefly review some of particular interest to the book's scope. The end of the section proposes a discussion on the ability of distributed systems to simultaneously maintain these good properties.

14.3.1 Reliability

Reliability denotes the ability of a distributed system to deliver its services even when one or several of its software of hardware components fail. It definitely constitutes one of the main expected advantages of a distributed solution, based on the assumption that a participating machine affected by a failure can always be replaced by another one, and not prevent the completion of a requested task. For instance, a common requirements of large electronic web sites is that a user transaction should never be canceled because of a failure of the particular machine that is running that transaction. An immediate and obvious consequence is that reliability relies on *redundancy* of both the software components and data. At the limit, should the entire data center be destroyed by an earthquake, it should be replaced by another one that has a replica of the shopping carts of the user. Clearly, this has a cost and depending of the application, one may more or less fully achieve such a resilience for services, by eliminating every *single point of failure*.

14.3.2 Scalability

The concept of scalability refers to the ability of a system to continuously evolve in order to support a growing amount of tasks. In our setting, a system may have to scale because of an increase of data volume, or because of an increase of work (e.g., number of transactions). We would like to achieve this scaling without performance loss. We will favor here *horizontal scalability* achieved by adding new servers. But,

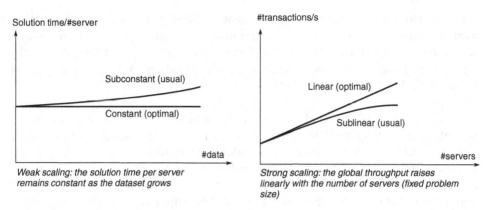

Figure 14.7. Dimensions of scalability.

one can also consider *vertical scalability* obtained by adding more resources to a single server.

To illustrate these options, suppose we have distributed the workload of an application between 100 servers, in a somehow perfect and abstract manner, with each holding 1/100 of the data and serving 1/100 of the queries. Now suppose we get 20% more data, or 20% more queries, we can simply get 20 new servers. This is horizontal scalability that is virtually limitless for very parallelizable applications. Now we could also add extra disk/memory to the 100 servers (to handle the increase in data), and add extra memory or change the processors to faster ones (to handle the increase in queries). This is vertical scalability that typically reaches rather fast the limits of the machine.

In parallel computing, one further distinguishes *weak scalability* from *strong scalability* (see Figure 14.7). The former analyzes how the time to obtain a solution varies with respect to the processor count with a fixed data set size per processor. In the perfect case, this time remains constant (per processor), indicating the ability of the system to maintain a perfect balance. Strong scalability refers to the global throughput of a system, for a fixed data set size. If the throughput raises linearly as new servers are added, the system does not suffer from an overhead due to the management tasks associated to a distributed job. (Note that the preceding discussion assumes a linear complexity of the system behavior, which is true at least for basic read/write/search operations.)

It is actually a common situation that the performance of a system, although designed (or claimed) to be scalable, declines with the system size, due to the management or environment cost. For instance, network exchanges may become slower because machines tend to be far apart from one another. More generally, it may happen that some tasks are not distributed, either because of their inherent atomic nature or because of some flaw in the system design. At some point, these tasks (if any) limit the speed-up obtained by distribution (a phenomenon known as Amdahl's law in the related context of parallel computing).

A scalable architecture avoids this situation and attempts to balance evenly the load on all the participating nodes. Let us consider the simple case of a server that would carry out 10% more work than the others, due to some special role.

This is a source of nonscalability. For small workloads, such a difference is unnoticeable, but eventually it will reach an importance that will make the "stressed" node a bottleneck. However, a node dedicated to some administrative tasks that is really negligible or that does not increase proportionally to the global workload is acceptable.

Many architectures presented in the rest of this chapter are of type "one Master—many Servers." The Master is a node that handles a few specific tasks (e.g., adding a new server to the cluster or connecting a client) but does not participate to the core functionalities of the application. The servers hold the data set, either via a full replication (each item is present on each each server) or, more commonly, via "sharding": the data set is partitioned, and each subset is stored on one server and replicated on a few others. This Master–Server approach is easier to manage than a cluster where all nodes play an equivalent role, and often remains valid on the long run.

14.3.3 Availability

A task that is partially allocated to a server may become idle if the server crashes or turns out to be unavailable for any reason. In the worst case, it can be delayed until the problem is fixed or the faulty server replaced by a replica. *Availability* is the capacity of a system to limit as much as possible this latency (note that this implicitly assumes that the system is already reliable: Failures can be detected and repair actions initiated). This involves two different mechanisms: The failure (crash, unavailability, etc.) must be detected as soon as possible, and a quick recovery procedure must be initiated. The process of setting up a protection system to face and fix quickly node failures is usually termed *failover*.

The first mechanism is handled by periodically monitoring the status of each server ("heartbeat"). It is typically assigned to the node dedicated to administrative tasks (the "master"). Implementing this mechanism in a fully distributed way is more difficult due to the absence of a well-identified manager. Structured P2P networks promote one of the nodes as "Super-peer" in order to take in charge this kind of background monitoring surveillance. Note that some P2P approaches assume that a node will kindly inform its companions when it needs to leave the network, an assumption (sometimes called "fail-stop") that facilitates the design. This may be possible for some kinds of failures, but is unrealistic in many cases (e.g., for hardware errors).

The second mechanism is achieved through replication (each piece of data is stored on several servers) and redundancy (there should be more than one connection between servers for instance). Providing failure management at the infrastructure level is not sufficient. As seen earlier, a service that runs in such an environment must also take care of adopting adapted recovery techniques for preserving the content of its volatile storage.

14.3.4 Efficiency

How do we estimate the efficiency of a distributed system? Assume an operation that runs in a distributed manner and delivers a set of items as a result. Two usual measures of its efficiency are the *response time* (or latency) that denotes the delay to obtain the first item and the *throughput* (or bandwidth) that denotes the number of items delivered in a given period unit (e.g., a second). These measures are useful to qualify the practical behavior of a system at an analytical level, expressed as a function of the network traffic. The two measures correspond to the following unit costs:

1. *Number of messages* globally sent by the nodes of the system, regardless of the message size;
2. *Size of messages* representing the volume of data exchanges.

The complexity of operations supported by distributed data structures (e.g., searching for a specific key in a distributed index) can be characterized as a function of one of these cost units.

Generally speaking, the analysis of a distributed structure in terms of number of messages is oversimplistic. It ignores the impact of many aspects, including the network topology, the network load and its variation, the possible heterogeneity of the software and hardware components involved in data processing and routing, among others. However, developing a precise cost model that would accurately take into account all these performance factors is a difficult task, and we have to live with rough but robust estimates of the system behavior.

14.3.5 Putting Everything Together: The CAP Theorem

We now come to the question of building systems that simultaneously satisfy all the properties expected from a large-scale distributed system. It should scale to an unbounded number of transactions on unlimited data repositories, always be available with high efficiency (say, a few milliseconds to serve each user's request), and provide strong consistency guarantees.

In a keynote speech given in 2000 at the *Symposium on Principles of Distributed Computing*, Eric Brewer proposed the following conjecture: No distributed system can simultaneously provide all three of the following properties: Consistency (all nodes see the same data at the same time), Availability (node failures do not prevent survivors from continuing to operate), and Partition tolerance (the system continues to operate despite arbitrary message loss). This conjecture, formalized and proved two years later, is now known as the CAP theorem, and strongly influences the design of Web-scale distributed systems.

The problem can be simply explained with a figure (Figure 14.8). Assume two applications A and B running on two distinct servers S_1 and S_2. A executes writes to a repository, whereas B reads from a replicated version of the repository. The synchronization is obtained by replication messages sent from S_1 to S_2.

When the Client application sends a *put(d)* to update a piece of data d, A receives the request and writes in its local repository; S_1 then sends the replication message that replaces d', the older replica, with d, and a subsequent *read(d)* sent by the Client retrieves from S_2 the updated version. So, the system seems consistent.

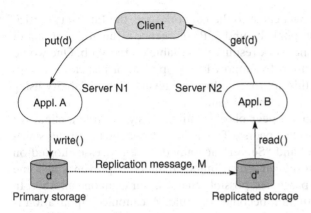

Figure 14.8. The CAP theorem illustrated.

Now, assume a failure in the system that entails a loss of messages. If we want the system to be fault-tolerant, it continues to run, and the replica is out of date: the Client receives an old version of its data (inconsistency). If S_1 synchronizes the write operation and the replication message M as an *atomic* transaction, this goes against availability, because waiting for the acknowledgment of S_2 may take an unpredictable amount of time.

The CAP theorem essentially says that there is a trade-off between availability and consistency (partition tolerance is something we have to deal with anyway) in large-scale distributed systems. In an "eventual consistency" model, the replication message is asynchronous, but S_1 resends the messages if it does not receive an acknowledgment until, *eventually*, the replica on S_2 is known to be consistent with S_1. Meanwhile, the Client may have to deal with an inconsistent state. In concrete terms, if you remove an item from your basket, it possibly reappears later in the transaction! Obviously, this is a better choice for the e-commerce site than a user who gives up her transaction due to high-system latency.

The CAP theorem gave rise to debates regarding its exact definition and consequences. We already noted that the partition tolerance property is not symmetric to the other ones, since we do not really have the choice to give it up. This leaves two possible combinations: CP (consistent and partition tolerant) and AP (available and partition tolerant). Moreover, the concept of availability (a transaction always terminates) ignores the efficiency aspect (how long does it take?) which is an important factor. Still, the theorem points out that consistency and availability are central, and somehow incompatible, issues in the design of distributed systems, and that a clear trade-off should be made explicit.

14.4 PARTICULARITIES OF P2P NETWORKS

A *peer-to-peer* network is a large network of nodes, called *peers*, that agree to cooperate in order to achieve a particular task. A P2P system is a distributed system, and as such it shares a lot of features with the settings previously presented.

What makes P2P systems particular with respect to the cluster systems examined so far is their very loose and flexible (not to say unstable) organization. Peers often consist of personal computers connected to the network (e.g., the Internet) participating in a specific task. The rationale behind P2P emergence is the huge amount of available CPU, memory, disk, network resources available on the Web. One would like to use these existing resources to support heavy applications as close to zero hardware cost. Furthermore, this approach allows achieving high scalability using massively distribution and parallel computation.

A second particularity is that a peer plays simultaneously the role a client (of other peers) and a server (to other peers). This is in fact not such a strong specificity, if we recall that "Client" and "Server" actually denote processes hosted on possibly the same computer. Nothing in a distributed architecture prevents the same machine from running several processes, possibly client/server from one another. In P2P systems, however, this situation becomes the rule. A canonical application is file-sharing: a Client (node) gets a file from another (Server) node, and the file, once stored on the Client disk, becomes available to other peers (so, the former Client becomes indeed a Server). In theory, this leads to high availability, reliability (due to large replication), and adequate load balancing.

P2P systems raise many problems, though, even if we set aside the somewhat illegal nature of their most popular applications. First, the behavior of each peer is fully autonomous. A peer owns its computing power and storage resource and can independently choose to allocate these resources to a particular task. A peer can also join or leave the system at will (as mentioned above, the fail-stop hypothesis hardly holds in practice). Second, P2P networks connect nodes via a possibly slow communication channel (usually, the Internet) and this may bring a quite high communication overhead compared to a cluster of machine on a very high-speed local network (See Table 14.1, page 291). Finally, the lack of control on the infrastructure makes P2P networks not adapted to very rapidly changing data and high quality of services, and in particular not adapted to transactional tasks.

Peers in a P2P network refer to each other by their IP addresses, forming a structure over the Internet called an *overlay network* (e.g., a graph laid over a physical infrastructure). A peer p in this structure is connected to a few other peers (often called its "friends"), which are its primary (and possibly) unique way to communicate with the rest of the system. P2P systems mostly differ by the topology of their overlay network, which dictates how dictionary operations (insert, search, update) can be implemented. We should be aware nevertheless that even if two peers p_1 and p_2 seem friends in the overlay, a message sent from p_1 to p_2 must actually follow a physical route in the underlying Internet graph, with possibly many hops. So, things may not work as nicely as expected when considering the overlay topology.

A general (although not very efficient) search technique is *flooding*: a peer p disseminates its request to all its friends, which flood in turn their own friends distinct from p, and so on until the target of the request (e.g., a peer holding the requested music file) is reached. A P2P system that only supports flooding is called an *unstructured P2P network*. The approach is simple and works as follows. A peer only needs to know some friends to join a network. From them, it can discover new friends. Queries are then supported using flooding typically limited by a "Time to live" bound (abbreviated TTL). The TTL limits the number of times a particular query is forwarded before it should be discarded to avoid using too much resource on a single query. Unstructured P2P networks are not very efficient. They are in particular inherently unstable. Because the peers in the community are autonomous and selfish, one can often observe a very high rate of peers going in and out of the system (one speaks of high *churn*). As a consequence, it is difficult to guarantee that a node stays connected to the system, or that the overall topology remains consistent.

More structured ways of looking up the network ("Structured P2P networks") have been designed to avoid the blind and uncontrolled nature of the flooding mechanism among which *Distributed Hash Tables* (DHTs) are probably the most popular. Joining the network becomes more involved, but the performance and stability are improved. We will consider DHTs in Chapter 15.

14.5 CASE STUDY: A DISTRIBUTED FILE SYSTEM FOR VERY LARGE FILES

To conclude this introductory part, we study a simple distributed service: a file system that serves very large data files (hundreds of Gigabytes or Terabytes). The architecture presented here is a slightly simplified description of the Google File System and of several of its descendants, including the HADOOP Distributed File System (HDFS) available as an open-source project. The technical environment is that of a high-speed local network connecting a cluster of servers. The file systems is designed to satisfy some specific requirements: (i) we need to handle very large collections of unstructured to semistructured documents, (ii) data collections are written once and read many times, and (iii) the infrastructure that supports these components consists of thousands of connected machines, with high failure probability. These particularities make common distributed system tools only partially appropriate.

14.5.1 Large-Scale File System

Why would we need a specialized architecture for distributing large files (DFS) in the first place? The answer is summarized by Figure 14.9 that shows, on the left side,

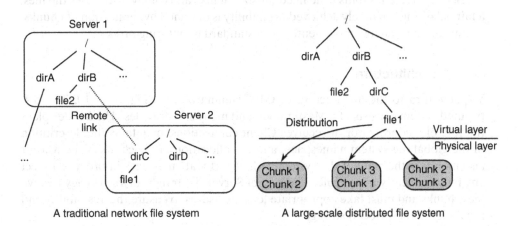

A traditional network file system   A large-scale distributed file system

Figure 14.9. Distributed file systems for large files.

a standard solution to share files among computers (a widespread implementation of this solution is NFS, the Network File System, in the UNIX world). Assume that server A needs to access the files located in the directory *dirC* on server B. The DFS allows *dirC* to be "mounted" in the local file system as, say, a subdirectory of *dirB*. From the user point of view, this is transparent: s/he can navigate to the files stored in */dirA/dirB/dirC* just as if it was fully located on its local computer. The network calls that maintain *dirC* as part of the Server A namespace are handled by the DFS.

Modern distributed systems like NFS care about reliability and availability and provide for instance mechanisms to replicate files and handle node failures. In the context of large-scale data-intensive applications, this solution is nevertheless not convenient because it breaks several of the principles mentioned so far and does not satisfy some of its expected properties. The main broken principle is data locality. A process running on Server A in charge of manipulating data stored on Server B will strongly solicit the network bandwidth. Regarding the properties, one notes that the approach is hardly scalable. If we store 10% of our data set in *file1* and 90% in *file2*, Server B will serve (assuming a uniform access pattern) 90% of the Client requests. One could carefully monitor the size and location of files to explicitly control load balancing, but this would lose the benefits of using a transparent file system namespace.

An NFS-like system is not natively designed to meet the specific requirements of a large-scale repository. The right-hand side of Figure 14.9 shows a different approach which explicitly addresses the challenge of very large files. Essentially, the difference lies in the fact that a file is no longer the storage unit, but is further decomposed in "chunks" of equal size, each allocated by the DFS to the participating nodes (of course, this works best for systems consisting of large files).

There exists a global file system namespace, shared by all the nodes in the cluster. It defines a hierarchy of directories and files that is "virtual" as it does not affect in any way the physical location of its components. Instead, the DFS maps the files, in a distributed manner, to the cluster nodes viewed as blind data repositories. File *file1* in the right-hand side of Figure 14.9 is for instance split in three chunks. Each chunk is duplicated and the two copies are each assigned to a distinct node.

Because the DFS splits a file in equal-size chunks and evenly distributes the files, a fair balancing is natively achieved. Reliability is obtained by replication of chunks, and availability can be implemented by a standard monitoring process.

14.5.2 Architecture

We now turn to the architecture of GFS, summarized on Figure 14.10. The distributed system consists of a Master node and many server nodes. The Master plays the role of a coordinator: it receives Client connections, maintains the description of the global file system namespace, and the allocation of file chunks. The Master also monitors the state of the system with "heartbeat" messages in order to detect any failure as early as possible. The role of Servers is straightforward. They receive files chunks and must take appropriate local measures to ensure the availability and reliability of their (local) storage.

A single-master architecture brings simplicity to the design of the system but gives rise to some concern for its scalability and reliability. The scalability concern

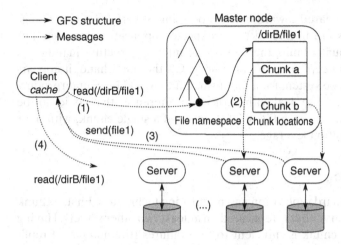

Figure 14.10. Architecture of the GFS system (after [71]).

is addressed by a Client cache, called *Client image* in the following. Let us examine in detail how the system handles a *read()* request, as illustrated on Figure 14.10 with dotted arrows:

1. The Client sends a first *read(/dirB/file1)* request; since it knows nothing about the file distribution, the request is routed to the Master (1).
2. The Master inspects the namespace and finds that *file1* is mapped to a list of chunks; their location is found in a local table (2).
3. Each server holding a chunk of *file1* is required to transmit this chunk to the Client (3).
4. The Client keeps in its cache the addresses of the nodes that serve *file1* (but *not* the file itself); this knowledge can be used for subsequent accesses to *file1* (4).

The approach is typical of distributed structures and will be met in several other distributed services further on. The Client cache avoids a systematic access to the Master, a feature that would make the structure nonscalable. By limiting the exchanges with the Master to messages that require metadata information, the coordination task is reduced and can be handled by a single computer.

From the Client point of view,[1] the distributed file system appears just like a directory hierarchy equipped with the usual UNIX navigation (chddir, ls) and access (read, write) commands.

Observe again that the system works best for a relatively small number of very large files. GFS (and similar systems) expects typical files of several hundreds of megabytes each, and sets accordingly the chunk size to 64 MB. This can be compared to the traditional block-based organization of centralized storage systems (e.g., databases) where is block size is a small multiple of the disk physical block (typically, 4–8 KB in a database block).

---

[1] We recall that "Client" here technically means a component integrated to the Client application and implementing the communication protocol with the system.

The design of GFS is geared toward batch processing of very large collections. The architectural choices are in line with the expected application features. For instance, having large chunks limits the size of the internal structure maintained by the Master and allows keeping them in memory. On the other hand, it appears clearly that using a GFS-like system for a lot of small files would be counterproductive. The Master would have to deal with a lot more references that could not be held in memory anymore, and each file would consist of a single chunk, with poor exploitation of the distribution leverage.

14.5.3 Failure Handling

Failure is handled by standard replication and monitoring techniques. First, a chunk is not written on a single server but is replicated on at least two other servers. Having three copies of the same chunk is sufficient to face failures (the number of replicas can be chosen by administrator to adapt to special applications). The Master is aware of the existing replicas because each server that joins the clusters initially sends the chunk that it is ready to serve.

Second, the Master is in charge of sending background heartbeat messages to each server. If a server does not answer to a heartbeat messages, the Master initiates a server replacement by asking to one of the (at least two) remaining servers to copy to a new server the chunks that fell under their replication factor.

The Master itself must be particularly protected because it holds the file namespace. A recovery mechanism is used for all the updates that affect the namespace structure, similar to that presented in Figure 14.5. We refer the reader to the original paper (see last section) for technical details on the management of aspects that fall beyond the scope of our limited presentation, in particular access rights and data consistency.

14.6 FURTHER READING

Distributed computing systems have constituted an intensive area of research for more than three decades, and the area has been boosted further by the success of the Internet and the profusion of distributed resources now available. A wide coverage of distributed systems issues and techniques is [29], with strong emphasis on the reliability of distributed applications. In a data management perspective, [131] is a general reference for distributed databases, while [78] specializes on transaction management. The notion of scalability is analyzed in [122]. Failure management is an essential topic in the context of large-scale distributed systems. Beyond the general principles that can be found in the textbooks already mentioned, the reader is referred to [84] for an in-depth approach. Replication protocols are ubiquitous in distributed systems design, along with the related problems of consistencies and availability: See [77], which clearly exposes the trade-offs involved in replication policies, and well as the recent survey in [142].

Properties expected from a cluster-based system are analyzed in [68]. A counterpart to ACID properties, called BASE (*Basically Available, Soft-state, Eventually consistent*) is proposed there. The CAP theorem has been conjectured during a keynote speech by Eric Brewer at PODC'2000, formalized in [72] (Figure 14.8 is a simplified illustration of the proof) and has been an active topic of discussion since then. The trade-off between consistency, availability, and fault-tolerance has been investigated in several research works; see for instance [186]. Eventual consistency is the level adopted by many Web-scale systems, including Ebay and Amazon [52]. See also the on-line text from Werner Voegels on consistency models.[2]

The necessity to adopt a trade-off between availability and consistency in large-scale distributed systems is often presented as a reason of the "NoSQL systems" emergence. Since relational DBMS are not designed to satisfy eventual consistency, storage systems specifically designed to operate at large-scale have been implemented by several Web companies. They often adopt a very simplified data model based on key-value pairs (hence the "key-value stores" term). See http://nosql-database.org/ site for a list of these systems.

Peer-to-peer networks emerged at the beginning of the millennium and have been since then mostly targeted toward file sharing. P2P systems are accountable for a major part of the Internet traffic (about 50%, sometimes more for certain parts of the world). P2P opponents argue that with P2P is mostly used to share illegal content. However, this is ignoring that P2P also has a growing number of legitimate uses (such as SKYPE).

A P2P system is deemed resilient to failures (due to the large replication factor) and scalable. This is probably true for basic applications (e.g., file management), but building complex and efficient data management systems over a P2P architecture is quite challenging. A major problem is the lack of control on nodes that appear and vanish at will. A trend in P2P system design is therefore to distinguish several classes of participants, ranging from the basic clients whose contributions to the overall computing effort are quite unreliable, to "super-peers" that provide dependable services that help stabilize the system.

The Google File System is presented in [71]. The paper contains detailed material on its internal design and implementation. Consistency issues in particular are presented in depth, as well as replicas management. Since its presentation, GFS inspired several other systems, often distributed in Open Source. HADOOP[3] is the most widely used (it is, for instance, adopted and supported by Yahoo!), free implementation of the GFS principles. KOSMOS FILESYSTEM (now available as CLOUDSTORE[4]) is another derivation of GFS, implemented in C++. The technical documentation of these system shows that they quite closely match the design of GFS. A consequence is that they also target the same application range: large, append-only data files mostly subject to batch analysis.

[2] http://www.allthingsdistributed.com/2008/12/eventually_consistent.html
[3] http://hadoop.apache.org/.
[4] http://kosmosfs.sourceforge.net/.

15

Distributed Access Structures

In large-scale file systems presented in Chapter 14, search operations are based on a *sequential scan* that accesses the whole data set. When it comes to finding a specific object, typically a tiny part of the data volume, direct access is much more efficient than a linear scan. The object is directly obtained using its physical address that may simply be the offset of the object's location with respect to the beginning of the file, or possibly a more sophisticated addressing mechanism.

An *index* on a collection C is a structure that maps the *key* of each object in C to its (physical) address. At an abstract level, it can be viewed as a set of pairs (k,a), called *entries*, where k is a key and a the address of an object. For the purpose of this chapter, an object is seen as raw (unstructured) data, its structure being of concern to the Client application only. You may want to think, for instance, of a relational tuple, an XML document, a picture or a video file. It may be the case that the key uniquely determines the object, as for keys in the relational model.

An index we consider here supports at least the following operations that we thereafter call the *dictionary operations*:

1. Insertion *insert(k,a)*,
2. Deletion *delete(k)*,
3. Key search *search(k): a*.

If the keys can be linearly ordered, an index may also support *range queries* of the form *range(k₁,k₂)* that retrieves all the keys (and their addresses) in that range. Finally, if the key space is associated to a metric (a distance function f), one may consider a nearest neighbor search *kNN(o)* that retrieves the k objects closest (in other words, most similar) to a query object o.

Given a cost unit, the efficiency of an index is expressed as the number of cost units required to execute an operation. In the centralized databases case, the cost unit is usually the disk access. We are more concerned here with communication, so we will assume that the cost unit is the transmission of one message, and this (to simplify), regardless of the message size.

For indexing, two main families of access structures have been considered, namely, *hash tables*, with constant search complexity, and *search trees*, with logarithmic search complexity. In the next two chapters, we consider in turn the distribution of these two kinds of access structures.

15.1 HASH-BASED STRUCTURES

Let us first recall the basics of hash-based indexing in centralized databases. The *hash file* structure consists of a memory-resident *directory D* and a set of M disk buckets $\{b_0, b_1, \ldots, b_{M-1}\}$. The directory is an array with M cells, each referring to one of the buckets (Figure 15.1).

The placement of objects in the buckets is determined by a *hash function h*. Consider a collection C of objects where each item I in it has a property $I.A$. (A is called the *hash field*.) Each item I in C is stored in the bucket b_j such that $j = h(I.A)$. So, note that the hash function takes as input a value from the hash field domain and outputs an integer in the range $[0, M-1]$. The hash function should also follow the requirement that it uniformly assigns objects to buckets.

Figure 15.1 shows a simple example. The hash file contains a collection of *Person* objects. The hash field is the name of each person. We find that $h('Suzan') = 3$ and $h('John') = 3$. To insert the Susan object in the hash file, one computes its hash value, namely 3, finds in the Directory the address of Bucket 3, and places the object there. To retrieve the Susan object, one similarly finds the hash value and retrieve Bucket 3. Observe that both Susan and John objects are put in Bucket b_3. Indeed, two objects with totally different hash field values may be mapped to the same bucket. This is called a *collision*. Collisions are quite acceptable in hash files because the purpose of a hash function is indeed to group objects to buckets independently from the hash field distribution. A problem only arises when a bucket is full and there is no place for new objects in this bucket. This is somewhat difficult to control, and may lead to degenerate hash structures. We will discuss further how to handle this issue.

Hash files support dictionary operations in constant time. In nondegenerated cases, one disk access is sufficient.

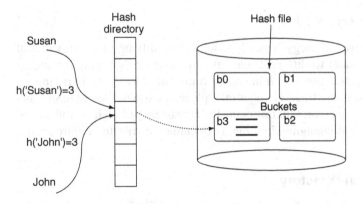

Figure 15.1. The hash file structure.

1. Insertion *insert(k,a)*: compute $h(k)$, find the address of $b_{h(k)}$ in $D[h(k)]$ and insert a there;
2. Deletion *delete(k)*: find the bucket as in search, remove from it all objects with key k;
3. Key search *search(k): {a}*: compute $h(k)$, find the address of $b_{h(k)}$ in the directory, read $b_{h(k)}$ and take all objects in the bucket with key k (if any).

In the simple variant presented so far, the number M of buckets must be chosen in advance so that the entire collection can be accommodated. If c_B is a bucket capacity, and $|C|$ the expected collection size, then M should be of the order $\lceil \frac{|C|}{c_B} \rceil$. In fact, it has to be somewhat greater because even if, in theory, the hash function does distribute uniformly the objects into the buckets, there will always be some buckets used more than others for a particular distribution.

Observe that the hash file is very efficient for point queries, but it does not support range search. If range search is required, search trees will be preferred. An important issue that affects the basic version presented so far is that it does not adapt easily to a dynamic collection that expands or shrinks rapidly. More sophisticated versions exist, but the previous simple presentation is enough to examine the main issues that must be addressed when we want to distribute a hash structure.

Dynamicity

The first issue we consider relates to *dynamicity*. A straightforward distribution strategy consists in assigning each bucket of the hash file to one of the participating servers. For this to work, all the nodes (Clients or Servers) that access the structure have to share the same hash function. In real life, though, data sets evolve, and servers must be added or removed. A naive solution would require the modification of the hash function. For instance, we use a function $\bar{h}$ here and throughout the chapter that maps the domain of keys to integer. Then we do as follows:

- Suppose the servers $S_0, ..., S_{N-1}$ for some N are available.
- We use the hash value $h(key) = modulo(\bar{h}(key), N)$.
- We assign each key of hash value i to server S_i for each $i \in [0, N-1]$.

If a server S_N is added, the hash function is modified to

$$h(key) = modulo(\bar{h}(key), N+1)$$

Observe that this "naive" strategy typically results in modifying the hash value of most objects, moving them to different buckets, thus essentially totally rebuilding the hash file. Also, the new function h has to be transmitted to all the participants, notably all the Clients. While these changes take place, the use of the old hash function is likely to result in an error. Guaranteeing the consistency of such an addressing when the hash function is changing, in a highly dynamic, distributed environment, is a challenging task.

Location of the Hash Directory

The second issue that needs to be considered when distributing a hash file is the location of the hash directory itself. Recall that this directory establishes a mapping between the hashed values and the physical locations of data repositories. Any operation on the structure requires an access to the directory, which therefore constitutes a potential bottleneck.

We present next two hash-based indexing techniques adapted to a distributed setting. The first one called *linear hashing* (an extension of the well-known dynamic hashing method) has been proposed a while ago in the context of centralized systems. We recall it and consider its distribution. The second one, called *consistent hashing*, is a direct attempt at instantiating the hashing paradigm in a distributed context. We will see that it is better adapted when servers enter and leave the system at a rapid pace. Both approaches provide interesting insights on common design patterns for data-centric distributed structures: caching, replication, routing tables, and lazy adjustment. Consistent hashing is further illustrated with the system CHORD, a Distributed Hash Tables (DHT) designed for P2P environments.

15.1.1 Distributed Linear Hashing

The goal of linear hashing (LH) is to maintain an efficient hash structure when the collection is very dynamic, and in particular when it may grow very rapidly. The maintenance involves a dynamic enlargement of the hash directory that entails an extension of the hash function, and the reorganization of the buckets. As we will see, *linear hashing* provides a linear growth of the file one bucket at a time. We first recall the method in a centralized case, then develop the distributed version.

Linear Hashing

The simple manner of expending a hash file, when the collection expands, and a bucket b become too small, consists in introducing an *overflow* bucket. More precisely, this consists in (i) adding a new bucket b' to the file, (ii) moving some items from b to b', adding a pointer from b to b'. In the worst case, if the collection keeps expanding, we have to perform more and more linear scans in the buckets corresponding to one hash value. To avoid this issue, in linear hashing, when we introduce an overflow bucket, we simultaneously augment the number of hash values. The LH innovative idea is to decouple the extension of the hash function from the overflowing bucket. More precisely, when a bucket b overflows, this triggers the following modifications:

1. An overflow bucket is linked from b, in order to accommodate the new items.
2. The bucket b_p (or the chain list of buckets) corresponding to the hash value p, *usually distinct from b*, is split, where p is a special index value maintained by the structure and called the *split pointer*.

Observe that a bucket that overflows is not split. It is just linked to an overflow bucket. This bucket together with the overflow bucket will eventually be split when the split pointer will point to it. Surprisingly, this behaves nicely. Hash values that raise problems are eventually dealt with and the number of hash values somewhat gracefully adapt to the size of the collection.

Initially, $p = 0$, so bucket b_0 is the first that must split, *even if it does not overflow*. The value of p is incremented after each split. Look at Figure 15.2. We abstractly represented the presence of an object of key k in a bucket by placing $\bar{h}(k)$ in it.

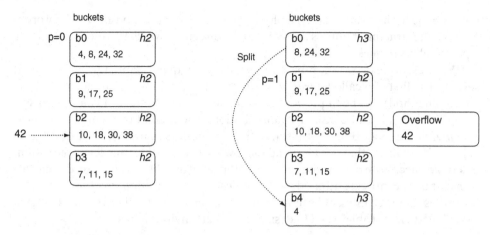

Bucket b2 receives a new object   Bucket b0 splits; bucket b2 is linked to a new one

Figure 15.2. Split process in linear hashing.

So, for instance, some object k with $h(k) = 17$ is in b_1. Here, the size of the hash directory is 4, and we assume that each bucket holds at most four objects (we only show $h(k)$ for each key k). For simplicity, we use the *mod()* function for hashing, so $h(k) = \bar{h}(k)\ mod\ N$, where N is the size of the hash directory.

An object with key 42 must be inserted in bucket b_2, which overflows its capacity. A bucket is linked to b_2, and receives object 42. At the same time, bucket b_0 (recall that $p = 0$) is split. Its content is partially reassigned to a new bucket added to the hash file, namely b_4.

This reassignment raises an issue: If we keep unchanged the hash function, all the objects moved to bucket b_4 cannot be found anymore. This is where the hash function extension occurs. Linear hashing actually relies on a *pair* of hash functions (h_n, h_{n+1}), where for each n:

1. $h_n : k \rightarrow \bar{h}(k)\ mod\ 2^n$, so in particular,
2. $h_{n+1} : k \rightarrow \bar{h}(k)\ mod\ 2^{n+1}$.

Initially, the pair is (h_0, h_1), $p = 0$ and h_0 applies to all the buckets. As the structure evolves, p is incremented, and h_0 applies to the buckets in the range $[p, N-1]$, while h_1 applies to all other buckets. (Recall that N is the size of the hash directory.) For the example of Figure 15.2, after the first split, we have

1. h_0 applies to buckets b_1, b_2, and b_3,
2. h_1 applies to buckets b_0 and b_4: the ones that just split.

It can be verified in the example that all objects such that $h_1(k) = \bar{h}(k)\ mod\ 2^3 = 4$ have been moved to bucket b_4, while those for which $h_1(k) = \bar{h}(k)\ mod\ 2^3 = 0$ stay in bucket b_0. This extension of the hash function is, therefore, consistent and allows for a limited reorganization of the hash file.

What happens next? Bucket b_1 is the next one to split, if *any* of the buckets (including b_1 itself) overflows. Then p will be set to 2, and b_2 becomes the split target. When the split of b_2 occurs, its content and that of its associated overflow bucket will be distributed in two first-range buckets, and this will likely eliminate the need for a linked chain. In this perspective, linear hashing can be seen as a delayed management of collision overflows.

Eventually, p will take the value 3. When b_3 splits in turn, the hash function h_1 is applied for all the buckets and h_0 is no longer used. The hash file is "switched" one level up, the pair of hash function becomes (h_1, h_2), p is reset to 0, and the process goes on gracefully. Observe that a large part of the hash directory is left unchanged when we modify the hash function. This is an important advantage of the technique since we avoid having to resend it entirely.

A dictionary operation on some key value k uses the following computation (called the *LH algorithm* in what follows) to obtain the address a of the bucket that contains k:

```
a := hₙ(k);
if  (a < p) a := hₙ₊₁(k)
```

In words: One applies first h_n, assuming that no split occurred, and obtains a hash value a in the range $[0, 2^n - 1]$. Next, one checks whether this value corresponds to a bucket that did split, in which case the correct address is obtained with h_{n+1}.

Distributed Linear Hashing

We now turn to LH*, a distributed version of LH. The mapping of a LH file structure to a cluster of servers is straightforward. Assume for the time being that there exists a global knowledge of the file level, n, with hash functions (h_n, h_{n+1}), and of the split pointer p. Suppose the cluster consists of the servers $\{S_0, S_1, \ldots, S_N\}$, $2^n \leq N < 2^{n+1}$, each holding a bucket. When the bucket of a server S_i overflows, the server referred to by the split pointer p, S_p, splits. This involves the allocation of new server S_{N+1} to the structure, and a transfer from S_p to S_{N+1} of objects, similar to the LH case. This results in a partition of data among servers, often denoted as "sharding," each bucket being a "data shard". To perform this split, we can either wait to have a new server available, or better, have each physical server plays the role of several "virtual servers."

Recall that, as already mentioned, the Linear Hashing technique does not require resending entirely the hash directory each time the hash function is modified. When this happens, we have to let the servers know:

■ The level n that determines the pair of hash functions (h_n, h_{n+1}) currently in use,
■ The current split pointer p,
■ Changes of the hash directory.

We meet again a standard trade-off in distributed data structures:

■ Either all the participants have an accurate and up-to-date view of the whole structure; then searches are fast, but changes to the structure involve a costly propagation of the update to each node (including Client nodes).

■ Or they only maintain a partial representation, possibly lagged with respect to the actual structure status; in that case, the maintenance cost is possibly much lighter, but searches may have to follow nontrivial paths before reaching their targets.

For LH*, for instance, each server and each Client could store a local copy of the localization information: the pair (n,p) as well as the list of all the server nodes addresses. Let us call *Loc* this information. Whenever the LH* evolves by adding or removing a server, an update must be sent to every participant. This yields a *gossiping system*, a perfectly valid choice in a rather controlled environment, assuming the set of participating peers does not evolve at a rapid pace.

Reducing Maintenance Cost by Lazy Adjustment

LH* provides a more flexible solution to cope with the maintenance problem. Each Client keeps its local copy *Loc'* of *Loc*, but this copy may be out of date with respect to the "true" *Loc* (e.g., p may have been incremented since *Loc'* was acquired). This may lead the Client to addressing errors: A dictionary operation with key k may be sent to a wrong server, due to some distributed file evolution ignored by the Client. LH* then applies a *forwarding path* algorithm that eventually leads to the correct server. This latter server carries out the required operations. Furthermore, with the acknowledgment, it sends back to the Client some information for Client to refresh its copy of *Loc*. The next client request, based on this refreshed information, will be more accurate than the initial one.

We call *client image* the knowledge maintained by a Client on the distributed structure. An image is some partial replication of the global structure in the client cache. It is *partial* because parts of the structure that the Client does not need are not mirrored in the image. Also, it may not record recent evolutions of the structure that followed the image acquisition.

Keeping an outdated replica is imposed for a number of reasons. First, a Client may be temporarily disconnected, and thus incapable of updating its image. Of course, one can imagine that the Client refreshes asynchronously its image when it reconnects. But this is complex and very expensive if Clients connect/reconnect often. Also, the maintenance of all Clients and Servers completely up to date is likely to represent an important traffic overhead. A (reasonably) outdated image represents a good trade-off, providing that the Client knows how to cope with referencing errors. We examine next how LH* adjusts to addressing errors.

Details on the LH* Algorithms

The adjustment mechanism principles are illustrated in Figure 15.3. Here, we assume that the Client image is $(n_C = 1, p_C = 1)$, whereas several splits led the LH* to the status $(n = 3, p = 2)$.

The Client sends a request *search(5)*. It computes the bucket address with the LH algorithm (see earlier):

1. $a = h_{n_C}(5) = 5 \bmod 2^1 = 1$
2. since $a \geq p_C$, we keep $a = 1$ and the request is sent to S_1.

When a LH* server receives a request, it first checks whether it is indeed the right recipient by applying the following algorithm (called *the forward algorithm*).

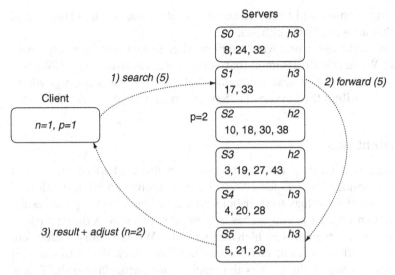

Figure 15.3. The LH* adjustment mechanism.

The algorithm attempts to find the correct hash value for key k, using the local knowledge of the server on the file structure.

```
// Here, j denotes the server level
a' := h_j(k)
if (a' ≠ a)
    a" := h_{j-1}(k)
    if (a" > a and a" < a') then a' := a"
```

$$a' := h_j(k)$$
$$\text{if } (a' \neq a)$$
$$a'' := h_{j-1}(k)$$
$$\text{if } (a'' > a \text{ and } a'' < a') \text{ then } a' := a''$$

If a', obtained by this algorithm is not the server address, then the Client made an addressing error. The request is then forwarded to server a'. In our example, S_1 receives the Client request. S_1 is the last server that split, and its level is 3. Therefore, $a' = h_3(5) = 5 \mod 2^3 = 5$. The request is forwarded to S_5 where the key is found.

It can be shown that the number of messages to reach the correct server is three in the worst case. This makes the structure fully decentralized, with one exception: when a Server overflows, the exact value of p, the (other) Server that splits, must be accurately determined. The LH* recommendation is to assign a special role to one of the servers, called the *Master*, to keep the value of p and inform the other nodes when necessary. Since this only happens during a split, the structure remains scalable. We omit the other technical details. For more, see the bibliographical notes at the end of the section; see also exercises.

The main lesson that can be learned from this design is that a relative inaccuracy of the information maintained by a component is acceptable, if associated to a stabilization protocol that guarantees that the structure eventually converges to a stable and accurate state. Note also that, in order to limit the number of messages, the "metadata" information related to the structure maintenance can be piggybacked with messages that answer Client requests.

We mentioned in the discussion what happens when some Client gets temporarily disconnected. We implicitly assumed that Servers are somewhat stable. We will remove this assumption in the next technique that also addresses settings where there is a high *churn* within the Servers (i.e. Servers come and go at a rapid pace).

15.1.2 Consistent Hashing

Consistent hashing is a method initially proposed in the context of distributed caching systems. Consider for instance a Web site that receives an intensive flow of HTTP requests. A useful strategy to distribute the query load is to keep the results of the most common queries in the *caches* of several servers. A dedicated proxy machine records which servers store which query results. When a query is received, the proxy detects whether its result has been cached, and when this is the case, it forwards the query to one of the servers that cached this particular result. This is where consistent hashing helps: The assignment of queries to servers is based on the hash value of the query, and the scheme is designed to gracefully adapt itself to a varying number of servers (see the http://memcached.org Web site for details).

Distributing Data with Consistent Hashing

In the context of data distribution, the same mechanism can be adopted, the only difference lying in the handling of the hash directory, discussed at the end of this section. The first idea is to use a simple, nonmutable hash function h that maps *both* the server address and the object keys to the same large address space A. Assume for instance that we choose a 64-bits addressing space A. The hash function can be implemented as follows: Take the server IP (resp., the object key) and apply the cryptographic MD5 algorithm that yields a 32-bytes string; then interpret the first 8 bytes of the MD5 value as an unsigned integer in the range $[0, 2^{64} - 1]$. Implement keys similarly. So, now, both the servers and the keys are mapped to the same very large domain, $[0, 2^{64} - 1]$.

The second idea is to organize A as a ring, scanned in clockwise order. That is, each element has a successor, the successor of $2^{64} - 1$ being 0. The situation is depicted in the left part of Figure 15.4. The large circle is A; small circles represent servers; and small squares represent objects. Clearly, we do not have 2^{64} available servers, the large size of A being merely intended to avoid collisions. We must therefore define a rule for assigning objects to servers. The consistent hashing mapping rule is as follows:

If S and S' are two adjacent servers on the ring,
all the keys in range $[h(S), h(S')[$ are mapped to S.

Looking again at Figure 15.4, Object a is hashed to a position of the ring that comes after (the hash value of) IP3-1 and before (the hash value of) IP1-2. Thus, a is mapped to the server IP3-1, and the object is stored there. By a similar mechanism, object b is mapped to IP1-1. One obtains a partition of the whole data set in "shards" where each server is fully responsible for a subset of the whole collection.

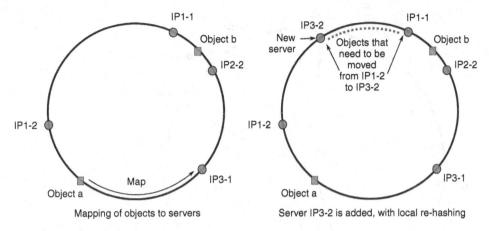

Figure 15.4. The ring of hash values in consistent hashing.

The scheme is often completed by a replication of shards on a few nodes for failure management purposes: see further.

What did we gain? The immediate advantage is that when a new server is added, we do not need to re-hash the whole data set. Instead, the new server takes place at a position determined by the hash value on the ring, and part of the objects stored on its successor must be moved. The reorganization is local, as all the other nodes remain unaffected. Figure 15.4, right, shows an example, with a new server IP3-2 inserted on the ring. The set of objects whose hash belongs to the arc between IP3-2 and IP1-1 were initially stored on IP1-2 and must be reallocated on IP3-2. A similar local process holds when a server leaves the ring. Because the hash function remains unaffected, the scheme maintains its consistency over the successive evolutions of the network configuration.

Refinements
The global scheme we just presented may be improved. The most important improvement aims at balancing the load between the servers, a concern that is not addressed by the basic approach. The example of Figure 15.4 shows that the size of the arcs allocated to servers may vary. Server IP3-1 for instance receives all the objects hashed to the arc between itself and its successor. If objects are uniformly hashed (as they should be with a correct hash function), the load of IP3-1 is likely to be much more important than that of, say, server IP1-1.

To fix this shortcoming, we extend consistent hashing with the concept of *virtual nodes*. Basically, the ring consists of a large number of virtual machines, and several virtual machines are hosted on a same physical server. This is illustrated in Figure 15.5. Server IP2-2 has been (virtually) split in three nodes assigned to multiple points of the ring. In practice, a physical server is assigned to hundreds of virtual nodes. This obviously helps balancing the storage and query load: a server may be "lucky" and get assigned a virtual machine with very little data, but it is unlikely to be randomly assigned many such virtual machines. So, the workload is more evenly distributed between the physical machines. Moreover, when a physical

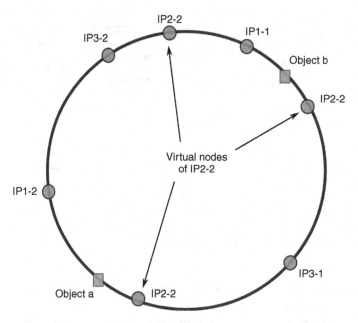

Figure 15.5. Load balancing with consistent hashing.

server is removed from the ring, all its objects are not assigned to a unique unlucky neighbor, but are split between all the successors of its virtual nodes. Similarly, when a server joins the ring, it takes a piece of the workload of many physical servers and not just some of one. Last but not least, observe that virtualization also helps dealing with heterogeneity of servers. A very powerful machine can support many more virtual servers than a very slow one.

A second useful refinement relates to failure management. Data must be replicated to prevent any loss due to server failure. There are many possible replication strategies. One may for instance use several hash functions, say h_1, h_2, h_3 for a *replication factor* of 3. An object of key k is replicated on the servers in charge of $h_i(k)$ for each i. One can fix the replication factor depending on the needs of the application.

The Hash Directory

A last question pertains to the location of the hash directory. Recall that this directory maintains the mapping between hash values and the location (i.e., IP address) of servers. As previously mentioned, consistent hashing was originally designed for distributing cache hits. In such an environment, a proxy server hosts the directory and routes requests to the appropriate node on the ring. The equivalent architecture in a large-scale data management system would be a single Master–many Servers organization, where a dedicated machine, the Master, receives queries and forward them to data servers. This is a simple choice, that raises concerns regarding its scalability.

Other solutions are possible, the choice depending mostly on the level of dynamicity of the system. We consider two solutions:

Full duplication. The hash directory is duplicated on each node. This enables a quite efficient structure because queries can be routed in one message to the correct server. It requires a notification of all the participants when a server joins or leaves the network, so this solution is better adapted when the network is stable.

Partial duplication. If the system is highly dynamic, in particular in a P2P context, the amount of "gossiping" required by the full duplication may become an important overhead. In that case, a partial duplication that only stores $O(\log N)$ entries of the hash directory on each server, N being the total number of servers, is a choice of interest. It allows in particular the routing of queries in $O(\log N)$ messages, and thus constitutes a convenient trade-off between the cost of network maintenance and the cost of dictionary operations.

Full duplication is used, for instance, in the DYNAMO system, a distributed hash table implemented by Amazon for its internal infrastructure needs (see Further Reading section). A typical example of partial duplication is CHORD, a distributed hash table, that we present next.

15.1.3 Case Study: CHORD

A *distributed hash table* is a hash structure distributed in a fully decentralized manner, and thus particularly adapted to unstable networks where nodes can leave or join at any moment. "Decentralized" in this context has a strong implication: There cannot be a node, or a group of nodes, responsible for any critical part of the system maintenance. DHTs are mostly used in P2P systems, and the presentation that follows explicitly adopts this context. We now call *peers* the server nodes, each peer being identified by a unique pId (e.g., URI).

Overview

A DHT supports the search, insert and delete dictionary operations. Range queries are not possible, although range structures can be "overlaid" upon a DHT infrastructure (see Section 15.1.2). Since a DHT is itself already overlaid over the Internet, a specialized range structure based on the search tree paradigm is better adapted to range searches. We will consider search trees in the next section.

A DHT must also handle the following operations related to the network topology:

- *join(pId)*: Let a peer *pId* join the network, and possibly transfer some objects to this new player;
- *leave(pId)*: Peer *pId* leaves the network; its objects are distributed to other peers.

CHORD is one of the first DHTs proposed at the beginning of the millennium as a complete solution to the problem of indexing items stored in a P2P network. CHORD is based on consistent hashing, as presented earlier. Figure 15.6 (left) shows a CHORD ring over an address space $A = 2^3$. Each peer with Id n is located at node n

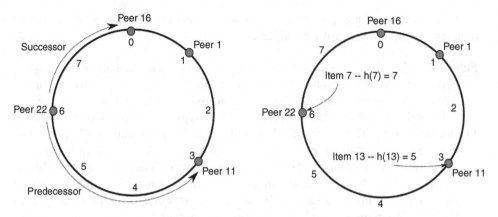

Figure 15.6. The CHORD ring, with $m = 3$ (left part), and key assignment in CHORD (right part).

mod 8 on the ring (e.g., peer 22 is assigned to location 6). Each peer has a *successor*, the next peer on the ring in clockwise order, and a *predecessor*.

Each peer p is *responsible* for a range of keys: An object is assigned to the server that *precedes* its hash value on the ring. Object 13, for instance, is hashed to $h(13) = 5$ and assigned to the peer p with the largest $h(p) \leq 5$. So far, this is a direct application of consistent hashing. A main contribution of CHORD comes from the design of its routing tables.

Routing Tables

Let $A = 2^m$ be the address space (i.e., the number of positions of the ring). Each peer maintains a routing table, called *friends*$_p$, that contains (at most) $\log 2^m = m$ peer addresses. For each i in $[1\ldots m]$, the ith friend p_i is such that

- $h(p_i) \leq h(p) + 2^{i-1}$;
- there is no p' such that $h(p_i) < h(p') \leq h(p) + 2^{i-1}$.

In other words, p_i is the peer responsible for key $h(p) + 2^{i-1}$. Figure 15.7 shows the friends of peer 16, with location 0 (note the collisions). Peer 16 does *not* know peer 22.

Example 15.1.1 Let $m = 10$, $2^m = 1,024$; consider peer p with $h(p) = 10$. The first friend p_1 is the peer responsible for $10 + 2^0 = 11$; the second friend p_2 is the peer responsible for $10 + 2^1 = 12$; finally, the last friend p_{10} is the peer responsible for $10 + 512 = 522$.

The CHORD routing tables imply some important useful properties. First, a peer's routing table contains at most m references. Each peer has no more than 16 friends in a ring with $m = 16$ and $2^{16} = 65,536$ nodes. Second, each peer knows better the peers close on the ring that the peers far away. Finally, a peer p cannot (in general) find directly the peer p' responsible for a key k, *but p can always find a friend that holds more accurate information about k.*

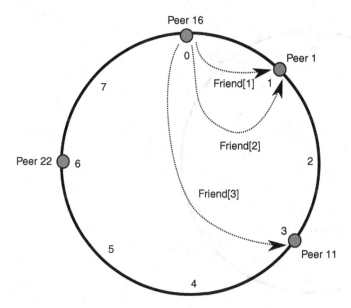

Figure 15.7. The friend nodes in CHORD.

CHORD Operations

We illustrate the operations supported by CHORD with the *search()* algorithm (the other can be easily inferred). Assume that p searches for key k. Two cases occur:

- If p is responsible for k, we are done;
- Else let i such that $h(p) + 2^{i-1} \leq h(k) < h(p) + 2^i$: p forwards the search to its friend p_i.

For instance, looking at Figure 15.8, peer 16 receives a request for item k, with $h(k) = 7$. First, peer 16 forwards the request to peer 11, its third friend; then peer 11 forwards to peer 22, its third friend; and, finally, peer 22 finds k locally. As a matter of fact, the search range is (at worst) halved at each step, and thus the search converges in $O(\log 2^m) = O(m)$ messages.

In a P2P network, nodes can join and leave at any time. When a peer p wants to join, it uses a *contact peer p'*, which helps p carry out three tasks: (i) determine the friends of p, (ii) inform the peers for which p becomes a friend, and (iii) move some objects to p.

Let N be the current number of nodes. To locate the friends of p, p' uses its own routing table. This involves $O(\log N)$ times (the number of friends) a lookup that costs $O(\log N)$ messages, hence a total cost of $O(\log^2 N)$ messages (see exercises).

Next, the routing table of the existing nodes must be updated to reflect the addition of p. This is the trickiest part of the process. We note first that p becomes the ith friend of a peer p' if and only if the following conditions hold:

1. $h(p) - 2^{i-1} \leq h(p') < h(p) - 2^{i-2}$;
2. The current i^{th} friend of p' is before p on the ring.

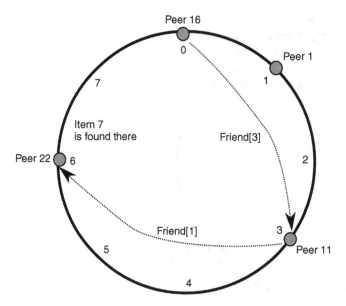

Figure 15.8. The *search()* operation in CHORD.

Finally, p takes from its predecessor all the items k such that $h(p) \le h(k)$. At this point, the join procedure is completed and the network is consistent.

Example 15.1.2 Consider the example of Figure 15.9, which shows how peer 13 joins the ring, taking the slot 5. We assume that its contact node is peer 22. First, peer 22 computes the routing table of peer 13. Next, one finds that peer 13 is the third friend of either a peer at slot 2 $(5 - 2^{3-2} - 1)$, or at slot 1 $(5 - 2^{3-1})$. Finally, peer 13 receives part of the data stored on peer 11. Details of the process are left to the reader as an exercise.

We do not elaborate the leaving procedure, which is essentially similar in its principles with the operations seen so far. As usual for failure handling, one distinguishes two cases:

Cold. Peer p leaves "cold" when it knows it is leaving and has the time to take appropriate measures. This case is sometimes called "fail-stop." The local part of the file stored at p must be transmitted to the predecessor, and the routing tables must be updated.

Hot. This is the more difficult case resulting from a failure, and all kinds of failures typically happen often. We want to reach eventually and as fast as possible a consistent state, with as in the cold case, the local part of the file stored at p transmitted to its predecessor, and the routing tables updated. For the local part of the file, we rely on replication. More precisely, the content of a peer is replicated on r predecessors, where the replication factor r depends on the expected network stability. The general rule to fix addressing errors to a peer

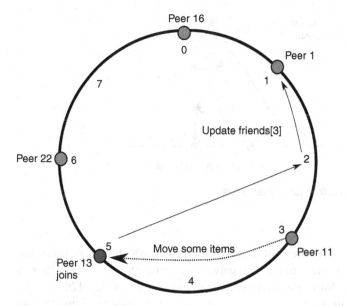

Figure 15.9. Joining a node in CHORD.

p that does not answer is to re-route the query to a predecessor of p which chooses another route.

This concludes our presentation of hash-based indexing structures. In short, these structures are very efficient. Both LH* and DHT are quite adapted to rapidly evolving collections. DHT also support very well high churn of the network.

15.2 DISTRIBUTED INDEXING: SEARCH TREES

Hash-based data structures do not support range queries or nearest-neighbors searches. This is a well-known limitation that justifies the coexistence, in centralized systems, of hash tables and tree indexes (generally, B+trees). We study in this section the design of distributed search trees.

15.2.1 Design Issues

A general problem with tree structures is that operations usually execute a top-down traversal of the tree. A naive distribution approach that would assign each tree node to a server would result in a very poor load balancing. The server hosting the root node, in particular, is likely to become overloaded. Figure 15.10 shows a tree structure, where each black dot represents both a node of the tree and the server where it resides. For the sake of illustration we assume a binary tree but the discussion holds for any node fanout.

Consider a query that searches for objects located on node (i.e., a server) e. The left-hand side of the figure illustrates what happens in a naive implementation.

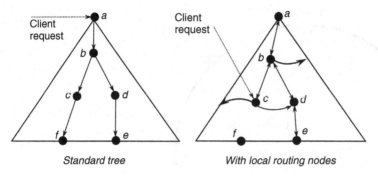

Standard tree   *With local routing nodes*

Figure 15.10. Design issues for distributed trees.

A client node always contacts the root node a which forwards the query down the tree, eventually reaching e. Statistically, a receives two times more messages that its children, and generally 2^h more messages than any node located at level h.

The design of distributed tree structures attempts to avoid such bottlenecks with a combination of three ideas:

1. *Caching* of the tree structure, or part of it, on the Client node, so that the Client node can directly access the server that can serve its request;
2. *Replication* of the upper levels of the tree, to avoid overloading servers in charge of nodes in these levels;
3. *Routing tables*, stored at each node, enabling horizontal and vertical navigation in the tree.

With respect to caching, a standard means of improving the search for a particular server is to keep in the Client cache an *image* that records the part of the tree already visited by the Client. If, for instance, a previous query led the client to node f through node c, this local part of the structure can be memorized in the client image. Any query in that Client addressing the same part of the key space can then directly access node c, avoiding a full traversal from the root to f. Otherwise, the client must still use the standard algorithm. If the client only knows c, the query must be first forwarded up from c to the nearest ancestor (here, b) that covers the query criteria, then down to the leaf. Thus, the use of such caching does not avoid an imbalance of the servers load.

A more drastic approach is to replicate the whole tree on each node of the cluster. This way, a client node can directly send its query to any server of the cluster and get an exact answer. It suffices to apply a protocol that evenly distributes the keys over all the servers to solve the load-balancing issue. As already seen with hash-based approaches, this clearly trades one problem for another, namely the maintenance of an exact replica of the whole tree at each node. For instance, in some variant, a server sends the whole tree image to the client at each request. In a system with say, hundreds of servers, hundreds of thousands of clients, and millions of queries every day, this represents a huge overhead.

Finally, assume that each node of the distributed tree stores the list of its siblings, along with the part of the key space covered by each (Figure 15.10, right). The navigation is not anymore limited to the "parent" and "child" axis (borrowing the XPath terminology). A search that targets node e can start from c (assuming the client identifies in its image this node as the closest to its query), which inspects its local routing table and forwards the query to its sibling d. From d, a short top-down path leads to the leaf.

We next present in detail two representative approaches to the distribution of a search tree. The first one, namely BATON, is tailored to P2P networks, whereas the second, namely BIGTABLE, is built for clusters of machines.

15.2.2 Case Study: BATON

BATON is a P2P tree structure that aims at efficiently supporting range queries. It is actually representative of several data structures designed to overcome the limitation of hash-based approaches regarding range queries. The goal is to index a collection of objects using keys from a linearly ordered domain. We assume a homogeneous collection of servers, each with maximal capacity of B entries (an entry is a pair $[k,o]$, k being the key and o an object).

Kernel Structure
The structure of the distributed tree is conceptually similar to that of a binary tree (e.g., AVL trees). It satisfies the following properties (for some fixed value B):

■ Each internal node, or *routing node*, has exactly two children.
■ To each node a of the tree is associated a range:
  – The range of the root is $]-\infty,+\infty[$.
  – The range of a nonleaf node is the union of the ranges of its children. The "cut" point is assigned to the right child. (For instance, a node of range $[12,72[$ may have children with ranges $[12,42[$ and $[42,72[$ with 42 belonging to the second.)
■ Each leaf node, or *data node*, stores the subset of the indexed objects whose keys belong to its range.
■ Each leaf node contains at least $B/2$ and at most B entries.

Observe that the definition is almost that of a standard binary tree, except for the leaves data storage. We note also that a binary tree with n leaves has exactly $n-1$ internal nodes. This permits a simple mapping of the conceptual structure to a set of n servers. Each server S_i (except server S_n) stores exactly a pair (r_i, l_i), r_i being a routing node and l_i a leaf node. As a leaf node, a server acts as an objects repository up to its maximal capacity.

Figure 15.11 shows a first example with three successive evolutions. Leaf nodes are shown with circles, internal (routing) nodes with rectangles, and each node, whether leaf or internal, is associated to the server where it resides. Initially (part 1) there is one node a on server S_0 storing the leaf l_0, and its range is $]-\infty,\infty[$. Any insert request will put the new entry on this server, whatever its key.

When S_0 gets full because it contains B entries, a split occurs (part 2). A new server S_1 stores the new leaf l_1. The entries initially stored in l_0 have been distributed

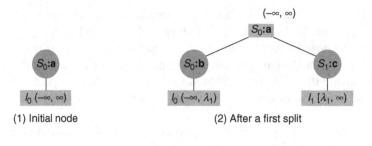

(1) Initial node   (2) After a first split

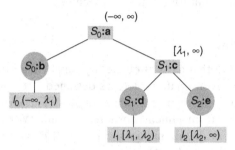

Figure 15.11. Evolution of the binary search tree.

among the two servers by considering the median value λ_1, or *pivot key*, just like the standard B-tree split.

A routing node a is stored on S_0. The range of this routing node is the union of the ranges of its children (e.g., $]-\infty,\infty[$). A routing node maintains links to its left and right children, and to its parent node, which is a difference with standard binary trees in the centralized context where upward pointers are rarely kept. A *link* is simply a pair (Id, range), where Id is the Id of the server that stores the referenced node, and range is its range. For our example, the left link of a is $\langle S_0 : b,]-\infty,\lambda_1[\rangle$ and its right link is $\langle S_1 : c, [\lambda_1,\infty[\rangle$. Links are used during top-down traversals of the distributed tree.

When it is the turn of server S_1 to split, its collection of entries is further divided and the objects distributed among S_1 and a new server S_2 that will store a new leaf node. A routing node c is created with range $[\lambda_1,\infty[$, and the ranges of its left and right children $S_1 : d$ and $S_2 : e$ are, respectively, $[\lambda_1,\lambda_2[$ and $[\lambda_2,\infty[$.

Performance

This basic distribution schema yields reasonable storage balancing. After a certain number of key insertions and assuming keys are not removed from the access structure, one can see that each server is at least half-full. However, as previously discussed, load balancing is not achieved: servers corresponding to upper levels of the tree get more work. To perform a dictionary operation, a client sends the query to the root node, that forwards the query to the appropriate nodes down the tree. Since all searches start from the root node, the server that hosts it, is both a bottleneck and a single point of failure. As the number of clients increases, so does the number of incoming requests that this root server must handle. As a result, the structure (as just described) does not scale.

What about efficiency? Any dictionary operation takes as input a key value, starts from the root node and follows a *unique* path down to a leaf. If the *insert()* requests are independently and uniformly distributed, the complexity is logarithmic in the number of servers *assuming the tree is balanced*. However, such a binary tree may degenerate to a worst case linear behavior for all dictionary operations. (This is left as an exercise). To fix this issue, some "rotation" operations are applied to maintain the balance of the tree. Rotations techniques for trees are standard and details may be found in textbooks. We rather focus now on the management of routing tables, which is more specific to the distributed context.

Routing Tables

In addition to the structural information already presented, nodes maintain *routing tables* that guide tree traversals to find the appropriate nodes. More precisely, each node stores the following information:

1. Its level l in the tree (starting from the root, at level 0);
2. Its position *pos* in this level, $0 \leq pos < 2^l$;
3. The addresses of its parent and left and right children;
4. The address of the previous and next adjacent nodes in in-order traversal;
5. Left and right routing tables that reference nodes at the same level and at position $pos + / - 2^i$ for $i = 0, 1, 2, \ldots.$

For instance, for the binary tree of Figure 15.12, node m is at level 3, and its position in this level, for the whole tree, is 6. The left routing table refers to nodes at respective positions $6 - 2^0 = 5$, $6 - 2^1 = 4$, and $6 - 2^4 = 2$. This is strongly reminiscent of the friends in CHORD. A node knows better the nodes that are close, and the number of friends is clearly logarithmic in the total number of nodes. BATON records the range and children of its friends. Note that, since the tree is not complete at each level, a friend may be set to null.

BATON Operations

First consider search. A client may send a *search(k)* request to any peer p in the tree; so, it suffices to know a single server to access information. A left or right traversal is first initiated, to find the node p' *at the same level as p* whose range covers k.

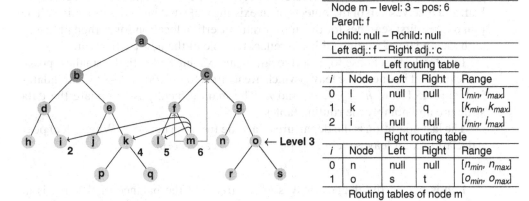

| Node m – level: 3 – pos: 6 |
| Parent: f |
| Lchild: null – Rchild: null |
| Left adj.: f – Right adj.: c |

Left routing table

i	Node	Left	Right	Range
0	l	null	null	$[l_{min}, l_{max}]$
1	k	p	q	$[k_{min}, k_{max}]$
2	i	null	null	$[i_{min}, i_{max}]$

Right routing table

i	Node	Left	Right	Range
0	n	null	null	$[n_{min}, n_{max}]$
1	o	s	t	$[o_{min}, o_{max}]$

Routing tables of node m

Figure 15.12. Routing information in BATON.

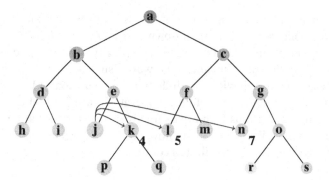

Figure 15.13. Searching with routing tables.

The process is somewhat similar to CHORD search: if p' is not part of the friends of p, p finds, among its friends, the one that is "closest" to p'. Specifically, assuming that k is larger than the upper bound of its range, p chooses the furthest friends p'' whose lower bound is smaller than k. The search continues until p' is found. Then the search continues downwards to the leaf in charge of k.

Looking at Figure 15.13, assume a request sent to node j for a key that belongs to node r. From the friends of j, the one that satisfies the horizontal search condition is n, the third friend in the right routing table. Then, the horizontal traversal continues with n forwarding the search to o, its first friend. From o, the top-down search phase leads to node r.

In summary, BATON proceeds with a CHORD-like search in a given tree level, and with a top-down search when the node at the current level whose subtree contains the searched key has been found. The first phase, enabled by the routing tables, enables a horizontal navigation in the tree that avoids to always have to access the root.

Recall that a P2P structure, in addition to dictionary operations (that include range search in the present case), must also provide *join()* and *leave()* operations that affect the network topology.

Just as in CHORD, a peer p that wants to join the network uses any *contact peer* p' to initiate the join in the structure. In BATON, a peer that joins always becomes a leaf, and receives half of the objects of an existing leaf (that becomes its sibling). The join process first searches for the appropriate insertion location for p, then proceeds with the update of routing tables to reflect the role of the new participant.

Intuitively, we choose for insert location, an existing leaf with the smallest possible level (that is, one of the leaves which are nearest to the root). Possible candidates in Figure 15.12 are h, i, j, l, m, and n. The main difficulty is to update the data structure and notably the routing tables.

The last operation is the departure of a node from the network. When a leaf peer p declares that it leaves ("cold" departure), two cases occur:

1. p is one of the deepest leaves in the tree and the balance of the tree is in principle not affected by the departure of p. The main task is then to distribute keys of p to neighbors.

2. p is one of the deepest leaves. We then need to find a replacement for p and for that we choose one of the deepest leaves in the tree that is moved from its previous location in the tree.

Again the difficulty is the maintenance of the routing tables, in particular in the second case.

If the BATON structure is difficult to maintain when new information is entered (possibly requiring tree balancing) and servers joining/leaving (possibly leading to moving servers in the tree), it is very efficient for search. Also, it clusters objects based on the values of their keys, and supports range queries. The two-phase mechanism based on horizontal navigation in the tree followed by some constant number of vertical navigation, leads to an $O(\log n)$ cost. A design principle that we can see at work in BATON is: Find an appropriate trade-off between the amount of replication (here by the number of "friends" at each node) and the efficiency of the structure.

To conclude with BATON, observe that "hot" departures in such a complex structure become very difficult to handle. Although the redundancy of routing tables provides the means of rebuilding the information of a lost peer, this comes at the cost of lots of work and in particular, lots of communications. As a consequence, it becomes difficult to guarantee robustness in a highly changing environment.

15.2.3 Case Study: BIGTABLE

In 2006, scientists working at Google published a paper on "BIGTABLE: A Distributed Storage System for Structured Data." It describes a distributed index designed to manage very large datasets ("petabytes of data") in a cluster of data servers. BIGTABLE supports key search, range search and high-throughput file scans. BIGTABLE also provides a flexible storage for structured data. As such, it can also be seen as a large distributed database system with a B-tree-like file organization.

The presentation that follows highlights the main architectural and technical aspects of BIGTABLE. Many details are omitted. Please refer to the Further Reading section at the end of the chapter.

Structure Overview

Figure 15.14 gives an overview of the structure. The data representation is roughly similar to the relational model. A *table* contains a list of *rows*. Each row consists of a key and a list of columns. The rows are sorted in lexicographic order by the key values. A large table is partitioned horizontally in "tablets" which constitute the leaves of the distributed tree. The size of a tablet is typically a few hundreds of megabytes.

The content of a row differs from those of standard relational tables. First, columns can be grouped in "families," which form the basic data management unit in BIGTABLE. The columns of a same family are stored independently from those of the other families. Hence, BIGTABLE captures both aspects of a row store (several columns in one family) and that of a column-oriented store, with the typical advantage that compression can benefit from the homogeneity of the values stored in a column. Moreover, a "cell" (i.e., the intersection of a row and a column) can store many versions of a same content (e.g., a Web page collected from the Web), each identified by a timestamp. This completes the multimap organization of BIGTABLE

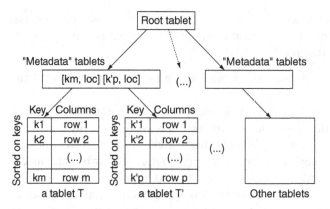

Figure 15.14. Overview of BIGTABLE structure.

which can therefore be summarized as a four-level access pattern:

$$key \rightarrow family \rightarrow column \rightarrow timestamp$$

It is possible to access each content independently from the others by combining those four criteria. Note finally that the data model is flexible enough to allow for the addition of new columns on a per-row basis.

The tablets of a table are distributed in a cluster. In order to perform efficient lookups during exact and range search, tablets are indexed on the range of the keys. At this point, the BIGTABLE organization differs from our generic search tree. Instead of a binary tree reflecting the split history of the structures, BIGTABLEs collects the tablet ranges and store them in another table, called the "metadata" table. One obtains what would be called, in a centralized context, a nondense index on a sorted file. Since the Metadata table is managed just like any other table, it is itself partitioned into tablets. The indexing process can be applied recursively by creating upper levels until the collection of ranges occupies a single tablet, the root of a distributed tree, quite similar to centralized B-trees.

Figure 15.14 shows the first level of metadata. Its rows consist of pairs (key, loc), where loc is a tablet location, and key is the key of the last row in the tablet. Note that, because the table is sorted, this is sufficient to determine the range of a table. The first pair in the metadata table represented on Figure 15.14 for instance refers to a tablet covering the range $] - \infty, k_m]$.

Conceptually, the number of levels in the distributed tree is unbounded. In practice, BIGTABLE limits the number of levels to 3: The root node is a tablet above the metadata table, which is never split. This suffices to potentially index very large data sets. Indeed, assume a (realistic) tablet size of $2^{28} = 268$ MB, and 1 KB entries in the metadata tablet. Then

1. A metadata tablet can index $268,000 \approx 2^{18}$ data tablets,
2. The root tablet can index in turn up to 2^{18} metadata tablets, hence 2^{36} data tablets.

Since the capacity of a tablet is 2^{28} bytes, this represents a maximal storage of 2^{64} bytes for a single table (16,384 petabytes!).

Note that a single metadata tablet is already sufficient to index a 2^{46} bytes data set. If this metadata tablet were stored without replication, and without using Client caches, it would likely become a bottleneck of the system. BIGTABLE uses caching and replication to distribute the load evenly over many servers.

Distribution Strategy

A BIGTABLE instance consists of a Master server, many (tablet) servers, and Client nodes. The Master acts as a coordinator for a few tasks that would be complicated to handle in a fully decentralized setting. This includes column

1. Maintenance of the table schemas (columns names, types, families, etc.),
2. Monitoring of servers and management of failures,
3. Assignment of tablets to server.

Each tablet server handles the storage and access to a set of tablets (100–1000) assigned by the Master. This involves persistence management, error recovery, concurrency, and split request when the server capacity is exhausted. The tablet server also provides search and update services on all the rows that belong to its range.

The evolution of the tree is rather different from that of a P2P structure like BATON. Three cases occur: (i) a tablet server decides to split and to distribute a part (about half) of its tablets to another server, (ii) a tablet server merges its content with another server, and (iii) a failure (of any kind) occurs and keeps the server from participating to the cluster.

The failure is handled by the Master, which sends heartbeat messages and initiates replacement, in a way similar to that already seen for GFS (see Section 14.5.2). The other two cases modify the range of the tablet server. At this point, we have two choices: Either the modification is reported to all the participants, including the Client nodes, or a lazy strategy is adopted. This is the same kind of trade-off already encountered with the LH* structure, CHORD, and BATON.

BIGTABLE relies on lazy updates. This may affect the result of operations required by other components of the system because their requests may fall "out of range" due to some discrepancy between their local information and the actual status of the structure. The system is always ready to handle such errors. An "internal" out-of-range can be met when the Master requires from a server a tablet, which does not correspond to its range. In that case, there is a discrepancy between the actual range covered by the server, and the range stored at the metadata level, which can be viewed as an replicated "image" of the tablet range. The tablet server then initiates an adjustment message that informs the Master of the past split. Another case of out-of-range affects Client nodes: The stabilization protocol in case of out-of-range is explained next.

Adjustment of the Client Image

A Client is a Google application that uses the BIGTABLE client library. A Client initially connects to the cluster through the Master, which sends back information regarding the tablet servers of interest to the Client initial requests. This information

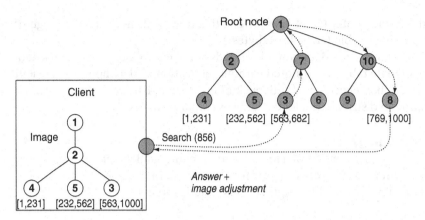

Figure 15.15. Example of an out-of-range request followed by an adjustment.

is stored in the Client local cache (its image in our terminology) and used to directly communicate with tablet servers later on. The Master is therefore rarely involved in the message exchanges, and this keeps it from being overloaded. So far, this is akin to GFS.

The Client maintains its image regardless of the changes that affect the tree. If a request is sent to a server that does no longer hold the required key, an out-of-range answer is sent back. The Client requires then the correct address to the metadata level. In the worst case, this induces a new out of range request, and another round-trip with the root is necessary. Assume that, initially, the situation is the one shown on Figure 15.15. The Client stores an outdated image of the tree with only five tablets (including one metadata tablet, and the root). Since the last refresh of the Client image, the tree has actually grown to the state shown on the right, with ten tablets. The figure gives the range owned by each leaf.

The Client sends a *search*(856) request. From its image, it determines that node **3** should own the key. When node **3** processes the message, it observes an out of range. The search is forwarded to node **7**, which forwards it to the root node. From there, a standard top-down traversal finally leads to the true owner of key 856. The Client image is then refreshed with the information collected during this process, so that the addressing error does not repeat (at least for this part of the tree). In case of an out of range request, 6 networks round trips may be necessary in the worse case (three for an upward path, three for a downward one).

Persistence

Each tablet server manages locally the persistence of its tablets. Figure 15.16 shows the components involved in *write()* and *read()* operations (the latter being a full scan) of a single tablet. Recall first that a tablet is sorted by its key. It would be very inefficient to attempt an insertion of each new row in a sorted file because of the time necessary to find its location and to the complicated space management incurred by the order maintenance. BIGTABLE uses a more sophisticated, yet rather classical strategy, which can be summarized as an incremental sort-merge with REDO

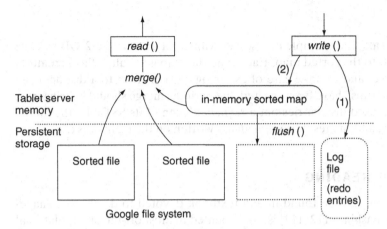

Figure 15.16. Persistence management in a tablet server.

logging. When a row must be inserted in the tablet, the *write()* operates in two steps:

1. The row is appended to a log file;
2. After the log has acknowledged the append operation, the row is put in an in-memory sorted table.

The log file belongs to the persistent storage, resilient to failures (and managed by GFS). As soon as a row has been written to the log, GFS guarantees that it can be recovered, even if the tablet server crashes. Moreover, the log is an append-only file. A row can be added with minimal overhead because it is always inserted right away at the end of the current log file.

The second step puts the row in a sorted table in memory. This does not require a disk access and can therefore be performed efficiently. Moreover, rows in this table can be merged very quickly with the rest of the tablet content to satisfy read requests. Thus, the row becomes immediately accessible even though it is still not in the sorted file.

The memory table grows and eventually reaches a predefined threshold. At this point, the sorted table is reconstructed and stored. The space of the memory table becomes available for subsequent *write()*. So, eventually, a tablet therefore consists in a set of files (called SSTables in Google terminology), each sorted by the key, and an in-memory collection also sorted by the key. Now, if a *read()* requests the content of the tablet, this content must be supplied in key order. This is achieved with a *merge()* of the files that constitutes the tablet, plus the current content of the in-memory table. Note that the hybrid process that involves persistent file and in-memory structures is reminiscent of the merge-based construction of an inverted index.

As the number of SSTables increases, so does the cost of their merging. A practical obstacle is that a merge, to be efficient, requires a sequential scan of the SSTables, which can only be achieved if each is stored on a distinct disk entirely devoted to the scan operation. Therefore, in order to limit the fan-in, merges are carried out periodically between the sorted files to limit their number.

Example 15.2.1 Take the example of a server with eight disks and a 2-GB volatile memory allocated to the sorted map. Each time the map gets full, a flush creates a new 2-GB SSTable, and we take care of assigning each of them to a distinct disk. When seven such "runs" have been created, the periodic merge should be triggered: Each of the seven used disk carries out a *sequential* scan of its SSTable, the merge occurs in memory, and the result is *sequentially* written on the eighth disk.

15.3 FURTHER READING

Centralized indexing can be found in any textbook devoted to database management [61]. Linear hashing [112, 114] is implemented in most off-the-shelf relational databases. LH* is presented in [116]. Consistent hashing is proposed and analyzed in [107]. The technique is used in the Open Source *memcached* library (http://memcached.org), in the Amazon's DYNAMO system [52] and in the CHORD DHT [150]. The authors of [52] describe in detail the design of DYNAMO, whose data structure is a large distributed hash table intended to provide fast and reliable answer to point queries. Beyond the indexing aspect, DYNAMO features many interesting aspects representative of the main issues that must be addressed during the design and implementation of a large-scale data-centric system. The data model for instance is limited to a "key store" (i.e., (*key*, *value*) pairs), and supports only a few basic operations: *put()* and *get()*. Several open-source implementation of Amazon's project now exist, including VOLDEMORT http://project-voldemort.com/ and CASSANDRA http://cassandra.apache.org/. DYNAMO has inspired many of the recent distributed key-value stores collectively known as "NoSQL" (Not Only SQL) databases (see http://nosql-databases.org/).

Distributed hash tables is a term coined by [53] who first proposed the extension of hash techniques to distributed systems. Several DHT structures have been proposed, notably, CHORD [150], Pastry [141], Tapestry [188], and CAN [140]. Distributed hash tables has been developed as a means of overcoming shortcomings of the flooding strategy used in early P2P systems such as Napster. The $O(\log N)$ number of messages required to route a query incurs a latency which may be deemed unsuitable for highly demanding application. Through extended replication, a $O(1)$ message cost can be reached: see [139] and the already mentioned DYNAMO paper. DHTs are widely used in P2P systems: BitTorrent, the Kad network, the Storm botnet, YaCy, and the Coral Content Distribution Network.

Distributed strategies for tree-based structures has been first tackled in [111, 115] which propose several important principles later adopted for Web-scale indexing. In particular, details on the maintenance of a tree image in the Client cache can be found in [111]. BATON is a P2P tree structure presented in [102]. See also [101] for a multiway tree structure based on the same principles and [103] for a multidimensional structure, the VBI-tree. Another proposal for offering range search is the P-tree [50] which is essentially a B+tree distributed over a CHORD network. Each node stores a leaf of the B+tree, as well as the path from the root to the leaf. Point and range queries can be answered in $O(\log N)$, but the maintenance of the structure as peers join or leave the network is costly: In addition to the $\log N + \log^2 N$ costs of adding the new peer to CHORD, information must be obtained on the tree structure to build the tree branch.

BIGTABLE has inspired several other projects outside Google, including the HYPERTABLE Open source project (http://www.hypertable.org/), the HBASE data structure of HADOOP, and CASSANDRA, which combines features from both DYNAMO and BIGTABLE. BIGTABLE is described in [44]. Its canonical usage is the storage of documents extracted from the Web and indexed by their URL. BIGTABLE (and its Open-source variants) is more than just an indexing mechanism, as it features a data model that can be roughly seen as an extension of the relational one, with flexible schema and versioning of cell values.

15.4 EXERCISES

Exercise 15.4.1 (static and extendible hashing) *The following is a list of French "départements":*

3 Allier	36 Indre	18 Cher	75 Paris
39 Jura	9 Ariege	81 Tarn	11 Aude
12 Aveyron	25 Doubs	73 Savoie	55 Meuse
15 Cantal	51 Marne	42 Loire	40 Landes
14 Calvados	30 Gard	84 Vaucluse	7 Ardeche

The first value is the key. We assume that a bucket contains up to five records.

1. *Propose a hash function and build a static hash file, taking the records in the proposed order (left-right, then top-bottom).*
2. *Same exercise, but now use an linear hash file based on the following hash values:*

Allier	1001	Indre	1000	Cher	1010	Paris	0101
Jura	0101	Ariege	1011	Tarn	0100	Aude	1101
Aveyron	1011	Doubs	0110	Savoie	1101	Meuse	1111
Cantal	1100	Marne	1100	Loire	0110	Landes	0100
Calvados	1100	Gard	1100	Vaucluse	0111	Ardeche	1001

Exercise 15.4.2 (LH*) *Consider Figure 15.3. What happens if we insert an object with key 47, still assuming that the maximal number of objects in a bucket is 4.*

Exercise 15.4.3 (LH*) *Prove that the number of messages for LH* insertion is three in the worst case.*

Exercise 15.4.4 (consistent hashing) *Assume that someone proposes the following solution to the problem of distributing the hash directory: Each node maintains the hash value and location of its successor. Discuss the advantage and disadvantages of this solution, and examine in particular the cost of the dictionary operation (insert, delete, search) and network maintenance operations (join and leave).*

Exercise 15.4.5 (CHORD friends) *Express the gap between friends[i] and friends[$i+1$] in the routing table of a CHORD peer, and and use the result to show formally that a search operations converges in logarithmic time.*

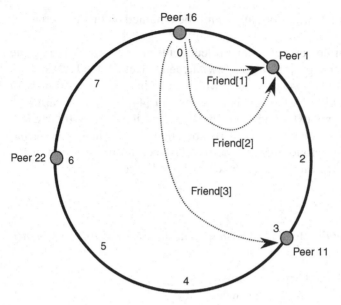

Figure 15.17. A CHORD ring.

Exercise 15.4.6 *Consider the* CHORD *ring of Figure 15.17. What are the friends of p11, located at 3?*

Exercise 15.4.7 *Develop an example of the worst case for the search() operation in* CHORD, *with* $m = 10$.

Exercise 15.4.8 (BATON range search) *Explain the range search algorithm of* BATON.

Exercise 15.4.9 (BATON range search) *Complete the description of the Join algorithm in* BATON *regarding the modification of routing tables in order to take into account the new node.*

Exercise 15.4.10 (BIGTABLE) *Describe the split algorithm of* BIGTABLE. *Compare with standard B-tree algorithms.*

Exercise 15.4.11 *Compare two of the index structures presented in the Chapter and identify, beyond their differences, some of the common design principles adopted to cope with the distribution problem. Take for instance distributed linear hashing and* BIGTABLE *and consider how a Client communicates with the structure.*

16

Distributed Computing with MAPREDUCE and PIG

So far, the discussion on distributed systems has been limited to data storage, and to a few data management primitives (e.g., *write()*, *read()*, *search()*, etc.). For real applications, one also needs to develop and execute more complex programs that process the available datasets and effectively exploit the available resources.

The naive approach that consists in getting all the required data at the Client in order to apply locally some processing, often looses in a distributed setting. First, some processing may not be available locally. Moreover, centralizing all the information then processing it, would simply miss all the advantages brought by a powerful cluster of hundreds or even thousands machines. We have to use distribution. One can consider two main scenarios for data processing in distributed systems.

Distributed processing and workflow: In the first one, an application disposes of large data sets and needs to apply to them some processes that are available on remote sites. When this is the case, the problem is to send the data to the appropriate locations, and then sequence the remote executions. This workflow scenario is typically implemented using *Web services* and some high-level coordination language.

Distributed data and MAPREDUCE: In a second scenario, the data sets are already distributed in a number of servers, and, conversely to the previous scenario, we "push" programs to these servers. Indeed, due to network bandwidth issues, it is often more cost-effective to send a small piece of program from the Client to Servers, than to transfer large data volumes to a single Client. This leads to the MAPREDUCE approach that we present in this chapter.

This second scenario is illustrated in Figure 16.1. Ideally, each piece of program running as a process on a server n should work only on the data stored locally at n, achieving an optimal reduction of network traffic. More practically, we should try to limit communications by applying local processing as much as possible. We refer to this as the *data locality principle* (i.e., *the distribution strategy must be such that a program component operates, as much as possible, on data stored on the local machine.*). In such a setting, the Client plays the role of a coordinator sending pieces

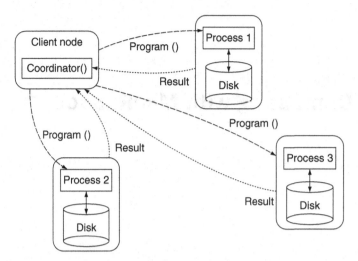

Figure 16.1. Distributed computing with distributed data storage.

of code to each server, initiating, and possibly coordinating, a fully decentralized computation.

Enabling a sound, efficient and reliable distributed data processing gives rise to the following complex issues:

Parallelization: Can we split a particular task into tasks executing concurrently on independent data sets and cooperating to compute a final result? It is not always clear how to answer that question and take advantage of distributed resources. The important word here is *independence*. If a relevant data set can be partitioned, and each part be processed independently, the answer is: yes. Also, if, on the other hand, a program can be split in several tasks that operate independently, the answer is also: yes. If both conditions are satisfied, this is even better. For complex tasks, the answer may not be that simple. In other words, it is not always obvious to see which part of a program can take advantage of parallelization.

Failure resilience: When there are a large number of participants involved in a complex task, it becomes necessary to cope with potential system failures. Trying to address them with traditional programming environments used in everyday application development would be a daunting task. What is called for is a programming model, and an associated software support, to facilitate the deployment, monitoring, and control of such distributed programs.

In the first part of the chapter, we introduce MAPREDUCE, a programming model for large-scale parallel computing that addresses these issues. Even if developing applications with MAPREDUCE greatly reduces the effort of applications programmers, the task remains very challenging. In the second part, we present the PIGLATIN language that, based on a rich model and high-level language primitives, further allows simplifying the design of distributed data processing applications.

At the time of writing, considerable research and development efforts are devoted to the design of high-level languages that express parallel and distributed data processing. MAPREDUCE is often nowadays taken as a kind of de facto standard for the robust execution of large data-oriented tasks on dozens of computer, at least at a low, "physical" level. However, MAPREDUCE is by no means the universal solution to parallel data processing problems. The area is still a moving territory subject to debates and alternative proposals. The last section of the chapter attempts, as usual, to provide useful references and discussions.

16.1 MAPREDUCE

Initially designed and used internally by Google, the MAPREDUCE distributed programming model is now promoted by several other major Web companies (e.g., Yahoo! and Amazon) and supported by many Open Source implementations (e.g., HADOOP, COUCHDB, MONGODB, and many others in the "NoSQL" world). It proposes a programming model strongly influenced by functional programming principles, a task being modeled as a sequential evaluation of stateless functions over nonmutable data. A function in a MAPREDUCE process takes as input an argument, outputs a result that only depends on its argument, and is side-effect free. All there properties are necessary to ensure an easy parallelization of the tasks.

Let us start by highlighting important features that help understand the scope of this programming model within the realm of data processing:

Semistructured data: MAPREDUCE is a programming paradigm for distributed processing of semistructured data (typically, data collected from the Web). The programming model is designed for self-contained "documents" without references to other pieces of data, or, at least, very few of them. The main assumption is that such documents can be processed *independently*, and that a large collection of documents can be partitioned at will over a set of computing machines without having to consider clustering constraints.

Not for joins: Joins (contrary to, say, in a relational engine) are not at the center of the picture. A parallel join-oriented computing model would attempt, in the first place, to put on the same server, documents that need to be joined. This design choice is deliberately ignored by MAPREDUCE. (We will nonetheless see how to process joins using simple tweaks of the model.)

Not for transactions: MAPREDUCE is inappropriate for transactional operations. In a typical MAPREDUCE computation, programs are distributed to various servers and a server computation typically involves a scan its input datasets. This induces an important latency, and thus is not adapted to a workload consisting of many small transactions.

So, how come such an approach that does not seem to address important data processing issues such as joins and transactions, could become rapidly very popular? Well, it turns out to be very adapted to a wide range of data processing applications consisting in analyzing large quantities of data (e.g., large collections of Web documents). Also, its attractiveness comes from its ability to natively support the key features of a distributed system, and in particular failure management, scalability, and the transparent management of the infrastructure.

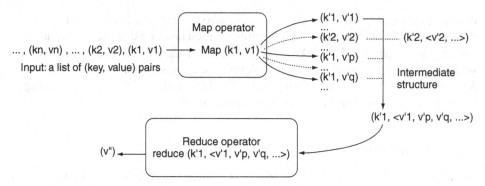

Figure 16.2. The programming model of MAPREDUCE.

16.1.1 Programming Model

Let us begin with the programming model, ignoring for the moment distribution aspects. As suggested by its name, MAPREDUCE operates in two steps (see Figure 16.2):

1. The first step, MAP, takes as input a list of pairs (k,v), where k belongs to a key space K_1 and v to a value space V_1. A *map()* operation, defined by the programmer, processes *independently* each pair and produces (for each pair), another *list* of pairs $(k',v') \in K_2 \times V_2$, called *intermediate pairs* in the following. Note that the key space and value space of the intermediate pairs, K_2 and V_2, may be different from those of the input pairs, K_1 and V_1.
2. Observe that the MAP phase may produce several pairs $(k'_1,v'_1),\ldots,(k'_1,v'_p),\ldots,$ for the same key value component. You should think that all the values for the same key as grouped in structures of type $(K_2, list(V_2))$, for instance $(k'_1, \langle v'_1, \ldots, v'_p, \ldots \rangle)$.
3. The second step, REDUCE, phase operates on the grouped instances of intermediate pairs. Each of these instances is processed by the procedure *independently* from the others. The user-defined *reduce()* function outputs a result, usually a single value. On Figure 16.2, the grouped pair $(k'_1, \langle v'_1, \ldots, v'_p, \ldots \rangle)$ is processed in the REDUCE phase and yields value v''.

Example 16.1.1 As a concrete example, consider a program *CountWords()* that counts the number of word occurrences in a collection of documents. More precisely, for each word w, we want to count how many times w occurs in the entire collection.

In the MAPREDUCE programming model, we will use a user-defined function *mapCW* that takes as input a pair (i, doc), where i is a document id, and *doc* its content. Given such a pair, the function produces a list of intermediate pairs (t, c), where t is a term occurring in the input document and c the number of occurrences of t in the document. The MAP function takes as input a list of (i, doc) pairs and applies *mapCW* to each pair in the list.

```
mapCW(String key, String value):
  // key: document name
  // value: document contents

  // Loop on the terms in value
  for each term t in value:
    let result be the number of occurrences of t in value
    // Send the result
    return (t, result);
```

Now as a result of the MAP phase, we have for each word w, a list of all the partial counts produced. Consider now the REDUCE phase. We use a user-defined function *reduceCW* that takes as input a pair $(t, list(c))$, t being a term and $list(c)$ a list of all the partial counts produced during the MAP phase. The function simply sums the counts.

```
reduceCW(String key, Iterator values):
  // key: a term
  // values: a list of counts
  int result = 0;

  // Loop on the values list; accumulate in result
  for each v in values:
    result += v;

  // Send the result
  return result;
```

The REDUCE function applies *reduceCW* to the pair $(t, list(c))$ for each t occurring in any document of the collection. Logically, this is all there is in MAPREDUCE. An essential feature to keep in mind is that each pair in the input of either the MAP or the REDUCE phase is processed independently from the other input pairs. This allows splitting an input in several parts, and assigning each part to a process, without affecting the program semantics. In other words, MAPREDUCE can naturally be split into independent tasks that are executed in parallel.

Now, the crux is the programming environment that is used to actually take advantage of a cluster of machines. This is discussed next.

16.1.2 The Programming Environment

The MAPREDUCE environment first executes the MAP function and stores the output of the MAP phase in an intermediate file. Let us ignore the distribution of this file first. An important aspect is that intermediate pairs (k', v') are clustered (via sorting or hashing) on the key value. This is illustrated in Figure 16.2. One can see that all the values corresponding to a key k are grouped together by the MAPREDUCE environment. No intervention from the programmer (besides optional parameters to tune or monitor the process) is required.

Programming in MAPREDUCE is just a matter of adapting an algorithm to this peculiar two-phase processing model. Note that it not possible to adapt any task to such a model, but that many large data processing tasks naturally fit this pattern (see Exercises). The programmer only has to implement the *map()* and *reduce()* functions, and then submits them to the MAPREDUCE environment that takes care of the replication and execution of processes in the distributed system. In particular, the programmer does not have to worry about any aspect related to distribution. The following code shows a program that creates a MAPREDUCE job based on the above two functions.[1]

```
// Include the declarations of Mapper and Reducer
// which encapsulate mapWC() and reduceWC()
#include "MapWordCount.h"
#include "ReduceWourdCount.h"

// A specification object for \mapreduce/ execution
MapReduceSpecification spec;

// Define input files
  MapReduceInput* input = spec.add_input();
  input-> set_filepattern ("documents.xml");
  input->set_mapper_class("MapWordCount");

// Specify the output files :
MapReduceOutput* out = spec.output();
out-> set_filebase ("wc.txt");
out->set_num_tasks(100);
out-> set_reducer_class ("ReduceWourdCount");

// Now run it
MapReduceResult result;
if (!MapReduce(spec, &result)) abort ();
  // Done: 'result' structure contains info
  // about counters, time taken, number of
  // machines used, etc.
  return 0;
```

---

[1] This piece of C++ code is a slightly simplified version of the full example given in the original Google paper on MAPREDUCE.

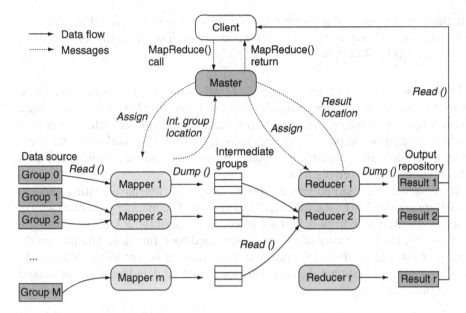

Figure 16.3. Distributed execution of a MAPREDUCE job.

The execution of a MAPREDUCE job is illustrated in Figure 16.3. The context should now be familiar to the reader. The job is distributed in a cluster of servers, and one of these servers plays the special role of a Master. The system is designed to cope with a failure of any of its components, as explained further.

The Client node is, as usual, a library incorporated in the Client application. When the *MapReduce()* function is called, it connects to a Master and transmits the *map()* and *reduce()* functions. The execution flow of the Client is then frozen. The Master considers then the input data set, which is assumed to be partitioned over a set of *M* nodes in the cluster. The *map()* function is distributed to these nodes and applies to the local subset of the data set (recall the data locality principle), called "bag" in what follows. These bags constitute the units of the distributed computation of the MAP: Each MAP task involved in the distributed computation works on one and only one bag. Note that the input of a MAPREDUCE job can be a variety of data sources, ranging from a relational database to a file system, with all possible semistructured representations in between. In the case of a relational system, each node hosts a DBMS server and a bag consists of one of the blocks in a partition of a relational table. In the case of a file system, a bag is a set of files stored on the node.

Whatever the data source, it must support an iterator-like mechanism that extracts pieces of data from the local bag. A piece of data may be a row in a relational DB, or a line from a file. More generally it is a self-contained object that we call *document* in the remainder of this chapter.

Example 16.1.2 Turning back to the *WordCount()* example, suppose the input consists of a collection of, say, one million 100-term documents of approximately 1 KB each. Suppose we use as data source a large-scale file system, say GFS, with bags of 64 MBs. So, each bag consists of 64,000 documents. Therefore the number M of bags is $\lceil 1,000,000/64,000 \rceil \approx 16,000$ bags.

The number of REDUCE tasks is supplied by the programmer, as a parameter R, along with a *hash()* partitioning function that can be used to hash the intermediate pairs in R bags for sharding purposes. If, for example, the intermediate keys consist of uniformly distributed positive integer values, the simple *modulo(key, R)* partitioning function is an acceptable candidate. In general, a more sophisticated hash function, robust to skewed distribution, is necessary.

At run-time, the MAPREDUCE Master assigns to the participating servers, called *Mappers*, the MAP task for their local chunks. The mapper generates a local list of (k_2, v_2) intermediate pairs that are placed into one of the R local intermediate bags based on the hash value of k_2 for the specified hash function. The intermediary bags are stored on the local disk, and their location is sent to the Master. At this point, the computation remains purely local, and no data has been exchanged between the nodes.

Example 16.1.3 Consider once more the *WordCount()* example in a GFS environment. Each chunk contains 64,000 documents, and 100 distinct terms can be extracted from each document. The (local) MAP phase over one bag produces 6,400,000 pairs (t,c), t being a term and c its count. Suppose $R = 1,000$. Each intermediate bag $i, 0 \leq i < 1,000$, contains approximately 6,400 pairs, consisting of terms t such that $hash(t) = i$.

At the end of the MAP phase, anyway, the intermediate result is globally split into R bags. The REDUCE phase then begins. The tasks corresponding to the intermediary bags are distributed between servers called *Reducers*. A REDUCE task corresponds to one of the R bags (i.e., it is specified by one of the values of the hash function). One such task is initiated by the Master that sends to an individual Reducer the id of the bag (the value of the hash function), the addresses of the different buckets of the bag, and the *reduce()* function. The Reducer processes its task as follows:

1. The Reducer reads the buckets of the bag from all the Mappers and sorts their union by the intermediate key; note that this now involves data exchanges between nodes.
2. Once this has been achieved, the intermediate result is sequentially scanned, and for each key k_2, the *reduce()* function is evaluated over the bag of values $\langle v_1, v_2, \ldots \rangle$ associated to k_2.
3. The result is stored either in a buffer, or in a file if its size exceeds the Reducer capacity.

Each Reducer must carry out a sort operation on its input in order to group the intermediate pairs on their key. The sort can be done in main memory or with the external sort/merge algorithm detailed in Chapter 12.

Example 16.1.4 Recall that we assumed $R = 1,000$. We need 1,000 REDUCE tasks $R_i, i \in [0,1000[$. Each R_i must process a bag containing all the pairs (t,c) such that $hash(t) = i$.

Let $i = 100$, and assume that $hash('call') = hash('mine') = hash('blog') = 100$. We focus on three Mappers M^p, M^q and M^r, each storing a bag G_i for hash key i with several occurrences of 'call', 'mine', or 'blog':

1. $G_i^p = (\langle \ldots, ('mine', 1), \ldots, ('call',1), \ldots, ('mine',1), \ldots, ('blog', 1) \ldots \rangle$
2. $G_i^q = (\langle \ldots, ('call',1), \ldots, ('blog',1), \ldots \rangle$
3. $G_i^r = (\langle \ldots, ('blog', 1), \ldots, ('mine',1), \ldots, ('blog',1), \ldots \rangle$

R_i reads G_i^p, G_i^q, and G_i^r from the three Mappers, sorts their unioned content, and groups the pairs with a common key:

$$\ldots, ('blog', \langle 1,1,1,1 \rangle), \ldots, ('call', \langle 1,1 \rangle), \ldots, ('mine', \langle 1,1,1 \rangle)$$

Our *reduceWC()* function is then applied by R_i to each element of this list. The output is *('blog', 4), ('call', 2) and ('mine', 3)*.

When all Reducers have completed their task, the Master collects the location of the R result files and sends them to the Client node, in a structure that constitutes the result of the local *MapReduce()* function. In our example, each term appears in exactly one of the R result files, together with the count of its occurrences.

As mentioned before, the ideal situation occurs when R servers are idle and each can process in parallel a REDUCE task. Because of the two-phases process, a server playing the role of a Mapper may become a Reducer, and process (sequentially) several REDUCE tasks. Generally, the model is flexible enough to adapt to the workload of the cluster at any time. The optimal (and usual) case is a fully parallel and distributed processing. At the opposite, a MAPREDUCE job can be limited to a single machine.

16.1.3 MapReduce Internals

A MAPREDUCE job should be resilient to failures. A first concern is that a Mapper or a Reducer may die or become laggard during a task, due to networks or hardware problems. In a centralized context, a batch job interrupted because of hardware problem can simply be reinstantiated. In a distributed setting, the specific job handled by a machine is only a minor part of the overall computing task. Moreover, because the task is distributed on hundreds or thousands of machines, the chances that a problem occurs somewhere are much larger. For these reasons, starting the job from the beginning is not a valid option.

The interrupted task must be reassigned to another machine. The Master periodically checks the availability and reacheability of the "Workers" (Mapper or Reducer) involved in a task. If the Worker does not answer after a certain period, the action depends on its role:

Reducer: If it is a Reducer, the REDUCE task is restarted by selecting a new server and assigning the task to it.

Mapper: If it is a Mapper, the problem is more complex, because of the intermediate files. Even if the Mapper finished computing these intermediary files, a failure prevents this server to serve these files as input to some reducers. The MAP task has to be reexecuted on another machine, and any REDUCE task that has not finished to read the intermediate files from this particular failed node must be reexecuted as well.

This leads to the second important concern: the central role of the Master. In summary,

1. It assigns MAP and REDUCE tasks to the Mappers and the Reducers, and monitors their progress.
2. It receives the location of intermediate files produced by the Mappers, and transmits these locations to the Reducers.
3. It collects the location of the result files and sends them to the Client.

The central role of the Master is a potential architectural weakness. If the Master fails, the MAPREDUCE task is jeopardized. However, there is only one Master, and many more workers. The odds for the Master to fail are low. So it may be tolerable for many applications that when a Master fails, its clients resubmit their jobs to a new master, simply ignoring all the processing that has already been achieved for that task. Alternatively, one can realize that the issue is not really the failure of a Master but the loss of all the information that had been gathered about the computation. Using standard techniques based on replication and log files, one can provide recovery from Master failure that will avoid redoing tasks already performed.

It should be clear to the reader how complex data processing tasks can be performed using MAPREDUCE. However, the reader may be somewhat afraid by the complexity of the task facing the application programmer. In a second part of this chapter, we present the PIGLATIN language. The goal is to use a rich model and high-level language primitives, to simplify the design of distributed data processing applications.

16.2 PIG

The MAPREDUCE processing model is low-level. The computation of complex tasks with MAPREDUCE typically requires combining several jobs. Frequently used operations such as **sort** or **group** must be repeatedly introduced in applications as **map/reduce** functions, and integrated with more application-specific operations. To design large-scale data processing applications, it would be definitely useful to dispose of a language that would save the burden of these low-level tasks while preserving the assets of MAPREDUCE. In some sense, this can be compared to introducing declarative languages such as SQL in databases, to facilitate the task of developing applications and thereby improve the productivity of application programmers.

To illustrate the use of high-level language primitives, we present the PIG environment and PIG (or PIGLATIN) language. In spite of sometimes clumsy ad hoc features, the language is in general quite adapted to standard large scale data processing tasks. Another advantage is that it can be tested with minimal installation overhead. PIG brings two important features with respect to the MAPREDUCE approach: (i) a richer data model, with nested data structures, and (ii) expressive data manipulation primitives that can be combined in *data flows* to obtain complex operations.

In brief, a PIG program takes as input a "bag" represented in a file. We will detail the bag data structure further, but it is a roughly speaking a *nested relation* (i.e., a relation where the entries may themselves be relations). A PIG program also produces a bag, either stored in a file or displayed on screen.

We begin with a short illustrative session, and then develop the data and processing model of PIG. The *Putting into Practice* chapter (Chapter 19) devoted to HADOOP gives practical hints and exercises to experiment with PIG.

16.2.1 A Simple Session

Consider the following simple example: Given a file with a list of publications in a scientific journal, determine the average number of papers published each year. We use data coming from DBLP, a large collection of information on scientific publications, publicly available[2] in XML.

The PIG loader accepts a variety of input formats. We use here the default file format that it accepts. Each line of the file is interpreted as an entry (here a publication). Within a line, the attributes are separated by *tabs*. Suppose the input consists of the following lines:

```
2005    VLDB J. Model-based approximate querying in sensor networks.
1997    VLDB J. Dictionary-Based Order-Preserving String Compression.
2003    SIGMOD Record   Time management for new faculty.
2001    VLDB J. E-Services - Guest editorial.
2003    SIGMOD Record   Exposing undergraduate students to system internals.
1998    VLDB J. Integrating Reliable Memory in Databases.
1996    VLDB J. Query Processing and Optimization in Oracle Rdb
1996    VLDB J. A Complete Temporal Relational Algebra.
1994    SIGMOD Record   Data Modelling in the Large.
2002    SIGMOD Record   Data Mining: Concepts and Techniques - Book Review.
...
```

Each line gives the year a publication was published, the journal it was published in (e.g., the *VLDB Journal*) and its title.

Here is the complete PIG program that computes the average number of publications per year in SIGMOD RECORD.

```
-- Load records from the journal-small.txt file (tab separated)
articles = load '../../ data/dblp/journal-small.txt'
    as (year: chararray, journal: chararray, title : chararray) ;
sr_articles = filter articles BY journal=='SIGMOD Record';
year_groups = group sr_articles by year;
```

2 http://www.sigmod.org/dblp/db/index.html.

```
avg_nb = foreach year_groups generate group, COUNT( sr_articles . title );
dump avg_nb;
```

When run on a sample file, the output may look as follows:

```
(1977,1)
(1981,7)
(1982,3)
(1983,1)
(1986,1)
...
```

The program is essentially a sequence of operations, each defining a temporary bag that can be used as input of the subsequent operations. It can be viewed as a flow of data transformation, that is linear in its simplest form but can more generally be an *acyclic workflow* (i.e., a directed acyclic graph).

We can run a step-by-step evaluation of this program with the *grunt* command interpreter to better figure out what is going on.

Load and filter The **load** operator produces as temporary result, a bag named articles. PIG disposes of a few atomic types (int, chararray, bytearray). To "inspect" a bag, the interpreter proposes two useful commands: **describe** outputs its type, and **illustrate** produces a sample of the relation's content.

```
grunt> DESCRIBE articles ;
articles : {year: chararray, journal: chararray, title : chararray}

grunt> ILLUSTRATE articles ;
---------------------------------------------------------------------------------
| articles | year: chararray | journal: chararray | title : chararray         |
---------------------------------------------------------------------------------
|          | 2003            | SIGMOD Record      | Call  for  Book Reviews.|
---------------------------------------------------------------------------------
```

The file contains a bag of tuples, where the tuple attributes are distinguished by position. After loading, articles also contains a bag of tuples, but the tuple attributes are now distinguished by name.

The filter operation simply selects the elements satisfying certain conditions, pretty much like a relational selection.

Group In the example, the bags resulting from the load or from the filter do not look different than standard relations. However, a difference is that they may have two identical elements. This would happen, in the example, if the file contains two identical lines. Note that this cannot happen in a relation that is a *set* of tuples. Bags allow the repetition of elements. Furthermore, like nested relations, PIG bags can be *nested*. The result of a **group** for instance is a nested bag. In the example, the group operation is used to create a bag with one element for each distinct year:

```
grunt> year_groups = GROUP sr_articles  BY year;

grunt> describe  year_groups;
year_groups: {group: chararray,
       sr_articles : {year: chararray, journal: chararray, title : chararray}}

grunt> illustrate  year_groups;
 group: 1990
  sr_articles :
  {
    (1990,  SIGMOD Record, An SQL-Based Query Language For Networks of  Relations .),
    (1990,  SIGMOD Record, New Hope on Data Models and Types.)
  }
```

PIG represents bags, nested or not, with curly braces {}. Observe the year_groups example provided by the **illustrate** command. Note that the grouping attribute is by convention named group. All the elements with the same year compose a nested bag.

Before detailing PIG, we summarize its main features essentially contrasting it with SQL:

- Bags in PIG allow repeated elements (therefore the term *bag*) unlike relations that are sets of elements.
- Bags in PIG allow nesting as in nested relations, but unlike classical relations.
- As we will see further, in the style of semistructured data, bags also allow further flexibility by not requiring any strict typing (i.e., by allowing heterogeneous collections).
- For processing, PIG is deliberately oriented toward batch transformations (from bags to bags) possibly in multiple steps. In this sense, it may be viewed as closer to a workflow engine than to an SQL processor.

Note that these design choices have clear motivations:

- The structure of a bag is flexible enough to capture the wide range of information typically found in large-scale data processing.
- The orientation toward read/write sequential data access patterns is, of course, motivated by the distributed query evaluation infrastructure targeted by PIG program, and (as we shall see) by the MAPREDUCE processing model.
- Because of the distributed processing, data elements should be processable independently from each other, to make parallel evaluation possible. So language primitives such as references or pointers are not offered. As a consequence, the language is not adapted to problems such as graph problems. (Note that such problems are notoriously difficult to parallelize.)

The rest of this section delves into a more detailed presentation of PIG's design and evaluation.

16.2.2 The Data Model

As shown by our simple session, a PIG *bag* is a bag of PIG tuples (i.e., a collection with possibly repeated elements). A PIG *tuple* consist of a sequence of values distinguished by their positions or a sequence of (attribute name, attribute value) pairs. Each value is either atomic or itself a bag.

To illustrate subtle aspects of nested representations, we briefly move away from the running example. Suppose that we obtain a nested bag (as a result of previous computations) of the form:

$$a : \{ b : chararray, c : \{ c' : chararray \}, d : \{ d' : chararray \} \}$$

Examples of tuples in this bag may be

$$\langle a : \{ \quad \langle b:1, c:\{\langle c':2\rangle, \langle c':3\rangle\}, d:\{\langle d':2\rangle\}\rangle, \quad \langle b:2, c:\emptyset, d:\{\langle d':2\rangle, \langle d':3\rangle\}\rangle \quad \}\rangle$$

Note that to represent the same bag in the relational model, we would need identifiers for tuples in the entire bag, and also for the tuples in the c and d bags. One could then use a relation over $b_{id}b$, one over $b_{id}c_{id}c$ and one over $b_{id}d_{id}d$:

b_{id}	b	b_{id}	c_{id}	c	b_{id}	d_{id}	d
i_1	1	i_1	j_1	2	i_1	j_2	2
i_2	2	i_1	j_3	3	i_2	j_4	2
					i_2	j_5	3

Observe that an association between some b, c, and d is obtained by sharing an id and requires a join to be computed. The input and output of a single PIG operation would correspond to several first-normal-form relations.[3] Joins would be necessary to reconstruct the associations. In very large data sets, join processing is very likely to be a serious bottleneck.

As already mentioned, more flexibility is obtained by allowing heterogeneous tuples to cohabit in a same bag. More precisely, the number of attributes in a bag (and their types) may vary. This gives to the programmer much freedom to organize her data flow by putting together results coming from different sources if necessary.

Returning to the running example, an intermediate structure created by our program (year_groups) represents tuples with an atomic group value (the year) and a nested article value containing the set of articles published that year.

Also, PIG bags introduce lots of flexibility by not imposing a strong typing. For instance, the following is a perfectly valid bag in PIG:

```
{
    (2005, {'SIGMOD Record', 'VLDB J.'},  {' article1 ',  article2 '} )
    (2003, 'SIGMOD Record', {' article1 ',  article2 '}, {'author1', 'author2'})
}
```

This is essentially semistructured data, and can be related to the specificity of applications targeted by PIG. Input data sets often come from a nonstructured source (log files, documents, e-mail repositories) that does not comply to a rigid

---

[3] A relation is in *first-normal-form*, 1NF for short, if each entry in the relation is atomic. Nested relations are also sometimes called not-first-normal-form relations.

Table 16.1. List of PIG Operators

Operator	Description
foreach	Apply one or several expression(s) to each of the input tuples
filter	Filter the input tuples with some criteria
order	Order an input
distinct	Remove duplicates from an input
cogroup	Associate two related groups from distinct inputs
cross	Cross product of two inputs
join	Join of two inputs
union	Union of two inputs (possibly heterogeneous, unlike in SQL)

data model and needs to be organized and processed on the fly. Recall also that the application domain is typically that of data analysis: intermediate results are not meant to be persistent, and they are not going to be used in transactions requiring stable and constrained structures.

PIG has a last data type to facilitate look-ups, namely *maps*. We mention it briefly. A map associates to a key, that is required to be a data atom, an arbitrary data value.

To summarize, every piece of data in PIG is one of the following four types:

■ An *atom* (i.e., a simple atomic value),
■ A *bag* of tuples (possibly heterogeneous and possibly with duplicates),
■ A PIG *tuple* (i.e., a sequence of values),
■ A PIG *map* from keys to values.

It should be clear that the model does not allow the definition of constraints commonly met in relational databases: key (primary key, foreign key), uniqueness, or any constraint that needs to be validated at the collection level. Thus, a collection can be partitioned at will, and each of its items can be manipulated independently from the others.

16.2.3 The Operators

Table 16.1 gives the list of the main PIG operators operating on bags. The common characteristic of the unary operations is that they apply on a flow of tuples that are independently processed one-at-a-time. The semantics of an operation applied to a tuple never depends on the previous or subsequent computations. Similarly, for binary operations: Elementary operations are applied to a pair of tuples, one from each bag, independently from the other tuples in the two bags. This guarantees that the input data sets can be distributed and processed in parallel without affecting the result.

We illustrate some important features with examples applied to the following tiny data file *webdam-books.txt*. Each line contains a publication date, a book title, and the name of an author.

```
-- Load records from the webdam-books.txt file (tab separated)
books = load '../../ data/dblp/webdam-books.txt'
     as (year: int, title : chararray, author: chararray) ;
group_auth = group books by title ;
authors = foreach group_auth generate group, books.author;
dump authors;
```

Figure 16.4. Example of **group** and **foreach**.

```
1995    Foundations of Databases Abiteboul
1995    Foundations of Databases Hull
1995    Foundations of Databases Vianu
2010    Web Data Management Abiteboul
2010    Web Data Management Manolescu
2010    Web Data Management Rigaux
2010    Web Data Management Rousset
2010    Web Data Management Senellart
```

The first example (Figure 16.4) shows a combination of **group** and **foreach** to obtain a bag with one tuple for each book, and a nested list of the authors.

The operator **foreach** applies some expressions to the attributes of each input tuple. PIG provides a number a predefined expressions (projection/flattening of nested sets, arithmetic functions, conditional expressions), and allows User Defined Functions (UDF) as well. In the example, a *projection* expressed as books.authors is applied to the nested set result of the **group** operator. The final authors nested bag is

```
(Foundations of Databases,
    {(Abiteboul),( Hull ),( Vianu)})
(Web Data Management,
    {(Abiteboul),( Manolescu),(Rigaux),(Rousset),( Senellart )})
```

The **flatten** expression serves to unnest a nested attribute.

```
-- Take the 'authors' bag and flatten the nested set
flattened = foreach authors generate group, flatten (author);
```

Applied to the nested bag computed earlier, **flatten** yields a relation in 1NF:

```
(Foundations of Databases,Abiteboul)
(Foundations of Databases,Hull)
(Foundations of Databases,Vianu)
(Web Data Management,Abiteboul)
(Web Data Management,Manolescu)
```

```
--- Load records from the webdam-publishers.txt file
publishers = load '../../ data/dblp/webdam-publishers.txt'
    as ( title : chararray , publisher : chararray ) ;
cogrouped = cogroup flattened by group, publishers by title ;
```

Figure 16.5. Illustration of the **cogroup** operator.

```
(Web Data Management,Rigaux)
(Web Data Management,Rousset)
(Web Data Management,Senellart)
```

The **cogroup** operator collects related information from different sources and gathers them as separate nested sets. Suppose for instance that we also have the following file *webdam-publishers.txt*:

```
Fundations of Databases Addison-Wesley  USA
Fundations of Databases Vuibert France
Web Data Management    Cambridge University Press   USA
```

We can run a PIG program that associates the set of authors and the set of publishers for each book (Figure 16.5).

The result (limited to *Foundations of databases*) is the following.

```
(Foundations of Databases,
   { (Foundations of Databases,Abiteboul),
     (Foundations of Databases,Hull),
     (Foundations of Databases,Vianu)
   },
   {(Foundations of Databases,Addison-Wesley),
    (Foundations of Databases,Vuibert)
   }
)
```

The result of a **cogroup** evaluation contains one tuple for each group with three attributes. The first one (named group) is the identifier of the group, the second and third attributes being nested bags with, respectively, tuples associated to the identifier in the first input bag, and tuples associated to the identifier in the second one. Cogrouping is close to joining the two (or more) inputs on their common identifier, which can be expressed as follows:

```
-- Take the 'flattened' bag, join with 'publishers'
joined = join flattened by group, publishers by title ;
```

The structure of the result is however different than the one obtained with **cogroup**.

> (Foundations of Databases,Abiteboul,Fundations of Databases,Addison-Wesley)
> (Foundations of Databases,Abiteboul,Fundations of Databases,Vuibert)
> (Foundations of Databases,Hull,Fundations of Databases,Addison-Wesley)
> (Foundations of Databases,Hull,Fundations of Databases,Vuibert)
> (Foundations of Databases,Vianu,Fundations of Databases,Addison-Wesley)
> (Foundations of Databases,Vianu,Fundations of Databases,Vuibert)

In this example, it makes sense to apply **cogroup** because the (nested) set of authors and the (nested) set of publishers are independent, and it may be worth considering them as separate bags. The **join** applies a cross product of these sets right away, which may lead to more complicated data processing later.

The difference between **cogroup** and **join** is an illustration of the expressiveness brought by the nested data model. The relational join operator must deliver flat tuples, and intermediate states of the result cannot be kept as first-class citizen of the data model, although this could sometimes be useful from a data processing point of view. As another illustration, consider the standard SQL **group by** operator in relational databases. It operates in two, nonbreakable steps that correspond to a PIG **group**, yielding a nested set, followed by a **foreach**, applying an aggregation function. The following example is a PIG program that computes a 1NF relation with the number of authors for each book.

```
-- Load records from the webdam-books.txt file (tab separated)
books = load 'webdam-books.txt'
     as (year: int, title : chararray, author: chararray) ;
group_auth = group books by title ;
authors = foreach group_auth generate group, COUNT(books.author);
dump authors;
```

The possible downside of this modeling flexibility is that the size of a tuple is unbounded: It can contain arbitrarily large nested bags. This may limit the parallel execution (the extreme situation is a bag with only one tuple and very large nested bags) and force some operators to flush their input or output tuple to the disk if the main memory is exhausted.

16.2.4 Using MAPREDUCE to Optimize PIG Programs

The starting point of this optimization is that a combination of **group** and **foreach** operators of PIG can be almost directly translated into a program using MAPRE-DUCE. In that sense, a MAPREDUCE job may be viewed as a group-by operator over large-scale data with build-in parallelism, fault tolerance and load-balancing features. The MAP phase produces grouping keys for each tuple. The shuffle phase of MAPREDUCE puts these keys together in intermediate pairs (akin to the nested

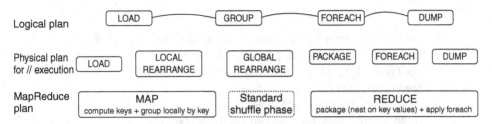

Figure 16.6. Compilation of a PIG program in MAPREDUCE.

bags, result of the PIG **group**). Finally, the REDUCE phase provides an aggregation mechanism to cluster intermediate pairs. This observation is at the core of using a MAPREDUCE environment as a support for the execution of PIG programs.

Basically, each **(co)group** operator in the PIG data flow yields a MAPREDUCE tasks that incorporates the evaluation of PIG operators surrounding the **(co)group**. As previously explained, a *join*, can be obtained using a **cogroup** followed by a flattening of the inner nested bags. So, joins can also benefit from the MAPREDUCE environment.

To conclude, we illustrate such a MAPREDUCE evaluation with two of the examples previously discussed.

Example: group and foreach In a first example, we use the program given in Figure 16.4. Following the classical query evaluation mechanism, the compilation transforms this program through several abstraction levels. Three levels are here represented. The "logical" level directly represents the data flow process. At this point, some limited reorganization may take place. For instance, a **filter** operator should be "pushed" as near as possible to the **load** to decrease the amount of data that needs to be processed.

The second level represents the sequence of physical operations that need to be executed in a parallel query processing environment. PIG targets several parallel execution models, and this intermediate level provides the means to describe and manipulate a physical plan independently from a specific infrastructure.

The blocks in the physical plan introduce some new operators, namely REAR-RANGE (LOCAL and GLOBAL), and PACKAGE. REARRANGE denotes a physical operator that groups tuples with the same key, via either hashing or sorting. The distinction between LOCAL and GLOBAL stems from the parallelization context. The LOCAL operator takes place on a single node, whereas the GLOBAL operator needs to collect and arrange tuples initially affected to many nodes. The algorithms that implement these variants may therefore be quite different.

PACKAGE relates to the PIG data model. Once a set of tuples sharing the same key are put together by a REARRANGE, a nested bag can be created and associated with the key value to form the typical nested structure produced by the **(co)group** operation. Expressions in the **foreach** operator can then be applied.

The lower level in Figure 16.4 shows the MAPREDUCE execution of this physical plan. There is only one MAPREDUCE job, and the physical execution proceeds as follows:

```
-- Load records from the webdam-books.txt file (tab separated)
books = load '../../ data/dblp/webdam-books.txt'
     as (year: int, title : chararray, author: chararray) ;
-- Keep only books from Victor Vianu
vianu = filter books by author == 'Vianu';
--- Load records from the webdam-publishers.txt file
publishers = load '../../ data/dblp/webdam-publishers.txt'
     as ( title : chararray, publisher: chararray) ;
-- Join on the book title
joined = join vianu by title , publishers by title ;
-- Now, group on the author name
grouped = group joined by vianu :: author;
-- Finally count the publishers (nb: we should remove duplicates !)
count = foreach grouped generate group, COUNT(joined.publisher);
```

Figure 16.7. A complex PIG program with **join** and **group**.

1. MAP generates the key of the input tuples (in general, this operation may involve the application of one or several functions) and groups the tuples associated to given key in intermediate pairs.
2. The GLOBAL REARRANGE operator is natively supported by the MAPRE-DUCE framework: Recall that intermediate pairs that hash to a same value are assigned to a single Reducer that performs a merge to "arrange" the tuples with a common key together.
3. The PACKAGE physical operator is implemented as part of the *reduce()* function that takes care of applying any expression required by the **foreach** loop.

Example: join and group Our second example involves a **join** followed by a **group**. It returns the number of publishers of Victor Vianu. Note that one might want to remove duplicates from the answer; this is left as an exercise.

Figure 16.8 shows the execution of this program using two MAPREDUCE jobs. The first one carries out the join. Both inputs (books and publishers) are loaded, filtered, sorted on the title, tagged with their provenance, and stored in intermediate pairs (MAP phase). Specifically, the *map()* function receives rows:

1. Either from the books input with year, title, and author
2. Or from the publishers input with title and publisher, again recording provenance.

Each row records its provenance, either books or publishers.

These intermediate pairs are sorted during the shuffle phase and submitted to the *reduce()* function. For each key (title), this function must take the set of authors (known by their provenance), the set of publishers (idem), and compute their cross

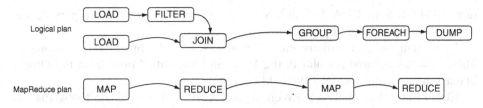

Figure 16.8. A multijobs MAPREDUCE execution.

product that constitutes a part of the join result. This output can then be transmitted to the next MAPREDUCE job in charge of executing the **group**.

Clearly, this complex query would require an important amount of work with MAPREDUCE programming, whereas it is here fulfilled by a few PIG instructions. The advantage is more related to the software engineering process than to the efficiency of the result. Due to the rather straighforward strategy applied by the PIG evaluator, early performance reports show that PIG execution is, not surprisingly, slightly worse than the equivalent MAPREDUCE direct implementation. This is notably due to the overhead introduced by the translation mechanism. The next section mentions alternative approaches that pursue similar goal that PIG.

16.3 FURTHER READING

Distributed computing now has a long history, with Web services as a recent popular outcome. We refer the reader to the general references [153] for distributed systems and [31] for parallel algorithms. At the center of distributed computing we find the possibility of activating some computation on a distant machine. This leads to *remote procedure call*, an abstraction that allows interacting with a remote program while ignoring its details. Some data are sent as argument of the call. The remote program is activated with this data as input. Its result is shipped back to the caller. Note that this involves transmission of data in both directions, from the caller to the callee (parameters of the call) and back (results).

To support such communications, one needs to provide endpoints for these communications (e.g. sockets). A communication happens between a local socket and a remote one. To understand each other, they need to use some common protocol for the messages (e.g., TCP, UDP, raw IP, or, in the Web Services realm, SOAP).

Based on such communications, middleware systems have been developed since the 1960s, the so-called *message-oriented* middleware. They are based on asynchronous calls (i.e., the call is made and the caller is not blocked waiting for an answers). The messages are managed in queues. Examples of such systems are IBM Websphere and Microsoft MQ series.

The object-oriented paradigm proved to be very successful for distributed computing. Indeed, it is very natural to see an external resource as an object (i.e., a black box with a set of methods as interface). This lead to very popular systems, *object brokers*.

From a data management perspective, one may want to support transactions between the distributed machines. This leads to *transaction processing monitors* (e.g., IBM CICS, or BEA Tuxedo). Such systems provide support for persistence, distributed transactions, logging, and error recovery.

By merging, object brokers and TP monitors, one obtains the *object monitors*. These systems became popular in the 1990s, notably with Corba from the Object Management Group and DCOM by Microsoft.

Closer to us and targeting the Web, we find XML-RPC (in the late 1990s) that, as indicated by its name, is based on remote procedure calls using XML as underlying data format. The calls are performed using HTTP-POST.

Finally, we briefly discuss Corba that had a very important influence in the evolution of distributed computing. Corba stands for *Common Object Request Broker Architecture*. As previously mentioned, it is based on RPC and the object-oriented paradigm. The development of Corba-based components is somewhat independent of the programming language (e.g., C++ or Java may be used). An implementation of Corba consists of the deployment of a system (called an ORB) that provides the interoperability between applications distributed on different machines. The ORB provides a large set of services (e.g., persistence, transaction, messaging, naming, security). Corba and DCOM were the main supports for distribution before Web services.

There is a long history of research on so-called nested relations (e.g., [4]), or complex objects (e.g., [3]), that somehow paved the way for semistructured data models. An algebra for bags vs. sets of tuples is considered in [79].

Parallel query processing is an old research topic. Issues related to scalable query execution in shared-nothing architecture have been investigated since the emergence of relational systems. See [55, 69] for important milestones and [56] for a position paper. The proposed techniques are now available in several commercial systems, including Teradata (http://www.teradata.com), a leading datawarehouse software company. The systems based on Google technology, and in particular MAPREDUCE have been criticized for ignoring previous advances in database technology [54]. A detailed discussion of the MAPREDUCE limits and contributions, viewed in a database perspective, is reported in [151]. MAPREDUCE is suitable for text processing and more generally for data sets where relational schema does not fit. It is also a convenient tool for cost-effective environments (e.g., commodity hardware) that allow an inexpensive horizontal scalability but lead to unreliable infrastructures where the resilience brought by MAPREDUCE is a valuable asset.

In practical terms, a major restriction of MAPREDUCE is the high latency that stems from both the initial dissemination of a program in the cluster prior to any execution and the need to fully achieve the MAP phase before running the REDUCE one. This is justified for batch analysis of large data sets but make it unsuitable for transactional applications [133]. Its attractiveness on the other hand lies in its scalability and fault-tolerance, two features where parallel databases arguably show their limits, at least for Web-scale data sets.

Recently, research attempts to benefit from the best of the two worlds have been undertaken. HADOOPDB [10] is a "hybrid" distributed data management system that uses a standard relational DBMS (e.g., PostgreSQL) at each node, and uses MAPREDUCE as a communication layer between nodes. The relational system instance acts as a source to MAPREDUCE jobs, with the advantage of being able to run complex SQL query plans that exploit database index, saving the otherwise mandatory full scan of the data sets. Other approaches aims at providing high-level data processing languages which can then be executed in a MAPREDUCE-like environment: SCOPE [40], PIG [70, 129], JAQL http://code.google.com/p/jaql/, and Hive [155] are examples of some recent or ongoing efforts.

16.4 EXERCISES

Exercise 16.4.1 (log processing with MAPREDUCE) *A big company stores all incoming e-mails in log files. How can you count the frequency of each e-mail address found in these logs with MAPREDUCE?*

Exercise 16.4.2 (optimizing the MAP and REDUCE phases) *The* REDUCE *phase needs to download intermediate pairs produced by the mappers. How can we reduce the cost of this exchange? The following gives some hints:*

1. *Consider again the WordCount example; Propose a post-processing step, running on the mapper, that reduces the size of the files sent to the reducers.*
2. *Now, consider a* MAPREDUCE *task aiming at retrieving the inverse document frequency; does the foregoing optimization still help?*
3. *Finally, one could sort the intermediate pairs before sending them to the reducer; discuss the pros and cons of this approach.*

Exercise 16.4.3 (SP relational queries) *A Selection-Projection-Aggregation relational query corresponds to the simple SQL syntax:*

```
SELECT <list-attributes>
FROM <someTable>
WHERE <list-conditions>
GROUP BY <attribute>
```

Propose a MAPREDUCE *job (using pseudo-code for map() and reduce()) for the following queries:*

1.
```
SELECT title, year
FROM paper
WHERE author='Jeff Ullman'
AND published='ACM'
```

2.
```
SELECT title, count(author)
FROM paper
WHERE year=2011
GROUP BY title
```

When is the reduce function really useful? How would you express these queries with PIG.

Exercise 16.4.4 (sorting with MAPREDUCE) *How can you obtain a parallel sort with* MAPREDUCE? *For instance, what would be the* MAPREDUCE *parallel execution of the following SQL query:*

SELECT *title*
FROM *paper*
ORDER BY year

Hint: *Partition the input in R intervals with map(), then sort each local interval with reduce().*

Exercise 16.4.5 (joins with MAPREDUCE) *And, finally, how can you express joins? For instance:*

SELECT *title, journalName*
FROM *paper p, journal j*
WHERE *p.idJournal = j. id*

Hint: *This requires to somewhat distord the* MAPREDUCE *principles. The reduce() function should receive pairs $(id, < p_1, \ldots, p_n >)$ where id is a journal id and each p_i is a row from paper. By unnesting the structure, one gets the expected result. Note that the reduce phase does not reduce at all the output in that case! Such a tweak may not be accepted by all* MAPREDUCE *environments.*

Exercise 16.4.6 (distributed Monte Carlo) *We want to create a distributed program that approximates π. The method is based on the inscription of a circle in a square (Figure 16.9).*

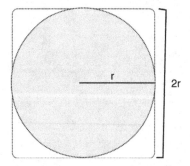

Figure 16.9. A method to computing π.

Note that the area of the square is $A_s = (2r)^2 = 4r^2$; the area of the circle is $A_c = \pi \times r^2$. Therefore,

$$\pi = 4 \times \frac{A_c}{A_s}$$

1. Propose a parallel program that computes an approximation of π; how can you express such a program in MAPREDUCE?
2. The previous computation of π is actually a simple instance of the classical Monte Carlo method. Assume now a very large data set of geographic regions. Each region is identified by a key, we know its contour and can test whether a point belongs to a region thanks to a point-in-polygon (PinP()) function. We can also obtain the minimal bounding box of aa region thanks to the mbb() function. We want to calculate their areas. Propose a distributed implementation based on MAPREDUCE.

Exercise 16.4.7 (distributed inverted file construction) Describe a MAPREDUCE job that constructs an inverted file for a very large data set of Web documents. Give the map() and reduce() functions in pseudo-code, and explain the data flow in a distributed system.

Exercise 16.4.8 (distributed PageRank) Describe a MAPREDUCE job that computes one iteration of the PageRank algorithm over a collection of documents. Some hints:

1. The map() function takes as input the doc id, the list of URLs that refer to the document, and the current rank;
2. The reduce() takes as input a URL and a list of ranks; you can assume that the damping factor is a constant in this function.

Exercise 16.4.9 (PIG) Refer to the Putting into Practice chapter on HADOOP for a list of PIG queries.

17

Putting into Practice: Full-Text Indexing with LUCENE (by Nicolas Travers)

LUCENE[1] is an open-source tunable indexing platform often used for full-text indexing of Web sites. It implements an inverted index, creating posting lists for each term of the vocabulary. This chapter proposes some exercises to discover the LUCENE platform and test its functionalities through its Java API.

17.1 PRELIMINARY: A LUCENE SANDBOX

We provide a simple graphical interface that lets you capture a collection of Web documents (from a given Web site), index it, and search for documents matching a keyword query. The tool is implemented with LUCENE (surprise!) and helps to assess the impact of the search parameters, including ranking factors.

You can download the program from our Web site. It consists of a Java archive that can be executed right away (provided you have a decent Java installation on your computer). Figure 17.1 shows a screenshot of the main page. It allows you to

1. Download a set of documents collected from a given URL (including local addresses),
2. Index and query those documents,
3. Consult the information used by LUCENE to present ranked results.

Use this tool as a preliminary contact with full text search and information retrieval. The projects proposed at the end of the chapter give some suggestions to realize a similar application.

17.2 INDEXING PLAIN TEXT WITH LUCENE – A FULL EXAMPLE

We embark now in a practical experimentation with LUCENE. First, download the Java packages from the Web site http://lucene.apache.org/java/docs/. The examples and exercises that follow have been tested with version 3.0.2, so check whether something changed if you use another version.

---

[1] http://lucene.apache.org/java/docs/.

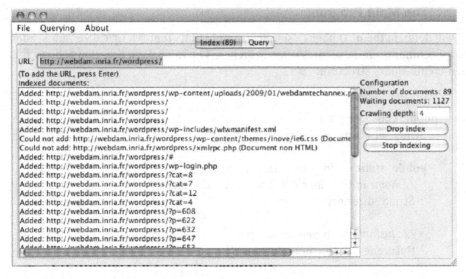

Figure 17.1. The LUCENE sandbox of WDM.

You will find several packages.

- *lucene-core-3.0.2.jar*. The main package; put it right away in your CLASSPATH or in your project environment if you use an IDE.
- *lucene-demos-3.0.2.jar*. A set of demonstration programs.
- *luceneWeb.war*. A simple LUCENE Web application installer based on a demonstrator.
- *contrib*. A set of packages that complement the core functions.
  - *analyzers*. Main languages analyzers (*lucene-analyzers-3.0.2.jar*); mandatory with most LUCENE indexing and querying applications.
  - *collation*. Change LUCENE analyzer to optimize ranking and range queries.
  - *db*. The berkeleyDB database management system.
  - *instantiated*. RAM-based LUCENE indexing.
  - *queryparser*. Tuning of the query parser.
  - *snowball*. Stemming package that extract stems over terms within a given language.
  - *spellchecker*. Word spell checking; suggests replacement by the nearest valid word.
  - *spatial*. Sort LUCENE results with distance based scoring.
  - *wordnet*. The Wordnet API is integrated to LUCENE in order to check words and synonyms in the dictionnary.

The packages *lucene-core-3.0.2.jar* (for indexing and querying) and *lucene-analyzers-3.0.2.jar* (for text analyzer features) are required for the examples and exercises below. We will use them in the following to create our LUCENE application.

17.2.1 The Main Program

We will detail in the next pages a simple example that creates a LUCENE index, adds a few documents, and executes some searches. The main Java program follows this open-create-query structure:

```java
public class Simple {
  String directory = "index";

  public static void main(String[] args) {
    // Name of the directory that holds the index
    String directory = "index";

    // Instantiate a new Lucene tool
    MyLucene lucene = new MyLucene();

    // Open the directory
    lucene.openIndex(directory, true);

    // Add a few documents
    lucene.addDoc("Web Data Management");
    lucene.addDoc("Data on the Web");
    lucene.addDoc("Spatial Databases -- with Application to GIS");

    // Close the index
    lucene.closeIndex ();

    // Now, search for some term
    String query[] = {"Web"};
    lucene.search(query);
  }
}
```

Everything is handled by the *MyLucene* class, which is now detailed (the full code can be found on the book's Web site). Note that the program is for illustration purposes, and thus makes a poor job at catching exceptions.

17.2.2 Create the Index

The *openIndex* method creates an index, or opens an existing index.

```java
public void openIndex(String directory, boolean newIndex) {
  try {
    // Link the directory on the FileSystem to the application
    index = FSDirectory.open(new File(directory));
```

```
    // Check whether the index has already been locked
    // (or not properly closed).
    if (IndexWriter.isLocked(index))
      IndexWriter.unlock(index);
    if (writer == null)
      // Link the repository to the IndexWriter
      writer = new IndexWriter(index, analyzer, newIndex,
          IndexWriter.MaxFieldLength.LIMITED);
  } catch (Exception e) {
    System.out.println ("Got an Exception: " + e.getMessage());
  }
}
```

The LUCENE index repository must be opened prior to any access. When the *newIndex* Boolean value is true, LUCENE creates the repository name directory. When *newIndex* is false, the previously created index is reused. Only one IndexWriter at a time can be access the repository. Be careful, each time newIndex is set to *true*, the index will be entirely replaced.

The *StandardAnalyzer* object is the document analyzer process (instantiated in the constructor). It takes into account the specifics of the input language. For consistency reasons, the same analyzer must be used for the creation and for searches.

Once an index is generated, you can look at the repository generated by LUCENE, which contains several files:

- *segments_X / segments.gen*. The segment index files.
- *write.lock*. Lock file, modified each time an IndexWriter instance works on the repository.
- *_X.cfs*. Compound files. Describe all indexed files.
- *_X.cfx*. Compound files for storing field values and term vectors.

The index must be closed when inserts and updates are finished.

```
public void closeIndex() {
    try {
      writer.optimize();
      writer.close ();
    } catch (Exception e) {
      System.out.println ("Got an Exception: " + e.getMessage());
    }
}
```

Each call to *optimize()* applies a compression and store the modified values in the repository.

17.2.3 Adding Documents

Once the index is created, we can populate it with documents. LUCENE defines an abstraction of documents as instances of the *Document* class. Such an instance contains several *Field*s that define which information will be stored, indexed and queried. The following example defines a single field, named content. You will be invited to create multifield documents in the labs.

```
public void addDoc(String value) {
    try {
        // Instantiate a new document
        Document doc = new Document();
        // Put the value in a field name content
        Field f = new Field("content", value, Field.Store.YES,
            Field.Index.ANALYZED);
        // Add the field to the document
        doc.add(f);
        // And add the document to the index
        writer.addDocument(doc);
    } catch (Exception e) {
        System.out.println("Got an Exception: " + e.getMessage());
    }
}
```

Modeling a document as a list of fields is tantamount to defining how the information is analyzed, indexed, and stored.

17.2.4 Searching the Index

We can instantiate the *IndexSearcher* class, giving as a parameter the index repository name. We also provide to the constructor an *Analyzer* object, which must be of the same type as the one used during the indexing process. The *QueryParser* instance applies the analyzer to the the query string, ensuring that the tokenization and other transformations applied to terms is consistent. We must also specify which fields will be queried by default for each query.

```
public void search(String[] args) {
    // Nothing given? Search for "Web".
    String querystr = args.length > 0 ? args[0] : "Web";
```

```
try {
    // Instantiate a query parser
    QueryParser parser = new QueryParser(Version.LUCENE_30, "content",
        analyzer );
    // Parse
    Query q = parser.parse(querystr);
    // We look for top-10 results
    int hitsPerPage = 10;
    // Instantiate a searcher
    IndexSearcher searcher = new IndexSearcher(index, true);
    // Ranker
    TopScoreDocCollector collector = TopScoreDocCollector.create(
        hitsPerPage, true);
    // Search!
    searcher.search(q, collector);
    // Retrieve the top-10 documents
    ScoreDoc[] hits = collector.topDocs().scoreDocs;

    // Display results
    System.out.println("Found " + hits.length + " hits.");
    for (int i = 0; i < hits.length; ++i) {
        int docId = hits[i].doc;
        Document d = searcher.doc(docId);
        System.out.println((i + 1) + ". " + d.get("content"));
    }

    // Close the searcher
    searcher.close();
} catch (Exception e) {
    System.out.println("Got an Exception: " + e.getMessage());
}
}
```

17.2.5 LUCENE Querying Syntax

The LUCENE querying syntax is almost simple. A query is composed of a set of words, each of which check in the index the posting lists and provide a *tf/idf* value. The global rank of the query is the sum of these values, as we saw previously. Here is a sketch of query:

```
Web Data Management
```

This query is composed of three words that will be searched into the index. The score of each document depends of the sum of scores for "Web," "Data," and "Management."

In order to complexify queries, LUCENE provides some more features that helps to creates richer queries. All these features follow a specific syntax. For each feature, we will illustrate it by modifying the previous query:

- **Negation:** *NOT xxx*
  The given word must not be present into the document. All documents containing this word will be removed from the result set (i.e., the score is equal to zero).

  ```
  Web Data NOT Management
  ```

  The document will contain "Web" and "Data" but never "Management."
- **Mandatory keywords:** *+xxx*
  The given word must be present in the document. In fact, although a word is asked in the query and its score in a document is equal to zero, this document could appear (other words bring a good score). This feature forbids documents that do not mention this word.

  ```
  +Web Data Management
  ```

  The word "*Web*" must be contained in the document; "*Data*" and "*Management*" may be present.
- **Exact matching:** *"xxx yyy"*
  Bringing a sentence into quotes makes an exact matching query, for which the document must contains this sentence:

  ```
  "Web Data" Management
  ```

  The document must contain the sentence "Web Data"; the word "Management" brings an additional score to the document.
- **Word importance:** *xxx^X*
  A word may be more important than others in a query; for this you can increase the scoring weight of this word in the document. This weight is applied on the score before making the sum of all scores.

  ```
  Web^3 Data Management
  ```

  The resulting score of the word "Web" in the documents is three times bigger than "Data" and "Management".
- **Wildcard search:** *xx**
  LUCENE will search for words that match with given letters, completing the wildcard with existing words in the index. A word must not begin with a wildcard.

  ```
  Web Data Manag*
  ```

  All documents that contain a words beginning with "Manag" will be returned (like *Management, Manage, Managing, Manager...*)
- **Querying fields:** *FFF:xxx*
  As we saw during indexing, we can specify fields (title, content, path). By default,

we specified that the "content" field is used for queries. By specifying a field, LUCENE searches the given word into it.

```
title:Web Data Management
```

The word "Web" will be searched into the *field* "title", while "Data" and "Management" will be searched into the default field.

■ **Similarity search:** *xxx~*
A similarity search corrects misspelling of a given word, LUCENE will search this words with different spelling. The tilda can optionally be followed by a numeric value, this value gives the distance of similarity between the given word and the proposed one.

```
Web Data ~ Management
```

Documents will contain "Web" and "Management", but also words similar to "data" (like *date, tata, sata*).

■ **Range queries:** *xxx TO yyy*
A query can ask for a range of values for corresponding documents. This range can be numeric values, dates, or words (with lexicographic orders).

```
title:"Web Data Management" title:{1 TO 3}
```

All documents must have the exact sentence "Web Data Management" and also a numeric (book's version) value between 1 and 3.

17.3 PUT IT INTO PRACTICE!

You should first make our simple example run and examine carefully all the methods. Note that the following improvements would be useful:

1. Handle more carefully the exceptions raised by LUCENE classes;
2. Implement an iterator-like mechanism that allows to retrieve the documents in the result one by one, instead of printing the result right away in the *search* method;
3. Add some optional, yet useful features, such as for instance a management of a list of stop words (this is a first opportunity to look at the LUCENE API).

Once these changes are effective, you should then be ready to implement your first search engine.

17.3.1 Indexing a Directory Content

A sample of several files with two "fields," respectively "title" and "content," can be found on the Web site (*lucene* directory). Download them in a *files* directory. Next, create a parsing function that takes as input a file path, open this file, and extracts title, content according to the following pattern:

```
title:XXXX
content:YYYY
```

Create a directory extractor to get all the files from the *files* directory and index them with Lucene (do not forget to call the *closeIndex()* function).

Your index is created. Now, implement a function that considers a list of words given on the standard input stream for querying the index. Here are some possible searches:

- *Information Research*
- *Research NOT Lucene*
- *+Research Information*
- *"Information Research"*
- *Research^3 Information*
- *Research Info**
- *title:Research*
- *Research Information~*
- *title:{Research TO Information}*

17.3.2 Web Site Indexing (Project)

To index the content of a whole Web site, create a class that "crawls" the document belonging to a given domain (e.g., http://Webdam.inria.fr/). Index the documents content, extract titles from the appropriate HTML tags (<title> or h1 — *Hint*: Use *java.util.regex.Matcher*.). Once a document is loaded, find the embedded links in order to recursively process the whole Web site (*Hint*: Look for href attributes).

Be careful to not index a document twice, and do *not* process external links (not belonging to the given domain) nor images or generally non-html documents.

17.4 Lucene – TUNING THE SCORING (PROJECT)

As previously discussed, Lucene computes a score values for each document with respect to the query terms. This score is based on the tf–idf measures. Here is the detailed scoring function used in Lucene:

$$score(q,d) = \sum tf(t_d) \times idf(t) \times boost(t.field_d)$$
$$\times lengthNorm(t.field_d) \times coord(q,d) \times qNorm(q)$$

where q is the query, d a document, t a term, and

1. *tf*: A function of the term frequency within the document (default: $\sqrt{freq}$);
2. *idf*: Inverse document frequency of t within the whole collection (default: $\log(\frac{numDocs}{docFreq+1}) + 1$);
3. *boost*: The boosting factor, if required in the query with the "^" operator on a given field (if not specified, set to the default field);
4. *lengthNorm*: Field normalization according to the number of terms (default: $\frac{1}{\sqrt{nbTerms}}$);
5. *coord*: Overlapping rate of terms of the query in the given document (default: $\frac{overlap}{maxOverlap}$);

6. *qNorm*: Query normalization according to its length; it corresponds to the sum of square values of terms' weight, the global value is multiplied by each term's weight.

Only underlined functions can be modified in LUCENE: *tf*, *idf*, *lengthNom* and *coord*. Default functions are given and can be modified by creating a new *Similarity* class with overloaded methods. specifically,

1. Create a new class that inherits the *org.apache.lucene.search.DefaultSimilarity* class;
2. Overload and implement default similarity functions:
   - **public float** tf(**float** freq),
   - **public float** idf(**int** docFreq, **int** numDocs),
   - **public float** lengthNorm(String fieldName, int numTerms),
   - **public float** coord(**int** overlap, **int** maxOverlap);
3. Add some parameters to allow changing the similarity functions as follows:
   - *tf*: $\sqrt{freq}, 1, freq, \sqrt{(1-freq)}$,
   - *idf*: $\log(\frac{numDocs}{docFreq+1})+1, 1, \frac{numDocs}{docFreq+1}, \log(1-\frac{numDocs}{docFreq+1})+1$,
   - *lengthNorm*: $\frac{1}{\sqrt{numTerms}}, 1, 1-\frac{1}{\sqrt{numTerms}}$,
   - *coord*: $\frac{overlap}{maxOverlap}, 1, 1-\frac{overlap}{maxOverlap}$;
4. Change the similarity function in the querying class previously created with *searcher.setSimilarity(similarity);*
5. Compute previous queries with different combinations of similarity functions.

18

Putting into Practice: Recommendation Methodologies (by Alban Galland)

This chapter proposes an introduction to recommendation techniques and suggests some exercises and projects. We do not present a recommendation system in particular but rather focus on the general methodology. As an illustrative example, we will use the MovieLens data set to construct movie recommendations.

The chapter successively introduces recommendation, user-based collaborative filtering and item-based collaborative filtering. It discusses different methods parameterizations and evaluates their result with respect to the quality of the data set. We show how to generate recommendations using SQL queries on the Movie-Lens data set. Finally, we suggest some projects for students who want to investigate further the realm of recommendation systems.

18.1 INTRODUCTION TO RECOMMENDATION SYSTEMS

Given a set of ratings of items by a set of users, a recommendation system produces a list of items for a particular user, possibly in a given context. Such systems are widely used in Web applications. For example, content sites like Yahoo! Movies (movies), Zagat (restaurants), LibraryThing (books), Pandora (music), StumbleUpon (Web site) suggest a list of items of interest by predicting the ratings of their users. E-commerce sites such as Amazon (books) or Netflix (movies) use recommendations to suggest new products to their users and construct bundle sales. Usually, they exploit the recent browsing history as a limited context. Finally, advertisement companies need to find a list of advertisements targeted for their users. Some of them, like Google AdSense, rely more on the context (e.g., keywords) than on an estimation of the user's taste based on her/his recent browsing history. Nevertheless, techniques close to recommendation methodologies are successfully used, for example, by DoubleClick or Facebook ads.

One usually distinguishes two kinds of tasks on data: information retrieval and information filtering. *Information retrieval* is the problem of answering dynamic queries on static content. Typical examples are answering keyword queries on the Web or SQL queries on a database. The general method relies on data modeling, providing structure and semantics to the data, that is then organized using indexes.

Information filtering is the problem of answering static queries on dynamic content. A typical example is the monitoring of Web server logs. The general method is to model the queries, which are then organized as filters. Under this general perspective, recommendation stands between information retrieval and information filtering: data (the set of ratings) varies slowly at the scale of a user but quickly at the scale of the system; queries (a user and possibly some context) depend on a few parameters, each having a wide domain.

Specifically, a recommendation system may either produce top-k ranking (list of "best" items) or prediction of ratings. The focus of the result may be generic (everyone receives the same recommendations), demographic (everyone in the same category receives the same recommendations), or personal. In the present chapter, we are mostly interested in personal recommendation. The context may rely on the user's current activity or on her/his long-term interests.

The information that serves as a basis to recommendation systems consists of the following components:

1. The users' description (e.g., sex, age, localization, profession of the user);
2. The items' description (e.g., genre, author, date, price of the item);
3. And the ratings matrix, giving the rating of each item by each user.

The ratings matrix is incomplete, being fed only either by acquiring data from the user (e.g., an item is bought, or a level of interest is explicitly collected) or by monitoring her/his activity (an item is visited, which gives some hint on the user's interests). Recommendation is indeed the process of filling empty cells of the matrix with *predicted ratings* derived from the other sources of information, including known ratings.

18.2 PREREQUISITES

This chapter uses SQL; we assume the reader is familiar with the language. You will need access to a relational database, for example by installing MYSQL on your computer: see http://www.mysql.com. Here is a very brief introduction to MYSQL commands (refer to the Web for information on any other SQL database systems). Assuming that you have an account on the MYSQL server, the connection is established with

```
mysql -h [servername] -P [port] -u [login] -p
```

The utility asks for your passwords and gives you access to the command-line interpreter. You may directly type SQL commands, or execute command(s) stored in a file myCom.sql:

```
mysql> source myCom.sql;
```

We will play with the MovieLens (http://www.movielens.org) data set to generate recommendations of movies. The data set must first be imported in your database. Create the following tables and indexes (the SQL scripts can be found on the book's site):

```
# Tables creation
create table ratingsdata (
    userid int,
    itemid int,
    rating int,
    timestamp int,
    primary key (userid, itemid));

create table items (
    itemid int primary key,
    title text,
    date text,
    videodate text,
    imdb text,
    unknown boolean,
    action boolean,
    adventure boolean,
    animation boolean,
    childrens boolean,
    comedy boolean,
    crime boolean,
    documentary boolean,
    drama boolean,
    fantasy boolean,
    noir boolean,
    horror boolean,
    musical boolean,
    mystery boolean,
    romance boolean,
    scifi boolean,
    thriller boolean,
    war boolean,
    western boolean);

create table users (
    userid int primary key,
    age int,
    gender char,
    occupation text,
    zip int );

# Indexes creation
create index usersdata_index on ratingsdata (userid);
create index itemsdata_index on ratingsdata (itemid);
```

You can get the MovieLens 100K Ratings Dataset from http://www.grouplens. org/node/73. The files are respectively named u.data, u.item, and u.user. They are loaded in the database as follows:

```
load data infile '[path to u.data]' into table ratingsdata;
load data infile '[path to u.item]' into table items fields
    terminated by '|';
load data infile '[path to u.user]' into table users fields
    terminated by '|';
```

The ratingsdata table now contains the list of ratings. Most of the computation presented further rely on its content. Table items and users contain respectively the list of movies and the list of users.

18.3 DATA ANALYSIS

The quality of a given recommendation method highly depends on the quality of the input. It can be characterized by the *support* (number of users and items, and distribution of the number of ratings by users and by items) and by the *rating quality* (distribution of the ratings by user and by movies). Let us first consider the support, which can be determined by the following SQL commands:

▪ Number of users, movies, and ratings:

```
select count(distinct userid) as nbusers,
    count(distinct itemid) as nbitems, count(*) as nbratings
from ratingsdata;
```

▪ Distribution of the number of ratings by user (histogram rounded to a precision of 10 ratings):

```
select count(userid) as nbusers, nbratings
from (select round(count(itemid)/10,0)*10 as nbratings, userid
        from ratingsdata
        group by userid
        ) as nbratingsbyusers
group by nbratings
order by nbratings desc;
```

■ Distribution of the number of ratings by movies (histogram rounded to 10 ratings):

```
select count(itemid) as nbitems, nbratings
from (select round(count(userid)/10,0)*10 as nbratings, itemid
      from ratingsdata
      group by itemid
      ) as nbratingsbyitems
group by nbratings
order by nbratings desc;
```

1. Run the queries and examine the result. Note first that there is no user with fewer than 20 ratings, since such users have already been filtered out by MoviesLens. However, one can find some movies with very few ratings. Recommending an item with a small support yields unreliable results. The problem is known as "cold-start" in the area of recommendation system and is difficult to solve: We will not elaborate further on this aspect.
2. Can you determine the law followed by these distributions? This law is frequently observed in practice and means that a few users are very productive and a few items are very famous, while the huge majority of items are hardly rated by any user. A good recommendation method should avoid giving more importance to items or users based on their number of ratings, since quantity does not always implies quality.

We now examine the quality of the ratings with the following SQL queries:

■ Average rating:

```
select avg(rating) as avgrating
from ratingsdata;
```

■ Ratings distribution:

```
select count(*) as nbratings, rating
from ratingsdata
group by rating
order by rating desc;
```

■ Distribution of the average ratings by users (histogram rounded to 0.1):

```
select count(userid) as nbusers, avgrating
from (select round(avg(rating),1) as avgrating, userid
    from ratingsdata
    group by userid
    ) as avgratingbyusers
group by avgrating
order by avgrating desc;
```

■ Distribution of the average ratings by movies (histogram rounded to 0.1):

```
select count(itemid) as nbitems, avgrating
from (select round(avg(rating),1) as avgrating, itemid
    from ratingsdata
    group by itemid
    ) as avgratingbyitems
group by avgrating
order by avgrating desc;
```

Run the queries and examine the result. Can you determine the distribution law? What happens regarding the distribution of the average ratings by movies, compared to the natural expectation? Try to figure out what would be the normal curve for such an application, and explain the "picks" associated with each rounded rating. Also note the curve behavior for extreme values, and provide an explanation. Finally note that the distribution of ratings is not centered. Why?

As for most data analysis tasks, raw data have to be cleaned up during a preprocessing step. We will limit ourselves to the centering of the ratings distribution. This normalization makes easier the comparison of the users' behavior. A more involved normalization would, among others, also correct the standard deviation. This is left as an exercise. The centering is obtained by the following query:

```
create table ratings (
    userid int,
    itemid int,
    rating int,
    timestamp int,
    primary key (userid, itemid));
create index usersratings_index on ratings (userid);
create index itemsratings_index on ratings (itemid);
insert into ratings (userid,itemid,rating,timestamp)
    (select ratingsdata.userid, ratingsdata.itemid,
```

```
        ratingsdata . rating - avgratingbyusers . avgrating ,
        ratingsdata .timestamp
    from ratingsdata,
        ( select  userid ,  avg(rating )
         from ratingsdata
         group by userid
        ) as avgratingbyusers
    where ratingsdata. userid=avgratingbyusers . userid
    );
```

18.4 GENERATING SOME RECOMMENDATIONS

18.4.1 Global Recommendation

Global recommendation roughly retrieves the movies with the best average rating. The query is straightforward:

```
    select  title ,  avgrating ,  nbratings
    from items,
        ( select  round(avg(rating),1) as  avgrating ,
             count(userid) as  nbratings ,  itemid
         from ratings
         group by itemid
         order by avgrating  desc
         limit 10
        ) as avgratingbyitems
    where items.itemid = avgratingbyitems.itemid
    order by avgrating  desc;
```

If you carefully look at the result, you should observe that items with the best average ratings are those with a very small support (only a few ratings are known). This is a classic problem in statistics: An estimation of the average cannot be accurate if the support is too small. Problems related to the low quality of the support are very common in recommendation. In practice, a safe rule is to base any estimation on at least ten measurements. How can you correct the query to obtain a better result? Write and run the corrected query.

The next query retrieves the 40 movies with the largest number of ratings.

```
    select  title ,  items.itemid,  avgrating ,  nbratings
    from items,
        ( select  round(avg(rating),1) as  avgrating ,
             count(userid) as  nbratings ,  itemid
```

```
        from ratings
        group by itemid
        order by nbratings desc
        limit 40
     ) as avgratingbyitems
where items.itemid = avgratingbyitems.itemid
order by nbratings desc;
```

Pick 20 of those movies (if possible those you know) and give them a rating using the command

```
create table me (
    itemid int primary key,
    rating int );
insert into me values (id1, rating1 ), (id2, rating2 ), ... (id20, rating20 );
```

You may want to check your updates with

```
select  title , me.itemid, rating
from me, items
where me.itemid=items.itemid;
```

We will use this table to compute some movie recommendations for you. Keep in mind that in a real recommendation system, one has to find recommendation for every user, so scaling is a real issue.

18.4.2 User-Based Collaborative Filtering

The collaborative filtering class of methods focuses on the ratings matrix and ignores the users or items description. It usually proceeds in two steps: First, the correlation step determines a similarity between users (for the user-based approach) or between items (item-based), then the aggregation step predicts new rating from this similarity information.

In the case of user-based collaborative filtering (Figure 18.1), the correlation between a pair of users is computed by comparing their ratings. For simplicity (and

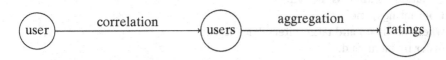

Figure 18.1. User-based collaborative filtering.

efficiency), we only compute the correlation between you and all the other users. Then the ratings of these users for a given item are aggregated to predict the rating of the initial user for this item.

Correlation

There exist several possible measures of correlations. Let U_i be the vector of ratings of user u_i (seen as a line), then

- The scalar product similarity is

$$sim(u_j, u_l) = U_j{}^t U_l$$

- The cosine similarity is

$$sim(u_j, u_l) = \frac{U_j{}^t U_l}{\|U_j\| \|U_l\|}$$

The cosine correlation is obtained by the following query:

```
select distances.userid as userid, dist/(sqrt(my.norm)*sqrt(users.norm))
    as score
from (select userid, sum((me.rating)*(ratings.rating)) as dist
        from ratings, me
        where me.itemid = ratings.itemid
        group by userid
    ) as distances,
    (select userid, sum((rating)*(rating)) as norm
     from ratings
     group by userid
    ) as users,
    (select sum((rating)*(rating)) as norm
     from me
    ) as my
where users.userid = distances.userid
order by score desc
limit 30;
```

You can compare the ratings of user u_i to yours with the following query:

```
select me.itemid as itemid, me.rating as myrating,
    ratings.rating as herrating
from ratings, me
where userid=ui and ratings.itemid=me.itemid
order by me.itemid;
```

You should observe that the estimation of the correlation is not accurate for pairs of users with a small support (i.e., users who rated only a few common items). How can you modify the correlation formula to take the support into account? You should in particular try the other formula suggested previously. This should lead to the conclusion that there is a trade-off regarding the support: Giving too much weight to the support may bias the result toward popular items, whereas simply ignoring it leads to a bad estimation quality.

We used the normalized table in the SQL commands. What could happen if we had used the initial, nonnormalized data?

We keep the correlated users whose behavior is close to yours, into the sim table, using the following command:

```
create table sim (
    userid int primary key,
      score double);
insert into sim (userid, score)
    (select  ...)
```

Recommendation

Let $\hat{r}(u_i, i_k)$ be the rating prediction of user u_i and item i_k and let $S_t(u_i)$ be the user highly correlated with u_i (the users that you put in the sim table). The following formula represent some possible ways of computing aggregated values:

- Means on the best users (the rating of a user for an item is considered to be equal to 0 if it does not exist in the rating matrix):

$$\hat{r}(u_j, i_k) = \frac{1}{|S_t(u_j)|} \sum_{u_l \in S_t(u_j)} r(u_l, i_k)$$

- Weighted average on the best users:

$$\hat{r}(u_j, i_k) = \frac{\sum_{u_l \in S_t(u_j)} sim(u_j, u_l) r(u_l, i_k)}{\sum_{u_l \in S_t(u_j)} sim(u_j, u_l)}$$

The means aggregation is obtained by

```
select  title , items.itemid, score, nbratings
from items,
    (select itemid, sum(ratings.rating)/simsize.size as score,
        count(sim.userid) as nbratings
    from sim, ratings ,
        (select  count(*) as size from sim) as simsize
    where sim.userid= ratings . userid
    group by itemid
```

```
order by score desc
limit 10
) as itemscores
where items.itemid = itemscores.itemid
order by score desc;
```

You probably want to remove the movies that you already know by adding the following filter to the where clause:

```
and itemid not in (select itemid from me)
```

You may also want to see the movies you probably dislike, replacing desc by asc in the previous command.

1. We used the normalized table. What may happen if you use the raw data?
2. You may have already observed that we kept only the 30 closest users. Try a different number as intermediate seeds (clean first the sim table with delete from sim;). Usually, the choice of $S_t(u_i)$ is very sensitive. If you are too selective, you get results with very small support (few aggregated ratings by items) and a bad estimation. If you are not selective enough, you get results very close to the global recommendation (the majority wins), and thus a bad precision. This is another illustration of the concerns related to the support: There is a trade-off between sparsity (bad estimation) and noise (bad precision).
3. To soften the previous problem, one may try to estimate the quality of the correlation. For example, try the weighted average (or even a quadratic weight). Try also to use a threshold on the value of the correlation

18.4.3 Item-Based Collaborative Filtering

For item-based collaborative filtering (Figure 18.2), we compute the correlation between any pairs of items by comparing their ratings. We then aggregate the ratings of a user for these items to predict the rating of this user for the initial item. To avoid too much computation time, you may only compute the correlation between all items and yours. Let I_k be the vector of ratings of item i_k (seen as a column). You may use

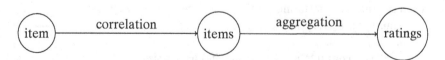

Figure 18.2. Item-based collaborative filtering.

$$sim(i_l, i_k) = {}^t I_l I_k$$

$$\hat{r}(u_j, i_k) = \frac{1}{|S_t(i_k)|} \sum_{i_l \in S_t(i_k)} r(u_j, i_l)$$

1. How can you rewrite the previous queries to do item-based collaborative filtering?
2. What is usually the benefit of using item-based collaborative filtering instead of user-based collaborative filtering, from the support point of view? In particular, what changes if some attacker in the system attempts to improve the recommendation of some items by adding new ratings?

18.5 PROJECTS

The following projects outline some suggestions to extend the basic recommendation scheme presented earlier.

18.5.1 Scaling

So far, we limited the computation to recommendations for a single user. In general, recommendation systems attempt to provide recommendations to every of their users. Several methods can be envisaged to achieve scalability:

1. Distribution,
2. Clustering methods to group similar users and similar items,
3. Reducing the dimension on the ratings matrix.

Any of these methods can be used as a starting point for a project aiming at scalable computation of the recommendations. Distribution is a suitable objective if you wish to investigate in the context of a practical project some of the main techniques described in the book. You could for instance design and experiment the computation of the correlation and aggregation indicators with the MAPREDUCE paradigm, taking the opportunity of implementing your functions in one of the systems that we present in other Putting into Practice chapters (e.g., HADOOP or COUCHDB).

18.5.2 The Probabilistic Way

Some recommendation methods are fully based on a probabilistic model. In general, they consist in choosing a probabilistic model of generation (e.g., using Markov chains), followed by an estimation of the model parameters (e.g., using expectation maximization). The project can be conducted by finding academic references to model-based recommendation. You should then choose a probabilistic model of generation and use the standard statistics methods to estimate the ratings.

18.5.3 Improving Recommendation

Many refinements can improve the recommendations obtained by the basic methods presented here. In particular, in some cases, *content filtering* (i.e., prediction of ratings given the description of items and users) provides some useful additional information. The description can also be used to increase diversity. For example, one may look for the list of items that maximize the sum of aggregated ratings under the constraint that the elements do not share all their attributes. The description of users and items are respectively in the files u.user and u.item of the MovieLens database. The imdb field of the item table can be used to get more attributes from the IMDB database.

Another standard improvement is to manage more precisely *serendipity* (i.e., to suggest items that are more risked). It may happen for instance that an item has been rated by only few users. If it turns out that all of them are enthusiastic, it may be worth proposing the item even if the support is low. For example, in user-based collaborative filtering, the first aggregation function can be modified to base the means only on users who have produced ratings. It yields the same problem of trade-off between sparsity and noise.

Taking context into account to filter the recommendation results is another interesting issue. For example, one may try to produce a recommendation for a given bag of keywords looked up in the attributes of the items. Explanation is another direction of improvement of recommendation (i.e., help the user to understand why s/he got this recommendation). The cold start problem (users or items with very few ratings) is also an important topic of research and can be easily experimented. Recommendation can benefit from interacting with the user to modify the recommendation process based on feedback. Finally, one may try to recommend to a group of users instead of a single user.

The project will try to improve the recommendation in some of these directions.

19

Putting into Practice: Large-Scale Data Management with HADOOP

The chapter proposes an introduction to HADOOP and suggests some exercises to initiate a practical experience of the system. The following assumes that you dispose of a UNIX-like system (Mac OS X works just fine; Windows requires Cygwin). HADOOP can run in a pseudo-distributed mode that does not require a cluster infrastructure for testing the software, and the main part of our instructions considers this mode. Switching to a real cluster requires some additional configurations that are introduced at the end of the chapter. Since HADOOP is a relatively young system that steadily evolves, looking at the online, up-to-date documentation is of course recommended if you are to use it on a real basis. We illustrate HADOOP, MAPREDUCE, and PIG manipulations on the DBLP data set, which can be retrieved from the following URL:

$http://dblp.uni-trier.de/xml/$

Download the *dblp.dtd* and *dblp.xml* files. The latter is, at the time of writing, almost 700 MB. Put both files in a *dblp* directory. In addition, you should take some smaller files extracted from the DBLP archive, that we make available on the book Web site.

The content of the *dblp* directory should be similar to the following:

```
ls -l dblp/
total 705716
-rw-r--r-- 1 webdam webdam    108366  author-medium.txt
-rw-r--r-- 1 webdam webdam     10070  author-small.txt
-rw-r--r-- 1 webdam webdam      7878  dblp.dtd
-rw-r--r-- 1 webdam webdam 720931885  dblp.xml
-rw-r--r-- 1 webdam webdam    130953  proceedings-medium.txt
-rw-r--r-- 1 webdam webdam     17151  proceedings-small.txt
```

19.1 INSTALLING AND RUNNING HADOOP

First, get a stable release from the HADOOP site (http://hadoop.apache.org/) and unpack the archive on your machine. To set up your environment, you need a HADOOP_HOME variable that refers to the HADOOP installation directory. For instance,

    export HADOOP_HOME=/users/webdam/hadoop

This can also be set up in the */path/to/hadoop/conf/hadoop-env.sh* script. HADOOP features a command-line interpreter, written in Java, named *hadoop*. Add the HADOOP_HOME/bin directory to your path, as follows:

    export PATH=$PATH:$HADOOP_HOME/bin

You should be able to run hadoop:

    bash-3.2$ hadoop version
    Hadoop 0.20.2

Now, you are ready to make some preliminary tests with HADOOP. We will begin with simple filesystem manipulations, in a mode called "pseudo-distributed," which runs the HADOOP servers on the local machine. To set up this mode, you need first to edit the *conf/core-site.xml* configuration file (all relative paths are rooted at $HADOOP_HOME) to add the following parameters.

```
<configuration>
  <property>
    <name>fs.default.name</name>
    <value>hdfs://localhost:9000</value>
  </property>
</configuration>
```

This tells HADOOP that the current installation runs with a local HDFS Master node (the "NameNode" in HADOOP termonilogy) on the port 9000. The filesystem is initialized with the format command:

    $ hadoop namenode -format

This initializes a directory in */tmp/hadoop-<username>/dfs/name*. The *hadoop* program is a Java command-line interpreter used to execute HADOOP commands. The general usage is

    $ hadoop <command> [parameters]

where command is one of namenode (commands sent to the Master node), fs (filesystem commands), job (commands that control MAPREDUCE jobs), and so on.

Once the file system is formatted, you must launch the HDFS Master node (*namenode*). The name node is a process responsible for managing file server nodes (called *datanodes* in HADOOP) in the cluster, and it does so with *ssh* commands. You must check that SSH is properly configured and, in particular, that you can log in the local machine with SSH without having to enter a passphrase. Try the following command:

```
$ ssh  localhost
```

If it does not work (or if you are prompted for a passphrase), you must execute the following commands:

```
$ ssh-keygen -t dsa -P " -f ~/.ssh/id_dsa
$ cat ~/.ssh/id_dsa.pub >> ~/.ssh/authorized_keys
```

This generates a new SSH key with an empty password. Now, you should be able to start the namenode server:

```
$ start-dfs.sh &
```

This launches a namenode process, and a datanode process on the local machine. You should get the following messages

```
starting  namenode, logging to  (...)
localhost :  starting  datanode, logging to  (...)
localhost :  starting  secondarynamenode, logging to  (...)
```

The secondary namenode is a mirror of the main one, used for failure recovery. At this point you can check that the HDFS is up and running with

```
$ hadoop fs -ls /
```

and look for errors. If anything goes wrong, you must look at the log files that contain a lot of report messages on the initialization steps carried out by the start procedure. Once the servers are correctly launched, we can copy the *dblp* directory in the HDFS filesystem with the following command:

```
$ hadoop fs -put dblp/ /dblp
```

This creates a *dblp* directory under the root of the HDFS filesystem hierarchy. All the basic filesystem commands can be invoked through the *hadoop* interface. Here is a short session that shows typical UNIX-like file manipulations.

```
$ hadoop fs -ls /dblp/dblp*
Found 2 items
-rw-r--r--    1 wdmd supergroup      7878 2010-03-29 10:40 /DBLP/dblp.dtd
-rw-r--r--    1 wdmd supergroup 719304448 2010-03-29 10:40 /DBLP/dblp.xml
$ hadoop fs -mkdir /DBLP/dtd
```

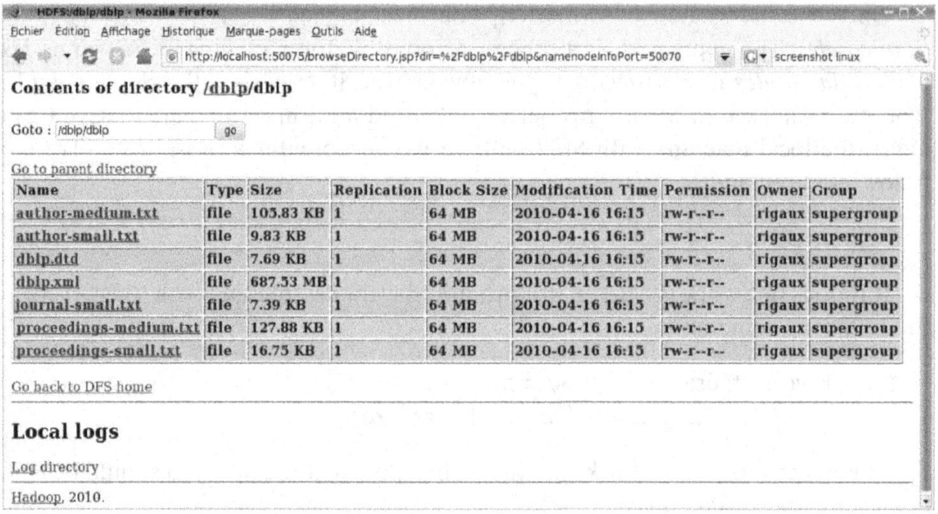

Figure 19.1. Browsing the HDFS filesystem.

```
$ hadoop fs -cp /DBLP/dblp.dtd /DBLP/dtd/
$ hadoop fs -ls /DBLP/dtd
Found 1 items
-rw-r--r--   1 wdmd supergroup      7878 2010-03-29 10:55 /DBLP/dtd/dblp.dtd
$ hadoop fs -get /DBLP/dtd/dblp.dtd my.dtd
bash-3.2$ ls -l my.dtd
-rw-r--r--   1 wdmd  staff   7878 29 mar 10:56 my.dtd
```

The output of the ls command is quite similar to the standard UNIX one, except for the second value of each line that indicates the replication factor in the distributed filesystem. The value is, here, 1 (no replication), the default parameter that can be set in the *conf/hdfs-site.xml* configuration file.

```
<?xml version="1.0"?>
<configuration>
  <property>
    <name>dfs.replication</name>
    <value>1</value>
  </property>
</configuration>
```

The Namenode also instantiates a rudimentary Web server at *http://localhost: 50070/*. It shows some information on the current status of the filesystem and provides a simple Web interface to browse the file hierarchy. Figure 19.1 shows a screen shot of this interface, with the list of our sample files loaded in the HDFS server. Note the replication factor (here, 1) and the large block size of 64 MB.

19.2 RUNNING MapReduce JOBS

We can now run MapReduce job to process data files stored in HDFS. The following gives first an example that scans text files extracted from the DBLP dataset. We then suggest some improvements and experiments. You must first start the MapReduce servers:

```
start -mapred.sh
```

Our example processes data files extracted from the DBLP data set and transformed in flat text files for simplicity. You can take these data inputs of various sizes, named *authors-xxx.txt* from the book Web site, along with the Java code. The smallest file size is a few kilobytes, the largest 300 MB. These are arguably small data sets for HADOOP, yet sufficient for an initial practice.

The file format is pretty simple. It consists of one line for each pair (author, title), with tab-separated fields, as follows:

```
<author name> < title > <year>
```

Our MapReduce job counts the number of publications found for each author. We decompose the code in two Java files, available as usual from the site. The first one, which follows, provides an implementation of both the Map and Reduce operations.

```java
package myHadoop;

/**
 * Import the necessary Java packages
 */

import java.io.IOException;
import java.util.Scanner;
import org.apache.hadoop.io.*;
import org.apache.hadoop.mapreduce.Mapper;
import org.apache.hadoop.mapreduce.Reducer;

/**
 * A Mapreduce example for Hadoop. It extracts some basic
 * information from a text file derived from the DBLP dataset.
 */
public class Authors {

    /**
     * The Mapper class -- it takes a line from the input file and
     * extracts the string before the first tab (= the author name)
     */
    public static class AuthorsMapper extends
```

```
Mapper<LongWritable, Text, Text, IntWritable> {

    private final static IntWritable one = new IntWritable(1);
    private Text author = new Text();

    public void map(LongWritable key, Text value, Context context)
        throws IOException, InterruptedException {

        /* Open a Java scanner object to parse the line */
        Scanner line = new Scanner(value.toString ());
        line.useDelimiter ("\t");
        author.set (line.next ());
        context.write(author, one);
    }
}


/**
 * The Reducer class -- receives pairs (author name, < list of counts>)
 * and sums up the counts to get the number of publications per author
 */
public static class CountReducer extends
    Reducer<Text, IntWritable, Text, IntWritable> {
    private IntWritable result = new IntWritable ();

    public void reduce(Text key, Iterable <IntWritable> values,
            Context context)
        throws IOException, InterruptedException {

        /* Iterate on the list to compute the count */
        int count = 0;
        for (IntWritable val : values) {
          count += val.get ();
        }
        result.set (count);
        context.write(key, result );
    }
  }
}
```

HADOOP provides two abstract classes, Mapper and Reducer, which must be
extended and specialized by the implementation of, respectively, a *map()* and
reduce() methods. The formal parameters of each abstract class describe, respectively, the types of the input key, input value, output key, and output value. The
framework also comes with a list of serializable data types that must be used to
represent the values exchanged in a MAPREDUCE workflow. Our example relies

on three such types: LongWritable (used for the input key, i.e., the line number), IntWritable (used for counting occurrences), and Text (a generic type for character strings). Finally, the Context class allows the user code to interact with the MAPREDUCE system.

So, consider first the *map()* method of our (extended) Mapper class AuthorMapper. It takes as input pairs *(key, value)*, *key* being here the number of the line from the input file (automatically generated by the system, and not used by our function), and *value* the line itself. Our code simply takes the part of the line that precedes the first tabulation, interpreted as the author name, and produces a pair *(author, 1)*.

The *reduce()* function is almost as simple. The input consists of a key (the name of an author) and a list of the publication counts found by all the mappers for this author. We simply iterate on this list to sum up these counts.

The second Java program shows how a job is submitted to the MAPREDUCE environment. The comments in the code should be explicit enough to inform the reader. An important aspect is the Configuration object that loads the configuration files that describe our MAPREDUCE setting. The same job can run indifferently in local or distributed mode, depending on the configuration chosen at run-time. This allows to test a (map, reduce) pair of functions on small, local data sets, before submitted a possibly long process.

```java
package myHadoop;

/**
 * Example of a simple MapReduce job: it reads
 * file  containing  authors and  publications ,  and
 * produce each author with  her  publication  count.
 */

import org.apache.hadoop.conf.Configuration;
import org.apache.hadoop.fs.Path;
import org.apache.hadoop.io.IntWritable;
import org.apache.hadoop.io.Text;
import org.apache.hadoop.mapreduce.Job;
import org.apache.hadoop.mapreduce.lib.input.FileInputFormat;
import org.apache.hadoop.mapreduce.lib.output.FileOutputFormat;

import myHadoop.Authors;

/**
 * The follozing  class implements the Job submission,  based on
 * the Mapper (AuthorsMapper) and the Reducer (CountReducer)
 */
public class AuthorsJob {

    public static void main(String[] args) throws Exception {
```

```
   /*
    * Load the Haddop configuration. IMPORTANT: the
    * $HADOOP_HOME/conf directory must be in the CLASSPATH
    */
   Configuration conf = new Configuration();

   /* We expect two arguments */

   if (args.length != 2) {
     System.err.println("Usage: AuthorsJob <in> <out>");
     System.exit(2);
   }

   /* Allright, define and submit the job */
   Job job = new Job(conf, "Authors count");

   /* Define the Mapper and the Reducer */
   job.setMapperClass(Authors.AuthorsMapper.class);
   job.setReducerClass(Authors.CountReducer.class);

   /* Define the output type */
   job.setOutputKeyClass(Text.class);
   job.setOutputValueClass(IntWritable.class);

   /* Set the input and the output */
   FileInputFormat.addInputPath(job, new Path(args[0]));
   FileOutputFormat.setOutputPath(job, new Path(args[1]));

   /* Do it! */
   System.exit(job.waitForCompletion(true) ? 0 : 1);
  }
}
```

The second object of importance is the instance of Job that acts as an interface with the MAPREDUCE environment for specifying the input, the output, and the *map()* and *reduce()* functions. Our example presents the bare minimal specification.

The Job can be directly run as java AuthorsJob <inputfile> <outputdir>. It produces an output directory outputdir (which must not exist prior to the job execution) with a set of files, one for each reducer, containing the result. Be sure to add all the HADOOP Jar files (found in HADOOP home directory) in your CLASSPATH before running the job. Here is for instance a part of the result obtained by processing the *author-small.txt* data file:

```
(...)
Dominique Decouchant   1
E. C. Chow        1
```

```
E. Harold Williams        1
Edward Omiecinski         1
Eric N. Hanson 1
Eugene J. Shekita         1
Gail E. Kaiser 1
Guido Moerkotte 1
Hanan Samet     2
Hector Garcia-Molina      2
Injun Choi      1
(...)
```

Note that the authors are alphabetically ordered, which is a desirable side effect of the map reduce framework. Sorting is done during the shuffle phase to bring together intermediate pairs that share the same key value.

19.3 PigLatin SCRIPTS

PIGLATIN can be found at *http://hadoop.apache.org/pig/*. Download a recent and stable archive, and uncompress it somewhere (say, in *$home/pig*). Add the *pig/bin* subdirectory to your path variable (change the directories to reflect your own setting):

```
$ export PATH=$HOME/pig/bin:$PATH
```

Check that the command-line interface is ready. The pig -x local should produce the following output.

```
$ pig -x local
[main] INFO  org.apache.pig.Main - Logging error messages to: xxx.log
grunt>
```

PIG accepts commands from an interpreter called grunt which runs either in "local" mode (files are read from the local filesystem) or "MAPREDUCE" mode. The former is sufficient to take a grasp on the main features of PIGLATIN. It is also useful for testing new scripts that could run for hours on large collections.

We refer to the presentation of PIGLATIN that can be found in the chapter devoted to distributed computing. Running PIGLATIN with the command-line interpreter is a piece of cake. As an initial step, we invite the reader to run a script equivalent to the MAPREDUCE Job described in the previous section.

19.4 RUNNING IN CLUSTER MODE (OPTIONAL)

We give now some hints to run HADOOP in a real cluster. As far as experimental data manipulations are involved, this is not really necessary, because neither the principles nor the code change depending on the pseudo-distributed mode. If you need to process really large data sets, and/or use HADOOP in real-life environment, a real cluster of machines is, of course, required. Understanding the architecture of a real HADOOP cluster may also be interesting on its own. You need, of course, at least two connected machines, preferably sharing a regular distributed filesystem like NFS, with system administration rights. Before going further, please note that if your objective is real-life processing of large data sets, you do not need to set up your own cluster, but can (at least for some noncommitting experiments) use a cloud computing environment supporting HADOOP (e.g., Amazon Web Services (*http://aws.amazon.com*) or Cloudera (*http://www.cloudera.com*) to name a few).

19.4.1 Configuring HADOOP in Cluster Mode

Most of the parameters that affect the running mode of HADOOP are controlled from the configuration files located in the *conf* directory. To switch easily from one mode to the other, you can simply copy *conf* as (say) *conf-cluster*. The choice between the two configurations is set by the environement variable HADOOP_CONF_DIR. Set this variable to the chosen value:

    export HADOOP_CONF_DIR=$HADOOP_HOME/conf-cluster

For simplicity, we assume that all the nodes in the cluster share the same configuration file (accessible thanks to a NFS-like distribution mechanism). If your machines are heterogeneous, you may have to refine the configuration for each machine.

The *slaves* file contains the list of nodes in the cluster, referred to by their name or IP. Here is for instance the content of *slaves* for a small 10-node cluster located at INRIA:

    node1.gemo.saclay. inria . fr
    node2.gemo.saclay. inria . fr
    node3.gemo.saclay. inria . fr
    ...
    node10.gemo.saclay. inria . fr

There exists a *masters* file, which contains the name of the secondary Nameserver. You can leave it unchanged.

Before attempting to start your cluster, you should look at the XML configuration file *core-site.xml*, *hdfs-site.xml* and *mapred-site.xml*. They contain parameter (or "properties") relative, respectively, to core HADOOP, HDFS, and MAPREDUCE. Here is for instance a self-commented *hdfs-site.xml* file with some important properties.

```
<?xml version="1.0"?>

<configuration>
  <! Amount of replication  of
            each data chunk -->
  <property>
      <name>dfs. replication </name>
      <value>3</value>
```

```
    </property>

    <!-- Disk(s) and directory/ies
              for filesystem info -->
    <property>
       <name>dfs.name.dir</name>
       <value>/disk1/hdfs/name</value>
    </property>

    <!-- Disk(s) and directory/ies
              for data chunks -->
    <property>
       <name>dfs.data.dir</name>
       <value>/disk1/hdfs/data</value>
    </property>
</configuration>
```

19.4.2 Starting, Stopping, and Managing HADOOP

HADOOP servers are launched with the *start-dfs.sh* script (located in *bin*). It starts the Namenode on the local machine (that is, the machine the script is run on), one datanode on each of the machines listed in the *slaves* file, and a secondary Namenode on the machine listed in the *masters* file. These scripts report error messages in log files located in the *HADOOP_HOME/logs* directory. Before your cluster is up and running, you will probably have to inspect these files more than once to find and correct the (hopefully small) problems specific to your environment. The HDFS system is, of course, halted with *stop-dfs.sh*.

A MAPREDUCE environment is launched with the *start-mapred.sh* script which starts a JobTracker (a MAPREDUCE Master node) on the local machine, and a tasktracker (the Workers in Google MAPREDUCE terminology) on the machines listed in *slaves*.

Another useful script is *hadoop-env.sh* where many parameters that affect the behavior of HADOOP can be set. The memory buffer used by each node is for instance determined by HADOOP_HEAPSIZE. The list of these parameters goes beyond the scope of this introduction: We refer the reader to the online documentation.

19.5 EXERCISES

If you succesfully managed to run the above examples, you are ready to go further in the discovery of HADOOP and its associated tools.

Exercise 19.5.1 (Combiner functions) *Once a map() function gets executed, it stores its result on the local filesystem. This result is then transferred to a Reducer. The performance of the Job may therefore be affected by the size of the data. A useful operation is thus to limit the size of the MAP result before network transmission:*

HADOOP *allows the specification of Combiner functions to this end. This can be seen as performing locally (that is, on the Mapper) a part of the* REDUCE *task at the end of the* MAP *phase.*

Not all Jobs are subject to Combiner optimization. Computing the average of the intermediate pairs value for instance can only be done by the Reducer. In the case of associate functions like count(), a Combiner is quite appropriate. The exercise consists in defining a Combiner function for the MAPREDUCE *job of Section 19.2. We let the reader investigate the* HADOOP *documentation (in particular Java APIs) to learn the interface that allows to define and run Combiner functions.*

Exercise 19.5.2 *Consider the XML files representing movies. Write* MAPREDUCE *jobs that take these files as input and produce the following flat text files with tab-separated fields:*

■ *title-and-actor.txt: each line contains the title, the actor's name, year of birth and role. Example:*

> The Social network   Jesse Eisenberg 1983 Mark Zuckerberg
> The Social network   Mara Rooney   1985 Erica Albright
> Marie Antoinette   Kirsten Dunst 1982 Marie-Antoinette

■ *director-and-title.txt: each line contains the director's name and the movie title. Example:*

> David Fincher   The Social network 2010
> Sofia Coppola   Lost in translation 2003
> David Fincher   Seven   1995

You must write an input function that reads an XML file and analyzes its content with either SAX or DOM: refer to the PiP chapter on the XML programming APIs.

Exercise 19.5.3 *Run the following* PIGLATIN *queries on the files obtained from the previous exercise.*

1. *Load title-and-actor.txt and group on the title. The actors (along with their roles) should appear as a nested bag.*
2. *Load director-and-title.txt and group on the director name. Titles should appear as a nested bag.*
3. *Apply the **cogroup** operator to associate a movie, its director and its actors from both sources.*
4. *Write a* PIG *program that retrieves the actors that are also director of some movie: Output a tuple for each artist, with two nested bags, one with the movies s/he played a role in, and one with the movies s/he directed.*
5. *write a modified version that looks for artists that were both actors and director of a same movie.*

Exercise 19.5.4 (inverted file project) *The goal of the project is to build a simple inverted file using a* MAPREDUCE *job. You can either use Java programming, or*

PIG *programs with a few additional functions used to process character strings and* compute tf *and* idf *indicators.*

Design and implement a process that takes as input a set of text files (consider for instance the abstracts of our movies collection) and outputs a list of the terms found in the texts, along with their frequency. Associate to each term the list of documents, along with the idf *indicator.*

Putting into Practice: COUCHDB, a JSON Semistructured Database

This chapter proposes exercises and projects based on COUCHDB, a recent database system which relies on many of the concepts presented so far in this book. In brief:

1. COUCHDB adopts a semistructured data model, based on the JSON (*JavaScript Object Notation*) format; JSON offers a lightweight alternative to XML;
2. A database in COUCHDB is schema-less: the structure of the JSON documents may vary at will depending on their specific features;
3. In order to cope with the absence of constraint that constitutes the counterpart of this flexibility, COUCHDB proposes an original approach, based on *structured materialized views* that can be produced from document collections;
4. Views are defined with the MAPREDUCE paradigm, allowing both a parallel computation and incremental maintenance of their content;
5. Finally, the system aspects of COUCHDB illustrate most of the distributed data management techniques covered in the last part of the present book: distribution based on consistent hashing, support for data replication and reconciliation, horizontal scalability, parallel computing, and so forth.

COUCHDB is representative of the emergence of so-called *key-value store* systems that give up many features of the relational model, including schema, structured querying, and consistency guarantees, in favor of flexible data representation, simplicity and scalability. It illustrates the "No[tOnly]SQL" trend with an original and consistent approach to large-scale management of "documents" viewed as autonomous, rich pieces of information that can be managed independently, in contrast with relational databases, which take the form of a rich graph of interrelated flat tuples. This chapter will help you to evaluate the pros and cons of such an approach.

We first introduce COUCHDB and develop some of its salient aspects. Exercises and projects follow. As usual, complementary material can be found on the Web site, including JSON data sets extracted from the DBLP source. We also provide an online testing environment that lets you play with COUCHDB, insert data, and run MAPREDUCE scripts.

20.1 INTRODUCTION TO THE CouchDB DOCUMENT DATABASE

This section is an introduction to the COUCHDB features that will be explored in the project and exercises. We left apart many interesting aspects (e.g., security, load balancing, view management) that fall beyond the scope of this introductory chapter. The presentation successively covers the data model, the definition of views, and data replication and distribution.

20.1.1 JSON, a Lightweight Semistructured Format

JSON is a simple text format initially designed for serializing Javascript objects. For the record, Javascript is a scripting language (distinct from Java), which is intensively used in Web browsers for "dynamic HTML" applications. In particular, a Javascript function can access and modify the DOM tree of the document displayed by a browser. Any change made to this document is instantaneously reflected in the browser window. This gives a means to react to user's actions without having to request a new page from the server (a development technique know as AJAX), and therefore enables the creation of rich, interactive client-side applications.

Although JSON comes from the Javascript world, the format is language-independent. There exist libraries in all programming languages to read and parse JSON documents, which makes it a simple alternative to XML. This is particularly convenient when persistent data must be tightly integrated in a programming environment because objects can be instantiated from the JSON serialization with minimal programming effort.

Key-Value Pairs
The basic construct of JSON is a key-value pair of the form *"key": value*. Here is a first example, where the value is a character string:

```
" title ":  "The  Social  network"
```

Usual escaping rules apply: The character ", for instance, must be escaped with '\'. Special characters like tabs and newlines are also escaped:

```
"summary": "On a fall  night in 2003, Harvard undergrad and computer\n
    programming genius Mark Zuckerberg sits  down at his  computer\n
    and heatedly  begins  working on a new idea.  (...) "
```

JSON accepts a limited set of basic data types: character strings, integers, floating-point numbers and Booleans (true or false). Nonstring values need not be surrounded by" "".

```
"year": 2010
```

Complex Values: Objects and Arrays

Complex values are built with two constructors: objects and arrays. An *object* is an unordered set of name/value pairs, separated by commas, and enclosed in braces. The types can be distinct, and a key can only appear once. The following is an object made of three key-value pairs.

```
{"last_name": "Fincher", "first_name": "David", "birth_date": 1962}
```

Since constructors can be nested, an object can be used as the (complex) value component of a key-value construct:

```
" director ": {
       "last_name": "Fincher",
       "first_name": "David",
       "birth_date": 1962
   }
```

An array is an ordered collection of values that need not be of the same type (JSON definitely does not care about types). The list of values is enclosed in square brackets []. The following key-value pairs represents a list of actors' names.

```
"actors": ["Eisenberg", "Mara", " Garfield ", "Timberlake"]
```

JSON Documents

A *document* is an object. It can be represented with an unbounded nesting of array and object constructs, as shown by the following example which provides a JSON representation of the movie *The Social Network*.

```
{
   " title ": "The Social network",
   "year": "2010",
```

```
    "genre": "drama",
    "summary": "On a fall night in 2003, Harvard undergrad and computer
    programming genius Mark Zuckerberg sits down at his computer
    and heatedly begins working on a new idea. In a fury of blogging
    and programming, what begins in his dorm room soon becomes a global
    social network and a revolution in communication. A mere six years
    and 500 million friends later, Mark Zuckerberg is the youngest
    billionaire in history ... but for this entrepreneur, success leads
    to both personal and legal complications.",
    "country": "USA",
  "director": {
      "last_name": "Fincher",
      "first_name": "David",
      "birth_date": "1962"
  },
  "actors": [
      {
          "first_name": "Jesse",
          "last_name": "Eisenberg",
          "birth_date": "1983",
          "role": "Mark Zuckerberg"
      },
      {
          "first_name": "Rooney",
          "last_name": "Mara",
          "birth_date": "1985",
          "role": "Erica Albright"
      },
      {
          "first_name": "Andrew",
          "last_name": "Garfield",
          "birth_date": "1983",
          "role": "Eduardo Saverin "
      },
      {
          "first_name": "Justin",
          "last_name": "Timberlake",
          "birth_date": "1981",
          "role": "Sean Parker"
      }
  ]
}
```

To summarize, JSON relies on a simple semistructured data model and shares
with XML some basic features: Data are self-described, encoded independently

from any application or system, and the representation supports simple but powerful constructs that allow building arbitrarily complex structures. It is obvious that any JSON document can be converted to an XML document. The opposite is not true, at least if we wish to maintain all the information potentially conveyed by XML syntax. Namespaces are absent from JSON, documents are always encoded in UTF-8, and the language lacks from a built-in support for references (the ID-IDREF mechanism in XML).

Moreover, at the time of writing, there is nothing like a "JSON schema" that could help to declare the structure of a JSON database (some initiatives are in progress: see the Further Reading section). The attractiveness from JSON comes primarily from its easy integration in a development framework, since a JSON document can directly be instantiated as an object in any programming language. The absence of typing constraint requires some complementary mechanisms to ensure that a JSON database presents a consistent and robust data interface to an application. Documents should be validated before insertion or update, and data access should retrieve documents whose structure is guaranteed to comply to at least some common structural pattern. CouchDB is an interesting attempt to provide answers to these issues.

20.1.2 CouchDB, Architecture, and Principles

A CouchDB instance is based on a Client/Server architecture, where the CouchDB server handles requests sent by the client, processes the requests on its database(s), and sends an answer (Figure 20.1). Unlike most of the database management systems that define their own, proprietary client-server communication protocol, CouchDB proposes a REST-based interface. Requests sent by the Client to the server are REST calls and take actually the form of an HTTP request, together with parameters transmitted with one of the basic HTTP method: GET, POST, PUT and DELETE.

It is probably worth recalling at this point the essential features of the HTTP requests that constitute a REST interface. First, we aim at manipulating *resources*, in our case, essentially JSON documents or collections of documents. Second, each resource is referenced by a *Universal Resource Identifier (URI)* (i.e., a character string that uniquely determines how and where we access the resource on the Internet). And, third, we apply *operations* to resources. Operations are defined by the HTTP protocol as follows:

GET retrieves the resource referenced by the URI.
PUT creates the resource at the given URI.
POST sends a message (along with some data) to an existing resource.
DELETE deletes the resource.

The difference between PUT and POST, often misunderstood, is that PUT creates a new resource, whereas POST sends some data to an existing resource (typically, a service that processes the data). The difference is harmless for many applications that ignore the specificities of REST operation semantics, and simply communicate with

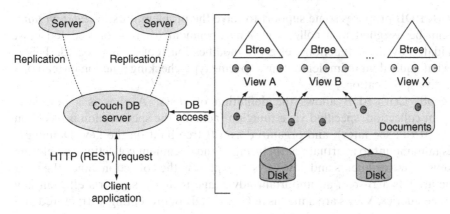

Figure 20.1. The architecture of CouchDB.

a Web server through HTTP. A so-called RESTful service takes care of the meaning of each operation and deliberately bases its design of the concept of resources manipulation.

This is the case of a COUCHDB server. It implements a REST interface to communicate with the client application. HTTP calls can be encapsulated either by a REST client library, or even expressed directly with a tool like *curl* (see later). The server answers through HTTP, with messages encoded in JSON. Here is a first, very simple communication with an hypothetical COUCHDB server located at, say, http://mycouch.org: We send a GET request and receive a JSON-encoded acknowledgment message.

```
$ curl -X GET http://mycouch.org
{"couchdb":"Welcome","version ":"1.0.1"}
```

A nice feature of the approach is that is quite easy to directly communicate with a server. Keeping in mind the three main REST concepts (resource, URI, and operation semantics) helps figuring out the purpose of each request.

The server maintains one or several collections of JSON *documents*. In addition to the JSON structure that constitutes the description of a document d, nonstructured files can be attached to d. COUCHDB adds to each document an *id* and a *revision number*. The id of a document is unique in the collection (an error is raised by COUCHDB if one attempts to create a document with an already existing id), and is stored as the value of the _id key in the JSON document. In case the value of _id is not part of the inserted document, COUCHDB automatically assigns a unique value (a long, obscure character string).

Revisions correspond to the versioning feature of COUCHDB: Each update to a document creates a new version, with the same _id but a new revision number, represented by the value of a _rev key.

A collection in a COUCHDB collection has no schema: A document d_1 with a structure A can cohabit with a document d_2 with a structure B, potentially completely different from A. Basically, this means that the application is in charge of checking the structural constraints before insertion or updates.

COUCHDB proposes some support to solve the problem. First, *validation functions* can be assigned to a collection: Any document inserted or updated must be validated by these functions; else the modification request is rejected. This is somewhat equivalent to implementing a specific type-checking function instead of a declarative specification.

Second, COUCHDB allows the definition of *views*. A view is a new key-document collection, specified via a function (actually the specification is based on MAPREDUCE: see later), and organized as a B-tree built on the key. Defining a view is tantamount to a virtual restructuring of the document collection, generating new keys, new documents and new ways of exploring the collection. Since the view is structured as a B-tree, an important advantage is that it supports efficient key and range queries. Views are a means in COUCHDB of presenting a structured and well-organized content to applications.

Finally, the last COUCHDB aspect illustrated by Figure 20.1 is data replication. It is possible to ask a COUCHDB instance to synchronize itself with another instance located anywhere on the Web. This enables a replication mechanism that copies each document to the remote servers. Replication is useful for security (replicated data is safer data) and for scalability. It also gives rise to consistency concerns, since two client applications may modify independently two replicas of a same document. COUCHDB detects update conflicts and reports them, but it does not attempt an automatic reconciliation.

These are the basics of COUCHDB principles. Let us now delve into practice.

20.1.3 Preliminaries: Set Up Your COUCHDB Environment

From now on, we will guide you through a step-by-step exploration of a few salient features of COUCHDB: creating data and views, replication and distribution. You are invited to download a sample of our *movies* data set, encoded in JSON, from the book Web site. You also need an access to a running COUCHDB server. You can set up your own environment (see the site http://couchdb.apache.org), or use our on-line environment. Please look at the site for details. In the following, $COUCHDB will refer to the IP of the COUCHDB server. In case you would use a UNIX console, this variable can be defined with

    export COUCHDB=http://<couchIP>:5984

where couchIP denotes the IP address of the host.[1] To communicate with the server, you need a client application that sends HTTP requests to your COUCHDB server. The universal command-line tool to do so is *curl*, which should be available on any UNIX-like system. For instance, the following command:

    curl $COUCHDB

sends an HTTP request GET (the default method) to the server, which should answer

    {"couchdb":"Welcome","version ":"1.0.1"}

---

[1] If you use our COUCHDB server, you must add you login/password to this IP.

Using the option *-v* unveils the details of the HTTP protocol.

```
$ curl -v  $COUCHDB
* About to connect() to xx.xxx.xxx port 5984 (#0)
*    Trying xx.xxx.xxx ... connected
* Connected to xx.xxx.xxx (xx.xxx.xxx) port 5984 (#0)
> GET / HTTP/1.1
> User-Agent: curl/7.19.7
> Host: xx.xxx.xxx:5984
> Accept: */*
>
< HTTP/1.1 200 OK
< Server: CouchDB/1.0.1 (Erlang OTP/R13B)
< Date: Tue, 09 Nov 2010 08:34:36 GMT
< Content-Type: text/plain;charset=utf-8
< Content-Length: 40
< Cache-Control: must-revalidate
<
{"couchdb":"Welcome","version ":"1.0.1"}
* Connection #0 to host xx.xxx.xxx left  intact
* Closing  connection #0
```

Every interaction with the server can in principle be handled by *curl*. Of course, a graphical interface is more pleasant that a command-line tool. Our site proposes such an interface. If you have your own installation of COUCHDB, Futon is an application, shipped with any COUCHDB environment, that lets you manage your databases. Futon is actually a Javascript application natively stored in a COUCHDB server, so that it works without any further installation step. It can be accessed at the following URL:

```
$COUCHDB/_utils
```

Figure 20.2 shows a screen shot of the Futon home page. In the following, we will describe the interactions with COUCHDB through the *curl* command-line interface. Most of them can also be expressed with Futon.

20.1.4 Adding Data

Let us create our first database. We simply send a PUT request to the COUCHDB server, asking for the creation of a resource. The following command creates the *movies* database.

```
$ curl -X PUT $COUCHDB/movies
{"ok":true}
```

Now the resource exists at the given URI, and a GET request will retrieve some information about the database.

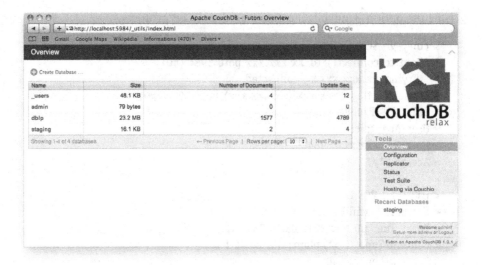

Figure 20.2. Futon, the admin interface of COUCHDB.

```
$ curl -X GET $COUCHDB/movies
{"db_name":"movies",
 "doc_count":0,
  "doc_del_count":0,
  "update_seq":0,
  "purge_seq":0,
  "compact_running":false,
  "disk_size":79,
  "instance_start_time":"1289290809351647",
  "disk_format_version":5,
  "committed_update_seq":0}
```

That's all: we send HTTP requests to COUCHDB, which answers with a JSON document. COUCHDB offers an "API" which takes the form of REST services whenever appropriate (not all services can be conveniently implemented as REST calls). The _all_dbs service for instance returns an array with the list of existing databases.

```
$ curl -X GET $COUCHDB/_all_dbs
["movies","_users"]
```

It is time now to add documents. Get the JSON-encoded documents of the movies database from the book's Web site. We shall first insert *The Social Network*.

```
$ curl -X PUT $COUCHDB/movies/tsn -d @The_Social_Network.json
{"ok":true,"id":"tsn","rev":"1-db1261d4b2779657875dafbed6c8f5a8"}
```

This deserves some explanations. First, we follow the very same logic as before, asking COUCHDB to create a new resource at URI $COUCHDB/movies/tsn. The resource content must be JSON-encoded: we transfer the content of the *The_Social_Network.json* file. Note the -d curl option, which must be followed by the content of the HTTP request message. Note also that this content can be extracted from a file with the special syntax @fileName.

CouchDB answers with a resource that contains several information. First, "ok":true means that the document has been successfully inserted. Then we get the id, and the revision number. The id (or key) of the document is the means by which it can be retrieved from the database. Try the following request:

```
$ curl -X GET $COUCHDB/movies/tsn
```

You should get the document just inserted. In this case, the document id, tsn is user-defined. We must be careful to ensure that the id does not already exist in the database. CouchDB generates an error if we attempt to do so:

```
$ curl -X PUT $COUCHDB/movies/tsn -d @The_Social_Network.json
{"error":"conflict","reason":"Document update conflict."}
```

A *conflict* has been detected. CouchDB uses an "eventually consistent" transaction model, to be described next.

If we want CouchDB to generate the id of the document, we must send a POST request, along with the content and its MIME encoding. Recall that POST sends some data to an existing resource, here the database in charge of inserting the document:

```
$ curl -X POST $COUCHDB/movies -d @The_Social_Network.json \
  -H "Content-Type: application/json"
{"ok":true,
 "id":"bed7271",
 "rev":"1-db126"}
```

A new id has been generated for us by CouchDB, and the document has been stored as a resource whose URI is determined by this id (e.g., $COUCHDB/-movies/bed7271).

To update a document, you must send a PUT request that refers to the modified document by its id *and* its revision number. The multiversion protocol of CouchDB requires that both values must be given to refer to a document value. The usual update mechanism involves thus (i) getting the document from the database, including its revision number, (ii) modifying locally the document, and (iii) putting back the document to CouchDB, which creates a new version with a new revision id.

Let us show how to update a document by adding an *attachment*. We execute a PUT request on the previous movie to associate its poster (a JPEG file). We must provide the file content in the request body, along with the MIME type. The version of the document which is modified is referred to by its revision number. Here is the curl command, which specifies the MIME type of the attachment:

```
$ curl -X PUT $COUCHDB/movies/tsn/poster?rev=1-db1261 -d
@poster-tsn.jpg   -H "Content-Type: image/jpg"
{"ok":true,"id":"tsn","rev":"2-26863"}
```

As a result, a new revision "2-26863" has been created. The poster can be retrieved from CouchDB with the URI $COUCHDB/movies/tsn/poster.

Finally, a document can be deleted with the REST DELETE command. The revision number must be indicated. Here is an example:

```
$ curl -X DELETE $COUCHDB/movies/tsn?rev=2-26863
{"ok":true ," id ":" tsn "," rev ":"3-48 e92b"}
```

A surprising aspect of the result is that a new revision is created! Indeed, the deletion is "logical": Old revisions still exist, but the latest one is marked as "deleted," as shown by the following query that attempts to retrieve the current version of tsn.

```
$ curl $COUCHDB/movies/tsn
{" error ":" not_found","reason ":" deleted "}
```

We invite you now to load in your collection the *movies* documents available on our Web site. The following section shows how to query COUCHDB databases with views.

20.1.5 Views

A *view* in COUCHDB is the result of a MAPREDUCE job. The main rationale behind this seemingly odd choice is, first, the ability to run in parallel the evaluation of view queries in a distributed environment, and, second, the incremental maintenance of view results. Both aspects are closely related: Because the MAP phase is applied to each document independently, the evaluation process is inherently scalable; and because COUCHDB records any change that affects a document in a collection, view results can be maintained by reevaluating the MAPREDUCE job only on changed documents.

Views definition are stored in the COUCHDB database as special documents called *design* documents. Temporary views can also be created using the Futon interface which provides a quite convenient tool for interactive view definition and testing. From your favorite browser, access the $COUCHDB/_utils URL, move to the *movies* database, and select the temporary views choice form the Views menu. You should obtain the form shown on Figure 20.3.

The form consists of two text windows: the left one (mandatory) for the MAP function and the right one (optional) for the REDUCE function. Functions are written in Javascript (we use simple examples that are self-explanatory). We begin with a simple MAP function that takes as input a document (i.e., a representation of a movie, see earlier) and produces a (*key, value*) pair consisting of the movie title (key) and the movie's director object (value). Write the following text in the left window and press the Run button: You should obtain the list of (*title, director*) pairs shown on Figure 20.3.

```
function(doc)
{
    emit(doc. title , doc. director )
}
```

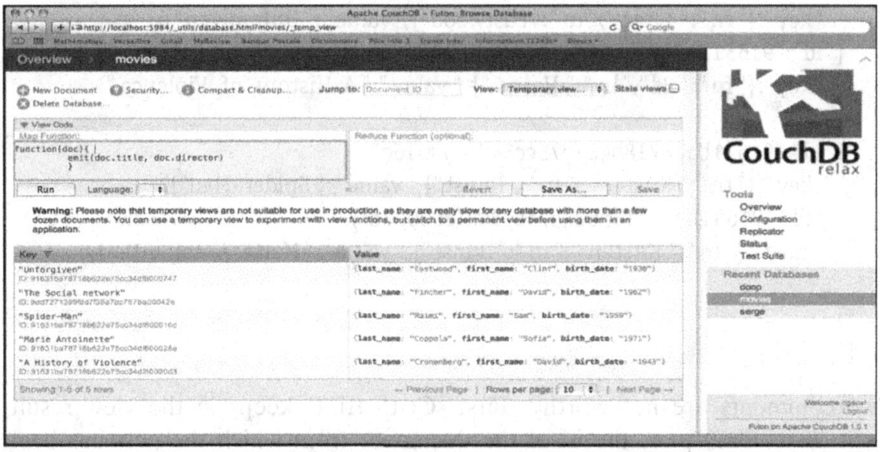

Figure 20.3. The view creation form in Futon.

A MAP function always takes as input a document of the collection. The reader is referred to Chapter 16 for a detailed description of the MAPREDUCE parallel computation principles. Essentially, the point is that the preceding function can be spread over all the nodes that participate to the storage of a COUCHDB database, and run on the local fragment of the database.

Here is a second example that shows how one can create a view that produces a list of actors (the key) along with the movie they play in (the value). Note that, for each document, several pairs are produced by the MAP function:

```
function(doc)
{
    for each (actor in doc.actors) {
        emit({"fn": actor.first_name, "ln": actor.last_name}, doc.title) ;
    }
}
```

Note that the key component may consist of a complex JSON object. From Futon, save the first function as "director" and the second one as "actors" in a design document called ("examples"). The views are now stored in the *movies* database and can be queried from the REST interface, as follows:

```
$ curl $COUCHDB/movies/_design/examples/_view/actors
{"total_rows":16," offset":0,
"rows":[
 {"id":"bed7271399fdd7f35a7ac767ba00042e",
   "key":{"fn":"Andrew","ln":"Garfield"}," value":"The Social network"},
 {"id":"91631ba78718b622e75cc34df8000747",
```

```
 "key":{"fn":" Clint "," ln ":" Eastwood"},"value ":" Unforgiven "},
{"id":"91631ba78718b622e75cc34df80020d3",
 "key":{"fn":" Ed"," ln ":" Harris "}," value ":" A History of Violence "},
 ...
{"id":"91631ba78718b622e75cc34df800016c",
 "key":{"fn":" Kirsten "," ln ":" Dunst"},"value ":" Spider-Man"},
 {"id":"91631ba78718b622e75cc34df800028e",
 "key":{"fn":" Kirsten "," ln ":" Dunst"},"value ":" Marie Antoinette"},
 ...
]
}
```

Two comments are noteworthy. First, COUCHDB keeps in the view result, for each (*key*, *value*) pair, the id of the document from which the pair has been produced. This might be useful for getting additional information if necessary.

Second, you will notice that the result is sorted on the key value. This relates to the underlying MAPREDUCE process: The (*key*, *value*) pairs produced by the MAP function are prepared to be merged and aggregated in the REDUCE phase, and this requires an intermediate "shuffle" phase that puts together similar key values. In the results samples, movies featuring Kirsten Dunst are consecutive in the list.

From this sorted representation, it is easy to derive "reduced" result by applying a REDUCE function. It takes as input a key value k and an array of values v, and returns a pair (k, v') where v' is a new value derived from v and, hopefully, smaller. Here is a first, generic example, that return the number of values associated to a key:

```
function (key, values) {
    return values.length;
}
```

Add this REDUCE function to the actors view, and compute the result (be sure to set the "reduce" option in Futon, or pass a group=true parameter to activate the reduction). You should see indeed with each actor's name the number of movies s/he features in.

```
$ curl $COUCHDB/movies/_design/examples/_view/actors?group=true
{"rows":[
{"key":{"fn":" Andrew","ln":" Garfield "}," value ":1},
{"key":{"fn":" Clint "," ln ":" Eastwood"},"value ":1},
...
{"key":{"fn":" Kirsten "," ln ":" Dunst"},"value ":2},
{"key":{"fn":" Maria "," ln ":" Bello "}," value ":1},
{"key":{"fn":" Morgan","ln":" Freeman"},"value":1}
...
]}
```

20.1.6 Querying Views

In COUCHDB, views are *materialized*. The MAPREDUCE job is run once, when the view is created, and the view content is maintained incrementally as documents are added, updated or deleted. In addition, this content is a represented as a B-tree which supports efficient search on either key value or ranges. Create a third view, called "genre", with the following definition.

```
function(doc)
{
    emit(doc.genre, doc. title ) ;
}
```

This is tantamount to issuing the following command in a relational database:

```
create index on movies (genre);
```

Now the database system (whether relational or COUCHDB) can efficiently evaluate a query that refers to the key value. Here is the REST request searching for all documents in genre with key value "Drama".

```
$ curl $COUCHDB/movies/_design/examples/_view/genre?key=\"Drama\"
{"total_rows ":5," offset ":2," rows ":[
{"id":"91631ba78718b622e75cc34df800028e",
  "key":"Drama","value ":"Marie Antoinette "},
{"id ":"bed7271399fdd7f35a7ac767ba00042e",
  "key":"Drama","value ":"The Social network"}
]}
```

Range queries can be expressed by sending two parameters startkey and endkey.

View creation (based on MAPREDUCE) and view querying (based on view materialization and B-tree indexing on the results' key) constitute in essence the solution proposed by COUCHDB to the challenge of satisfying both the flexible data structuring of semistructured models and the robust data representation needed by applications. Views provide a means to clean up and organize a collection of documents according to the regular representation expected by application programs. MAP and REDUCE functions act first as filters that check the content of input documents and second as data-structuring tools that create the virtual document representation put as values in a view.

The cost of computing the view representation each time a query is submitted by such a program is avoided thanks to the incremental materialization strategy.

The design is also strongly associated with the distribution features of a COUCHDB instance, described next.

20.1.7 Distribution Strategies: Master–Master, Master–Slave, and Shared–Nothing

Several distribution strategies can be envisaged with COUCHDB. The system does not impose any of them but rather provides a simple and powerful *replication* functionality, which lies at the core of any distribution solution.

Replication

Replication is specified in COUCHDB with a POST request sent to the _replicate utility. The following example requires a replication from local database *movies* to the local database *backup*. The *continuous* option is necessary to ensure that any future update to a document in *movies* will be reflected in *backup* (otherwise a one-shot replication is made).

```
curl  -X POST $COUCHDB/_replicate \
    -d '{" source ": "movies",  " target ": "backup", "continuous": true }' \
    -H "Content-Type:  application/json"
```

Futon proposes actually an interface that makes the specification of a replication trivial. Note that the command defines a one-way copy of the content of a database. Full, symmetric replication can be obtained by submitting a second command inverting the target and source roles.

You are invited to experiment right away the replication feature: create a second database on one of your available COUCHDB server, and replicate your *movies* database there. You should be able to verify that the content of *movies* can be found in the replica, as well as any subsequent change. Replication is basically useful for security purposes, as it represents a backup of the database (preferably on a remote server). It also serves as a basic service of the distribution options, presented next.

Distribution Options

A first distribution strategy, called *master–slave*, is illustrated on Figure 20.4, left part (refer also to the introduction given in Chapter 14). It relies on a *master* server and one or several *slaves* (for the sake of simplicity we illustrate the ideas with a two-machines scenario, but the extension to any number of participants is straightforward). The master receives all write requests of the form $w(d)$ by Clients. A replication service at the master's site monitors all the writes and replicates them to the slave(s). Replication in COUCHDB is asynchronous: the Client does not have to wait for the completion of the write on the slave.

Read requests, on the other hand, can be served either by the master or by the slave. This approach avoids inconsistencies, because writes are handled by a single process, and therefore implicitly serialized. On the other hand, it may happen that a Client issues a $w(d)$ to the master, then a read $r(d)$ to the slave, and receives an outdated version of d because the replication has not yet been carried out. The system is said to be *eventually consistent* (see, again, Chapter 14).

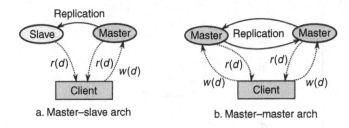

a. Master–slave arch   b. Master–master arch

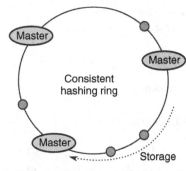

c. Shared-nothing (consistent hashing)

Figure 20.4. Distribution strategies with COUCHDB.

Remark 20.1.1 *Recall that "Client" in our terminology refers to any software component in charge of communicating with the distributed storage system. It may take the form of a library incorporated in the client application, of a proxy that receives network requests, and so on.*

A second strategy, called *master–master*, allows write operations to take place at any node of the distributed system. So, each server plays the role of a "Master", as defined above, and the replication now works both sides. In a cluster with n machines, each COUCHDB servers replicates its write request to the $n-1$ other nodes. This avoids the bottleneck of sending writes to a single machine, but raises consistency issues. It may happen that a same document d is modified concurrently on two distinct sites S_1 and S_2, thereby creating two *conflicting* versions.

Conflict Management

When a replication is attempted from, say, S_1 to S_2, COUCHDB detects the conflict. The detection is based on a classical transaction protocol called Multi-Versions Concurrency Control (MVCC) that relies heavily on the revision numbers. The protocol is simple and easily understood from an example (summarized in Figure 20.5). Assume a document d with revision number r, denoted $d_{(r)}$. This document is replicated on S_1 and S_2, and each replica is going to be modified by two client transactions denoted respectively T_1 and T_2.

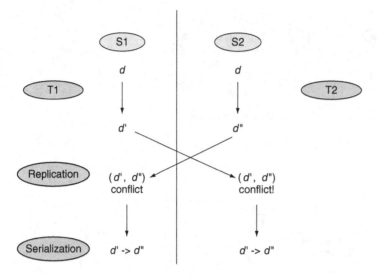

Figure 20.5. Multiversion concurrency in CouchDB.

1. T_1: $d_{(r)}$ is modified on S_1 by the local CouchDB server which assigns a new revision, r'; the current version becomes $d_{(r')}$.
2. T_2: $d_{(r)}$ is modified on S_2 by the local CouchDB server which assigns a new revision, r''; the current version becomes $d_{(r'')}$.
3. Now, the replication mechanism must be triggered; S_1 sends to S_2 a transaction request specifying that d evolves from revision r to revision r'; S_2 detects that its current revision is *not* r but r'' and concludes that there is an update conflict.

A conflict is also detected when S_2 attempts a replication of its own transaction to S_1. Basically, the protocol describes the modification of a document d by specifying the initial and final revisions, and each replica must check that it is able to execute the very same transaction, which is only possible if its own current revision is the initial one specified by the transaction. Else, the document has been modified meanwhile by another application and we are in presence of two conflicting versions.

What happens then? CouchDB takes two actions. First, a current version is chosen with a deterministic algorithm that operates similarly for each replica. For instance, each local CouchDB server chooses $d_{(r'')}$ as the current revision, both at S_1 and S_2. No communication is required: The decision algorithm is guaranteed to make the same decision at each site. This can be seen as a serialization a posteriori of the concurrent transactions $T_1 \rightarrow T_2$, resulting in a revision sequence $d_{(r)} \rightarrow d_{(r')} \rightarrow d_{(r'')}$. Second, the conflict is recorded in both $d_{(r')}$ and $d_{(r'')}$ with a _conflict attribute added to the document.

CouchDB does not attempt any automatic reconciliation, since the appropriate strategy is clearly application dependent. A specific module should be in charge on searching for conflicting documents versions (i.e, those featuring a _conflicts attribute) in order to apply an ad hoc reconciliation mechanism.

Conflict management is easy to investigate. Run the following simple scenario: in your replicated, *backup*, database, edit and modify with Futon one of the movies (say, *The Social Network*). Then change (in a different way) the same movie in the original database *movies*. The continuous replication from *movies* to *backup* will generate a conflict in the latter. Conflicts can be reported with the following view:

```
function(doc) {
  if(doc._conflicts) {
    emit(doc._conflicts, null);
  }
}
```

It returns an array of the conflicting versions. A reconciliation-aware application should implement a module that monitors conflicts and determines the correct current version content, based on the specific application needs.

Shared-Nothing architecture

The third replication option is an implementation of the shared-nothing architecture presented in Chapter 15, based on consistent hashing and data partition (often called "sharding"). A set of COUCHDB servers is (logically) assigned to a position on a ring, and documents are stored on the server that follows their hash value on the ring. The topology of the ring is replicated on each server, so that Client requests can be forwarded in one message to the relevant server. We do not further elaborate the design that closely follows that presented in Chapter 15 and tends to become a standard in the world of distributed storage system (see CASSANDRA, VOLDEMORT, MONGODB, and other "NoSQL" emerging platforms).

20.2 PUTTING CouchDB INTO PRACTICE!

We now propose several exercises and projects to further discover the features of COUCHDB that relate to the book scope, namely data representation, semistructured data querying, and distribution features. Recall that you can create an account on our COUCHDB server and one or several database to play with the system.

20.2.1 Exercises

The following exercises apply to the *movies* database. You should first load the JSON documents available on our site. Then create and query MAPREDUCE views to obtain the required results. Views can be created with Futon and searched with the following HTTP request:

/database/_design/application/_view/viewname?key=value

Many of these queries are similar to those suggested in the chapter devoted to EXIST:

1. Give all titles.
2. Titles of the movies published after 2000.
3. Summary of *Spider-Man*.
4. Who is the director of *Heat*?
5. Title of the movies featuring Kirsten Dunst.
6. What was the role of Clint Eastwood in *Unforgiven*?
7. Get the movies whose cast consists of exactly three actors?
8. Create a flat list of all the title-role pairs. (*Hint*: Recall that you can emit several pairs in a MAP function.)
9. Get a movie given its title. (*Hint*: Create a view where movies are indexed by their title, then query the view.)
10. Get the movies featuring an actor's name.
11. Get the title of movies published a given year or in a year range.
12. Show the movies where the director is also an actor.
13. Show the directors, along with the list of their films.
14. Show the actors, along with the list of directors of the film they played in.

Note: Some of the above queries are *joins*. Expressing joins in MAPREDUCE is not the most natural operation, but it can be achieved with a few tricks. *Hint*: Recall that the result of the MAP phase is sorted on the key because it is stored in a B-tree (and because this can be convenient if a subsequent REDUCE operation must be carried out). The order thereby defined on the MAP results helps to obtain the join result.

20.2.2 Project: Build a Distributed Bibliographic Database with CouchDB

The proposed project consists in building a (simple) distributed bibliographic database based on a master–master architecture. Here are the full specifications:

1. There should be several (at least two!, up to the number of participants) COUCHDB instances (or "master"), storing a fully replicated collection of bibliographic entries; each update on one master should be replicated to all the other masters;
2. There should be a view that produces the Bibtex entry;
3. PDF files can be associated with entries (COUCHDB uses "attachments" to associate file in any format with a JSON document: see the documentation for details);
4. Several views should be created to allow the presentation (and search) of the bibliographic collection with respect to the following criteria: title, author, journal or publisher, year.
5. (advanced) COUCHDB manages a log of changes that records all the modifications affecting a database; use this log to create (with a view) a notification mechanism showing all the recently created entries of interest to a user (e.g., all the entries referring to a publication in JACM).

We provide a collection of JSON bibliographic entries extracted from the DBLP datasets as a starting point. The project could include the development of an interface to add/update/remove entries.

20.3 FURTHER READING

The main source of information on COUCHDB is the Wiki available at http://couchdb.apache.org. The book [17], available on-line at http://wiki.apache.org/couchdb/, covers the main practical aspects of the system. The incremental maintenance of views built using MapReduce is inspired from the Sawzall language presented in [135].

Bibliography

1. N. Abdallah, F. Goasdoué, and M.-C. Rousset. DL-LITE$_\mathcal{R}$ in the Light of Propositional Logic for Decentralized Data Management. In *Proc. Intl. Joint Conference on Artificial Intelligence (IJCAI)*, 2009.
2. S. Abiteboul, S. Alstrup, H. Kaplan, T. Milo, and T. Rauhe. Compact labeling scheme for ancestor queries. *SIAM J. Comput.*, 35(6):1295–1309, 2006.
3. S. Abiteboul and C. Beeri. The power of languages for the manipulation of complex values. *Very Large Databases Journal (VLDBJ)*, 4(4):727–794, 1995.
4. S. Abiteboul and N. Bidoit. Non first normal form relations: An algebra allowing data restructuring. *J. Comput. Syst. Sci.*, 33(3):361–393, 1986.
5. S. Abiteboul, P. Buneman, and D. Suciu. *Data on the Web: From Relations to Semistructured Data and XML*. Morgan-Kaufman, 1999.
6. S. Abiteboul, S. Cluet, V. Christophides, T. Milo, G. Moerkotte, and J. Simeon. Querying documents in object databases. *Intl. J. Digital Libraries*, 1:5–19, 1997.
7. S. Abiteboul, M. Preda, and G. Cobena. Adaptive on-line page importance computation. In *Proc. Intl. World Wide Web Conference (WWW)*, 2003.
8. S. Abiteboul, D. Quass, J. McHugh, J. Widom, and J. Wiener. The Lorel query language for semistructured data. *Intl. J. Digital Libraries*, 1:68–88, 1997.
9. S. Abiteboul, R.Hull, and V. Vianu. *Foundations of Databases*. Addison-Wesley, 1995.
10. A. Abouzeid, K. Bajda-Pawlikowski, D. J. Abadi, A. Rasin, and A. Silberschatz. HadoopDB: An Architectural Hybrid of MAPREDUCE and DBMS Technologies for Analytical Workloads. *Proc. VLDB Endowment (PVLDB)*, 2(1):922–933, 2009.
11. A. Cali, G. Gottlob, and T. Lukasiewicz. Datalog+-: A Unified Approach to Ontologies and Integrity Constraints. In *Proc. Intl. Conf. on Database Theory (ICDT)*, 2009.
12. A.Cali, G.Gottlob, and T. Lukasiewicz. A General Datalog-Based Framework for Tractable Query Answering over Ontologies. In *Proc. ACM Symp. on Principles of Database Systems (PODS)*, 2009.
13. A. Acciarri, D. Calvanese, G. D. Giacomo, D. Lembo, M. Lenzerini, M. Palmieri, and R. Rosati. Quonto: Querying Ontologies. In *Proc. Intl. Conference on Artificial Intelligence (AAAI)*, 2005.
14. P. Adjiman, P. Chatalic, F. Goasdoué, M.-C. Rousset, and L. Simon. Distributed reasoning in a peer-to-peer setting. *J. Artificial Intelligence Research*, 25, 2006.

15. S. Al-Khalifa, H. V. Jagadish, J. M. Patel, Y. Wu, N. Koudas, and D. Srivastava. Structural Joins: A Primitive for Efficient XML Query Pattern Matching. In *Proc. Intl. Conf. on Data Engineering (ICDE)*, 2002.

16. D. Allemang and J. Hendler. *Semantic Web for the Working Ontologist: Effective Modeling in RDFS and OWL*. Morgan-Kaufman, 2008.

17. J. C. Anderson, J. Lehnardt, and N. Slater. *CouchDB: the Definitive Guide*. O'Reilly, 2010. Available at http://wiki.apache.org/couchdb/.

18. V. N. Anh and A. Moffat. Inverted index compression using word-aligned binary codes. *Inf. Retrieval*, 8(1):151–166, 2005.

19. V. N. Anh and A. Moffat. Improved Word-Aligned Binary Compression for Text Indexing. *IEEE Trans. Knowledge and Data Engineering*, 18(6):857–861, 2006.

20. G. Antoniou and F. van Harmelen. *A Semantic Web Primer*. The MIT Press, 2008.

21. A. Arasu and H. Garcia-Molina. Extracting structured data from Web pages. In *Proc. ACM Intl. Conf. Management of Data (SIGMOD)*, pages 337–348, June 2003.

22. F. Baader, D. Calvanese, D. McGuinness, D. Nardi, and P. F. Patel-Schneider, editors. *The Description Logic Handbook: Theory, Implementation, and Applications*. Cambridge University Press, 2003.

23. J.-F. Baget, M. Croitoru, A. Gutierrez, M. Leclre, and M.-L. Mugnier. Translations between rdf(s) and conceptual graphs. In *Proc. Intl. Conference on Conceptual Structures (ICCS)*, pages 28–41, 2010.

24. M. Benedikt and C. Koch. XPath leashed. *ACM Computing Surveys*, 41(1), 2008.

25. M. Benedikt and C. Koch. From XQuery to relational logics. *ACM Trans. Database Systems*, 34(4), 2009.

26. V. Benzaken, G. Castagna, and A. Frisch. Cduce: An XML-centric general-purpose language. *SIGPLAN Notices*, 38(9):51–63, 2003.

27. G. J. Bex, F. Neven, T. Schwentick, and S. Vansummeren. Inference of concise regular expressions and DTDs. *ACM Trans. Database Systems*, 35(2), 2010.

28. G. J. Bex, F. Neven, and S. Vansummeren. Inferring XML Schema Definitions from XML Data. In *Proc. Intl. Conf. Very Large Databases (VLDB)*, pages 998–1009, 2007.

29. K. P. Birman, editor. *Reliable Distributed Systems: Technologies, Web Services, and Applications*. Springer, 2005.

30. P. Blackburn, J. V. Benthem, and F. Wolter. *Handbook of Modal Logic*. Springer, 2006.

31. G. E. Blelloch. Programming parallel algorithms. *Commun. ACM*, 39(3):85–97, 1996.

32. P. A. Boncz, T. Grust, M. van Keulen, S. Manegold, J. Rittinger, and J. Teubner. MonetDB/XQuery: A Fast XQuery Processor Powered by a Relational Engine. In *Proc. ACM Intl. Conf. Management of Data (SIGMOD)*, pages 479–490, 2006.

33. BrightPlanet. The Deep Web: Surfacing Hidden Value. White Paper, July 2000.

34. S. Brin and L. Page. The anatomy of a large-scale hypertextual Web search engine. *Computer Networks*, 30(1–7):107–117, Apr. 1998.

35. A. Z. Broder, S. C. Glassman, M. S. Manasse, and G. Zweig. Syntactic clustering of the Web. *Computer Networks*, 29(8–13):1157–1166, 1997.

36. J. D. Bruijn, E. Franconi, and S. Tessaris. Logical reconstruction of normative RDF. In *Proc. OWL: Experiences and Directions Workshop (OWLED'05)*, 2005.

37. N. Bruno, N. Koudas, and D. Srivastava. Holistic twig joins: optimal XML pattern matching. In *Proc. ACM Intl. Conf. Management of Data (SIGMOD)*, 2002.

38. D. Calvanese, G. D. Giacomo, D. Lembo, M. Lenzerini, and R. Rosati. Tractable reasoning and efficient query answering in description logics: The DL-LITE family. *J. Automated Reasoning*, 39(3):385–429, 2007.

39. R. G. G. Cattell, editor. *The Object Database Standard: ODMG-93*. Morgan Kaufmann, 1994.

40. R. Chaiken, B. Jenkins, P.-Å. Larson, B. Ramsey, D. Shakib, S. Weaver, and J. Zhou. SCOPE: Easy and Efficient Parallel Processing of Massive Data Sets. *Proc. Intl. Conf. Very Large Databases (VLDB)*, 1(2):1265–1276, 2008.

41. S. Chakrabarti. *Mining the Web: Discovering Knowledge from Hypertext Data.* Morgan Kaufmann, 2003.

42. A. Chandra and M. Vardi. The implication problem for functional and inclusion dependencies is undecidable. *SIAM J. Computing*, 14(3):671–677, 1985.

43. C.-H. Chang, M. Kayed, M. R. Girgis, and K. F. Shaalan. A survey of Web information extraction systems. *IEEE Trans. Knowledge and Data Engineering*, 18(10):1411–1428, Oct. 2006.

44. F. Chang, J. Dean, S. Ghemawat, W. C. Hsieh, D. A. Wallach, M. Burrows, T. Chandra, A. Fikes, and R. E. Gruber. Bigtable: A Distributed Storage System for Structured Data. In *Intl. Symp. on Operating System Design and Implementation (OSDI)*, 2006.

45. K. C.-C. Chang, B. He, C. Li, M. Patel, and Z. Zhang. Structured databases on the Web: Observations and implications. *SIGMOD Record*, 33(3):61–70, 2004.

46. K. C.-C. Chang, B. He, and Z. Zhang. Toward Large Scale Integration: Building a MetaQuerier over Databases on the Web. In *Proc. Intl. Conference on Innovative Data Systems Research (CIDR)*, Jan. 2005.

47. M. Chein and M.-L. Mugnier. *Graph-based Knowledge Representation.* Springer, 2008.

48. H. Comon, M. Dauchet, R. Gilleron, C. Löding, F. Jacquemard, D. Lugiez, S. Tison, and M. Tommasi. Tree automata techniques and applications. http://www.grappa. univ-lille3.fr/tata, 2007.

49. T. H. Cormen, C. E. Leiserson, and R. L. Rivest. *Introduction to Algorithms.* The MIT Press, 1990.

50. A. Crainiceanu, P. Linga, J. Gehrke, and J. Shanmugasundaram. Querying Peer-to-Peer Networks Using P-Trees. In *Proc. Intl. Workshop on the Web and Databases (WebDB)*, pages 25–30, 2004.

51. V. Crescenzi, G. Mecca, and P. Merialdo. RoadRunner: Towards Automatic Data Extraction from Large Web Sites. In *Proc. Intl. Conf. Very Large Databases (VLDB)*, 2001.

52. G. DeCandia, D. Hastorun, M. Jampani, G. Kakulapati, A. Lakshman, A. Pilchin, S. Sivasubramanian, P. Vosshall, and W. Vogels. Dynamo: Amazon's highly available key-value store. In *Proc. ACM Symp. Operating Systems Principles (SOSP)*, pages 205–220, 2007.

53. R. Devine. Design and Implementation of DDH: A Distributed Dynamic Hashing Algorithm. In *Intl. Conf. Foundations of Data Organization and Algorithms (FODO)*, pages 101–114, 1993.

54. D. DeWitt and M. Stonebraker. MAPREDUCE, a Major Step Backward. DatabaseColumn blog, 1987. http://databasecolumn.vertica.com/database-innovation/mapreduce-a-major-step-backwards/.

55. D. J. DeWitt, R. H. Gerber, G. Graefe, M. L. Heytens, K. B. Kumar, and M. Muralikrishna. GAMMA — A High Performance Dataflow Database Machine. In *Proc. Intl. Conf. Very Large Databases (VLDB)*, 1996.

56. D. J. DeWitt and J. Gray. Parallel Database Systems: The Future of High Performance Database Systems. *Commun. ACM*, 35(6):85–98, 1992.

57. P. Dietz. Maintaining Order in a Linked List. In *Proc. ACM SIGACT Symp. Theory of Computing (STOC)*, 1982.

58. Document Object Model. w3.org/DOM.

59. O. Duschka, M. Genesereth, and A. Y. Levy. Recursive query plans for data integration. *J. Logic Programming*, 43(1):49–73, 2000.

60. P. Elias. Universal code word sets and representations of the integers. *IEEE Trans. Information Theory*, 21(2):194–203, 1975.
61. R. Elmasri and S. B. Navathe. *Fundamentals of Database Systems*. Addison-Wesley, 2003.
62. FaCT++. http://owl.cs.manchester.ac.uk/fact++/.
63. R. Fagin. Combining fuzzy information from multiple systems. *J. Computer System Sciences*, 58:83–99, 1999. Abstract published in PODS'96.
64. R. Fagin, A. Lotem, and M. Naor. Optimal aggregation algorithms for middleware. *J. Computer System Sciences*, 66:614–656, 2003. Abstract published in PODS'2001.
65. G. Flake, S. Lawrence, and C. L. Giles. Efficient Identification of Web Communities. In *Proc. ACM Intl. Conf. on Knowledge and Data Discovery (SIGKDD)*, pages 150–160, 2000.
66. G. W. Flake, S. Lawrence, C. L. Giles, and F. Coetzee. Self-organization of the web and identification of communities. *IEEE Computer*, 35(3):66–71, 2002.
67. D. Florescu and D. Kossmann. Storing and querying XML data using an RDMBS. *IEEE Data Eng. Bull.*, 22(3):27–34, 1999.
68. A. Fox, S. D. Gribble, Y. Chawathe, E. A. Brewer, and P. Gauthier. Cluster-Based Scalable Network Services. In *Proc. ACM Symposium on Operating Systems Principles (SOSP)*, pages 78–91, 1997.
69. S. Fushimi, M. Kitsuregawa, and H. Tanaka. An Overview of the System Software of a Parallel Relational Database Machine Grace. In *Proc. Intl. Conf. on Very Large Databases (VLDB)*, pages 209–219, 1986.
70. A. Gates, O. Natkovich, S. Chopra, P. Kamath, S. Narayanam, C. Olston, B. Reed, S. Srinivasan, and U. Srivastava. Building a High-Level Dataflow System on top of MAPREDUCE: The PIG Experience. *Proce. VLDB Endowment (PVLDB)*, 2(2):1414–1425, 2009.
71. S. Ghemawat, H. Gobioff, and S.-T. Leung. The Google File System. In *Proc. Intl. ACM Symp. on Operating Systems Principles (SOSP)*, 2003.
72. S. Gilbert and N. A. Lynch. Brewer's conjecture and the feasibility of consistent, available, partition-tolerant web services. *SIGACT News*, 33(2):51–59, 2002.
73. F. Goasdoué and M.-C. Rousset. Querying distributed data through distributed ontologies: A simple but scalable approach. *IEEE Intelligent Systems (IS)*, 18(5): 60–65, 2003.
74. C. Goldfarb. *The SGML Handbook*. Calendon Press, 1990.
75. R. Goldman and J. Widom. Dataguides: Enabling Query Formulation and Optimization in Semistructured Databases. In *Proc. Intl. Conf. on Very Large Databases (VLDB)*, pages 436–445, 1997.
76. G. Gottlob, C. Koch, and R. Pichler. Efficient algorithms for processing XPath queries. *ACM Trans. Database Systems*, 30(2):444–491, 2005.
77. J. Gray, P. Helland, P. E. O'Neil, and D. Shasha. The Dangers of Replication and a Solution. In *Proc. ACM Intl. Conf. on the Management of Data (SIGMOD)*, pages 173–182, 1996.
78. J. Gray and A. Reuter. *Transaction Processing: Concepts and Techniques*. Morgan Kaufmann, 1993.
79. S. Grumbach and T. Milo. An algebra for pomsets. *Inf. Comput.*, 150(2):268–306, 1999.
80. T. Grust. Accelerating XPath Location Steps. In *Proc. ACM Intl. Conf. Management of Data (SIGMOD)*, pages 109–120, 2002.
81. T. Grust, S. Sakr, and J. Teubner. XQuery on SQL Hosts. In *Proc. Intl. Conf. Very Large Databases (VLDB)*, pages 252–263, 2004.
82. T. Grust, M. van Keulen, and J. Teubner. Staircase Join: Teach a Relational DBMS to Watch Its (Axis) Steps. In *Proc. Intl. Conf. on Very Large Databases (VLDB)*, pages 524–525, 2003.

83. T. Grust, M. van Keulen, and J. Teubner. Accelerating XPath Evaluation in Any RDBMS. *ACM Trans. Database Systems*, 29:91–131, 2004.

84. I. Gupta, T. D. Chandra, and G. S. Goldszmidt. On Scalable and Efficient Distributed Failure Detectors. In *Proc. ACM Intl. Symposium on Principles of Distributed Computing (PODC)*, 2001.

85. Z. Gyöngyi, H. Garcia-Molina, and J. O. Pedersen. Combating Web Spam with TrustRank. In *Proc. Intl. Conf. on Very Large Databases (VLDB)*, 2004.

86. A. Halevy, Z. Ives, D. Suciu, and I. Tatarinov. Schema Mediation for Large-Scale Semantic Data Sharing. *Very Large Databases J. (VLDBJ)*, 14(1):68–83, 2005.

87. A. Y. Halevy. Answering queries using views: A survey. *Very Large Databases J. (VLDBJ)*, 10(4):270–294, 2001.

88. A. Y. Halevy, Z. G. Ives, D. Suciu, and I. Tatarinov. Schema mediation in peer data management systems. In *Proc. Intl. Conf. Data Engineering (ICDE)*, 2003.

89. E. R. Harold. *Effective XML*. Addison-Wesley, 2003.

90. S. Heinz and J. Zobel. Efficient single-pass index construction for text databases. *J. American Society for Information Science and Technology (JASIST)*, 54(8):713–729, 2003.

91. J. Hopcroft, R. Motwani, and J. Ullman. *Introduction to Automata Theory, Languages, and Computation*. Addison-Wesley, 2006.

92. H. Hosoya and B. C. Pierce. Xduce: A statically Typed XML Processing Language. *ACM Trans. Internet Techn.*, 3(2):117–148, 2003.

93. H. Hosoya, J. Vouillon, and B. C. Pierce. Regular expression types for xml. *ACM Trans. Program. Lang. Syst.*, 27(1):46–90, 2005.

94. IETF. Request For Comments 1034. Domain Names—Concepts and Facilities. http://www.ietf.org/rfc/rfc1034.txt, June 1999.

95. IETF. Request For Comments 2616. Hypertext transfer protocol—HTTP/1.1. http://www.ietf.org/rfc/rfc2616.txt, June 1999.

96. ISO. Specification of astraction syntax notation one (asn.1), 1987. Standard 8824, Information Processing System.

97. ISO. *ISO/IEC 19757-2: Document Schema Definition Language (DSDL). Part 2: Regular-grammar-based validation. RELAX NG*. International Standards Organization, 2008.

98. ISO. *ISO/IEC 19757-3: Document Schema Definition Language (DSDL). Part 3: Rule-based validation. Schematron*. International Standards Organization, 2008.

99. ISO/IEC 9075-14:2003, Information technology—Database languages—SQL—Part 14: XML-Related Specifications (SQL/XML), 2003.

100. P. Jaccard. Étude comparative de la distribution florale dans une portion des Alpes et du Jura. *Bulletin de la Société Vaudoise des Sciences Naturelles*, 37, 1901.

101. H. V. Jagadish, B. C. Ooi, K.-L. Tan, Q. H. Vu, and R. Zhang. Speeding up search in peer-to-peer networks with a multi-way tree structure. In *Proc. ACM Intl. Conf. Management of Data (SIGMOD)*, pages 1–12, 2006.

102. H. V. Jagadish, B. C. Ooi, and Q. H. Vu. BATON: A Balanced Tree Structure for Peer-to-Peer Networks. In *Proc. Intl. Conf. Very Large Databases (VLDB)*, pages 661–672, 2005.

103. H. V. Jagadish, B. C. Ooi, Q. H. Vu, R. Zhang, and A. Zhou. VBI-Tree: A Peer-to-Peer Framework for Supporting Multi-Dimensional Indexing Schemes. In *Proc. Intl. Conf. Data Engineering (ICDE)*, 2006.

104. Jena—A semantic web framework for java. http://jena.sourceforge.net/.

105. H. Jiang, H. Lu, W. Wang, and J. X. Yu. XParent: An Efficient RDBMS-Based XML Database System. In *Proc. Intl. Conf. Data Engineering (ICDE)*, pages 335–336, 2002.

106. H. Kaplan, T. Milo, and R. Shabo. Compact labeling scheme for XML ancestor queries. *Theory Comput. Syst.*, 40(1):55–99, 2007.

107. D. R. Karger, E. Lehman, F. T. Leighton, R. Panigrahy, M. S. Levine, and D. Lewin. Consistent Hashing and Random Trees: Distributed Caching Protocols for Relieving Hot Spots on the World Wide Web. In *Proc. ACM SIGACT Symp. Theory of Computing (STOC)*, pages 654–663, 1997.

108. M. Kay. *XSLT 2.0 and XPath 2.0 Programmer's Reference*, fourth edition. Wrox, May 2008.

109. J. M. Kleinberg. Authoritative Sources in a Hyperlinked Environment. *J. ACM*, 46(5):604–632, 1999.

110. M. Koster. A Standard for Robot Exclusion. http://www.robotstxt.org/orig.html, June 1994.

111. B. Kröll and P. Widmayer. Distributing a Search Tree Among a Growing Number of Processors. In *Proc. ACM Intl. Conf. Management of Data (SIGMOD)*, pages 265–276, 1994.

112. P.-Å. Larson. Dynamic hash tables. *Commun. ACM*, 31(4):446–457, 1988.

113. A. Y. Levy, A. Rajaraman, and J. Ordille. Querying heterogeneous information sources using source descriptions. In *Proc. Intl. Conf. Very Large Databases (VLDB)*, 1996.

114. W. Litwin. Linear Hashing, a New Tool for File and table addressing. In *Proc. Intl. Conf. Very Large Databases (VLDB)*, 1980.

115. W. Litwin, M.-A. Neimat, and D. Schneider. RP*: A Family of Order-Preserving Scalable Distributed Data Structures. In *Proc. Intl. Conf. Very Large Databases (VLDB)*, 1994.

116. W. Litwin, M.-A. Neimat, and D. A. Schneider. LH*—A Scalable, Distributed Data Structure. *ACM Trans. Database Syst.*, 21(4):480–525, 1996.

117. B. Liu, R. L. Grossman, and Y. Zhai. Mining Web Pages for Data Records. *IEEE Intelligent Systems*, 19(6):49–55, 2004.

118. J. Lu, T. W. Ling, C. Y. Chan, and T. Chen. From region encoding to extended Dewey: On efficient processing of XML twig pattern matching. In *Proc. Intl. Conf. Very Large Databases (VLDB)*, 2005.

119. J. Madhavan, A. Y. Halevy, S. Cohen, X. Dong, S. R. Jeffery, D. Ko, and C. Yu. Structured Data Meets the Web: A Few Observations. *IEEE Data Engineering Bulletin*, 29(4):19–26, Dec. 2006.

120. C. D. Manning, P. Raghavan, and H. Schütze. *Introduction to Information Retrieval*. Cambridge University Press, 2008. Online version at http://informationretrieval.org/.

121. J. Melton and S. Buxton. *Querying XML: XQuery, XPath, and SQL/XML in Context*. Morgan Kaufmann, Mar. 2006.

122. M. Michael, J. Moreira, D. Shiloach, and R. Wisniewski. Scale-up x Scale-out: A Case Study Using Nutch/Lucene. In *Proc. Intl. Parallel Processing Symposium (IPPS)*, 2007.

123. P. Michiels, I. Manolescu, and C. Miachon. Toward microbenchmarking XQuery. *Inf. Systems*, 33(2):182–202, 2008.

124. T. D. Millstein, A. Y. Halevy, and M. Friedman. Query containment for data integration systems. *J. Computer and System Sciences*, 66(1):20–39, 2003.

125. T. Milo, D. Suciu, and V. Vianu. Typechecking for XML transformers. *J. Computer and System Sciences*, 66(1):66–97, 2003.

126. M. E. J. Newman and M. Girvan. Finding and evaluating community structure in networks. *Physical Review E*, 69(2), 2004.

127. OASIS. RELAX NG specification. http://www.relaxng.org/spec-20011203.html, Dec. 2001.

128. OASIS. RELAX NG compact syntax. http://www.relaxng.org/compact-20021121.html, Nov. 2002.

129. C. Olston, B. Reed, U. Srivastava, R. Kumar, and A. Tomkins. Pig Latin: A Not-so-Foreign Language for Data Processing. In *Proc. ACM Intl. Conf. Management of Data (SIGMOD)*, pages 1099–1110, 2008.

130. P. E. O'Neil, E. J. O'Neil, S. Pal, I. Cseri, G. Schaller, and N. Westbury. ORD-PATHs: Insert-friendly XML node labels. In *Proc. ACM Intl. Conf. on the Management of Data (SIGMOD)*, pages 903–908, 2004.

131. M. T. Özsu and P. Valduriez. *Principles of Distributed Database Systems*, third edition. Prentice-Hall, 2010.

132. Y. Papakonstantinou, H. Garcia-Molina, and J. Widom. Object exchange across heterogeneous information sources. In *Proc. Intl. Conf. Data Engineering (ICDE)*, 1995.

133. A. Pavlo, E. Paulson, A. Rasin, D. J. Abadi, D. J. DeWitt, S. Madden, and M. Stonebraker. A comparison of approaches to large-scale data analysis. In *Proc. ACM Intl. Conf. Management of Data (SIGMOD)*, pages 165–178, 2009.

134. P.Buneman, S. Davidson, and D. Suciu. Programming constructs for unstructured data. In *Proc. Intl. Workshop Database Programming Languages (DBLP)*, 1995.

135. R. Pike, S. Dorward, R. Griesemer, and S. Quinlan. Interpreting the data: Parallel analysis with sawzall. *Scientific Programming Journal, Special Issue on Grids and Worldwide Computing Programming Models and Infrastructure*, 13(4):227–298, 2005.

136. M. F. Porter. An algorithm for suffix stripping. *Program*, 14(3):130–137, July 1980.

137. R. Pottinger and A. Y. Halevy. Minicon: A scalable algorithm for answering queries using views. *Very Large Databases J. (VLDBJ)*, 10(2–3):182–198, 2001.

138. Racerpro. http://www.racer-systems.com/.

139. V. Ramasubramanian and E. G. Sirer. Beehive: O(1) Lookup Performance for Power-Law Query Distributions in Peer-to-Peer Overlays. In *Intl. Symposium on Networked Systems Design and Implementation (NSDI)*, pages 99–112, 2004.

140. S. Ratnasamy, P. Francis, M. Handley, R. M. Karp, and S. Shenker. A scalable content-addressable network. In *ACM-SIGCOMM*, pages 161–172, 2001.

141. A. I. T. Rowstron and P. Druschel. Pastry: Scalable, Decentralized Object Location, and Routing for Large-Scale Peer-to-Peer Systems. In *Middleware 2001, IFIP/ACM International Conference on Distributed Systems Platforms Heidelberg*, volume 2218 of *Lecture Notes in Computer Science*, pages 329–350. Springer, 2001.

142. Y. Saito and M. Shapiro. Optimistic replication. *ACM Computing Surveys*, 37(1):42–81, 2005.

143. S. E. Schaeffer. Graph clustering. *Computer Science Review*, 1(1):27–64, 2007.

144. F. Scholer, H. E. Williams, J. Yiannis, and J. Zobel. Compression of inverted indexes for fast query evaluation. In *Proc. ACM Symp. Information Retrieval*, pages 222–229, 2002.

145. P. Senellart, A. Mittal, D. Muschick, R. Gilleron, and M. Tommasi. Automatic Wrapper Induction from Hidden-Web Sources with Domain Knowledge. In *Proc. Intl. Workshop on Web Information and Data Management (WIDM)*, pages 9–16, Oct. 2008.

146. J. Shanmugasundaram, E. J. Shekita, R. Barr, M. J. Carey, B. G. Lindsay, H. Pirahesh, and B. Reinwald. Efficiently Publishing Relational Data as XML Documents. In *Proc. Intl. Conf. Very Large Databases (VLDB)*, pages 65–76, 2000.

147. J. Shanmugasundaram, K. Tufte, C. Zhang, G. He, D. J. DeWitt, and J. F. Naughton. Relational Databases for Querying XML Documents: Limitations and Opportunities. In *Proc. Intl. Conf. on Very Large Databases (VLDB)*, 1999.

148. E. Sirin, B. Parsia, B. C. Grau, A. Kalyanpur, and Y. Katz. Pellet: A practical OWL-DL reasoner. *J. Web Semantics*, 5(2):51–53, 2007.

149. sitemaps.org. Sitemaps XML format. http://www.sitemaps.org/protocol.php, Feb. 2008.

150. I. Stoica, R. Morris, D. Liben-Nowell, D. R. Karger, M. F. Kaashoek, F. Dabek, and H. Balakrishnan. Chord: A scalable peer-to-peer lookup protocol for internet applications. *IEEE/ACM Trans. Netw.*, 11(1):17–32, 2003.

151. M. Stonebraker, D. J. Abadi, D. J. DeWitt, S. Madden, E. Paulson, A. Pavlo, and A. Rasin. MAPREDUCE and parallel DBMSs: friends or foes? *Commun. ACM*, 53(1):64–71, 2010.

152. D. Suciu. The XML typechecking problem. *SIGMOD Record*, 31(1):89–96, 2002.

153. A. S. Tanenbaum and M. van Steen. *Distributed Systems: Principles and Paradigms*. Prentice Hall, 2001.

154. B. ten Cate and M. Marx. Navigational XPath: Calculus and algebra. *SIGMOD Record*, 36(2):19–26, 2007.

155. A. Thusoo, J. S. Sarma, N. Jain, Z. Shao, P. Chakka, S. Anthony, H. Liu, P. Wyckoff, and R. Murthy. Hive — A warehousing solution over a map-reduce framework. *Proc. VLDB Endowment (PVLDB)*, 2(2):1626–1629, 2009.

156. J. Ullman. *Principles of Database and Knowledge Base Systems, volume I*. Computer Science Press, 1988.

157. U.S. National Archives and Records Administration. The Soundex Indexing System. http://www.archives.gov/genealogy/census/soundex.html, May 2007.

158. S. M. van Dongen. *Graph Clustering by Flow Simulation*. PhD thesis, University of Utrecht, May 2000.

159. M. Vardi. The Complexity of Relational Query Languages. In *Proc. ACM SIGACT Symp. Theory of Computing (STOC)*, pages 137–146, 1982.

160. J. S. Vitter. External memory algorithms and data structures. *ACM Computing Surveys*, 33(2):209–271, 2001.

161. W3C. http://www.w3.org/.

162. W3C. HTML 4.01 Specification, Sept. 1999. http://www.w3.org/TR/REC-html40/.

163. W3C. XML Path Language (XPath). http://www.w3.org/TR/xpath/, Nov. 1999.

164. W3C. XHTML 1.0: The Extensible Hypertext Markup Language, second edition. http://www.w3.org/TR/xhtml1/, Aug. 2002.

165. W3C. XML Schema Part 0: Primer. http://www.w3.org/TR/xmlschema-0/, Oct. 2004.

166. W3C. XML Schema Part 1: Structures. http://www.w3.org/TR/xmlschema-1/, Oct. 2004.

167. W3C. XML Schema Part 2: Datatypes. http://www.w3.org/TR/xmlschema-2/, Oct. 2004.

168. W3C. XML Path Language (XPath) 2.0. http://www.w3.org/TR/xpath20/, Jan. 2007.

169. W3C. XQuery 1.0: An XML query language. http://www.w3.org/TR/xquery/, Jan. 2007.

170. W3C. XQuery 1.0 and XPath 2.0 data model (XDM). http://www.w3.org/TR/xpath-datamodel/, Jan. 2007.

171. W3C. XQuery 1.0 and XPath 2.0 Formal Semantics. http://www.w3.org/TR/xquery-semantics/, Jan. 2007.

172. W3C. XQuery 1.0 and XPath 2.0 Functions and Operators. http://www.w3.org/TR/xquery-operators/, Jan. 2007.

173. W3C. XSLT 2.0 and XQuery 1.0 Serialization. http://www.w3.org/TR/xslt-xquery-serialization/, Jan. 2007.

174. W3C. Extensible markup language (XML) 1.0. http://www.w3.org/TR/REC-xml/, Nov. 2008.

175. W3C. SPARQL Query Language for RDF. http://www.w3.org/TR/rdf-sparql-query/, Jan. 2008.

176. W3C. Owl 2 Web Ontology Language Profiles. http://www.w3.org/2004/OWL/, 2009.

177. W3C. HTML5, 2010. Working draft available at http://dev.w3.org/html5/spec/Overview.html.

178. P. Walmsley. *XQuery*. O'Reilly, Mar. 2007.

179. I. Witten, A. Moffat, and T. Bell. *Managing Gigabytes: Compressing and Indexing Documents and Images*. Morgan-Kaufmann, 1999.

180. X. Wu, M. L. Lee, and W. Hsu. A Prime Number Labeling Scheme for Dynamic Ordered XML trees. In *Proc. Intl. Conf. Data Engineering (ICDE)*, 2004.

181. Y. Wu, J. M. Patel, and H. V. Jagadish. Structural join order selection for XML query optimization. In *Proc. Intl. Conf. Data Engineering (ICDE)*, pages 443–454, 2003.

182. XML Query (XQuery). http://www.w3.org/XML/Query.

183. The Extensible Stylesheet Language Family. http://www.w3.org/Style/XSL.

184. L. Xu, T. W. Ling, H. Wu, and Z. Bao. DDE: From Dewey to a Fully Dynamic XML Labeling scheme. In *Proc. ACM Intl. Conf. Management of Data (SIGMOD)*, 2009.

185. M. Yoshikawa, T. Amagasa, T. Shimura, and S. Uemura. XRel: A Path-Based Approach to Storage and Retrieval of XML Documents Using Relational Databases. *ACM Trans. on Internet Technology*, 1(1):110–141, 2001.

186. H. Yu and A. Vahdat. Design and evaluation of a continuous consistency model for replicated services. *ACM Trans. Comput. Syst.*, 20(3):239–282, 2002.

187. Y. Zhai and B. Liu. Web Data Extraction Based on Partial Tree Alignment. In *Proc. Intl. World Wide Web Conference (WWW)*, 2005.

188. B. Y. Zhao, L. Huang, J. Stribling, S. C. Rhea, A. D. Joseph, and J. Kubiatowicz. Tapestry: A resilient global-scale overlay for service deployment. *IEEE J. Selected Areas in Communications*, 22(1):41–53, 2004.

189. J. Zobel and A. Moffat. Inverted Files for Text Search Engines. *ACM Computing Surveys*, 38(2), 2006.

Index

Printed in the United States
by Baker & Taylor Publisher Services